WITHDRAWN

MySQL®

Certification Study Guide

Paul DuBois, Stefan Hinz, and Carsten Pedersen

MySQL
Press

800 East 96th Street, Indianapolis, Indiana 46240 USA

MySQL® Certification Study Guide

The world sample database: Copyright Statistics Finland, http://www.stat.fi/worldinfigures

International Standard Book Number: 0-672-32632-9

Library of Congress Catalog Card Number: 2003095797

Printed in the United States of America

First Printing: April 2004

07   06   05   04   4   3   2

Trademarks

Warning and Disclaimer

Bulk Sales

Pearson offers excellent discounts on this book when ordered in quantity for bulk purchases or special sales. For more information, please contact

U.S. Corporate and Government Sales
1-800-382-3419
corpsales@pearsontechgroup.com

For sales outside of the U.S., please contact

International Sales
1-317-428-3341
international@pearsontechgroup.com

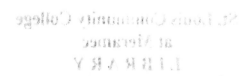

ASSOCIATE PUBLISHER	MANAGING EDITOR	INDEXER	COVER & INTERIOR DESIGNER
Mark Taber	Charlotte Clapp	Rebecca Salerno	Gary Adair
ACQUISITIONS EDITOR	SENIOR PROJECT EDITOR	PROOFREADER	PAGE LAYOUT
Shelley Johnston	Tricia Liebig	Wendy Ott	Michelle Mitchell
DEVELOPMENT EDITOR	COPY EDITOR	MARKETING MANAGER	PUBLISHING COORDINATOR
Damon Jordan	Mike Henry	Randi Roger	Vanessa Evans

MySQL® **Press** is the exclusive publisher of technology books and materials that have been authorized by MySQL AB. MySQL Press books are written and reviewed by the world's leading authorities on MySQL technologies, and are edited, produced, and distributed by the Que/Sams Publishing group of Pearson Education, the worldwide leader in integrated education and computer technology publishing. For more information on MySQL Press and MySQL Press books, please go to **www.mysqlpress.com**.

MYSQL HQ
MySQL AB
Bangårdsgatan 8
S-753 20 Uppsala
Sweden

GERMANY, AUSTRIA, AND SWITZERLAND
MySQL GmbH
Schlosserstraße 4
D-72622 Nürtingen
Germany

FRANCE
MySQL AB (France)
123, rue du Faubourg St. Antoine
75011, Paris
France

UNITED STATES
MySQL Inc.
2510 Fairview Avenue East
Seattle, WA 98102
USA

FINLAND
MySQL Finland Oy
Tekniikantie 21
FIN–02150 Espoo
Finland

MySQL® **AB** develops, markets, and supports a family of high-performance, affordable database servers and tools. MySQL AB is the sole owner of the MySQL server source code, the MySQL trademark, and the mysql.com domain. For more information on MySQL AB and MySQL AB products, please go to **www.mysql.com** or the following areas of the MySQL Web site:

- Training information: **www.mysql.com/training**
- Support services: **www.mysql.com/support**
- Consulting services: **www.mysql.com/consulting**

About the Authors

Paul DuBois is a member of the MySQL documentation team, a database administrator, and a leader in the Open Source and MySQL communities. He contributed to the online documentation for MySQL and is the author of *MySQL Developer's Library*, *MySQL and Perl for the Web* (New Riders Publishing), and *MySQL Cookbook*, *Using csh and tcsh*, and *Software Portability with imake* (O'Reilly and Associates).

Stefan Hinz is a member of the MySQL documentation team, a MySQL trainer and consultant, and the German translator of the *MySQL Reference Manual*. He is also the translator of Paul's *MySQL Cookbook* (O'Reilly and Associates) and translator and author of MySQL-related German books. Stefan passed the MySQL Certification exam before he joined MySQL AB.

Carsten Pedersen is the MySQL AB Certification Manager, and has led the development of the MySQL Certification Program. He has taught several MySQL courses in a number of countries. Before joining MySQL AB, he administered MySQL databases in several production systems and maintained a very popular "MySQL FAQ and Tools" Internet site.

Acknowledgments

We would like to thank all of our colleagues at MySQL who have helped build the certification program over the past 18 months, and without whom this book wouldn't have come into existence. A special thank you to Kaj Arnö, who was the person to conceive and initiate the MySQL Certification program.

References

The MySQL Reference Manual is the primary source of information on MySQL. It is available online in several formats and languages from the MySQL AB Web site (http://www.mysql.com/).

The portals section at the MySQL AB Web site provides descriptions of a number of MySQL-related books. These might be helpful in supplementing the material in the *MySQL Reference Manual*, and many of them also deal with specific topics not extensively covered by the manual, such as Web site development, e-commerce, and application programming using the C client library or other APIs.

Contents at a Glance

Table of Contents

We Want to Hear from You!

As the reader of this book, *you* are our most important critic and commentator. We value your opinion and want to know what we're doing right, what we could do better, what areas you'd like to see us publish in, and any other words of wisdom you're willing to pass our way.

You can email or write me directly to let me know what you did or didn't like about this book—as well as what we can do to make our books stronger.

Please note that I cannot help you with technical problems related to the topic of this book, and that due to the high volume of mail I receive, I might not be able to reply to every message.

When you write, please be sure to include this book's title and author as well as your name and phone or email address. I will carefully review your comments and share them with the author and editors who worked on the book.

Email: mysqlpress@pearsoned.com

Mail: Mark Taber
            Associate Publisher
            Pearson Education
            800 East 96th Street
            Indianapolis, IN 46240 USA

Introduction

Foreword

Although the MySQL™ Relational Database Management System (RDBMS) has existed for many years, it's only within the last two years that MySQL has gained official recognition in many enterprise settings. The growth has been tremendous—in just a few years, the number of MySQL installations worldwide has risen from a few hundred thousand to an estimated four million in early 2003.

The growth of MySQL in the enterprise, paired with downturn in the economy at the turn of the century, has created a new phenomenon: There are more companies than ever looking specifically for people with MySQL skills. At the same time, many people with MySQL knowledge are out looking for a job after the burst of the dot-com bubble, which means that companies interested in hiring can pick and choose at will.

MySQL AB, the company behind the MySQL RDBMS (yes, even though the MySQL RDBMS is an open source product, there's a thriving company behind it) developed the MySQL Certification Program to help companies identify individuals with the skillset they need and expect from their employees. The certification program also helps individuals by setting them apart from hobbyists, increasing their prospects for finding challenging new tasks.

MySQL AB currently offers certification at two levels:

- The Core Certification tests basic MySQL knowledge and usage, knowledge that's sufficient to maintain a basic MySQL installation and to create application programs that use MySQL as a backend database.
- The Professional Certification goes into more detail regarding such topics as large table maintenance, storage engines, and optimizations.

This book meets the demand that was created by the introduction of the MySQL Certification Program. How do you prepare for the exams? Reading this study guide is the best way to enhance your chances of passing the demanding MySQL Core and Professional exams.

Although the topics covered by each exam (as listed in the "MySQL Certification Candidate Guide") might seem basic, the exams aren't easy, and they require a combination of study and practical experience. This book will help you understand many of these topics in-depth. Combined with real-world experience, this will help you pass the exams.

Another means of gaining skills and knowledge to both help you pass the exams and be successful in the field of MySQL administration and usage is to attend one or more of the courses provided by MySQL AB.

More information on the MySQL training and certification programs may be found on the MySQL AB Web site (see http://www.mysql.com).

I would like to thank Paul DuBois, Stefan Hinz, and Carsten Pedersen for bringing this book into existence. Thank you to Trudy Pelzer, who reviewed and edited all exercises as well as large parts of the text. Also thank you to the following people, each of whom has reviewed and given extensive comments on the text: Thomas Bassel, Jeremy Cole, Bob Donahue, Jason Frisvold, Peter Gulutzan, Mike Hillyer, Arjen Lentz, Max Mether, Heikki Tuuri, Nils Valentin, and Peter Zaitsev.

I am happy the book is now out. MySQL AB now has an excellent answer to the most frequent question we get about certification, namely, "How do I best prepare for it?"

Good luck on your exam!

—Kaj Arnö, MySQL AB, Vice President, Professional Services

About This Book

This is a study guide for the MySQL Core and Professional Certification exams. It contains both the "Core Study Guide" and the "Professional Study Guide." It should be seen as a primer for the exams, but not as a replacement for the *MySQL Reference Manual*. This guide is not meant as an exhaustive exposition of everything there is to know about MySQL. Instead, it focuses specifically on topics that appear on the exams and in MySQL training classes. As part of your preparation for an exam, you should of course make sure that you're thoroughly familiar with the *MySQL Reference Manual*. In addition, the "Professional Study Guide" assumes that you're familiar with everything in the "Core Study Guide."

You might find that the wording of a topic covered in this guide corresponds exactly to the wording of a question on an exam. However, that is the exception, so rote memorization of the material in this guide will not be effective. You'll need to *understand* the principles discussed herein so that you can apply them to the exam questions. If you find the material difficult, you might want to consider the training classes offered by MySQL AB. These classes are presented in a format that facilitates understanding by allowing you to interact with the instructor.

Some features in MySQL are version specific. The current exam and this book cover MySQL 4, and you should consider a feature available if it's available as of MySQL 4. For example, UNION statements were implemented for MySQL 4. For purposes of the exam, you should consider UNION a topic upon which you might be tested. More specifically, you should expect to be tested on a given feature shortly after it appears in a gamma version of a

MySQL release. In practice, however, the features tested in exams are likely to lag a month or two behind the release date of such a gamma version.

Because the study guide is targeted to MySQL 4, it doesn't normally point out when features are unavailable in earlier versions. This differs from what you might be used to in the *MySQL Reference Manual*. For example, the InnoDB storage engine requires explicit configuration in MySQL 3.23, but not in MySQL 4. The *MySQL Reference Manual* points out that difference. In contrast, this study guide simply indicates that InnoDB uses default configuration values if you do not provide them explicitly because that is always true in MySQL 4.

This introduction provides some general hints on what to expect from the exam, what to do in order to take the exam, what happens on the day of the exam, and what happens once you have passed the exam.

The remainder of this study guide covers each section of the exams, as defined in the "MySQL Certification Candidate Guide." The appendixes include the "Candidate Guide" itself and a "Quick Reference."

Each chapter ends with a number of sample exercises. It's essential that you work through the exercises to test your knowledge. Doing so will prepare you to take the exam far better than just reading the text. Another reason to read the exercises is that occasionally they augment a topic with more detail than is given in the body of the chapter.

Note that the exercises are not always in the same format as the exam questions. The exam questions are in a format that is suited for *testing* your knowledge. The exercises are designed to help you get a better *understanding* of the contents of this book, and to help you prove to yourself that you really grasp the topics covered.

Conventions Used in This Book

This section explains the conventions used in this study guide.

Text in this style is used for program and shell script names, SQL keywords, and command output.

Text in this style represents input that you would type while entering a command or statement.

Text in this style represents variable input for which you're expected to enter a value of your own choosing. Some examples show commands or statements that aren't meant to be entered exactly as shown. Thus, in an example such as the following, you would substitute the name of some particular table for *table_name*:

```
SELECT * FROM table_name;
```

In syntax descriptions, square brackets indicate optional information. For example, the following syntax for the SHOW TABLES statement indicates that you can invoke the statement with or without a FROM clause that specifies a database name:

```
SHOW TABLES [FROM db_name]
```

In most cases, SQL statements are shown with a trailing semicolon character (;). The semi-colon indicates where the statement ends and is useful particularly in reading multiple-statement examples. However, the semicolon is not part of the statement itself.

If a statement is shown together with the output that it produces, it's shown preceded by a mysql> prompt. An example shown in this manner is meant to illustrate the output you would see were you to issue the statement using the mysql client program. For example, a section that discusses the use of the VERSION() function might contain an example like this:

```
mysql> SELECT VERSION();
+------------------+
| VERSION()        |
+------------------+
| 4.0.16-gamma-log |
+------------------+
```

Some commands are intended to be invoked from the command line, such as from a Unix shell prompt or from a Windows console window prompt. In this guide, these commands are shown preceded by a shell> prompt. Some Windows-specific examples use a prompt that begins with C:. The prompt you will actually see on your own system depends on your command interpreter and the prompt settings you use. (The prompt is likely to be % or $ for a Unix shell and C:\> for a Windows console.)

SQL keywords such as SELECT or ORDER BY aren't case sensitive in MySQL and may be speci-fied in any lettercase when you issue queries. However, for this guide, keywords are written in uppercase letters to help make it clear when they're being used as keywords and not in a merely descriptive sense. For example, "UPDATE statement" refers to a particular kind of SQL statement (one that begins with the keyword UPDATE), whereas "update statement" is a descriptive term that refers more generally to any kind of statement that updates or modifies data. The latter term includes UPDATE statements, but also other statements such as INSERT, REPLACE, and DELETE.

Example commands generally omit options for specifying connection parameters, such as --host or --user to specify the server host or your MySQL username. It's assumed that you'll supply such options as necessary. The "Core Study Guide" discusses connection parameter options.

Other Related Documents

Although this book was thoroughly checked for correctness prior to publication, errors might remain. Any errors found after publication are noted at http://www.mysql.com/certification/studyguides.

Before going to the exam, you should ensure that you're fully up-to-date with the MySQL Certification Program information available at http://www.mysql.com/certification.

The Certification area of the MySQL Web site provides comprehensive information on the certifications offered, upcoming certifications and betas, training offers, and so forth. After you've taken a certification exam, the Web site is also where you will be able to check the status of your certification.

The MySQL Certification Candidate Guide

The "MySQL Certification Candidate Guide" contains the overall description of the MySQL Certification program, as well as all the practical information you will need in order to write an exam. The current version of the "Candidate Guide" as of study guide publication time is included in an appendix. However, the "Candidate Guide" is subject to revision and certain details might have changed by the time this book reaches you. You should make sure that you've read the most current version of the "Candidate Guide" before going to an exam. The latest version can be found at http://www.mysql.com/certification/candguide.

The "Candidate Guide" contains a list of items providing practical advice to you as the candidate, an overview of the entire certification program, prices, policies, practical details regarding going to the exam, and so forth. It also details the kinds of information you will be responsible for knowing for each exam.

One item found at the end of the "Candidate Guide" that you should note particularly is the "Non-Disclosure and Logo Usage Agreement" (NDA/LUA). You'll be asked to agree to the agreement when you go to take the exam. At that point, legal agreements will probably be the last thing on your mind, so reading the agreement *before* you go will save you some distraction and also some exam time.

The NDA/LUA consists of two main parts. The "Non-Disclosure Agreement" defines the information you may pass on to others about the exams you have attended (actually, it's mostly about what you're *not* allowed to tell). The "Logo Usage Agreement" defines how you may use the MySQL certification logos after you've passed an exam and attained a MySQL Certification title.

The Certification Mailing List

As an alternative to frequently checking the Web site for new developments in MySQL certification, you can subscribe to the certification announcement mailing list. This is a low-volume list to which MySQL AB posts news related to the certification program. The subscription address for the mailing list is certification-subscribe@lists.mysql.com. To subscribe, send an empty message to that address.

About the Exams

To take a MySQL certification exam, you must go to a VUE test center. MySQL AB creates the exams and defines the content, the passing score, and so forth. VUE is responsible for delivering the exams to candidates worldwide.

Registering for an Exam

There are three ways to register for an exam:

- You can use the VUE Web site, http://www.vue.com/mysql. Note that you must preregister on the Web site to set up an account with VUE. VUE processes your application and notifies you when your account is ready. This process usually takes about 24 hours. After your account has been set up, you can register for the exam you want to take.

- You can call one of the VUE call centers. The telephone numbers are listed in Appendix D, "MySQL Certification Candidate Guide" and at http://www.vue.com/contact/mysql.

- You can register directly at your local VUE test center on the day of the exam. A complete list of the test centers can be found on the Web at http://www.vue.com/mysql. Click on the Test Centers link about halfway down the page. Note that many test centers have limited hours of operation, so it's always a good idea to call ahead to ensure that you can be accommodated at the time you want to take the exam.

MySQL AB recommends that you use the VUE Web site for exam registration and payment, but you're welcome to use any method you choose.

If you register through the Web or a call center, a receipt will be sent to you as soon as the registration process is completed. If you register directly at the test center, please ask for your receipt when you submit payment.

Going to the Exam

On the day of your exam, you should ensure that you arrive at the test center well ahead of the appointed time (at least 15 minutes early is recommended). As you register, test center personnel will provide information on how much time you can expect to spend to complete all steps necessary for testing.

At the test center, you must do the following:

1. Sign the test log.
2. Provide two forms of identification. One must contain your address and one must be a photo ID.
3. Sign a page explaining the test center rules and procedures.

After you've completed these steps, you'll be taken to your testing station, where you'll be required to accept the MySQL AB Certification "Non-Disclosure and Logo Usage Agreement." You'll find this agreement in the "MySQL Certification Candidate Guide."

The Certification Non-Disclosure and Logo Usage Agreement as it will be presented at the testing station.

Taking the Exam

Each MySQL Certification Exam lasts $1\frac{1}{2}$ hours. In that time, you must answer 70 questions.

The questions and answers in any particular exam are drawn from a large question pool. Each section of the exam will have a different number of questions, proportional to the percentages shown in the "MySQL Certification Candidate Guide."

This study guide organizes topic material into the sections shown in the "Candidate Guide," but you shouldn't expect the exam to follow the same format. While you're taking the exam, questions may occur in any order. For example, on the Core Certification Exam, you might be presented with a question on a data import operation, followed by a question pertaining to the Data Definition Language.

Learning to Read Questions

The single most important factor in answering any exam question is first to *understand* what the question is asking. The questions are written in very concise language and are thoroughly checked for readability. But you also need to know how to interpret any additional information presented with the question.

One type of information that's often provided is a display of the structure of a table. Instructions for interpreting this information are given later in this introduction (see the section "Interpreting DESCRIBE Output").

Answering Questions

You should attempt to answer all exam questions, because an unanswered question counts as an incorrect answer. When taking the exam, you'll be able to move back and forth between questions. This makes it possible to initially skip questions you're unsure of and return to them as time permits. You'll also be able to mark a question "for review," if you want to spend more time on it later. When you've gone through all questions, a review screen will be presented that contains any questions that you've marked for review, as well as all unanswered questions.

Each exam question falls into one of three categories:

- A multiple-choice question with a *single* correct answer
- A multiple-choice question with *multiple* correct answers
- A question requiring a textual answer, for which you must *type in* one or more words in response

For a multiple-choice question, you can select an answer either by clicking with the mouse on the field to the left of the answer or by pressing the corresponding letter on the keyboard.

For a multiple-choice/single-answer question, only one response is correct and you must identify the correct answer from among the possible responses. Some of the responses provided might be partially correct, but only one will be completely correct. In a single-answer question, the fields that you can select are circles ("radio buttons") and the text in the status bar below the question says "select the best possible answer."

For a multiple-choice/multiple-answer question, you must choose *all* correct answers to get credit for your response. As with single-answer questions, there might be subtle differences between correct and incorrect answers; take your time to read each possible answer carefully before deciding whether it is correct. In multiple-answer questions, the fields that you can select are square ("check boxes") and the status line says "Select between 1 and *n* answers," where *n* is the total number of possible answers.

For a question requiring a textual answer, you must respond by filling in a text box with one or more words in the text box provided. You must spell each word correctly. However, you need not worry about lettercase or spacing. Uppercase and lowercase are considered the same, and multiple whitespace characters are considered to be equivalent to a single space character.

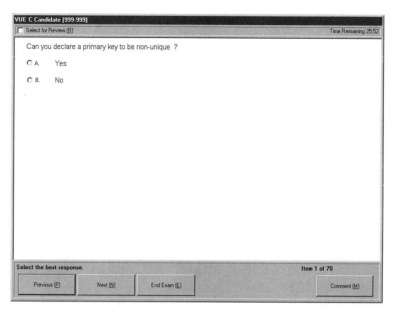

A multiple-choice/single-answer question. Note that each answer key has a circle ("radio button") beside it, and the status bar says "select the best response."

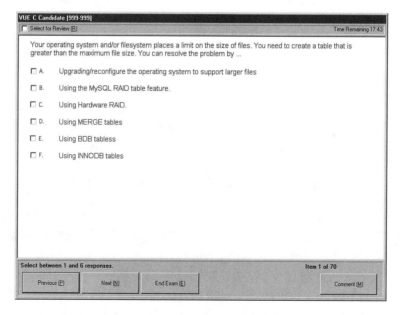

A multiple-choice/multiple-answer question. Note that each answer key has a square ("check box") beside it, and the status bar says "select between 1 and 6 responses."

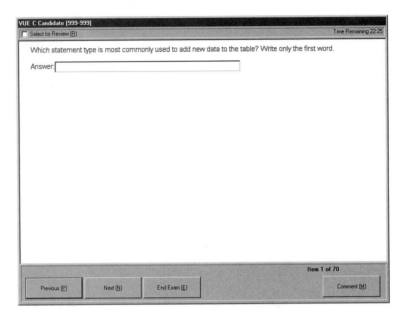

A question requiring a textual answer.

For some text questions, you might be able to think of several possible answers; however, you should *always* follow the onscreen instructions. If the instructions tell you to use only one word, use only one word. Otherwise, you're certain to receive no credit for your response.

After the Exam

Unless you're taking part in a Beta exam, you'll receive your grade as soon as you complete the exam. The test center will provide you with a score report.

If you pass, MySQL AB will mail your certificate shortly after receiving your exam results from the test center.

If you get a failing grade on the exam, you have the option of retaking it. Although MySQL AB does not place restrictions on how soon you can retake an exam, doing so is not advised until you've done some further study.

Whether you pass or fail, after you've taken any MySQL certification exam, you'll receive a letter from MySQL AB telling you how to gain access to extra information at `http://www.mysql.com`. Two main entry points into this area are

- The candidate area: `http://www.mysql.com/certification/candidate`

  Here, you will find information specially set aside for MySQL certification candidates. For example, there might be special offers, information on prereleases of new certifications, and so on.

- The results area: http://www.mysql.com/certification/results

   In this area, potential clients and employers can confirm that your certificate is valid. Access for others to this area is controlled by you, using the candidate area.

Warning

For every popular certification exam, there are always enterprising individuals who set up so-called "braindump" Internet sites, where people anonymously post questions and answers purported to be from the exam. Please note these cautions about using or contributing to these sites:

- If you use such a site, you might be misled. The answers they provide are often *wrong*. Most of the questions have never been in an exam; they exist only in the submitter's head. As a result, instead of being helpful, such sites lead to confusion.

- If you contribute to such a site by posting your own exam questions and answers, you risk forfeiting not only the certification for the exam about which you have posted details, but your involvement in the entire MySQL Certification program. You might thus never be able to regain MySQL certification credentials.

Interpreting DESCRIBE Output

You should understand how to interpret the output of the DESCRIBE *table_name* statement. This is of particular importance both for this study guide and for taking certification exams. In both cases, when it's necessary that you know the structure of a table, it will be shown as the output of a DESCRIBE statement in the same format as that displayed by the mysql program. For example, assume that a question requires you to know about a table named City. The table's structure will be presented as follows:

```
mysql> DESCRIBE City;
+-------------+----------+------+-----+---------+----------------+
| Field       | Type     | Null | Key | Default | Extra          |
+-------------+----------+------+-----+---------+----------------+
| ID          | int(11)  |      | PRI | NULL    | auto_increment |
| Name        | char(35) |      |     |         |                |
| CountryCode | char(3)  |      |     |         |                |
| District    | char(20) |      |     |         |                |
| Population  | int(11)  |      |     | 0       |                |
+-------------+----------+------+-----+---------+----------------+
```

The output of the DESCRIBE statement contains one row for each column in the table. The most important features of the output are as follows:

- The Field value indicates the name of the column.
- The Type value shows the column datatype.

- The Null indicator is the word YES if the column can contain NULL values and is empty if it cannot. In the example shown, Null is empty for all columns of the City table. This indicates that none of that table's columns can contain NULL values.

- The Key indicator may be empty or contain one of three nonempty values:

  - An empty Key value indicates that the column in question either isn't indexed or is indexed only as a secondary column in a multiple-column, nonunique index. For purposes of the exam, you should assume that if Key is empty, it's because the column is not indexed at all.

  - If the Key value is the keyword PRI (as in the output shown for the ID column), this indicates that the column is a PRIMARY KEY or is one of the columns in a multiple-column PRIMARY KEY.

  - If the Key value is the keyword UNI, this indicates that the column is the first column of a unique-valued index that cannot contain NULL values.

  - If the Key value is the keyword MUL, this indicates that the column is the first column of a nonunique index or a unique-valued index that can contain NULL values.

  It's possible that more than one of the Key values may apply to a given column of a table. For example, a column that is a PRIMARY KEY might also be part of other indexes. When it's possible for more than one of the Key values to describe an index, DESCRIBE displays the one with the highest priority, in the order PRI, UNI, MUL.

  Because a column can be part of several indexes, the Key values do not necessarily provide an exhaustive description of a table's indexes. However, for purposes of the exam, you should assume that the table descriptions given provide all the information needed to correctly answer the question.

- Default shows the column's default value. This is the value that MySQL assigns to the column when a statement that creates a new record does not provide an explicit value for the column. (For example, this can happen with the INSERT, REPLACE, and LOAD DATA INFILE statements.)

- The Extra value displays other details about the column. The only Extra detail about which you need be concerned for the exam is the value auto_increment. This value indicates that the column has the AUTO_INCREMENT attribute. (The ID column shown in the example is such an instance.)

You can read more about indexing, column datatypes, default values, and the AUTO_INCREMENT column option in Chapter 4, "Data Definition Language."

Sample Tables

This study guide uses several different database and table names in examples. However, one set of tables occurs repeatedly: the tables in a database named world. This section discusses the structure of these tables. Throughout this study guide, you're assumed to be familiar with them.

The `world` database contains three tables, `Country`, `City`, and `CountryLanguage`:

- The `Country` table contains a row of information for each country in the database:

```
mysql> DESCRIBE Country;
+----------------+------------------+------+-----+---------+-------+
| Field          | Type             | Null | Key | Default | Extra |
+----------------+------------------+------+-----+---------+-------+
| Code           | char(3)          |      | PRI |         |       |
| Name           | char(52)         |      |     |         |       |
| Continent      | enum('Asia', ...)|      |     | Asia    |       |
| Region         | char(26)         |      |     |         |       |
| SurfaceArea    | float(10,2)      |      |     | 0.00    |       |
| IndepYear      | smallint(6)      | YES  |     | NULL    |       |
| Population     | int(11)          |      |     | 0       |       |
| LifeExpectancy | float(3,1)       | YES  |     | NULL    |       |
| GNP            | float(10,2)      | YES  |     | NULL    |       |
| GNPOld         | float(10,2)      | YES  |     | NULL    |       |
| LocalName      | char(45)         |      |     |         |       |
| GovernmentForm | char(45)         |      |     |         |       |
| HeadOfState    | char(60)         | YES  |     | NULL    |       |
| Capital        | int(11)          | YES  |     | NULL    |       |
| Code2          | char(2)          |      |     |         |       |
+----------------+------------------+------+-----+---------+-------+
```

The entire output of the DESCRIBE statement is too wide to display on the page, so the Type value for the Continent line has been shortened. The value enum('Asia', …) as shown actually stands for enum('Asia', 'Europe', 'North America', 'Africa', 'Oceania', 'Antarctica', 'South America').

- The `City` table contains rows about cities located in countries listed in the `Country` table:

```
mysql> DESCRIBE City;
+-------------+----------+------+-----+---------+----------------+
| Field       | Type     | Null | Key | Default | Extra          |
+-------------+----------+------+-----+---------+----------------+
| ID          | int(11)  |      | PRI | NULL    | auto_increment |
| Name        | char(35) |      |     |         |                |
| CountryCode | char(3)  |      |     |         |                |
| District    | char(20) |      |     |         |                |
| Population  | int(11)  |      |     | 0       |                |
+-------------+----------+------+-----+---------+----------------+
```

- The CountryLanguage table describes languages spoken in countries listed in the Country table:

```
mysql> DESCRIBE CountryLanguage;
+-------------+---------------+------+-----+---------+-------+
| Field       | Type          | Null | Key | Default | Extra |
+-------------+---------------+------+-----+---------+-------+
| CountryCode | char(3)       |      | PRI |         |       |
| Language    | char(30)      |      | PRI |         |       |
| IsOfficial  | enum('T','F') |      |     | F       |       |
| Percentage  | float(3,1)    |      |     | 0.0     |       |
+-------------+---------------+------+-----+---------+-------+
```

The Name column in the Country table contains full country names. Each country also has a three-letter country code stored in the Code column. The City and CountryLanguage tables each have a column that contains country codes as well, though the column is named CountryCode in those tables.

In the CountryLanguage table, note that each country may have multiple languages. For example, Finnish, Swedish, and several other languages are spoken in Finland. For this reason, CountryLanguage has a composite (multiple-column) index consisting of both the Country and Language columns.

Summary

This introduction provided background information and general hints on what to expect from the exam, what to do in order to take the exam, what happens on the day of the exam, and what happens once you have passed the test. Advice on how to understand the questions was provided as well.

When you are done studying the chapters (and answering all the example questions!), and are ready to sign up for the exam, you should return to this introduction and re-read the sections on taking the exam. That way, you are fully prepared for the exam when the day arrives.

1

MySQL and MySQL AB

This chapter covers the following exam topics:

- The difference between MySQL and MySQL AB
- How MySQL AB operates
- MySQL core values
- MySQL dual licensing
- Organization and structure of the MySQL reference manual
- The MySQL mailing lists

Questions on the material in this chapter make up approximately 10% of the exam.

Among the things you need to understand about MySQL is the difference between the *product MySQL* and the *company MySQL AB*. This chapter describes the nature of this difference. It also provides some general information about MySQL AB, licensing issues for MySQL, and how to get information about MySQL.

1.1 The Difference Between MySQL and MySQL AB

The name "MySQL" is sometimes used to refer to the MySQL database management system and sometimes to the company behind it. The company is more properly known as MySQL AB. MySQL is the DBMS product that MySQL AB owns, develops, and sells— that is, the database server software called "MySQL" and related products, such as client programs for communicating with the server and programming interfaces for developing new clients.

As a side note, the "AB" part of the company name is the acronym for the Swedish "aktiebolag," or "stock company." Thus, the name translates to "MySQL Inc." In fact, MySQL Inc. and MySQL GmbH are examples of MySQL AB subsidiaries. They're located in the USA and Germany, respectively. This isn't something you need to know for the exam.

1.2 How MySQL AB Operates

It might seem odd for a certification exam to require you to know about the company behind the product. However, MySQL AB *is* a company that does things differently, and in order to understand how licenses work and how to make use of MySQL most effectively, knowledge of how the company operates is considered essential for anyone working with the products provided by the company.

To understand MySQL AB's business model, it's important to realize that all the software MySQL AB creates is distributed using one of two licenses:

- The *GNU General Public License* (GPL), which allows anyone to use the software without restrictions provided they either do not redistribute the software *or* that they redistribute the software under the same license. Usage of MySQL under the GPL comes at no cost.

- A *Commercial License*, which allows the license holder to redistribute the software in a less restricted manner. Commercial licenses must be paid for, but are relatively inexpensive.

Section 1.4, "MySQL Dual Licensing," covers the different license types in greater detail. The largest number of installations of MySQL are used under the GPL.

In addition to selling commercial licenses, MySQL AB also provides professional services, such as the following:

- Selling *support services* to companies that use MySQL. Companies purchase these services as insurance to make sure that they have a MySQL developer available if needed.

- Selling *consulting services* to companies that have a need for assistance outside the scope provided by the support services.

- Selling *training services* to companies and individuals who want to gain a better understanding of the MySQL products.

1.3 MySQL Core Values

MySQL the product and MySQL AB the company owe their success to a few core values that are very different from those of other leading DBMS and software development companies. These values have to do with the roots of MySQL and the Open Source community.

The mission statement of MySQL AB is summed up in a single sentence: *To make superior data management software available and affordable for all.* This goal is achieved by three means:

- Adhering to a set of *server development goals* when authoring the MySQL software

- Identifying a number of *core values* that MySQL AB, its employees, and any partners are expected to adhere to

- *Dual Licensing,* as outlined earlier in this chapter, and described in more detail in section 1.4, "MySQL Dual Licensing"

These core values direct how MySQL AB works with the MySQL server software:

- To be the best and the most widely used database in the world
- To be available and affordable for all
- To be easy to use
- To be continuously improved while remaining fast and safe
- To be fun to use and improve
- To be free from bugs

These are the core values of the company MySQL AB and its employees:

- We subscribe to the Open Source philosophy
- We aim to be good citizens
- We prefer partners that share our values and mindset
- We answer email and provide support
- We are a virtual company, networking with others

Dual licensing is described in more detail in section 1.4, "MySQL Dual Licensing."

1.4 MySQL Dual Licensing

MySQL AB software is covered by licenses that govern the conditions under which it can be used. This section describes those conditions.

MySQL AB owns the copyright to the MySQL source code. This means that MySQL AB can distribute MySQL under several different licenses, depending on the needs of the user. Currently, two types of licenses are used to distribute the MySQL database server:

- The *GNU General Public License* (GPL) is intended for open source usage of MySQL, where applications based on MySQL are also distributed under the GPL.
- *Commercial licensing* is intended for commercial usage of MySQL, where applications based on MySQL can be distributed without publishing the source.

In some cases, most notably for programs released under Open Source licenses other than the GPL, exceptions are granted. However, the two license types discussed here are the ones used in almost all cases. They are the ones you need to understand for purposes of studying for the exam.

The MySQL dual licensing covers these products:

- All the MySQL-specific sources in the server.
- The MySQL client interfaces: the libmysqlclient C client library, MySQL Connector/ODBC, and MySQL Connector/J.
- Client programs such as MySQLCC (MySQL Control Center), mysql, mysqladmin, and mysqldump.

Dual licensing does not cover documentation produced by MySQL AB. Documentation is covered by copyright.

1.4.1 Use of MySQL Under the General Public License

The GNU General Public License (GPL) was created to govern the rules of using free software (where "free" refers to liberty, not price). For more information on the GPL, refer to `http://www.gnu.org/licenses`.

Quoting the philosophy of free software from `http://www.gnu.org/philosophy/free-sw.html`:

Free software is a matter of the users' freedom to run, copy, distribute, study, change and improve the software. More precisely, it refers to four kinds of freedom, for the users of the software:

- *The freedom to run the program, for any purpose (freedom 0).*
- *The freedom to study how the program works, and adapt it to your needs (freedom 1). Access to the source code is a precondition for this.*
- *The freedom to redistribute copies so you can help your neighbor (freedom 2).*
- *The freedom to improve the program, and release your improvements to the public, so that the whole community benefits (freedom 3). Access to the source code is a precondition for this.*

Many developers want to pose restrictions on the usage of their programs with regard to the freedoms of software as defined by `http://www.gnu.org`. In such cases, the developers prefer not to abide by the GPL in their usage of MySQL and must therefore purchase commercial licenses from MySQL AB.

You can think of MySQL AB offering you two choices when it comes to the cost of a MySQL license:

- You pay a price in money, as for other commercial software.
- You pay a price in offering your users the same freedoms to use your programs that MySQL AB offers you through the GPL.

As a consequence of the GPL, MySQL is also free of charge for those who never copy, modify, or distribute the MySQL software. As long as you never distribute (internally or externally) the MySQL Software in any way, you're free to use it for powering your application, whether or not your application is under GPL license.

1.4.2 Use of MySQL with a Commercial License

If you use MySQL software but don't want to adhere to the GPL, you can purchase a commercial license from MySQL AB.

If your application isn't licensed under GPL or a compatible Open Source Initiative (OSI) license approved by MySQL AB and you intend to distribute MySQL software (either internally or externally), you must first obtain a commercial license for the MySQL software in question. More specifically:

- If you include the MySQL server in your non-open source application, you need a commercial license for the MySQL server.

n If you include one or more of the MySQL drivers in your non-open source application so that your application can run with MySQL, you need a commercial license for the drivers in question. The MySQL drivers currently include the `libmysqlclient` C client library, MySQL Connector/ODBC, and MySQL Connector/J.

- If you use MySQL software within your organization and you don't want to risk having it fall under the GPL license, you should purchase a commercial license.

- Many users opt for the commercial license simply because, under it, MySQL AB takes responsibility for its products. Under the GPL license, there are no warranties or representations from the developer, which is MySQL AB in this case.

1.5 Organization and Structure of the MySQL Reference Manual

The *MySQL Reference Manual* is MySQL AB's primary documentation for the MySQL server and related products. It's included with distributions of MySQL software and is also available in several forms and languages online.

There are two main methods of accessing the online documentation:

- By going to the address `http://www.mysql.com/doc`.
- By using your browser to request the page `http://www.mysql.com/`*keyword*, where *keyword* is a section name from the reference manual. For example, typing **INSERT** in place of *keyword* will take you to the section of the manual that describes the INSERT statement.

1.5.1 General Reference Manual Organization

The *MySQL Reference Manual* consists of the following main sections:

- General description of MySQL (the product) and MySQL AB (the company).
  - Information on licensing of the MySQL software.
  - Information on the MySQL server development roadmap (features planned for future versions).
  - Notes on MySQL and the SQL standards. To which standards does MySQL adhere? Which extensions to the standards does MySQL provide?

- How to install and upgrade MySQL.
    - Configuring and administering the MySQL server.
    - Server utilities. What scripts are available for starting and stopping the server? How do I set up multiple servers on the same machine?
    - Security issues. How do I make MySQL secure against crackers? How does the privilege system work? How do I add and remove users?

- A short MySQL tutorial.
- Database administration.
    - Backup and recovery of data.
    - Database administration. How do I create a database or a table? How do I repair broken tables? How do I optimize the tables?

- International support. How do I make MySQL sort strings according to my preferred language's alphabetic sort order?
- Optimization. How do I make my queries run faster?
- Client-side programs and scripts. How do I use the command-line client? How do I import and export data? How do I find out what those pesky error codes mean?
- Using MySQL.
    - Language reference. How do I write SQL statements?
    - Column datatypes. What's the correct datatype for the data that I want to store? What are the limits of each datatype?
    - Storage engines. Which table type is the correct one to use for my task?

- Programming interfaces. How do I interface my PHP, Perl, or C/C++ program to a MySQL server? How do I use ODBC with MySQL?
- Error handling. How do I track down the causes of errors?

1.5.2 MySQL Reference Manual Change Notes

One appendix in the *MySQL Reference Manual* contains the MySQL Change Notes. This list of changes and updates for each version of MySQL is one of the more important sections of the manual, especially if you work with MySQL installations over which you have no control (for example, if you have an account with a Web hosting provider).

By checking the Change Notes, you can find the changes and bug fixes that have been made to MySQL over time. If you cannot otherwise track down an error, this might be the place to look. For example, a common problem is that a statement does not work because it relies on a feature that was introduced more recently than the version of MySQL you're using. The Change Notes can help clarify this.

1.6 The MySQL Mailing Lists

MySQL AB provides several mailing lists in various languages. You can use these lists to obtain information and help on all things related to MySQL. Messages that are sent to a list via email are distributed to each subscriber to the list. The general mailing list is a good way to ask questions and get answers. The list takes advantage of, and provides access to, the aggregate knowledge and experience of the subscriber base. More specific lists exist for purposes such as distributing announcements of new software releases.

The most important English language mailing lists are:

- *announce*—This list is for announcements of new versions of MySQL and related programs. It is a moderated low-volume list to which all MySQL users should subscribe.

- *mysql*—This is the main list for general MySQL discussion. Please note that some topics are better discussed on the more specialized lists. If you post to the wrong list, you might not get an answer.

- *win32*—This list is for discussions about the MySQL software on Microsoft Windows operating systems.

- *mysqlcc*—This list is for discussions about MySQL Control Center (MySQLCC), the MySQL graphical client.

- *myodbc*—This list is for discussions about connecting to the MySQL server with ODBC.

- *java*—This list is for discussions about MySQL Connector/J and using the MySQL server from Java programs.

To subscribe to any of these lists, visit `http://lists.mysql.com`.

1.7 Exercises

Question 1:

Is the following statement true or false?

MySQL AB can distribute MySQL software under a commercial license because it holds software patents for its software.

Question 2:

Is the following statement true or false?

The MySQL dual licensing covers only the source in the server.

Question 3:

Is the following statement true or false?

MySQL software can be used at no cost only for private purposes, and within small companies with fewer than 500 employees.

Question 4:

Assume that you have a problem installing MySQL software. Which of the following procedures would you choose to solve that problem?

   a. Send an email to `developers@mysql.com` asking for help.

   b. Send an email to `docs@mysql.com` asking for help.

   c. Send an email to `mysql@lists.mysql.com` asking for help.

Answers to Exercises

Answer 1:

False. The reason why MySQL AB can offer commercial licenses is because the company owns the copyright to the MySQL source code.

Answer 2:

False. MySQL dual licensing also covers the MySQL client interfaces, such as the C client library, and client programs, such as `mysqladmin`.

Answer 3:

False. MySQL software can be used at no cost by anyone, provided they adhere to the restrictions imposed by the GNU General Public License (GPL).

Answer 4:

`mysql@lists.mysql.com` is the main list for general MySQL discussion. It's the right place to ask for help when you encounter general problems, such as installation problems.

You should not contact the MySQL developers if you have an installation problem. However, if you have purchased commercial support from MySQL AB, a support person might get you in contact with a MySQL developer.

`docs@mysql.com` is the public address of the MySQL documentation team. You should report your problem to that address only if you find that the MySQL documentation is unclear.

2

MySQL Software

This chapter covers the following exam topics:

- Major program components used in MySQL
- Major operating system families supported by MySQL
- Differences between major MySQL distributions
- Available MySQL client interfaces

Questions on the material in this chapter make up approximately 10% of the exam.

This chapter provides a general overview of MySQL software. It describes the major components of MySQL software distributions, the type of systems on which you can expect to run MySQL successfully, the kinds of distributions available, and the client programming interfaces available.

2.1 Major Program Components Used in MySQL

MySQL operates in a networked environment using a client/server architecture. As you read the following, please keep in mind the difference between a server and a host as used in this guide: The server is software (the MySQL server program `mysqld` or a derivative name, as explained in the following text) and is defined both by the version number and whether certain features are included in or excluded from that particular version. The host is the physical machine on which the server runs. The host is defined by hardware, the operating system running on the machine, its network addresses, and so forth.

The major components of a MySQL installation are:

- `mysqld`, the server program. The database server manages access to the actual databases on disk and in memory. `mysqld` comes in several configurations, the most notable being `mysqld-max`, which contains support for BDB tables, as well as for features that have not yet proven to be totally stable and mature. On Windows, the `mysqld-nt` and `mysql-max-nt` servers provide support for named pipe connections on Windows NT, 2000, and XP.

The exact configuration of the `mysqld` versions might change over time, so whenever you download a new version, it's wise to check the documentation. For the purposes of the exam, the preceding information suffices.

- A number of `client programs`. Client programs are the programs used by the programmer or user to communicate with the server, in order to manipulate the information in the databases that the server manages. MySQL includes several standard client programs.

    - `MySQL Control Center` (also known as `MySQLCC`) is a graphical front end to the server.

    - `mysql` is a command-line program that acts as a text-based front end for the server. It's the most commonly used standard client for issuing queries and viewing the results interactively.

    - There are other command-line clients as well. These include `mysqlimport` for importing datafiles, `mysqldump` for making backups, `mysqladmin` for server administration, and `mysqlcheck` for checking the health of the database files. These are described in more detail later in this study guide.

- A few MySQL utilities that operate independently of the server. `myisamchk` is an example. It performs table checking and repair operations. Another is `myisampack`, which creates compressed read-only versions of MyISAM tables. Both utilities operate by accessing MyISAM table files directly, independent of the `mysqld` database server.

More information on using MySQL client programs and utilities is given in Chapter 3, "Using MySQL Client Programs."

2.2 Major Operating System Families Supported by MySQL

Because the server and clients communicate over network connections, it isn't necessary to run them all on the same host. Nor is it necessary that server and clients be run on hosts that use the same operating system because MySQL supports several major families of operating systems. This means that MySQL can be used in heterogeneous environments. For example, a server running on a Unix host can be accessed by clients running on Windows machines.

The major operating system families supported by MySQL include Windows, Unix, Linux, and NetWare.

- Under Windows, MySQL runs both on NT-based systems (Windows NT, Windows 2000, and Windows XP), and on non-NT systems (Windows 95, Windows 98, and Windows Me). MySQL does not run on Windows 3.1 or earlier, or on MS-DOS. (You can invoke MySQL programs from within a console window under Windows, but MySQL does not run on DOS-only systems.)

- Within the Unix family, MySQL runs on BSD-based systems such as FreeBSD, NetBSD, OpenBSD, and Mac OS X. It also runs on System V versions of Unix, such as Solaris and HP-UX.

- Within the Linux family, MySQL runs on varieties such as SuSE, RedHat, Debian, and Caldera.

- Novell and MySQL have partnered to make MySQL available on Novell NetWare. MySQL is distributed as part of NetWare 6.5.

For most purposes, Unix and Linux are identical as far as MySQL use is concerned. Therefore, unless explicitly stated otherwise, any reference to Unix elsewhere in this study guide should be taken to include Linux as well.

Although there are technical differences between the distributions of MySQL released for each operating system, cross-platform support is such that differences are usually small enough to be unnoticeable in daily use. Some operating systems are supported more extensively than others.

- For many operating systems, MySQL AB provides precompiled ("binary") distributions that are ready to be installed. In general, MySQL AB recommends that you use a binary distribution if one is available for your system.

- In some cases, binary distributions are made available by third parties. For example, SGI Irix binary distributions are provided by SGI.

- There are sometimes no binary distributions available for an operating system upon which MySQL can run. If you want to run MySQL on such an operating system, you can download the source code and compile it yourself.

Note that although binary distributions are recommended, you aren't required to use them. The source code is available to anyone, for those who prefer to compile MySQL themselves.

Another area in which distributions differ is in the level of support you can get from MySQL AB. Factors such as your operating system and the version of MySQL that you run are likely to affect your choice of support options.

2.3 Differences Between Major MySQL Distributions

In addition to supporting several operating systems, MySQL AB ships versions of MySQL that are at different stages of development.

A release series of MySQL goes through a development cycle in the following stages. The series numbers in parentheses indicate which series happens to be at a particular stage as of November 2003.

- *Pre-alpha*: No binaries are available; source code is first developed internally within MySQL AB, and then made publicly available. At this stage, new features are added, internal tests are applied, and bugs are fixed. (MySQL 5.0)

- *Alpha*: Binaries are available; new features are still added and bugs fixed based on both internal and external input. (MySQL 4.1)

- *Beta*: Binaries are available; no new features are added while the program stabilizes (that is, while reported bugs are being fixed).

- *Gamma*: Binaries are available and no major bugs have been found for over a month.

- *Production*: All known bugs, major and minor, have been fixed. (MySQL 4.0)

A given version of MySQL is available in different distribution formats. You can always download the source code and compile it yourself. For many systems, you can also download a precompiled binary distribution. Binary distributions vary according to their feature set. For example, there is a stripped-down distribution (MySQL Classic) that doesn't support the InnoDB storage engine, and a standard MySQL distribution that does support InnoDB. For the convenience of users who want to test recent features that have been omitted from MySQL to make the distribution smaller, MySQL AB provides the MySQL Max distribution. MySQL Max includes features such as support for geographical data (GIS), the BDB storage engine, and so on.

2.4 Available MySQL Client Interfaces

MySQL AB provides several application programming interfaces (APIs) for accessing the MySQL server:

- The C client library, `libmysqlclient`. This API may be used for writing MySQL-based C programs. It's also the basis for all higher-level APIs written for other languages (other than Java).

- MySQL Connector/ODBC provides a MySQL-specific driver for ODBC; it allows ODBC-compliant programs to access MySQL databases.

- MySQL Connector/J is a JDBC driver for use in Java programs; it allows JDBC-compliant programs to access MySQL databases.

In addition to the preceding APIs, each of which is officially supported by MySQL AB, many other client APIs are available. Most of them are based on the C client library and provide a binding for some other language. These include the PHP interface to MySQL, the DBD::mysql driver for the Perl DBI module, and interfaces for other languages such as Python, Ruby, Pascal, and Tcl. Although you can download these client APIs from the MySQL Web site and members of the MySQL AB development team often work closely with the developers of these products, the APIs do not receive official support from MySQL AB. If you're embarking on a project that involves these APIs, you should contact the developers to determine whether future support will be available.

2.5 Exercises

Question 1:

Which of the following MySQL 4.x distributions include support for InnoDB tables? Under which license are those distributions shipped?

  a. Standard

  b. Max

  c. Pro

  d. Classic

Question 2:

Is the following statement true or false?

All of the MySQL client programs and utilities communicate with the MySQL server.

Question 3:

Is the following statement true or false?

When running a MySQL server under Windows, client programs accessing that server must also run under Windows.

Question 4:

Is the following statement true or false?

A command-line program commonly used to communicate with the server is called `mysqld`.

Question 5:

Is the following statement true or false?

MySQL client programs and utilities can only be obtained from the binary distributions, as the MySQL source distributions contain only the server.

Answers to Exercises

Answer 1:

Except for the commercially licensed Classic distribution, all distributions include support for InnoDB tables. Like Classic, the Pro distribution is shipped under a commercial license, whereas Standard and Max are available under the GNU General Public License.

Answer 2:

False. There are MySQL utilities that don't communicate with the server, but work directly on MyISAM tables. Examples include `myisamchk` and `myisampack`.

Answer 3:

False. MySQL can be used in heterogeneous environments. For example, a server running on a Unix host can be accessed by clients running on Windows machines.

Answer 4:

False. The most commonly used command-line program is called `mysql`, not `mysqld`. The latter is the MySQL server.

Answer 5:

False. MySQL client programs, utilities, and the server all can be obtained both in source and in binary form.

Using MySQL Client Programs

This chapter covers the following exam topics:

- Invoking command-line client programs
- Specifying command-line options
- The `mysql` client
    - Using `mysql` interactively
    - Using script files with `mysql`
    - `mysql` client commands and SQL statements
    - Using the `---safe-updates` option
- Using `mysqlimport`
- Using `mysqldump` and reloading the dump
- Checking tables with `mysqlcheck` and `myisamchk`
- Using `MySQLCC`
- Using MySQL Connector/ODBC and MySQL Connector/J

Questions on the material in this chapter make up approximately 10% of the exam.

This chapter discusses general principles that are common to most MySQL client programs. It also describes how to use several specific types of clients:

- The interactive graphical client `MySQLCC` (MySQL Control Center). This general-purpose client provides a graphical interface to the MySQL server. It can be thought of as an extended graphical version of the character-based `mysql` client.

    `MySQLCC` is still being actively developed at the time of publication of the first Core exam. For that reason, you are expected to be familiar with the general properties and capabilities of `MySQLCC`, but you are *not* expected to know all the ins and outs of the program.

- The character-based client programs. These run either interactively or perform their job based on command-line arguments with no further input from the user. Character-based clients discussed in this chapter include:
  - mysql, a general-purpose client for issuing queries and retrieving their results. It can be used interactively or in batch mode to read queries from a file.
  - mysqladmin, an administrative client that helps you manage the server.
  - mysqlimport, a program for importing text files into databases. It provides a command-line interface to the LOAD DATA INFILE SQL statement.
  - mysqldump, a program for dumping the contents of databases. It can be used to make database backups or to copy databases to other machines.
  - mysqlcheck and myisamchk, programs for checking and repairing tables. They're useful for checking and maintaining the integrity of certain types of tables.
- The MySQL Connector drivers. These drivers provide connectivity to the MySQL server for client programs:
  - MySQL Connector/ODBC, the MySQL driver for programs that use the ODBC (Open Database Connectivity) interface.
  - MySQL Connector/J, the MySQL driver for JDBC connectivity to Java programs.

3.1 Invoking Command-Line Client Programs

MySQL client programs can be invoked from the command line; for example, from a Windows console prompt or from a Unix shell prompt. When you invoke a client program, you can specify options to control its behavior. Some options tell the client how to connect to the MySQL server. Other options tell the program what actions to perform.

This section discusses the following option-related topics:

- The general syntax for specifying options
- How to use connection parameter options
- How to specify options in an option file

Most examples in this section use the mysql program, but the general principles apply to other MySQL client programs as well.

To determine the options supported by any MySQL program, invoke the program with the --help option. For example, to find out how to use mysql, use this command:

```
shell> mysql --help
```

To determine the version of a program, use the --version option. For example:

```
shell> mysql --version
mysql  Ver 12.22 Distrib 4.0.18, for apple-darwin7.2.0 (powerpc)
```

This output indicates that the mysql client is from MySQL version 4.0.18.

3.1.1 Specifying Command-Line Options

Typically, you invoke MySQL client programs with options that indicate to the program what you want it to do. This section describes the general syntax for specifying options, as well as some of the options that are common to most MySQL clients.

3.1.1.1 Command Option Syntax

Options to MySQL programs have two general forms:

- Long options consist of a word preceded by double dashes.
- Short options consist of a single letter preceded by a single dash.

In many cases, a given option has both a long and a short form. For example, to display a program's version number, you can use the long --version option or the short -V option. These two commands are equivalent:

```
shell> mysql --version
shell> mysql -V
```

Options are case sensitive. --version is recognized by MySQL programs, but lettercase variations such as --Version or --VERSION are not. This applies to short options as well. -V and -v are both legal options, but mean different things.

Some options are followed by values. For example, when you specify the --host or -h option to indicate the host machine where the MySQL server is running, you must follow the option with the machine's hostname. For a long option, separate the option and the value by an equal sign (=). For short options, the option and the value can be, but need not be, separated by a space. The following three option formats are equivalent; each one specifies myhost.example.com as the host machine where the MySQL server is running:

```
--host=myhost.example.com
-h myhost.example.com
-hmyhost.example.com
```

In most cases, if you don't specify an option explicitly, a program will use a default value. Default values make it easier to invoke MySQL client programs because you need specify only those options for which the defaults are unsuitable. For example, the default server hostname is localhost, so if the MySQL server to which you want to connect is running on the local host, you need not specify --host or -h at all.

Exceptions to these option syntax rules are noted in the following discussion wherever relevant. The most important exception is that password options have a slightly different behavior than other options.

3.1.1.2 Connection Parameter Options

To connect to a server using a client program, the client must know upon which host the server is running. A connection may be established locally to a server running on the same host as the client program, or remotely to a server running on a different host. To connect, you must also identify yourself to the server with a username and password.

Each MySQL client has its own program-specific options, but all clients support a common set of options for making a connection to the MySQL server. This section describes the options that specify connection parameters, and how to use them if the default values aren't appropriate.

For command-line clients, all connection parameters are specified after the command name. The following discussion lists each option's long form and short form, as well as its default value. (You'll need to specify connection parameters for other types of client programs as well, such as the graphical MySQLCC client. Such a client might allow you to specify connection parameters on the command line, but might also provide an additional method of allowing you to indicate them, such as a dialog box.)

There are three options that indicate to the client where the server is running, as well as the type of connection to establish:

- --host=*host_name* or -h *host_name*

  This option specifies the machine where the MySQL server is running. The value can be a hostname or an IP number. The hostname localhost means the local host (that is, the computer on which you're running the client program). On Unix, localhost is treated in a special manner. On Windows, the value . also means the local host and is treated in a special manner as well. For a description of this special treatment, refer to the discussion of the --socket option.

  The default host value is localhost.

- --port=*port_number* or -P *port_number*

  This option indicates the port number to which to connect on the server host; it applies only to TCP/IP connections. TCP/IP is used unless you connect using a hostname value of . on Windows or localhost on Unix.

  The default MySQL port number is 3306.

- --socket=*socket_name* or -S *socket_name*

  This option's name comes from its original use for specifying a Unix domain socket file. On Unix, for a connection to the host localhost, a client connects to the server using a Unix socket file. This option specifies the pathname of that file.

On Windows, the `--socket` option is used for specifying a named pipe. For Windows NT-based systems that support named pipes, a client can connect using a pipe by specifying . as the hostname. In this case, `--socket` specifies the name of the pipe. Pipe names aren't case sensitive. (Note that NT-specific MySQL servers don't enable named pipe connections by default; the server must be started with the `--enable-named-pipe` option.)

If this option is omitted, the default Unix socket file pathname is `/tmp/mysql.sock` and the default Windows pipe name is `MySQL`.

Two options provide identification information. These are the username and password of the account that you want to use for accessing the server. The server will reject a connection attempt unless you provide values for these parameters that correspond to an account that the server recognizes:

- `--user=user_name` or `-u user_name`

  This option specifies the username for your MySQL account. To determine which account applies, the server uses the username value in conjunction with the name of the host from which you connect. This means that there can be different accounts with the same username, which can be used for connections from different hosts.

  On Unix, client programs use your system login name as your default MySQL account username. On Windows, the default MySQL account name is `ODBC`.

- `--password=pass_value` or `-ppass_value`

  This option specifies the password for your MySQL account. There is no default password. If you omit this option, your MySQL account must be set up to allow you to connect without a password.

MySQL accounts are set up using the `GRANT` statement, which is discussed in the "Professional Study Guide."

Password options are special in two ways, compared to the other connection parameter options:

- You can omit the password value after the option name. This differs from the other connection parameter options, each of which requires a value after the option name. If you omit the password value, the client program will prompt you interactively for a password, as shown here:

  ```
  shell> mysql -p
  Enter password:
  ```

  When you see the `Enter password:` prompt, type in your password and press Enter. The password isn't echoed as you type, to prevent other people from seeing it.

- If you use the short form of the password option (-p) and give the password value on the command line, there must be no space between the -p and the value. That is, -p*pass_val* is correct, but -p *pass_val* is not. This differs from the short form for other connection parameter options, where a space is allowed between the option and its value. (For example, -h*host_name* and -h *host_name* are both valid.) This exceptional requirement that there be no space between -p and the password value is a logical necessity of allowing the option parameter to be omitted.

Another option that affects how the connection setup occurs is --compress (or -C). This option causes data sent between the client and the server to be compressed before transmission and uncompressed upon receipt. The result is a reduction in the number of bytes sent over the connection, which can be helpful on slow networks. The cost is additional computational overhead for both the client and server to perform compression and uncompression. --compress and -C take no value after the option name.

Here are some examples that show how to specify connection parameters:

- Connect to the server using the default hostname and username values with no password:

```
shell> mysql
```

- Connect to the server on the local host with a username of myname, asking mysql to prompt you for a password:

```
shell> mysql --host=localhost --password --user=myname
```

- Connect with the same options as the previous example, but using the corresponding short option forms:

```
shell> mysql -h localhost -p -u myname
```

- Connect to the server at a specific IP address, with a username of myname and password of mypass:

```
shell> mysql --host=192.168.1.33 --user=myname --password=mypass
```

- Connect to the server on the local host, using the default username and password and compressing client/server traffic:

```
shell> mysql --host=localhost --compress
```

3.1.1.3 Using Option Files

As an alternative to specifying options on the command line, you can place them in an option file. The standard MySQL client programs look for option files at startup time and use any appropriate options they find there. Putting an option in an option file saves you time: You need not specify the option on the command line each time you invoke a program.

Options in option files are organized into groups, with each group preceded by a [*group-name*] line that names the group. Typically, the group name is the name of the program to which the group of options applies. For example, the [mysql] and [mysqldump] groups are for options to be used by mysql and mysqldump, respectively. The special [client] group can be used to specify options that you want all client programs to use. A common use for the [client] group is to specify connection parameters.

To write an option in an option file, use the long option format that you would use on the command line, but omit the leading dashes. Here's a sample option file:

```
[client]
host = myhost.example.com
compress

[mysql]
safe-updates
```

In this example, the [client] group specifies the server hostname and indicates that the client/server protocol should use compression for traffic sent over the network. Options in this group apply to all standard clients. The [mysql] group applies only to the mysql program. The group shown indicates that mysql should use the --safe-updates option.

Note that if an option takes a value, spaces are allowed around the = sign, something that isn't true for options specified on the command line.

Where an option file should be located depends on your operating system. The standard option files are as follows:

- On Windows, programs use the my.ini file in the Windows directory and the C:\my.cnf file.
- On Unix, the file /etc/my.cnf serves as a global option file used by all users. You can set up your own option file by creating a file named .my.cnf in your home directory.

To use an option file, create it as a plain text file using an editor. Client programs can access options from multiple option files, if they exist. It isn't an error for an option file to be missing.

To create or modify an option file, you must have write permission for it. Client programs need only read access.

To tell a program to read a specific option file instead of the standard option files, use the --defaults-file option. For example, to use the file C:\my-opts for mysql on Windows, invoke the program like this:

```
shell> mysql --defaults-file=C:\my-opts
```

If you use --defaults-file, it must be the first option after the command name.

If a program finds that an option is specified multiple times, either in the same option file or in multiple option files, the option value that occurs last takes precedence. Options specified on the command line take precedence over options found in option files.

3.1.2 Selecting a Default Database

For most client programs, you must specify a database so that the program knows where to find the tables that you want to use. The conventional way to do this is to name the database on the command line following any options. For example, to dump the contents of the world database to an output file named world.sql, you might run mysqldump like this:

```
shell> mysqldump --password --user=user_name world > world.sql
```

For the mysql client, a database name on the command line is optional. This is because you can explicitly indicate the database name for any table when you issue queries. For example, the following statement selects rows from the table Country in the world database:

```
mysql> SELECT * FROM world.Country;
```

To select or change the default database while running mysql, issue a USE db_name statement, where db_name is the name of the database you'd like to use. For example, the following statement makes world the default database:

```
mysql> USE world;
```

The advantage of selecting a default database with USE is that in subsequent queries you can refer to tables in that database without having to specify the database name. For example, with world selected as the default database, the following SELECT statements are equivalent, but the second is easier to write because the table name doesn't need to be qualified with the database name:

```
mysql> SELECT * FROM world.Country;
mysql> SELECT * FROM Country;
```

The default database is sometimes called the current database.

3.2 The mysql Client Program

The mysql client program enables you to send queries to the MySQL server and receive their results. It can be used interactively or it can read query input from a file in batch mode:

- Interactive mode is useful for day-to-day usage, for quick one-time queries, and for testing how queries work.
- Batch mode is useful for running queries that have been prewritten. It's especially valuable for issuing a complex series of queries that's difficult to enter manually, or queries that need to be run automatically by a job scheduler without user intervention.

3.2.1 Using mysql Interactively

To invoke mysql interactively from the command line, specify any necessary connection parameters after the command name:

```
shell> mysql -u user_name -p -h host_name
```

You can also provide a database name to select that database as the default database:

```
shell> mysql -u user_name -p -h host_name database_name
```

After mysql has connected to the MySQL server, it prints a mysql> prompt to indicate that it's ready to accept queries. To issue a query, enter it at the prompt. Complete the query with a statement terminator (typically a semicolon). The terminator tells mysql that the statement has been entered completely and should be executed. When mysql sees the terminator, it sends the query to the server and then retrieves and displays the result. For example:

```
mysql> SELECT DATABASE();
+------------+
| DATABASE() |
+------------+
| world      |
+------------+
```

A terminator is necessary after each statement because mysql allows several queries to be entered on a single input line. mysql uses the terminators to distinguish where each query ends, and then sends each one to the server in turn and displays its results:

```
mysql> SELECT DATABASE(); SELECT VERSION();
+------------+
| DATABASE() |
+------------+
| world      |
+------------+
+------------+
| VERSION()  |
+------------+
| 4.0.18-log |
+------------+
```

Statement terminators are necessary for another reason as well: mysql allows a single query to be entered using multiple input lines. This makes it easier to issue a long query because you can enter it over the course of several lines. mysql will wait until it sees the statement terminator before sending the query to the server to be executed. For example:

```
mysql> SELECT Name, Population FROM City
    -> WHERE Country = 'IND'
    -> AND Population > 3000000;
```

```
+--------------------+-----------+
| Name               | Population |
+--------------------+-----------+
| Mumbai (Bombay)    |  10500000 |
| Delhi              |   7206704 |
| Calcutta [Kolkata] |   4399819 |
| Chennai (Madras)   |   3841396 |
+--------------------+-----------+
```

More information about statement terminators can be found in section 3.2.3, "Statement Terminators."

In the preceding example, notice what happens when you don't complete the query on a single input line: mysql changes the prompt from mysql> to -> to indicate that it's still waiting to see the end of the statement. The full set of mysql prompts is discussed in section 3.2.4, "The mysql Prompts."

If a statement results in an error, mysql displays the error message returned by the server:

```
mysql> This is an invalid statement;
ERROR 1064: You have an error in your SQL syntax.
```

If you change your mind about a statement that you're composing, enter \c and mysql will return you to a new prompt:

```
mysql> SELECT Name, Population FROM City
    -> WHERE \c
mysql>
```

To quit mysql, use \q, QUIT, or EXIT:

```
mysql> \q
```

3.2.2 Using Editing Keys in mysql

mysql supports input-line editing, which enables you to recall and edit input lines. For example, you can use the up-arrow and down-arrow keys to move up and down through previous input lines, and the left-arrow and right-arrow keys to move back and forth within a line. Other keys, such as Backspace and Delete, erase characters from the line, and you can type in new characters at the cursor position. To submit an edited line, press Enter.

On Windows, you might find that input-line editing does not work for Windows 95, 98, or Me.

mysql also supports tab-completion to make it easier to enter queries. With tab-completion, you can enter part of a keyword or identifier and complete it using the Tab key. This feature is supported on Unix only.

3.2.3 Statement Terminators

You may use any of several statement terminators to end a query. Two statement terminators are the semicolon character (;) and the \g sequence. They're equivalent and may be used interchangeably:

```
mysql> SELECT VERSION(), DATABASE();
+-----------+-----------+
| VERSION() | DATABASE() |
+-----------+-----------+
| 4.0.18-log | world     |
+-----------+-----------+
mysql> SELECT VERSION(), DATABASE()\g
+-----------+-----------+
| VERSION() | DATABASE() |
+-----------+-----------+
| 4.0.18-log | world     |
+-----------+-----------+
```

The \G sequence also terminates queries, but causes mysql to display query results in a different style. The new style shows each output row with each column value on a separate line:

```
mysql> SELECT VERSION(), DATABASE()\G
*************************** 1. row ***************************
 VERSION(): 4.0.18-log
DATABASE(): world
```

The \G terminator is especially useful if a query produces very wide output lines. It can make the result much easier to read.

3.2.4 The mysql Prompts

The mysql> prompt displayed by mysql is just one of several different prompts that you might see when entering queries. Each type of prompt has a functional significance because mysql varies the prompt to provide information about the status of the statement you're entering. The following table shows each of these prompts:

Prompt	Meaning of Prompt
mysql>	Ready for new statement
->	Waiting for next line of statement
'>	Waiting for end of single-quoted string
">	Waiting for end of double-quoted string or identifier
`>	Waiting for end of backtick-quoted identifier

The mysql> prompt is the main (or primary) prompt. It signifies that mysql is ready for you to begin entering a new statement.

The other prompts are continuation (or secondary) prompts. mysql displays them to indicate that it's waiting for you to finish entering the current statement. The -> prompt is the most generic continuation prompt. It indicates that you have not yet completed the current statement, for example, by entering ; or \G. The '>, ">, and `> prompts are more specific. They indicate not only that you're in the middle of entering a statement, but that you're in the middle of entering a single-quoted string, a double-quoted string, or a backtick-quoted identifier, respectively. When you see one of these prompts, you'll often find that you have entered an opening quote on the previous line without also entering the proper closing quote.

If in fact you did mistype the current query by forgetting to close a quote, you can cancel the query by entering the closing quote followed by the \c clear-query command.

3.2.5 Using Script Files with mysql

When used interactively, mysql reads queries entered at the keyboard. mysql can also accept input from a file. An input file containing SQL statements to be executed is known as a "script file" or a "batch file." A script file should be a plain text file containing statements in the same format that you would use to enter the statements interactively. In particular, each statement must end with a terminator.

One way to process a script file is to execute it with a SOURCE command from within mysql:

```
mysql> SOURCE input_file;
```

Notice that there are no quotes around the name of the file.

mysql executes the queries in the file and displays any output produced.

The file must be located on the client host where you're running mysql. The filename must either be an absolute pathname listing the full name of the file, or a pathname that's specified relative to the directory in which you invoked mysql. For example, if you started mysql on a Windows machine in the C:\mysql\ directory and your script file is my_commands in the C:\scripts directory, either of the following SOURCE commands would tell mysql to run the file:

```
mysql> SOURCE C:\scripts\my_commands;
mysql> SOURCE ..\scripts\my_commands;
```

The other way to execute a script file is by naming it on the mysql command line. Invoke mysql and use the < input redirection operator to specify the file from which to read query input:

```
shell> mysql db_name < input_file
```

If a statement in a script file fails with an error, mysql ignores the rest of the file. To execute the entire file regardless of whether errors occur, invoke mysql with the --force or -f option.

A script file can itself contain SOURCE commands to execute other files. But be careful not to create a SOURCE loop. For example, if file1 contains a SOURCE file2 command, file2 should not contain a SOURCE file1 command.

3.2.6 mysql **Output Formats**

By default, mysql produces output in one of two formats, depending on whether you use it in interactive or batch mode:

- When invoked interactively, mysql displays query output in a tabular format that uses bars and dashes to display values lined up in boxed columns.
- When you invoke mysql with a file as its input source on the command line, mysql runs in batch mode with query output displayed using tab characters between data values.

To override the default output format, use these options:

- --batch or -B

  Produce batch mode (tab-delimited) output, even when running interactively.

- --table or -t

  Produce tabular output format, even when running in batch mode.

In batch mode, you can use the --raw or -r option to suppress conversion of characters such as newline and carriage return to escape-sequences like \n or \r. In raw mode, the characters are printed literally.

To select a different output format than either of the default formats, use these options:

- --html or -H

  Produce output in HTML format.

- --xml or -X

  Produce output in XML format.

3.2.7 mysql **Client Commands and SQL Statements**

When you issue an SQL statement while running mysql, the program sends the statement to the MySQL server to be executed. SELECT, INSERT, UPDATE, and DELETE are examples of this type of input. mysql also understands a number of its own commands that aren't SQL statements. The QUIT and SOURCE commands that have already been discussed are examples of mysql commands. Another example is STATUS, which displays information about the current connection to the server, as well as status information about the server itself. Here is what a status display might look like:

```
mysql> STATUS;
--------------
mysql  Ver 12.22 Distrib 4.0.18, for apple-darwin7.2.0 (powerpc)


Connection id:          14498
Current database:       world
Current user:           myname@localhost
SSL:                    Not in use
Current pager:          stdout
Using outfile:          ''
Server version:         4.0.18-log
Protocol version:       10
Connection:             Localhost via UNIX socket
Client characterset:    latin1
Server characterset:    latin1
UNIX socket:            /tmp/mysql.sock
Uptime:                 15 days 1 hour 9 min 27 sec

Threads: 4  Questions: 78712  Slow queries: 0  Opens: 786  Flush tables: 1
Open tables: 64  Queries per second avg: 0.061
--------------
```

A full list of mysql commands can be obtained using the HELP command.

mysql commands have both a long form and a short form. The long form is a full word (such as SOURCE, STATUS, or HELP). The short form consists of a backslash followed by a single character (such as \., \s, or \h). The long forms may be given in any lettercase. The short forms are case sensitive.

Unlike SQL statements, mysql commands cannot be entered over multiple lines. For example, if you issue a SOURCE file_name command to execute statements stored in a file, file_name must be given on the same line as SOURCE. It may not be entered on the next line.

By default, the short command forms are recognized on any input line, except within quoted strings. The long command forms aren't recognized except at the mysql> primary prompt. For example, CLEAR and \c both clear (cancel) the current command, which is useful if you change your mind about issuing the statement that you're currently entering. But CLEAR isn't recognized after the first line of a multiple-line statement, so you should use \c instead. To have mysql recognize the long command names on any input line, invoke it with the --named-commands option.

3.2.8 Using the --safe-updates Option

It's possible to inadvertently issue statements that modify many rows in a table or that return extremely large result sets. The --safe-updates option helps prevent these problems. The option is particularly useful for people who are just learning to use MySQL. --safe-updates has the following effects:

- UPDATE and DELETE statements are allowed only if they include a WHERE clause that specifically identifies which records to update or delete by means of a key value, or if they include a LIMIT clause.

- Output from single-table SELECT statements is restricted to no more than 1,000 rows unless the statement includes a LIMIT clause.

- Multiple-table SELECT statements are allowed only if MySQL will examine no more than 1,000,000 rows to process the query.

The --i-am-a-dummy option is a synonym for --safe-updates.

3.3 Using mysqlimport

The mysqlimport client program loads datafiles into tables. It provides a command-line interface to the LOAD DATA INFILE statement. That is, mysqlimport examines the options given on the command line and builds a LOAD DATA INFILE statement that corresponds to the actions specified by those options. It then connects to the server and, for each input file, issues the LOAD DATA INFILE statement that correctly loads the file into the appropriate table.

Because mysqlimport works this way, to use it most effectively, you should be familiar with the LOAD DATA INFILE statement. This section describes mysqlimport invocation syntax and how its options correspond to various clauses of the LOAD DATA INFILE statement. For a discussion specifically about LOAD DATA INFILE, you should also read Chapter 9, "Importing and Exporting Data." The details in that chapter aren't repeated here.

Invoke mysqlimport from the command line as follows:

```
shell> mysqlimport options db_name input_file
```

db_name names the database containing the table to be loaded and input_file names the file that contains the data to be loaded.

mysqlimport uses the filename to determine the name of the table into which the data should be loaded. The program does this by stripping off any filename extension (the last period and anything following it); the result is then used as the table name. For example, mysqlimport treats a file named City.txt or City.dat as input to be loaded into a table named City.

If you name multiple files on the command line after the database name, `mysqlimport` issues a `LOAD DATA INFILE` statement for each file.

Each table to be loaded by `mysqlimport` must already exist, and each input file should contain only data values. `mysqlimport` isn't intended for processing files that consist of SQL statements (such files can be created with the `mysqldump` program). For instructions on processing an SQL-format dump file produced by `mysqldump` that contains SQL statements, see section 3.4, "Using `mysqldump`."

The *options* part of the `mysqlimport` command may include any of the standard connection parameter options, such as `--host` or `--user`. You'll need to supply these options if the default connection parameters aren't appropriate. `mysqlimport` also understands options specific to its own operation. Invoke `mysqlimport` with the `--help` option to see a complete list of the options that can be used to tell `mysqlimport` the actions you want it to perform.

By default, input files for `mysqlimport` are assumed to contain lines terminated by newlines, with each line containing tab-separated data values. For an input file that's in a different format, use the following options to tell `mysqlimport` how to interpret the file:

- `--lines-terminated-by=string`

  string specifies the character sequence that each input line ends with. The default is \n (linefeed, also known as newline); other common line terminators are \r (carriage return) and \r\n (carriage return/linefeed pairs).

- `--fields-terminated-by=string`

  string specifies the delimiter between data values within input lines. The default delimiter is \t (tab).

- `--fields-enclosed-by=char` or `--fields-optionally-enclosed-by=char`

  char indicates a quote character that surrounds data values in the file. By default, values are assumed not to be quoted. Use this option if values are quoted. A common value for *char* is the double quote character ("). If quote characters enclose a data value, they're removed before the value is loaded into the table.

- `--fields-escaped-by=char`

  By default, \ within the input is taken as an escape character that signifies a special sequence. For example, if the \N sequence occurs alone in a field, it's interpreted as a NULL value. Use this option to specify a different escape character. To turn escaping off (no escape character), specify an empty value for *char*.

The preceding options give you the flexibility to load input files containing data in a variety of formats. Some examples follow; each one loads an input file named `City.txt` into the `City` table in the `world` database. Commands that are shown on multiple lines should be entered on a single line.

The following command loads a file that has lines ending in carriage return/linefeed pairs:

```
shell> mysqlimport --lines-terminated-by="\r\n" world City.txt
```

Note that the `--lines-terminated-by` value is quoted with double quotes. Format option values often contain special characters, such as backslash, that might have special meaning to your command interpreter. It might be necessary to quote such characters to tell your command interpreter to pass them, unchanged, to `mysqlimport`.

The syntax for specifying a double quote is trickier and depends on which command interpreter you use. The following command loads a datafile containing values quoted by double quote characters:

```
shell> mysqlimport --fields-terminated-by='"' world City.txt
```

This command should work on most Unix shells, which allow the double quote character to be quoted within single quotes. This doesn't work on Windows, where you must specify a double quote within a double-quoted string by escaping it:

```
shell> mysqlimport --fields-terminated-by="\"" world City.txt
```

The following command loads a file that has data values separated by commas, and lines ending with carriage returns:

```
shell> mysqlimport --fields-terminated-by=,
          --lines-terminated-by="\r" world City.txt
```

Other `mysqlimport` options provide additional control over datafile loading. The following list discusses some of those you're likely to find useful:

- `--ignore` or `--replace`

  These options tell `mysqlimport` how to handle input records that contain unique key values that are already present in the table. Such records result in duplicate-key errors and cannot be loaded by default. `--ignore` causes duplicates in the input file to be ignored. `--replace` causes existing records in the table to be replaced by duplicates in the input file.

- `--local`

  By default, a datafile to be loaded into a table is assumed to reside on the server host, allowing the server to read the file directly. This is very efficient, but requires the user running `mysqlimport` to have the `FILE` privilege (a powerful privilege normally reserved for administrators). The `--local` option allows use of a datafile that's located locally on the client host where `mysqlimport` is invoked. With `--local`, `mysqlimport` reads the datafile and sends it over the network to the server. This allows `mysqlimport` to read any file on the client host to which the invoker has access, without requiring the invoker to have the `FILE` privilege. For the `--local` option to work, the server must be configured to allow local files to be transferred to it.

3.4 Using `mysqldump`

The `mysqldump` client program dumps table contents to files. The program is useful for making database backups or for transferring database contents to another server. `mysqldump` can produce SQL-format dump files that contain CREATE TABLE and INSERT statements for re-creating the dumped files or it can produce tab-delimited datafiles. This section describes how to produce SQL-format dump files. Knowledge of tab-delimited dump files is not needed for the Core exam; that topic is discussed in the "Professional Study Guide."

3.4.1 General `mysqldump` Operation

`mysqldump` has three general modes of operation, depending on how it's invoked:

- By default, `mysqldump` interprets its first nonoption argument as a database name and dumps all the tables in that database. If any other arguments follow the database name, `mysqldump` interprets them as table names and dumps just those tables. The following command dumps the contents of all the tables in the `world` database into a file named `world.sql`:

```
shell> mysqldump world > world.sql
```

The contents of the `world.sql` file will begin something like this (statements to create and load the other tables in the database would follow the partial display shown here):

```
-- MySQL dump 9.10
--
-- Host: localhost    Database: world
-------------------------------------------------------------
-- Server version    4.0.18-log


--
-- Table structure for table 'City'
--

CREATE TABLE City (
  ID int(11) NOT NULL auto_increment,
  Name char(35) NOT NULL default '',
  CountryCode char(3) NOT NULL default '',
  District char(20) NOT NULL default '',
  Population int(11) NOT NULL default '0',
  PRIMARY KEY  (ID)
) TYPE=MyISAM;


--
-- Dumping data for table 'City'
--
```

```
INSERT INTO City VALUES (1,'Kabul','AFG','Kabol',1780000);
INSERT INTO City VALUES (2,'Qandahar','AFG','Qandahar',237500);
INSERT INTO City VALUES (3,'Herat','AFG','Herat',186800);
INSERT INTO City VALUES (4,'Mazar-e-Sharif','AFG','Balkh',127800);
INSERT INTO City VALUES (5,'Amsterdam','NLD','Noord-Holland',731200);
INSERT INTO City VALUES (6,'Rotterdam','NLD','Zuid-Holland',593321);
...
```

The following command names just the City and Country tables after the database name, so mysqldump dumps just those tables to a file called city_country.sql:

```
shell> mysqldump world City Country > city_country.sql
```

- With the --databases (or -B) option, mysqldump interprets any nonoption argument as a database name and dumps all the tables in each of the named databases. For example, the following command dumps both the world and test databases into a single file:

```
shell> mysqldump --databases world test > world_and_test.sql
```

- With the --all-databases (or -A) option, mysqldump dumps all tables in all databases. For example, this command writes a backup for all databases to the file alldb.sql:

```
shell> mysqldump --all-databases > alldb.sql
```

If you manage a lot of data, alldb.sql will be very large. Be sure that you have sufficient free disk space before issuing such a command.

mysqldump understands the standard connection parameter options, such as --host and --user. You'll need to supply these options if the default connection parameters aren't appropriate. mysqldump also understands options that provide more specific control over the dump operation. Invoke mysqldump with the --help option to see a list of available options. Those options described here are ones you're likely to find most useful:

- --add-drop-table

  Instructs mysqldump to precede the dump output for each table with a DROP TABLE statement that drops the table. This option ensures that when you reload the dump output, the reload operation removes any existing copy of the table before re-creating it.

- --all or -a

  Instructs mysqldump to produce CREATE TABLE statements that include all the MySQL-specific options (such as the table type and table comment) with which each table was created. By default, mysqldump does not include all these options, resulting in dump files that might be more portable for loading with a DBMS other than MySQL. With the --all option, tables created during reloading into MySQL will have the same options as the original tables.

- `--extended-insert` or `-e`

  By default, `mysqldump` writes each row as a separate `INSERT` statement. This option produces multiple-row `INSERT` statements that add several rows to the table at a time. Multiple-row statements can be reloaded more efficiently, although they're less readable than single-row statements if you examine the dump output. They're also less portable and might not be understood by other database systems.

- `--no-create-db` or `-n`

  Normally, when you run `mysqldump` with the `--all-databases` or `--databases` option, the program precedes the dump output for each database with a `CREATE DATABASE` statement to ensure that the database is created if it doesn't already exist. The `--no-create-db` option causes `CREATE DATABASE` statements not to be written. Note that their presence in the file is usually not a problem. They include an `IF NOT EXISTS` clause, so they're ignored when reloading the dump file for any database that does exist.

- `--no-create-info` or `-t`

  This option suppresses the `CREATE TABLE` statement that normally precedes the `INSERT` statements containing a table's data. Use this option when you're interested in dumping only a table's data. The option is useful mostly when you plan to reload the data into tables that already exist.

- `--no-data` or `-d`

  This option suppresses the `INSERT` statements containing table data. Use this option when you're interested in dumping only the `CREATE TABLE` statements that describe table structures. The `--no-data` option provides an easy way to get a dump file that can be processed to create empty tables with the same structure as the original tables.

- `--opt`

  This option turns on a set of additional options to make the dump and reload operations more efficient. Specifically, it's equivalent to using the `--add-drop-table`, `--add-locks`, `--all`, `--quick`, `--extended-insert`, `--lock-tables`, and `--disable-keys` options together. Note that this option makes the output less portable and less likely to be understood by other database systems.

- `--quick`

  This option tells `mysqldump` to write dump output as it reads each row from the server, which might be useful for large tables. By default, `mysqldump` reads all rows from a table into memory before writing the output; for large tables, this requires large amounts of memory, possibly causing the dump to fail.

3.4.2 Reloading `mysqldump` Output

To reload an SQL-format dump file produced by `mysqldump`, process it with `mysql`. For example, to make a copy of the `Country` table from the `world` database in the `test` database, you could issue these commands:

```
shell> mysqldump --opt world Country > dump.sql
shell> mysql test < dump.sql
```

mysql can read from a pipe, so you can combine the use of mysqldump and mysql into a single command. The preceding example can thus be written as one command:

```
shell> mysqldump --opt world Country | mysql test
```

This technique also can be used to copy databases or tables over the network to another server. For example, the following command uses a pipe to copy the Country table from the world database on the local host to the world database on the remote host other.host.com:

```
shell> mysqldump --opt world Country | mysql -h other.host.com world
```

3.5 Checking Tables with mysqlcheck and myisamchk

The mysqlcheck and myisamchk programs are used to check and repair tables (primarily MyISAM tables). They can help you keep your tables free from problems, or repair them if problems do occur—for example, if a MyISAM table becomes damaged as the result of a server crash.

mysqlcheck and myisamchk are similar in purpose, but they do have some differences. Here's a comparison of the two programs:

Both programs can check, repair, and analyze MyISAM tables. mysqlcheck also can optimize MyISAM tables, as well as check InnoDB tables and analyze BDB tables. There are certain operations that myisamchk can perform that mysqlcheck cannot, such as disabling or enabling indexes, although these operations aren't discussed in this study guide.

The two programs differ significantly in their mode of operation. mysqlcheck is a client program that communicates with the MySQL server over a network connection. It provides a command-line interface to the table-maintenance SQL statements supported by the server, such as CHECK TABLE and REPAIR TABLE. mysqlcheck determines which options were given on the command line, and then sends appropriate SQL statements to the MySQL server to perform the requested operation. This means that mysqlcheck requires the server to be running. It also means that you can use mysqlcheck to connect to remote servers. In contrast, myisamchk isn't a client program. It's a utility that operates directly on the files that represent MyISAM tables. This means that you must run myisamchk on the server host where those files are located. In addition, you need filesystem read privileges on those files for table checking operations, and write privileges for table repair operations.

The two programs also differ in their relationship with the server while they're running. With mysqlcheck, there's no problem of interaction with the server because mysqlcheck asks the server itself to do the work of checking and repairing the tables. With myisamchk, you need to make sure that the server doesn't have the tables open and isn't using them at the same time. It's possible to get incorrect results or even to cause table damage if table files are used by myisamchk and the server simultaneously. The most certain way to avoid conflict is to bring the server down while running myisamchk. It's also possible to lock the tables while checking or repairing them with myisamchk, but the procedure is not described here. You can find the details in the *MySQL Reference Manual*.

The rest of this section describes how to use mysqlcheck and myisamchk.

mysqlcheck has three general modes of operation, depending on how it is invoked:

- By default, mysqlcheck interprets its first nonoption argument as a database name and checks all the tables in that database. If any other arguments follow the database name, mysqlcheck treats them as table names and checks just those tables. For example, the first of the following commands checks all the tables in the world database; the second checks just the City and Country tables in that database:

```
shell> mysqlcheck world
shell> mysqlcheck world City Country
```

- With the --databases (or -B) option, mysqlcheck interprets its nonoption arguments as database names and checks all the tables in each of the named databases. The following command checks the tables in both the world and test databases:

```
shell> mysqlcheck --databases world test
```

- With the --all-databases (or -A) option, mysqlcheck checks all tables in all databases:

```
shell> mysqlcheck --all-databases
```

The procedure for using myisamchk is quite different, due to the need to avoid using tables at the same time the server might be accessing them. Use myisamchk as follows:

1. Stop the server so that it cannot access the tables while you're working with them.
2. From a command prompt, change location into the database directory where the tables are located. This will be the subdirectory of the server's data directory that has the same name as the database containing the tables you would like to check. (The reason for changing location is to make it easier to refer to the table files. You can skip this step if you like, but you'll have to specify to myisamchk the directory where the tables are located.)
3. Invoke myisamchk with options indicating the operation you want performed, followed by arguments that name the tables on which myisamchk should operate. Each of these arguments can be either a table name or the name of the table's index file. An index file-name is the same as the table name, plus an .MYI suffix.

The default myisamchk operation is to check tables. If that's what you want to do, no options are necessary and you need only name the table or tables to be checked. For example, to check a table named City, either of these commands will do:

```
shell> myisamchk City
shell> myisamchk City.MYI
```

To repair a table, use the `--recover` option:

```
shell> myisamchk --recover City
```

`mysqlcheck` and `myisamchk` both take many options to control the type of table maintenance operation performed. The following list summarizes some of the more commonly used options. For the most part, the list contains options that are understood by both programs. Where this isn't the case, it's noted in the relevant option description.

- `--analyze` or `-a`

  Analyze the distribution of key values in the table. This can improve performance of queries by speeding up index-based lookups.

- `--auto-repair` (`mysqlcheck` only)

  Repair tables automatically if a check operation discovers problems.

- `--check` or `-c`

  Check tables for problems. This is the default action if no other operation is specified.

- `--check-only-changed` or `-C`

  Skip table checking except for tables that have been changed since they were last checked or tables that haven't been properly closed. The latter condition might occur if the server crashes while a table is open.

- `--fast` or `-F`

  Skip table checking except for tables that haven't been properly closed.

- `--extended` (for `mysqlcheck`), `--extend-check` (for `myisamchk`), or `-e` (for both programs)

  Run an extended table check. For `mysqlcheck`, when this option is given in conjunction with a repair option, a more thorough repair is performed than when the repair option is given alone. That is, the repair operation performed by `mysqlcheck --repair --extended` is more thorough than the operation performed by `mysqlcheck --repair`.

- `--medium-check` or `-m`

  Run a medium table check.

- `--quick` or `-q`

  For `mysqlcheck`, `--quick` without a repair option causes only the index file to be checked, leaving the datafile alone. For both programs, `--quick` in conjunction with a repair option causes the program to repair only the index file, leaving the datafile alone.

- `--repair` (for `mysqlcheck`), `--recover` (for `myisamchk`), or `-r` (for both programs)

  Run a table repair operation.

3.6 Using MySQLCC

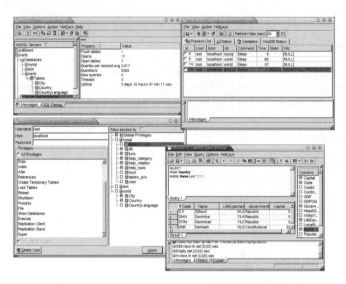

The MySQL Control Center (MySQLCC).

The MySQLCC (MySQL Control Center) program provides a graphical interface to the MySQL server. Precompiled binaries are currently available for Windows and Linux. MySQLCC can also be compiled from source.

The design goals of the MySQLCC graphical client are:

- To create a cross-platform client program that's as easy to use for novice users as the market-leading graphical database front ends.

- To create a client program that's as practical to use for experienced mysql client users as it is for novices, so that all users will prefer MySQLCC whenever the operating system provides them with a graphical user interface.

- To cover all common functions of the character-based clients while adding some frequently needed analysis tools.

MySQLCC is downloaded separately from MySQL Server and was at Version 0.9.4 (Beta) at the beginning of 2004.

The following list describes some of the features offered by MySQLCC:

- Interactive query entry and editing, including syntax highlighting and tab-completion. Syntax highlighting helps you see and understand the structure of queries more readily. With tab-completion, you can enter part of a keyword or identifier and complete it using the Tab key.

- A status window that provides easy access to the server's variables and status indicators. The window displays the output from the SHOW VARIABLES and SHOW STATUS statements.

- Capabilities for administering the server. For example, if you connect to the server using an account that has the appropriate privileges, you can flush logs, kill client connections, or tell the server to shut down.
- Capabilities for managing and administering user accounts.

3.7 MySQL Connectivity Drivers

MySQL AB provides drivers that aren't programs in themselves, but act as bridges to the MySQL server for client programs that speak a particular protocol. This section discusses Connector/ODBC and Connector/J, two drivers that provide connectivity to the MySQL server for programs that communicate using ODBC and JDBC, respectively.

The MySQL connectors are available for Windows and Unix. To use a connector, you must install it on the client host. It isn't necessary for the server to be running on the same machine or for the server to be running the same operating system as the client. This means that MySQL connectors are very useful for providing MySQL connectivity in heterogeneous environments. For example, people who use Windows machines can run ODBC or JDBC applications as clients that access MySQL databases located on a Linux server host.

3.7.1 MySQL Connector/ODBC

MySQL Connector/ODBC acts as a bridge between the MySQL server and client programs that use the ODBC standard. It provides a MySQL-specific driver for ODBC so that ODBC-based clients can access MySQL databases.

MySQL Connector/ODBC is based on the C client library. It converts ODBC calls made by the client program into C API operations that communicate with the server.

3.7.2 MySQL Connector/J

MySQL Connector/J is similar in spirit to Connector/ODBC, but is used by JDBC-based Java programs. It implements the client/server communication protocol directly and isn't based on the C client library. MySQL Connector/J converts JDBC calls made by the client program into the appropriate protocol operations.

3.8 Exercises

Question 1:

If you connect to a local server on a Unix machine using the hostname `localhost`, will the connection be made using TCP/IP or a Unix socket file? How will the connection be made if you use the local host's actual name?

Question 2:

Which connection parameters identify you to the MySQL server?

Question 3:

You want to execute a number of prewritten queries using the MySQL server running on the host db.myexample.com. Your mysql username is juan and you want to be prompted for your password. The prewritten queries are stored in the file /tmp/queries.sql and you want world to be the default database. What command do you issue?

Question 4:

Having connected to a server with the mysql client program, you want to run a query and display its output vertically. What statement terminator do you use to end the query?

Question 5:

Using mysql, you're about to enter a record into a table that has only one column. You've typed INSERT INTO tbl VALUES ('teststring and pressed Enter. Now the prompt looks like this: '>. What do you enter to perform the following operations?

a. Send a valid query to the server

b. Cancel the query

Question 6:

In an interactive session using mysql, you want to insert records into a table in the test database using a text file containing INSERT statements. The file is named tbl_import.sql and resides in /tmp. What command do you use to process the file in the following ways?

a. Within the mysql session

b. From the shell of your operating system

Question 7:

You're in the process of entering a long SQL statement in mysql and you decide not to send it to the server. What do you type to cancel the statement?

Question 8:

How do you back up the tables City and Country from the world database into the file /tmp/world_backup.sql using a single mysqldump command?

Question 9:

How do you back up the databases db1 and db2 into the file /tmp/db1_db2_backup.sql with a single mysqldump command that ensures existing tables will be overwritten when you restore them?

Question 10:

What are the advantages and disadvantages of the multiple-row INSERT statements `mysqldump` can produce?

Question 11:

You want to produce a backup of the `test` database into the file `/backups/structure.sql` using `mysqldump`. However, the purpose of the backup file is to create an empty copy of each table on another server. What command do you issue?

Question 12:

How do you restore a backup of tables in the `test` database from a backup file called `/backups/back.sql`? What options can you use with `mysqldump` to ensure existing tables will be overwritten when the tables are restored? If you don't use this `mysqldump` option, what option can you use when you restore the tables to ensure that the restore operation doesn't stop when it finds that a table already exists in the database?

Question 13:

Describe the main difference between `mysqlcheck` and `myisamchk`.

Question 14:

For which table types can you use `mysqlcheck`?

Question 15:

For which table types can you use `myisamchk`?

Question 16:

In addition to providing access to your database, `MySQLCC` serves as a graphical tool for server administration.

   a. What administrative actions does `MySQLCC` enable you to perform?

   b. What types of information about the server does `MySQLCC` provide?

   c. Besides the server, what else can you administer with `MySQLCC`?

Answers to Exercises

Answer 1:

   1. A Unix socket file will be used.

   2. When using the actual hostname, TCP/IP will be used.

Answer 2:

`--user` (or `-u`) and `--password` (or `-p`).

Answer 3:

```
shell> mysql -h db.example.com -p -u juan world < /tmp/queries.sql
```

Answer 4:

Use the \G sequence to display query output in vertical format.

Answer 5:

a. One possibility is ');

b. Another is to use the clear-query sequence: '\c

The '> prompt indicates that you began a single-quoted string but haven't finished it. Thus, you *must* enter the terminating single quote to finish the string regardless of whether you then want to enter the rest of the query or enter the cancel-query command.

Answer 6:

a. To process the file within the mysql session, use the SOURCE command:

```
mysql> SOURCE /tmp/tbl_import.sql;
```

(Note that the semicolon is optional for the SOURCE command.) If test isn't the default database, you must first issue a USE test statement before processing the file.

b. To process the file from the shell of the operating system, invoke mysql and direct it to read from the file:

```
shell> mysql test < /tmp/tbl_import.sql
```

You might also have to specify hostname, username, and password.

Answer 7:

To cancel a statement that you are entering, use the \c sequence.

Answer 8:

```
shell> mysqldump world City Country > /tmp/world_backup.sql
```

You might also have to specify hostname, username, and password.

Answer 9:

```
shell> mysqldump --add-drop-table --databases db1 db2 > /tmp/db1_db2_backup.sql
```

You might also have to specify hostname, username, and password.

Answer 10:

Advantages: Multiple-row statements can be reloaded more efficiently.

Disadvantages: Multiple-row statements are less readable and less easily ported to other database management systems.

Answer 11:

```
shell> mysqldump --no-data test > /backups/structure.sql
```

You might also have to specify hostname, username, and password.

Answer 12:

To restore tables, you can use this command:

```
shell> mysql test < /backups/back.sql
```

You might also have to specify hostname, username, and password.

To ensure that existing tables will be overwritten for the restore operation, you can use this command when dumping the tables:

```
shell> mysqldump --add-drop-table test > /backups/back.sql
```

To restore backups made without the --add-drop-table option, you can use the mysql --force, which will continue processing queries in batch mode even if errors occur.

Answer 13:

The main difference between mysqlcheck and myisamchk lies in how they access tables:

- mysqlcheck is a client program; it determines which options were given on the command line, and then sends appropriate SQL statements to the MySQL server to perform the requested operation.
- myisamchk is not a client program for the server. It performs operations on tables by accessing the table files directly.

Answer 14:

mysqlcheck can perform operations on MyISAM, InnoDB, and BDB tables.

Answer 15:

myisamchk works only for MyISAM tables.

Answer 16:

a. MySQLCC enables you to kill client connections, issue flush commands, and shut down the server.

b. MySQLCC has a server information window that provides single-click access to the same system and status variables that you get when issuing SHOW VARIABLES and SHOW STATUS statements manually.

c. MySQLCC also enables you to administer user accounts.

4

Data Definition Language

This chapter covers the following exam topics:

- General database and table properties
- Storage engines and table types
- Limits on number and size of database components
- Identifier syntax
- The CREATE DATABASE and DROP DATABASE statements
- The CREATE TABLE, ALTER TABLE, and DROP TABLE statements
- The CREATE INDEX and DROP INDEX statements; specifying indexes at table-creation time
- Creating and using primary keys
- Column types
- Using AUTO_INCREMENT
- String and number formats
- Using SHOW and DESCRIBE to review table structures

Questions on the material in this chapter make up approximately 20% of the exam.

Several of MySQL's SQL statements comprise the Data Definition Language (DDL) that is used to define the structural characteristics of your databases. The following statements create or remove databases and tables or modify the structure of tables:

- CREATE DATABASE creates a new database.
- DROP DATABASE removes a database and any tables it contains.
- CREATE TABLE creates a new table.
- DROP TABLE removes a table and any data it contains.
- ALTER TABLE modifies the structure of an existing table.
- CREATE INDEX adds an index to a table.
- DROP INDEX removes an index from a table.

Several of the table-related DDL statements require you to provide column definitions. MySQL allows several different types of data to be stored, and it's important to understand what column datatypes are available so that you can define your tables appropriately for the information they'll contain.

This chapter provides a general overview of how MySQL manages databases and tables and a discussion of the syntax of legal names that can be used to refer to them. It also describes how to use each of the DDL statements and discusses the available column datatypes, their properties, how to use them, and the syntax for writing column definitions.

Related to the DDL statements, MySQL supports several statements that are helpful for checking what databases or tables exist and for getting information about the internal column and index structure of tables. These statements include SHOW and DESCRIBE; they are discussed at the end of this chapter.

4.1 General Database and Table Properties

Every MySQL server has a data directory under which it manages the contents of databases and tables. The server represents these using directories and files under the data directory as follows:

- MySQL associates each database with a directory under the data directory. (This means that the data directory is the parent of all database directories.) A database directory has the same name as the database that it represents. For example, a database named world corresponds to a directory named world under the data directory. MySQL uses the database directory to manage the components of the database—that is, its tables and indexes. A database may be empty, or have one or more tables. Databases cannot be nested; one database cannot contain another.

- Each table in a database consists of rows and columns. A table can be empty (it can have zero rows of data), but it must have at least one column. A table may also be indexed to improve query performance. Every table is associated with a format file in the database directory that contains the definition, or structure, of the table. The format filename is the same as the table name, plus an .frm suffix. For example, the format file for a table named Country in the world database is named Country.frm and is located in the world directory under the server's data directory. Depending on the table type, the storage engine for a table might create additional files for the table. If Country is a MyISAM table, the MyISAM storage engine creates data and index files named Country.MYD and Country.MYI to store data rows and indexes (respectively) for the table. If Country is an InnoDB table, MySQL still creates a Country.frm format file in the database directory, but the InnoDB storage engine stores the table data and index information elsewhere, in the InnoDB tablespace.

4.2 Storage Engines and Table Types

The MySQL server uses storage engines to manage data in tables. Each storage engine handles a particular table type. Each table type has differing characteristics and features; these are summarized in this section as an overview. Elsewhere, this study guide concentrates primarily on the MyISAM and InnoDB table types, which are also discussed in more detail in the "Professional Study Guide." For additional information on all table types, see the *MySQL Reference Manual*.

4.2.1 MyISAM Tables

The MyISAM storage engine manages tables that have the following characteristics:

- Each MyISAM table is represented on disk by an `.frm` format file, as well as an `.MYD` datafile and an `.MYI` index file. All these files are located in the database directory.

- MyISAM has the most flexible `AUTO_INCREMENT` column handling of all the table types.

- MyISAM tables can be used to set up MERGE tables.

- MyISAM tables can be converted into fast, compressed, read-only tables.

- MyISAM supports `FULLTEXT` searching.

- MySQL manages contention between queries for MyISAM table access using table-level locking. Query performance is very fast for retrievals. Multiple queries can read the same table simultaneously. For a write query, an exclusive table-level lock is used to prevent use of the table by other read or write queries, leading to reduced performance in environments with a mix of read and write queries. Deadlock cannot occur with table-level locking. (Deadlock occurs when two or more queries are blocked, or stopped from completing, because each is waiting for one of the others to finish.)

4.2.2 InnoDB Tables

The InnoDB storage engine manages tables that have the following characteristics:

- Each InnoDB table is represented on disk by an `.frm` format file in the database directory, as well as data and index storage in the InnoDB tablespace. The InnoDB tablespace is a logical single storage area that is made up of one or more files or partitions on disk. The tablespace is shared by all InnoDB tables.

- InnoDB supports transactions (using the SQL `COMMIT` and `ROLLBACK` statements) with full ACID compliance.

- InnoDB provides auto-recovery after a crash of the MySQL server or the host where the server runs.

- InnoDB supports foreign keys and referential integrity, including cascaded deletes and updates.

- MySQL manages query contention for InnoDB tables using multi-versioning and row-level locking. Multi-versioning gives each transaction its own view of the database. This, combined with row-level locking, keeps contention to a minimum. The result is good concurrency even in an environment consisting of mixed reads and writes. However, it's possible for deadlock to occur. Multi-versioning is discussed further in the "Professional Study Guide."

4.2.3 MERGE Tables

The MERGE storage engine manages tables that have the following characteristics:

- A MERGE table is a collection of identically structured MyISAM tables. Each MERGE table is represented on disk by an `.frm` format file and an `.MRG` file that lists the names of the constituent MyISAM files. Both files are located in the database directory.
- Logically, a query on a MERGE table acts as a query on all the MyISAM tables of which it consists.
- A MERGE table creates a logical entity that can exceed the maximum MyISAM table size.

4.2.4 BDB (Berkeley DB) Tables

The BDB storage engine manages tables that have the following characteristics:

- Each BDB table is represented on disk by an `.frm` format file and a `.db` file that stores data and index information. Both files are located in the database directory.
- BDB supports transactions (using the SQL COMMIT and ROLLBACK statements) with full ACID compliance.
- BDB provides auto-recovery after a crash of the MySQL server or the host where the server runs.
- MySQL manages query contention for BDB tables using page-level locking. This locking level provides concurrency performance that is intermediate to that of row-level and table-level locking. It's possible for deadlock to occur.

4.2.5 HEAP (MEMORY) Tables

The HEAP storage engine manages tables that have the following characteristics:

- Each HEAP table is represented on disk by an `.frm` format file in the database directory. Table data and indexes are stored in memory.
- In-memory storage results in very fast performance.
- HEAP table contents do not survive a restart of the server. The table structure itself survives, but the table contains zero data rows after a restart.

- HEAP tables use up memory, so they should not be used for large tables.
- MySQL manages query contention for HEAP tables using table-level locking. Deadlock cannot occur.

4.3 Limits on Number and Size of Database Components

The MySQL server can manage multiple databases, each of which may contain multiple tables. MySQL does not place any limits on the number of databases, although your operating system or filesystem might. Each database is represented as a directory under the server's data directory, so if the filesystem on which the data directory resides has a limit on the number of subdirectories a directory may contain, MySQL can create no more than that number of databases.

The MySQL server places no limits on the number of tables in a database. The InnoDB storage engine, on the other hand, allows a maximum of two billion tables to exist within the InnoDB tablespace. This places a limit (albeit a rather high one) on the number of InnoDB tables that can be created among all databases combined. (The limit isn't enforced on a per-database basis because the InnoDB tablespace is shared among all databases.)

Your operating system or filesystem might also impose limits on the maximum number of tables allowed. For example, the MyISAM storage engine places no limits on the number of tables in a database. However, MyISAM tables are represented by files in the directory that MySQL associates with the database, so a limit on the number of tables in the database might arise from factors external to MySQL:

- If the operating system or filesystem places a limit on the number of files in a directory, MySQL is bound by that constraint.
- The efficiency of the operating system in handling large numbers of files in a directory can place a practical limit on the number of tables in a database. If the time required to open a file in the directory increases significantly as the number of files increases, database performance can be adversely affected.
- The amount of available disk space limits the number of tables.

MySQL storage engines do place limits on the allowable maximum size of individual tables. These limits vary per storage engine, but they tend to be rather high. Another factor that limits table size is the maximum file size allowed by your operating system or filesystem. An operating system may support different types of filesystems, each of which may have a different maximum file size.

For large tables, you might find that you run up against operating system or filesystem limits on file sizes before you reach MySQL's internal table size limits. Several strategies can be used for working around file size limits:

- Exploit any features allowed by a given table storage manager for increasing table size. For example, the contents of a MyISAM table can sometimes be distributed into several smaller tables, which can then be treated as a single logical unit by combining them into a MERGE table. This effectively multiplies the maximum table size by the number of component MyISAM tables in the MERGE table.

- The MyISAM storage engine supports a software RAID feature that partitions data storage for a table into a set of files under the database directory. This has the effect of breaking the single-file size barrier, although only for the datafile. Indexes are still stored in a single file, so software RAID might not be feasible for a heavily indexed table.

- Convert the table for use with a storage engine that allows larger tables. For example, convert a MyISAM table to an InnoDB table. The InnoDB storage engine manages tables within a tablespace that can be configured to be much larger than the size of a single file, and InnoDB tables can grow as large as the available storage within the tablespace.

- Modify your operating system. A factor external to MySQL that can be used to allow larger tables is to modify your operating system to support larger files. This might be possible by using a different filesystem type, or by using a newer version of the operating system that relaxes the limits on file sizes compared to an older version. You might also consider switching to an operating system that supports larger files than does your current operating system.

4.4 Identifier Syntax

When you write SQL statements, you use names to refer to databases and tables as well as to elements of tables such as columns and (sometimes) indexes. It's also possible to create aliases, which act as synonyms for table and column names. All of these types of names are known as identifiers; they identify a specific database element. This section describes the rules for writing identifiers.

4.4.1 Legal Characters for Identifiers

Identifiers for databases, tables, columns, and indexes may be unquoted or quoted. An unquoted identifier must follow these rules:

- An identifier may contain all alphanumeric characters, the underline character (_), and the dollar sign ($).

- An identifier may begin with any of the legal characters, even a digit. However, it's best to avoid identifiers that might be misinterpreted as constants. For example, 1e3 might be taken as a number in scientific notation, whereas 0x1 might be interpreted as a hex constant, so neither is a good choice for an identifier.

- An identifier cannot consist entirely of digits.

An identifier may be quoted, in which case it can contain characters such as spaces or dashes that aren't otherwise legal. To quote an identifier, you may enclose it within backtick (`` ` ``) characters. If the server was started with the `--ansi` or `--sql-mode=ANSI_QUOTES` option, you may also quote an identifier by enclosing it within double quotes (`"`). Quoting causes the identifier syntax rules to be relaxed as follows:

- Any character may be used in a quoted identifier except characters with a numeric value of 0 or 255. For database and table names, other illegal characters are `.`, `/`, and `\`.
- A quoted identifier may consist entirely of digits.

An alias identifier can include any character, but should be quoted if it's a reserved word (such as `SELECT` or `DESC`), contains special characters, or consists entirely of digits. Aliases may be quoted within single quotes (`'`), double quotes, or backticks.

4.4.2 Using Qualifiers for Table and Column Names

Column and table identifiers can be written in qualified form—that is, together with the identifier of a higher-level element, with a period (.) separator.

A table name may be qualified with the name of the database to which it belongs. For example, the `Country` table in the `world` database may be referred to as `world.Country` (note the `.` separating the two identifiers in the name). If `world` is the default database, these statements are equivalent:

```
SELECT * FROM Country;
SELECT * FROM world.Country;
```

A column name may be qualified with the name of the table to which it belongs. For example, the `Name` column in the `Country` table may be referred to as `Country.Name`.

A further level of column qualification is possible because a table name may be qualified with a database name. So, another way to refer to the `Name` column is `world.Country.Name`. If `world` is the default database, the following statements are equivalent. They differ only in having successively more specific levels of name qualification:

```
SELECT Name FROM Country;
SELECT Country.Name FROM Country;
SELECT world.Country.Name FROM world.Country;
```

Sometimes qualifiers are necessary to resolve ambiguity. Other times you may elect to use them to make a statement clearer or more precise.

4.5 CREATE DATABASE **and** DROP DATABASE

To create a new database, use the `CREATE DATABASE` statement. The following statement creates a database named `mydb`:

```
CREATE DATABASE mydb;
```

After a database has been created, you can create new tables in it using the CREATE TABLE statement, which is described in section 4.6, "CREATE TABLE."

If you try to create a database that already exists, an error occurs. If you simply want to ensure that the database exists, add an IF NOT EXISTS clause to the statement:

```
CREATE DATABASE IF NOT EXISTS mydb;
```

With the additional clause, the statement creates the database only if it does not already exist. Otherwise, the statement does nothing and no error occurs. This can be useful in applications that need to ensure that a given database is available, without disrupting any existing database with the same name.

Creating a database has no effect on the database that's currently selected as the default database. To make the new database the default database, issue a USE statement:

```
USE mydb;
```

To see a list of available databases, use the SHOW DATABASES statement. This statement will not show the names of databases to which you have no access. To see a list of tables in a database, use SHOW TABLES FROM *db_name* (or just SHOW TABLES if *db_name* is the name of the current database). The SHOW command is described in more detail in section 4.11, "Using SHOW and DESCRIBE to Review Table Structures."

When you no longer need a database, you can remove it with DROP DATABASE:

```
DROP DATABASE mydb;
```

It's unnecessary to remove the tables in a database before dropping it. DROP DATABASE does not require the database to be empty, so it does not fail if the database contains tables. DROP DATABASE removes the tables in the process of removing the database.

DROP DATABASE is a dangerous statement and you should use it with care. There is no statement to "undo" DROP DATABASE. If you drop a database by mistake, your only option is to recover it from your backups.

4.6 CREATE TABLE

Use the CREATE TABLE statement to create a new table. A table's definition includes its name and a list of columns, each of which has a name and a definition. The table definition may also include index definitions.

This section describes basic CREATE TABLE syntax using simple column definitions. More information on column datatypes and properties can be found in section 4.10, "Column Types."

To create a table, give its name followed by a list of column definitions within parentheses:

```
CREATE TABLE table_name (definition1, definition2, ...);
```

In the simplest case, a table contains only one column. The following statement creates a table named t with a single column named id that will contain INT (integer) values:

```
CREATE TABLE t (id INT);
```

A column definition may include options to define the column data more precisely. For example, to disallow NULL values in the column, include NOT NULL in the definition:

```
CREATE TABLE t (id INT NOT NULL);
```

More complex tables have multiple columns, with the column definitions separated by commas. The following table definition includes, in addition to the id column, two 30-byte character columns for storing last names and first names, and a column for storing date values. All columns are declared NOT NULL to indicate that they require non-NULL values.

```
CREATE TABLE t
(
    id         INT NOT NULL,
    last_name  CHAR(30) NOT NULL,
    first_name CHAR(30) NOT NULL,
    d          DATE NOT NULL
);
```

Every table must belong to a database. That is, you cannot create a table that is not located within some database. If the table named in the CREATE TABLE statement isn't qualified with a database name, the table is created in the default database. To indicate explicitly where to create the table, you can qualify the table name with the name of the desired database, using *db_name.table_name* syntax. For example, if you want to create a table called mytable in the test database, write the CREATE TABLE statement like this:

```
CREATE TABLE test.mytable (i INT);
```

The qualified identifier syntax is helpful when there's no default database or when some other database is currently selected as the default. (If test happens to be the default database, the statement still works. In that case, the database name is unnecessary but harmless.)

When you create a table, you can provide index definitions in addition to the column definitions. Indexes are useful for increasing query performance by reducing lookup time. Here's a simple example that includes two index definitions. The first creates an index on the id column and requires each id value to be unique. The second index definition creates a two-column index on the last_name and first_name columns of the table:

```
CREATE TABLE t
(
    id         INT NOT NULL,
    last_name  CHAR(30) NOT NULL,
    first_name CHAR(30) NOT NULL,
    UNIQUE (id),
    INDEX (last_name, first_name)
);
```

Section 4.9, "Creating and Dropping Indexes," discusses index creation further.

If you try to create a table that already exists, an error occurs. If you simply want to ensure that the table exists, add an IF NOT EXISTS clause to the statement:

```
CREATE TABLE IF NOT EXISTS t (i INT);
```

Note, however, that MySQL does not perform any check on the table structure when you add this clause. In particular, MySQL will issue no warning if a table with the given name exists but has a structure different from the one you've defined in the CREATE TABLE statement.

A temporary table can be created by adding the keyword TEMPORARY to the CREATE TABLE statement:

```
CREATE TEMPORARY TABLE t (i INT);
```

Temporary tables exist only for the duration of the current connection. The server drops temporary tables when you disconnect, if you haven't already dropped them explicitly. This is convenient because you need not remember to remove the table yourself. A temporary table is visible only to the client that creates it, so different clients can create temporary tables in the same database, using the same name, without conflicting with one another.

4.7 DROP TABLE

When you no longer need a table, you can destroy it with the DROP TABLE statement:

```
DROP TABLE t;
```

In MySQL, a single DROP TABLE statement can name several tables to be dropped simultaneously:

```
DROP TABLE t1, t2, t3;
```

Normally, an error occurs if you attempt to drop a table that does not exist:

```
mysql> DROP TABLE no_such_table;
ERROR 1051: Unknown table 'no_such_table'
```

To prevent an error from occurring if a table does not exist when you attempt to drop it, add an IF EXISTS clause to the statement:

```
mysql> DROP TABLE IF EXISTS no_such_table;
```

If you drop a table by mistake, you must recover it from backups, so be careful. (This is the same principle as the one mentioned earlier for databases: If you drop a database, you cannot undo the action. A dropped database can only be recovered from your backups.)

4.8 ALTER TABLE

After creating a table, you might discover that its structure is not quite right for its intended use. If that happens, you can change the table's structure. One way to do this is to remove the table with DROP TABLE and then issue another CREATE TABLE statement that defines the table correctly. This can be a drastic method: If the table already contains data, dropping and re-creating the table destroys its contents unless you first make a backup. To change a table "in place," use the ALTER TABLE statement. With ALTER TABLE, you can modify a table's structure in the following ways:

- Add or drop columns
- Change the name or definition of a column
- Add or drop indexes
- Sort the table's rows in a particular order
- Rename the table

This section describes how to perform all the possible changes except for adding and dropping indexes. Adding and dropping of indexes is covered in a later section that focuses specifically on indexing issues. (See section 4.9, "Creating and Dropping Indexes.")

Most of the examples shown in this section use a table named HeadOfState, designed to keep track of world leaders. Assume that the table initially has the following structure:

```
CREATE TABLE HeadOfState
(
    ID          INT NOT NULL,
    LastName    CHAR(30) NOT NULL,
    FirstName   CHAR(30) NOT NULL,
    CountryCode CHAR(3) NOT NULL,
);
```

The corresponding DESCRIBE output for the table is as follows:

```
mysql> DESCRIBE HeadOfState;
+-------------+----------+------+-----+---------+-------+
| Field       | Type     | Null | Key | Default | Extra |
+-------------+----------+------+-----+---------+-------+
| ID          | int(11)  |      |     | 0       |       |
| LastName    | char(30) |      |     |         |       |
| FirstName   | char(30) |      |     |         |       |
| CountryCode | char(3)  |      |     |         |       |
+-------------+----------+------+-----+---------+-------+
```

4.8.1 Adding and Dropping Columns

To add a new column to a table, use ALTER TABLE with an ADD clause that specifies the column's definition. A column definition uses the same syntax for ALTER TABLE as for CREATE TABLE. For example, to add a DATE column named Inauguration to record the date the leaders listed in the table assumed office, you can issue this statement:

```
ALTER TABLE HeadOfState ADD Inauguration DATE NOT NULL;
```

This ALTER TABLE changes the table structure as follows:

```
mysql> DESCRIBE HeadOfState;
+-------------+----------+------+-----+------------+-------+
| Field       | Type     | Null | Key | Default    | Extra |
+-------------+----------+------+-----+------------+-------+
| ID          | int(11)  |      |     | 0          |       |
| LastName    | char(30) |      |     |            |       |
| FirstName   | char(30) |      |     |            |       |
| CountryCode | char(3)  |      |     |            |       |
| Inauguration| date     |      |     | 0000-00-00 |       |
+-------------+----------+------+-----+------------+-------+
```

As shown in the DESCRIBE output, when you add a new column to a table, MySQL places it after all existing columns. This is the default placement unless you specify otherwise. To indicate that MySQL should place the new column in a specific position within the table, append either the keyword FIRST or the keyword-identifier combination AFTER *column_name* to the column definition. For example, assume that you had executed this ALTER TABLE statement instead of the previous one:

```
ALTER TABLE HeadOfState ADD Inauguration DATE NOT NULL FIRST;
```

The FIRST keyword tells ALTER TABLE to place the new column before all existing columns (in the "first" position), resulting in the following table structure:

```
mysql> DESCRIBE HeadOfState;
+-------------+----------+------+-----+------------+-------+
| Field       | Type     | Null | Key | Default    | Extra |
+-------------+----------+------+-----+------------+-------+
| Inauguration| date     |      |     | 0000-00-00 |       |
| ID          | int(11)  |      |     | 0          |       |
| LastName    | char(30) |      |     |            |       |
| FirstName   | char(30) |      |     |            |       |
| CountryCode | char(3)  |      |     |            |       |
+-------------+----------+------+-----+------------+-------+
```

Using AFTER *column_name* tells ALTER TABLE to place the new column after a specific existing column. For example, to place the new Inauguration column after the existing FirstName column, you would issue this statement:

```
ALTER TABLE HeadOfState ADD Inauguration DATE NOT NULL AFTER FirstName;
```

This ALTER TABLE statement would result in a table structure that looks like this:

```
mysql> DESCRIBE HeadOfState;
+-------------+----------+------+-----+------------+-------+
| Field       | Type     | Null | Key | Default    | Extra |
+-------------+----------+------+-----+------------+-------+
| ID          | int(11)  |      |     | 0          |       |
| LastName    | char(30) |      |     |            |       |
| FirstName   | char(30) |      |     |            |       |
| Inauguration| date     |      |     | 0000-00-00 |       |
| CountryCode | char(3)  |      |     |            |       |
+-------------+----------+------+-----+------------+-------+
```

You cannot add a column with the same name as one that already exists in the table; column names within a table must be unique. Column names are not case sensitive, so if the table already contains a column named ID, you cannot add a new column using any of these names: ID, id, Id, or iD. They all are considered to be the same name.

To drop a column, use a DROP clause. In this case, it's necessary only to name the column you want to drop:

```
ALTER TABLE table_name DROP column_name;
```

4.8.2 Modifying Existing Columns

There are two ways to change the definition of an existing column within a table. One of these also enables you to rename the column.

The first way to alter a column definition is to use a MODIFY clause. You must specify the name of the column that you want to change, followed by its new definition. Assume that you want to change the ID column's datatype from INT to BIGINT, to allow the table to accommodate larger identification numbers. You also want to make the column UNSIGNED to disallow negative values. The following statement accomplishes this task:

```
ALTER TABLE HeadOfState MODIFY ID BIGINT UNSIGNED NOT NULL;
```

DESCRIBE now shows the table structure to be as follows:

```
mysql> DESCRIBE HeadOfState;
+-------------+--------------------+------+-----+------------+-------+
| Field       | Type               | Null | Key | Default    | Extra |
+-------------+--------------------+------+-----+------------+-------+
| ID          | bigint(20) unsigned|      |     | 0          |       |
| LastName    | char(30)           |      |     |            |       |
| FirstName   | char(30)           |      |     |            |       |
| Inauguration| date               |      |     | 0000-00-00 |       |
| CountryCode | char(3)            |      |     |            |       |
+-------------+--------------------+------+-----+------------+-------+
```

Note that if you want to disallow NULL in the column, the column definition provided for MODIFY must include the NOT NULL option, even if the column was originally defined with NOT NULL. This is true for other column options as well; if you don't specify them explicitly, the new definition won't carry them over from the old definition.

The second way to alter a column definition is to use a CHANGE clause. CHANGE enables you to modify both the column's definition and its name. To use this clause, specify the CHANGE keyword, followed by the column's existing name, its new name, and its new definition, in that order. Note that this means you must specify the existing name twice if you want to change only the column definition (and not the name). For example, to change the LastName column from CHAR(30) to CHAR(40) without renaming the column, you'd do this:

```
ALTER TABLE HeadOfState CHANGE LastName LastName CHAR(40) NOT NULL;
```

To change the name as well (for example, to Surname), provide the new name following the existing name:

```
ALTER TABLE HeadOfState CHANGE LastName Surname CHAR(40) NOT NULL;
```

4.8.3 Renaming a Table

Renaming a table changes neither a table's structure nor its contents. The following statement renames table t1 to t2:

```
ALTER TABLE t1 RENAME TO t2;
```

Another way to rename a table is by using the RENAME TABLE statement:

```
RENAME TABLE t1 TO t2;
```

RENAME TABLE has an advantage over ALTER TABLE in that it can perform multiple table renaming operations in a single statement. One use for this feature is to swap the names of two tables:

```
RENAME TABLE t1 TO tmp, t2 TO t1, tmp TO t2;
```

4.8.4 Specifying Multiple Alterations

You can specify multiple alterations for a table with a single ALTER TABLE statement. Just separate the actions by commas:

```
ALTER TABLE HeadOfState RENAME TO CountryLeader,
    MODIFY ID BIGINT UNSIGNED NOT NULL,
    ORDER BY LastName, FirstName;
```

4.9 Creating and Dropping Indexes

Tables in MySQL can grow very large, but as a table gets bigger, retrievals from it become slower. To keep your queries performing efficiently, it's essential to index your tables. Indexes allow column values to be found more quickly, so retrievals based on indexes are faster than those that are not. Another reason to use indexes is that they can enforce unique-ness to ensure that duplicate values do not occur and that each row in a table can be distin-guished from every other row.

MySQL supports four types of indexes:

- A nonunique index is an index in which any key value may occur multiple times.
- A UNIQUE index is unique-valued; that is, every key value is required to be different from all other keys.
- A PRIMARY KEY is a unique-valued index that's similar to a UNIQUE index but has addition-al restrictions (the major one being that no NULL values are allowed).
- A FULLTEXT index is specially designed for text searching.

This section discusses the following index-related topics:

- Defining indexes at table creation time with CREATE TABLE
- Using primary keys
- Adding indexes to existing tables with ALTER TABLE or CREATE INDEX
- Dropping indexes from tables with ALTER TABLE or DROP INDEX

The discussion here does not consider in any depth indexing topics such as query optimiza-tion, assessing how well indexes are used, or FULLTEXT searching. The "Professional Study Guide" covers those topics in more detail.

4.9.1 Defining Indexes at Table-Creation Time

To define indexes for a table at the time you create it, include the index definitions in the CREATE TABLE statement along with the column definitions. An index definition consists of the appropriate keyword or keywords to indicate the index type, followed by a list in paren-theses that names the column or columns that comprise the index. Suppose that the defini-tion of a table HeadOfState without any indexes looks like this:

```
CREATE TABLE HeadOfState
(
    ID          INT NOT NULL,
    LastName    CHAR(30) NOT NULL,
    FirstName   CHAR(30) NOT NULL,
    CountryCode CHAR(3) NOT NULL,
    Inauguration DATE NOT NULL
);
```

To create the table with the same columns but with a nonunique index on the date-valued column Inauguration, include an INDEX clause in the CREATE TABLE statement as follows:

```
CREATE TABLE HeadOfState
(
    ID          INT NOT NULL,
    LastName    CHAR(30) NOT NULL,
    FirstName   CHAR(30) NOT NULL,
    CountryCode CHAR(3) NOT NULL,
    Inauguration DATE NOT NULL,
    INDEX (Inauguration)
);
```

The keyword KEY may be used instead of INDEX.

To include multiple columns in an index (that is, to create a composite index), list all the column names within the parentheses, separated by commas. For example, a composite index that includes both the LastName and FirstName columns can be defined as follows:

```
CREATE TABLE HeadOfState
(
    ID          INT NOT NULL,
    LastName    CHAR(30) NOT NULL,
    FirstName   CHAR(30) NOT NULL,
    CountryCode CHAR(3) NOT NULL,
    Inauguration DATE NOT NULL,
    INDEX (LastName, FirstName)
);
```

Composite indexes can be created for any type of index.

For all index types other than PRIMARY KEY, you can name an index by including the name just before the column list. If you don't provide a name, MySQL assigns a name for you based on the name of the first column in the index. For a PRIMARY KEY, you don't specify a name because its name is always PRIMARY. (A consequence of this fact is that you cannot define more than one PRIMARY KEY per table.)

The preceding indexing examples each include just one index in the table definition, but a table can have multiple indexes. The following table definition includes two indexes:

```
CREATE TABLE HeadOfState
(
    ID          INT NOT NULL,
    LastName    CHAR(30) NOT NULL,
    FirstName   CHAR(30) NOT NULL,
    CountryCode CHAR(3) NOT NULL,
    Inauguration DATE NOT NULL,
    INDEX (LastName, FirstName),
    INDEX (Inauguration)
);
```

To create a unique-valued index, use the UNIQUE keyword instead of INDEX. For example, if you want to prevent duplicate values in the ID column, create a UNIQUE index on it like this:

```
CREATE TABLE HeadOfState
(
    ID           INT NOT NULL,
    LastName     CHAR(30) NOT NULL,
    FirstName    CHAR(30) NOT NULL,
    CountryCode  CHAR(3) NOT NULL,
    Inauguration DATE NOT NULL,
    UNIQUE (ID)
);
```

There's one exception to the uniqueness of values in a UNIQUE index: If a column in the index may contain NULL values, multiple NULL values are allowed. This differs from the behavior for all non-NULL values.

A PRIMARY KEY is a type of index that's similar to a UNIQUE index. The differences between the two are as follows:

- A UNIQUE index can contain NULL values; a PRIMARY KEY cannot. If a unique-valued index might be required to contain NULL values, you must use a UNIQUE index, not a PRIMARY KEY.

- It's possible to have multiple UNIQUE indexes for a table, but each table may have only one index defined as a PRIMARY KEY. (The internal name for a PRIMARY KEY is always PRIMARY, and there can be only one index with a given name.)

To index a column as a PRIMARY KEY, just use the keywords PRIMARY KEY rather than UNIQUE and declare the column NOT NULL to make sure that it cannot contain NULL values.

The use of PRIMARY KEY and UNIQUE to create indexes that ensure unique identification for any row in a table is discussed in the next section.

4.9.2 Creating and Using Primary Keys

The most common reason for creating an index is that it decreases lookup time for operations that search the indexed columns, especially for large tables. Another important use for indexing is to create a restriction that requires indexed columns to contain only unique values.

An index with unique values allows you to identify each record in a table as distinct from any other. This kind of index provides a primary key for a table. Without a primary key, there might be no way to identify a record that does not also identify other records at the same time. That is a problem when you need to retrieve, update, or delete a specific record in a table. A unique ID number is a common type of primary key.

Two of MySQL's index types can be used to implement the concept of a primary key:

- An index created with a `PRIMARY KEY` clause
- An index created with the `UNIQUE` keyword

In both cases, the column or columns in the index should be declared as `NOT NULL`. For a `PRIMARY KEY`, this is a requirement; MySQL won't create a `PRIMARY KEY` from any column that may be `NULL`. For a `UNIQUE` index, declaring columns as `NOT NULL` is a logical requirement if the index is to serve as a primary key. If a `UNIQUE` index is allowed to contain `NULL` values, it may contain multiple `NULL` values. As a result, some rows might not be distinguishable from others and the index cannot be used as a primary key.

A `PRIMARY KEY` is a type of unique-valued index, but a `UNIQUE` index isn't necessarily a primary key unless it disallows `NULL` values. If it does, a `UNIQUE` index that cannot contain `NULL` is functionally equivalent to a `PRIMARY KEY`.

The following definition creates a table `t` that contains an `id` column that's `NOT NULL` and declared as a primary key by means of a `PRIMARY KEY` clause:

```
CREATE TABLE t
(
    id   INT NOT NULL,
    name CHAR(30) NOT NULL,
    PRIMARY KEY (id)
);
```

A primary key on a column also can be created by replacing `PRIMARY KEY` with `UNIQUE` in the table definition, provided that the column is declared `NOT NULL`:

```
CREATE TABLE t
(
    id   INT NOT NULL,
    name CHAR(30) NOT NULL,
    UNIQUE (id)
);
```

An alternative syntax is allowed for the preceding two statements. For a single-column primary key, you can add the keywords `PRIMARY KEY` or `UNIQUE` directly to the end of the column definition. The following `CREATE TABLE` statements are equivalent to those just shown:

```
CREATE TABLE t
(
    id   INT NOT NULL PRIMARY KEY,
    name CHAR(30) NOT NULL
);
```

```
CREATE TABLE t
(
    id   INT NOT NULL UNIQUE,
    name CHAR(30) NOT NULL
);
```

Like other indexes, you can declare a PRIMARY KEY or UNIQUE index as a composite index that spans multiple columns. In this case, the index must be declared using a separate clause. (You cannot add the PRIMARY KEY or UNIQUE keywords to the end of a column definition because the index would apply only to that column.) The following definition creates a primary key on the last_name and first_name columns using a PRIMARY KEY clause:

```
CREATE TABLE people
(
    last_name  CHAR(30) NOT NULL,
    first_name CHAR(30) NOT NULL,
    PRIMARY KEY (last_name, first_name)
);
```

This primary key definition allows any given last name or first name to appear multiple times in the table, but no combination of last and first name can occur more than once.

You can also create a multiple-column primary key using UNIQUE, if the columns are declared NOT NULL:

```
CREATE TABLE people
(
    last_name  CHAR(30) NOT NULL,
    first_name CHAR(30) NOT NULL,
    UNIQUE (last_name, first_name)
);
```

Primary keys are an important general database design concept because they allow unique identification of each row in a table. For MySQL in particular, primary keys are frequently defined as columns that are declared with the AUTO_INCREMENT option. AUTO_INCREMENT columns provide a convenient way to automatically generate a unique sequence number for each row in a table and are described in section 4.10, "Column Types."

4.9.3 Modifying Indexes of Existing Tables

To add an index to a table, you can use ALTER TABLE or CREATE INDEX. To drop an index from a table, you can use ALTER TABLE or DROP INDEX. Of these statements, ALTER TABLE is the most flexible, as will become clear in the following discussion.

To add an index to a table with ALTER TABLE, use ADD followed by the appropriate index-type keywords and a parenthesized list naming the columns to be indexed. For example, assume that the HeadOfState table used earlier in this chapter is defined without indexes as follows:

```
CREATE TABLE HeadOfState
(
    ID          INT NOT NULL,
    LastName    CHAR(30) NOT NULL,
    FirstName   CHAR(30) NOT NULL,
    CountryCode CHAR(3) NOT NULL,
    Inauguration DATE NOT NULL
);
```

To create a PRIMARY KEY on the ID column and a composite index on the LastName and FirstName columns, you would issue these statements:

```
ALTER TABLE HeadOfState ADD PRIMARY KEY (ID);
ALTER TABLE HeadOfState ADD INDEX (LastName,FirstName);
```

MySQL allows multiple actions to be performed with a single ALTER TABLE statement. One common use for multiple actions is to add several indexes to a table at the same time, which is more efficient than adding each one separately. The preceding two ALTER TABLE statements can be combined as follows:

```
ALTER TABLE HeadOfState ADD PRIMARY KEY (ID), ADD INDEX (LastName,FirstName);
```

To drop an index with ALTER TABLE, use a DROP clause and name the index to be dropped. Dropping a PRIMARY KEY is easy:

```
ALTER TABLE HeadOfState DROP PRIMARY KEY;
```

To drop another kind of index, you must specify its name. If you don't know the name, you can use SHOW CREATE TABLE to see the table's structure, including any index definitions, as shown here:

```
mysql> SHOW CREATE TABLE HeadOfState\G
*************************** 1. row ***************************
       Table: HeadOfState
Create Table: CREATE TABLE `HeadOfState` (
  `ID` int(11) NOT NULL default '0',
  `LastName` char(30) NOT NULL default '',
  `FirstName` char(30) NOT NULL default '',
  `CountryCode` char(3) NOT NULL default '',
  `Inauguration` date NOT NULL default '0000-00-00',
  PRIMARY KEY  (`ID`),
  KEY `LastName` (`LastName`,`FirstName`)
) TYPE=MyISAM
```

The KEY clause of the output shows that the index name is LastName, so you can drop the index using the following statement:

```
ALTER TABLE HeadOfState DROP INDEX LastName;
```

After you've dropped an index, you can recover it merely by re-creating it. This differs from dropping a database or a table, which cannot be undone except by recourse to backups. The distinction is that when you drop a database or a table, you're removing data. When you drop an index, you aren't removing table data, you're merely removing a structure that's derived from the data. The act of removing an index is a reversible operation as long as the columns from which the index was constructed have not been removed.

CREATE INDEX and DROP INDEX provide alternatives to ALTER TABLE for index manipulation.

The syntax for CREATE INDEX is as follows, where the statements shown create a single-column UNIQUE index and a multiple-column nonunique index, respectively:

```
CREATE UNIQUE INDEX IDIndex ON HeadOfState (ID);
CREATE INDEX NameIndex ON HeadOfState (LastName,FirstName);
```

Note that with CREATE INDEX, it's necessary to provide a name for the index, whereas ALTER TABLE creates an index name automatically if you don't provide one.

To drop an index with DROP INDEX, indicate the index name and table name:

```
DROP INDEX IDIndex ON t;
DROP INDEX NameIndex ON t;
```

Unlike ALTER TABLE, the CREATE INDEX and DROP INDEX statements can operate only on a single index per statement. In addition, neither statement supports the use of PRIMARY KEY. This is the reason that ALTER TABLE is more flexible.

4.10 Column Types

MySQL can work with many different kinds of data. Generally speaking, data values can be grouped into three categories:

- Numeric values. Numbers may or may not have a fractional part and may have a leading sign. For example, 14, -428.948, and +739 all are legal numbers. Integer values have no fractional part; columns for values with a fractional part can be declared to have either a fixed or variable number of decimal places. Numeric columns can be declared to be unsigned to prevent negative values from being accepted in the column.
- String values. Strings may be case sensitive or case insensitive. Strings may store characters or raw data values that contain arbitrary byte values. Strings are written within quotes (for example, 'I am a string' or "I am a string"). String columns can be declared as either fixed length or variable length.
- Temporal values. Temporal values include dates (such as '2005-11-03'), times (such as '14:23:00'), and values that have both a date and a time part ('2005-11-03 14:23:00'). MySQL also supports a special temporal type that represents year-only values efficiently. Date and time values can be written as quoted strings and may sometimes be written as numbers in contexts where numeric temporal values are understood.

When you create a table, the declaration for each of its columns includes the column name, a datatype specification that indicates what kind of values the column may hold, and possibly some options that more specifically define how MySQL should handle the column. For example, the following statement creates a table named people, which contains a numeric column named id and two 30-byte string columns named first_name and last_name:

```
CREATE TABLE people
(
```

```
    id          INT,
    first_name CHAR(30),
    last_name  CHAR(30)
);
```

The column definitions in this CREATE TABLE statement contain only names and column datatype specifications. To control the use of a column more specifically, options may be added to its definition. For example, to disallow negative values in the id column, add the UNSIGNED option. To disallow NULL (missing or unknown) values in any of the columns, add NOT NULL to the definition of each one. The modified CREATE TABLE statement looks like this:

```
CREATE TABLE people
(
    id          INT UNSIGNED NOT NULL,
    first_name CHAR(30) NOT NULL,
    last_name  CHAR(30) NOT NULL
);
```

For each of the general datatype categories (number, string, date, and time), MySQL has several specific column types from which to choose. It's important to properly understand the datatypes that are available for representing data, to avoid choosing a column type that isn't appropriate. The following sections provide a general description of the column datatypes and their properties. For additional details, the *MySQL Reference Manual* provides an extensive discussion on column datatypes.

4.10.1 Numeric Column Types

MySQL provides numeric column types for integer values, values with a fixed number of decimal places, and floating-point values that have a variable number of decimal places. When you choose a numeric column datatype, consider the following factors:

- The range of values the datatype represents
- The amount of storage space that column values require
- The display width indicating the maximum number of characters to use when presenting column values in query output
- The column precision (number of digits before the decimal) for values with a scale

4.10.1.1 Integer Column Types

Integer datatypes include TINYINT, SMALLINT, MEDIUMINT, INT, and BIGINT. Smaller datatypes require less storage space, but are more limited in the range of values they represent. For example, a TINYINT column has a small range (–128 to 127), but its values take only one byte each to store. INT has a much larger range (–2,147,483,648 to 2,147,483,647) but its values require four bytes each. The integer datatypes are summarized in the following table, which indicates the amount of storage each type requires as well as its range. For integer values declared with the UNSIGNED option, negative values are not allowed, and the high end of the range shifts upward to approximately double the maximum value.

Type	Storage Required	Signed Range	Unsigned Range
TINYINT	1 byte	-128 to 127	0 to 255
SMALLINT	2 bytes	-32,768 to 32,767	0 to 65,535
MEDIUMINT	3 bytes	-8,388,608 to 8,388,607	0 to 16,777,215
INT	4 bytes	-2,147,683,648 to 2,147,483,647	0 to 4,294,967,295
BIGINT	8 bytes	-9,223,372,036,854,775,808 to 9,223,372,036,854,775,807	0 to 18,446,744,073,709,551,615

Integer datatypes may be declared with a display width, which affects the number of characters used to display column values in query output. For example, assume that you declare an INT column with a display width of 4 like this:

```
century INT(4)
```

The result is that values in the century column will usually be displayed four digits wide.

It's important to remember that the display width is unrelated to the range of the datatype. The display width you define for a column affects only the maximum number of digits MySQL will use to display column values. Values shorter than the display width are padded with spaces as necessary. Note also that the display width is not a hard limit; it won't cause output truncation of a value that's too long to fit within the width. Instead, the full value will be shown. For example, assume that you've inserted the number 57622 into the century column. When you SELECT the column in a query, MySQL will display the entire value (57622) rather than just the first four digits of the value.

If you don't specify a display width for an integer type, MySQL chooses a default based on the number of characters needed to display the full range of values for the type (including the minus sign). For example, SMALLINT has a default display width of 6 because the widest possible value is -32768.

4.10.1.2 Floating-Point and Fixed-Decimal Column Types

The floating-point datatypes include FLOAT and DOUBLE. The fixed-point datatype is DECIMAL. Each of these types may be used to represent numeric values that have a scale, or fractional part. FLOAT and DOUBLE datatypes represent floating-point values in the native binary format used by the server host's CPU. This is a very efficient type for storage and computation, but values are subject to rounding error. DECIMAL uses a fixed-decimal storage format: All values in a DECIMAL column have the same number of decimal places. Values are stored in string format using one byte per digit. Numbers represented as strings cannot be processed as quickly as numbers represented in binary, so operations on DECIMAL columns are slower than operations on FLOAT and DOUBLE columns. DECIMAL values are not subject to rounding error when stored, which makes the DECIMAL column type a popular choice for financial applications involving currency calculations. However, be aware that currently MySQL does internal calculations using floating-point arithmetic, which can produce rounding error in the result.

FLOAT and DOUBLE are used to represent single-precision and double-precision floating-point values. They use 4 and 8 bytes each for storage, respectively. By default, MySQL represents values stored in FLOAT and DOUBLE columns to the maximum precision allowed by the hardware, but you can specify a display width and precision in the column definition. The following single-precision column definition specifies a display width of 10 digits, with a precision of 4 decimals:

```
avg_score FLOAT(10,4)
```

DECIMAL columns may also be declared with a display width and scale. If you omit them, the defaults are 10 and 0, so the following declarations are equivalent:

```
total DECIMAL
total DECIMAL(10)
total DECIMAL(10,0)
```

If you want to represent values such as dollar-and-cents currency figures, you can do so using a two-digit scale:

```
total DECIMAL(10,2)
```

The amount of storage required for DECIMAL column values depends on the type. Normally, the number of bytes of storage required per value is equal to the display width plus 2. For example, DECIMAL(6,3) requires 8 bytes: the display width is 6 and 2 bytes are needed to store the sign and decimal point. If the scale is 0, no decimal point needs to be stored, so one fewer byte is required. If the column is UNSIGNED, no sign character needs to be stored, also requiring one fewer byte.

4.10.2 String Column Types

The string column types are listed in the following table:

Type	Description
CHAR	Fixed-length string
VARCHAR	Variable-length string
BLOB	Variable-length binary string
TEXT	Variable-length nonbinary string
ENUM	Enumeration consisting of a fixed set of legal values
SET	Set consisting of a fixed set of legal values

When you choose a string datatype, consider the following factors:

- The maximum length of values you need to store.
- Whether to use a fixed or variable amount of storage.
- Whether you need to store binary or nonbinary strings.
- The number of distinct values required; ENUM or SET may be useful if the set of values is fixed.

The following discussion first describes the general differences between binary and nonbinary strings, and then the specific characteristics of each of the string column datatypes.

4.10.2.1 Binary and Nonbinary String Characteristics

Strings in MySQL may be treated as binary or nonbinary. The two types are each most suited to different purposes.

Binary strings have the following characteristics:

- A binary string is treated as a string of byte values.
- Comparisons of binary strings are performed on the basis of those byte values. This has the following implications:
  - Uppercase and lowercase versions of a given character have different byte values, so binary string comparisons are case sensitive.
  - Versions of a character that have different accent marks have different byte values, so binary string comparisons are also accent sensitive.
- A multi-byte character, if stored as a binary string, is treated simply as multiple individual bytes. Character boundaries of the original data no longer apply.

Nonbinary strings are associated with a character set. The character set affects interpretation of string contents and sorting as follows:

- A nonbinary string is a string of characters, all of which must belong to a specific character set. Characters may consist of a single byte, or multiple bytes if the character set allows it. For example, each character in the MySQL default character set (Latin-1, also known as ISO-8859-1) requires one byte to store. In contrast, the Japanese SJIS character set contains so many characters that they cannot all be represented in a single byte, so each character requires multiple bytes to store.
- Nonbinary comparisons are based on the collating (sorting) order of the character set associated with the string.
- Collating orders, or collations, sometimes treat uppercase and lowercase versions of a given character as equivalent. This means that comparisons using such collations are not case sensitive, so that, for example, 'ABC', 'Abc', and 'abc' are all considered equal.

- Collations may also treat a given character with different accent marks as equivalent. The result is that comparisons of nonbinary strings may not be accent sensitive. For example, an **a** with no accent may be considered the same as the á and à characters.

- Multi-byte character comparisons are performed in character units, not in byte units.

The preceding remarks regarding case and accent sensitivity are not absolute, just typical. A given character set can be defined with a collating order that's case or accent sensitive, or both. MySQL takes care to create character sets that correspond to the sorting order rules of different languages.

String comparison rules are addressed in more detail in section 6.1.1, "Case Sensitivity in String Comparisons."

The different treatment of binary and nonbinary strings in MySQL is important when it comes to choosing datatypes for table columns. If you want column values to be treated as case and accent insensitive, you should choose a nonbinary column type. Conversely, if you want case and accent sensitive values, choose a binary type. You should also choose a binary type for storing raw data values that consist of untyped bytes.

The CHAR and VARCHAR string column types are nonbinary by default, but can be made binary by including the keyword BINARY in the column definition. Other string types are inherently binary or nonbinary. BLOB columns are always binary, whereas TEXT columns are always nonbinary.

You can mix binary and nonbinary string columns within a single table. For example, assume that you want to create a table named auth_info, to store login name and password authorization information for an application. You want login names to match in any lettercase but passwords to be case sensitive. This statement would accomplish the task:

```
CREATE TABLE auth_info
(
    login    CHAR(16),           # not case sensitive
    password CHAR(16) BINARY     # case sensitive
);
```

4.10.2.2 The CHAR and VARCHAR Column Types

The CHAR and VARCHAR column types hold strings up to the maximum length specified in the column definition. To define a column with either of these datatypes, provide the column name, the keyword CHAR or VARCHAR, the maximum length of acceptable values in parentheses, and possibly the keyword BINARY. The maximum length should be a number from 0 to 255. (One of the sample exercises at the end of this chapter discusses why you might declare a zero-length column.) By default, CHAR and VARCHAR columns contain nonbinary strings. The BINARY modifier causes the values they contain to be treated as binary strings.

The CHAR datatype is a fixed-length type. Values in a CHAR column always take the same amount of storage. A column defined as CHAR(30), for example, requires 30 bytes for each value, even empty values. In contrast, VARCHAR is a variable-length datatype. A VARCHAR column takes only the number of bytes required to store each value, plus one byte per value to record the value's length.

For MySQL 4.0, the length for CHAR and VARCHAR columns is measured in bytes, not characters. There's no difference for single-byte character sets, but the two measures are different for multi-byte character sets. In MySQL 4.1, this will change; column lengths will be measured in characters. For example, CHAR(30) will mean 30 characters, even for multi-byte character sets.

4.10.2.3 The BLOB and TEXT Column Types

The BLOB and TEXT datatypes each come in four different sizes, differing in the maximum length of values they can store. All are variable-length types, so an individual value requires storage equal to the length (in bytes) of the value, plus 1 to 4 bytes to record the length of the value. The following table summarizes these datatypes; L represents the length of a given value.

Type	Storage Required	Maximum Length
TINYBLOB, TINYTEXT	L + 1 byte	255 bytes
BLOB, TEXT	L + 2 bytes	65,535 bytes
MEDIUMBLOB, MEDIUMTEXT	L + 3 bytes	16,777,215 bytes
LONGBLOB, LONGTEXT	L + 4 bytes	4,294,967,295 bytes

BLOB column values are always binary and TEXT column values are always nonbinary. When deciding which of the two to choose for a column, you would normally base your decision on whether you want to treat column values as case sensitive or whether they contain raw bytes rather than characters. BLOB columns are more suitable for case-sensitive strings or for raw data such as images or compressed data. TEXT columns are more suitable for case-insensitive character strings such as textual descriptions.

4.10.2.4 The ENUM and SET Column Types

Two of the string column types, ENUM and SET, are used when the values to be stored in a column are chosen from a fixed set of values. You define columns for both types in terms of string values, but MySQL represents them internally as integers. This leads to very efficient storage, but can have some surprising results unless you keep this string/integer duality in mind.

ENUM is an enumeration type. An ENUM column definition includes a list of allowable values; each value in the list is called a "member" of the list. Every value stored in the column must equal one of the values in the list. A simple (and very common) use for ENUM is to create a two-element list for columns that store yes/no or true/false choices. The following table shows how to declare such columns:

```
CREATE TABLE booleans
(
    yesno     ENUM('Y','N'),
    truefalse ENUM('T','F')
);
```

Enumeration values aren't limited to being single letters or uppercase. The columns could also be defined like this:

```
CREATE TABLE booleans
(
    yesno     ENUM('yes','no'),
    truefalse ENUM('true','false')
);
```

An ENUM column definition may list up to 65,535 members. Enumerations with up to 255 members require one byte of storage per value. Enumerations with 256 to 65,535 members require two bytes per value. The following table contains an enumeration column continent that lists continent names as valid enumeration members:

```
CREATE TABLE Countries
(
    name char(30),
    continent ENUM ('Asia','Europe','North America','Africa',
                    'Oceania','Antarctica','South America')
);
```

The values in an ENUM column definition are given as a comma-separated list of quoted strings. Internally, MySQL stores the strings as integers, using the values 1 through n for a column with n enumeration members. The following statement assigns the enumeration value 'Africa' to the continent column; MySQL actually stores the value 4 because 'Africa' is the fourth continent name listed in the enumeration definition:

```
INSERT INTO Countries (name,continent) VALUES('Kenya','Africa');
```

MySQL reserves the internal value 0 as an implicit member of all ENUM columns. It's used to represent illegal values assigned to an enumeration column. For example, if you assign 'USA' to the continent column, MySQL will store the value 0, rather than any of the values 1 through 7, because 'USA' is not a valid enumeration member. If you select the column later, MySQL displays 0 values as '' (the empty string).

The SET datatype, like ENUM, is declared using a comma-separated list of quoted strings that define its valid members. But unlike ENUM, a given SET column may be assigned a value consisting of any combination of those members. The following definition contains a list of symptoms exhibited by allergy sufferers:

```
CREATE TABLE allergy
(
    symptom SET('sneezing','runny nose','stuffy head','red eyes')
);
```

A patient may have any or all (or none) of these symptoms, and `symptom` values therefore might contain zero to four individual SET members, separated by commas. The following statements set the `symptom` column to the empty string (no SET members), a single SET member, and multiple SET members, respectively:

```
INSERT INTO allergy (symptom) VALUES('');
INSERT INTO allergy (symptom) VALUES('stuffy head');
INSERT INTO allergy (symptom) VALUES('sneezing,red eyes');
```

MySQL represents SET columns as a bitmap using one bit per member, so the elements in the `symptom` definition have internal values of 1, 2, 4, and 8 (that is, they have the values of bits 0 through 3 in a byte). Internally, MySQL stores the values shown in the preceding INSERT statements as 0 (no bits set), 4 (bit 2 set), and 9 (bits 0 and 3 set; that is, 1 plus 8).

A SET definition may contain up to 64 members. The internal storage required for set values varies depending on the number of SET elements (1, 2, 3, 4, or 8 bytes for sets of up to 8, 16, 24, 32, or 64 members).

If you try to store an invalid list member into a SET column, it's ignored because it does not correspond to any bit in the column definition. For example, setting a `symptom` value to `'coughing,sneezing,wheezing'` results in an internal value of 1 (`'sneezing'`). The `'coughing'` and `'wheezing'` elements are ignored because they aren't listed in the column definition as legal set members.

As mentioned earlier in this section, the conversion between string and numeric representations of ENUM and SET values can result in surprises if you aren't careful. For example, although you would normally refer to an enumeration column using the string forms of its values, you can also use the internal numeric values. The effect of this can be very subtle if the string values look like numbers. Suppose that you define a table t like this:

```
CREATE TABLE t (age INT, siblings ENUM('0','1','2','3','>3'));
```

In this case, the enumeration values are the strings `'0'`, `'1'`, `'2'`, `'3'`, and `'>3'`, and the matching internal numeric values are 1, 2, 3, 4, and 5, respectively. Now suppose that you issue the following statement:

```
INSERT INTO t (age,siblings) VALUES(14,'3');
```

The `siblings` value is specified here as the string `'3'`, and that is the value assigned to the column in the new record. However, you can also specify the `siblings` value as a number, as follows:

```
INSERT INTO t (age,siblings) VALUES(14,3);
```

But in this case, 3 is interpreted as the internal value, which corresponds to the enumeration value `'2'`! The same principle applies to retrievals. Consider the following two statements:

```
SELECT * FROM t WHERE siblings = '3';
SELECT * FROM t WHERE siblings = 3;
```

In the first case, you get records that have an enumeration value of '3'. In the second case, you get records where the internal value is 3; that is, records with an enumeration value of '2'.

4.10.3 Date and Time Column Types

MySQL provides column types for storing different kinds of temporal information. In the following descriptions, the terms *YYYY*, *MM*, *DD*, *hh*, *mm*, and *ss* stand for a year, month, day of month, hour, minute, and second value, respectively.

The storage requirements and ranges for the date and time datatypes are summarized in the following table:

Type	Storage Required	Range
DATE	3 bytes	'1000-01-01' to '9999-12-31'
TIME	3 bytes	'-838:59:59' to '838:59:59'
DATETIME	8 bytes	'1000-01-01 00:00:00' to '9999-12-31 23:59:59'
TIMESTAMP	4 bytes	'1970-01-01 00:00:00' to mid-year 2037
YEAR	1 byte	1901 to 2155 (YEAR(4)), 1970 to 2069 (YEAR(2))

For TIMESTAMP, MySQL 4.0 displays values such as '1970-01-01 00:00:00' as 19700101000000. In MySQL 4.1, this changes so that TIMESTAMP display format is the same as DATETIME.

Each of these temporal datatypes also has a "zero" value that's used when you attempt to store an illegal value. The "zero" value is represented in a format appropriate for the type (such as '0000-00-00' for DATE and '00:00:00' for TIME).

4.10.3.1 The DATE and TIME Column Types

The DATE datatype represents date values in 'YYYY-MM-DD' format. This representation corresponds to the ANSI SQL date format, also known as ISO 8601 format.

The supported range of DATE values is '1000-01-01' to '9999-12-31'. You might be able to use earlier dates than that, but it's better to stay within the supported range to avoid unexpected behavior.

MySQL always represents DATE values in ISO 8601 format when it displays them. If necessary, you can reformat DATE values into other display formats using the DATE_FORMAT() function.

For date entry, MySQL also expects to receive dates in ISO format, or at least close to ISO format. That is, date values must be given in year-month-day order, but some deviation from strict ISO format is allowed:

- Leading zeros on month and day values may be omitted. For example, '2000-1-1' and '2000-01-01' are both accepted as legal.

- The delimiter between date parts need not be -; you can use other punctuation characters, such as /.

- Two-digit years are converted to four-digit years. You should be aware that this conversion is done based on the rule that year values from 70 to 99 represent the years 1970 to 1999, whereas values from 00 to 69 represent the years 2000 to 2069. It's better to provide values with four-digit years to avoid problems with conversion of values for which the rule does not apply.

Instead of attempting to load values that aren't in an acceptable format into a DATE column, you should convert them into ISO format. An alternative approach that's useful in some circumstances is to load the values into a string column and perform reformatting operations using SQL string functions to produce ISO format values that can be assigned to a DATE column.

The TIME datatype represents time values in 'hh:mm:ss' format. TIME values may represent elapsed time, and thus might be outside the range of time-of-day values. They may even be negative values. (The actual range of TIME values is '-838:59:59' to '838:59:59'.)

MySQL represents TIME values in 'hh:mm:ss' format when displaying them. If necessary, you can reformat TIME values into other display formats using the TIME_FORMAT() function.

For TIME value entry, some variation on this format is allowed. For example, leading zeros on TIME parts may be omitted.

4.10.3.2 The TIMESTAMP and DATETIME Column Types

The DATETIME column type stores date-and-time values in 'YYYY-MM-DD hh:mm:ss' format. It's similar to a combination of DATE and TIME values, but the TIME part represents time of day rather than elapsed time and has a range limited to '00:00:00' to '23:59:59'. The date part of DATETIME columns has the same range as DATE columns; combined with the TIME part, this results in a DATETIME range from '1000-01-01 00:00:00' to '9999-12-31 23:59:59'.

The TIMESTAMP type, like DATETIME, stores date-and-time values, but has a different range and some special properties that make it especially suitable for tracking data modification times. TIMESTAMP also has a different display format from DATETIME prior to MySQL 4.1:

- Until MySQL 4.1, TIMESTAMP values are represented as numbers in YYYYMMDDhhmmss format. The default display width is 14 digits, but you can specify an explicit width of any even number from 2 to 14. The display width affects only how MySQL displays TIMESTAMP values, not how it stores them. Stored values always include the full 14 digits.

- From MySQL 4.1 on, the TIMESTAMP format is 'YYYY-MM-DD hh:mm:ss', just like DATETIME. Display widths are not supported.

The range of TIMESTAMP values begins at 1970-01-01 00:00:00 (GMT) and extends partway into the year 2037. TIMESTAMP values actually represent the number of seconds elapsed since the beginning of 1970 and are stored using four bytes. This provides room for sufficient seconds to represent a date in the year 2037. Note that TIMESTAMP values are stored using the server's local timezone.

TIMESTAMP columns have the following special properties:

- Storing NULL into a TIMESTAMP column sets it to the current date and time. Updating a TIMESTAMP column to NULL also sets it to the current date and time.

- If you omit a TIMESTAMP column from an INSERT statement, MySQL inserts the current date and time if the column is the first TIMESTAMP column in the table, and inserts zero if it is not.

- MySQL automatically updates the first TIMESTAMP column in a table to the current date and time when you update (change the existing data in) any other column in the table. (Setting a column to its current value doesn't count as updating it.) Only the first TIMESTAMP column is subject to automatic updating. All other TIMESTAMP columns do not change unless you update them explicitly.

It's important to know about the automatic-update property. It's what makes TIMESTAMP columns useful for tracking record modification times, but is a source of confusion if you're not aware of it. People who choose TIMESTAMP for a column on the basis of the fact that it stores date-and-time values become dismayed and mystified when they discover that the column's values change unexpectedly.

4.10.3.3 The YEAR Column Type

The YEAR column type represents year-only values. You can declare such columns as YEAR(4) or YEAR(2) to obtain a four-digit or two-digit display format. If you don't specify any display width, the default is four digits.

If you don't need a full date and the range of values you need to store falls into the YEAR range, consider using YEAR to store temporal values. It's a very space-efficient datatype because values require only one byte of storage each.

4.10.4 Column Options

The final part of a column definition (following the datatype) can include optional modifiers. These options are described in the following list. Note that many of them apply only to certain column types.

- UNSIGNED applies to numeric datatypes and causes negative values to be disallowed. If you attempt to store a negative value in an UNSIGNED column, MySQL stores zero instead.

- ZEROFILL applies to integer numeric column types. It causes retrieved values to be left-padded with leading zeros up to the column's display width. For example, if you store the values 0, 14, and 1234 in a column that's defined as INT(5) ZEROFILL, MySQL displays them as 00000, 00014, and 01234 when you retrieve them.

  Using the ZEROFILL option for a column causes it to be UNSIGNED as well.

- AUTO_INCREMENT applies to integer numeric column types. It's used to generate sequences of successive unique values. Defining a column with AUTO_INCREMENT causes a special behavior: When you insert NULL into the column, MySQL generates the next value in the sequence automatically and stores that in the column instead. Use of AUTO_INCREMENT carries with it other requirements: There may be only one AUTO_INCREMENT column per table, the column must be indexed, and the column must be defined as NOT NULL. Section 4.10.5, "Using the AUTO_INCREMENT Column Option," provides specific details on the use of AUTO_INCREMENT columns.

- BINARY applies to the CHAR and VARCHAR datatypes. CHAR and VARCHAR columns are nonbinary by default; adding BINARY to the definition causes column values to be treated as binary strings.

  Beginning with MySQL 4.1, BINARY may also be applied to ENUM and SET columns to cause case-sensitive treatment of column values.

- NULL and NOT NULL apply to all column types. They indicate whether or not a column can contain NULL values. If you specify neither option, the default is NULL, which allows NULL values in the column.

- DEFAULT *value* provides the column with a default value to be used when you create a new record but don't explicitly specify a value for the column (for example, when you execute an INSERT statement that doesn't provide values for all columns in the table). This attribute applies to all column types except BLOB and TEXT. A default value must be a constant; it cannot be an expression whose value is calculated at record-creation time.

  If you don't specify a DEFAULT value for a column, MySQL chooses a default for you. The value is NULL if the column may contain NULL; otherwise, the value depends on the column type:

  - For numeric columns, the default is zero.
  - For string columns other than ENUM, the default is the empty string. For ENUM columns, the default is the first enumeration member.
  - For temporal columns, the default value is the "zero" value for the datatype, represented in whatever format is appropriate to the column type (for example, '0000-00-00' for DATE and '00:00:00' for TIME).

The exceptions to the preceding are the first TIMESTAMP column in a table and integer columns that have the AUTO_INCREMENT attribute. For such columns, MySQL uses a default value of the current date and time, and the next sequence number, respectively. Furthermore, if you supply a DEFAULT option for these column types, MySQL ignores it or produces an error.

It's an error to specify a default value of NULL for a NOT NULL column.

- PRIMARY KEY and UNIQUE may be given at the end of a column definition, for all datatypes except BLOB and TEXT. They cause the creation of a PRIMARY KEY or UNIQUE index for the column. Adding either of these options to a column definition is the same as defining the index in a separate clause. For example, the following table definitions are equivalent:

```
CREATE TABLE t (i INT NOT NULL PRIMARY KEY);

CREATE TABLE t (i INT NOT NULL, PRIMARY KEY (i));
```

4.10.5 Using the AUTO_INCREMENT Column Option

The AUTO_INCREMENT option may be added to an integer column definition to create a column for which MySQL automatically generates a new sequence number each time you create a new row. The option is used in conjunction with an index (usually a primary key) and provides a mechanism whereby each value is a unique identifier that can be used to refer unambiguously to the row in which it occurs. MySQL also provides a LAST_INSERT_ID() function that returns the most recently generated AUTO_INCREMENT value. This function is useful for determining the identifier when you need to look up the record just created, or when you need to know the identifier to create related records in other tables.

The following scenario illustrates how you can set up and use an AUTO_INCREMENT column. Assume that you're organizing a conference and need to keep track of attendees and the seminars for which each attendee registers. (When someone submits a registration form for the conference, the form must indicate which of the available seminars the person wants to attend.)

Your task is to record seminar registrations and associate them with the appropriate attendee. Unique ID numbers provide a way to keep track of attendees and an AUTO_INCREMENT column makes the implementation for the task relatively easy:

1. Set up an attendee table to record information about each person attending the conference. The table shown here includes columns for ID number, name, and job title:

```
mysql> CREATE TABLE attendee
    -> (
    ->     att_id       INT UNSIGNED NOT NULL AUTO_INCREMENT,
    ->     att_name     CHAR(100),
    ->     att_title    CHAR(40),
    ->     PRIMARY KEY (att_id)
    -> );
```

The att_id column is created as a PRIMARY KEY because it must contain unique values, and as an AUTO_INCREMENT column because it's necessary for MySQL to generate values for the column automatically.

2. Set up a `seminar` table to record the seminars for which each attendee registers. Assume that there are four seminars: Database Design, Query Optimization, SQL Standards, and Using Replication. There are various ways in which these seminars can be represented; an `ENUM` column is one that works well because the seminar titles form a small fixed list of values. The table must also record the ID of each attendee taking part in the seminar. The table can be created with this statement:

```
mysql> CREATE TABLE seminar
    -> (
    ->     att_id    INT UNSIGNED NOT NULL,
    ->     sem_title ENUM('Database Design','Query Optimization',
    ->                    'SQL Standards','Using Replication'),
    ->     INDEX (att_id)
    -> );
```

Note both the differences and similarities of the `att_id` column declarations in the two tables. In `attendee`, `att_id` is an `AUTO_INCREMENT` column and is indexed as a `PRIMARY KEY` to ensure that each value in the column is unique. In `seminar`, `att_id` is indexed for faster lookups, but it isn't indexed as a `PRIMARY KEY`. (There might be multiple records for a given attendee and a `PRIMARY KEY` does not allow duplicates.) Nor is the column declared in the `seminar` table with the `AUTO_INCREMENT` option because ID values should be tied to existing IDs in the `attendee` table, not generated automatically. Aside from these differences, the column is declared using the same datatype (`INT`) and options (`UNSIGNED`, `NOT NULL`) as the `att_id` column in the `attendee` table.

3. Each time a conference registration form is received, enter the attendee information into the `attendee` table. For example:

```
mysql> INSERT INTO attendee (att_name,att_title)
    -> VALUES('Charles Loviness','IT Manager');
```

Note that the `INSERT` statement doesn't include a value for the `att_id` column. Because `att_id` is an `AUTO_INCREMENT` column, MySQL generates the next sequence number (beginning with 1) and sets the `att_id` column in the new row to that value. You can use the new `att_id` value to look up the record just inserted, but how do you know what value to use? The answer is that you don't need to know the exact value. Instead, you can get the ID by invoking the `LAST_INSERT_ID()` function, which returns the most recent `AUTO_INCREMENT` value generated during your current connection with the server. Thus, the record for Charles Loviness can be retrieved like this:

```
mysql> SELECT * FROM attendee WHERE att_id = LAST_INSERT_ID();
+--------+------------------+------------+
| att_id | att_name         | att_title  |
+--------+------------------+------------+
|      3 | Charles Loviness | IT Manager |
+--------+------------------+------------+
```

This output indicates that the Loviness form was the third one entered.

4. Next, enter new records into the `seminar` table for each seminar marked on the entry form. The `att_id` value in each of these records must match the `att_id` value in the newly created `attendee` record. Here again, the `LAST_INSERT_ID()` value can be used. If Loviness will participate in Database Design, SQL Standards, and Using Replication, create records for those seminars as follows:

```
mysql> INSERT INTO seminar (att_id,sem_title)
    -> VALUES(LAST_INSERT_ID(),'Database Design');
mysql> INSERT INTO seminar (att_id,sem_title)
    -> VALUES(LAST_INSERT_ID(),'SQL Standards');
mysql> INSERT INTO seminar (att_id,sem_title)
    -> VALUES(LAST_INSERT_ID(),'Using Replication');
```

To see what the new `seminar` records look like, use the `LAST_INSERT_ID()` value to retrieve them:

```
mysql> SELECT * FROM seminar WHERE att_id = LAST_INSERT_ID();
+--------+-------------------+
| att_id | sem_title         |
+--------+-------------------+
|      3 | Database Design   |
|      3 | SQL Standards     |
|      3 | Using Replication |
+--------+-------------------+
```

5. When you receive the next registration form, repeat the process just described. For every new `attendee` record, the value of `LAST_INSERT_ID()` will change to reflect the new value in the `att_id` column.

The preceding description shows how to use an `AUTO_INCREMENT` column—how to declare the column, how to generate new ID values when inserting new records, and how to use the ID values to tie together related tables. However, the description glosses over some of the details. These are presented in the following discussion, beginning with declaration syntax and then providing further information about how `AUTO_INCREMENT` columns work.

The `att_id`-related declarations in the `attendee` table look like this:

```
att_id INT UNSIGNED NOT NULL AUTO_INCREMENT,
PRIMARY KEY (att_id)
```

These declarations involve the following factors, which you should consider when creating an `AUTO_INCREMENT` column:

- The column must be an integer type. Choose the specific datatype based on the number of values the column must be able to hold. For the largest range, use `BIGINT`. However, `BIGINT` requires 8 bytes per value. If you want to use less storage, `INT` requires only 4 bytes per value and provides a range that's adequate for many applications. You can use integer types smaller than INT as well, but it's a common error to choose one that's *too* small. For example, TINYINT has a range that allows very few unique numbers, so you'll almost certainly run into problems using it as an AUTO_INCREMENT column for identification purposes.

- An AUTO_INCREMENT sequence contains only positive values. For this reason, it's best to declare the column to be UNSIGNED. Syntactically, it isn't strictly required that you declare the column this way, but doing so doubles the range of the sequence because an UNSIGNED integer column has a larger maximum value. Defining the column as UNSIGNED also serves as a reminder that you should never store negative values in an AUTO_INCRE-MENT column.

- The most common way to use an AUTO_INCREMENT column is as a primary key, which ensures unique values and prevents duplicates. The column should thus be defined to contain unique values, either as a PRIMARY KEY or a UNIQUE index. (MySQL allows you to declare an AUTO_INCREMENT column with a nonunique index, but this is less common.)

- An AUTO_INCREMENT column defined as a PRIMARY KEY must also be NOT NULL.

After setting up an AUTO_INCREMENT column, use it as follows:

- Inserting NULL into an AUTO_INCREMENT column causes MySQL to generate the next sequence value and store it in the column. Omitting the AUTO_INCREMENT column from an INSERT statement is the same as inserting NULL explicitly. In other words, an INSERT statement that does not provide an explicit value for an AUTO_INCREMENT column also generates the next sequence value for the column. For example, if id is an AUTO_INCREMENT column in the table t, the following two statements are equivalent:

```
INSERT INTO t (id,name) VALUES(NULL,'Hans');
INSERT INTO t (name) VALUES('Hans');
```

- Currently, inserting 0 into an AUTO_INCREMENT column has the same effect as inserting NULL: the next sequence value is generated. However, it isn't recommended that you rely on this behavior because it might change in the future.

- A positive value can be inserted explicitly into an AUTO_INCREMENT column if the value isn't already present in the column. If this value is larger than the current sequence counter, subsequent automatically generated values begin with the value plus one:

```
mysql> CREATE TABLE t (id INT AUTO_INCREMENT, PRIMARY KEY (id));
mysql> INSERT INTO t (id) VALUES(NULL),(NULL),(17),(NULL),(NULL);
mysql> SELECT id FROM t;
+----+
| id |
+----+
|  1 |
|  2 |
| 17 |
| 18 |
```

```
| 19 |
+----+
```

- After an AUTO_INCREMENT value has been generated, the LAST_INSERT_ID() function returns the generated value. LAST_INSERT_ID() will continue to return the same value, regardless of the number of times it's invoked, until another AUTO_INCREMENT value is generated.

- The value returned by LAST_INSERT_ID() is specific to the client that generates the AUTO_INCREMENT value. That is, it's connection-specific, so the LAST_INSERT_ID() value is always correct for the current connection, even if other clients also generate AUTO_INCREMENT values of their own. Another client cannot change the value that LAST_INSERT_ID() returns to you, nor can one client use LAST_INSERT_ID() to determine the AUTO_INCREMENT value generated by another.

- AUTO_INCREMENT behavior is the same for REPLACE as it is for INSERT. Any existing record is deleted, and then the new record is inserted. Consequently, replacing an AUTO_INCREMENT column with NULL or 0 causes it to be set to the next sequence value.

- If you update an AUTO_INCREMENT column to NULL or 0 in an UPDATE statement, the column is set to 0.

- If you delete rows containing values at the high end of a sequence, those values are not reused for MyISAM or InnoDB tables when you insert new records. For example, if an AUTO_INCREMENT column contains the values from 1 to 10 and you delete the record containing 10, the next sequence value is 11, not 10. (This differs from ISAM and BDB tables, for which values deleted from the high end of a sequence *are* reused.)

The MyISAM storage engine supports composite indexes that include an AUTO_INCREMENT column. This allows creation of independent sequences within a single table. Consider the following table definition:

```
CREATE TABLE multisequence
(
    name     CHAR(10) NOT NULL,
    name_id  INT UNSIGNED NOT NULL AUTO_INCREMENT,
    PRIMARY KEY (name, name_id)
);
```

Inserting name values into the multisequence table generates separate sequences for each distinct name:

```
mysql> INSERT INTO multisequence (name)
    -> VALUES('Petr'),('Ilya'),('Ilya'),('Yuri'),('Ilya'),('Petr');
mysql> SELECT * FROM multisequence ORDER BY name, name_id;
+------+---------+
| name | name_id |
+------+---------+
| Ilya |       1 |
```

```
| Ilya |      2 |
| Ilya |      3 |
| Petr |      1 |
| Petr |      2 |
| Yuri |      1 |
+------+--------+
```

Note that for this kind of AUTO_INCREMENT column, values deleted from the high end of any sequence are reused. This differs from MyISAM behavior for single-column AUTO_INCREMENT sequences.

4.10.6 Automatic Type Conversion and Value Clipping

For historical reasons, MySQL is forgiving about signaling an error if a given value doesn't match the datatype of the column that is the insert target. Instead, MySQL does its best to perform automatic type conversion. For example, if you attempt to store a negative value in an UNSIGNED integer column, MySQL silently converts it to zero, which is the nearest legal value for the column. In other words, the MySQL server converts input values to the types expected from the column definitions, inserts the result, and continues on its way.

If you need to prevent attempts to insert invalid values into a table, you should first validate the values on the client side; however, because that isn't an exam topic, it isn't discussed further here.

This section describes the kinds of conversions that MySQL performs and the circumstances under which they occur. After you know these principles, you'll know what types of validation are necessary before trying to store your data in a MySQL database.

In many cases, type conversion affords you the flexibility to write a statement different ways and get the same result. For example, if i is an integer column, the following statements both insert 43 into it, even though the value is specified as a number in one statement and as a string in the other:

```
INSERT INTO t (i) VALUES(43);
INSERT INTO t (i) VALUES('43');
```

MySQL performs automatic string-to-number conversion for the second statement.

In other cases, the effects of type conversion might be surprising, particularly if you're unaware that these conversions occur. You can avoid such surprises by understanding the conditions under which conversion takes place. In general, MySQL performs type conversion based on the constraints implied by a column's definition. These constraints apply in several contexts:

- When you insert or update column values with statements such as INSERT, REPLACE, UPDATE, or LOAD DATA INFILE.

- When you change a column definition with ALTER TABLE.

- When you specify a default value using a DEFAULT *value* option in a column definition. (For example, if you specify a negative default for an UNSIGNED column, the value is converted, resulting in a default of zero.)

The following list discusses some of the conversions that MySQL performs. It isn't exhaustive, but is sufficiently representative to provide you with a good idea of how MySQL treats input values and what you'll be tested on in the exam. Circumstances under which automatic type conversion occurs include the following:

- *Conversion of out-of-range values to in-range values.* If you attempt to store a value that's smaller than the minimum value allowed by the range of a column's datatype, MySQL stores the minimum value in the range. If you attempt to store a value that's larger than the maximum value in the range, MySQL stores the range's maximum value. Some examples of this behavior are as follows:

  - TINYINT has a range of –128 to 127. If you attempt to store values less than –128 in a TINYINT column, MySQL stores –128 instead. Similarly, MySQL stores values greater than 127 as 127.

  - If you insert a negative value into an UNSIGNED integer column, MySQL converts the value to 0.

  - When you reach the upper limit of an AUTO_INCREMENT column, an attempt to generate the next sequence value results in a duplicate-key error. This is a manifestation of MySQL's general out-of-range value clipping behavior. For example, assume that you have a TINYINT UNSIGNED column as an AUTO_INCREMENT column and that it currently contains 254 as the maximum sequence value. The upper limit for this column type is 255, so the next insert generates a sequence value of 255 and successfully stores it in the new record. However, the insert after that fails because MySQL generates the next sequence value, which is 256. Because 256 is higher than the column's upper limit of 255, MySQL clips 256 down to 255 and attempts to insert that value. But because 255 is already present in the table, a duplicate-key error occurs.

- *Conversion to datatype default.* If you attempt to store a value for which MySQL cannot decide on an appropriate conversion, it stores the default value for the datatype of the target column. For example, if you try to store the value 'Sakila' in an INT column, MySQL stores the value 0. For dates, the "zero" value is 0000-00-00 and for time columns 00:00:00. More details on the default for each column type are given in section 4.10.4, "Column Options."

- *String truncation.* If you attempt to store a string value into a VARCHAR or CHAR column with a defined length that's shorter than the string, the string is truncated to fit the column's length. That is, only the leading characters that fit into the column are stored. The remaining characters are discarded. For example, if you try to store the value 'Sakila' into a column defined as CHAR(4), MySQL stores the value 'Saki'.

- *Date and time interpretation.* The server performs streamlined checking of temporal values. It looks at individual components of date and time values, but does not perform an exhaustive check of the value as a whole. For example, day values may be considered valid as long as they're within the range 1 to 31. This means you can specify a date such as '2000-04-31' and MySQL will store it as given. However, a DATETIME value such as '2000-01-01 24:00:00' contains an hour value of 24, which is never valid as a time of day. Consequently, MySQL stores the "zero" value in DATETIME format ('0000-00-00 00:00:00').

- *Addition of century for two-digit years.* Like many other computer programs, MySQL converts two-digit years to four-digit years. Values 00 to 69 are converted to 2000-2069; values 70 to 99 are converted to 1970-1999.

- *Enumeration and set value conversion.* If a value that's assigned to an ENUM column isn't listed in the ENUM definition, MySQL converts it to '' (the empty string). If a value that's assigned to a SET column contains elements that aren't listed in the SET definition, MySQL discards those elements, retaining only the legal elements.

- *Handing assignment of NULL to NOT NULL columns.* The effect of assigning NULL to a NOT NULL column depends on whether the assignment occurs in a single-row or multiple-row INSERT statement. For a single-row INSERT, the statement fails. For a multiple-row INSERT, the column is assigned the default value for the column type.

- *Conversion of fixed-point values.* Conversion, into numbers, of string values that can be interpreted as numbers is different for DECIMAL than for other numeric datatypes. This occurs because DECIMAL values are represented as strings rather than in native binary format. For example, if you assign '0003' to an INT or FLOAT, it's stored as 3 in integer or floating-point binary format. In contrast, if you assign '0003' to a DECIMAL column, it's stored without change, including the leading zeros, even though it will behave identically to a '3' in mathematical operations. If the DECIMAL column isn't wide enough to accommodate the leading zeros, as many are stored as possible. If you store '0003' into a DECIMAL(2,0) UNSIGNED column, it's converted to '03'.

Using ALTER TABLE to change a column's datatype maps existing values to new values according to the constraints imposed by the new datatype. This might result in some values being changed. For example, if you change a TINYINT to an INT, no values are changed because all TINYINT values fit within the INT range. However, if you change an INT to a TINYINT, any values that lie outside the range of TINYINT are clipped to the nearest endpoint of the TINYINT range. Similar effects occur for other types of conversions, such as TINYINT to TINYINT UNSIGNED (negative values are converted to zero), and converting a long string column to a shorter one (values that are too long are truncated to fit the new size).

If a column is changed to NOT NULL using ALTER TABLE, MySQL converts NULL values to the default value for the column type.

The following table shows how several types of string values are handled when converted to date or numeric datatypes. It demonstrates several of the points just discussed. Note that only string values that look like dates or numbers convert properly without loss of information. Note too that leading zeros are retained for the DECIMAL column during conversion.

String Value	Converted to DATE	Converted to INT	Converted to DECIMAL
'2010-12-03'	'2010-12-03'	2010	2010
'zebra'	'0000-00-00'	0	0
'500 hats'	'0000-00-00'	500	500
'1978-06-12'	'1978-06-12'	1970	1970
'06-12-1978'	'0000-00-00'	6	06
'0017'	'0000-00-00'	17	0017

4.11 Using SHOW and DESCRIBE to Review Table Structures

The SELECT statement retrieves the information *contained* in your databases. You can also ask MySQL to show you information *about* your databases, such as database and table names or information about the columns or indexes in a table. This section discusses the SHOW and DESCRIBE statements, which provide the following types of information:

```
SHOW DATABASES;
SHOW TABLES [FROM db_name];
SHOW CREATE TABLE table_name;
DESCRIBE table_name;
```

You're already familiar with the DESCRIBE statement. Its output format was discussed in the "Introduction" and it has been used in several examples earlier in this study guide.

4.11.1 Listing Database or Table Names

To determine the databases or tables that exist on your server, use the SHOW statement. SHOW is a versatile statement that has several variations for displaying many types of information.

SHOW DATABASES displays a list of the databases that your server manages:

```
mysql> SHOW DATABASES;
+-------------+
| Database    |
+-------------+
| menagerie   |
| mysql       |
| test        |
| world       |
+-------------+
```

The mysql and test databases are created during MySQL installation, so you're likely to see both of them in the output from the SHOW DATABASES statement. The mysql database contains the grant tables and should always be present because the grant tables contain user account information that the server uses to control access to the databases. The test database will be present unless someone has removed it.

The output of the SHOW DATABASES statement depends on whether you have the SHOW DATABASES privilege. If you have the privilege, the statement shows the names of all existing databases. Otherwise, it shows only those databases to which you have access.

To determine the tables a particular database contains, use SHOW TABLES:

```
mysql> SHOW TABLES FROM world;
+-----------------+
| Tables_in_world |
+-----------------+
| City            |
| Country         |
| CountryLanguage |
+-----------------+
```

The FROM clause names the database whose table names you want to determine. With no FROM clause, SHOW TABLES displays the names of the tables in the default database. If there is no default database, an error occurs:

```
mysql> SHOW TABLES;
ERROR 1046: No Database Selected
```

SHOW DATABASES and SHOW TABLES can each take a LIKE 'pattern' clause (note the quotes). With LIKE, the statement performs a pattern-matching operation and displays information only about databases or tables with names that match the pattern. Pattern matching is discussed in section 6.2, "Using LIKE for Pattern Matching."

```
mysql> SHOW DATABASES LIKE 'm%';
+---------------+
| Database (m%) |
+---------------+
| menagerie     |
| mysql         |
+---------------+
mysql> SHOW TABLES FROM world LIKE '%tr%';
+-----------------------+
| Tables_in_world (%tr%) |
+-----------------------+
| Country               |
| CountryLanguage       |
+-----------------------+
```

4.11.2 Getting Table Information

To obtain information about the structure of a given table, use DESCRIBE or one of the forms of the SHOW statement that displays the kind of table information in which you're interested.

Information about a table's columns can be obtained using DESCRIBE. For example:

```
mysql> DESCRIBE CountryLanguage;
+------------+--------------+------+-----+---------+-------+
| Field      | Type         | Null | Key | Default | Extra |
+------------+--------------+------+-----+---------+-------+
| Country    | char(3)      |      | PRI |         |       |
| Language   | char(30)     |      | PRI |         |       |
| IsOfficial | enum('T','F')|      |     | F       |       |
| Percentage | float(3,1)   |      |     | 0.0     |       |
+------------+--------------+------+-----+---------+-------+
```

The format of DESCRIBE was discussed in the "Introduction." DESCRIBE *table_name* is a synonym for SHOW COLUMNS FROM *table_name* or SHOW FIELDS FROM *table_name*. These statements are equivalent:

```
DESCRIBE CountryLanguage;
SHOW COLUMNS FROM CountryLanguage;
SHOW FIELDS FROM CountryLanguage;
```

SHOW CREATE TABLE shows the CREATE TABLE statement that corresponds to a table's definition, including its columns, indexes, and any table options the table has:

```
mysql> SHOW CREATE TABLE CountryLanguage\G
*************************** 1. row ***************************
       Table: CountryLanguage
Create Table: CREATE TABLE `countrylanguage` (
  `Country` char(3) NOT NULL default '',
  `Language` char(30) NOT NULL default '',
  `IsOfficial` enum('T','F') NOT NULL default 'F',
  `Percentage` float(3,1) NOT NULL default '0.0',
  PRIMARY KEY  (`Country`,`Language`)
) TYPE=MyISAM
```

4.12 Exercises

Question 1:

What statement do you use to drop the test database? How can you undo, or cancel, this statement?

Question 2:

Which statements can you use to drop the index idx_id on table tbl? How can you recover the index?

Question 3:

Name the four kinds of indexes that MySQL supports.

Question 4:

List the differences between a UNIQUE index and a PRIMARY KEY.

Question 5:

What must be true of the columns named in a UNIQUE index for the index to be functionally equivalent to a PRIMARY KEY on the same columns?

Question 6:

Which type of index cannot be created with CREATE INDEX or dropped with DROP INDEX?

Question 7:

If you want a table to include a column that will automatically record the current date and time when rows are inserted or modified, what column datatype should you use?

Question 8:

If you want to store monetary values (for example, values representing U.S. dollar-and-cent amounts such as $48.99), which column datatype should you use to avoid rounding errors?

Question 9:

Which column datatype is more space-efficient: CHAR(100) or VARCHAR(100)?

Question 10:

How do you make a CHAR or VARCHAR column case sensitive?

Question 11:

Which column datatype is case sensitive: TEXT or BLOB? Why?

Question 12:

What's the difference between a string value that consists of characters and a string value that consists of bytes?

Question 13:

When you use DROP TABLE to remove a table, how do you tell MySQL not to report an error if the table doesn't exist?

Question 14:

Is the following statement true or false?

A database must contain at least one table.

Question 15:

Is the following statement true or false?

A table must contain at least one column.

Question 16:

Is the following statement true or false?

A table must contain at least one row.

Question 17:

Is the following statement true or false?

To create a table, you must first issue a statement to choose a default database in which to store the table.

Question 18:

Is the following statement true or false?

MySQL itself imposes no limit on the number of databases you can create on the server.

Question 19:

Is the following statement true or false?

InnoDB imposes no limit on the number of tables that can be held in the InnoDB tablespace.

Question 20:

Is the following statement true or false?

In a MySQL database, every table has an .frm file in the appropriate database directory, regardless of the table type used.

Question 21:

Name four ways to work around a table size limitation that's imposed by the file size limitation of the operating system.

Question 22:

Which of the following statements are true for HEAP tables?

  a. Table structure, data, and indexes are held in memory only.

  b. They are read-only.

  c. They support row-level locking.

  d. They have extremely high performance.

Question 23:

Which clause can you add to a CREATE DATABASE or CREATE TABLE statement to ensure that no error occurs if the database or table already exists?

Question 24:

Which clause can you add to a DROP DATABASE or DROP TABLE statement to ensure that no error occurs if the database or table doesn't exist?

Question 25:

The test database is your default database. You want to create a table named cats in the friends database without changing the default database. What statement do you issue? (Leave out the column specifications for your answer.)

Question 26:

You want to create a table, but you want to decide later the database to which it should belong. How do you do accomplish this?

Question 27:

Why does the following SQL statement fail?

```
CREATE TABLE cats (
    id   INT       UNSIGNED NOT NULL AUTO_INCREMENT PRIMARY KEY
    name CHAR(10)
);
```

Question 28:

Provide the SQL statement that will create a table with the following structure:

```
mysql> DESCRIBE mytbl;
+-------+-----------------+------+-----+---------+
| Field | Type            | Null | Key | Default |
+-------+-----------------+------+-----+---------+
| col1  | int(10) unsigned |     | PRI | 0       |
| col2  | char(50)        |      | UNI |         |
| col3  | char(50)        |      | MUL |         |
+-------+-----------------+------+-----+---------+
```

Question 29:

Is the following statement true or false?

You can add a column to a table with a single ALTER TABLE statement.

Question 30:

Is the following statement true or false?

You can add multiple columns to a table with a single ALTER TABLE statement.

Question 31:

Is the following statement true or false?

You can add one or more rows to a table with a single ALTER TABLE statement.

Question 32:

Is the following statement true or false?

You can change the datatype of a column with a single ALTER TABLE statement.

Question 33:

Is the following statement true or false?

You can change the name of a column with a single ALTER TABLE statement.

Question 34:

Is the following statement true or false?

You can drop indexes with a single ALTER TABLE statement.

Question 35:

Is the following statement true or false?

You can create indexes with a single ALTER TABLE statement.

Question 36:

Is the following statement true or false?

You can drop all columns of a table (thus dropping the table itself) with a single ALTER TABLE statement.

Question 37:

Is the following statement true or false?

Using a single ALTER TABLE statement, you can add a new column as the first column in a table.

Question 38:

Is the following statement true or false?

You can change existing data in the table with a single ALTER TABLE statement.

Question 39:

Suppose that you have the following table structure:

```
+-------+---------+
| Field | Type    |
+-------+---------+
| col   | int(11) |
+-------+---------+
```

You want to add another column with the name COL (all uppercase letters). How can you do this?

Question 40:

There are two ways to rename table tbl to tbl_new with SQL statements. What statements can you use?

Question 41:

Name the two most common reasons to create an index on a table.

Question 42:

The table `mytable` has the following structure, with a UNIQUE index on its only column, `col`:

```
mysql> DESCRIBE mytable;
+-------+----------+------+-----+---------+-------+
| Field | Type     | Null | Key | Default | Extra |
+-------+----------+------+-----+---------+-------+
| col   | char(10) | YES  | MUL | NULL    |       |
+-------+----------+------+-----+---------+-------+
```

The table is empty. Will the following INSERT statement fail?

```
mysql> INSERT INTO mytable VALUES (NULL),(NULL),('data'),('test'),(NULL);
```

Question 43:

Table `mytable` has a composite PRIMARY KEY consisting of both `col1` and `col2`. Is it possible to declare one of the two columns as NULL, like this?

```
mysql> CREATE TABLE mytable (
    -> col1 CHAR(5) NOT NULL,
    -> col2 CHAR(5) NULL,
    -> PRIMARY KEY (col1,col2)
    -> );
```

Question 44:

Table `mytable` contains the data shown in the following listing. The data should remain unchanged. Is it possible to add a PRIMARY KEY to table `mytable`? If it's possible, what SQL statement would you use to create a composite PRIMARY KEY for `col1` and `col2` on the table?

```
mysql> SELECT * FROM mytable;
+------+------+
| col1 | col2 |
+------+------+
| yoo  | doo  |
| doo  | yoo  |
| doo  | doo  |
| yoo  | yoo  |
+------+------+
```

Question 45:

You have a table `mytable` that looks like this:

```
mysql> DESCRIBE mytable;
+-------+---------+
| Field | Type    |
+-------+---------+
| col1  | int(11) |
| col3  | int(11) |
+-------+---------+
```

You want to add three more columns: col0 as the first column in the table, col2 between col1 and col3, and col4 as the last column. All new columns should be of type INT. What SQL statement do you issue?

Question 46:

You want to see what indexes you have in table tbl, but DESCRIBE tbl does not show sufficient information. What other statement can you issue to obtain additional information about the table structure?

Question 47:

What happens if you don't provide an index name when creating an index with ALTER TABLE or with CREATE INDEX?

Question 48:

Can you drop multiple indexes with a single DROP INDEX statement?

Question 49:

To declare a primary key on only one column (col1, with datatype INT) of table tbl at creation time, you can use the following syntax:

```
mysql> CREATE TABLE tbl (col1 INT NOT NULL PRIMARY KEY);
```

What's the correct syntax if you want to declare a composite primary key for this table on two INT columns col1 and col2?

Question 50:

In a table population, you want to store the number of inhabitants of cities. Storage is at a premium. You expect the maximum population to be 15,000,000 for a city. Which column datatype (and desired column options) would you use? What's the storage requirement for this column datatype for each row in the table?

Question 51:

In a table user, you have a comment column to store remarks. For each remark, you want to be able to store up to 2,000 characters. What column datatype would you use, and what's the storage requirement for each row if the average remark is 300 characters long?

Question 52:

You have a table in which you want to store birthdays of historical persons, and you decide to use the DATE datatype to store the information. What's the earliest birthday you can store?

Question 53:

Here's the structure of a table datetest with a single column d of datatype DATE. This table will be used for the next seven questions.

```
mysql> DESCRIBE datetest;
+-------+------+------+-----+---------+
| Field | Type | Null | Key | Default |
+-------+------+------+-----+---------+
| d     | date | YES  |     | NULL    |
+-------+------+------+-----+---------+
```

You perform the following INSERT operation on table datetest:

```
INSERT INTO datetest VALUES ('2002-02-31');
```

What data value will actually be stored in the table? Provide a short explanation.

Question 54:

You perform the following INSERT operations on table datetest, which has a single DATE column called d with a default value of NULL:

```
INSERT INTO datetest VALUES (NULL);

INSERT INTO datetest VALUES ('NULL');
```

What data value will actually be stored in the table for each statement? Provide a short explanation.

Question 55:

You perform the following INSERT operation on table datetest, which has a single DATE column called d with a default value of NULL:

```
INSERT INTO datetest VALUES ('10000-01-01');
```

What data value will actually be stored in the table? Provide a short explanation.

Question 56:

You perform the following INSERT operations on table datetest, which has a single DATE column called d with a default value of NULL:

```
INSERT INTO datetest VALUES ('10-02-08');

INSERT INTO datetest VALUES ('69-12-31');

INSERT INTO datetest VALUES ('70-01-01');
```

What data value will actually be stored in the table for each statement? Provide a short explanation.

Question 57:

You perform the following INSERT operation on table datetest, which has a single DATE column called d with a default value of NULL:

```
INSERT INTO datetest VALUES ('12:00:00');
```

What data value will actually be stored in the table? Provide a short explanation.

Question 58:

You perform the following INSERT operation on table datetest, which has a single DATE column called d with a default value of NULL:

```
INSERT INTO datetest VALUES ('12:00');
```

What data value will actually be stored in the table? Provide a short explanation.

Question 59:

You perform the following INSERT operation on table datetest, which has a single DATE column called d with a default value of NULL:

```
INSERT INTO datetest VALUES ('2002-02-08 21:39');
```

What data value will actually be stored in the table? Provide a short explanation.

Question 60:

Here's the structure of a table typetest with three columns (number, string, and dates), which will be used for the next five questions.

```
mysql> DESCRIBE typetest;
+--------+---------------------+------+
| Field  | Type                | Null |
+--------+---------------------+------+
| number | tinyint(3) unsigned | YES  |
| string | char(5)             | YES  |
| dates  | date                | YES  |
+--------+---------------------+------+
```

You perform the following INSERT operation on table typetest:

```
INSERT INTO typetest VALUES (1,22,333);
```

What data values will actually be stored in the table? Provide a short explanation.

Question 61:

You perform the following INSERT operation on table typetest:

```
INSERT INTO typetest VALUES (1000,'yoodoo','999-12-31');
```

What data values will actually be stored in the table? Provide a short explanation. (Reminder: The table has three columns. number is a TINYINT column, string is a CHAR(5) column, and dates is a DATE column. All three allow NULL values.)

Question 62:

You perform the following INSERT operation on table typetest:

```
INSERT INTO typetest VALUES (NULL,NULL,NULL);
```

What data values will actually be stored in the table? Provide a short explanation. (Reminder: The table has three columns. number is a TINYINT column, string is a CHAR(5) column, and dates is a DATE column. All three allow NULL values.)

Question 63:

You perform the following INSERT operation on table typetest:

```
INSERT INTO typetest VALUES ('string',5+5,'string');
```

What data values will actually be stored in the table? Provide a short explanation. (Reminder: The table has three columns. number is a TINYINT column, string is a CHAR(5) column, and dates is a DATE column. All three allow NULL values.)

Question 64:

You perform the following INSERT operation on table typetest:

```
INSERT INTO typetest VALUES (-1,-1,'2000-02-32');
```

What data values will actually be stored in the table? Provide a short explanation. (Reminder: The table has three columns. number is a TINYINT column, string is a CHAR(5) column, and dates is a DATE column. All three allow NULL values.)

Question 65:

Here's the structure of a table timetest with three columns (alteration, creation, and entry), which will be used for the next six questions.

```
mysql> DESCRIBE timetest;
+------------+------------------+------+-----+---------+
| Field      | Type             | Null | Key | Default |
+------------+------------------+------+-----+---------+
| alteration | timestamp(14)    | YES  |     | NULL    |
| creation   | timestamp(14)    | YES  |     | NULL    |
| entry      | int(10) unsigned | YES  |     | NULL    |
+------------+------------------+------+-----+---------+
```

You perform the following INSERT operation on table timetest:

```
INSERT INTO timetest VALUES (NULL,NULL,1);
```

What data values will actually be stored in the two TIMESTAMP columns? Provide a short explanation. *Note:* Because the values are dependent on the system date and time, you cannot know exactly which values will result. For this and the next five questions, what you can say is whether TIMESTAMP values will be entered or changed, and whether NULL values will be entered.

Question 66:

You now perform the following UPDATE operation on table timetest:

```
UPDATE timetest SET entry=1 WHERE entry=1;
```

What data values will actually be stored in the two TIMESTAMP columns? Provide a short explanation. (Reminder: The table has three columns. alteration is a TIMESTAMP column, creation is a TIMESTAMP column, and entry is an INT column. All three allow NULL values. Assume a system date of February 13, 2003 and system time of 22:23:37.)

Question 67:

You now perform the following UPDATE operation on table timetest:

```
UPDATE timetest SET entry=2 WHERE entry=1;
```

What data values will actually be stored in the two TIMESTAMP columns? Provide a short explanation. (Reminder: The table has three columns. alteration is a TIMESTAMP column, creation is a TIMESTAMP column, and entry is an INT column. All three allow NULL values. Assume a system date of February 13, 2003 and system time of 22:32:09.)

Question 68:

You now perform the following UPDATE operation on table timetest:

```
UPDATE timetest SET alteration=NULL, creation=NULL, entry=3
WHERE entry=2;
```

What data values will actually be stored in the two TIMESTAMP columns? Provide a short explanation. (Reminder: The table has three columns. alteration is a TIMESTAMP column, creation is a TIMESTAMP column, and entry is an INT column. All three allow NULL values. Assume a system date of February 13, 2003 and system time of 22:53:17.)

Question 69:

You now perform the following INSERT operation on table timetest:

```
INSERT INTO timetest (entry) VALUES (4);
```

What data values will actually be stored in the two TIMESTAMP columns? Provide a short explanation. (Reminder: The table has three columns. alteration is a TIMESTAMP column, creation is a TIMESTAMP column, and entry is an INT column. All three allow NULL values. Assume a system date of February 13, 2003 and system time of 22:55:44.)

Question 70:

You now perform the following INSERT operation on table timetest:

INSERT INTO timetest VALUES('2002-02-08',200202082139,5);

What data values will actually be stored in the two TIMESTAMP columns? Provide a short explanation. (Reminder: The table has three columns. alteration is a TIMESTAMP column, creation is a TIMESTAMP column, and entry is an INT column. All three allow NULL values. Assume a system date of February 13, 2003 and system time of 22:55:55.)

Question 71:

Here's the structure of the table datetimetest with one column (dt), which will be used for the next six questions.

```
mysql> DESCRIBE datetimetest;
+-------+----------+------+
| Field | Type     | Null |
+-------+----------+------+
| dt    | datetime | YES  |
+-------+----------+------+
```

You perform the following INSERT operation on table datetimetest:

INSERT INTO datetimetest VALUES (NULL);

What data value will actually be stored in the DATETIME column? Provide a short explanation.

Question 72:

You perform the following INSERT operation on table datetimetest:

INSERT INTO datetimetest VALUES ('string');

What data value will actually be stored in the DATETIME column? Provide a short explanation. (Reminder: The table has one column. dt is a DATETIME column that allows NULL values.)

Question 73:

You perform the following INSERT operation on table datetimetest:

INSERT INTO datetimetest VALUES (200202082139);

What data value will actually be stored in the DATETIME columns? Provide a short explanation. (Reminder: The table has one column. dt is a DATETIME column that allows NULL values.)

Question 74:

You perform the following INSERT operation on table datetimetest:

INSERT INTO datetimetest VALUES (20020208213900);

What data value will actually be stored in the DATETIME columns? Provide a short explanation. (Reminder: The table has one column. dt is a DATETIME column that allows NULL values.)

Question 75:

You perform the following INSERT operation on table datetimetest:

```
INSERT INTO datetimetest VALUES ('2002-02-31 23:59:59');
```

What data value will actually be stored in the DATETIME columns? Provide a short explanation. (Reminder: The table has one column. dt is a DATETIME column that allows NULL values.)

Question 76:

You perform the following INSERT operation on table datetimetest:

```
INSERT INTO datetimetest VALUES ('2002-02-31 23:59:60');
```

What data value will actually be stored in the DATETIME columns? Provide a short explanation. (Reminder: The table has one column. dt is a DATETIME column that allows NULL values.)

Question 77:

MySQL will make context-specific datatype conversions not only when working with column values, but also when working with functions and operators that expect specific datatypes. For example, the CONCAT() function expects data of a string type, whereas the + operator expects data of a numeric type. What value will result from the following operation? Give a short explanation.

```
SELECT CONCAT(1,1,1);
```

Question 78:

Based on MySQL's capability to make context-specific datatype conversions when working with functions and operators, what value will result from the following operation? Give a short explanation.

```
SELECT CONCAT(NULL,'Lennart');
```

Question 79:

Based on MySQL's capability to make context-specific datatype conversions when working with functions and operators, what value will result from the following operation? Give a short explanation.

```
SELECT CONCAT(1,' plus ',1,' equals ',2);
```

Question 80:

Based on MySQL's capability to make context-specific datatype conversions when working with functions and operators, what value will result from the following operation? Give a short explanation.

```
SELECT 1 + 1 + ' equals 2';
```

Question 81:

Based on MySQL's capability to make context-specific datatype conversions when working with functions and operators, what value will result from the following operation? Give a short explanation.

```
SELECT 1 + 1 + '1.1 equals GUESS!';
```

Question 82:

Based on MySQL's capability to make context-specific datatype conversions when working with functions and operators, what value will result from the following operation? Give a short explanation.

```
SELECT 1 + NULL;
```

Question 83:

What's the largest value you can store in a TINYINT(2) column?

Question 84:

Which numeric datatype is slowest in regard to processing time?

Question 85:

Which numeric datatype is a common choice for financial applications? Why?

Question 86:

What's the explanation for the following datatype conversion in a MyISAM table?

```
mysql> CREATE TABLE convtest (
    ->   mychar      CHAR(3),
    ->   myotherchar CHAR(4),
    ->   myvarchar   VARCHAR(10)
    -> ) TYPE=MyISAM;
mysql> DESCRIBE convtest;
+-------------+-------------+------+
| Field       | Type        | Null |
+-------------+-------------+------+
| mychar      | char(3)     | YES  |
| myotherchar | varchar(4)  | YES  |
| myvarchar   | varchar(10) | YES  |
+-------------+-------------+------+
```

Question 87:

What's the explanation for the following datatype conversion in a MyISAM table?

```
mysql> CREATE TABLE convtest2 (
    -> mychar       CHAR(3),
    -> myotherchar CHAR(2),
    -> myvarchar    VARCHAR(3)
    -> ) TYPE=MyISAM;
mysql> DESCRIBE convtest2;
+-------------+---------+------+-----+---------+-------+
| Field       | Type    | Null | Key | Default | Extra |
+-------------+---------+------+-----+---------+-------+
| mychar      | char(3) | YES  |     | NULL    |       |
| myotherchar | char(2) | YES  |     | NULL    |       |
| myvarchar   | char(3) | YES  |     | NULL    |       |
+-------------+---------+------+-----+---------+-------+
```

Question 88:

How do you define columns with the CHAR, VARCHAR, TEXT, or BLOB datatypes to ensure that their values will be compared in a case-sensitive manner?

Question 89:

What column types would you choose for a table that contains pictures with a maximum data length of 10 megabytes, and remarks with a maximum length of 250 characters?

Question 90:

You want to store user IDs and passwords in a table. You know you'll need to store up to 1,000 users. User IDs need be nothing more than serial numbers, but MySQL should ensure that no number is ever stored more than once for the table. Each password will be exactly eight characters long, and passwords that differ in lettercase (such as secret and SECRET) are considered different passwords. What would your table structure look like?

Question 91:

Is it possible to declare a column as CHAR(0)? What would be the use of such a column?

Question 92:

How much space is required to store a value that is 2,000 bytes long in a BLOB column?

Question 93:

Here's the structure of a table continent that has only one column (name, which stores names of continents). This table will be used for the next seven questions.

```
mysql> DESCRIBE continent\G
*************************** 1. row ***************************
  Field: name
```

```
   Type: enum('Africa','America','Antarctica','Asia','Australia','Europe')
   Null: YES
    Key:
Default: NULL
  Extra:
```

What string value will be stored by the following INSERT operation? What integer value will be stored internally?

```
INSERT INTO continent VALUES ('Africa');
```

Question 94:

Recall that table continent has only one column (name, with a datatype of ENUM) that stores names of continents, with NULL values allowed. A DESCRIBE of the table shows the following (partial data only):

```
Field: name
 Type: enum('Africa','America','Antarctica','Asia','Australia','Europe')
```

What string value will be stored by the following INSERT operation? What integer value will be stored internally?

```
INSERT INTO continent VALUES ('Europa');
```

Question 95:

Recall that table continent has only one column (name, with a datatype of ENUM) that stores names of continents, with NULL values allowed. A DESCRIBE of the table shows the following (partial data only):

```
Field: name
 Type: enum('Africa','America','Antarctica','Asia','Australia','Europe')
```

What string value will be stored by the following INSERT operation? What integer value will be stored internally?

```
INSERT INTO continent VALUES ('');
```

Question 96:

Recall that table continent has only one column (name, with a datatype of ENUM) that stores names of continents, with NULL values allowed. A DESCRIBE of the table shows the following (partial data only):

```
Field: name
 Type: enum('Africa','America','Antarctica','Asia','Australia','Europe')
```

What string value will be stored by the following INSERT operation? What integer value will be stored internally?

```
INSERT INTO continent VALUES (0);
```

Question 97:

Recall that table continent has only one column (name, with a datatype of ENUM) that stores names of continents, with NULL values allowed. A DESCRIBE of the table shows the following (partial data only):

```
Field: name
 Type: enum('Africa','America','Antarctica','Asia','Australia','Europe')
```

What string value will be stored by the following INSERT operation? What integer value will be stored internally?

```
INSERT INTO continent VALUES (1);
```

Question 98:

Recall that table continent has only one column (name, with a datatype of ENUM) that stores names of continents, with NULL values allowed. A DESCRIBE of the table shows the following (partial data only):

```
Field: name
 Type: enum('Africa','America','Antarctica','Asia','Australia','Europe')
```

What string value will be stored by the following INSERT operation? What integer value will be stored internally?

```
INSERT INTO continent VALUES ('1');
```

Question 99:

Recall that table continent has only one column (name, with a datatype of ENUM) that stores names of continents, with NULL values allowed. A DESCRIBE of the table shows the following (partial data only):

```
Field: name
 Type: enum('Africa','America','Antarctica','Asia','Australia','Europe')
```

What string value will be stored by the following INSERT operation? What integer value will be stored internally?

```
INSERT INTO continent VALUES (NULL);
```

Question 100:

The following CREATE TABLE statement shows the definition for table defaults, which will be used for the next seven questions.

```
mysql> CREATE TABLE defaults (
    ->   id INT UNSIGNED NOT NULL UNIQUE,
    ->   col1 INT NULL,
    ->   col2 INT NOT NULL,
```

```
    -> col3 INT DEFAULT 42,
    -> col4 CHAR(5) NULL,
    -> col5 CHAR(5) NOT NULL,
    -> col6 CHAR(5) DEFAULT 'yoo',
    -> col7 TEXT NULL,
    -> col8 TEXT NOT NULL,
    -> col9 TIME NOT NULL,
    -> col10 DATE NULL,
    -> col11 DATE NOT NULL,
    -> col12 DATE DEFAULT '2002-02-08',
    -> col13 ENUM('doo','yoo'),
    -> col14 SET('blabla','yooyoo'),
    -> col15 ENUM('doo','yoo') NOT NULL,
    -> col16 SET('blabla','yooyoo') NOT NULL
    -> );
```

What's the effect on the other columns with an INT datatype if you issue the following INSERT statement? Why?

```
mysql> INSERT INTO defaults (id) VALUES (1);
```

Question 101:

Refer to the definition of the defaults table, shown in the previous question. What's the effect on the columns with a CHAR datatype if you issue this INSERT statement? Why?

```
mysql> INSERT INTO defaults (id) VALUES (1);
```

Question 102:

Refer to the definition of the defaults table, shown two questions earlier. What's the effect on the columns with a TEXT datatype if you issue this INSERT statement? Why?

```
mysql> INSERT INTO defaults (id) VALUES (1);
```

Reminder: Table defaults has two TEXT columns, shown in this partial table definition:

```
mysql> CREATE TABLE defaults (
    -> id INT UNSIGNED NOT NULL UNIQUE,
    -> . . .
    -> col7 TEXT NULL,
    -> col8 TEXT NOT NULL,
    -> . . .
    -> );
```

Question 103:

Refer to the definition of the defaults table, shown three questions earlier. What's the effect on the columns with a TIME datatype if you issue this INSERT statement? Why?

```
mysql> INSERT INTO defaults (id) VALUES (1);
```

Reminder: Table `defaults` has one TIME column, shown in this partial table definition:

```
mysql> CREATE TABLE defaults (
    -> id INT UNSIGNED NOT NULL UNIQUE,
    -> . . .
    -> col9 TIME NOT NULL,
    -> . . .
    -> );
```

Question 104:

Refer to the definition of the `defaults` table, shown four questions earlier. What's the effect on the columns with a DATE datatype if you issue this INSERT statement? Why?

```
mysql> INSERT INTO defaults (id) VALUES (1);
```

Reminder: Table `defaults` has three DATE columns, shown in this partial table definition:

```
mysql> CREATE TABLE defaults (
    -> id INT UNSIGNED NOT NULL UNIQUE,
    -> . . .
    -> col10 DATE NULL,
    -> col11 DATE NOT NULL,
    -> col12 DATE DEFAULT '2002-02-08',
    -> . . .
    -> );
```

Question 105:

Refer to the definition of the `defaults` table, shown five questions earlier. What's the effect on the columns with an ENUM datatype if you issue this INSERT statement? Why?

```
mysql> INSERT INTO defaults (id) VALUES (1);
```

Reminder: Table `defaults` has two ENUM columns, shown in this partial table definition:

```
mysql> CREATE TABLE defaults (
    -> id INT UNSIGNED NOT NULL UNIQUE,
    -> . . .
    -> col13 ENUM('doo','yoo'),
    -> col15 ENUM('doo','yoo') NOT NULL,
    -> . . .
    -> );
```

Question 106:

Refer to the definition of the `defaults` table, shown six questions earlier. What's the effect on the columns with a SET datatype if you issue this INSERT statement? Why?

```
mysql> INSERT INTO defaults (id) VALUES (1);
```

Reminder: Table `defaults` has two `SET` columns, shown in this partial table definition:

```
mysql> CREATE TABLE defaults (
    -> id INT UNSIGNED NOT NULL UNIQUE,
    -> . . .
    -> col14 SET('blabla','yooyoo'),
    -> col16 SET('blabla','yooyoo') NOT NULL
    -> . . .
    -> );
```

Question 107:

The table `myauto` looks like this:

```
mysql> DESCRIBE myauto;
+-------+---------+------+-----+---------+----------------+
| Field | Type    | Null | Key | Default | Extra          |
+-------+---------+------+-----+---------+----------------+
| id    | int(11) |      | PRI | NULL    | auto_increment |
+-------+---------+------+-----+---------+----------------+
```

No records have been inserted into the table so far. Now, a value is inserted like this:

```
mysql> INSERT INTO myauto (id) VALUES (NULL);
```

Which SQL function would you use to retrieve the last inserted value for `id` and what would be that value? When you invoke this function over and over again without inserting new values, and some other user on another connection inserts new rows into the table, what would your function call return?

Question 108:

The table `cliptest` has the following columns and rows:

```
mysql> DESCRIBE cliptest;
+--------+--------------+------+-----+---------+-------+
| Field  | Type         | Null | Key | Default | Extra |
+--------+--------------+------+-----+---------+-------+
| number | int(11)      | YES  |     | NULL    |       |
| string | varchar(255) | YES  |     | NULL    |       |
+--------+--------------+------+-----+---------+-------+
mysql> SELECT * FROM cliptest;
+---------+------------------------------------+
| number  | string                             |
+---------+------------------------------------+
| 1000000 | The Hitchhiker's Guide to the Galaxy |
|    NULL | NULL                               |
+---------+------------------------------------+
```

The table structure is modified with this statement:

```
mysql> ALTER TABLE cliptest
    ->  MODIFY number TINYINT UNSIGNED NOT NULL,
    ->  MODIFY string TINYINT UNSIGNED NOT NULL
    -> ;
```

What will the table data look like afterward?

Question 109:

The table mytiny has the following structure:

```
mysql> DESCRIBE mytiny;
+-------+------------+------+-----+---------+----------------+
| Field | Type       | Null | Key | Default | Extra          |
+-------+------------+------+-----+---------+----------------+
| id    | tinyint(4) |      | PRI | NULL    | auto_increment |
+-------+------------+------+-----+---------+----------------+
```

An application attempting to insert data with a program loop issues the following statement during every iteration of the loop:

```
INSERT INTO mytiny (id) VALUES (NULL);
```

How many times will this loop run without error? When an error occurs, what will be the reason?

Question 110:

Which SHOW statement will retrieve a list of all tables in the current database with a table name that contains the string 'test'?

Question 111:

Which SHOW statement will retrieve a list of tables in the database test, even if test isn't the current database?

Question 112:

Which SHOW statement will retrieve a list of the columns in the table mytest, found in the test database?

Question 113:

Which SHOW statement will retrieve a list of columns in the table test.mytest, where the column names begin with id?

Question 114:

Which SHOW statement will retrieve a statement that could be used to re-create the table test.mytest in an arbitrary database? Assume that test is not the default database.

Answers to Exercises

Answer 1:

DROP DATABASE test. This statement cannot be undone, so be careful with it.

Answer 2:

DROP INDEX idx_id ON tbl or ALTER TABLE tbl DROP INDEX idx_id. You can recover the index by rebuilding it with a CREATE INDEX or ALTER TABLE … ADD INDEX statement.

Answer 3:

PRIMARY KEY, UNIQUE, INDEX (nonunique), and FULLTEXT.

Answer 4:

A UNIQUE index can contain NULL values; a PRIMARY KEY cannot. It's possible to have multiple UNIQUE indexes for a table, but there can be only one index defined as a PRIMARY KEY for each table.

Answer 5:

The columns must be declared NOT NULL.

Answer 6:

PRIMARY KEY

Answer 7:

TIMESTAMP

Answer 8:

DECIMAL

Answer 9:

CHAR(100) stores 100 bytes for every record, whereas VARCHAR(100) only stores the number of bytes actually inserted, plus one byte to store the length of the entry. This means that VARCHAR(100) is normally more space-efficient. However, in the special case that you consistently insert 100-byte values into the column, CHAR(100) is more space-efficient because the byte used by VARCHAR to store the length of the entry is unneeded.

Answer 10:

By using the keyword BINARY when specifying the column, for example, codeName CHAR(10) BINARY.

Answer 11:

BLOB is case sensitive because it stores binary strings.

Answer 12:

Binary values are sequences of arbitrary bytes. Nonbinary values are sequences of characters. Characters might require one or more bytes each to store, whereas byte values require only a single byte each.

Answer 13:

By using the IF EXISTS clause; for example, DROP TABLE IF EXISTS tbl.

Answer 14:

False. A database can be empty.

Answer 15:

True. There cannot be a table with zero columns.

Answer 16:

False. Tables do not have to contain data, they may be empty.

Answer 17:

False. You can specify the database in which to create the table by using a fully qualified table name—that is, *database_name.table_name* (for example, mydb.mytable).

Answer 18:

True. Such a limit could, however, be imposed by the operating system.

Answer 19:

False. InnoDB allows for a maximum of two billion tables in its tablespace.

Answer 20:

True. However, depending on the table type, other files may also be present in the database directory.

Answer 21:

    a. Use features of the table storage manager, such as MERGE tables for the MyISAM storage manager.

    b. Use the RAID feature for MyISAM tables to partition the datafile (the .MYD file).

    c. Convert the table for use with a storage engine that allows larger tables. For example, convert MyISAM tables to InnoDB tables. The InnoDB tablespace can consist of several files and InnoDB can spread a table's contents over more than one of these files. This allows the table to be larger than any single file.

    d. Use another filesystem or a newer version of the operating system that allows for larger files.

Answer 22:

a. False. Although the data and index information is stored in memory, the format (.frm) file is stored on disk.

b. False. You can insert, update, and delete data, just as you can with other tables.

c. False. HEAP tables support table locking only.

d. True. The table's contents are always stored in memory and never need to be read from, or written to, disk.

Answer 23:

`IF NOT EXISTS`

Answer 24:

`IF EXISTS`

Answer 25:

`CREATE TABLE friends.cats (...);`

Answer 26:

It's not possible. All tables must belong to a database, and therefore must be created within a database.

Answer 27:

Column specifications must be separated by commas. In this case, there must be a comma between the words `KEY` and `name`.

Answer 28:

```
mysql> CREATE TABLE mytbl (
    -> col1 INT UNSIGNED NOT NULL,
    -> col2 CHAR(50) NOT NULL,
    -> col3 CHAR(50) NOT NULL,
    -> PRIMARY KEY(col1),
    -> UNIQUE(col2),
    -> INDEX(col3)
    -> );
```

Other variations are possible. For example, the indexes created by the `PRIMARY KEY` and `UNIQUE` clauses could be specified by adding `PRIMARY KEY` to the end of the col1 definition and `UNIQUE` to the end of the col2 definition.

Answer 29:

True.

Answer 30:

True. MySQL supports multiple actions for a single ALTER TABLE statement.

Answer 31:

False. Rows cannot be added with an SQL statement that changes the table structure.

Answer 32:

True. MySQL will convert existing data if necessary.

Answer 33:

True.

Answer 34:

True.

Answer 35:

True.

Answer 36:

False. MySQL will tell you to use the DROP TABLE command for this action.

Answer 37:

True. To do so, specify the keyword FIRST at the end of the ADD clause that provides the column definition.

Answer 38:

True, although this will happen only as a side effect. You could truncate existing data by shortening the length of a CHAR or VARCHAR column, or you could convert data by changing the datatype.

Answer 39:

You cannot do this. Column names in a table must be unique no matter what the lettercase is.

Answer 40:

Either of the following statements renames the table:

```
ALTER TABLE tbl RENAME TO tbl_new;
RENAME TABLE tbl TO tbl_new;
```

Answer 41:

Indexes can speed up table scans, especially for large tables, and they can be used to place restrictions on columns to ensure that a column or a set of columns may contain only unique-valued entries.

Answer 42:

The Key value in DESCRIBE output for a UNIQUE index will be UNI or PRI if the index does not allow NULL values. The Key value is MUL if the index does allow NULL values because NULL in a UNIQUE index is a special case: Multiple NULL values are allowed, unlike any other value. For mytable, the Key value is MUL, which indicates that the UNIQUE index on col allows multiple NULL values. Consequently, the INSERT statement will not fail, even though it inserts several NULL values.

Answer 43:

No, it isn't possible. A PRIMARY KEY can only contain columns that are specified as NOT NULL.

Answer 44:

Yes. Because the combination of col1 and col2 has unique and non-NULL values only, it's possible to create a PRIMARY KEY with this SQL statement:

```
ALTER TABLE mytable ADD PRIMARY KEY (col1, col2);
```

Answer 45:

```
mysql> ALTER TABLE mytable
    -> ADD col0 INT FIRST,
    -> ADD col2 INT AFTER col1,
    -> ADD col4 INT
    -> ;
```

Answer 46:

SHOW CREATE TABLE tbl will display all index information for the table, including composite indexes. SHOW INDEX FROM tbl also shows index information, although the output might not be as easy to interpret.

Answer 47:

With ALTER TABLE … ADD INDEX, if you don't explicitly provide a name for the index, MySQL creates an index name based on the name of the first indexed column. With CREATE INDEX, an error occurs if you don't provide a name for the index.

Answer 48:

No. If you want to drop more than one index at the same time, you must use ALTER TABLE … DROP INDEX.

Answer 49:

```
mysql> CREATE TABLE tbl (
    -> col1 INT NOT NULL,
    -> col2 INT NOT NULL,
    -> PRIMARY KEY (col1, col2)
    -> );
```

Answer 50:

MEDIUMINT UNSIGNED can hold numbers up to 16,777,215. The UNSIGNED option ensures that you don't store negative numbers by accident. Without UNSIGNED, the maximum positive number would only be 8,388,607. The storage requirement is 3 bytes per row.

Answer 51:

TEXT is the column datatype best suited to this situation. It can hold up to 65,535 characters. For 300 characters, the storage requirement is 302 bytes (300 bytes for a remark plus 2 bytes to store the actual length of the entry).

Answer 52:

'1000-01-01' (January 1, 1000) is the earliest date that can be stored in a DATE column. You might be able to store earlier dates, but doing so isn't recommended because unexpected results from date operations might result.

Answer 53:

The value inserted is '2002-02-31'. MySQL performs only elementary checking on the validity of a date.

Answer 54:

   a. The value inserted is NULL. Because NULL values are permitted for column d, they'll be accepted.

   b. The value inserted is '0000-00-00' because 'NULL' is a string value which is an invalid date. MySQL converts this to the default date value '0000-00-00'.

Answer 55:

The value inserted is '2010-00-00' (this could differ in your MySQL version). The valid DATE range is from '1000-01-01' to '9999-12-31'. If you insert values outside of this range, you'll get unpredictable results.

Answer 56:

If a date is entered with a two-digit year value, MySQL converts it to a date between '1970-01-01' and '2069-12-31'. For each of the three examples, then, the results are as follows:

   a. The value inserted is '2010-02-08'.

   b. The value inserted is '2069-12-31'.

   c. The value inserted is '1970-01-01'.

Answer 57:

The value inserted is '2012-00-00'. MySQL interprets the inserted value as a date, '12-00-00', which is interpreted as the year '2012'.

Answer 58:

The value inserted is '0000-00-00'. '12:00' is considered to be an invalid date and so gets converted to the "zero" date value '0000-00-00'.

Answer 59:

The value inserted is '2002-02-08'. '2002-02-08 21:39' is a DATETIME value. When inserted into a DATE column, the time portion of a DATETIME value is truncated.

Answer 60:

```
+--------+--------+------------+
| number | string | dates      |
+--------+--------+------------+
|      1 | 22     | 0000-00-00 |
+--------+--------+------------+
```

22 is converted to the string value '22'. The number 333 is interpreted as an invalid date, so the "zero" date is stored.

Answer 61:

```
+--------+--------+------------+
| number | string | dates      |
+--------+--------+------------+
|    255 | yoodo  | 0000-00-00 |
+--------+--------+------------+
```

The inserted number 1000 is too big to fit in the TINYINT UNSIGNED column, so the highest possible value (255) is inserted. 'yoodoo' is too long for a CHAR(5) column and is thus truncated to five characters. '999-12-31' is a date which is earlier than the earliest possible DATE value ('1000-01-01'). This is interpreted as an invalid date, so the "zero" date is stored.

Answer 62:

```
+--------+--------+------------+
| number | string | dates      |
+--------+--------+------------+
|   NULL | NULL   | NULL       |
+--------+--------+------------+
```

All columns are declared NULL (by not specifying them as NOT NULL), so they accept NULL values.

Answer 63:

```
+--------+--------+------------+
| number | string | dates      |
+--------+--------+------------+
|      0 | 10     | 0000-00-00 |
+--------+--------+------------+
```

'string' is converted to a number for the number column; because there are no digit characters at the beginning of the string, the result is 0. 5+5 is evaluated to 10, which is converted
to the string '10' before it is stored in the string column. 'string' is converted to a date
before it is stored in the dates column; because it is invalid as a date, the "zero" date is
stored.

Answer 64:

```
+--------+--------+------------+
| number | string | dates      |
+--------+--------+------------+
|      0 | -1     | 0000-00-00 |
+--------+--------+------------+
```

-1 is lower than the lowest possible value for any unsigned integer column, so it's converted
to 0 before it's stored. -1 is converted to the corresponding string value ('-1') before it's
stored. The inserted date has an invalid day portion (32); because this is interpreted as an
invalid date, the "zero" date is stored.

Answer 65:

Note: The values displayed for the alteration and creation columns are examples only,
given for a system date of February 13, 2003 (20030213) and a system time sometime after 22
hours (10 p.m.) (22).

```
+----------------+----------------+-------+
| alteration     | creation       | entry |
+----------------+----------------+-------+
| 20030213222337 | 20030213222337 |     1 |
+----------------+----------------+-------+
```

When an attempt is made to insert a NULL value into a TIMESTAMP column, a timestamp
consisting of the system date and time is inserted instead, regardless of whether the column
definition includes NULL or NOT NULL. (In fact, it isn't really possible to define a TIMESTAMP
column as NULL; the declaration will be ignored.)

Answer 66:

```
+----------------+----------------+-------+
| alteration     | creation       | entry |
+----------------+----------------+-------+
| 20030213222337 | 20030213222337 |     1 |
+----------------+----------------+-------+
```

Because the UPDATE statement doesn't actually change any data, the table row remains
unchanged.

Answer 67:

```
+----------------+----------------+-------+
| alteration     | creation       | entry |
+----------------+----------------+-------+
| 20030213223209 | 20030213222337 |     2 |
+----------------+----------------+-------+
```

This UPDATE statement actually changes data in the row, so the *first* TIMESTAMP column is set to the system date and time, even though column alteration isn't explicitly mentioned in the list of columns to update. The other TIMESTAMP column remains untouched.

Answer 68:

```
+----------------+----------------+-------+
| alteration     | creation       | entry |
+----------------+----------------+-------+
| 20030213225317 | 20030213225317 |     3 |
+----------------+----------------+-------+
```

When any TIMESTAMP column is explicitly set to a value, it gets updated, so column alteration is updated as well. If the value is NULL, the column is set to the current date and time.

Answer 69:

The newly inserted row looks like this:

```
+----------------+----------------+-------+
| alteration     | creation       | entry |
+----------------+----------------+-------+
| 20030213225544 | 00000000000000 |     4 |
+----------------+----------------+-------+
```

None of the TIMESTAMP columns is mentioned in the INSERT statement, so creation is set to the standard default value. (Although creation is declared as NOT NULL, MySQL will never assign a NULL value to a TIMESTAMP column, but use the "zero" value instead.) alteration is set to the system date and time.

Answer 70:

The newly inserted row looks like this:

```
+----------------+----------------+-------+
| alteration     | creation       | entry |
+----------------+----------------+-------+
| 20020208000000 | 20200202082139 |     5 |
+----------------+----------------+-------+
```

For alteration, the DATE value given is converted appropriately (with the time portion set to 0). For creation, the conversion of the 12-digit number 200202082139 produces a puzzling result. The value is interpreted as a DATETIME, with the leftmost two digits treated as the year portion of the DATETIME. 20 thus becomes the year value 2020, and the rest of the digits (0202082139) are interpreted as month (02), day (02), hour (08), minute (21), and second (39). The rules for interpretation of "short" TIMESTAMP values are detailed in the *MySQL Reference Manual*.

Answer 71:

```
+------+
| dt   |
+------+
| NULL |
+------+
```

Because dt isn't explicitly declared NOT NULL, it can hold NULL values.

Answer 72:

```
+---------------------+
| dt                  |
+---------------------+
| 0000-00-00 00:00:00 |
+---------------------+
```

'string' is converted into a DATETIME value before it's inserted. Because the result of the conversion is an invalid DATETIME of 0, the "zero" value is inserted instead.

Answer 73:

```
+---------------------+
| dt                  |
+---------------------+
| 2020-02-02 08:21:39 |
+---------------------+
```

The conversion of the 12-digit number 200202082139 produces a puzzling result. The value is interpreted as a DATETIME, with the leftmost two digits treated as the year portion of the DATETIME. 20 becomes the year value 2020, and the rest of the digits (0202082139) are interpreted as month (02), day (02), hour (08), minute (21), and second (39).

Answer 74:

```
+---------------------+
| dt                  |
+---------------------+
| 2002-02-08 21:39:00 |
+---------------------+
```

20020208213900 looks like a 14-digit TIMESTAMP value and is interpreted as a DATETIME on insertion, where the rightmost 00 is the seconds portion of the value.

Answer 75:

```
+---------------------+
| dt                  |
+---------------------+
| 2002-02-31 23:59:59 |
+---------------------+
```

2002-02-31 23:59:59 is a valid DATETIME value although it isn't a valid calendar date. MySQL regards the value as valid because all parts of it (year, month, day, hour, minute, second) are within a valid range.

Answer 76:

```
+---------------------+
| dt                  |
+---------------------+
| 0000-00-00 00:00:00 |
+---------------------+
```

2002-02-31 23:59:60 isn't a valid DATETIME value because the seconds portion (60) isn't within the valid range. MySQL thus converts the value to the "zero" DATETIME value.

Answer 77:

'111'. The three arguments to CONCAT() are converted into strings before they're concatenated.

Answer 78:

NULL. If any argument to CONCAT() is NULL, the result is NULL as well.

Answer 79:

'1 plus 1 equals 2'. All arguments to CONCAT() are converted to strings before they're concatenated.

Answer 80:

2. The string ' equals 2' is interpreted as a number. It evaluates to 0 because it has no leftmost numeric part. Thus, the operation performed is 1 + 1 + 0.

Answer 81:

3.1. The leftmost part of the string '1.1 equals GUESS' contains the floating point number 1.1. Thus, all numbers are converted to floats, so the operation performed is 1.0 + 1.0 + 1.1.

Answer 82:

NULL. The result of an arithmetic operation is indeterminate with a NULL operand, so the result is NULL.

Answer 83:

127. The display width of (2) in the column type indicates only that values should be displayed in a two-digit format when they have only one digit. It doesn't restrict the range of values that can be stored in a TINYINT column.

Answer 84:

DECIMAL columns cannot be processed as fast as FLOAT and DOUBLE columns because values are stored as strings, and strings cannot be processed as quickly as numbers represented in binary.

Answer 85:

DECIMAL values are not subject to rounding errors when they are stored, so, despite their speed disadvantages, they're a common choice in financial applications where accuracy is of prime importance.

Answer 86:

MySQL converts myotherchar to VARCHAR because this datatype is more often space efficient than CHAR. Because VARCHAR columns are usually slower in table scans, MySQL will do a datatype change like this only if the table will become variable length, anyway. In the example, myvarchar is the column that will cause the table to become variable length. Thus, MySQL can save disk space if the datatype of myotherchar is changed to VARCHAR. For mychar, however, this does not hold true because this column is shorter than 3 bytes. If the mychar column was converted to VARCHAR, MySQL would waste disk space, not save it; therefore, the column definition remains unchanged.

Answer 87:

MySQL changes the datatype of myvarchar to CHAR because a VARCHAR that is 3 bytes long is less space efficient than a CHAR(3). As a side effect, the datatype change also keeps the table fixed length, which provides a speed advantage over variable-length MyISAM tables during a table scan.

Answer 88:

You can only do this for CHAR and VARCHAR columns by adding the keyword BINARY when defining the columns in a CREATE TABLE or ALTER TABLE statement. BLOB column values are always case sensitive, so no special declaration is necessary. TEXT column values are always case insensitive; you cannot declare a TEXT column to be case sensitive.

Answer 89:

For the pictures, you would choose MEDIUMBLOB, which can store almost 16 megabytes. For the remarks, you would choose VARCHAR(250), which can store up to 250 characters and is more space-efficient than CHAR(250). (If you happened to choose CHAR(250), MySQL would convert it to VARCHAR(250) anyway. The MEDIUMBLOB column is a variable-length type, so MySQL automatically converts other fixed-length types in the table to their corresponding variable-length types to save space.)

Answer 90:

```
mysql> DESCRIBE passwords;
+---------+---------------------+------+-----+---------+----------------+
| Field   | Type                | Null | Key | Default | Extra          |
+---------+---------------------+------+-----+---------+----------------+
| user_id | smallint(5) unsigned |     | PRI | NULL    | auto_increment |
| user_pw | char(8) binary      |      |     |         |                |
+---------+---------------------+------+-----+---------+----------------+
```

For up to 1,000 users, SMALLINT provides a sufficiently large range. This column should be declared UNSIGNED to ensure that you don't accidentally enter negative values, which would lead to confusion. The UNSIGNED option is also a prerequisite for the AUTO_INCREMENT option to work as expected; if you store negative values in an AUTO_INCREMENT column this might produce unexpected results.

AUTO_INCREMENT will take care of the numbering of new users when they're inserted into the table. To be able to use this option, the column must be declared as a primary key (that is, as a NOT NULL column that is indexed with either PRIMARY KEY or as a UNIQUE index). The primary key index ensures that every entry is unique-valued, and NOT NULL ensures that you have no NULL users in the table.

When all passwords are exactly eight characters long, a CHAR column is better suited than a VARCHAR because a VARCHAR would require one additional byte per row to store the actual length of the entry. As a side effect, passwords stored as CHAR are faster to retrieve (although one would not recognize the difference in speed with such a small table). To make comparisons of password column values case sensitive, the column should be specified with the BINARY option.

Answer 91:

CHAR(0) is not defined in ANSI SQL, but in MySQL it's possible to define a column with this datatype specification. This is mainly useful when you have to be compliant with older applications that depend on the existence of a column but that do not actually use the value. It is also useful when you need a column that can accept only two values. A CHAR(0) that isn't defined as NOT NULL will occupy only one bit and can take only two values: NULL or ' ' (the empty string).

Answer 92:

2,002 bytes; 2,000 bytes for the value and 2 bytes to store the length of the value.

Answer 93:

String value: 'Africa'. Internal number: 1 because Africa is the first member in the ENUM list.

Answer 94:

String value: ' ' (the empty string). Internal number: 0. Because 'Europa' isn't a member of the ENUM list, the special error value of ' ' (or 0 as the internal representation) is stored.

Answer 95:

String value: ' ' (the empty string). Internal number: 0. The empty string (internally, 0) is the special error value that is stored if the inserted value isn't a member of the ENUM list, or if the empty string (or 0) is explicitly stored, as in this case.

Answer 96:

String value: ' ' (the empty string). Internal number: 0. The empty string (internally, 0) is the special error value that is stored if the inserted value isn't a member of the ENUM list, or if the empty string (or 0) is explicitly stored, as in this case.

Answer 97:

String value: 'Africa'. Internal number: 1. 'Africa' is the first member in the ENUM list. The value can be inserted by giving the element number instead of the string value.

Answer 98:

String value: 'Africa'. Internal number: 1. 'Africa' is the first member in the ENUM list. MySQL first converts the string '1' to a number before it's inserted.

Answer 99:

NULL can be inserted into the name column because the column definition allows NULL values.

Answer 100:

These values will be inserted into the table's other INT columns (partial listing only):

```
mysql> SELECT * FROM defaults\G
*********** 1. row
   id: 1
 col1: NULL
 col2: 0
 col3: 42
...
```

- col1: Because this column has no defined DEFAULT value and can accept NULL values, the value inserted is NULL.
- col2: This column is declared NOT NULL and has no defined DEFAULT value. Because the INSERT provides no explicit value for this column, MySQL assigns the standard default value, in this case 0.
- col3: This column was explicitly defined with a DEFAULT value (42), so this value is inserted.

Answer 101:

These values will be inserted into the table's CHAR columns (partial listing only):

```
mysql> SELECT * FROM defaults\G
*********** 1. row
   id: 1
...
col14: NULL
col15:
col16: yoo
...
```

- col14: Because this column has no defined DEFAULT value and can accept NULL values, the value inserted is NULL.
- col15: This column is declared NOT NULL and has no defined DEFAULT value. Because the INSERT provides no explicit value for this column, MySQL assigns the standard default value, in this case ' ' (the empty string).
- col16: This column was explicitly declared with a DEFAULT value ('yoo'), so this value is inserted.

Answer 102:

These values will be inserted into the table's TEXT columns (partial listing only):

```
mysql> SELECT * FROM defaults\G
*********** 1. row
   id: 1
...
col17: NULL
col18:
...
```

- col17: Because this column can accept NULL values, the value inserted is NULL.
- col18: This column is declared NOT NULL. Because the INSERT provides no explicit value for this column, MySQL assigns the standard default value, in this case ' ' (the empty string). (You cannot declare a DEFAULT value for a TEXT column.)

Answer 103:

This value will be inserted into the table's TIME column (partial listing only):

```
mysql> SELECT * FROM defaults\G
*********** 1. row
   id: 1
...
col19: 00:00:00
...
```

col19: This column is declared NOT NULL and has no defined DEFAULT value. Because the INSERT provides no explicit value for this column, MySQL assigns the standard default value, in this case '00:00:00'.

Answer 104:

These values will be inserted into the table's DATE columns (partial listing only):

```
mysql> SELECT * FROM defaults\G
*********** 1. row
    id: 1
 ...
col10: NULL
col11: 0000-00-00
col12: 2002-02-08
 ...
```

- col10: Because this column has no defined DEFAULT value and can accept NULL values, the value inserted is NULL.

- col11: This column is declared NOT NULL and has no defined DEFAULT value. Because the INSERT provides no explicit value for this column, MySQL assigns the standard default value, in this case '0000-00-00'.

- col12: This column was explicitly defined with a DEFAULT value ('2002-02-08'), so this value is inserted.

Answer 105:

These values will be inserted into the table's ENUM columns (partial listing only):

```
mysql> SELECT * FROM defaults\G
*********** 1. row
    id: 1
 ...
col13: NULL
col15: doo
 ...
```

- col13: Because this column has no defined DEFAULT value and can accept NULL values, the value inserted is NULL.

- col15: The ENUM column is declared NOT NULL and has no defined DEFAULT value. Because the INSERT provides no explicit value for this column, MySQL uses the first list member as the standard default value.

Answer 106:

These values will be inserted into the table's SET columns (partial listing only):

```
mysql> SELECT * FROM defaults\G
*********** 1. row
    id: 1
 ...
```

```
col14: NULL
col16:

  ...
```

- col14: Because this column has no defined DEFAULT value and can accept NULL values, the value inserted is NULL.
- col16: The SET column is declared NOT NULL and has no defined DEFAULT value. Because the INSERT provides no explicit value for this column, MySQL uses the empty string as the standard default value.

Answer 107:

You could use the SQL function LAST_INSERT_ID(). The inserted value is 1. If you call LAST_INSERT_ID() repeatedly within the same connection, it will continue to return the same value (1), even if other connections insert new rows into the table.

Answer 108:

```
mysql> SELECT * FROM cliptest;
+--------+--------+
| number | string |
+--------+--------+
|    255 |      0 |
|      0 |      0 |
+--------+--------+
```

1000000 is clipped to the maximum value of TINYINT UNSIGNED. The string is converted to an integer number, and because it doesn't begin with an integer part, the result of the conversion is the number 0. The NULL entries are converted to values that match the new option NOT NULL, and because there are no DEFAULT values specified in the ALTER TABLE statement, MySQL uses the standard default values for integers, which is 0.

Answer 109:

The loop will run 127 times without error. With the first loop run, 1 is inserted, with the second run, 2 is inserted, and so on. 127 is the maximum value for a TINYINT column. An error will occur when the application tries to insert id number 128. This number will be clipped to 127, and MySQL will try to insert this value once again. Because of the PRIMARY KEY restriction that allows for only unique values in the id column, this will result in a duplicate-key error. With the mysql client, the error would be displayed as follows:

```
ERROR 1062: Duplicate entry '127' for key 1
```

Answer 110:

Either of the following statements provides the desired information:

```
SHOW TABLES LIKE '%test';
SHOW TABLE STATUS LIKE '%test%';
```

SHOW TABLES lists just the table names. SHOW TABLE STATUS displays the names and additional table information.

Answer 111:

Either of the following statements provides the desired information:

```
SHOW TABLES FROM test;
SHOW TABLE STATUS FROM test;
```

Answer 112:

```
SHOW COLUMNS FROM mytest FROM test;
```

Answer 113:

```
SHOW COLUMNS FROM mytest FROM test LIKE 'id%';
```

Answer 114:

```
SHOW CREATE TABLE test.mytest;
```

5

The SELECT Statement

This chapter covers the following exam topics:

- Selecting which columns to display
- Restricting a selection using WHERE
- Using ORDER BY to sort query results
- Limiting a selection using LIMIT
- Aggregate functions, GROUP BY, and HAVING
- Using DISTINCT to eliminate duplicates
- Concatenating SELECT results with UNION

Questions on the material in this chapter make up approximately 10% of the exam.

The SELECT statement retrieves information from one or more tables. Retrievals tend to be the most common database operation, so it's important to understand how SELECT works and what you can do with it.

This chapter provides the basic background on how to write SELECT statements and how to use the various parts of its syntax to get the results you want. The examples in this chapter use SELECT statements for retrievals involving no more than a single table. Joins (retrievals that select information from multiple tables in the same query) are covered in a later chapter.

A representative syntax for the SELECT statement is as follows:

```
SELECT values_to_display
    FROM table_name
    WHERE expression
    GROUP BY how_to_group
    HAVING expression
    ORDER BY how_to_sort
    LIMIT row_count;
```

Note that the syntax shown here has been simplified; full SELECT syntax includes additional clauses that aren't covered in this chapter.

All clauses following the output column list are optional. For example, you don't need to include a LIMIT clause when writing a SELECT statement. However, any clauses that you do include must be specified in the order shown.

This chapter discusses several clauses of the SELECT statement that allow control over many aspects of query processing:

- What values to display and the table from which to retrieve them
- How to identify the characteristics that define which records to retrieve
- How to sort output rows
- How to limit the output to a specific number of the rows retrieved
- How to arrange rows into groups and calculate aggregate values such as sums or averages for each group
- How to remove duplicates from query output
- How to combine results from multiple queries into a single result set

In most cases, the sample queries shown assume that you've already selected a default database. If that isn't true, you can select a database named *db_name* by issuing a USE *db_name* statement.

5.1 Identifying What Values to Display

To indicate what values to display, name them following the SELECT keyword. In the simplest case, you specify an expression or list of expressions. MySQL evaluates each expression and returns its value. Expressions may return numbers, strings, temporal values, or NULL. The following SELECT statement returns a value of each of those types:

```
mysql> SELECT 2+2, REPEAT('x',5), DATE_ADD('2001-01-01',INTERVAL 7 DAY), 1/0;
+-----+---------------+---------------------------------------+------+
| 2+2 | REPEAT('x',5) | DATE_ADD('2001-01-01',INTERVAL 7 DAY) | 1/0  |
+-----+---------------+---------------------------------------+------+
|   4 | xxxxx         | 2001-01-08                            | NULL |
+-----+---------------+---------------------------------------+------+
```

The first expression is a sum of numbers and returns the number 4. The second expression returns a string ('xxxxx') consisting of the character x repeated five times. The third expression returns a date value. The fourth expression returns NULL because it involves a divide-by-zero condition and cannot be evaluated. In general, if MySQL finds it impossible to evaluate an expression because it involves some exceptional condition, the result is NULL.

SELECT can serve to evaluate expressions, but it's more commonly used to retrieve values from a table. To retrieve information from a table, it's necessary to identify the table by adding a FROM `table_name` clause following the list of values to display. Suppose that you have a table named personnel that contains three columns named id, name, and salary, in that order:

```
mysql> DESCRIBE personnel;
+--------+---------------+------+-----+---------+-------+
| Field  | Type          | Null | Key | Default | Extra |
+--------+---------------+------+-----+---------+-------+
| id     | int(11)       |      | PRI | 0       |       |
| name   | char(20)      | YES  |     | NULL    |       |
| salary | decimal(10,2) | YES  |     | NULL    |       |
+--------+---------------+------+-----+---------+-------+
```

To display the contents of these columns, write the SELECT statement as follows:

```
SELECT id, name, salary FROM personnel;
```

MySQL returns a result set consisting of one row of output for each row in the table. (The term "result set" refers to the set of rows resulting from a SELECT statement.) If the table is empty, the result will be empty, too. An empty result set is perfectly legal; a syntactically valid SELECT that returns no rows is not considered erroneous.

For a SELECT operation that retrieves every column from a table, the shortcut * may be used to specify the output columns. The * stands for "all columns in the table," so for the sample table, the following statements are equivalent:

```
SELECT id, name, salary FROM personnel;
SELECT * FROM personnel;
```

The * shorthand notation is clearly more convenient to type than a list of column names. However, you should understand when it is useful and when it isn't:

- If you want to retrieve all columns from a table and you don't care about the order in which they appear from left to right, * is appropriate. If you want to ensure that the columns appear left to right in a particular order, * cannot be used because it gives you no control over the order in which columns will appear.
- If you don't want to retrieve all the columns from the table, you cannot use *. Instead, name the columns to display in the order they should appear.

As an example of when * is inapplicable, assume that you want to retrieve all columns from personnel, but in the order salary, id, and name. In this case, instead of using *, you should name the columns explicitly in the order you want them displayed:

```
SELECT salary, id, name FROM personnel;
```

Note that you cannot issue a SELECT * query to find out the left-to-right display order for the columns in a table and then assume that for future queries they will always be displayed in the same order. That strategy depends implicitly on the internal structure of the table because the actual left-to-right column order used for SELECT * retrievals is determined by the order of the columns in the table definition. However, the table's internal structure can be changed with ALTER TABLE, so the strategy is unsafe. A SELECT * statement might return different results before and after an ALTER TABLE statement.

5.1.1 Using Aliases to Name Output Columns

Output column names, by default, are the same as the column or expression selected. To give a specific name to a column, provide an alias following the column in the output list:

```
mysql> SELECT 1 AS One, 4*3 'Four Times Three';
+-----+------------------+
| One | Four Times Three |
+-----+------------------+
|   1 |               12 |
+-----+------------------+
```

Columns aliases can be used as follows:

- The keyword AS is optional.
- An alias may be quoted. If it consists of multiple words, it must be quoted.
- You can refer to a column alias elsewhere in the query, in the GROUP BY, HAVING, or ORDER BY clause. You cannot refer to it in the WHERE clause.

5.1.2 Identifying the Database Containing a Table

When you name a table in a SELECT statement, it's normally assumed to be a table in the default database. (This is true for other statements as well.) For example, if world is the default database, the following statement selects rows from the Country table in the world database:

```
SELECT * FROM Country;
```

If there's no default database, the statement results in an error because MySQL cannot tell where to find the table:

```
mysql> SELECT * FROM Country;
ERROR 1046: No Database Selected
```

To specify a database explicitly, qualify the table name—that is, precede the table name with the database name and a period:

```
SELECT * FROM world.Country;
```

The database name acts as a qualifier for the table name. It provides to the server a context for locating the table. Qualified table names are useful under several circumstances:

- When there's no default database. In this case, a qualifier is necessary for accessing the table.

- When you want to select information from a table that's located somewhere other than the default database. In this situation, it's possible to issue a USE statement to select the other database as the default, a SELECT that uses the unqualified table name, and then another USE to select the original database as the default. However, qualifying the table name is simpler because it allows the two USE statements to be avoided.

- When you aren't sure what the default database is. If the default isn't the database in which the table is located, the qualifier allows the server to locate the table. If the default happens to be the same as the named database, the qualifier is unnecessary, but harmless.

5.1.3 Retrieving Records from Multiple Tables

It's possible to retrieve records from more than one table in a single query. One way to do this is by means of a join, which selects records from multiple tables simultaneously. Joins are covered in Chapter 8, "Joins." Another way is to select records from one table after the other with multiple SELECT statements and concatenate the results using the UNION operator. UNION is covered in section 5.7, "Concatenating SELECT Results with UNION."

5.2 Restricting a Selection Using WHERE

If you don't specify any criteria for selecting records from a table, a SELECT statement will retrieve every record in the table. This is often more information than you need, particularly for large tables. To be more specific about the rows that are of interest, include a WHERE clause that describes the characteristics of those rows.

A WHERE clause can be as simple or complex as necessary to identify the rows that are relevant for your purposes. For example, to return only those rows from a table personnel that have id values less than 100, it's sufficient to use a WHERE clause that specifies a single condition:

```
SELECT * FROM personnel WHERE id < 100;
```

More complex WHERE clauses specify multiple conditions, which may be combined using logical operators such as AND and OR. The following statement returns rows with id values in the range from 10 to 20:

```
SELECT * FROM t WHERE id >= 10 AND id <= 20;
```

For testing values in a range, you can also use the BETWEEN operator:

```
SELECT * FROM t WHERE id BETWEEN 10 AND 20;
```

Some operators have higher precedence than others. For example, AND has a higher precedence than OR. To control the order of evaluation of terms within a complex expression (or simply to make the evaluation order explicit), you can use parentheses to group expression terms. Consider the following WHERE clause:

```
WHERE id < 3 AND name = 'Wendell' OR name = 'Yosef'
```

Because AND has a higher precedence than OR, the preceding expression is equivalent to the following one:

```
WHERE (id < 3 AND name = 'Wendell') OR name = 'Yosef'
```

This expression finds all records with an id value less than 3 that also have a name value of 'Wendell', as well as all records with a name value of 'Yosef' (regardless of their id value).

A different placement of parentheses results in a very different meaning:

```
WHERE id < 3 AND (name = 'Wendell' OR name = 'Yosef')
```

This expression finds records that have an id value less than 3 and a name value of either 'Wendell' or 'Yosef'.

More information on writing expressions can be found in section 6.1, "Using SQL Expressions and Functions." Detailed descriptions of the operators and functions that you can use in expressions are provided in the *MySQL Reference Manual*.

It's possible to prevent SELECT statements that might generate a great deal of output from returning more than 1,000 rows. The mysql client supports this feature if you invoke it with the --safe-updates option. For more information, see section 3.2.8, "Using the --safe-updates Option."

5.3 Using ORDER BY to Sort Query Results

By default, the rows in the result set produced by a SELECT statement are returned by the server to the client in no particular order. When you issue a query, the server is free to return the rows in any convenient order. This order can be affected by a factor such as the order in which rows are actually stored in the table or which indexes are used to process the query. If you require output rows to be returned in a specific order, include an ORDER BY clause that indicates how to sort the results.

The examples in this section use a table t that has the following contents (id is numeric, last_name and first_name are strings, and d contains dates):

```
mysql> SELECT id, last_name, first_name, d FROM t;
+------+-----------+------------+------------+
| id   | last_name | first_name | d          |
+------+-----------+------------+------------+
|    1 | Brown     | Bill       | 1972-10-14 |
|    2 | Larsson   | Sven       | 1965-01-03 |
|    3 | Brown     | Betty      | 1971-07-12 |
|    4 | Larsson   | Selma      | 1968-05-29 |
+------+-----------+------------+------------+
```

ORDER BY provides a great deal of flexibility for sorting result sets. It has the following characteristics:

- You can name one or more columns, separated by commas, to use for sorting. With a single sort column, rows are sorted using the values in that column:

```
mysql> SELECT id, last_name, first_name, d FROM t
    -> ORDER BY d;
+------+-----------+------------+------------+
| id   | last_name | first_name | d          |
+------+-----------+------------+------------+
|    2 | Larsson   | Sven       | 1965-01-03 |
|    4 | Larsson   | Selma      | 1968-05-29 |
|    3 | Brown     | Betty      | 1971-07-12 |
|    1 | Brown     | Bill       | 1972-10-14 |
+------+-----------+------------+------------+
```

If there are additional sort columns, rows with the same value in the first sort column are sorted together, and are then further sorted using the values in the second and remaining sort columns. The following query sorts the Browns before the Larssons, and then within each group of rows with the same last name, sorts them by first name:

```
mysql> SELECT id, last_name, first_name, d FROM t
    -> ORDER BY last_name, first_name;
+------+-----------+------------+------------+
| id   | last_name | first_name | d          |
+------+-----------+------------+------------+
|    3 | Brown     | Betty      | 1971-07-12 |
|    1 | Brown     | Bill       | 1972-10-14 |
|    4 | Larsson   | Selma      | 1968-05-29 |
|    2 | Larsson   | Sven       | 1965-01-03 |
+------+-----------+------------+------------+
```

- By default, ORDER BY sorts values in ascending order (smallest to largest). Any sort column may be followed with ASC if you want to specify ascending order explicitly. These ORDER BY clauses are equivalent:

```
ORDER BY last_name, first_name
ORDER BY last_name ASC, first_name ASC
```

To sort values in descending order (largest to smallest), follow the sort column name with DESC:

```
mysql> SELECT id, last_name, first_name, d FROM t
    -> ORDER BY id DESC;
+------+-----------+------------+------------+
| id   | last_name | first_name | d          |
+------+-----------+------------+------------+
|    4 | Larsson   | Selma      | 1968-05-29 |
|    3 | Brown     | Betty      | 1971-07-12 |
|    2 | Larsson   | Sven       | 1965-01-03 |
|    1 | Brown     | Bill       | 1972-10-14 |
+------+-----------+------------+------------+
```

When you name a column followed by ASC or DESC, the sort direction specifier applies only to that column. It doesn't affect sort direction for any other columns listed in the ORDER BY clause.

- ORDER BY typically refers to table columns by name:

```
SELECT last_name, first_name FROM t ORDER BY last_name, first_name;
```

However, it's possible to refer to columns in other ways. If a column is given an alias in the output column list, you can refer to that column by its alias:

```
SELECT last_name AS last, first_name AS first FROM t ORDER BY last, first;
```

Or you can specify a number corresponding to the column's position in the column output list (1 for the first output column, 2 for the second, and so forth):

```
SELECT last_name, first_name FROM t ORDER BY 1, 2;
```

One caution against specifying columns by position is that this syntax has been removed from the SQL Standard (in SQL:1999) and should be considered obsolete. Application developers should keep this in mind and consider using one of the other column specification methods.

- It's possible to perform a sort using an expression result. If the expression appears in the output column list, you can use it for sorting by repeating it in the ORDER BY clause. Alternatively, you can refer to the expression by an alias given to it or by its column position (although the latter isn't recommended). The following queries each sort the output rows by month of the year:

```
SELECT id, last_name, first_name, MONTH(d) FROM t ORDER BY MONTH(d);
SELECT id, last_name, first_name, MONTH(d) AS m FROM t ORDER BY m;
SELECT id, last_name, first_name, MONTH(d) FROM t ORDER BY 3;
```

- You can sort output using values that don't appear in the output at all. The following statement displays month names in the output, but sorts the rows using the numeric month value:

```
mysql> SELECT id, last_name, first_name, MONTHNAME(d) FROM t
    -> ORDER BY MONTH(d);
+------+-----------+------------+--------------+
| id   | last_name | first_name | MONTHNAME(d) |
+------+-----------+------------+--------------+
|    2 | Larsson   | Sven       | January      |
|    4 | Larsson   | Selma      | May          |
|    3 | Brown     | Betty      | July         |
|    1 | Brown     | Bill       | October      |
+------+-----------+------------+--------------+
```

- ORDER BY doesn't require the sorted columns to be indexed, although a query might run faster if such an index does exist.

- ORDER BY is useful together with LIMIT for selecting a particular section of a set of sorted rows. (See section 5.4, "Limiting a Selection Using LIMIT.")

- ORDER BY may be used with DELETE or UPDATE to force rows to be deleted or updated in a certain order. These uses of ORDER BY are covered in Chapter 7, "Update Statements."

5.3.1 The Natural Sort Order of Column Types

Each type of data managed by MySQL has its own natural sort order. For the most part, these orders are fairly intuitive, except that the rules for string sorting depend on whether the strings are binary or nonbinary, and whether they come from ENUM or SET columns.

- Numeric columns sort in ascending numeric order by default, or descending order if DESC is specified.

- DECIMAL columns are numeric, so they sort numerically, even though DECIMAL values are stored in string form.

- Date and time columns sort in ascending temporal order by default, with oldest values first and most recent values last. The order is reversed if DESC is specified.

- The sort order for string columns other than ENUM and SET depends on whether the column contains binary or nonbinary values. Binary strings sort based on the numeric values of the bytes that make up the strings. This means that the sort order is case sensitive. Nonbinary strings sort in lexical order, which is defined by the collating sequence of the server's character set. Typically, this means that nonbinary string sorts aren't case sensitive. For example, assume that a table t has a CHAR column c that contains the following values:

```
mysql> SELECT c FROM t;
+------+
| c    |
+------+
| D    |
| a    |
```

```
| c    |
| B    |
+------+
```

A CHAR column is nonbinary by default, so its contents sort lexically without regard to lettercase:

```
mysql> SELECT c FROM t ORDER BY c;
+------+
| c    |
+------+
| a    |
| B    |
| c    |
| D    |
+------+
```

You can force a string column sort to be case sensitive by using the BINARY keyword:

```
mysql> SELECT c FROM t ORDER BY BINARY c;
+------+
| c    |
+------+
| B    |
| D    |
| a    |
| c    |
+------+
```

- The sort order for members of an ENUM or SET column is based on their internal numeric values. These values correspond to the order in which the enumeration or set members are listed in the column definition. Suppose that a table t contains a column mon that is an ENUM listing abbreviations for months of the year:

```
CREATE TABLE t
(
    mon ENUM('Jan','Feb','Mar','Apr','May','Jun',
             'Jul','Aug','Sep','Oct','Nov','Dec')
);
```

Assume that table t has 12 rows, one for each of the possible enumeration values. When you sort this column, the values come out in month-of-year order:

```
mysql> SELECT mon FROM t ORDER BY mon;
+------+
| mon  |
+------+
| Jan  |
| Feb  |
```

```
| Mar |
| Apr |
| May |
| Jun |
| Jul |
| Aug |
| Sep |
| Oct |
| Nov |
| Dec |
+------+
```

This is because 'Jan' through 'Dec' are assigned internal values 1 through 12 based on their order in the column definition, and those values determine the sort order. To produce a lexical sort using the string values, use CAST() to convert the enumeration values to CHAR values:

```
mysql> SELECT mon FROM t ORDER BY CAST(mon AS CHAR);
+------+
| mon |
+------+
| Apr |
| Aug |
| Dec |
| Feb |
| Jan |
| Jul |
| Jun |
| Mar |
| May |
| Nov |
| Oct |
| Sep |
+------+
```

SET columns also sort using the internal values of the set's legal members. The ordering is more complex than with ENUM because values may consist of multiple SET members. For example, the following SET column contains three members:

```
CREATE TABLE t (hue SET('red','green','blue'));
```

Assume that t contains the following rows:

```
mysql> SELECT hue FROM t;
+----------------+
| hue            |
+----------------+
| red,green      |
```

```
| red,green,blue |
| red,blue       |
| green,blue     |
+----------------+
```

The SET members 'red', 'green', and 'blue' have internal values of 1, 2, and 4, respectively. Thus, the rows of the table have internal numeric values of 3 (1+2), 7 (1+2+8), 5 (1+4), and 6 (2+4). An ORDER BY on the column sorts using these numeric values:

```
mysql> SELECT hue FROM t ORDER BY hue;
+----------------+
| hue            |
+----------------+
| red,green      |
| red,blue       |
| green,blue     |
| red,green,blue |
+----------------+
```

- NULL values in a column sort together at one end or the other of the sort order. For MySQL, NULL values sort at the beginning for ascending sorts and at the end for descending sorts. (However, MySQL does not fully implement this behavior until version 4.0.11. In most earlier MySQL 4 releases, NULL values sort at the beginning, regardless of sort direction.)

5.4 Limiting a Selection Using LIMIT

MySQL supports a LIMIT clause in SELECT statements that tells the server to return only some of the rows selected by the statement. This is useful for retrieving records based on their position within the set of selected rows.

LIMIT may be given with either one or two arguments, which must be integer constants:

```
LIMIT row_count
LIMIT skip_count, row_count
```

When followed by a single integer, row_count, LIMIT returns the first row_count rows from the beginning of the result set. To select just the first 10 rows of a table t, use the following query:

```
SELECT * FROM t LIMIT 10;
```

When followed by two integers, skip_count and row_count, LIMIT skips the first skip_count rows from the beginning of the result set, and then returns the next row_count rows. To skip the first 20 rows and then return the next 10 rows, do this:

```
SELECT * FROM t LIMIT 20,10;
```

The single-argument form of LIMIT is applicable only when the rows you want to retrieve appear at the beginning of the result set. The two-argument form is more general and can be used to select an arbitrary section of rows from anywhere in the result set.

When you need only some of the rows selected by a query, LIMIT is an efficient way to obtain them. For an application that fetches rows from the server, you get better performance by adding LIMIT to the query than by fetching all the rows and discarding all but the ones of interest. By using LIMIT, the unwanted rows never cross the network at all.

It's often helpful to include an ORDER BY clause to put the rows in a particular order when you use LIMIT. When ORDER BY and LIMIT are used together, MySQL applies ORDER BY first and then LIMIT. One common use for this is to find the row containing the smallest or largest values in a particular column. For example, to find the row in a table t containing the smallest id value, use this statement:

```
SELECT * FROM t ORDER BY id LIMIT 1;
```

To find the largest value instead, use DESC to sort the rows in reverse:

```
SELECT * FROM t ORDER BY id DESC LIMIT 1;
```

The two-argument form of LIMIT is useful in conjunction with ORDER BY for situations in which you want to process successive sections of a result set. For example, in Web applications, it's common to display the result of a large search across a series of pages that each present one section of the result. To retrieve sections of the search result this way, issue a series of statements that all specify the same number of rows to return in the LIMIT clause, but vary the number of initial rows to skip:

```
SELECT * FROM t ORDER BY id LIMIT  0, 20;
SELECT * FROM t ORDER BY id LIMIT 20, 20;
SELECT * FROM t ORDER BY id LIMIT 40, 20;
SELECT * FROM t ORDER BY id LIMIT 60, 20;
...
```

It's possible to abuse the LIMIT feature. For example, it isn't a good idea to use a clause such as LIMIT 1000000, 10 to return 10 rows from a query that normally would return more than a million rows. The server must still process the query to determine the first million rows before returning the 10 rows. It's better to use a WHERE clause to reduce the query result to a more manageable size and use LIMIT to pull rows from that result. This also makes the use of ORDER BY with LIMIT more efficient because the server need not sort as large a row set before applying the limit.

In addition to their uses with SELECT, the UPDATE and DELETE statements also support a LIMIT clause, to cause only a certain number of rows to be updated or deleted. See Chapter 7, "Update Statements."

5.5 Aggregate Functions, GROUP BY, and HAVING

A SELECT statement can produce a list of rows that match a given set of conditions. The list provides the details about the selected rows, but if you want to know about the overall characteristics of the rows, you'll be more interested in getting a summary instead. When that's your goal, use aggregate functions to calculate summary values, possibly combined with a GROUP BY clause to arrange the selected rows into groups so that you can get summaries for each group.

Grouping can be based on the values in one or more columns of the selected rows. For example, the Country table indicates which continent each country is part of, so you can group the records by continent and calculate the average population of countries in each continent:

```
SELECT Continent, AVG(Population) FROM Country GROUP BY Continent;
```

Functions such as AVG() that calculate summary values for groups are known as "aggregate" functions because they're based on aggregates or groups of values.

This section describes the aggregate functions available to you and shows how to use GROUP BY to group rows appropriately for the type of summary you want to produce. It also discusses the HAVING clause that enables you to select only groups that have certain characteristics.

5.5.1 Computing Summary Values

An aggregate function calculates a summary value from a group of individual values. There are several types of aggregate functions. Those discussed here are as follows:

- SUM() and AVG() summarize numeric values to produce sums (totals) and averages.
- MIN() and MAX() find smallest and largest values.
- COUNT() counts rows, values, or the number of distinct values.

Aggregate functions may be used with or without a GROUP BY clause that places rows into groups. Without a GROUP BY clause, an aggregate function calculates a summary value based on the entire set of selected rows. (That is, MySQL treats all the rows as a single group.) With a GROUP BY clause, an aggregate function calculates a summary value for each group. For example, if a WHERE clause selects 20 rows and the GROUP BY clause arranges them into four groups of five rows each, a summary function produces a value for each of the four groups.

5.5.1.1 The SUM() and AVG() Aggregate Functions

The SUM() and AVG() functions calculate sums and averages. For example, the Country table in the world database contains a Population column, so we can calculate the total world population and the average population per country like this:

```
mysql> SELECT SUM(Population), AVG(Population) FROM Country;
+-----------------+-----------------+
| SUM(Population) | AVG(Population)  |
+-----------------+-----------------+
|      6078749450 |    25434098.1172 |
+-----------------+-----------------+
```

SUM() and AVG() are most commonly used with numeric values. If you use them with other types of values, those values are subjected to numeric conversion, which might not produce a sensible result:

```
mysql> SELECT SUM(Name), SUM(Continent) FROM Country;
+-----------+----------------+
| SUM(Name) | SUM(Continent) |
+-----------+----------------+
|         0 |            754 |
+-----------+----------------+
```

In this case, the Name values are strings that don't look like numbers. Each converts to zero, so the sum is zero as well. The Continent column is an ENUM, so its values are summed according to their internal numeric representation. In neither case are the results meaningful.

SUM() and AVG() ignore NULL values.

5.5.1.2 The MIN() and MAX() Aggregate Functions

MIN() and MAX() are comparison functions. They return smallest or largest numeric values, lexically first or last string values, and earliest or latest temporal values. The following queries determine the smallest and largest country populations and the lexically first and last country names:

```
mysql> SELECT MIN(Population), MAX(Population) FROM Country;
+-----------------+-----------------+
| MIN(Population) | MAX(Population) |
+-----------------+-----------------+
|               0 |      1277558000 |
+-----------------+-----------------+
mysql> SELECT MIN(Name), MAX(Name) FROM Country;
+-------------+-----------+
| MIN(Name)   | MAX(Name) |
+-------------+-----------+
| Afghanistan | Zimbabwe  |
+-------------+-----------+
```

For string values, the behavior of MIN() and MAX() depends on whether the strings are binary (case sensitive) or nonbinary (not case sensitive). Consider a table t containing the following string values:

```
mysql> SELECT name FROM t;
+--------+
| name   |
+--------+
| Calvin |
| alex   |
+--------+
```

If the names are nonbinary strings (for example, if they're CHAR values), MAX(name) returns 'Calvin' because C is greater than a in a collating order that isn't case sensitive:

```
mysql> SELECT MAX(name) FROM t;
+-----------+
| MAX(name) |
+-----------+
| Calvin    |
+-----------+
```

But if the values are binary strings (for example, CHAR BINARY values), the values are compared using the actual numeric byte values of the characters and thus are treated as case sensitive. If lowercase letters have larger byte values than uppercase letters (as is true for the default character set), a has a larger byte value than C and MAX(name) returns 'alex':

```
mysql> ALTER TABLE t MODIFY name CHAR(20) BINARY;
mysql> SELECT MAX(name) FROM t;
+-----------+
| MAX(name) |
+-----------+
| alex      |
+-----------+
```

MIN() and MAX()ignore NULL values.

5.5.1.3 The COUNT() Aggregate Function

The COUNT() function can be used in several ways to count either rows or values. To illustrate, the examples here use the following table that has several rows containing various combinations of NULL and non-NULL values:

```
mysql> SELECT i, j FROM t;
+------+------+
| i    | j    |
+------+------+
|    1 | NULL |
| NULL |    2 |
|    1 |    1 |
|    1 |    1 |
|    1 |    3 |
```

```
| NULL | NULL |
|    1 | NULL |
+------+------+
```

COUNT() may be used as follows:

- COUNT(*) counts the total number of rows:

  ```
  mysql> SELECT COUNT(*) FROM t;
  +----------+
  | COUNT(*) |
  +----------+
  |        7 |
  +----------+
  ```

- COUNT(*expression*) counts the number of non-NULL values of the given expression. It's common for *expression* to be a column name, in which case, COUNT() counts the number of non-NULL values in the column:

  ```
  mysql> SELECT COUNT(i), COUNT(j) FROM t;
  +----------+----------+
  | COUNT(i) | COUNT(j) |
  +----------+----------+
  |        5 |        4 |
  +----------+----------+
  ```

- COUNT(DISTINCT *expression*) counts the number of distinct (unique) non-NULL values of the given expression. *expression* can be a column name to count the number of distinct non-NULL values in the column:

  ```
  mysql> SELECT COUNT(DISTINCT i), COUNT(DISTINCT j) FROM t;
  +-------------------+-------------------+
  | COUNT(DISTINCT i) | COUNT(DISTINCT j) |
  +-------------------+-------------------+
  |                 1 |                 3 |
  +-------------------+-------------------+
  ```

  It's also possible to give a list of expressions separated by commas. In this case, COUNT() returns the number of distinct combinations of values that contain no NULL values. The following query counts the number of distinct rows that have non-NULL values in both the i and j columns:

  ```
  mysql> SELECT COUNT(DISTINCT i, j) FROM t;
  +----------------------+
  | COUNT(DISTINCT i, j) |
  +----------------------+
  |                    2 |
  +----------------------+
  ```

5.5.1.4 Aggregate Values for an Empty Set

A SELECT statement might produce an empty result set if the table is empty or the WHERE clause selects no rows from it. If the set of values passed to an aggregate function is empty, the function computes the most sensible value. For COUNT(), the result is zero. But functions such as SUM(), MIN(), MAX(), and AVG() return NULL. They also return NULL if a nonempty result contains only NULL values. These behaviors occur because there is no way for such functions to compute results without at least one non-NULL input value.

5.5.2 Grouping Rows with GROUP BY

If the query does not contain a GROUP BY clause to place rows of the result set into groups, an aggregate function result is based on all the selected rows. A GROUP BY clause may be added to generate a more fine-grained summary that produces values for subgroups within a set of selected rows.

Suppose that a table named personnel contains the following information about company employees:

```
mysql> SELECT * FROM personnel;
+---------+--------+---------+-------------+----------+
| pers_id | name   | dept_id | title       | salary   |
+---------+--------+---------+-------------+----------+
|       1 | Wendy  |      14 | Supervisor  | 38000.00 |
|       2 | Wally  |       7 | Stock clerk | 28000.00 |
|       3 | Ray    |       7 | Programmer  | 41000.00 |
|       4 | Burton |      14 | Secretary   | 32000.00 |
|       5 | Gordon |      14 | President   | 78000.00 |
|       6 | Jeff   |       7 | Stock clerk | 29000.00 |
|       7 | Doris  |       7 | Programmer  | 48000.00 |
|       8 | Daisy  |       7 | Secretary   | 33000.00 |
|       9 | Bea    |       7 | Accountant  | 40000.00 |
+---------+--------+---------+-------------+----------+
```

A count for a query with no GROUP BY produces a single value for the entire set of rows:

```
mysql> SELECT COUNT(*) FROM personnel;
+----------+
| COUNT(*) |
+----------+
|        9 |
+----------+
```

Adding a GROUP BY clause arranges rows using the values in the grouping column or columns with the result that COUNT(*) produces a count for each group. To find out how many times each title occurs, do this:

```
mysql> SELECT title, COUNT(*) FROM personnel
    -> GROUP BY title;
+------------+----------+
| title      | COUNT(*) |
+------------+----------+
| Accountant |        1 |
| President  |        1 |
| Programmer |        2 |
| Secretary  |        2 |
| Stock clerk|        2 |
| Supervisor |        1 |
+------------+----------+
```

To count the number of people in each department, group by department number:

```
mysql> SELECT dept_id, COUNT(*) FROM personnel
    -> GROUP BY dept_id;
+---------+----------+
| dept_id | COUNT(*) |
+---------+----------+
|       7 |        6 |
|      14 |        3 |
+---------+----------+
```

A GROUP BY that names multiple columns arranges rows according to the combinations of values in those columns. For example, to find out how many times each job title occurs in each department, group by both department and title:

```
mysql> SELECT dept_id, title, COUNT(*) FROM personnel
    -> GROUP BY dept_id, title;
+---------+------------+----------+
| dept_id | title      | COUNT(*) |
+---------+------------+----------+
|       7 | Accountant |        1 |
|       7 | Programmer |        2 |
|       7 | Secretary  |        1 |
|       7 | Stock clerk|        2 |
|      14 | President  |        1 |
|      14 | Secretary  |        1 |
|      14 | Supervisor |        1 |
+---------+------------+----------+
```

The preceding queries use COUNT(*) to count rows, but you can also use summary functions to compute results based on values in specific columns of the rows in each group. For example, numeric functions can tell you about the salary characteristics of each title or department:

```
mysql> SELECT title, MIN(salary), MAX(salary), AVG(salary)
    -> FROM personnel
    -> GROUP BY title;
+------------+-------------+-------------+--------------+
| title      | MIN(salary) | MAX(salary) | AVG(salary)  |
+------------+-------------+-------------+--------------+
| Accountant |    40000.00 |    40000.00 | 40000.000000 |
| President  |    78000.00 |    78000.00 | 78000.000000 |
| Programmer |    41000.00 |    48000.00 | 44500.000000 |
| Secretary  |    32000.00 |    33000.00 | 32500.000000 |
| Stock clerk|    28000.00 |    29000.00 | 28500.000000 |
| Supervisor |    38000.00 |    38000.00 | 38000.000000 |
+------------+-------------+-------------+--------------+
mysql> SELECT dept_id, MIN(salary), MAX(salary), AVG(salary)
    -> FROM personnel
    -> GROUP BY dept_id;
+---------+-------------+-------------+--------------+
| dept_id | MIN(salary) | MAX(salary) | AVG(salary)  |
+---------+-------------+-------------+--------------+
|       7 |    28000.00 |    48000.00 | 36500.000000 |
|      14 |    32000.00 |    78000.00 | 49333.333333 |
+---------+-------------+-------------+--------------+
```

Note that in each of these queries, the output columns consist only of the columns listed in the GROUP BY clause, and values produced by summary functions. If you try to display table columns other than those listed in the GROUP BY clause, the values displayed for the extra columns are unpredictable.

5.5.3 GROUP BY and Sorting

In MySQL, a GROUP BY clause has the side effect of sorting rows. If you already have a GROUP BY clause in your query that produces the desired sort order, there's no need for an ORDER BY. Use of ORDER BY is necessary with GROUP BY only to produce a different sort order than that resulting from the GROUP BY. However, this isn't a portable behavior; for database engines other than MySQL, GROUP BY might not sort rows. To write more portable queries, add an ORDER BY even if MySQL does not require it.

For examples that show the effect of using ORDER BY in conjunction with GROUP BY to produce a different sort order than the grouping does, see the sample exercises at the end of the chapter.

5.5.4 Selecting Groups with HAVING

It could be when you use GROUP BY that you're interested only in groups that have particular summary characteristics. To retrieve just those groups and eliminate the rest, use a HAVING clause that identifies the required group characteristics. HAVING acts in a manner somewhat similar to WHERE, but occurs at a different stage of query processing:

1. WHERE, if present, identifies the initial set of records to be selected from a table.

2. GROUP BY arranges the selected records into groups.

3. Aggregate functions compute summary values for each group.

4. HAVING identifies which groups to retrieve for the final result set.

The following example shows how this progression works, using the personnel table from the previous section:

1. A query with no GROUP BY clause or aggregate functions selects a list of records. This list provides details, not overall characteristics:

```
mysql> SELECT title, salary
    -> FROM personnel WHERE dept_id = 7;
+-------------+----------+
| title       | salary   |
+-------------+----------+
| Stock clerk | 28000.00 |
| Programmer  | 41000.00 |
| Stock clerk | 29000.00 |
| Programmer  | 48000.00 |
| Secretary   | 33000.00 |
| Accountant  | 40000.00 |
+-------------+----------+
```

2. Adding GROUP BY and aggregate functions arranges rows into groups and computes summary values for each.

```
mysql> SELECT title, COUNT(*), AVG(salary)
    -> FROM personnel WHERE dept_id = 7
    -> GROUP BY title;
+-------------+----------+--------------+
| title       | COUNT(*) | AVG(salary)  |
+-------------+----------+--------------+
| Accountant  |        1 | 40000.000000 |
| Programmer  |        2 | 44500.000000 |
| Secretary   |        1 | 33000.000000 |
| Stock clerk |        2 | 28500.000000 |
+-------------+----------+--------------+
```

3. Finally, adding HAVING places an additional constraint on the output rows. In the following query, only those groups consisting of two or more people are displayed:

```
mysql> SELECT title, salary, COUNT(*), AVG(salary)
    -> FROM personnel WHERE dept_id = 7
```

```
    -> GROUP BY title
    -> HAVING COUNT(*) > 1;
+-------------+----------+----------+--------------+
| title       | salary   | COUNT(*) | AVG(salary)  |
+-------------+----------+----------+--------------+
| Programmer  | 41000.00 |        2 | 44500.000000 |
| Stock clerk | 28000.00 |        2 | 28500.000000 |
+-------------+----------+----------+--------------+
```

Sometimes you can place selection criteria in either the WHERE clause or in the HAVING clause. In such cases, it's better to do so in the WHERE clause because that eliminates rows from consideration sooner and allows the query to be processed more efficiently. Choosing values in the HAVING clause might cause the query to perform group calculations on groups in which you have no interest.

5.6 Using DISTINCT to Eliminate Duplicates

If a query returns a result that contains duplicate rows, you can remove duplicates and produce a result set in which every row is unique. To do this, include the keyword DISTINCT after SELECT and before the output column list.

Suppose that a query returns a result set that contains duplicated rows:

```
mysql> SELECT last_name FROM t;
+-----------+
| last_name |
+-----------+
| Brown     |
| Larsson   |
| Brown     |
| Larsson   |
+-----------+
```

Adding DISTINCT removes the duplicates and returns only unique rows:

```
mysql> SELECT DISTINCT last_name FROM t;
+-----------+
| last_name |
+-----------+
| Brown     |
| Larsson   |
+-----------+
```

Duplicate elimination for string values happens differently for binary and nonbinary strings. The strings 'ABC', 'Abc', and 'abc' are considered distinct if they're binary strings, but the same if they are nonbinary. (Stated another way, strings that vary only in lettercase are considered the same unless they're binary.)

Distinctiveness of rows is assessed taking NULL values into account. Suppose that a table t contains the following rows:

```
mysql> SELECT i, j FROM t;
+------+------+
| i    | j    |
+------+------+
|    1 |    2 |
|    1 | NULL |
|    1 | NULL |
+------+------+
```

For purposes of DISTINCT, the NULL values in the second column are considered the same, so the second and third rows are identical. Adding DISTINCT to the query eliminates one of them as a duplicate:

```
mysql> SELECT DISTINCT i, j FROM t;
+------+------+
| i    | j    |
+------+------+
|    1 |    2 |
|    1 | NULL |
+------+------+
```

Using DISTINCT is equivalent to using GROUP BY on all selected columns with no aggregate function. For such a query, GROUP BY just produces a list of distinct grouping values. If you display and group by a single column, the query produces the distinct values in that column. If you display and group by multiple columns, the query produces the distinct combinations of values in the column. For example, the following two queries are equivalent:

```
SELECT DISTINCT id FROM t;
SELECT id FROM t GROUP BY id;
```

As are these:

```
SELECT DISTINCT id, name FROM t;
SELECT id, name FROM t GROUP BY id, name;
```

Another correspondence between the behavior of DISTINCT and GROUP BY is that for purposes of assessing distinctness, DISTINCT considers all NULL values the same. This is analogous to the way that GROUP BY groups together NULL values.

A difference between DISTINCT and GROUP BY is that DISTINCT doesn't cause row sorting the way that GROUP BY does.

DISTINCT can be used with the COUNT() function to count how many distinct values a column contains. However, in this case, NULL values are ignored:

```
mysql> SELECT j FROM t;
+------+
| j    |
+------+
|    2 |
| NULL |
| NULL |
+------+
mysql> SELECT COUNT(DISTINCT j) FROM t;
+-------------------+
| COUNT(DISTINCT j) |
+-------------------+
|                 1 |
+-------------------+
```

COUNT(DISTINCT) is discussed further in section 5.5, "Aggregate Functions, GROUP BY, and HAVING."

5.7 Concatenating SELECT Results with UNION

The UNION keyword enables you to concatenate the results from two or more SELECT statements. The syntax for using it is as follows:

```
SELECT ... UNION SELECT ... UNION SELECT ...
```

The result of such a statement consists of the rows retrieved by the first SELECT, followed by the rows retrieved by the second SELECT, and so on. Each SELECT must produce the same number of columns.

By default, UNION eliminates duplicate rows from the result set. If you want to retain all rows, replace the first instance of UNION with UNION ALL. (UNION ALL also is more efficient for the server to process because it need not perform duplicate removal.)

UNION is useful under the following circumstances:

- You have similar information in multiple tables and you want to retrieve rows from all of them at once.
- You want to select several sets of rows from the same table, but the conditions that characterize each set aren't easy to write as a single WHERE clause. UNION allows retrieval of each set with a simpler WHERE clause in its own SELECT statement; the rows retrieved by each are combined and produced as the final query result.

Suppose that you run three mailing lists, each of which is managed using a different MySQL-based software package. Each package uses its own table to store names and email addresses, but they have slightly different conventions about how the tables are set up. The tables used by the list manager packages look like this:

```
CREATE TABLE list1
(
    subscriber  CHAR(60),
    email       CHAR(60)
);

CREATE TABLE list2
(
    name        CHAR(255),
    address     CHAR(255)
);

CREATE TABLE list3
(
    email       CHAR(50),
    real_name   CHAR(30)
);
```

Note that each table contains similar types of information (names and email addresses), but they don't use the same column names or types, and they don't store the columns in the same order. How do you write a query that produces the combined subscriber list? Use UNION. It doesn't matter that the tables don't have exactly the same structure. To select their combined contents, name the columns from each table in the order you want to see them. A query to retrieve names and addresses from the tables looks like this:

```
SELECT subscriber, email FROM list1
UNION SELECT name, address FROM list2
UNION SELECT real_name, email FROM list3;
```

The first column of the result contains names and the second column contains email addresses. The names of the columns resulting from a UNION are taken from the names of the columns in the first SELECT statement. This means the result set column names are subscriber and email. If you provide aliases for columns in the first SELECT, the aliases are used as the output column names.

The types of the output columns also are taken from the values retrieved by the first SELECT. For the query shown, the types will be CHAR(60). (Note that because the list2 table contains CHAR(255) columns, it's possible for values retrieved from that table to be truncated in the UNION result. This limitation on UNION is removed in MySQL 4.1; column types are determined based on all retrieved values. In MySQL 4.0, you can avoid the problem by selecting from the table with the widest columns first.)

ORDER BY and LIMIT clauses can be placed at the end of a UNION to sort or limit the result set as a whole. Columns named in such an ORDER BY should refer to columns in the first SELECT of the statement. (This is a consequence of the fact that the first SELECT determines the result set column names.) The following statement sorts the result of the UNION by email address and returns the first 10 rows of the combined result:

```
SELECT subscriber, email FROM list1
UNION SELECT name, address FROM list2
UNION SELECT real_name, email FROM list3
ORDER BY email LIMIT 10;
```

ORDER BY and LIMIT clauses also can be applied to individual SELECT statements within a UNION: Add the clauses to the appropriate SELECT and surround the resulting SELECT with parentheses. In this case, an ORDER BY should refer to columns of the particular SELECT with which it's associated. The following query sorts the result of each SELECT by email address and returns the first five rows from each one:

```
(SELECT subscriber, email FROM list1 ORDER BY email LIMIT 5)
UNION (SELECT name, address FROM list2 ORDER BY address LIMIT 5)
UNION (SELECT real_name, email FROM list3 ORDER BY email LIMIT 5);
```

5.8 Exercises

Question 1:

Assume that a table t contains a DATE column d. How would you find the oldest date? How would you find the most recent date?

Question 2:

Assume that a table t contains a date-valued column d as well as other columns. How would you find the row that contains the oldest date? How would you find the row containing the most recent date? (Note that these are different problems than finding the oldest and most recent date.)

Question 3:

Consider the following table structure and partial listing of its contents:

```
mysql> DESCRIBE CountryList;
+-----------+-------------+------+-----+---------+-------+
| Field     | Type        | Null | Key | Default | Extra |
+-----------+-------------+------+-----+---------+-------+
| Code      | char(3)     |      |     |         |       |
| Name      | char(52)    |      |     |         |       |
| IndepYear | smallint(6) | YES  |     | NULL    |       |
+-----------+-------------+------+-----+---------+-------+
mysql> SELECT * FROM CountryList;
+------+-------------+-----------+
| Code | Name        | IndepYear |
+------+-------------+-----------+
| AFG  | Afghanistan |      1919 |
| AGO  | Angola      |      1975 |
| ALB  | Albania     |      1912 |
...
```

a. How can you find out which country was the last to become independent?

b. How can you find out which country was the first to become independent?

Question 4:

Here's an alphabetical list of some basic clauses for the SELECT statement:

- FROM
- GROUP BY
- HAVING
- LIMIT
- ORDER BY
- WHERE

These clauses must be used in a specific order. What's this order?

Question 5:

In general, which of the SELECT statement clauses shown in the previous question are optional? Which of them are optional when retrieving data from a table?

Question 6:

You want to retrieve data from a table users in the project1 database. Your current database is test. How can you refer to the users table in the FROM clause of SELECT statements without changing the default database beforehand?

Question 7:

The City table looks like this:

```
mysql> DESCRIBE City;
+-------------+----------+------+-----+---------+----------------+
| Field       | Type     | Null | Key | Default | Extra          |
+-------------+----------+------+-----+---------+----------------+
| ID          | int(11)  |      | PRI | NULL    | auto_increment |
| Name        | char(35) |      |     |         |                |
| CountryCode | char(3)  |      |     |         |                |
| District    | char(20) |      |     |         |                |
| Population  | int(11)  |      |     | 0       |                |
+-------------+----------+------+-----+---------+----------------+
```

You want to find cities whose names start with letters B to F and K to M, and that have more than a million inhabitants. The output should be sorted in ascending name order. What query will produce this result?

Question 8:

The table petbirth has the following structure and contents:

```
mysql> DESCRIBE petbirth; SELECT * FROM petbirth;
+-------+----------+------+-----+---------+-------+
| Field | Type     | Null | Key | Default | Extra |
+-------+----------+------+-----+---------+-------+
| name  | char(20) | YES  |     | NULL    |       |
| birth | date     | YES  |     | NULL    |       |
+-------+----------+------+-----+---------+-------+
+----------+------------+
| name     | birth      |
+----------+------------+
| Fluffy   | 1993-02-04 |
| Claws    | 1994-03-17 |
| Buffy    | 1989-05-13 |
| Fang     | 1990-08-27 |
| Bowser   | 1995-07-29 |
| Chirpy   | 1998-09-11 |
| Whistler | 1997-12-09 |
| Slim     | 1996-04-29 |
| Puffball | 1999-03-30 |
| Lucy     | 1988-05-08 |
| Macie    | 1997-05-08 |
| Myra     | 1997-06-09 |
| Cheep    | 1998-05-08 |
+----------+------------+
```

Using the SQL functions MONTH() and YEAR(), you want to produce an ordered list that's sorted by year and month of birth:

```
+----------+-------+------+
| Pet      | Month | Year |
+----------+-------+------+
| Puffball |     3 | 1999 |
| Chirpy   |     9 | 1998 |
| Cheep    |     5 | 1998 |
| Whistler |    12 | 1997 |
| Myra     |     6 | 1997 |
| Macie    |     5 | 1997 |
| Slim     |     4 | 1996 |
| Bowser   |     7 | 1995 |
| Claws    |     3 | 1994 |
| Fluffy   |     2 | 1993 |
| Fang     |     8 | 1990 |
| Buffy    |     5 | 1989 |
| Lucy     |     5 | 1988 |
+----------+-------+------+
```

What's the appropriate SQL statement to produce this result?

Question 9:

The table sortorder has the following structure and contents:

```
mysql> DESCRIBE sortorder; SELECT * FROM sortorder;
+-------+----------+------+-----+---------+-------+
| Field | Type     | Null | Key | Default | Extra |
+-------+----------+------+-----+---------+-------+
| cs    | tinyblob | YES  |     | NULL    |       |
| ci    | tinytext | YES  |     | NULL    |       |
+-------+----------+------+-----+---------+-------+
+-------+-------+
| cs    | ci    |
+-------+-------+
| Anton | Anton |
| anton | anton |
| Berta | Berta |
| berta | berta |
+-------+-------+
```

What's the output of this statement?

```
SELECT cs FROM sortorder ORDER BY cs;
```

Question 10:

Refer to the structure and contents shown for table sortorder in the previous question. What is the output of these two statements?

```
SELECT ci FROM sortorder ORDER BY ci;
SELECT ci FROM sortorder ORDER BY BINARY ci;
```

Question 11:

The table petbirth has the following structure and contents:

```
mysql> DESCRIBE petbirth; SELECT * FROM petbirth;
+-------+----------+------+-----+---------+-------+
| Field | Type     | Null | Key | Default | Extra |
+-------+----------+------+-----+---------+-------+
| name  | char(20) | YES  |     | NULL    |       |
| birth | date     | YES  |     | NULL    |       |
+-------+----------+------+-----+---------+-------+
+----------+------------+
| name     | birth      |
+----------+------------+
| Fluffy   | 1993-02-04 |
| Claws    | 1994-03-17 |
```

```
| Buffy     | 1989-05-13 |
| Fang      | 1990-08-27 |
| Bowser    | 1995-07-29 |
| Chirpy    | 1998-09-11 |
| Whistler  | 1997-12-09 |
| Slim      | 1996-04-29 |
| Puffball  | 1999-03-30 |
| Lucy      | 1988-05-08 |
| Macie     | 1997-05-08 |
| Myra      | 1997-06-09 |
| Cheep     | 1998-05-08 |
+----------+------------+
```

You want to display name and birthday of the oldest pet. What's the appropriate SQL statement?

Question 12:

The table pet has the following structure and contents:

```
mysql> DESCRIBE pet; SELECT * FROM pet;
+---------+----------+------+-----+---------+-------+
| Field   | Type     | Null | Key | Default | Extra |
+---------+----------+------+-----+---------+-------+
| name    | char(20) | YES  |     | NULL    |       |
| owner   | char(20) | YES  |     | NULL    |       |
| species | char(20) | YES  |     | NULL    |       |
| gender  | char(1)  | YES  |     | NULL    |       |
+---------+----------+------+-----+---------+-------+

+----------+--------+---------+--------+
| name     | owner  | species | gender |
+----------+--------+---------+--------+
| Fluffy   | Harold | cat     | f      |
| Claws    | Gwen   | cat     | m      |
| Buffy    | Harold | dog     | f      |
| Fang     | Benny  | dog     | m      |
| Bowser   | Diane  | dog     | m      |
| Chirpy   | Gwen   | bird    | f      |
| Whistler | Gwen   | bird    | NULL   |
| Slim     | Benny  | snake   | m      |
| Puffball | Diane  | hamster | f      |
+----------+--------+---------+--------+
```

What statements would you use to produce the following results?

a. The number of male and female pets (discarding the pets whose gender is unknown)

b. The number of pets of each species, with the species having the highest number of individuals appearing first

c. The number of dogs and cats, with the species that has the highest number of individuals to appear first, using the WHERE clause

d. The number of dogs and cats, with the species which has the highest number of individuals to appear first, using the HAVING clause

The table headings for the results should be Species, Gender, and Total.

Question 13:

The table personnel has the following structure and contents:

```
mysql> DESCRIBE personnel; SELECT * FROM personnel;
+--------+----------------------+
| Field  | Type                 |
+--------+----------------------+
| pid    | smallint(5) unsigned |
| unit   | tinyint(3) unsigned  |
| salary | decimal(9,2)         |
+--------+----------------------+
+-----+------+---------+
| pid | unit | salary  |
+-----+------+---------+
|   1 |   42 | 1500.00 |
|   2 |   42 | 1700.00 |
|   3 |   42 | 1950.00 |
|   4 |   42 | 2300.00 |
|   5 |   42 | 1900.00 |
|   6 |   23 |  850.00 |
|   7 |   23 | 1250.00 |
|   8 |   23 | 1450.00 |
|   9 |   23 | 1920.00 |
|  10 |   42 | 2200.00 |
|  11 |   23 | 2900.00 |
|  12 |   23 | 1000.00 |
|  13 |   42 | 2850.00 |
+-----+------+---------+
```

What statements would you use to retrieve the following information?

a. Find the number of employees, the salary total, and the average salary per employee for the two company units, with the highest total salary appearing first. The output should have headings that should look like this:

```
+------+-----------+----------+-------------+
| Unit | Employees | Total    | Average     |
+------+-----------+----------+-------------+
```

b. Identify the employees with the highest and the lowest salary per unit. The output should have headings that should look like this:

```
+------+---------+---------+
| Unit | High    | Low     |
+------+---------+---------+
```

Question 14:

The table pet has the following structure and contents:

mysql> **DESCRIBE pet; SELECT * FROM pet;**

```
+---------+----------+------+-----+---------+-------+
| Field   | Type     | Null | Key | Default | Extra |
+---------+----------+------+-----+---------+-------+
| name    | char(20) | YES  |     | NULL    |       |
| owner   | char(20) | YES  |     | NULL    |       |
| species | char(20) | YES  |     | NULL    |       |
| gender  | char(1)  | YES  |     | NULL    |       |
+---------+----------+------+-----+---------+-------+
```

```
+----------+--------+---------+--------+
| name     | owner  | species | gender |
+----------+--------+---------+--------+
| Fluffy   | Harold | cat     | f      |
| Claws    | Gwen   | cat     | m      |
| Buffy    | Harold | dog     | f      |
| Fang     | Benny  | dog     | m      |
| Bowser   | Diane  | dog     | m      |
| Chirpy   | Gwen   | bird    | f      |
| Whistler | Gwen   | bird    | NULL   |
| Slim     | Benny  | snake   | m      |
| Puffball | Diane  | hamster | f      |
+----------+--------+---------+--------+
```

How many rows will the following statements return?

```
SELECT COUNT(*) FROM pet;

SELECT COUNT(gender) FROM pet;

SELECT COUNT(DISTINCT gender) FROM pet;

SELECT COUNT(DISTINCT species) FROM pet;
```

Question 15:

The table pet has the following structure and contents:

mysql> **DESCRIBE pet; SELECT * FROM pet;**

```
+---------+----------+------+-----+---------+-------+
| Field   | Type     | Null | Key | Default | Extra |
+---------+----------+------+-----+---------+-------+
| name    | char(20) | YES  |     | NULL    |       |
```

```
| owner   | char(20) | YES |     | NULL    |       |
| species | char(20) | YES |     | NULL    |       |
| gender  | char(1)  | YES |     | NULL    |       |
+---------+----------+-----+-----+---------+-------+
```

```
+----------+--------+---------+--------+
| name     | owner  | species | gender |
+----------+--------+---------+--------+
| Fluffy   | Harold | cat     | f      |
| Claws    | Gwen   | cat     | m      |
| Buffy    | Harold | dog     | f      |
| Fang     | Benny  | dog     | m      |
| Bowser   | Diane  | dog     | m      |
| Chirpy   | Gwen   | bird    | f      |
| Whistler | Gwen   | bird    | NULL   |
| Slim     | Benny  | snake   | m      |
| Puffball | Diane  | hamster | f      |
+----------+--------+---------+--------+
```

Write an SQL statement to produce the following output:

```
+---------+--------+-------+
| Species | Gender | Total |
+---------+--------+-------+
| bird    | NULL   |     1 |
| bird    | f      |     1 |
| cat     | f      |     1 |
| cat     | m      |     1 |
| dog     | f      |     1 |
| dog     | m      |     2 |
| hamster | f      |     1 |
| snake   | m      |     1 |
+---------+--------+-------+
```

Question 16:

An e-commerce company has a different database for each project. For each project, it has a table that holds the team members. Unluckily, this information is not organized consistently, so there are three tables in three different databases that look like this:

```
mysql> SELECT * FROM project1.user;
+-------+-------------+
| name  | job         |
+-------+-------------+
| John  | Manager     |
| Steve | Programmer  |
| Andy  | Webdesigner |
+-------+-------------+
mysql> SELECT * FROM project2.users;
```

```
+-------+------------+
| nick  | task       |
+-------+------------+
| Jim   | Manager    |
| Steve | Programmer |
+-------+------------+
mysql> SELECT * FROM project3.members;
+--------+------------+
| member | job        |
+--------+------------+
| John   | Manager    |
| Steve  | Programmer |
| Carol  | Webdesigner |
+--------+------------+
```

Assume that you want output with headings that look like this:

```
+------------+-------------+
| TeamMember | TeamTask    |
+------------+-------------+
```

What SQL statement will give you a list of all team members, sorted by their names? What would the statement be if you don't want team members to appear more than once in the list?

Answers to Exercises

Answer 1:

The following queries find the oldest and most recent dates in the column d:

```
SELECT MIN(d) FROM t;
SELECT MAX(d) FROM t;
```

Answer 2:

To find the rows containing the oldest and most recent dates in the column d, sort the dates in ascending or descending date order and return the first row of the result:

```
SELECT * FROM t ORDER BY d LIMIT 1;
SELECT * FROM t ORDER BY d DESC LIMIT 1;
```

Answer 3:

a. Here's the last country that became independent:

```
mysql> SELECT * FROM CountryList ORDER BY IndepYear DESC LIMIT 1;
+------+-------+-----------+
| Code | Name  | IndepYear |
+------+-------+-----------+
| PLW  | Palau |      1994 |
+------+-------+-----------+
```

b. Here's the first country that became independent:

```
mysql> SELECT * FROM CountryList ORDER BY IndepYear ASC LIMIT 1;
+------+-------+-----------+
| Code | Name  | IndepYear |
+------+-------+-----------+
| CHN  | China |     -1523 |
+------+-------+-----------+
```

Answer 4:

The clauses must be used in this order:

- FROM
- WHERE
- GROUP BY
- HAVING
- ORDER BY
- LIMIT

Answer 5:

All the SELECT clauses shown in the previous question are optional. When you retrieve data from a table, the FROM clause is mandatory; all other clauses are optional.

Answer 6:

You can use a fully qualified table name. That is, precede the table name with the database name as a qualifier. The users table would be referred to as project1.users.

Answer 7:

The following query retrieves cities having names that begin with B, C, D, E, F, K, L, or M and that have more than a million inhabitants:

```
mysql> SELECT Name, Population FROM City
    -> WHERE (
    ->         (Name >= 'B' AND Name < 'G')
    ->       OR
    ->         (Name >= 'K' AND Name < 'N')
    ->       )
    ->         AND Population > 1000000
    -> ORDER BY Name ASC
    -> ;
```

Other solutions are possible.

Answer 8:

Birthdays of pets (months and years only) in descending order:

```
mysql> SELECT
    -> name          AS Pet,
    -> MONTH(birth) AS Month,
    -> YEAR(birth)  AS Year
    -> FROM petbirth
    -> ORDER BY Year DESC, Month DESC
    -> ;
```

Answer 9:

```
mysql> SELECT cs FROM sortorder ORDER BY cs;
+-------+
| cs    |
+-------+
| Anton |
| Berta |
| anton |
| berta |
+-------+
```

For string columns, the sort order depends on whether the strings are binary or nonbinary. The TINYBLOB column cs is binary, so it sorts in a case-sensitive manner. The byte values of A and B are lower than the byte values of a and b in the server's default character set.

Answer 10:

```
mysql> SELECT ci FROM sortorder ORDER BY ci;
+-------+
| ci    |
+-------+
| Anton |
| anton |
| Berta |
| berta |
+-------+
mysql> SELECT ci FROM sortorder ORDER BY BINARY ci;
+-------+
| ci    |
+-------+
| Anton |
| Berta |
| anton |
| berta |
+-------+
```

For string columns, the sort order depends on whether the strings are binary or nonbinary. In the first query, the TINYTEXT column ci is nonbinary, so it sorts in the lexical order defined by the server's default character set. In the second query, the keyword BINARY makes the sort order for ci case-sensitive, so the result is the same as for the case-sensitive column cs in the previous question.

Answer 11:

To retrieve information for the oldest animal, sort the table in birth order and limit the result to the first row:

```
mysql> SELECT
    ->  name, birth
    -> FROM petbirth
    -> ORDER BY birth ASC
    -> LIMIT 1
    -> ;
+-------+------------+
| name  | birth      |
+-------+------------+
| Lucy  | 1988-05-08 |
+-------+------------+
```

Answer 12:

The following queries produce the desired results:

a. Number of pets by gender:

```
mysql> SELECT
    ->  gender AS Gender,
    ->  COUNT(*) AS Total
    -> FROM pet
    -> WHERE gender IS NOT NULL
    -> GROUP BY Gender;
+--------+-------+
| Gender | Total |
+--------+-------+
| f      |     4 |
| m      |     4 |
+--------+-------+
```

b. Number of pets by species:

```
mysql> SELECT
    ->  species AS Species,
    ->  COUNT(*) AS Total
    -> FROM pet
    -> GROUP BY Species
    -> ORDER BY Total DESC;
```

```
+---------+-------+
| Species | Total |
+---------+-------+
| dog     |     3 |
| cat     |     2 |
| bird    |     2 |
| snake   |     1 |
| hamster |     1 |
+---------+-------+
```

c. Number of dogs and cats, using a WHERE clause:

```
mysql> SELECT
    ->  species AS Species,
    ->  COUNT(*) AS Total
    -> FROM pet
    -> WHERE Species='dog' OR Species='cat'
    -> GROUP BY Species
    -> ORDER BY Total DESC;
+---------+-------+
| Species | Total |
+---------+-------+
| dog     |     3 |
| cat     |     2 |
+---------+-------+
```

d. Number of dogs and cats, using a HAVING clause:

```
mysql> SELECT
    ->  species AS Species,
    ->  COUNT(*) AS Total
    -> FROM pet
    -> GROUP BY Species
    -> HAVING Species='dog' OR Species='cat'
    -> ORDER BY Total DESC;
+---------+-------+
| Species | Total |
+---------+-------+
| dog     |     3 |
| cat     |     2 |
+---------+-------+
```

Answer 13:

a. Number of employees, total, and average salary per unit:

```
mysql> SELECT
    ->  unit AS Unit,
    ->  COUNT(*) AS Employees,
```

```
        -> SUM(salary) AS Total,
        -> AVG(salary) AS Average
        -> FROM personnel
        -> GROUP BY Unit
        -> ORDER BY Total DESC
        -> ;
+------+-----------+----------+-------------+
| Unit | Employees | Total    | Average     |
+------+-----------+----------+-------------+
|   42 |         7 | 14400.00 | 2057.142857 |
|   23 |         6 |  9370.00 | 1561.666667 |
+------+-----------+----------+-------------+
```

b. Highest and lowest salary per unit:

```
mysql> SELECT
        -> unit AS Unit,
        -> MAX(salary) AS High,
        -> MIN(salary) AS Low
        -> FROM personnel
        -> GROUP BY Unit
        -> ;
+------+---------+---------+
| Unit | High    | Low     |
+------+---------+---------+
|   23 | 2900.00 |  850.00 |
|   42 | 2850.00 | 1500.00 |
+------+---------+---------+
```

Answer 14:

a. This statement produces the total number of pets in the table:

```
mysql> SELECT COUNT(*) FROM pet;
+----------+
| COUNT(*) |
+----------+
|        9 |
+----------+
```

b. COUNT(gender) counts only non-NULL values, so the statement counts only those rows containing a known gender. Because there's one NULL value in the gender column, that row isn't counted:

```
mysql> SELECT COUNT(gender) FROM pet;
+---------------+
| COUNT(gender) |
+---------------+
|             8 |
+---------------+
```

c. The statement counts the number of distinct known genders. The NULL gender of the bird isn't counted:

```
mysql> SELECT COUNT(DISTINCT gender) FROM pet;
+------------------------+
| COUNT(DISTINCT gender) |
+------------------------+
|                      2 |
+------------------------+
```

d. The statement counts the number of distinct known species:

```
mysql> SELECT COUNT(DISTINCT species) FROM pet;
+-------------------------+
| COUNT(DISTINCT species) |
+-------------------------+
|                       5 |
+-------------------------+
```

Answer 15:

The output counts the number of individuals for each combination of species and gender. It's displayed sorted by species and by gender within species. The following statement produces the output:

```
mysql> SELECT
    ->   species AS Species,
    ->   gender  AS Gender,
    ->   COUNT(*) AS Total
    -> FROM pet
    -> GROUP BY Species, Gender
    -> ;
```

Answer 16:

To display all team members, issue this statement:

```
mysql> SELECT
    ->   name AS TeamMember,
    ->   job  AS TeamTask
    ->   FROM project1.user
    -> UNION ALL
    ->   SELECT * FROM project2.users
    -> UNION
    ->   SELECT * FROM project3.members
    -> ORDER BY TeamMember
    -> ;
+------------+-------------+
| TeamMember | TeamTask    |
+------------+-------------+
```

```
| Andy       | Webdesigner |
| Carol      | Webdesigner |
| Jim        | Manager     |
| John       | Manager     |
| John       | Manager     |
| Steve      | Programmer  |
| Steve      | Programmer  |
| Steve      | Programmer  |
+------------+-------------+
```

To remove duplicates of team members, the statement is the same, with the exception that you omit the ALL keyword:

```
mysql> SELECT
    ->   name AS TeamMember,
    ->   job  AS TeamTask
    -> FROM project1.user
    -> UNION
    ->   SELECT * FROM project2.users
    -> UNION
    ->   SELECT * FROM project3.members
    -> ORDER BY TeamMember
    -> ;
+------------+-------------+
| TeamMember | TeamTask    |
+------------+-------------+
| Andy       | Webdesigner |
| Carol      | Webdesigner |
| Jim        | Manager     |
| John       | Manager     |
| Steve      | Programmer  |
+------------+-------------+
```

6

Basic SQL

This chapter covers the following exam topics:

- Using SQL expressions and functions
- Using LIKE for pattern matching
- Using IN() to test membership
- Case sensitivity in string comparisons
- Case sensitivity in database, table, column, and function names
- Using reserved words as identifiers
- NULL values in SELECT statements
- Comments in SQL statements

Questions on the material in this chapter make up approximately 10% of the exam.

> **Note**
> In studying for the Core exam, you should familiarize yourself with all the SQL functions listed in Appendix A, "Quick Reference." For the exam, you're not expected to know every little detail about each function listed there, but you'll be expected to know its general behavior.

6.1 Using SQL Expressions and Functions

Expressions are a common element of SQL statements, and they occur in many contexts. For example, expressions often occur in the WHERE clause of SELECT, DELETE, and UPDATE statements to identify which records to retrieve, delete, or update. But expressions may be used in many other places; for example, in the output column list of a SELECT statement, or in ORDER BY or GROUP BY clauses.

Terms of expressions consist of constants (literal numbers, strings, dates, and times), NULL values, references to table columns, and function calls. Terms may be combined using operators into more complex expressions. Many types of operators are available, such as those for arithmetic, comparison, logical, and pattern-matching operations.

Here are some examples of expressions:

- The following statement refers to table columns to select country names and populations from the Country table:

```
SELECT Name, Population FROM Country;
```

- You can work directly with literal data values that aren't stored in a table. The following statement refers to literal integer, floating-point number, and string values:

```
SELECT 14, -312.82, 'I am a string';
```

- Another way to produce data values is by invoking functions. This statement calls functions that return the current date and a server version string:

```
SELECT CURDATE(), VERSION();
```

All these types of values can be combined into more complex expressions to produce other values of interest. The following statement demonstrates this:

```
mysql> SELECT Name,
    -> TRUNCATE(Population/SurfaceArea,2) AS 'people/sq. km',
    -> IF(GNP > GNPOld,'Increasing','Not increasing') AS 'GNP Trend'
    -> FROM Country ORDER BY Name LIMIT 10;
+---------------------+---------------+----------------+
| Name                | people/sq. km | GNP Trend      |
+---------------------+---------------+----------------+
| Afghanistan         |         34.84 | Not increasing |
| Albania             |        118.31 | Increasing     |
| Algeria             |         13.21 | Increasing     |
| American Samoa      |        341.70 | Not increasing |
| Andorra             |        166.66 | Not increasing |
| Angola              |         10.32 | Not increasing |
| Anguilla            |         83.33 | Not increasing |
| Antarctica          |          0.00 | Not increasing |
| Antigua and Barbuda |        153.84 | Increasing     |
| Argentina           |         13.31 | Increasing     |
+---------------------+---------------+----------------+
```

The expressions in the preceding statement refer to these types of values:

- Table columns: Name, Population, SurfaceArea, GNP, and GNPOld. ("GNP" means "gross national product.")
- Literal values: 'Increasing', 'Not increasing', and the column aliases are all string constants.

- Functions: TRUNCATE() is used to format the population/area ratio to two decimals, and IF() is a logical function that tests the expression in its first argument and returns the second or third argument depending on whether the expression is true or false.

Many functions are available in MySQL. This study guide uses several of them for examples, but they make up only a fraction of the number available. Consult the *MySQL Reference Manual* for a complete list of functions and how to use them. For the purpose of testing, Appendix C, "Quick Reference," lists a subset of functions with which you should familiarize yourself before going to the exam.

Note that when you invoke a function, there must be no space after the function name and before the opening parenthesis. (It's possible to change this default behavior by starting the server with a special option; see section 6.5, "Using Reserved Words as Identifiers.")

More examples of SQL expressions can be found in the sample exercises at the end of the chapter.

6.1.1 Case Sensitivity in String Comparisons

String comparisons are somewhat more complex than numeric or temporal comparisons. Numbers sort in numeric order and dates and times sort in temporal order, but string comparisons depend not only on the specific content of the strings, but on whether they are binary or nonbinary and on the character set of the server. A letter in uppercase may compare as the same or different than the same letter in lowercase, and a letter with one type of accent may be considered the same or different than that letter with another type of accent.

The earlier discussion in Chapter 4, "Data Definition Language," on data and column types described how strings may be binary or nonbinary, and how the properties of these two types of strings differ. To summarize:

- Binary strings are treated as raw bytes. Nonbinary strings are treated as characters. Characters may consist of single or multiple bytes, depending on the character set.
- Because binary strings have no character set, they have no collating (sorting) order. Comparisons between binary strings are based on the numeric values of the raw bytes. This results in case sensitive comparisons. Nonbinary strings contain characters in a particular character set, and each character set has a collating order that determines sorting behavior. Typically, collating orders treat uppercase and lowercase versions of a given character the same, which results in case-insensitive comparisons.

The rules that govern string comparison apply in several ways. They determine the result of comparisons performed explicitly with operators such as = and <, and comparisons performed implicitly by ORDER BY, GROUP BY, and DISTINCT operations.

Literal strings are nonbinary by default, and thus are not case sensitive. You can see this by comparing strings that differ only in lettercase:

```
mysql> SELECT 'Hello' = 'hello';
+-------------------+
| 'Hello' = 'hello' |
+-------------------+
|                 1 |
+-------------------+
```

Depending on the character set, strings might not be accent sensitive, either. If the German sorting order is in use, ue and ü are the same:

```
mysql> SELECT 'Mueller' = 'Müller';
+---------------------+
| 'Mueller' = 'Müller' |
+---------------------+
|                   1 |
+---------------------+
```

A nonbinary string can be treated as a binary string by preceding it with the BINARY keyword. If either string in a comparison is binary, both strings are treated as binary:

```
mysql> SELECT BINARY 'Hello' = 'hello';
+------------------------+
| BINARY 'Hello' = 'hello' |
+------------------------+
|                      0 |
+------------------------+
mysql> SELECT 'Hello' = BINARY 'hello';
+------------------------+
| 'Hello' = BINARY 'hello' |
+------------------------+
|                      0 |
+------------------------+
```

The same principles apply to CHAR and VARCHAR table columns. By default, they're nonbinary, but you can add BINARY to a column definition to make the column binary. Suppose that a table t contains a CHAR column c and has the following rows (each of which means "good-bye"):

```
mysql> SELECT c FROM t;
+-----------+
| c         |
+-----------+
| Hello     |
| goodbye   |
| Bonjour   |
| au revoir |
+-----------+
```

Because c is a nonbinary CHAR column, its character set collating order controls how its values are sorted. For the default character set (Latin-1, also known as ISO-8859-1), the collating order isn't case sensitive, so uppercase and lowercase are treated as identical and a sort operation that uses ORDER BY produces results like this:

```
mysql> SELECT c FROM t ORDER BY c;
+-----------+
| c         |
+-----------+
| au revoir |
| Bonjour   |
| goodbye   |
| Hello     |
+-----------+
```

If c is declared as a CHAR BINARY column instead, ORDER BY sorts based on raw byte codes and produces a different result. Assuming that values are stored on a machine that uses ASCII codes, uppercase precedes lowercase and the results look like this:

```
mysql> SELECT c FROM t ORDER BY c;
+-----------+
| c         |
+-----------+
| Bonjour   |
| Hello     |
| au revoir |
| goodbye   |
+-----------+
```

String comparison rules also apply to GROUP BY and DISTINCT operations. Suppose that t has a column c with the following contents:

```
mysql> SELECT c FROM t;
+---------+
| c       |
+---------+
| Hello   |
| hello   |
| Goodbye |
| goodbye |
+---------+
```

If c is a CHAR column, GROUP BY and DISTINCT do not make lettercase distinctions:

```
mysql> SELECT c, COUNT(*) FROM t GROUP BY c;
+---------+----------+
| c       | COUNT(*) |
+---------+----------+
```

```
| Goodbye |        2 |
| Hello   |        2 |
+---------+----------+
mysql> SELECT DISTINCT c FROM t;
+---------+
| c       |
+---------+
| Hello   |
| Goodbye |
+---------+
```

On the other hand, if c is a CHAR BINARY column, those operations do take lettercase into account:

```
mysql> SELECT c, COUNT(*) FROM t GROUP BY c;
+---------+----------+
| c       | COUNT(*) |
+---------+----------+
| Goodbye |        1 |
| Hello   |        1 |
| goodbye |        1 |
| hello   |        1 |
+---------+----------+
mysql> SELECT DISTINCT c FROM t;
+---------+
| c       |
+---------+
| Hello   |
| hello   |
| Goodbye |
| goodbye |
+---------+
```

The preceding discussion shows that to understand sorting and comparison behavior for literal strings or string columns, it's important to know whether they are binary or nonbinary. This is important when using string functions as well. String functions may treat their arguments as binary or nonbinary strings, or return binary or nonbinary results. It depends on the function. Here are some examples:

- LENGTH() returns the length of a string in bytes, whereas CHAR_LENGTH() returns the length in characters. For single-byte character sets, the two functions return identical results, but for multi-byte character sets, you should choose the function that is appropriate for the type of result you want. For example, the SJIS character set includes characters that require two bytes to represent. The value of LENGTH() for any string containing such characters will be greater than the value of CHAR_LENGTH().

- The LOCATE() function determines whether a substring is present in another string and returns 1 or 0 depending on whether it is or is not. The comparison rules depend on the arguments. LOCATE() performs a case-sensitive comparison if at least one of its arguments is a binary string. Otherwise, the comparison is not case sensitive:

```
mysql> SELECT LOCATE('A','abc');
+-------------------+
| LOCATE('A','abc') |
+-------------------+
|                 1 |
+-------------------+
mysql> SELECT LOCATE('A',BINARY 'abc');
+--------------------------+
| LOCATE('A',BINARY 'abc') |
+--------------------------+
|                        0 |
+--------------------------+
```

- MD5() takes a string argument and produces a 32-byte byte checksum represented as a string of hexadecimal digits. It treats its argument as a binary string:

```
mysql> SELECT MD5('a');
+----------------------------------+
| MD5('a')                         |
+----------------------------------+
| 0cc175b9c0f1b6a831c399e269772661 |
+----------------------------------+
mysql> SELECT MD5('A');
+----------------------------------+
| MD5('A')                         |
+----------------------------------+
| 7fc56270e7a70fa81a5935b72eacbe29 |
+----------------------------------+
```

However, the result from MD5() is *not* a binary string, as can be seen by using LOWER() and UPPER() to convert a given MD5() result to lowercase and uppercase and comparing the two values:

```
mysql> SELECT LOWER(MD5('a'));
+----------------------------------+
| LOWER(MD5('a'))                  |
+----------------------------------+
| 0cc175b9c0f1b6a831c399e269772661 |
+----------------------------------+
mysql> SELECT UPPER(MD5('a'));
+----------------------------------+
| UPPER(MD5('a'))                  |
+----------------------------------+
| 0CC175B9C0F1B6A831C399E269772661 |
+----------------------------------+
```

```
mysql> SELECT LOWER(MD5('a')) = UPPER(MD5('a'));
+-----------------------------------+
| LOWER(MD5('a')) = UPPER(MD5('a')) |
+-----------------------------------+
|                                 1 |
+-----------------------------------+
```

These examples demonstrate that you must take into account the properties of the particular function you want to use. If you don't, you might be surprised at the results you get. See the *MySQL Reference Manual* for details on specific functions.

6.2 Using LIKE for Pattern Matching

Operators such as = and != are useful for finding values that are equal to or not equal to a specific exact comparison value. When it's necessary to find values based on similarity instead, a pattern match is useful. To perform a pattern match, use *value* LIKE '*pattern*', where *value* is the value you want to test and '*pattern*' is a pattern string that describes the general form of values that you want to match.

Patterns used with the LIKE pattern-matching operator can contain two special characters (called "metacharacters" or "wildcards") that stand for something other than themselves:

- The % character matches any sequence of characters. For example, the pattern 'a%' matches any string that begins with **a**, '%b' matches any string that ends with **b**, and '%c%' matches any string that contains a **c**. The pattern '%' matches any string, including empty strings.

- The _ (underscore) character matches any single character. 'd_g' matches strings such as 'dig', 'dog', and 'd@g'. Because _ matches any single character, it matches itself and the pattern 'd_g' also matches the string 'd_g'.

A pattern can use these metacharacters in combination. For example, '_%' matches any string containing at least one character. Other examples can be found in the sample exercises at the end of the chapter.

LIKE evaluates to NULL if either operand is NULL, but any non-NULL literal value matches itself. Likewise, a function call that produces a non-NULL value matches itself (with one exception). Thus, the following expressions evaluate as true:

```
'ABC' LIKE 'ABC'
column_name LIKE column_name
VERSION() LIKE VERSION()
```

The exception is that different invocations of the RAND() random-number function might return different values, even within the same query:

```
mysql> SELECT RAND(), RAND();
+------------------+------------------+
| RAND()           | RAND()           |
+------------------+------------------+
| 0.15430032289987 | 0.30666533979277 |
+------------------+------------------+
```

As a result, the expression RAND() LIKE RAND() normally will be false.

LIKE is not case sensitive unless at least one operand is a binary string:

```
mysql> SELECT 'ABC' LIKE 'abc', 'ABC' LIKE BINARY 'abc';
+------------------+------------------------+
| 'ABC' LIKE 'abc' | 'ABC' LIKE BINARY 'abc' |
+------------------+------------------------+
|                1 |                      0 |
+------------------+------------------------+
```

MySQL, unlike some other database systems, allows use of LIKE with nonstring values. This can be useful in some cases. For example, the expression d LIKE '19%' is true for date values d that occur during the 1900s. MySQL evaluates such comparisons by converting nonstring values to strings before performing the pattern match.

It's possible to specify the pattern in a LIKE expression using a table column. In this case, the actual pattern that a value is compared to can vary for every row of a result set. The following table has one column containing patterns and another column that characterizes the type of string each pattern matches:

```
mysql> SELECT pattern, description FROM patlist;
+---------+-------------------------------+
| pattern | description                   |
+---------+-------------------------------+
|         | empty string                  |
| _%      | non-empty string              |
| ___     | string of exactly 3 characters |
+---------+-------------------------------+
```

The patterns in the table can be applied to specific values to characterize them:

```
mysql> SELECT description, IF('' LIKE pattern,'YES','NO')
    -> FROM patlist;
+-------------------------------+--------------------------------+
| description                   | IF('' LIKE pattern,'YES','NO') |
+-------------------------------+--------------------------------+
| empty string                  | YES                            |
| non-empty string              | NO                             |
| string of exactly 3 characters | NO                            |
+-------------------------------+--------------------------------+
```

```
mysql> SELECT description, IF('abc' LIKE pattern,'YES','NO')
    -> FROM patlist;
+-----------------------------+-----------------------------------+
| description                 | IF('abc' LIKE pattern,'YES','NO') |
+-----------------------------+-----------------------------------+
| empty string                | NO                                |
| non-empty string            | YES                               |
| string of exactly 3 characters | YES                            |
+-----------------------------+-----------------------------------+
mysql> SELECT description, IF('hello' LIKE pattern,'YES','NO')
    -> FROM patlist;
+-----------------------------+-----------------------------------+
| description                 | IF('hello' LIKE pattern,'YES','NO') |
+-----------------------------+-----------------------------------+
| empty string                | NO                                |
| non-empty string            | YES                               |
| string of exactly 3 characters | NO                             |
+-----------------------------+-----------------------------------+
```

To match a literal pattern metacharacter and only that character, escape it by preceding it by a backslash:

```
mysql> SELECT 'AA' LIKE 'A%', 'AA' LIKE 'A\%', 'A%' LIKE 'A\%';
+---------------+----------------+----------------+
| 'AA' LIKE 'A%' | 'AA' LIKE 'A\%' | 'A%' LIKE 'A\%' |
+---------------+----------------+----------------+
|             1 |              0 |              1 |
+---------------+----------------+----------------+
mysql> SELECT 'AA' LIKE 'A_', 'AA' LIKE 'A\_', 'A_' LIKE 'A\_';
+---------------+----------------+----------------+
| 'AA' LIKE 'A_' | 'AA' LIKE 'A\_' | 'A_' LIKE 'A\_' |
+---------------+----------------+----------------+
|             1 |              0 |              1 |
+---------------+----------------+----------------+
```

To specify a particular character as the escape character, use an ESCAPE clause:

```
mysql> SELECT 'AA' LIKE 'A@%' ESCAPE '@', 'A%' LIKE 'A@%' ESCAPE '@';
+---------------------------+---------------------------+
| 'AA' LIKE 'A@%' ESCAPE '@' | 'A%' LIKE 'A@%' ESCAPE '@' |
+---------------------------+---------------------------+
|                         0 |                         1 |
+---------------------------+---------------------------+
```

To invert a pattern match, use NOT LIKE rather than LIKE:

```
mysql> SELECT 'ABC' LIKE 'A%', 'ABC' NOT LIKE 'A%';
+----------------+--------------------+
| 'ABC' LIKE 'A%' | 'ABC' NOT LIKE 'A%' |
+----------------+--------------------+
|              1 |                  0 |
+----------------+--------------------+
```

6.3 Using IN() to Test Membership in a List of Values

It's sometimes necessary to determine whether a value is equal to any of several specific values. One way to accomplish this is to combine several equality tests into a single expression with the OR logical operator:

```
... WHERE id = 13 OR id = 45 OR id = 97 OR id = 142
... WHERE name = 'Tom' OR name = 'Dick' OR name = 'Harry'
```

However, MySQL provides an IN() operator that performs the same kind of comparison and that is more concise and easier to read. To use it, provide the comparison values as a comma-separated list of arguments to IN():

```
... WHERE id IN(13,45,97,142)
... WHERE name IN('Tom','Dick','Harry')
```

Using IN() is equivalent to writing a list of comparisons with OR, but IN() is much more efficient.

Arguments to IN() may be of any type (numeric, string, or temporal), although generally all values given within a list are all the same type.

Elements in a list may be given as expressions that are evaluated to produce a value. If the expression references a column name, the column is evaluated for each row.

IN() always returns NULL when used to test NULL. That is, NULL IN(list) is NULL for any list of values, even if NULL is included in the list. This occurs because NULL IN(NULL) is equivalent to NULL = NULL, which evaluates to NULL.

IN() tests membership within a set of individual values. If you're searching for a range of values, a range test might be more suitable. The BETWEEN operator takes the two endpoint values of the range and returns true if a comparison value lies between them:

```
... WHERE id BETWEEN 5 AND 10
```

The comparison is inclusive, so the preceding expression is equivalent to this one:

```
... WHERE id >= 5 AND id <= 10
```

6.4 Case Sensitivity of Identifiers and Reserved Words

Identifiers are used in several ways in SQL statements: They refer to databases, tables, columns, indexes, and aliases. One property that affects how you use identifiers is whether they're case sensitive; some identifiers are case sensitive and others are not. You should understand which is which and use them accordingly.

The rules that determine whether an identifier is case sensitive depend on what kind of identifier it is, and are described in the following items:

- For database and table names, case sensitivity depends on the operating system and filesystem of the server host, and on the setting of the `lower_case_table_names` system variable. Databases and tables are represented by directories and files, so if the operating system has case-sensitive filenames, MySQL treats database and table names as case sensitive. If filenames aren't case sensitive, database and table names are not either. Windows systems do not have case-sensitive filenames, but most Unix systems do. However, if the `lower_case_table_names` system variable is set to 1, database and table names are forced to lowercase before being used, which effectively results in case-insensitive behavior. (If you plan to use this variable, you should set it before creating any databases and tables.)

  Regardless of the case-sensitive properties of your filesystem, database and table names must be written consistently with the same lettercase throughout a query.

- Column names and index names are not case sensitive.

- Aliases are not case sensitive except aliases on table names.

Words such as SELECT, DELETE, WHERE, LIMIT, and VARCHAR are special in MySQL and are reserved as keywords. Reserved words are not case sensitive. They can be given in uppercase, lowercase, or even mixed case, and need not be written the same way throughout a query. The same is true for function names.

6.5 Using Reserved Words as Identifiers

Reserved words are special. For example, function names cannot be used as identifiers such as table or column names, and an error occurs if you try to do so. The following statement fails because it attempts to create a column named order, which is erroneous because order is a reserved word (it's used in ORDER BY clauses):

```
mysql> CREATE TABLE t (order INT NOT NULL UNIQUE, d DATE NOT NULL);
ERROR 1064: You have an error in your SQL syntax.  Check the
manual that corresponds to your MySQL server version for the
right syntax to use near 'order INT NOT NULL UNIQUE, d DATE
NOT NULL)' at line 1
```

Similarly, this statement fails because it uses a reserved word as an alias:

```
mysql> SELECT 1 AS INTEGER;
ERROR 1064: You have an error in your SQL syntax.  Check the
manual that corresponds to your MySQL server version for the
right syntax to use near 'INTEGER' at line 1
```

The solution to these problems is to quote the identifiers properly. Quoting rules depend on the type of identifier you're quoting:

- To use a reserved word as a database, table, column, or index identifier, there are either one or two allowable quoting styles, depending on the mode in which the server is running. By default, quoting a reserved word within backtick (`) characters allows it to be used as an identifier:

  ```
  mysql> CREATE TABLE t (`order` INT NOT NULL UNIQUE, d DATE NOT NULL);
  Query OK, 0 rows affected (0.00 sec)
  ```

  If the server was started with the --ansi or --sql-mode=ANSI_QUOTES option, it's also allowable to quote using double quotes:

  ```
  mysql> CREATE TABLE t ("order" INT NOT NULL UNIQUE, d DATE NOT NULL);
  Query OK, 0 rows affected (0.00 sec)
  ```

  If an identifier must be quoted in a CREATE TABLE statement, it's also necessary to quote it in any subsequent statements that refer to the identifier.

- To use a reserved word as an alias, quote it using either single quotes, double quotes, or backticks. (The server mode doesn't make any difference; all three are legal in any mode.) To use INTEGER as an alias, you can write it like this:

  ```
  mysql> SELECT 1 AS 'INTEGER';
  +---------+
  | INTEGER |
  +---------+
  |       1 |
  +---------+
  ```

  It can also be written in either of these ways, with the same result:

  ```
  SELECT 1 AS "INTEGER";
  SELECT 1 AS `INTEGER`;
  ```

Quoting is useful not only for identifiers that are reserved words; a given name might be illegal because it contains characters that normally are not allowed in names, such as dashes or spaces. Such names can be used as identifiers by applying the same quoting rules. If you aren't sure whether a name is legal, quote it. It's harmless to put quotes around a name that's legal without them. For a discussion of the legal syntax for identifiers, see Chapter 4, "Data Definition Language."

It's a good idea to avoid using function names as identifiers. Normally, they aren't reserved, but there are circumstances under which this isn't true:

- Some functions have names that are also keywords and thus are reserved. CHAR() is one example.

- By default, a function name and the opening parenthesis that follows it must be written with no intervening space. This allows the query parser to distinguish a name in a function invocation from the same name used for another purpose, such as an identifier. However, the server may be run in a mode that allows spaces between function names and the following parenthesis. (This happens if you start it with the --ansi or --sql-mode=IGNORE_SPACE option.) A side effect of running the server in this mode is that all function names become ambiguous in certain contexts because the query parser no longer can distinguish reliably whether a function name represents a function invocation or an identifier. Consider the following query:

```
INSERT INTO COUNT (id) VALUES(43);
```

In ignore-spaces mode, this query might mean "create a new row in the COUNT table, setting the id column to 43," or it might simply be a malformed INSERT statement that has an invocation of the COUNT function where a table name ought to be. The parser cannot tell.

If you do want to use an identifier that's a function name, it should be quoted to prevent the possibility of it being interpreted as a reserved word.

6.6 NULL Values

NULL is unusual because it doesn't represent a specific value the way that numeric, string, or temporal values do. Instead, NULL stands for the absence of a known value. The special nature of NULL means that it often is handled differently than other values. This section describes how MySQL processes NULL values in various contexts.

Syntactically, NULL values are written in SQL statements without quotes. Writing NULL is different from writing 'NULL' or "NULL". The latter two values are actually strings that contain the word "NULL". Also, because it is an SQL keyword, NULL is not case sensitive. NULL and null both mean "a NULL value," whereas the string values 'NULL' and 'null' may be different or the same depending on whether or not they are binary strings.

Note that some database systems treat the empty string and NULL as the same value. In MySQL, the two values are different.

6.6.1 NULL Values and Column Definitions

NULL can be stored into columns of any type, except columns that are defined as NOT NULL. Allowing NULL values in a column complicates column processing somewhat because the query processor has to treat NULL values specially in some contexts. This results in a slight speed penalty.

If you specify no DEFAULT option, defining a column as NULL or NOT NULL affects how MySQL assigns the default value. For a column that allows NULL values, NULL becomes the default value as well. Otherwise, the default depends on the column type, as described in section 4.10.4, "Column Options."

6.6.2 NULL Values and NOT NULL Columns

A column that is defined as NOT NULL may not be set to NULL. An attempt to do so has different effects depending on the context in which the attempt occurs:

- In a CREATE TABLE statement, specifying a DEFAULT value of NULL for a NOT NULL column results in an error, and the table is not created.
- In a single-row INSERT statement, inserting NULL into a NOT NULL column causes the statement to fail with an error, and no record is created.
- In a multiple-row INSERT statement, inserting NULL into a NOT NULL column has these effects:
    - The column is set to zero, an empty string, or the "zero" temporal value, depending on the column type.
    - The record is created.
    - The warning count is incremented.

The preceding rules do not apply to TIMESTAMP columns or to integer columns defined with the AUTO_INCREMENT option. These types of columns can never contain a NULL value. However, setting them to NULL does not result in an error; instead, they're set to the current date and time or the next sequence number.

6.6.3 NULL Values in Expressions and Comparisons

Expressions that cannot be evaluated (such as 1/0) produce NULL as a result.

Use of NULL values in arithmetic or comparison operations normally produces NULL results:

```
mysql> SELECT NULL + 1, NULL < 1;
+----------+----------+
| NULL + 1 | NULL < 1 |
+----------+----------+
|     NULL |     NULL |
+----------+----------+
```

Even comparing NULL to itself results in NULL, because you cannot tell whether one unknown value is the same as another:

```
mysql> SELECT NULL = 1, NULL != NULL;
+----------+-------------+
| NULL = 1 | NULL != NULL |
+----------+-------------+
|     NULL |         NULL |
+----------+-------------+
```

LIKE evaluates to NULL if either operand is NULL:

```
mysql> SELECT NULL LIKE '%', 'abc' LIKE NULL;
+--------------+-----------------+
| NULL LIKE '%' | 'abc' LIKE NULL |
+--------------+-----------------+
|         NULL |            NULL |
+--------------+-----------------+
```

The proper way to determine whether a value is NULL is to use the IS NULL or IS NOT NULL operators, which produce a true (nonzero) or false (zero) result:

```
mysql> SELECT NULL IS NULL, NULL IS NOT NULL;
+-------------+------------------+
| NULL IS NULL | NULL IS NOT NULL |
+-------------+------------------+
|           1 |                0 |
+-------------+------------------+
```

You can also use the special <=> operator, which is like = except that it works with NULL operands by treating them as any other value:

```
mysql> SELECT 1 <=> NULL, 0 <=> NULL, NULL <=> NULL;
+-----------+-----------+--------------+
| 1 <=> NULL | 0 <=> NULL | NULL <=> NULL |
+-----------+-----------+--------------+
|         0 |         0 |            1 |
+-----------+-----------+--------------+
```

ORDER BY, GROUP BY, and DISTINCT all perform comparisons implicitly. For purposes of these operations, NULL values are considered identical. That is, NULL values sort together, group together, and are not distinct.

Functions intended specifically for use with NULL values include ISNULL() and IFNULL(). ISNULL() is true if its argument is NULL and false otherwise:

```
mysql> SELECT ISNULL(NULL), ISNULL(0), ISNULL(1);
+-------------+----------+----------+
| ISNULL(NULL) | ISNULL(0) | ISNULL(1) |
+-------------+----------+----------+
|           1 |        0 |        0 |
+-------------+----------+----------+
```

IFNULL() takes two arguments. If the first argument is not NULL, that argument is returned; otherwise, the function returns its second argument:

```
mysql> SELECT IFNULL(NULL,'a'), IFNULL(0,'b');
+-----------------+---------------+
| IFNULL(NULL,'a') | IFNULL(0,'b') |
+-----------------+---------------+
| a               | 0             |
+-----------------+---------------+
```

Other functions handle NULL values in various ways, so you have to know how a given function behaves. In many cases, passing a NULL value to a function results in a NULL return value. For example, any NULL argument to CONCAT() causes it to return NULL:

```
mysql> SELECT CONCAT('a','b'), CONCAT('a',NULL,'b');
+-----------------+----------------------+
| CONCAT('a','b') | CONCAT('a',NULL,'b') |
+-----------------+----------------------+
| ab              | NULL                 |
+-----------------+----------------------+
```

But not all functions behave that way. CONCAT_WS() (concatenate with separator) simply ignores NULL arguments entirely:

```
mysql> SELECT CONCAT_WS('/','a','b'), CONCAT_WS('/','a',NULL,'b');
+------------------------+-----------------------------+
| CONCAT_WS('/','a','b') | CONCAT_WS('/','a',NULL,'b') |
+------------------------+-----------------------------+
| a/b                    | a/b                         |
+------------------------+-----------------------------+
```

For information about the behavior of specific functions, consult the *MySQL Reference Manual*.

6.6.4 NULL Values and Aggregate Functions

NULL values are ignored by all aggregate functions except COUNT(*), which counts rows and not values. Suppose that you have the following table:

```
mysql> SELECT * FROM t;
+------+------+------+
| i    | j    | k    |
+------+------+------+
|    0 |    1 | NULL |
| NULL |    2 | NULL |
|    2 | NULL | NULL |
|    3 |    4 | NULL |
|    4 | NULL | NULL |
+------+------+------+
```

COUNT(*) counts rows, including those that contain NULL values:

```
mysql> SELECT COUNT(*) FROM t;
+----------+
| COUNT(*) |
+----------+
|        5 |
+----------+
```

COUNT(*expression*) ignores NULL values:

```
mysql> SELECT COUNT(i), COUNT(j), COUNT(k) FROM t;
+----------+----------+----------+
| COUNT(i) | COUNT(j) | COUNT(k) |
+----------+----------+----------+
|        4 |        3 |        0 |
+----------+----------+----------+
```

COUNT(DISTINCT) also ignores NULL values:

```
mysql> SELECT COUNT(DISTINCT j), COUNT(DISTINCT k) FROM t;
+-------------------+-------------------+
| COUNT(DISTINCT j) | COUNT(DISTINCT k) |
+-------------------+-------------------+
|                 3 |                 0 |
+-------------------+-------------------+
```

The other aggregate functions always ignore NULL values:

```
mysql> SELECT SUM(i), SUM(j), SUM(k), SUM(i+j+k) FROM t;
+--------+--------+--------+------------+
| SUM(i) | SUM(j) | SUM(k) | SUM(i+j+k) |
+--------+--------+--------+------------+
|      9 |      7 |      0 |          0 |
+--------+--------+--------+------------+
mysql> SELECT AVG(i), AVG(j), AVG(k) FROM t;
+--------+--------+--------+
| AVG(i) | AVG(j) | AVG(k) |
+--------+--------+--------+
| 2.2500 | 2.3333 |   NULL |
+--------+--------+--------+
mysql> SELECT MIN(i), MIN(j), MIN(k) FROM t;
+--------+--------+--------+
| MIN(i) | MIN(j) | MIN(k) |
+--------+--------+--------+
|      0 |      1 |   NULL |
+--------+--------+--------+
mysql> SELECT MAX(i), MAX(j), MAX(k) FROM t;
```

```
+--------+--------+--------+
| MAX(i) | MAX(j) | MAX(k) |
+--------+--------+--------+
|      4 |      4 |   NULL |
+--------+--------+--------+
```

Note that SUM(), AVG(), MIN(), and MAX() produce a result of NULL when given a set of input values that contain no non-NULL values (such as the column k in the preceding examples).

6.7 Comments in SQL Statements

MySQL supports three forms of comment syntax. One of those forms has some variants that allow special instructions to be passed through to the MySQL server.

- A # character begins a comment that extends to the end of the line. This commenting style is like that used by several other programs, such as Perl, Awk, and several Unix shells.

- A /* sequence begins a comment that ends with a */ sequence:

```
/* this is a comment */
```

This style is the same as that used for writing comments in the C programming language. A C-style comment may span multiple lines:

```
/*
  this
  is a
  comment
*/
```

- A -- (double dash) sequence followed by a space begins a comment that extends to the end of the line. This syntax requires a space and thus differs from standard ANSI SQL syntax, which allows comments to be introduced by -- without the space. MySQL disallows a double dash without a space as a comment because it's ambiguous. (For example, does 1--3 mean "one minus negative three" or "one followed by a comment"?)

C-style comments can contain embedded SQL text that's treated specially by the MySQL server, but ignored by other database engines. This is an aid to writing more portable SQL; it enables you to write comments that are treated as part of the surrounding statement if executed by MySQL and ignored if executed by other database servers. There are two ways to write embedded SQL in a C-style comment:

- If the comment begins with /*! rather than with /*, MySQL executes the body of the comment as part of the surrounding query. The following statement creates a table named t, but for MySQL creates it as a HEAP table:

```
CREATE TABLE t (i INT) /*! TYPE = HEAP */;
```

- If the comment begins with /*! followed by a version number, the embedded SQL is version specific. The server executes the body of the comment as part of the surrounding query if its version is at least as recent as that specified in the query. Otherwise, it ignores the comment. For example, HEAP tables appeared in MySQL 3.23.0. To write a comment that's understood only by servers from MySQL 3.23.0 and up and ignored by older servers, write it as follows:

```
CREATE TABLE t (i INT) /*!32300 TYPE = HEAP */;
```

6.8 Exercises

Question 1:

An SQL expression can consist of constants. What kind of constants are there? What else could an SQL expression consist of?

Question 2:

Give an example of a SELECT statement that contains an expression using numeric constants.

Question 3:

Give an example of a SELECT statement that contains an expression using string constants.

Question 4:

Give an example of a SELECT statement that contains an expression using date constants.

Question 5:

Give an example of a SELECT statement that contains an expression using time constants.

Question 6:

Give an example of a SELECT statement that contains an expression using a column reference.

Question 7:

Give an example of a SELECT statement that contains an expression using a function call.

Question 8:

Give an example of a SELECT statement that contains an expression using both a temporal value and a function call.

Question 9:

The table personnel has the following data for employees in two organizational units:

```
mysql> SELECT * FROM personnel;
+-----+------+---------+
| pid | unit | salary  |
+-----+------+---------+
|   1 |   42 | 1500.00 |
```

```
|    2 |   42 | 1700.00 |
|    3 |   42 | 1950.00 |
|    4 |   42 | 2300.00 |
|    5 |   42 | 1900.00 |
|    6 |   23 |  850.00 |
|    7 |   23 | 1250.00 |
|    8 |   23 | 1450.00 |
|    9 |   23 | 1920.00 |
|   10 |   42 | 2200.00 |
|   11 |   23 | 2900.00 |
|   12 |   23 | 1000.00 |
|   13 |   42 | 2850.00 |
+-----+------+---------+
```

What SQL statement would you issue to retrieve a list showing tax deductions for each employee? Assume that the deduction is 40% of the salary. Gross salary, deduction, and net salary should be displayed with descriptive, instead of mathematical, headings (for example, use Deduction as a heading, not the expression used to calculate the deduction).

Question 10:

Refer to the data shown for the personnel table in the previous question. What SQL statement would you issue to retrieve a list showing tax deductions for each unit (displayed with descriptive headings instead of mathematical headings)? Assume that the deduction is 40% of the salary.

Question 11:

Refer to the data shown for the personnel table two questions earlier. What SQL statement would you issue to retrieve a list showing tax deductions for each employee? Assume that the deduction is 40% of the salary for employees with a salary of 2,000 or more, and 30% for those who earn less. The result should show descriptive headings.

Question 12:

The table personnel has the following data for employees in two organizational units:

```
mysql> SELECT * FROM personnel;
+-----+------+---------+
| pid | unit | salary  |
+-----+------+---------+
|   1 |   42 | 1500.00 |
|   2 |   42 | 1700.00 |
|   3 |   42 | 1950.00 |
|   4 |   42 | 2300.00 |
|   5 |   42 | 1900.00 |
|   6 |   23 |  850.00 |
|   7 |   23 | 1250.00 |
|   8 |   23 | 1450.00 |
```

```
|   9 |   23 | 1920.00 |
|  10 |   42 | 2200.00 |
|  11 |   23 | 2900.00 |
|  12 |   23 | 1000.00 |
|  13 |   42 | 2850.00 |
+-----+------+---------+
```

What SQL statement would you issue to retrieve a list showing the cost rise for the organization if employee salaries are increased by 10%? The result should show descriptive headings instead of mathematical headings (for example, use Cost Rise as a heading, not the expression used to calculate the cost rise).

Question 13:

Refer to the data shown for the personnel table in the previous question. What SQL statement would you issue to retrieve a list showing the cost rise for the units if employee salaries are increased by 10% for unit 23 and by 5% for unit 42 (displayed with descriptive headings instead of mathematical headings)?

Question 14:

The table leonardo has the following structure and contents:

```
mysql> DESCRIBE leonardo;
+-------+---------+
| Field | Type    |
+-------+---------+
| name  | char(7) |
+-------+---------+
mysql> SELECT * FROM leonardo;
+---------+
| name    |
+---------+
| Lennart |
| lennart |
| LENNART |
| lEnNaRt |
+---------+
```

What output will the following statements yield?

```
SELECT DISTINCT name FROM leonardo;

SELECT name, COUNT(*) FROM leonardo GROUP BY name;

SELECT name, COUNT(*) FROM leonardo;
```

Question 15:

The table leonardo has the following structure and contents:

```
mysql> DESCRIBE leonardo;
+-------+---------------+
| Field | Type          |
+-------+---------------+
| name  | char(7) binary |
+-------+---------------+
mysql> SELECT * FROM leonardo;
+---------+
| name    |
+---------+
| Lennart |
| lennart |
| LENNART |
| lEnNaRt |
+---------+
```

What output will the following statements yield?

```
SELECT DISTINCT name FROM leonardo;

SELECT name, COUNT(*) FROM leonardo GROUP BY name;

SELECT name, COUNT(*) FROM leonardo;
```

Question 16:

The SQL functions LENGTH() and CHAR_LENGTH() both return the length of a string. Why are there two functions for the same apparent functionality?

Question 17:

What's the result of the following string comparison?

```
SELECT BINARY 'LENNART' = UPPER('Lennart');
```

Question 18:

What's the result of the following string comparison?

```
SELECT BINARY LOWER('LeNNaRT') = LOWER('lEnnArt');
```

Question 19:

What's the result of the following string comparison?

```
SELECT MD5('lennart') = MD5('LENNART');
```

Question 20:

The IF() function returns the second argument if the condition in the first argument evaluates to true; otherwise, it returns the third argument. Knowing this, what do you expect IF() to return for the following comparisons?

a. `SELECT IF('ABC' = 'abc','TRUE','FALSE');`

b. `SELECT IF('ABC' = BINARY 'abc','TRUE','FALSE');`

c. `SELECT IF(BINARY 'ABC' = BINARY 'abc','TRUE','FALSE');`

Question 21:

Name an SQL function that treats its argument as a binary string and thus operates in a case-sensitive manner.

Question 22:

Will the following query evaluate to true (1), false (0), or NULL? (The pattern contains three underscores.)

```
SELECT 'abc' LIKE '%___%';
```

Question 23:

Will the following query evaluate to true (1), false (0), or NULL? (The pattern contains five underscores.)

```
SELECT 'abc' LIKE '%_____%';
```

Question 24:

Will the following query evaluate to true (1), false (0), or NULL?

```
SELECT '' LIKE '%';
```

Question 25:

Will the following query evaluate to true (1), false (0), or NULL?

```
SELECT '' LIKE ' % ';
```

Question 26:

Will the following query evaluate to true (1), false (0), or NULL?

```
SELECT '%' LIKE ' % ';
```

Question 27:

Will the following query evaluate to true (1), false (0), or NULL?

```
SELECT ' % ' LIKE '%';
```

Question 28:

Will the following query evaluate to true (1), false (0), or NULL?

```
SELECT 'Lennart' LIKE '_e%_t';
```

Question 29:

Will the following query evaluate to true (1), false (0), or NULL?

```
SELECT 'Lennart' LIKE '_e%';
```

Question 30:

Will the following query evaluate to true (1), false (0), or NULL?

```
SELECT NULL LIKE NULL;
```

Question 31:

Will the following query evaluate to true (1), false (0), or NULL?

```
SELECT NULL LIKE '%';
```

Question 32:

Will the following query evaluate to true (1), false (0), or NULL?

```
SELECT 'NULL' LIKE '%';
```

Question 33:

Will the following query evaluate to true (1), false (0), or NULL?

```
SELECT BINARY 'NULL' LIKE 'null';
```

Question 34:

Will the following query evaluate to true (1), false (0), or NULL?

```
SELECT '2002-02-08' LIKE '2002%';
```

Question 35:

Will the following query evaluate to true (1), false (0), or NULL?

```
SELECT 23.42 LIKE '2%2';
```

Question 36:

Will the following query evaluate to true (1), false (0), or NULL?

```
SELECT 023.420 LIKE '2%2';
```

Question 37:

The table `CityList` has the following structure:

```
mysql> DESCRIBE CityList;
+------------+----------+------+-----+---------+----------------+
| Field      | Type     | Null | Key | Default | Extra          |
+------------+----------+------+-----+---------+----------------+
| ID         | int(11)  |      | PRI | NULL    | auto_increment |
| Name       | char(35) |      |     |         |                |
| Country    | char(3)  |      |     |         |                |
| District   | char(20) |      |     |         |                |
| Population | int(11)  |      |     | 0       |                |
+------------+----------+------+-----+---------+----------------+
```

You want to retrieve the list of cities in the United States of America (USA), Denmark (DNK), and Germany (DEU) that have a number of inhabitants between 400,000 and 500,000, sorted from largest to smallest. Use the IN() operator to perform this query. The list should look like this:

```
+----------------+---------+------------+
| City           | Country | Population |
+----------------+---------+------------+
| Koebenhavn     | DNK     |     495699 |
| Leipzig        | DEU     |     489532 |
| Tucson         | USA     |     486699 |
| Nuernberg      | DEU     |     486628 |
| New Orleans    | USA     |     484674 |
| Las Vegas      | USA     |     478434 |
| Cleveland      | USA     |     478403 |
| Dresden        | DEU     |     476668 |
| Long Beach     | USA     |     461522 |
| Albuquerque    | USA     |     448607 |
| Kansas City    | USA     |     441545 |
| Fresno         | USA     |     427652 |
| Virginia Beach | USA     |     425257 |
| Atlanta        | USA     |     416474 |
| Sacramento     | USA     |     407018 |
+----------------+---------+------------+
```

Question 38:

Using the client tool `mysql`, the following statements are issued:

```
mysql> CREATE DATABASE CaseTest;
Query OK, 1 row affected (0.00 sec)
mysql> USE casetest;
Database changed
```

Sometime later, the database is moved to another MySQL server. Trying to select the database as before results in an error message:

```
mysql> USE casetest;
ERROR 1049: Unknown database 'casetest'
```

What's the reason for this error message? How could this problem be solved? What could you do to prevent problems like this?

Question 39:

The table personnel has the following structure:

```
mysql> DESCRIBE personnel;
+--------+----------------------+
| Field  | Type                 |
+--------+----------------------+
| pid    | smallint(5) unsigned |
| unit   | tinyint(3) unsigned  |
| salary | decimal(9,2)         |
+--------+----------------------+
```

Which of the following statements will produce an error?

```
mysql> SELECT
    ->  pid AS 'Employee ID',
    ->  salary AS Salary
    -> FROM personnel
    -> WHERE Salary > 2000
    -> ;
```

```
mysql> SELECT
    ->  p.pid,
    ->  p.salary
    -> FROM personnel AS P
    -> WHERE Salary > 2000
    -> ;
```

```
mysql> SELECT
    ->  PERSONNEL.pid AS 'Employee ID',
    ->  PERSONNEL.salary
    -> FROM personnel AS PERSONNEL
    -> WHERE PID > 10
    -> ;
```

Question 40:

Will the following SQL statement succeed or result in an error? Assume that the table to be created doesn't already exist.

```
CREATE TABLE select (id INT);
```

Question 41:

Will the following SQL statement succeed or result in an error? Assume that the table to be created doesn't already exist.

```
CREATE TABLE `select` (id INT);
```

Question 42:

Will the following SQL statement succeed or result in an error? Assume that the table to be created doesn't already exist.

```
CREATE TABLE 'select' (id INT);
```

Question 43:

Will the following SQL statement succeed or result in an error? Assume that the table to be created doesn't already exist.

```
CREATE TABLE `select-me, please!` (id INT);
```

Question 44:

Will the following SQL statement succeed or result in an error? Assume that the table to be created doesn't already exist.

```
CREATE TABLE `select.me.please` (id INT);
```

Question 45:

Will the following SQL statement succeed or result in an error? Assume that the table to be created doesn't already exist.

```
CREATE TABLE MD5 (id INT);
```

Question 46:

Will the following SQL statement succeed or result in an error? Assume that the table to be created doesn't already exist.

```
CREATE TABLE `MD5()` (id INT);
```

Question 47:

Will the following SQL statement succeed or result in an error? Assume that the table to be created doesn't already exist.

```
CREATE TABLE `MD5('Lennart')` (id INT);
```

Question 48:

Will the following SQL statement succeed or result in an error? Assume that the table to be created doesn't already exist.

```
CREATE TABLE `COUNT(*)` (id INT);
```

Question 49:

Will the following SQL statement succeed or result in an error? Assume that the table to be created doesn't already exist.

```
CREATE TABLE `0123456789` (id INT);
```

Question 50:

Will the following SQL statement succeed or result in an error? Assume that the database to be created doesn't already exist.

```
CREATE DATABASE `0123456789`;
```

Question 51:

Will the following statement work?

```
mysql> CREATE TABLE nulltest (
    -> test1 INT NOT NULL,
    -> test2 INT NULL,
    -> test3 INT NOT NULL DEFAULT 123,
    -> test4 INT NULL DEFAULT 456
    -> );
```

Question 52:

What are the default values for the column of the following table?

```
mysql> CREATE TABLE nulltest (
    -> test1 INT NOT NULL,
    -> test2 INT NULL,
    -> test3 INT NOT NULL DEFAULT 123
    -> );
```

Question 53:

The table nulltest has the following structure:

```
mysql> DESCRIBE nulltest;
+-------+---------+------+-----+---------+-------+
| Field | Type    | Null | Key | Default | Extra |
+-------+---------+------+-----+---------+-------+
| test1 | int(11) |      |     | 0       |       |
+-------+---------+------+-----+---------+-------+
```

What results will the following INSERT statements yield?

```
INSERT INTO nulltest VALUES (NULL);

INSERT INTO nulltest VALUES (NULL),(NULL),(NULL);
```

Question 54:

Will the following statement evaluate to true (1), false (0), NULL, or result in an error?

```
SELECT NULL == NULL;
```

Question 55:

Will the following statement evaluate to true (1), false (0), NULL, or result in an error?

```
SELECT NULL = NULL = NULL;
```

Question 56:

Will the following statement evaluate to true (1), false (0), NULL, or result in an error?

```
SELECT NULL = NULL = 0;
```

Question 57:

Will the following statement evaluate to true (1), false (0), NULL, or result in an error?

```
SELECT NULL IS NOT 0;
```

Question 58:

Will the following statement evaluate to true (1), false (0), NULL, or result in an error?

```
SELECT 0 IS NOT NULL;
```

Question 59:

Will the following statement evaluate to true (1), false (0), NULL, or result in an error?

```
SELECT 0 <=> 1;
```

Question 60:

The table personnel has the following structure and contents:

```
mysql> DESCRIBE personnel; SELECT * FROM personnel;
+-------+---------------------+------+-----+---------+
| Field | Type                | Null | Key | Default |
+-------+---------------------+------+-----+---------+
| pid   | smallint(5) unsigned |     | PRI | NULL    |
| unit  | tinyint(3) unsigned | YES  |     | NULL    |
| grade | tinyint(3) unsigned | YES  |     | NULL    |
+-------+---------------------+------+-----+---------+
+-----+------+-------+
| pid | unit | grade |
+-----+------+-------+
|   1 |   42 |     1 |
|   2 |   42 |     2 |
|   3 |   42 |  NULL |
```

```
|   4 |   42 | NULL |
|   5 |   42 | NULL |
|   6 |   23 |    1 |
|   7 |   23 |    1 |
|   8 |   23 |    1 |
|   9 |   23 | NULL |
|  10 |   42 | NULL |
|  11 |   23 | NULL |
|  12 |   23 |    1 |
|  13 |   42 | NULL |
+-----+------+-------+
```

What result will the following statement yield?

```
SELECT unit, COUNT(grade) FROM personnel GROUP BY unit;
```

Question 61:

Refer to the structure and contents shown for the personnel table in the previous question. What result will the following statement yield?

```
SELECT unit, SUM(grade) FROM personnel GROUP BY unit;
```

Question 62:

Refer to the structure and contents shown for the personnel table two questions earlier. What result will the following statement yield?

```
SELECT unit, AVG(grade) FROM personnel GROUP BY unit;
```

Question 63:

The table personnel has the following structure and contents:

```
mysql> DESCRIBE personnel; SELECT * FROM personnel;
+-------+---------------------+------+-----+---------+
| Field | Type                | Null | Key | Default |
+-------+---------------------+------+-----+---------+
| pid   | smallint(5) unsigned |      | PRI | NULL    |
| unit  | tinyint(3) unsigned | YES  |     | NULL    |
| grade | tinyint(3) unsigned | YES  |     | NULL    |
+-------+---------------------+------+-----+---------+

+-----+------+-------+
| pid | unit | grade |
+-----+------+-------+
|   1 |   42 |    1 |
|   2 |   42 |    2 |
|   3 |   42 | NULL |
|   4 |   42 | NULL |
|   5 |   42 | NULL |
```

```
|    6 |   23 |      1 |
|    7 |   23 |      1 |
|    8 |   23 |      1 |
|    9 |   23 |   NULL |
|   10 |   42 |   NULL |
|   11 |   23 |   NULL |
|   12 |   23 |      1 |
|   13 |   42 |   NULL |
+-----+------+-------+
```

What result will the following statement yield?

```
SELECT unit, COUNT(*) FROM personnel GROUP BY unit;
```

Question 64:

Refer to the structure and contents shown for the `personnel` table in the previous question. What result will the following statement yield?

```
SELECT unit, COUNT(DISTINCT grade) FROM personnel GROUP BY unit;
```

Question 65:

Is the comment in the following statement legal in MySQL?

```
INSERT /*! DELAYED */ INTO mytable VALUES (5);
```

Question 66:

Is the comment in the following statement legal in MySQL?

```
SELECT * FROM mytable WHERE id < 100 /*!40000 FOR UPDATE */;
```

Question 67:

Is the comment in the following statement legal in MySQL?

```
CREATE /*32303 TEMPORARY */ TABLE tbl (col INT);
```

Question 68:

Is the comment in the following statement legal in MySQL?

```
SELECT * FROM mytable; // * is not good style, though
```

Question 69:

Is the comment in the following statement legal in MySQL?

```
SELECT a, b, c FROM tbl; --different column list needed?
```

Answers to Exercises

Answer 1:

Constants are either literal numbers, strings, or temporal values. An SQL expression can consist of constants, NULL values, references to table columns, and function calls.

Answer 2:

```
SELECT 1 + 1;
```

Answer 3:

```
SELECT 'Hello ', 'world!';
```

Answer 4:

```
SELECT '2002-02-08', '2003-02-08';
```

Answer 5:

```
SELECT '21:39:00';
```

Answer 6:

```
SELECT name, age FROM mytable;
```

Answer 7:

```
SELECT NOW();
```

Answer 8:

```
SELECT DATE_FORMAT(NOW(),'%m/%d/%Y');
```

Answer 9:

```
mysql> SELECT
    -> pid AS PID,
    -> salary AS 'Gross Salary',
    -> salary * 0.4 AS Deduction,
    -> salary * 0.6 AS 'Net Salary'
    -> FROM personnel
    -> ;
+-----+--------------+-----------+------------+
| PID | Gross Salary | Deduction | Net Salary |
+-----+--------------+-----------+------------+
|   1 |      1500.00 |    600.00 |     900.00 |
|   2 |      1700.00 |    680.00 |    1020.00 |
|   3 |      1950.00 |    780.00 |    1170.00 |
|   4 |      2300.00 |    920.00 |    1380.00 |
|   5 |      1900.00 |    760.00 |    1140.00 |
```

```
|    6 |        850.00 |     340.00 |      510.00 |
|    7 |       1250.00 |     500.00 |      750.00 |
|    8 |       1450.00 |     580.00 |      870.00 |
|    9 |       1920.00 |     768.00 |     1152.00 |
|   10 |       2200.00 |     880.00 |     1320.00 |
|   11 |       2900.00 |    1160.00 |     1740.00 |
|   12 |       1000.00 |     400.00 |      600.00 |
|   13 |       2850.00 |    1140.00 |     1710.00 |
+------+---------------+------------+-------------+
```

Answer 10:

```
mysql> SELECT
    ->   unit AS Unit,
    ->   SUM(salary) AS 'Gross Salary',
    ->   SUM(salary) * 0.4 AS Deduction,
    ->   SUM(salary) * 0.6 AS 'Net Salary'
    -> FROM personnel
    -> GROUP BY unit
    -> ;
+------+--------------+-----------+------------+
| Unit | Gross Salary | Deduction | Net Salary |
+------+--------------+-----------+------------+
|   23 |      9370.00 |   3748.00 |    5622.00 |
|   42 |     14400.00 |   5760.00 |    8640.00 |
+------+--------------+-----------+------------+
```

Answer 11:

```
mysql> SELECT
    ->   pid AS PID,
    ->   salary as 'Gross Salary',
    ->   IF(salary < 2000, salary * 0.3, salary * 0.4) AS Deduction,
    ->   IF(salary < 2000, salary * 0.7, salary * 0.6) AS 'Net Salary'
    -> FROM personnel
    -> ;
+-----+--------------+-----------+------------+
| PID | Gross Salary | Deduction | Net Salary |
+-----+--------------+-----------+------------+
|   1 |      1500.00 |    450.00 |    1050.00 |
|   2 |      1700.00 |    510.00 |    1190.00 |
|   3 |      1950.00 |    585.00 |    1365.00 |
|   4 |      2300.00 |    920.00 |    1380.00 |
|   5 |      1900.00 |    570.00 |    1330.00 |
|   6 |       850.00 |    255.00 |     595.00 |
|   7 |      1250.00 |    375.00 |     875.00 |
|   8 |      1450.00 |    435.00 |    1015.00 |
|   9 |      1920.00 |    576.00 |    1344.00 |
```

```
| 10 |     2200.00 |    880.00 |    1320.00 |
| 11 |     2900.00 |   1160.00 |    1740.00 |
| 12 |     1000.00 |    300.00 |     700.00 |
| 13 |     2850.00 |   1140.00 |    1710.00 |
+-----+-------------+----------+------------+
```

Answer 12:

```
mysql> SELECT
    ->   SUM(salary) AS Salary,
    ->   SUM(salary) * 1.1 AS 'New Salary',
    ->   SUM(salary) * 0.1 AS 'Cost Rise'
    -> FROM personnel
    -> ;
+----------+------------+-----------+
| Salary   | New Salary | Cost Rise |
+----------+------------+-----------+
| 23770.00 |   26147.00 |   2377.00 |
+----------+------------+-----------+
```

Answer 13:

```
mysql> SELECT
    ->   SUM(salary) AS Salary,
    ->   SUM(salary) * IF(unit = 23, 1.1, 1.05) AS 'New Salary',
    ->   SUM(salary) * IF(unit = 23, 0.1, 0.05) AS 'Cost Rise'
    -> FROM personnel
    -> GROUP BY unit
    -> ;
+----------+------------+-----------+
| Salary   | New Salary | Cost Rise |
+----------+------------+-----------+
|  9370.00 |   10307.00 |    937.00 |
| 14400.00 |   15120.00 |    720.00 |
+----------+------------+-----------+
```

Answer 14:

Each statement yields output as follows:

```
mysql> SELECT DISTINCT name FROM leonardo;
+---------+
| name    |
+---------+
| Lennart |
+---------+
```

Different lettercases aren't regarded as distinct in a nonbinary context.

```
mysql> SELECT name, COUNT(*) FROM leonardo GROUP BY name;
+----------+
| COUNT(*) |
+----------+
|        4 |
+----------+
```

Different lettercases aren't regarded as distinct in a nonbinary context.

```
mysql> SELECT name, COUNT(*) FROM leonardo;
ERROR 1140: Mixing of GROUP columns (MIN(),MAX(),COUNT()...)
with no GROUP columns is illegal if there is no GROUP BY clause
```

As the error message indicates, this isn't a legal SQL statement.

Answer 15:

Each statement yields output as follows:

```
mysql> SELECT DISTINCT name FROM leonardo;
+---------+
| name    |
+---------+
| Lennart |
| lennart |
| LENNART |
| lEnNaRt |
+---------+
```

Different lettercases are regarded as distinct in a binary context.

```
mysql> SELECT name, COUNT(*) FROM leonardo GROUP BY name;
+---------+----------+
| name    | COUNT(*) |
+---------+----------+
| LENNART |        1 |
| Lennart |        1 |
| lEnNaRt |        1 |
| lennart |        1 |
+---------+----------+
```

Different lettercases are regarded as distinct in a binary context.

```
mysql> SELECT name, COUNT(*) FROM leonardo;
ERROR 1140: Mixing of GROUP columns (MIN(),MAX(),COUNT()...)
with no GROUP columns is illegal if there is no GROUP BY clause
```

As the error message indicates, this isn't a legal SQL statement.

Answer 16:

LENGTH() counts string length in bytes, CHAR_LENGTH() counts string length in characters. For single-byte character sets, the two functions return identical results, but for multi-byte character sets, LENGTH() returns a different (higher) number than CHAR_LENGTH().

Answer 17:

The UPPER() function makes the second string equal to the first string, even when comparison is performed in a case-sensitive manner (BINARY):

```
+-----------------------------------+
| BINARY 'LENNART' = UPPER('Lennart') |
+-----------------------------------+
|                                 1 |
+-----------------------------------+
```

Answer 18:

The LOWER() function makes both strings equal, even when comparison is performed in a case-sensitive manner with BINARY:

```
+-------------------------------------------+
| BINARY LOWER('LeNNaRT') = LOWER('lEnnArt') |
+-------------------------------------------+
|                                         1 |
+-------------------------------------------+
```

Answer 19:

The MD5() function produces unequal values for the two strings:

```
+---------------------------------+
| MD5('lennart') = MD5('LENNART') |
+---------------------------------+
|                               0 |
+---------------------------------+
```

However, this result can be guessed only if you're able to anticipate the results of the MD5() function calls in advance (which is rather improbable):

```
mysql> SELECT MD5('lennart'), MD5('LENNART');
+----------------------------------+----------------------------------+
| MD5('lennart')                   | MD5('LENNART')                   |
+----------------------------------+----------------------------------+
| a6894e0c24b247a33b0de7e3fcd2b53f | d63445ebdc53cabe60ef708beafb39f0 |
+----------------------------------+----------------------------------+
```

Answer 20:

a. TRUE. A regular string comparison is performed in a case-insensitive manner.

b. FALSE. The keyword BINARY for one of the terms makes the string comparison case sensitive.

c. FALSE. The keyword BINARY for one (or both) of the terms makes the string comparison case sensitive.

Answer 21:

MD5() is an example of a function that operates in a case-sensitive manner. Other examples include the encryption functions in addition to MD5(); for example, ENCRYPT(), AES_ENCRYPT(), DES_ENCODE(), SHA(), and PASSWORD(). (Note that the PASSWORD() function also performs encryption, but it's a special-purpose function for user authentication and shouldn't be used for your own applications.)

Answer 22:

Three underscore metacharacters match any three characters, so they match the entire string 'abc'. That leaves nothing left to be matched, but because % also matches nothing, the expression evaluates to true.

```
+-------------------+
| 'abc' LIKE '%___%' |
+-------------------+
|                 1 |
+-------------------+
```

Answer 23:

'abc' doesn't match the five underscore metacharacters, so the expression evaluates to false.

```
+---------------------+
| 'abc' LIKE '%_____%' |
+---------------------+
|                   0 |
+---------------------+
```

Answer 24:

The '%' metacharacter also matches the empty string, so the expression evaluates to true.

```
+-------------+
| '' LIKE '%' |
+-------------+
|           1 |
+-------------+
```

Answer 25:

The space characters surrounding '%' do not match the empty string, so the expression evaluates to false.

```
+---------------+
| '' LIKE ' % ' |
+---------------+
|             0 |
+---------------+
```

Answer 26:

The '%' character is matched by '%', but not by the space characters surrounding it, so the expression evaluates to false.

```
+----------------+
| '%' LIKE ' % ' |
+----------------+
|              0 |
+----------------+
```

Answer 27:

Any non-NULL string is matched by the '%' metacharacter, so the expression evaluates to true.

```
+----------------+
| ' % ' LIKE '%' |
+----------------+
|              1 |
+----------------+
```

Answer 28:

The expression evaluates to true. '_e' at the start of the pattern matches 'Le', '_t' at the end matches 'rt', and the rest of the string is matched by the '%' metacharacter.

```
+-----------------------+
| 'Lennart' LIKE '_e%_t' |
+-----------------------+
|                     1 |
+-----------------------+
```

Answer 29:

The expression evaluates to true. _e matches Le and the rest of the string is matched by the '%' metacharacter.

```
+---------------------+
| 'Lennart' LIKE '_e%' |
+---------------------+
|                   1 |
+---------------------+
```

Answer 30:

If either operand is NULL, the expression evaluates to NULL.

```
+----------------+
| NULL LIKE NULL |
+----------------+
|           NULL |
+----------------+
```

Answer 31:

If either operand is NULL, the expression evaluates to NULL. '%' matches anything (including the empty string) except NULL.

```
+---------------+
| NULL LIKE '%' |
+---------------+
|          NULL |
+---------------+
```

Answer 32:

In this case, 'NULL' is just a string like any other string, not the NULL value, so the expression evaluates to true.

```
+----------------+
| 'NULL' LIKE '%' |
+----------------+
|              1 |
+----------------+
```

Answer 33:

In both operands, 'NULL' is just a string (in different lettercases). The comparison is performed in a case-sensitive way due to the BINARY keyword, so the expression evaluates to false.

```
+------------------------+
| BINARY 'NULL' LIKE 'null' |
+------------------------+
|                      0 |
+------------------------+
```

Answer 34:

Although it appears that the pattern match is performed on a date value rather than a string, the expression evaluates to true. The reason for this is that the "date" is actually a string value in this context.

```
+--------------------------+
| '2002-02-08' LIKE '2002%' |
+--------------------------+
|                        1 |
+--------------------------+
```

Answer 35:

Pattern-matching operations can be performed with numbers, too. Because 23.42 starts and ends with 2, it's matched by '2%2', so the expression evaluates to true.

```
+------------------+
| 23.42 LIKE '2%2' |
+------------------+
|                1 |
+------------------+
```

Answer 36:

Pattern-matching operations can be performed with numbers, too. However, because 023.420 does not start and end with 2, it isn't matched by '2%2'. The expression evaluates to false.

```
+--------------------+
| 023.420 LIKE '2%2' |
+--------------------+
|                  0 |
+--------------------+
```

Answer 37:

```
mysql> SELECT Name AS City, Country, Population
    ->    FROM CityList
    -> WHERE Country IN('DEU','DNK','USA')
    ->    AND POPULATION BETWEEN 400000 AND 500000
    -> ORDER BY Population DESC
    -> ;
```

Answer 38:

The database CaseTest was created under an operating system that does not have case-sensitive filenames, such as Windows. The database was then moved to a machine running an operating system that has case-sensitive filenames, such as Linux. To solve this problem, the database should be selected as follows:

```
mysql> USE CaseTest;
Database changed
```

To prevent problems with database and table names under different operating systems, you could start the MySQL server on all operating systems you're using with the lower_case_table_names variable set. (However, you should do this before creating any databases or tables.)

Answer 39:

Aliases are not case sensitive except table aliases. Only the second statement will result in an error because the table alias is P and it is referred to as p for the columns to be retrieved.

Answer 40:

An error will result. It isn't possible to use a reserved word as an identifier without quoting the identifier.

```
mysql> CREATE TABLE select (id INT);
ERROR 1064: You have an error in your SQL syntax.
```

Answer 41:

The statement succeeds. When a reserved word is quoted, it can be used as an identifier. In this example, backticks are used; this works under all circumstances.

```
mysql> CREATE TABLE `select` (id INT);
Query OK, 0 rows affected
```

Answer 42:

An error will result. Single quotes can be used as quotes for aliases, but they cannot be used for identifiers such as table names.

```
mysql> CREATE TABLE 'select' (id INT);
ERROR 1064: You have an error in your SQL syntax.
```

Answer 43:

The statement succeeds. Almost every character, including dash, comma, space, and exclamation mark, is legal in a table identifier when the identifier is properly quoted.

```
mysql> CREATE TABLE `select-me, please!` (id INT);
Query OK, 0 rows affected
```

Answer 44:

An error will result. Periods cannot be used in a table identifier even when the identifier is quoted. Because periods are used to separate database names from table names, and table names from column names, they aren't acceptable within an identifier.

```
mysql> CREATE TABLE `select.me.please` (id INT);
ERROR 1103: Incorrect table name 'select.me.please'
```

Answer 45:

The statement results in an error if the MySQL server has been started in ANSI mode (with the option `--ansi` or `--sql-mode=IGNORE_SPACE`). In that case, the statement would return an error because `MD5` is a function name, and in ANSI mode all function names become reserved words. If the MySQL server hasn't been started in ANSI mode, the statement succeeds.

```
mysql> CREATE TABLE MD5 (id INT);
Query OK, 0 rows affected
```

Answer 46:

The statement succeeds. Parentheses are legal characters in an identifier as long as it is quoted.

```
mysql> CREATE TABLE `MD5()` (id INT);
Query OK, 0 rows affected
```

Answer 47:

The statement succeeds. Single quotes are legal characters in an identifier as long as it is quoted.

```
mysql> CREATE TABLE `MD5('Lennart')` (id INT);
Query OK, 0 rows affected
```

Answer 48:

Whether this statement succeeds is dependent on the operating system under which the MySQL server is running. If the operating system doesn't allow certain characters in filenames, the characters cannot be used for database and table names even when the identifier is quoted.

```
mysql> CREATE TABLE `COUNT(*)` (id INT);
ERROR 1: Can't create/write to file '.\test\COUNT(*).frm'
(Errcode: 22)
```

Answer 49:

The statement succeeds. Identifiers consisting solely of numbers are accepted, provided they're quoted.

```
mysql> CREATE TABLE `0123456789` (id INT);
Query OK, 0 rows affected
```

Answer 50:

The statement succeeds. Quoted identifiers consisting solely of numbers are accepted for database names.

```
mysql> CREATE DATABASE `0123456789`;
Query OK, 1 row affected
```

Answer 51:

The statement will create the table nulltest. All the column specifications are legal:

```
mysql> CREATE TABLE nulltest (
    -> test1 INT NOT NULL,
    -> test2 INT NULL,
    -> test3 INT NOT NULL DEFAULT 123,
    -> test4 INT NULL DEFAULT 456
    -> );
mysql> DESCRIBE nulltest;
+-------+---------+------+-----+---------+-------+
| Field | Type    | Null | Key | Default | Extra |
+-------+---------+------+-----+---------+-------+
| test1 | int(11) |      |     | 0       |       |
| test2 | int(11) | YES  |     | NULL    |       |
| test3 | int(11) |      |     | 123     |       |
| test4 | int(11) | YES  |     | 456     |       |
+-------+---------+------+-----+---------+-------+
```

Answer 52:

The default values can be displayed with the DESCRIBE statement in mysql:

```
mysql> DESCRIBE nulltest;
+-------+---------+------+-----+---------+-------+
| Field | Type    | Null | Key | Default | Extra |
+-------+---------+------+-----+---------+-------+
| test1 | int(11) |      |     | 0       |       |
| test2 | int(11) | YES  |     | NULL    |       |
| test3 | int(11) |      |     | 123     |       |
+-------+---------+------+-----+---------+-------+
```

If no default value is explicitly assigned to a column in the CREATE TABLE statement, MySQL will assign its standard default value, depending on the datatype of the column. For integer column types, the standard default value is 0.

Answer 53:

Single-row insert operations cannot insert NULL into a table column declared as NOT NULL; an error occurs, as the first of the following listings shows. For multiple-row insert operations, however, this doesn't hold true. Instead, MySQL inserts the standard default value (0 in the case of integer columns), as shown in the second of the following listings:

```
mysql> INSERT INTO nulltest VALUES (NULL);
ERROR 1048: Column 'test1' cannot be null

mysql> INSERT INTO nulltest VALUES (NULL),(NULL),(NULL);
Query OK, 3 rows affected
Records: 3  Duplicates: 0  Warnings: 3
```

```
mysql> SELECT * FROM nulltest;
+-------+
| test1 |
+-------+
|     0 |
|     0 |
|     0 |
+-------+
3 rows in set
```

Answer 54:

The statement returns an error. It's a common error of programmers to mix up the == comparison operator used in many programming languages with the = comparison operator used in SQL.

```
mysql> SELECT NULL == NULL;
ERROR 1064: You have an error in your SQL syntax.
```

Answer 55:

The statement evaluates to NULL. If any operand in an equality comparison is NULL, the expression evaluates to NULL.

```
mysql> SELECT NULL = NULL = NULL;
+--------------------+
| NULL = NULL = NULL |
+--------------------+
|               NULL |
+--------------------+
```

Answer 56:

The statement evaluates to NULL. If any operand in an equality comparison is NULL, the expression evaluates to NULL.

```
mysql> SELECT NULL = NULL = 0;
+-----------------+
| NULL = NULL = 0 |
+-----------------+
|            NULL |
+-----------------+
```

Answer 57:

The statement returns an error. The IS NULL and IS NOT NULL operators must be followed by NULL.

```
mysql> SELECT NULL IS NOT 0;
ERROR 1064: You have an error in your SQL syntax.
```

Answer 58:

The statement evaluates to true (1) because 0 is not NULL.

```
mysql> SELECT 0 IS NOT NULL;
+---------------+
| 0 IS NOT NULL |
+---------------+
|             1 |
+---------------+
```

Answer 59:

The statement evaluates to false. The special <=> operator can be used for regular comparisons (exactly like the = operator). The only difference is that it's NULL-safe.

```
mysql> SELECT 0 <=> 1;
+---------+
| 0 <=> 1 |
+---------+
|       0 |
+---------+
```

Answer 60:

The statement provides the number of grades assigned for each unit. It counts only assigned grades; that is, grades that are not NULL:

```
mysql> SELECT unit, COUNT(grade) FROM personnel GROUP BY unit;
+------+--------------+
| unit | COUNT(grade) |
+------+--------------+
|   23 |            4 |
|   42 |            2 |
+------+--------------+
```

Answer 61:

For each unit, the statement sums up grades that aren't NULL:

```
mysql> SELECT unit, SUM(grade) FROM personnel GROUP BY unit;
+------+------------+
| unit | SUM(grade) |
+------+------------+
|   23 |          4 |
|   42 |          3 |
+------+------------+
```

Answer 62:

For each unit, the statement calculates the average value of grades that aren't NULL:

```
mysql> SELECT unit, AVG(grade) FROM personnel GROUP BY unit;
+------+------------+
| unit | AVG(grade) |
+------+------------+
|   23 |     1.0000 |
|   42 |     1.5000 |
+------+------------+
```

Answer 63:

The statement counts the number of rows for each unit:

```
mysql> SELECT unit, COUNT(*) FROM personnel GROUP BY unit;
+------+----------+
| unit | COUNT(*) |
+------+----------+
|   23 |        6 |
|   42 |        7 |
+------+----------+
```

Answer 64:

The statement counts how many different non-NULL grades there are for each unit:

```
mysql> SELECT unit, COUNT(DISTINCT grade) FROM personnel GROUP BY unit;
+------+----------------------+
| unit | COUNT(DISTINCT grade) |
+------+----------------------+
|   23 |                    1 |
|   42 |                    2 |
+------+----------------------+
```

Answer 65:

This is a legal comment in MySQL. The /*! part of the comment ensures that MySQL will not treat this as a comment, but other database servers will.

Answer 66:

This is a legal comment in MySQL. Other database servers will regard this as a comment; MySQL, however, will interpret the contents of the comment as part of the statement if the server version is 4.0.0 or higher.

Answer 67:

This is a legal comment in MySQL, but it is not a version-specific comment because it begins with /*, not /*!. For that purpose, it should be written as /*!32303 TEMPORARY */.

Answer 68:

This isn't a legal comment in MySQL.

Answer 69:

This SQL Standard-style comment isn't legal in MySQL because -- must be followed by a space character.

7

Update Statements

This chapter covers the following exam topics:

- The INSERT and REPLACE statements
- The UPDATE statement
- The DELETE and TRUNCATE statements
- Handling duplicate key values
- Using ORDER BY and LIMIT with UPDATE and DELETE statements

Questions on the material in this chapter make up approximately 10% of the exam.

This chapter discusses SQL statements that modify the contents of database tables:

- INSERT adds new records to a table.
- REPLACE is similar to INSERT, except that if a new record contains a value that duplicates a unique key value in an existing record, it deletes the old record first.
- UPDATE modifies existing table records.
- DELETE and TRUNCATE TABLE remove records from a table. DELETE can remove some or all records; TRUNCATE TABLE completely empties a table.

Another statement that modifies table contents is LOAD DATA INFILE, which reads records from a datafile and loads them into a table. It's discussed in Chapter 9, "Importing and Exporting Data."

Note that for purposes of discussion here, the term "update statement" is used in a collective sense to refer to various kinds of statements that modify tables. "UPDATE statement" refers specifically to statements that begin with the UPDATE keyword. Also, keep in mind the following terminology with regard to indexes:

- "UNIQUE index" means specifically a unique-valued index created using the keyword UNIQUE.
- "PRIMARY KEY" means specifically a unique-valued index created using the keywords PRIMARY KEY.

- The term "unique-valued index" is a generic term meaning any index that contains only unique values. A UNIQUE index or a PRIMARY KEY is a unique-valued index.

- The term "primary key" means a unique-valued index that cannot contain NULL values.

Much of the discussion in this chapter uses the following table as a source of examples:

```
CREATE TABLE people
(
    id      INT UNSIGNED NOT NULL AUTO_INCREMENT,
    name    CHAR(40) NOT NULL,
    age     INT NOT NULL,
    PRIMARY KEY (id)
);
```

7.1 The INSERT and REPLACE Statements

The INSERT and REPLACE statements add new records to a table. The two have very similar syntax. The primary difference between them lies in how they handle duplicate records.

7.1.1 The INSERT Statement

The INSERT statement adds new records to a table. It has two basic formats, one of which allows for insertion of multiple rows using a single statement:

```
INSERT INTO table_name (column_list) VALUES (value_list);
INSERT INTO table_name SET column_name1 = value1, column_name2 = value2, ... ;
```

The first syntax for INSERT uses separate column and value lists following the name of the table into which you want to add the record. The number of columns and values must be the same. The statement shown here uses this syntax to create a new record in the people table with id set to 12, name set to 'William', and age set to 25:

```
INSERT INTO people (id,name,age) VALUES(12,'William',25);
```

The second INSERT syntax follows the table name by a SET clause that lists individual column assignments separated by commas:

```
INSERT INTO people SET id = 12, name = 'William', age = 25;
```

The SET clause must assign a value to at least one column.

For any column not assigned an explicit value by an INSERT statement, MySQL sets it to its default value. For example, to have MySQL set the id column to its default, you can simply omit it from the statement. The following example shows statements using each INSERT syntax that assign no explicit id value:

```
INSERT INTO people (name,age) VALUES('William',25);
INSERT INTO people SET name = 'William', age = 25;
```

In both statements, the effect is the same: The id column is set to its default value. id is an AUTO_INCREMENT column, so its default is the next sequence number.

The VALUES form of INSERT has some variations:

- If both the column list and the VALUES list are empty, MySQL creates a new record with each column set to its default:

```
INSERT INTO people () VALUES();
```

The preceding statement creates a record with id, name, and age set to their defaults (the next sequence number, the empty string, and 0, respectively).

- It's allowable to omit the list of column names and provide only the values. In this case, the VALUES list must contain one value for every column in the table. Furthermore, the values must be listed in the same order in which the columns are named in the table's definition. (This is the order in which the columns appear in the output from DESCRIBE table_name.) The following INSERT statement satisfies these conditions because it provides three column values in id, name, age order:

```
INSERT INTO people VALUES(12,'William',25);
```

On the other hand, this statement is illegal because it provides only two values for a three-column table:

```
INSERT INTO people VALUES('William',25);
```

The following INSERT statement is syntactically legal because it provides a value for every column, but it assigns 25 to name and 'William' to age, which is not likely to serve any useful purpose:

```
INSERT INTO people VALUES(12,25,'William');
```

- You can insert multiple records with a single statement by providing several values lists after the VALUES keyword. This is discussed in section 7.1.1.1, "Adding Multiple Records with a Single INSERT Statement."

As noted, for an INSERT statement that provides data values in the VALUES list, it's permissible to omit the list of column names if the statement contains a data value for every column. However, it isn't necessarily advisable to do so. When you don't include the list of column names, the VALUES list must not only be complete, the data values must be in the same order as the columns in the table. If it's possible that you'll alter the structure of the table by adding, removing, or rearranging columns, such alterations might require any application that inserts records into the table to be modified. This is much more likely if the INSERT statements don't include a list of column names because they're more sensitive to the structure of the table. When you use an INSERT statement that names the columns, rearranging the table's columns has no effect. Adding columns has no effect, either, if it's appropriate to set the new columns to their default values.

7.1.1.1 Adding Multiple Records with a Single INSERT Statement

A single INSERT … VALUES statement can add multiple records to a table if you provide multiple VALUES lists. To do this, provide a parenthesized list of values for each record and separate the lists by commas. For example:

```
INSERT INTO people (name,age)
VALUES('William',25),('Bart',15),('Mary',12);
```

The statement shown creates three new people records, assigning the name and age columns in each record to the values listed. The id column is not listed explicitly, so MySQL assigns a sequence value to that column in each record.

Note that a multiple-row INSERT statement requires a *separate* parenthesized list for each row. Suppose that you have a table t with a single integer column i:

```
CREATE TABLE t (i INT);
```

To insert into the table five records with values of 1 through 5, the following statement will *not* work:

```
mysql> INSERT INTO t (i) VALUES(1,2,3,4,5);
ERROR 1136: Column count doesn't match value count at row 1
```

The error occurs because the number of values between parentheses in the VALUES list isn't the same as the number of columns in the column list. To write the statement properly, provide five separate parenthesized lists:

```
mysql> INSERT INTO t (i) VALUES(1),(2),(3),(4),(5);
Query OK, 5 rows affected (0.00 sec)
Records: 5  Duplicates: 0  Warnings: 0
```

It's allowable to omit the list of column names in multiple-row INSERT statements. In this case, each parenthesized list of values must contain a value for every table column.

The preceding example illustrates something about multiple-row INSERT statements that isn't true for single-row statements: MySQL returns an extra information string containing several counts. The counts in each field of this string will vary per INSERT statement. They have the following meanings:

- Records indicates the number of records inserted.
- Duplicates indicates how many records were ignored because they contained duplicate unique key values. This value can be nonzero if the statement includes the IGNORE keyword. The action of this keyword is described in section 7.1.4, "Handling Duplicate Key Values."

- Warnings indicates the number of problems found in the data values. These can occur if values are converted. For example, the warning count is incremented if an empty string is converted to 0 before being stored in a numeric column.

A multiple-row INSERT statement is logically equivalent to a set of individual single-row statements. However, the multiple-row statement is more efficient because the server can process all the rows at once rather than as separate operations. When you have many records to add, multiple-row statements provide better performance and reduce the load on the server. On the other hand, such statements are more likely to reach the maximum size of the communication buffer used to transmit information to the server. (This size is controlled by the max_allowed_packet variable, which has a default value of 1MB.)

MySQL treats single-row and multiple-row INSERT statements somewhat differently for purposes of error-handling. These differences are described in section 4.10.6, "Automatic Type Conversion and Value Clipping."

7.1.2 The REPLACE Statement

If a table contains a unique-valued index and you attempt to insert a record containing a key value that already exists in the index, a duplicate-key violation occurs and the row is not inserted. What if you want the new record to take priority over the existing one? You could remove the existing record with DELETE and then use INSERT to add the new record. However, MySQL provides REPLACE as an alternative that is easier to use and is more efficient because it performs both actions with a single statement. REPLACE is like INSERT except that it deletes old records as necessary when a duplicate unique key value is present in a new record. Suppose that you're inserting a record into the people table, which has id as a PRIMARY KEY:

- If the new record doesn't duplicate an existing id value, MySQL just inserts it.
- If the new record does duplicate an existing id value, MySQL deletes the old records first before inserting the new one.

An advantage of using REPLACE instead of an equivalent DELETE (if needed) and INSERT is that REPLACE is performed as a single atomic operation. There's no need to do any explicit table locking as there might be were you to issue separate DELETE and INSERT statements.

For a comparison of REPLACE with UPDATE, see section 7.2, "The UPDATE Statement."

The action of REPLACE in replacing rows with duplicate keys depends on the table having a unique-valued index:

- In the absence of any such indexes, REPLACE is equivalent to INSERT because no duplicates will ever be detected.
- Even in the presence of a unique-valued index, if an indexed column allows NULL values, it allows multiple NULL values. A new record with a NULL value in that column does not cause a duplicate-key violation and no replacement occurs.

REPLACE returns an information string indicating how many rows it affected. If the count is one, the row was inserted without replacing an existing row. If the count is two, a row was deleted before the new row was inserted. If the count is greater than two, it means the table has multiple unique-valued indexes and the new record matched key values in multiple rows, resulting in multiple duplicate-key violations. This causes multiple rows to be deleted, a situation that's described in more detail later in this section.

REPLACE statement syntax is similar to that for INSERT. The following are each valid forms of REPLACE. They're analogous to examples shown earlier in the chapter for INSERT:

- A single-record REPLACE with separate column and value lists:

```
REPLACE INTO people (id,name,age) VALUES(12,'William',25);
```

- A multiple-record REPLACE that inserts several rows:

```
REPLACE INTO people (id,name,age)
VALUES(12,'William',25),(13,'Bart',15),(14,'Mary',12);
```

  The rows-affected count for a multiple-row REPLACE often is greater than two because the statement may insert (and delete) several records in a single operation.

- A single-record REPLACE with a SET clause that lists column assignments:

```
REPLACE INTO people SET id = 12, name = 'William', age = 25;
```

If a table contains multiple unique-valued indexes, a new record added with REPLACE might cause duplicate-key violations for multiple existing records. In this case, REPLACE replaces each of those records. The following table has three columns, each of which has a UNIQUE index:

```
CREATE TABLE multikey
(
    i INT NOT NULL UNIQUE,
    j INT NOT NULL UNIQUE,
    k INT NOT NULL UNIQUE
);
```

Suppose that the table has these contents:

```
mysql> SELECT * FROM multikey;
+---+---+---+
| i | j | k |
+---+---+---+
| 1 | 1 | 1 |
| 2 | 2 | 2 |
| 3 | 3 | 3 |
| 4 | 4 | 4 |
+---+---+---+
```

Using REPLACE to add a record that duplicates a row in each column causes several records to be replaced with the new row:

```
mysql> REPLACE INTO multikey (i,j,k) VALUES(1,2,3);
Query OK, 4 rows affected (0.00 sec)
mysql> SELECT * FROM multikey;
+---+---+---+
| i | j | k |
+---+---+---+
| 1 | 2 | 3 |
| 4 | 4 | 4 |
+---+---+---+
```

The REPLACE statement reports a row count of four because it deletes three records and inserts one.

7.1.3 Handling Illegal Values

If you insert an invalid value into a row, MySQL normally attempts to convert it to the closest valid value, rather than generating an error:

- A numeric value that's out of range for the column type is clipped to the nearest value that's in range. For example, TINYINT has a range from –128 to 127. If you attempt to insert –1000 and 1000 into a TINYINT column, MySQL stores them as –128 and 127. A similar conversion is applied to temporal values: Out-of-range values are converted to the nearest value that's in range.

- String values that are too long are truncated to fit in the column. If you attempt to store 'Goodbye' into a CHAR(4) column, MySQL stores it as 'Good'.

- Values that are completely invalid are converted to the default value for the column type: 0 for numeric columns, the empty string for string columns, and the "zero" temporal value for temporal columns.

- For a single-row INSERT statement, an attempt to insert NULL into a NOT NULL column results in an error. For a multiple-row INSERT, MySQL treats NULL like any other invalid value and converts it to the default value for the column type. In addition, the warning count is incremented.

See section 4.10.6, "Automatic Type Conversion and Value Clipping," for additional discussion about data value conversion.

7.1.4 Handling Duplicate Key Values

If a table has a unique-valued index, it might not be possible to use INSERT to add a given record to the table. This happens when the new record contains a key value for the index that's already present in the table. Suppose that every person in the people table has a unique value in the `id` column. If an existing record has an `id` value of 347 and you attempt to insert a new record that also has an `id` of 347, it duplicates an existing key value. MySQL provides three ways to deal with duplicate values in a unique-valued index when adding new records to a table:

- With `INSERT`, if you don't indicate explicitly how to handle a duplicate, MySQL aborts the statement with an error and discards the new record. This is the default behavior. (For multiple-record `INSERT` statements, treatment of records inserted before a record that causes a duplicate-key violation is dependent on the storage engine. For MyISAM, the records are inserted. For InnoDB, the entire statement fails and no records are inserted.)

- With `INSERT`, you can tell MySQL to ignore the new record without producing an error. To do this, modify the statement so that it begins with `INSERT IGNORE` rather than with `INSERT`. If the record does not duplicate a unique key value, MySQL inserts it as usual. If the record does contain a duplicate key, MySQL ignores it. Clients that terminate on statement errors will abort with `INSERT` but not with `INSERT IGNORE`.

- With `REPLACE`, MySQL deletes the old record and inserts the new one.

These three behaviors also apply in another context: The `LOAD DATA INFILE` statement performs bulk insert operations and supports `IGNORE` and `REPLACE` modifiers to control how to handle records with duplicate key values. See Chapter 9, "Importing and Exporting Data."

Note that for a unique-valued index that can contain `NULL` values, inserting `NULL` into an indexed column that already contains `NULL` doesn't cause a duplicate-key violation. This is because such an index can contain multiple `NULL` values.

7.2 The UPDATE Statement

The `UPDATE` statement modifies the contents of existing records. To use it, name the table you want to update, provide a `SET` clause that lists one or more column value assignments, and optionally specify a `WHERE` clause that identifies which records to update:

```
UPDATE table_name SET column_name1 = value1, column_name2 = value2, ...
WHERE ... ;
```

For example, to set the age column to 30 for the `people` table record that has an `id` value of 12, use this statement:

```
UPDATE people SET age = 30 WHERE id = 12;
```

To update multiple columns, separate the column value assignments in the `SET` clause by commas:

```
UPDATE people SET age = 30, name = 'Wilhelm' WHERE id = 12;
```

The WHERE clause specifies the conditions that records must satisfy to be selected for updating. If you omit the WHERE clause, MySQL updates every row in the table.

The effects of column assignments made by an UPDATE are subject to column type constraints, just as they are for an INSERT or REPLACE. If you attempt to update a column to a value that doesn't match the column definition, MySQL converts the value. Values that lie outside the range of a numeric column are converted to the nearest in-range value. String values that are too long for a string column are truncated to fit. Updating a NOT NULL column to NULL sets it to the default value for the column type: 0 for numeric columns, the empty string for string columns, and the "zero" temporal value for temporal columns.

It's possible for an UPDATE statement to have no effect. This can occur under the following conditions:

- When the statement matches no records for updating. This always occurs if the table is empty, of course. It might also occur if no records match the conditions specified in the WHERE clause.
- When the statement does not actually change any column values. For example, if you set a date-valued column to '2000-01-01' and the column already has that date as its value, MySQL ignores the assignment.

UPDATE reports a rows-affected count to indicate how many rows actually were changed. This count doesn't include rows that were selected for updating but for which the update didn't change any columns from their current values. The second of the following statements produces a row count of zero because it doesn't actually change any values:

```
mysql> UPDATE people SET age = age + 1 WHERE id = 12;
Query OK, 1 row affected (0.02 sec)
mysql> UPDATE people SET age = age WHERE id = 12;
Query OK, 0 rows affected (0.00 sec)
```

Note that if a table contains a TIMESTAMP column, that column is updated automatically only if another column changes value. An UPDATE that sets columns to their current values does not change the TIMESTAMP. If you need the TIMESTAMP to be updated for every UPDATE, you can set it explicitly to the value of the NOW() function.

Some clients or APIs enable you to ask MySQL to return a rows-matched count rather than a rows-affected count. This causes the row count to include all rows selected for updating, even if their columns weren't changed from their present values. The C API provides an option for selecting the type of count you want. The MySQL Connector/J Java driver tells MySQL to operate in rows-matched mode by default because that behavior is mandated by the JDBC specification.

UPDATE is similar to REPLACE in some respects, but the two aren't equivalent:

- UPDATE does nothing if there's no existing record containing the specified key values in the table. REPLACE doesn't require an existing record with the key values and adds one if none exists.

- UPDATE can be used to change some columns in an existing record while leaving others unchanged. REPLACE entirely discards the existing record. To achieve the effect of leaving some columns unchanged with REPLACE, the new record must specify the same values in those columns that the existing record has.

7.2.1 Preventing Dangerous UPDATE Statements

As mentioned earlier, an UPDATE statement that includes no WHERE clause updates every row in the table. Normally, this isn't what you want. It's much more common to update only a specific record or small set of records. An UPDATE with no WHERE is likely to be accidental, and the results can be catastrophic.

It's possible to prevent UPDATE statements from executing unless the records to be updated are identified by key values or a LIMIT clause is present. This might be helpful in preventing accidental overly broad table updates. The mysql client supports this feature if you invoke it with the --safe-updates option. See section 3.2.8, "Using the --safe-updates Option," for more information.

7.2.2 Using UPDATE with ORDER BY and LIMIT

UPDATE by default makes no guarantee about the order in which rows are updated. This can sometimes result in problems. Suppose that the people table contains two rows, where id is a PRIMARY KEY:

```
mysql> SELECT * FROM people;
+----+--------+------+
| id | name   | age  |
+----+--------+------+
|  2 | Victor |   21 |
|  3 | Susan  |   15 |
+----+--------+------+
```

If you want to renumber the id values to begin at 1, you might issue this UPDATE statement:

```
UPDATE people SET id = id - 1;
```

The statement succeeds if it updates id values first by setting 2 to 1 and then 3 to 2. However, it fails if it first tries to set 3 to 2. That would result in two records having an id value of 2, so a duplicate-key violation occurs. To solve this problem, add an ORDER BY clause to cause the row updates to occur in a particular order:

```
UPDATE people SET id = id - 1 ORDER BY id;
```

UPDATE also allows a LIMIT clause, which places a limit on the number of records updated. For example, if you have two identical people records with a name value of 'Nicolas' and you want to change just one of them to 'Nick', use this statement:

```
UPDATE people SET name = 'Nick' WHERE name = 'Nicolas' LIMIT 1;
```

ORDER BY and LIMIT may be used together in the same UPDATE statement.

7.2.3 Multiple-Table UPDATE Statements

UPDATE supports a multiple-table syntax that enables you to update a table using the contents of another table. This syntax also allows multiple tables to be updated simultaneously. The syntax has much in common with that used for writing multiple-table SELECT statements, so it's discussed in Chapter 8, "Joins."

7.3 The DELETE and TRUNCATE TABLE Statements

To remove records from tables, use a DELETE statement or a TRUNCATE TABLE statement. The DELETE statement allows a WHERE clause that identifies which records to remove, whereas TRUNCATE TABLE always removes all records. DELETE therefore can be more precise in its effect.

To empty a table entirely by deleting all its records, you can use either of the following statements:

```
DELETE FROM table_name;
TRUNCATE TABLE table_name;
```

The word TABLE in TRUNCATE TABLE is optional.

To remove only specific records in a table, TRUNCATE TABLE cannot be used. You must issue a DELETE statement that includes a WHERE clause that identifies which records to remove:

```
DELETE FROM table_name WHERE ...;
```

When you omit the WHERE clause from a DELETE statement, it's logically equivalent to a TRUNCATE TABLE statement in its effect, but there is an operational difference: If you need to know how many records were deleted, DELETE returns a true row count, but TRUNCATE TABLE might return 0.

If a table contains an AUTO_INCREMENT column, emptying it completely with either TRUNCATE TABLE or a DELETE that includes no WHERE clause might have the side effect of resetting the sequence. In this case, the next record inserted into the table is assigned an AUTO_INCREMENT value of 1. If this side effect is undesirable, empty the table using a WHERE clause that always evaluates to true:

```
DELETE FROM table_name WHERE 1;
```

In this statement, because the WHERE clause is present, MySQL evaluates it for each row. WHERE 1 is always true, so the effect of the statement is to produce a row-by-row table-emptying operation. Note that although this form of DELETE avoids the side effect of resetting the AUTO_INCREMENT sequence when performing a complete-table deletion, the cost is that the statement will execute much more slowly than a DELETE with no WHERE.

The following comparison summarizes the differences between DELETE and TRUNCATE TABLE:

DELETE:

- Can delete specific rows from a table, if a WHERE clause is included
- Usually executes more slowly
- Returns a true row count indicating the number of records deleted

TRUNCATE TABLE:

- Cannot delete just certain rows from a table; always completely empties it
- Usually executes more quickly
- Might return a row count of zero rather than the actual number of records deleted

7.3.1 Using DELETE with ORDER BY and LIMIT

DELETE supports ORDER BY and LIMIT clauses, which provides finer control over the way records are deleted. For example, LIMIT can be useful if you want to remove only some instances of a given set of records. Suppose that the people table contains five records where the name column equals 'Emily'. If you want only one such record, use the following statement to remove four of the duplicated records:

```
DELETE FROM people WHERE name = 'Emily' LIMIT 4;
```

Normally, MySQL makes no guarantees about which four of the five records selected by the WHERE clause it will delete. An ORDER BY clause in conjunction with LIMIT provides better control. For example, to delete four of the records containing 'Emily' but leave the one with the lowest id value, use ORDER BY and LIMIT together as follows:

```
DELETE FROM people WHERE name = 'Emily' ORDER BY id DESC LIMIT 4;
```

7.3.2 Multiple-Table DELETE Statements

DELETE supports a multiple-table syntax that enables you to delete records from a table based on the contents of another table. This syntax also allows records to be deleted from multiple tables simultaneously. The syntax has much in common with that used for writing multiple-table SELECT statements, so it's discussed in Chapter 8, "Joins."

7.4 Exercises

Question 1:

MySQL provides three ways to handle new rows that would cause duplicate-key errors for unique index values in a table. Specifically, (a) with the standard form of INSERT, the new rows can be rejected; (b) with INSERT IGNORE, you can force MySQL to discard the new rows that duplicate existing unique-key values; and (c) with the REPLACE statement, you can force MySQL to delete the existing rows before inserting the new rows. For each of these three options, give an example of the effect of its use on the following table:

```
mysql> DESCRIBE twounique; SELECT * FROM twounique;
+-------+--------------------+------+-----+---------+-------+
| Field | Type               | Null | Key | Default | Extra |
+-------+--------------------+------+-----+---------+-------+
| id1   | tinyint(3) unsigned |      | PRI | 0       |       |
| id2   | tinyint(3) unsigned |      | UNI | 0       |       |
+-------+--------------------+------+-----+---------+-------+

+-----+-----+
| id1 | id2 |
+-----+-----+
|   1 |   2 |
+-----+-----+
```

Question 2:

Consider this table:

```
mysql> DESCRIBE twounique; SELECT * FROM twounique;
+-------+--------------------+------+-----+---------+-------+
| Field | Type               | Null | Key | Default | Extra |
+-------+--------------------+------+-----+---------+-------+
| id1   | tinyint(3) unsigned |      | PRI | 0       |       |
| id2   | tinyint(3) unsigned |      | UNI | 0       |       |
+-------+--------------------+------+-----+---------+-------+

+-----+-----+
| id1 | id2 |
+-----+-----+
|   1 |   2 |
|   3 |   4 |
|   5 |   6 |
+-----+-----+
```

What are the contents of table twounique after executing each of the following SQL statements?

```
mysql> REPLACE INTO twounique VALUES (2,2);
```

```
mysql> REPLACE INTO twounique VALUES (2,6);
```

Question 3:

How do you add multiple records to a table with a single INSERT statement?

Question 4:

INSERT supports an IGNORE modifier, but REPLACE does not. Why is that?

Question 5:

To completely empty a table, what statement or statements can you use?

Question 6:

To partially empty a table, what statement or statements can you use?

Question 7:

What's a difference in the way that MySQL handles errors for single-row and multiple-row INSERT statements when inserting NULL into a NOT NULL column?

Question 8:

What are the reasons why an UPDATE statement might have no effect (that is, not change any values)?

Question 9:

Why is the number of affected rows in the following UPDATE statement 0, although the number of rows matched by the WHERE clause is 5? Why is the number of matched rows 5 and not rather 10?

```
mysql> SELECT pid, grade FROM personnel;
+-----+-------+
| pid | grade |
+-----+-------+
|   1 |     1 |
|   2 |     2 |
|   3 |  NULL |
|   4 |  NULL |
|   5 |  NULL |
|   6 |     1 |
|   7 |     1 |
|   8 |     1 |
|   9 |  NULL |
|  10 |  NULL |
|  11 |  NULL |
|  12 |     1 |
|  13 |  NULL |
+-----+-------+
13 rows in set
mysql> UPDATE personnel SET grade = 1 WHERE grade != 2;
```

```
Query OK, 0 rows affected (0.00 sec)
Rows matched: 5  Changed: 0  Warnings: 0
```

Question 10:

Is the following statement true or false?

To prevent accidental UPDATE statements that would change all rows in a table, you can start the mysql program with the --safe-updates option.

Question 11:

Is the following statement true or false?

To prevent accidental UPDATE statements that would change all rows in a table, you can start the mysql program with the --i-am-a-dummy option.

Question 12:

Is the following statement true or false?

To prevent accidental UPDATE statements that would change all rows in a table, you can start the mysql program with the --safe-updates-and-deletes option.

Question 13:

Is the following statement true or false?

To prevent accidental UPDATE statements that would change all rows in a table, you can start any client program with the --safe-updates option.

Question 14:

Is the following statement true or false?

To prevent accidental UPDATE statements that would change all rows in a table, you can start any client program with the --safe-changes option.

Question 15:

Is the following statement true or false?

To prevent accidental UPDATE statements that would change all rows in a table, you can start the mysql command-line tool with the --safe-updates option.

Question 16:

Is the following statement true or false?

To prevent accidental UPDATE statements that would change all rows in a table, you can start the mysql command-line tool with the --i-am-a-dummy option.

Question 17:

Consider the following listing of a table named personnel that has a primary key on the pid column:

```
mysql> SELECT * FROM personnel;
+-----+------+-------+
| pid | unit | grade |
+-----+------+-------+
|   1 |  42  |     1 |
|   2 |  42  |     2 |
|   3 |  42  | NULL  |
|   4 |  42  | NULL  |
|   5 |  42  | NULL  |
|   6 |  23  |     1 |
|   7 |  23  |     1 |
|   8 |  23  |     1 |
|   9 |  23  | NULL  |
|  10 |  42  | NULL  |
|  11 |  23  | NULL  |
|  12 |  23  |     1 |
|  13 |  42  | NULL  |
+-----+------+-------+
```

What single UPDATE statement would you use to set all rows with no grade to 3?

Question 18:

Refer to the structure and contents shown for the personnel table in the previous question. What REPLACE statement would you use to set the grade column to 4 and the unit column to 45, for all rows where the pid column has the value 10?

Question 19:

The table personnel has the following structure and data:

```
mysql> DESCRIBE personnel; SELECT * FROM personnel;
+-------+--------------------+------+-----+---------+----------------+
| Field | Type               | Null | Key | Default | Extra          |
+-------+--------------------+------+-----+---------+----------------+
| pid   | smallint(5) unsigned |    | PRI | NULL    | auto_increment |
| unit  | tinyint(3) unsigned | YES |     | NULL    |                |
| grade | tinyint(3) unsigned | YES |     | NULL    |                |
+-------+--------------------+------+-----+---------+----------------+

+-----+------+-------+
| pid | unit | grade |
+-----+------+-------+
|   1 |  42  |     1 |
|   2 |  42  |     2 |
|   3 |  42  |     3 |
|   4 |  42  |     3 |
|   5 |  42  |     3 |
|   6 |  23  |     1 |
|   7 |  23  |     1 |
```

```
|   8 |  23 |     1 |
|   9 |  23 |     3 |
|  10 |  42 |     3 |
|  11 |  23 |     3 |
|  12 |  23 |     1 |
|  13 |  42 |     3 |
+-----+------+-------+
```

What UPDATE statement would you use to multiply the grade column values by 1,000? What values would the statement produce?

Question 20:

In the table personnel, the unit numbers were interchanged for some reason. Unit 23 is supposed to be 42, and 42 is supposed to be 23. What statement would you use to resolve this problem? Currently the table looks like this:

```
mysql> SELECT * FROM personnel;
+-----+------+-------+
| pid | unit | grade |
+-----+------+-------+
|   1 |  42 |   255 |
|   2 |  42 |   255 |
|   3 |  42 |   255 |
|   4 |  42 |   255 |
|   5 |  42 |   255 |
|   6 |  23 |   255 |
|   7 |  23 |   255 |
|   8 |  23 |   255 |
|   9 |  23 |   255 |
|  10 |  42 |   255 |
|  11 |  23 |   255 |
|  12 |  23 |   255 |
|  13 |  42 |   255 |
+-----+------+-------+
```

Question 21:

The table petnames contains the following data:

```
mysql> SELECT * FROM petnames;
+--------+
| name   |
+--------+
| Lucy   |
| Macie  |
| Myra   |
| Cheep  |
| Lucy   |
```

```
| Myra   |
| Cheep  |
| Macie  |
| Pablo  |
| Stefan |
+--------+
```

Assume that you issue the following statement:

```
mysql> UPDATE petnames SET name = CONCAT(name, 1) ORDER BY name LIMIT 1;
```

What will the table's contents be after the UPDATE?

Question 22:

Will the following statement delete all rows from the table `mytable`?

```
TRUNCATE TABLE mytable;
```

Question 23:

Will the following statement delete all rows from the table `mytable`?

```
DELETE FROM mytable;
```

Answers to Exercises

Answer 1:

There are three ways to handle records that would cause duplicate-key errors for unique indexes:

a. Use the IGNORE option in INSERT. IGNORE silently ignores the attempt to insert a duplicate unique key value:

```
mysql> INSERT IGNORE INTO twounique VALUES (1,42)
    -> /* Note the number of affected rows */;
Query OK, 0 rows affected
mysql> SELECT * FROM twounique;
+-----+-----+
| id1 | id2 |
+-----+-----+
|   1 |   2 |
+-----+-----+
```

b. Use REPLACE instead of INSERT. REPLACE replaces any row that would otherwise duplicate a unique key value. The existing row will first be deleted, and then the new row will be inserted (with the result that the otherwise duplicated key value remains the same):

```
mysql> REPLACE INTO twounique VALUES (1,42)
    -> /* Note the number of affected rows */;
Query OK, 2 rows affected
mysql> SELECT * FROM twounique;
+-----+-----+
| id1 | id2 |
+-----+-----+
|   1 |  42 |
+-----+-----+
```

c. Use an INSERT without the IGNORE option. An error occurs and the new record is not inserted:

```
mysql> INSERT INTO twounique VALUES (1,42);
ERROR 1062: Duplicate entry '1' for key 1
```

Answer 2:

The REPLACE statements change the table data as follows:

a. This statement replaces the first record rather than duplicating the existing unique value of 2 in the id2 column:

```
mysql> REPLACE INTO twounique VALUES (2,2);
Query OK, 2 rows affected (0.00 sec)
mysql> SELECT * FROM twounique;
+-----+-----+
| id1 | id2 |
+-----+-----+
|   2 |   2 |
|   3 |   4 |
|   5 |   6 |
+-----+-----+
```

Because the original record is deleted before the new row is inserted, the server reports 2 rows affected.

b. This statement replaces the first record (containing the value set 2,2 prior to the change), rather than duplicating the value in the id1 column:

```
mysql> REPLACE INTO twounique VALUES (2,6);
Query OK, 3 rows affected (0.00 sec)
mysql> SELECT * FROM twounique;
+-----+-----+
| id1 | id2 |
+-----+-----+
|   3 |   4 |
|   2 |   6 |
+-----+-----+
```

The result is that the first record then contains the value set 2,6. The statement also replaces the third record (containing the value set 5,6 prior to the change), rather than duplicating the value in the id2 column. The result is that the third record *also* contains the value set 2,6. Because this result is identical to the value set of the first record, the first record is then deleted. The server optimizes the REPLACE statement to avoid doing more work than necessary. Thus, the first record is deleted but not reinserted, and then the third record is deleted and then reinserted. For that reason, the server reports 3 rows affected.

Answer 3:

You can add multiple records with a single INSERT statement using multiple VALUES lists (this is an ANSI SQL-99 feature). The syntax is as follows:

```
INSERT INTO tbl [(col1, col2, ...)]
VALUES (value1, value2, ...), (value1, value2, ...), ...
```

Answer 4:

The point of REPLACE is to replace old records, not ignore new ones. If you specify the keyword IGNORE in an INSERT with multiple rows, any rows that duplicate an existing PRIMARY or UNIQUE key in the table are ignored, which means they aren't inserted. If you don't specify IGNORE, the insert is aborted if there is any row that duplicates an existing unique key value. With REPLACE, you explicitly want to replace records that would violate a PRIMARY or UNIQUE key constraint, so ignoring duplicates would make no sense.

Answer 5:

TRUNCATE TABLE, or DELETE with no WHERE clause, or DELETE with a WHERE clause that's always true. Assume that you have the following table:

```
mysql> SELECT * FROM tbl1;
+----+----------+
| id | sometext |
+----+----------+
|  1 | boo      |
|  2 | bar      |
|  3 | booboo   |
|  4 | barbar   |
+----+----------+
```

You could empty this table as follows:

- Use TRUNCATE TABLE:

  ```
  TRUNCATE TABLE tbl1;
  ```

- Use DELETE with no WHERE clause:

  ```
  DELETE FROM tbl1;
  ```

This will not work when mysql has been started with the ---safe-updates option, though.

- Use DELETE with a WHERE clause that's always true. The following statements use expressions that are true for every record in the table tbl1:

```
DELETE FROM tbl1 WHERE id < 5;
DELETE FROM tbl1 WHERE 1 = 1;
```

Answer 6:

Use a DELETE statement that includes a WHERE clause that selects only the records to be deleted. Assume that you have the following table:

```
mysql> SELECT * FROM tbl1;
+----+----------+
| id | sometext |
+----+----------+
|  1 | boo      |
|  2 | bar      |
|  3 | booboo   |
|  4 | barbar   |
+----+----------+
```

To delete records with id values of 2 and 3, statements that accomplish that goal include the following:

```
mysql> DELETE FROM tbl1 WHERE id > 1 AND id < 4;
mysql> DELETE FROM tbl1 WHERE id BETWEEN 2 AND 3;
```

Answer 7:

Attempting to insert NULL into a column that must not contain NULL is handled differently with single-row and multiple-row inserts:

- With single-row inserts, this attempt results in an error and the row isn't inserted.
- With multiple-row inserts, this attempt results in a warning, but the row is inserted. The NULL value is converted to the default value for the column type. This is 0 for numbers, ' ' (the empty string) for strings, and the "zero" value for temporal columns.

Answer 8:

An UPDATE statement changes no values if any of the following is true:

a. The table has no rows.

b. No rows match the conditions specified in the WHERE clause of the statement.

c. The updated columns are set to their current values.

Answer 9:

The number of affected rows is 0 because the WHERE clause matches only the rows where the grade column values are set to 1 already. Thus, the values are not changed. The number of matched rows is 5 rather than 10 because for grade values of NULL, the condition grade != 2 is not true (the != operator is never true for NULL values).

Answer 10:

True. To prevent accidental UPDATE (and DELETE) statements that don't contain a WHERE clause that uses a key, you can start the mysql command-line tool with the --safe-updates option:

```
C:\mysql\bin>mysql --safe-updates menagerie
Welcome to the MySQL monitor. Commands end with ; or \g.
mysql> DELETE FROM personnel;
ERROR 1175: You are using safe update mode and you tried to
update a table without a WHERE that uses a KEY column
```

Answer 11:

True. To prevent accidental UPDATE (and DELETE) statements that don't use a WHERE clause that uses a key, you can start the mysql command-line tool with the --i-am-a-dummy option, which is synonymous with the --safe-updates option:

```
C:\mysql\bin>mysql --i-am-a-dummy menagerie
Welcome to the MySQL monitor. Commands end with ; or \g.
mysql> UPDATE personnel SET grade = 42;
ERROR 1175: You are using safe update mode and you tried to
update a table without a WHERE that uses a KEY column
```

Answer 12:

False. There is no such option as --safe-updates-and-deletes to the mysql command-line tool. (In fact, there's no such option to any MySQL program.)

Answer 13:

False. The --safe-updates option is supported only by the mysql client program.

Answer 14:

False. There is no such option as --safe-changes to the mysql command-line tool. (In fact, there's no such option to any MySQL program.)

Answer 15:

True. To prevent accidental UPDATE (and DELETE) statements that don't use a WHERE clause that uses a key, you can start the mysql command-line tool with either the --safe-updates or the --i-am-a-dummy option (they're synonymous).

Answer 16:

True. To prevent accidental UPDATE (and DELETE) statements that don't use a WHERE clause that uses a key, you can start the mysql command-line tool with either the --safe-updates or the --i-am-a-dummy option (they're synonymous).

Answer 17:

The rows with no grade are those containing NULL in the grade column. The following UPDATE statement sets the grade column to 3 in all rows where grade is NULL:

```
mysql> UPDATE personnel SET grade = 3 WHERE grade IS NULL;
Query OK, 7 rows affected
Rows matched: 7  Changed: 7  Warnings: 0
```

Answer 18:

To make the required changes, you would issue this REPLACE:

```
mysql> REPLACE INTO personnel VALUES (10,45,4);
Query OK, 2 rows affected
mysql> SELECT * FROM personnel WHERE pid=10;
+-----+------+-------+
| pid | unit | grade |
+-----+------+-------+
|  10 |  45  |    4  |
+-----+------+-------+
```

Answer 19:

The following statement multiplies values in the grade column by 1,000:

```
mysql> UPDATE personnel SET grade = grade * 1000;
```

In this case, however, the statement would not produce the desired result. This is because the grade column has a datatype of TINYINT UNSIGNED and thus has a maximum value of 255. The result of the UPDATE statement would be as follows:

```
mysql> SELECT grade FROM personnel;
+-------+
| grade |
+-------+
|   255 |
|   255 |
|   255 |
|   255 |
|   255 |
|   255 |
|   255 |
|   255 |
```

```
|   255 |
|   255 |
|   255 |
|   255 |
|   255 |
+-------+
```

Answer 20:

To swap unit numbers 23 and 42, you would issue this statement:

```
mysql> UPDATE personnel
    ->   SET unit = IF(unit=23, 42, 23)
    -> ;
Query OK, 13 rows affected
Rows matched: 13   Changed: 13   Warnings: 0
mysql> SELECT * FROM personnel;
+-----+------+-------+
| pid | unit | grade |
+-----+------+-------+
|   1 |   23 |   255 |
|   2 |   23 |   255 |
|   3 |   23 |   255 |
|   4 |   23 |   255 |
|   5 |   23 |   255 |
|   6 |   42 |   255 |
|   7 |   42 |   255 |
|   8 |   42 |   255 |
|   9 |   42 |   255 |
|  10 |   23 |   255 |
|  11 |   42 |   255 |
|  12 |   42 |   255 |
|  13 |   23 |   255 |
+-----+------+-------+
```

Answer 21:

The UPDATE changes the row that is first when they're sorted by name. The first name is Cheep. It occurs twice, but LIMIT constrains the change to include just one of the rows. The resulting table contents are as follows:

```
mysql> SELECT * FROM petnames;
+--------+
| name   |
+--------+
| Lucy   |
| Macie  |
| Myra   |
```

```
| Cheep1 |
| Lucy   |
| Myra   |
| Cheep  |
| Macie  |
| Pablo  |
| Stefan |
+--------+
```

Answer 22:

Yes, TRUNCATE TABLE mytable will delete all records. The number of affected rows this statement returns will not necessarily be exact.

Answer 23:

Yes, DELETE FROM mytable will delete all records. It will also return the exact number of deleted records.

8

Joins

This chapter covers the following exam topics:

- Writing inner joins using the comma (',') operator and INNER JOIN
- Writing outer joins using LEFT JOIN and RIGHT JOIN
- Converting subqueries to inner and outer joins
- Resolving name clashes using qualifiers and aliases
- Multiple-table UPDATE and DELETE statements

Questions on the material in this chapter make up approximately 15% of the exam.

The SELECT queries shown thus far in this study guide retrieve information from a single table at a time. However, not all questions can be answered using just one table. When it's necessary to draw on information that is stored in multiple tables, use a join—a SELECT operation that produces a result by combining (joining) information in one table with information in another.

A join between tables is an extension of a single-table SELECT statement, but involves the following additional complexities:

- The FROM clause names all the tables needed to produce the query result, not just one table. The examples in this chapter focus on two-table joins, although in MySQL a join can be extended up to 31 tables as necessary.
- A join that matches records in one table with records in another must specify how to match up the records. These conditions often are given in the WHERE clause, but the particular syntax depends on the type of join.
- The list of columns to display can include columns from any or all of the tables involved in the join.
- If a join refers to a column name that appears in more than one table, the name is ambiguous and you must indicate which table you mean each time you refer to the column.

These complications are addressed in this chapter, which covers the following join-related topics:

- Writing inner joins, which find matches between tables. Inner joins are written using either the comma operator or the INNER JOIN keywords.

- Writing outer joins, which can find matches between tables, but also can identify mismatches (rows in one table not matched by any rows in the other). Outer joins include left and right joins, written using the LEFT JOIN and RIGHT JOIN keywords.

- Converting SELECT statements that involve subqueries (nested queries) to equivalent statements that use joins instead. MySQL 4.1 supports subqueries, but MySQL 4.0 does not, so this technique is useful for converting subqueries to run under 4.0.

- Using qualifiers and aliases to resolve ambiguity between identifiers that have the same name. Some queries involve tables or columns that have identical names (for example, if two tables each have an id column). Under these circumstances, it's necessary to provide the appropriate database or table name to specify the query more precisely. Aliasing can also be useful in some cases to resolve ambiguities.

- Multiple-table UPDATE and DELETE statements. These involve some of the same join concepts as multiple-table SELECT statements.

The material here builds directly on the single-table SELECT concepts described earlier in this guide, and it's assumed that you're familiar with those concepts.

The examples in this chapter are based primarily on the tables in the world database. These tables contain information that can be combined using joins to answer questions that cannot be answered using a single table. For example, you might ask, "What are the names of the countries where people speak Swedish?" The CountryLanguage table lists languages per country, but it contains three-letter country codes, not full names. The Country table lists three-letter codes and full names, so you can use the codes to match up records in the tables and associate a country name with each language.

8.1 Writing Inner Joins

A join that identifies combinations of rows from two tables is called an inner join. Inner joins may be written using two different syntaxes. One syntax lists the tables to be joined separated by a comma. The other uses the INNER JOIN keywords.

8.1.1 Writing Inner Joins with the Comma Operator

A simple question you might ask about the information in the world database is, "What languages are spoken in each country?" That question has a trivial answer if you don't mind listing countries by code. Just select the information from the CountryLanguage table. Two of its columns list three-letter country codes and language names:

```
mysql> SELECT CountryCode, Language FROM CountryLanguage;
+-------------+------------------+
| CountryCode | Language         |
+-------------+------------------+
| ABW         | Dutch            |
| ABW         | English          |
| ABW         | Papiamento       |
| ABW         | Spanish          |
| AFG         | Balochi          |
| AFG         | Dari             |
| AFG         | Pashto           |
| AFG         | Turkmenian       |
| AFG         | Uzbek            |
| AGO         | Ambo             |
| AGO         | Chokwe           |
| AGO         | Kongo            |
| AGO         | Luchazi          |
| AGO         | Luimbe-nganguela |
| AGO         | Luvale           |
...
```

That result would be more meaningful and easier to understand if it displayed countries identified by full name. However, that cannot be done using just the CountryLanguage table, which contains country codes and not names. Country names are available in the world database, but they're stored in the Country table that contains both the three-letter codes and the names:

```
mysql> SELECT Code, Name FROM Country;
+------+----------------------+
| Code | Name                 |
+------+----------------------+
| AFG  | Afghanistan          |
| NLD  | Netherlands          |
| ANT  | Netherlands Antilles |
| ALB  | Albania              |
| DZA  | Algeria              |
| ASM  | American Samoa       |
| AND  | Andorra              |
| AGO  | Angola               |
| AIA  | Anguilla             |
| ATG  | Antigua and Barbuda  |
| ARE  | United Arab Emirates |
| ARG  | Argentina            |
| ARM  | Armenia              |
| ABW  | Aruba                |
| AUS  | Australia            |
...
```

A query to display languages and full country names can be written as a join that matches the country codes in the `CountryLanguage` table with those in the `Country` table. To do that, modify the `CountryLanguage` query in the following ways:

- Change the `FROM` clause to name both the `CountryLanguage` and `Country` tables. This tells MySQL that it must consult multiple tables to process the query.

- Add a `WHERE` clause that indicates how to match records in the two tables. A join has the potential to generate all combinations of rows from the two tables; the `WHERE` clause tells MySQL which of these combinations you're interested in. To choose the proper matches, use the country code values that are common to the two tables. That is, match `CountryCode` values in the `CountryLanguage` table with `Code` values in the `Country` table.

- Change the output column list to display the `Name` column from the `Country` table rather than the `CountryCode` column from the `CountryLanguage` table.

The query that results from these changes is as follows:

```
mysql> SELECT Name, Language FROM CountryLanguage, Country
    -> WHERE CountryCode = Code;
+---------------------+------------+
| Name                | Language   |
+---------------------+------------+
| Afghanistan         | Balochi    |
| Afghanistan         | Dari       |
| Afghanistan         | Pashto     |
| Afghanistan         | Turkmenian |
| Afghanistan         | Uzbek      |
| Netherlands         | Arabic     |
| Netherlands         | Dutch      |
| Netherlands         | Fries      |
| Netherlands         | Turkish    |
| Netherlands Antilles | Dutch     |
| Netherlands Antilles | English   |
| Netherlands Antilles | Papiamento |
| Albania             | Albaniana  |
| Albania             | Greek      |
| Albania             | Macedonian |
...
```

Essentially what this query does is treat `Country` as a lookup table. For any given country code in the `CountryLanguage` table, the query uses that code to find the corresponding row in the `Country` table and retrieves the country name from that row.

Note several things about this query and the result that it produces:

- For an inner join, the order in which the `FROM` clause names the tables doesn't matter. Either of these `FROM` clauses would work:

```
FROM CountryLanguage, Country
FROM Country, CountryLanguage
```

- The output column list of the join displays one column from each table: Name from Country and Language from CountryLanguage. The list can name any columns that are appropriate for your purposes, from any of the joined tables. Suppose that you want to show both country code and name, as well as the continent in which each country is located. The following query does that by adding two columns to the output column list:

```
mysql> SELECT Code, Name, Continent, Language
    -> FROM CountryLanguage, Country
    -> WHERE CountryCode = Code;
+------+---------------------+---------------+------------+
| Code | Name                | Continent     | Language   |
+------+---------------------+---------------+------------+
| AFG  | Afghanistan         | Asia          | Balochi    |
| AFG  | Afghanistan         | Asia          | Dari       |
| AFG  | Afghanistan         | Asia          | Pashto     |
| AFG  | Afghanistan         | Asia          | Turkmenian |
| AFG  | Afghanistan         | Asia          | Uzbek      |
| NLD  | Netherlands         | Europe        | Arabic     |
| NLD  | Netherlands         | Europe        | Dutch      |
| NLD  | Netherlands         | Europe        | Fries      |
| NLD  | Netherlands         | Europe        | Turkish    |
| ANT  | Netherlands Antilles | North America | Dutch     |
| ANT  | Netherlands Antilles | North America | English   |
| ANT  | Netherlands Antilles | North America | Papiamento |
| ALB  | Albania             | Europe        | Albaniana  |
| ALB  | Albania             | Europe        | Greek      |
| ALB  | Albania             | Europe        | Macedonian |
...
```

Or suppose that you want to display each language together with the percentage of people who speak it. Select the Percentage column from the CountryLanguage table:

```
mysql> SELECT Name, Language, Percentage FROM CountryLanguage, Country
    -> WHERE CountryCode = Code;
+----------------------+----------------+------------+
| Name                 | Language       | Percentage |
+----------------------+----------------+------------+
| Afghanistan          | Pashto         |       52.4 |
| Netherlands          | Dutch          |       95.6 |
| Netherlands Antilles | Papiamento     |       86.2 |
| Albania              | Albaniana      |       97.9 |
| Algeria              | Arabic         |       86.0 |
| American Samoa       | Samoan         |       90.6 |
| Andorra              | Spanish        |       44.6 |
| Angola               | Ovimbundu      |       37.2 |
| Anguilla             | English        |        0.0 |
```

```
| Antigua and Barbuda | Creole English |    95.7 |
| United Arab Emirates | Arabic        |    42.0 |
| Argentina           | Spanish        |    96.8 |
| Armenia             | Armenian       |    93.4 |
| Aruba               | Papiamento     |    76.7 |
| Australia           | English        |    81.2 |
...
```

- As with any other SELECT, the output from a join does not appear in any particular order by default. To sort the results, add an ORDER BY clause. Output from the preceding query would be more easily understood with the rows sorted by country name and language percentage. Then for a country in which multiple languages are spoken, you can see which languages are most prevalent:

```
mysql> SELECT Name, Language, Percentage FROM CountryLanguage, Country
    -> WHERE CountryCode = Code ORDER BY Name, Percentage;
+----------------+------------+------------+
| Name           | Language   | Percentage |
+----------------+------------+------------+
| Afghanistan    | Balochi    |        0.9 |
| Afghanistan    | Turkmenian |        1.9 |
| Afghanistan    | Uzbek      |        8.8 |
| Afghanistan    | Dari       |       32.1 |
| Afghanistan    | Pashto     |       52.4 |
| Albania        | Macedonian |        0.1 |
| Albania        | Greek      |        1.8 |
| Albania        | Albaniana  |       97.9 |
| Algeria        | Berberi    |       14.0 |
| Algeria        | Arabic     |       86.0 |
| American Samoa | English    |        3.1 |
| American Samoa | Tongan     |        3.1 |
| American Samoa | Samoan     |       90.6 |
| Andorra        | French     |        6.2 |
| Andorra        | Portuguese |       10.8 |
...
```

Syntactically, the WHERE clause in a join is optional. However, it's usually necessary in practice to include a WHERE clause to keep the join from producing output far in excess of what you really want to see and to make sure that the output contains only information that's meaningful for the question you're asking.

A join can produce every combination of rows from the two tables, which is in fact what you'll get from an unrestricted join that includes no WHERE clause. This is called a Cartesian product, and the number of rows in the result is the product of the number of rows in the individual tables. For example, the Country and CountryLanguage tables contain approximately 240 and 1,000 rows, respectively, so a Cartesian product between them produces about

240,000 rows. But much of such output is irrelevant because most of the combinations aren't meaningful.

The following query shows what happens if you join records in the CountryLanguage and Country tables without a WHERE clause. The query displays the code from both tables to show that even nonmatching combinations are produced by an unrestricted join:

```
mysql> SELECT Code, Name, CountryCode, Language
    -> FROM CountryLanguage, Country;
+------+-------------+-------------+------------------+
| Code | Name        | CountryCode | Language         |
+------+-------------+-------------+------------------+
| AFG  | Afghanistan | ABW         | Dutch            |
| AFG  | Afghanistan | ABW         | English          |
| AFG  | Afghanistan | ABW         | Papiamento       |
| AFG  | Afghanistan | ABW         | Spanish          |
| AFG  | Afghanistan | AFG         | Balochi          |
| AFG  | Afghanistan | AFG         | Dari             |
| AFG  | Afghanistan | AFG         | Pashto           |
| AFG  | Afghanistan | AFG         | Turkmenian       |
| AFG  | Afghanistan | AFG         | Uzbek            |
| AFG  | Afghanistan | AGO         | Ambo             |
| AFG  | Afghanistan | AGO         | Chokwe           |
| AFG  | Afghanistan | AGO         | Kongo            |
| AFG  | Afghanistan | AGO         | Luchazi          |
| AFG  | Afghanistan | AGO         | Luimbe-nganguela |
| AFG  | Afghanistan | AGO         | Luvale           |
...
```

If you're using the mysql client program and want to guard against the possibility of generating huge result sets due to forgetting a WHERE clause, invoke the program with the --safe-updates option (which, despite its name, also affects output from joins). See section 3.2.8, "Using the --safe-updates Option," for more information.

The WHERE clause for a join specifies how to match records in the joined tables and eliminates noncorresponding combinations of rows from the output. The WHERE clause also can include additional conditions to further restrict the output and answer more specific questions. Here are some examples:

- In which countries is the Swedish language spoken? To answer this, include a condition that identifies the language you want to know about:

```
mysql> SELECT Name, Language FROM CountryLanguage, Country
    -> WHERE CountryCode = Code AND Language = 'Swedish';
+---------+----------+
| Name    | Language |
+---------+----------+
| Norway  | Swedish  |
```

```
| Sweden  | Swedish |
| Finland | Swedish |
| Denmark | Swedish |
+---------+---------+
```

- What languages are spoken in the country of Sweden? This question is the complement of the previous one, and can be answered by using a condition that identifies the country of interest rather than the language:

```
mysql> SELECT Name, Language FROM CountryLanguage, Country
    -> WHERE CountryCode = Code AND Name = 'Sweden';
+--------+--------------------------+
| Name   | Language                 |
+--------+--------------------------+
| Sweden | Arabic                   |
| Sweden | Finnish                  |
| Sweden | Norwegian                |
| Sweden | Southern Slavic Languages |
| Sweden | Spanish                  |
| Sweden | Swedish                  |
+--------+--------------------------+
```

Joins can use any of the constructs allowed for single-table SELECT statements. The following join uses the COUNT() function and a GROUP BY clause to summarize the number of languages spoken per country, and a HAVING clause to restrict the output to include only those countries where more than 10 languages are spoken:

```
mysql> SELECT COUNT(*), Name
    -> FROM CountryLanguage, Country
    -> WHERE CountryCode = Code
    -> GROUP BY Name
    -> HAVING COUNT(*) > 10;
+----------+--------------------+
| COUNT(*) | Name               |
+----------+--------------------+
|       12 | Canada             |
|       12 | China              |
|       12 | India              |
|       12 | Russian Federation |
|       11 | South Africa       |
|       11 | Tanzania           |
|       12 | United States      |
+----------+--------------------+
```

8.1.2 Writing Inner Joins with INNER JOIN

As described in the previous section, one form of inner join syntax uses the comma operator to name the joined tables. Another inner join syntax uses the INNER JOIN keywords. With this syntax, those keywords replace the comma operator between table names in the FROM clause. Also, with INNER JOIN, the conditions that indicate how to perform record matching for the tables move from the WHERE clause to become part of the FROM clause.

There are two syntaxes for specifying matching conditions with INNER JOIN queries:

- Add ON and an expression that states the required relationship between tables. Suppose that a join performs a country code match between the CountryLanguage and CountryLanguage tables. With the comma operator, you write the join as follows:

```
SELECT Name, Language
FROM CountryLanguage, Country WHERE CountryCode = Code;
```

  With INNER JOIN and ON, write the query like this instead:

```
SELECT Name, Language
FROM CountryLanguage INNER JOIN Country ON CountryCode = Code;
```

- If the name of the joined column is the same in both tables, you can add USING() rather than ON after the table names, and list the name within the parentheses. For example, if the country code column happened to be named Code in both tables, you could write the query like this:

```
SELECT Name, Language
FROM CountryLanguage INNER JOIN Country USING(Code);
```

  If you're joining the tables using more than one pair of like-named columns, list the column names within the parentheses of the USING() clause separated by commas.

8.2 Writing Outer Joins

An inner join produces results by selecting combinations of rows from the joined tables. However, it cannot find nonmatches; that is, instances where a row in one table has no match in another table. For example, an inner join can associate country names listed in the Country table with the languages spoken in those countries through a join based on country codes with the CountryLanguage table. But it cannot tell you which countries aren't associated with any language in the CountryLanguage table. Answering the latter question is a matter of identifying which country codes present in the Country table are *not* present in the CountryLanguage table.

To write a join that provides information about mismatches or missing records, use an outer join. An outer join can find matches (just like an inner join), but also can identify mismatches. Furthermore, with an appropriate WHERE clause, an outer join can filter out matches to display only the mismatches.

Two common forms of outer joins are left joins and right joins. These are written using the LEFT JOIN or RIGHT JOIN keywords rather than the comma operator or the INNER JOIN keywords.

Left and right joins can answer the same kinds of questions and differ only slightly in their syntax. That is, a left join can always be rewritten into an equivalent right join.

8.2.1 Writing LEFT JOIN Queries

A left join is a type of outer join, written using the LEFT JOIN keywords. A left join treats the left table (the first one named) as a reference table and produces output for each row selected from it, whether or not the row is matched by rows in the right table. Like a join written with the INNER JOIN keywords, a LEFT JOIN is written using either ON or USING() after the table names in the FROM clause. The examples here use the ON syntax. See the INNER JOIN section earlier in the chapter for details on USING() syntax.

To see the difference between an inner join and a left join, begin with the former. An inner join between the CountryLanguage and Country tables might be written like this:

```
mysql> SELECT Name, Language
    -> FROM Country INNER JOIN CountryLanguage ON Code = CountryCode;
+-------------------------------------+--------------------------+
| Name                                | Language                 |
+-------------------------------------+--------------------------+
| Afghanistan                         | Balochi                  |
| Afghanistan                         | Dari                     |
| Afghanistan                         | Pashto                   |
| Afghanistan                         | Turkmenian               |
| Afghanistan                         | Uzbek                    |
| Netherlands                         | Arabic                   |
| Netherlands                         | Dutch                    |
| Netherlands                         | Fries                    |
| Netherlands                         | Turkish                  |
...
| Palestine                           | Arabic                   |
| Palestine                           | Hebrew                   |
| United States Minor Outlying Islands | English                 |
+-------------------------------------+--------------------------+
```

That query displays information from table row combinations that have matching country code values. A LEFT JOIN has a similar syntax (replace INNER JOIN with LEFT JOIN), but produces a different result:

```
mysql> SELECT Name, Language
    -> FROM Country LEFT JOIN CountryLanguage ON Code = CountryCode;
+-----------------------------------------------+---------------------------+
| Name                                          | Language                  |
+-----------------------------------------------+---------------------------+
| Afghanistan                                   | Balochi                   |
| Afghanistan                                   | Dari                      |
| Afghanistan                                   | Pashto                    |
| Afghanistan                                   | Turkmenian                |
| Afghanistan                                   | Uzbek                     |
| Netherlands                                   | Arabic                    |
| Netherlands                                   | Dutch                     |
| Netherlands                                   | Fries                     |
| Netherlands                                   | Turkish                   |
| ...                                                                       |
| Palestine                                     | Arabic                    |
| Palestine                                     | Hebrew                    |
| Antarctica                                    | NULL                      |
| Bouvet Island                                 | NULL                      |
| British Indian Ocean Territory                | NULL                      |
| South Georgia and the South Sandwich Islands  | NULL                      |
| Heard Island and McDonald Islands             | NULL                      |
| French Southern territories                   | NULL                      |
| United States Minor Outlying Islands          | English                   |
+-----------------------------------------------+---------------------------+
```

In this query, the left table is the one named first (Country) and the right table is the one named second (CountryLanguage).

Notice that the LEFT JOIN finds both matches and nonmatches. That is, it displays all the rows produced by the inner join, plus a few more besides:

- If a row from the left table matches any right table rows, the result includes for each match a row containing the left table columns and the right table columns. These are rows that an inner join also will produce.

- If the left table row doesn't match any right table rows, the result includes a row containing the left table column values and NULL for any columns from the right table. These are rows that an outer join will produce but an inner join will not.

For the LEFT JOIN just shown, rows in Country not matched by any CountryLanguage rows correspond to countries for which no language is listed. These are the extra rows not produced by an inner join. Any columns that come from CountryLanguage are set to NULL. The NULL values serve two purposes. First, for a query such as the preceding one that displays both matches and nonmatches, the NULL values identify which output rows represent nonmatches. Second, if you're interested *only* in nonmatches, you can add a condition that restricts the output to only those rows that contain these NULL values. For example, the question, "Which countries have no languages listed?" is equivalent to asking which country codes in the Country table aren't matched by codes in the CountryLanguage table. To answer the question, write a LEFT JOIN and require row combinations to have NULL in the right table column:.

```
mysql> SELECT Name, Language
    -> FROM Country LEFT JOIN CountryLanguage ON Code = CountryCode
    -> WHERE CountryCode IS NULL;
+-----------------------------------------------+----------+
| Name                                          | Language |
+-----------------------------------------------+----------+
| Antarctica                                    | NULL     |
| Bouvet Island                                 | NULL     |
| British Indian Ocean Territory                | NULL     |
| South Georgia and the South Sandwich Islands  | NULL     |
| Heard Island and McDonald Islands             | NULL     |
| French Southern territories                   | NULL     |
+-----------------------------------------------+----------+
```

In this case, Language is always NULL in the output, so you probably would not bother displaying it:

```
mysql> SELECT Name
    -> FROM Country LEFT JOIN CountryLanguage ON Code = CountryCode
    -> WHERE CountryCode IS NULL;
+-----------------------------------------------+
| Name                                          |
+-----------------------------------------------+
| Antarctica                                    |
| Bouvet Island                                 |
| British Indian Ocean Territory                |
| South Georgia and the South Sandwich Islands  |
| Heard Island and McDonald Islands             |
| French Southern territories                   |
+-----------------------------------------------+
```

As mentioned earlier, the order in which you name the tables in the FROM clause doesn't matter for an inner join. The query results are the same regardless of which table you name first. For an outer join, the output depends very much on the order in which the tables are named. With a LEFT JOIN, the reference table should be listed on the left and the table from which rows might be missing should be listed on the right.

8.2.2 Writing RIGHT JOIN Queries

A right join is another type of outer join, written using the RIGHT JOIN keywords. Every right join corresponds to an equivalent left join. The only difference is that the roles of the tables in a right join are reversed relative to the roles in a left join. That is, the right table is the reference table, so a RIGHT JOIN produces a result for each row in the right table, whether or not it has any match in the left table. Thus, if you write a LEFT JOIN as follows:

```
SELECT ... FROM t1 LEFT JOIN t2 ON t1_column = t2_column ...
```

You can convert it to a RIGHT JOIN like this:

```
SELECT ... FROM t2 RIGHT JOIN t1 ON t2_column = t1_column ...
```

For example, a LEFT JOIN query to display countries in the Country table that have no languages listed in the CountryLanguage table can be written this way:

```
mysql> SELECT Name
    -> FROM Country LEFT JOIN CountryLanguage ON Code = CountryCode
    -> WHERE CountryCode IS NULL;
+---------------------------------------------+
| Name                                        |
+---------------------------------------------+
| Antarctica                                  |
| Bouvet Island                               |
| British Indian Ocean Territory              |
| South Georgia and the South Sandwich Islands |
| Heard Island and McDonald Islands           |
| French Southern territories                 |
+---------------------------------------------+
```

The corresponding RIGHT JOIN looks like this:

```
mysql> SELECT Name
    -> FROM CountryLanguage RIGHT JOIN Country ON CountryCode = Code
    -> WHERE CountryCode IS NULL;
+---------------------------------------------+
| Name                                        |
+---------------------------------------------+
| Antarctica                                  |
| Bouvet Island                               |
| British Indian Ocean Territory              |
| South Georgia and the South Sandwich Islands |
| Heard Island and McDonald Islands           |
| French Southern territories                 |
+---------------------------------------------+
```

Syntactically, converting a left join to a right join requires only that you reverse the order in which you name the tables. It isn't necessary to also reverse the order in which you name the columns in the ON clause, but it can help make the query clearer to name the columns in the same order as the tables in which they appear.

If you're looking only for matches between tables, you can do so with either an inner or outer join. In such cases, it's better to use an inner join because that allows the MySQL optimizer to choose the most efficient order for processing the tables. Outer joins require that the reference table be processed first, which might not be the most efficient order.

8.3 Converting Subqueries to Joins

Standard SQL allows a SELECT statement to contain a nested SELECT, which is known as a subquery. MySQL implements subqueries as of version 4.1. For MySQL 4.0, subqueries sometimes can be rewritten as joins, which provides a workaround for lack of subqueries in many cases. A join could also be more efficient than an equivalent statement expressed as a subquery.

A subquery that finds matches between tables often can be rewritten as an inner join. A subquery that finds mismatches often can be rewritten as an outer join.

8.3.1 Converting Subqueries to Inner Joins

One form of SELECT that uses subqueries finds matches between tables. For example, an IN subquery that identifies countries for which languages are listed in the CountryLanguage table looks like this:

```
mysql> SELECT Name FROM Country
    -> WHERE Code IN (SELECT CountryCode FROM CountryLanguage);
+---------------------------------------+
| Name                                  |
+---------------------------------------+
| Afghanistan                           |
| Netherlands                           |
| Netherlands Antilles                  |
| Albania                               |
| Algeria                               |
| American Samoa                        |
| Andorra                               |
| Angola                                |
| Anguilla                              |
| Antigua and Barbuda                   |
| United Arab Emirates                  |
| Argentina                             |
...
```

To convert this into an inner join, do the following:

1. Move the CountryLanguage table named in the subquery to the FROM clause.

2. The WHERE clause compares the Code column to the country codes returned from the subquery. Convert the IN expression to an explicit direct comparison between the country code columns of the two tables.

These changes result in the following inner join:

```
mysql> SELECT Name FROM Country, CountryLanguage
    -> WHERE Code = CountryCode;
+--------------------------------------+
| Name                                 |
+--------------------------------------+
| Afghanistan                          |
| Afghanistan                          |
| Afghanistan                          |
| Afghanistan                          |
| Afghanistan                          |
| Netherlands                          |
| Netherlands                          |
| Netherlands                          |
| Netherlands                          |
| Netherlands Antilles                 |
| Netherlands Antilles                 |
| Netherlands Antilles                 |
...
```

Note that this output is not quite the same as that from the subquery, which lists each
matched country just once. The output from the join lists each matched country once each
time its country code occurs in the CountryLanguage table. To list each name just once, as in
the subquery, add DISTINCT to the join:

```
mysql> SELECT DISTINCT Name FROM Country, CountryLanguage
    -> WHERE Code = CountryCode;
+--------------------------------------+
| Name                                 |
+--------------------------------------+
| Afghanistan                          |
| Netherlands                          |
| Netherlands Antilles                 |
| Albania                              |
| Algeria                              |
| American Samoa                       |
| Andorra                              |
| Angola                               |
| Anguilla                             |
| Antigua and Barbuda                  |
| United Arab Emirates                 |
| Argentina                            |
...
```

8.3.2 Converting Subqueries to Outer Joins

Another form of SELECT that uses subqueries finds mismatches between tables. For example, a NOT IN subquery that identifies countries for which no languages are listed in the CountryLanguage table looks like this:

```
mysql> SELECT Name FROM Country
    -> WHERE Code NOT IN (SELECT CountryCode FROM CountryLanguage);
+---------------------------------------------+
| Name                                        |
+---------------------------------------------+
| Antarctica                                  |
| Bouvet Island                               |
| British Indian Ocean Territory              |
| South Georgia and the South Sandwich Islands |
| Heard Island and McDonald Islands           |
| French Southern territories                 |
+---------------------------------------------+
```

This subquery can be rewritten as an outer join. For example, to change the preceding subquery into a left join, modify it as follows:

1. Move the CountryLanguage table named in the subquery to the FROM clause and join it to Country using LEFT JOIN.

2. The WHERE clause compares the Code column to the country codes returned from the subquery. Convert the IN expression to an explicit direct comparison between the country code columns of the two tables in the FROM clause.

3. In the WHERE clause, restrict the output to those rows having NULL in the CountryLanguage table column.

These changes result in the following LEFT JOIN:

```
mysql> SELECT Name
    -> FROM Country LEFT JOIN CountryLanguage ON Code = CountryCode
    -> WHERE CountryCode IS NULL;
+---------------------------------------------+
| Name                                        |
+---------------------------------------------+
| Antarctica                                  |
| Bouvet Island                               |
| British Indian Ocean Territory              |
| South Georgia and the South Sandwich Islands |
| Heard Island and McDonald Islands           |
| French Southern territories                 |
+---------------------------------------------+
```

Because any left join may be written as an equivalent right join, the subquery also can be written as a right join:

```
mysql> SELECT Name
    -> FROM CountryLanguage RIGHT JOIN Country ON CountryCode = Code
    -> WHERE CountryCode IS NULL;
+----------------------------------------------+
| Name                                         |
+----------------------------------------------+
| Antarctica                                   |
| Bouvet Island                                |
| British Indian Ocean Territory               |
| South Georgia and the South Sandwich Islands |
| Heard Island and McDonald Islands            |
| French Southern territories                  |
+----------------------------------------------+
```

8.4 Resolving Name Clashes Using Qualifiers and Aliases

When you join tables, it's often the case that the tables contain columns with the same names. If you refer to such a column in the query, it's ambiguous which table the column reference applies to. This ambiguity usually can be addressed by qualifying column names with table names. However, if you join a table to itself, even the table name is ambiguous and it's necessary to use aliases to disambiguate table references. This section describes how to address naming issues in queries by qualifying column and table names and by using aliases.

8.4.1 Qualifying Column Names

In each of the joins shown earlier in this chapter, the column names are unambiguous because no query refers to a column that appears in more than one of the joined tables. But it will often be the case that a join involves tables that have similarly named columns. If a column name used in the query appears in more than one table, the name is ambiguous and it's necessary to provide information that identifies which table you mean. To do this, qualify the column name with the appropriate table name.

Suppose that you want to list, for each country named in the Country table, all of its cities named in the City table. In principle, this is a simple query that associates country names and city names based on the country codes that are common to the two tables. In practice, there is a small complication:

```
mysql> SELECT Name, Name FROM Country, City
    -> WHERE Code = CountryCode;
ERROR 1052: Column: 'Name' in field list is ambiguous
```

The problem here is that the country name column in the Country table and the city name column in the City table both are called Name. MySQL has no way to know which instance of Name in the query goes with which table.

To resolve this ambiguity, qualify the references to Name with the appropriate table name so that MySQL can tell which table to use for each reference:

```
mysql> SELECT Country.Name, City.Name FROM Country, City
    -> WHERE Code = CountryCode;
+-------------+----------------+
| Name        | Name           |
+-------------+----------------+
| Afghanistan | Kabul          |
| Afghanistan | Qandahar       |
| Afghanistan | Herat          |
| Afghanistan | Mazar-e-Sharif |
| Netherlands | Amsterdam      |
| Netherlands | Rotterdam      |
| Netherlands | Haag           |
| Netherlands | Utrecht        |
| Netherlands | Eindhoven      |
| Netherlands | Tilburg        |
| Netherlands | Groningen      |
| Netherlands | Breda          |
| Netherlands | Apeldoorn      |
| Netherlands | Nijmegen       |
| Netherlands | Enschede       |
...
```

Note that although it might not always be necessary to provide table qualifiers in a join, it's always allowable to do so. Thus, although Code and CountryCode in the preceding example are unambiguous because each appears in only one table, you can qualify them explicitly if you want to do so:

```
mysql> SELECT Country.Name, City.Name FROM Country, City
    -> WHERE Country.Code = City.CountryCode;
+-------------+----------------+
| Name        | Name           |
+-------------+----------------+
| Afghanistan | Kabul          |
| Afghanistan | Qandahar       |
| Afghanistan | Herat          |
| Afghanistan | Mazar-e-Sharif |
| Netherlands | Amsterdam      |
| Netherlands | Rotterdam      |
| Netherlands | Haag           |
| Netherlands | Utrecht        |
```

```
| Netherlands | Eindhoven   |
| Netherlands | Tilburg     |
| Netherlands | Groningen   |
| Netherlands | Breda       |
| Netherlands | Apeldoorn   |
| Netherlands | Nijmegen    |
| Netherlands | Enschede    |
...
```

Adding qualifiers even when they aren't necessary for MySQL to understand a query often can make the query easier for people to understand, particularly people unfamiliar with the tables. Without the qualifiers, it might not be evident which table each column comes from.

More complex queries might involve multiple ambiguous columns. For example, the Country and City tables each have a Population column, and you can compare them to identify cities that contain more than 75% of their country's population:

```
mysql> SELECT Country.Name, Country.Population, City.Name, City.Population
    -> FROM City, Country
    -> WHERE City.CountryCode = Country.Code
    -> AND Country.Population * .75 < City.Population;
+---------------------------+------------+-------------+------------+
| Name                      | Population | Name        | Population |
+---------------------------+------------+-------------+------------+
| Falkland Islands          |       2000 | Stanley     |       1636 |
| Gibraltar                 |      25000 | Gibraltar   |      27025 |
| Cocos (Keeling) Islands   |        600 | Bantam      |        503 |
| Macao                     |     473000 | Macao       |     437500 |
| Pitcairn                  |         50 | Adamstown   |         42 |
| Saint Pierre and Miquelon |       7000 | Saint-Pierre|       5808 |
| Singapore                 |    3567000 | Singapore   |    4017733 |
+---------------------------+------------+-------------+------------+
```

Both Name and Population require table qualifiers in this query because both are ambiguous.

8.4.2 Qualifying and Aliasing Table Names

Table qualifiers resolve many column name ambiguities, but sometimes even the table name is ambiguous. This happens in two ways.

First, you might perform a join between tables that have the same name but come from different databases. In this case, you provide not only table names as qualifiers, but database names as well. Suppose that two databases world1 and world2 both have a table named Country and that you want to determine which names are present in both tables. The query can be written like this:

```
SELECT world1.Country.Name
FROM world1.Country, world2.Country
WHERE world1.Country.Name = world2.Country.Name;
```

Second, a table name is always ambiguous when you join the table to itself using a self-join. For example, the Country table in the world database contains an IndepYear column indicating the year in which each country achieved independence. To find all countries that have the same year of independence as some given country, you can use a self-join. However, you cannot write the query like this:

```
mysql> SELECT IndepYear, Name, Name
    -> FROM Country, Country
    -> WHERE IndepYear = IndepYear AND Name = 'Qatar';
ERROR 1066: Not unique table/alias: 'Country'
```

Furthermore, you cannot remove the ambiguity from column references by preceding them with table name qualifiers because the names remain identical:

```
mysql> SELECT Country.IndepYear, Country.Name, Country.Name
    -> FROM Country, Country
    -> WHERE Country.IndepYear = Country.IndepYear
    -> AND Country.Name = 'Qatar';
ERROR 1066: Not unique table/alias: 'Country'
```

It doesn't even help to add a database name qualifier because the database is the same for both tables. To address this naming issue, create an alias for one or both table references and refer to the aliases elsewhere in the query. The aliases give you alternative unambiguous names by which to refer to each instance of the table in the query. Here is one solution that aliases both tables:

```
mysql> SELECT t1.IndepYear, t1.Name, t2.Name
    -> FROM Country AS t1, Country AS t2
    -> WHERE t1.IndepYear = t2.IndepYear AND t1.Name = 'Qatar';
+-----------+-------+----------------------+
| IndepYear | Name  | Name                 |
+-----------+-------+----------------------+
|      1971 | Qatar | United Arab Emirates |
|      1971 | Qatar | Bahrain              |
|      1971 | Qatar | Bangladesh           |
|      1971 | Qatar | Qatar                |
+-----------+-------+----------------------+
```

8.5 Multiple-Table UPDATE and DELETE Statements

MySQL 4 supports the use of multiple tables in UPDATE and DELETE statements. Such statements can be used to perform the following operations:

- Update rows in one table by transferring information from another table
- Update rows in one table, determining which rows to update by referring to another table
- Update rows in multiple tables with a single statement
- Delete rows from one table, determining which rows to delete by referring to another table
- Delete rows from multiple tables with a single statement

Some of the principles involved in writing joins in SELECT statements also apply to multiple-table UPDATE and DELETE statements. This section provides a brief overview of their syntax.

A multiple-table UPDATE is an extension of a single-table statement:

- Name the tables involved in the operation following the UPDATE keyword, separated by commas. (You must name all the tables used in the query, even if you aren't updating all of them.)
- In the WHERE clause, describe the conditions that determine how to match records in the tables.
- In the SET clause, assign values to the columns to be updated. These assignments can refer to columns from any of the joined tables.

For example, to update one table based on another, do this:

```
UPDATE t1, t2 SET t1.name = t2.name WHERE t1.id = t2.id;
```

Multiple-table DELETE statements can be written in two formats. The following example demonstrates one syntax, for a query that deletes rows from a table t1 where the id values match those in a table t2:

```
DELETE t1 FROM t1,t2 WHERE t1.id = t2.id;
```

The second syntax is slightly different:

```
DELETE FROM t1 USING t1, t2 WHERE t1.id = t2.id;
```

The ORDER BY and LIMIT clauses normally supported by UPDATE and DELETE aren't allowed when these statements are used for multiple-table operations.

8.6 Exercises

Question 1:

What kind of join can find matches (values that are present in both tables involved in the join)?

Question 2:

What kind of join or joins find mismatches (values that are present in only one of the tables involved in the join)?

Question 3:

Here's the structure and contents for two tables, client and project, which will be used for the next two questions.

```
mysql> DESCRIBE client; DESCRIBE project;
+-------+----------------------+------+-----+---------+-------+
| Field | Type                 | Null | Key | Default | Extra |
+-------+----------------------+------+-----+---------+-------+
| cid   | smallint(5) unsigned |      | PRI | 0       |       |
| name  | char(20)             |      |     |         |       |
+-------+----------------------+------+-----+---------+-------+
+-------+----------------------+------+-----+---------+-------+
| Field | Type                 | Null | Key | Default | Extra |
+-------+----------------------+------+-----+---------+-------+
| pid   | int(10) unsigned     |      | PRI | 0       |       |
| cid   | smallint(5) unsigned |      |     | 0       |       |
| name  | char(30)             |      |     |         |       |
| start | date                 | YES  |     | NULL    |       |
| end   | date                 | YES  |     | NULL    |       |
+-------+----------------------+------+-----+---------+-------+
mysql> SELECT * FROM client; SELECT * FROM project;
+-----+---------------+
| cid | name          |
+-----+---------------+
| 101 | Seamen's      |
| 103 | Lennart AG    |
| 110 | MySQL AB      |
| 115 | Icoaten & Co. |
| 125 | Nittboad Inc  |
+-----+---------------+
+-------+-----+-------------+------------+------------+
| pid   | cid | name        | start      | end        |
+-------+-----+-------------+------------+------------+
| 10000 | 103 | New CMS     | 2003-01-00 | 2003-05-00 |
| 10010 | 110 | Texi2XML    | 2002-04-00 | 2003-09-00 |
| 10020 | 100 | Studyguides | 2002-09-00 | 2003-03-30 |
| 10030 | 115 | PDC Server  | 2003-01-00 | 2003-01-00 |
| 10040 | 103 | Intranet    | 2009-02-00 | NULL       |
| 10050 | 101 | Intranet    | NULL       | NULL       |
| 10060 | 115 | SMB Server  | 2003-05-00 | NULL       |
| 10070 | 115 | WLAN        | NULL       | 2003-07-00 |
+-------+-----+-------------+------------+------------+
```

How many rows will the following join statements return?

```
mysql> SELECT client.name, project.name, project.start, project.end
    ->  FROM client, project
    -> ;

mysql> SELECT client.name, project.name, project.start, project.end
    ->  FROM client, project
    ->  WHERE project.cid = client.cid
    -> ;
```

Question 4:

Refer to the client and project tables shown in the previous question. How many rows will the following join statements return?

```
mysql> SELECT client.name, project.name, project.start, project.end
    ->  FROM client, project
    ->  WHERE project.cid = client.cid
    ->  AND project.start IS NOT NULL
    -> ;

mysql> SELECT client.name, project.name, project.start, project.end
    ->  FROM client, project
    ->  WHERE project.cid = client.cid
    ->  AND project.start IS NOT NULL
    ->  AND project.end IS NOT NULL
    -> ;
```

Question 5:

Here's the structure and sample data for two tables, client and project, which will be used for the next three questions.

```
mysql> DESCRIBE client; DESCRIBE project;
```

Field	Type	Null	Key	Default	Extra
id	smallint(5) unsigned		PRI	0	
name	char(20)				

Field	Type	Null	Key	Default	Extra
pid	int(10) unsigned		PRI	0	
id	smallint(5) unsigned			0	
name	char(30)				
start	date	YES		NULL	
end	date	YES		NULL	

```
+-------+--------------------+------+-----+---------+-------+
mysql> SELECT * FROM client; SELECT * FROM project;
+-----+---------------+
| id  | name          |
+-----+---------------+
| 101 | Seamen's      |
| 103 | Lennart AG    |
| 110 | MySQL AB      |
| 115 | Icoaten & Co. |
| 125 | Nittboad Inc  |
+-----+---------------+

+-------+-----+-------------+------------+------------+
| pid   | id  | name        | start      | end        |
+-------+-----+-------------+------------+------------+
| 10000 | 103 | New CMS     | 2003-01-00 | 2003-05-00 |
| 10010 | 110 | Texi2XML    | 2002-04-00 | 2003-09-00 |
| 10020 | 100 | Studyguides | 2002-09-00 | 2003-03-30 |
| 10030 | 115 | PDC Server  | 2003-01-00 | 2003-01-00 |
| 10040 | 103 | Intranet    | 2009-02-00 | NULL       |
| 10050 | 101 | Intranet    | NULL       | NULL       |
| 10060 | 115 | SMB Server  | 2003-05-00 | NULL       |
| 10070 | 115 | WLAN        | NULL       | 2003-07-00 |
+-------+-----+-------------+------------+------------+
```

Using the client and project tables, you want to retrieve a list of clients that have no projects for a report with these headings:

```
+----------+---------+-------+------+
| CLIENT   | PROJECT | START | END  |
+----------+---------+-------+------+
```

What SQL statement will you issue?

Question 6:

Refer to the structure and sample data for the client and project tables, shown in the previous question. Using these two tables, you want to retrieve a list of clients that have projects starting in the year 2003, sorted by start date, for a report with these headings:

```
+----------+---------+-------+------+
| CLIENT   | PROJECT | START | END  |
+----------+---------+-------+------+
```

What SQL statement will you issue?

Question 7:

Refer to the structure and sample data for the client and project tables, shown two questions earlier. Using these two tables, you want to retrieve a list of clients that have intranet projects, using the LEFT JOIN syntax, for a report with these headings:

```
+----------+---------+-------+------+
| CLIENT   | PROJECT | START | END  |
+----------+---------+-------+------+
```

What SQL statement will you issue?

Question 8:

Here's the structure and sample data for two tables, client and project, which will be used for the next three questions.

```
mysql> DESCRIBE client; DESCRIBE project;
+-------+---------------------+------+-----+---------+-------+
| Field | Type                | Null | Key | Default | Extra |
+-------+---------------------+------+-----+---------+-------+
| id    | smallint(5) unsigned |      | PRI | 0       |       |
| name  | char(20)            |      |     |         |       |
+-------+---------------------+------+-----+---------+-------+
+-------+---------------------+------+-----+---------+-------+
| Field | Type                | Null | Key | Default | Extra |
+-------+---------------------+------+-----+---------+-------+
| pid   | int(10) unsigned    |      | PRI | 0       |       |
| id    | smallint(5) unsigned |     |     | 0       |       |
| name  | char(30)            |      |     |         |       |
| start | date                | YES  |     | NULL    |       |
| end   | date                | YES  |     | NULL    |       |
+-------+---------------------+------+-----+---------+-------+
mysql> SELECT * FROM client; SELECT * FROM project;
+-----+---------------+
| id  | name          |
+-----+---------------+
| 101 | Seamen's      |
| 103 | Lennart AG    |
| 110 | MySQL AB      |
| 115 | Icoaten & Co. |
| 125 | Nittboad Inc  |
+-----+---------------+
+-------+-----+------------+------------+------------+
| pid   | id  | name       | start      | end        |
+-------+-----+------------+------------+------------+
| 10000 | 103 | New CMS    | 2003-01-00 | 2003-05-00 |
| 10010 | 110 | Texi2XML   | 2002-04-00 | 2003-09-00 |
| 10020 | 100 | Studyguides | 2002-09-00 | 2003-03-30 |
| 10030 | 115 | PDC Server | 2003-01-00 | 2003-01-00 |
| 10040 | 103 | Intranet   | 2009-02-00 | NULL       |
| 10050 | 101 | Intranet   | NULL       | NULL       |
| 10060 | 115 | SMB Server | 2003-05-00 | NULL       |
| 10070 | 115 | WLAN       | NULL       | 2003-07-00 |
+-------+-----+------------+------------+------------+
```

Using the client and project tables, you want to retrieve a list of clients that have intranet projects, using the INNER JOIN syntax, for a report with these headings:

```
+----------+---------+-------+------+
| CLIENT   | PROJECT | START | END  |
+----------+---------+-------+------+
```

What SQL statement will you issue?

Question 9:

Refer to the structure and sample data for the client and project tables, shown in the previous question. Using these two tables, you want to retrieve a list of clients that have intranet projects, using an inner join with the WHERE clause, for a report with these headings:

```
+----------+---------+-------+------+
| CLIENT   | PROJECT | START | END  |
+----------+---------+-------+------+
```

What SQL statement will you issue?

Question 10:

Refer to the structure and sample data for the client and project tables, shown two questions earlier. Using these two tables, you want to retrieve a list of clients and their projects, sorted by client name, and within client name, sorted by start date, for a report with these headings:

```
+----------+---------+-------+------+
| CLIENT   | PROJECT | START | END  |
+----------+---------+-------+------+
```

What SQL statement will you issue? Clients without projects should also be displayed.

Question 11:

Here's the structure and sample data for two tables, client and project.

```
mysql> DESCRIBE client; DESCRIBE project;
+-------+---------------------+------+-----+---------+-------+
| Field | Type                | Null | Key | Default | Extra |
+-------+---------------------+------+-----+---------+-------+
| id    | smallint(5) unsigned |     | PRI | 0       |       |
| name  | char(20)            |      |     |         |       |
+-------+---------------------+------+-----+---------+-------+
+-------+---------------------+------+-----+---------+-------+
| Field | Type                | Null | Key | Default | Extra |
+-------+---------------------+------+-----+---------+-------+
| pid   | int(10) unsigned    |      | PRI | 0       |       |
| id    | smallint(5) unsigned |     |     | 0       |       |
| name  | char(30)            |      |     |         |       |
```

```
| start | date                 | YES |    | NULL   |      |        |
| end   | date                 | YES |    | NULL   |      |        |
+-------+----------------------+------+-----+---------+-------+
mysql> SELECT * FROM client; SELECT * FROM project;
+-----+---------------+
| id  | name          |
+-----+---------------+
| 101 | Seamen's      |
| 103 | Lennart AG    |
| 110 | MySQL AB      |
| 115 | Icoaten & Co. |
| 125 | Nittboad Inc  |
+-----+---------------+

+-------+-----+-------------+------------+------------+
| pid   | id  | name        | start      | end        |
+-------+-----+-------------+------------+------------+
| 10000 | 103 | New CMS     | 2003-01-00 | 2003-05-00 |
| 10010 | 110 | Texi2XML    | 2002-04-00 | 2003-09-00 |
| 10020 | 100 | Studyguides | 2002-09-00 | 2003-03-30 |
| 10030 | 115 | PDC Server  | 2003-01-00 | 2003-01-00 |
| 10040 | 103 | Intranet    | 2009-02-00 | NULL       |
| 10050 | 101 | Intranet    | NULL       | NULL       |
| 10060 | 115 | SMB Server  | 2003-05-00 | NULL       |
| 10070 | 115 | WLAN        | NULL       | 2003-07-00 |
+-------+-----+-------------+------------+------------+
```

Using the client and project tables, you want to retrieve a list of clients and their projects, sorted by client name, and within client name, sorted by start date, for a report with these headings:

```
+----------+---------+-------+------+
| CLIENT   | PROJECT | START | END  |
+----------+---------+-------+------+
```

What SQL statement will you issue? Clients without projects should be displayed, but projects that don't have a start date and projects that don't have an end date should not be displayed.

Question 12:

The following sample data from two tables, client and project, will be used for the next three questions.

```
mysql> SELECT * FROM client; SELECT * FROM project;
+-----+---------------+
| id  | name          |
+-----+---------------+
| 101 | Seamen's      |
```

```
| 103 | Lennart AG    |
| 110 | MySQL AB      |
| 115 | Icoaten & Co. |
| 125 | Nittboad Inc  |
+-----+---------------+
```

```
+-------+-----+------------+------------+------------+
| pid   | id  | name       | start      | end        |
+-------+-----+------------+------------+------------+
| 10000 | 103 | New CMS    | 2003-01-00 | 2003-05-00 |
| 10010 | 110 | Texi2XML   | 2002-04-00 | 2003-09-00 |
| 10020 | 100 | Studyguides | 2002-09-00 | 2003-03-30 |
| 10030 | 115 | PDC Server | 2003-01-00 | 2003-01-00 |
| 10040 | 103 | Intranet   | 2009-02-00 | NULL       |
| 10050 | 101 | Intranet   | NULL       | NULL       |
| 10060 | 115 | SMB Server | 2003-05-00 | NULL       |
| 10070 | 115 | WLAN       | NULL       | 2003-07-00 |
| 10080 | 135 | Intranet   | 2003-08-00 | NULL       |
| 10090 | 145 | PDC Server | NULL       | NULL       |
+-------+-----+------------+------------+------------+
```

The `client` and `project` tables are related through their common column (`id`). Thus, the following statement could be used to determine which projects have clients (that is, which projects have an `id` whose value is the same as one of the `id` values found in the `client` table):

```
SELECT ... FROM project WHERE project.id IN
  (SELECT client.id FROM client)
```

Prior to version 4.1, MySQL doesn't support subqueries such as this. How would you rewrite the statement using the LEFT JOIN operator? Your output should have headers like this:

```
+------------+--------------+-----------+--------------+
| Project ID | Project Name | Client No | Client Name  |
+------------+--------------+-----------+--------------+
```

Question 13:

Recall that the `client` and `project` tables shown in the previous question are related through their common column (`id`). This SQL statement produces a list of projects that have an `id` whose value is the same as one of the `id` values found in the `client` table:

```
SELECT ... FROM project WHERE project.id IN
  (SELECT client.id FROM client)
```

Prior to version 4.1, MySQL doesn't support subqueries such as this. How would you rewrite the statement using the RIGHT JOIN operator? Your output should have headers like this:

```
+------------+--------------+-----------+---------------+
| Project ID | Project Name | Client No | Client Name   |
+------------+--------------+-----------+---------------+
```

Question 14:

Recall that the `client` and `project` tables shown two questions earlier are related through their common column (`id`). This SQL statement produces a list of projects that have an `id` whose value is the same as one of the `id` values found in the `client` table:

```
SELECT ... FROM project WHERE project.id IN
  (SELECT client.id FROM client)
```

Prior to version 4.1, MySQL doesn't support subqueries such as this. How would you rewrite the statement using the `INNER JOIN` operator? Your output should have headers like this:

```
+------------+--------------+-----------+---------------+
| Project ID | Project Name | Client No | Client Name   |
+------------+--------------+-----------+---------------+
```

Question 15:

The following sample data from two tables, `client` and `project`, will be used for the next three questions.

```
mysql> SELECT * FROM client; SELECT * FROM project;
+-----+---------------+
| id  | name          |
+-----+---------------+
| 101 | Seamen's      |
| 103 | Lennart AG    |
| 110 | MySQL AB      |
| 115 | Icoaten & Co. |
| 125 | Nittboad Inc  |
+-----+---------------+
+-------+-----+------------+------------+------------+
| pid   | id  | name       | start      | end        |
+-------+-----+------------+------------+------------+
| 10000 | 103 | New CMS    | 2003-01-00 | 2003-05-00 |
| 10010 | 110 | Texi2XML   | 2002-04-00 | 2003-09-00 |
| 10020 | 100 | Studyguides| 2002-09-00 | 2003-03-30 |
| 10030 | 115 | PDC Server | 2003-01-00 | 2003-01-00 |
| 10040 | 103 | Intranet   | 2009-02-00 | NULL       |
| 10050 | 101 | Intranet   | NULL       | NULL       |
| 10060 | 115 | SMB Server | 2003-05-00 | NULL       |
| 10070 | 115 | WLAN       | NULL       | 2003-07-00 |
| 10080 | 135 | Intranet   | 2003-08-00 | NULL       |
| 10090 | 145 | PDC Server | NULL       | NULL       |
+-------+-----+------------+------------+------------+
```

The client and project tables are related through their common column (id). Thus, the following statement could be used to determine which projects don't have clients (that is, which projects have an id whose value is not the same as one of the id values found in the client table):

```
SELECT ... FROM project WHERE project.id NOT IN
  (SELECT client.id FROM client)
```

Prior to version 4.1, MySQL doesn't support subqueries such as this. How would you rewrite the statement using the LEFT JOIN operator? Your output should have headers like this:

```
+------------+--------------+-----------+---------------+
| Project ID | Project Name | Client No | Client Name   |
+------------+--------------+-----------+---------------+
```

Question 16:

Recall that the client and project tables shown in the previous question are related through their common column (id). This SQL statement produces a list of projects that have an id whose value is not the same as one of the id values found in the client table:

```
SELECT ... FROM project WHERE project.id NOT IN
  (SELECT client.id FROM client)
```

Prior to version 4.1, MySQL doesn't support subqueries such as this. How would you rewrite the statement using the RIGHT JOIN operator? Your output should have headers like this:

```
+------------+--------------+-----------+---------------+
| Project ID | Project Name | Client No | Client Name   |
+------------+--------------+-----------+---------------+
```

Question 17:

Recall that the client and project tables shown two questions earlier are related through their common column (id). This SQL statement produces a list of projects that have an id whose value is not the same as one of the id values found in the client table:

```
SELECT ... FROM project WHERE project.id NOT IN
  (SELECT client.id FROM client)
```

Prior to version 4.1, MySQL doesn't support subqueries such as this. How would you rewrite the statement using the INNER JOIN operator? Your output should have headers like this:

```
+------------+--------------+-----------+---------------+
| Project ID | Project Name | Client No | Client Name   |
+------------+--------------+-----------+---------------+
```

Question 18:

Consider the following record from the Country table:

```
mysql> SELECT
    ->   Name, Region, Continent, SurfaceArea, Population
    ->   FROM Country
    ->   WHERE Name = 'Paraguay'
    ->   ;
+----------+---------------+---------------+-------------+------------+
| Name     | Region        | Continent     | SurfaceArea | Population |
+----------+---------------+---------------+-------------+------------+
| Paraguay | South America | South America |   406752.00 |    5496000 |
+----------+---------------+---------------+-------------+------------+
```

What statement would you issue to retrieve a list of countries whose surface area is larger than that of Paraguay, when you consider countries on the same continent (South America) only? The headings of the result should look like this:

```
+----------+-----------------+---------------+--------------+
| Country  | Other Countries | Continent     | Surface Area |
+----------+-----------------+---------------+--------------+
```

Question 19:

Consider the following record from the Country table:

```
mysql> SELECT
    ->   Name, Region, Continent, SurfaceArea, Population
    ->   FROM Country
    ->   WHERE Name = 'Germany'
    ->   ;
+---------+----------------+-----------+-------------+------------+
| Name    | Region         | Continent | SurfaceArea | Population |
+---------+----------------+-----------+-------------+------------+
| Germany | Western Europe | Europe    |   357022.00 |   82164700 |
+---------+----------------+-----------+-------------+------------+
```

What statement would you issue to retrieve a list of the countries worldwide with a population at least as large as that of Germany? Germany should be included in the list, which should be sorted by descending population. The headings of the result should look like this:

```
+---------+--------------------+------------+
| Country | Other Countries    | Population |
+---------+--------------------+------------+
```

Question 20:

Consider the following record from the Country table:

```
mysql> SELECT
    -> Name, Region, Continent, SurfaceArea, Population
    -> FROM Country
    -> WHERE Name = 'Nepal'
    -> ;
+-------+--------------------------+-----------+-------------+------------+
| Name  | Region                   | Continent | SurfaceArea | Population |
+-------+--------------------------+-----------+-------------+------------+
| Nepal | Southern and Central Asia | Asia     |   147181.00 |   23930000 |
+-------+--------------------------+-----------+-------------+------------+
```

What statement would you issue to retrieve a list of countries in the same region with a population and surface area at least as large as that of Nepal? Nepal should be included in the list, which should be sorted by descending population. The headings of the result should look like this, with all region names cut to a maximum length of 10 characters:

```
+---------+-----------------+-----------------+------------+------------+
| Country | Other Countries | Region          | Population | Surface    |
+---------+-----------------+-----------------+------------+------------+
```

Answers to Exercises

Answer 1:

Any kind of join can find matches between tables.

Answer 2:

Outer joins, that is, LEFT JOIN and RIGHT JOIN.

Answer 3:

The statements will return the following result sets:

```
+---------------+-------------+------------+------------+
| name          | name        | start      | end        |
+---------------+-------------+------------+------------+
| Seamen's      | New CMS     | 2003-01-00 | 2003-05-00 |
| Lennart AG    | New CMS     | 2003-01-00 | 2003-05-00 |
| MySQL AB      | New CMS     | 2003-01-00 | 2003-05-00 |
| Icoaten & Co. | New CMS     | 2003-01-00 | 2003-05-00 |
| Nittboad Inc  | New CMS     | 2003-01-00 | 2003-05-00 |
| Seamen's      | Texi2XML    | 2002-04-00 | 2003-09-00 |
| Lennart AG    | Texi2XML    | 2002-04-00 | 2003-09-00 |
| MySQL AB      | Texi2XML    | 2002-04-00 | 2003-09-00 |
| Icoaten & Co. | Texi2XML    | 2002-04-00 | 2003-09-00 |
| Nittboad Inc  | Texi2XML    | 2002-04-00 | 2003-09-00 |
```

```
| Seamen's      | Studyguides | 2002-09-00 | 2003-03-30 |
| Lennart AG    | Studyguides | 2002-09-00 | 2003-03-30 |
| MySQL AB      | Studyguides | 2002-09-00 | 2003-03-30 |
| Icoaten & Co. | Studyguides | 2002-09-00 | 2003-03-30 |
| Nittboad Inc  | Studyguides | 2002-09-00 | 2003-03-30 |
| Seamen's      | PDC Server  | 2003-01-11 | 2003-01-00 |
| Lennart AG    | PDC Server  | 2003-01-11 | 2003-01-00 |
| MySQL AB      | PDC Server  | 2003-01-11 | 2003-01-00 |
| Icoaten & Co. | PDC Server  | 2003-01-11 | 2003-01-00 |
| Nittboad Inc  | PDC Server  | 2003-01-11 | 2003-01-00 |
| Seamen's      | Intranet    | 2009-02-00 | NULL       |
| Lennart AG    | Intranet    | 2009-02-00 | NULL       |
| MySQL AB      | Intranet    | 2009-02-00 | NULL       |
| Icoaten & Co. | Intranet    | 2009-02-00 | NULL       |
| Nittboad Inc  | Intranet    | 2009-02-00 | NULL       |
| Seamen's      | Intranet    | NULL       | NULL       |
| Lennart AG    | Intranet    | NULL       | NULL       |
| MySQL AB      | Intranet    | NULL       | NULL       |
| Icoaten & Co. | Intranet    | NULL       | NULL       |
| Nittboad Inc  | Intranet    | NULL       | NULL       |
| Seamen's      | SMB Server  | 2003-05-00 | NULL       |
| Lennart AG    | SMB Server  | 2003-05-00 | NULL       |
| MySQL AB      | SMB Server  | 2003-05-00 | NULL       |
| Icoaten & Co. | SMB Server  | 2003-05-00 | NULL       |
| Nittboad Inc  | SMB Server  | 2003-05-00 | NULL       |
| Seamen's      | WLAN        | NULL       | 2003-07-00 |
| Lennart AG    | WLAN        | NULL       | 2003-07-00 |
| MySQL AB      | WLAN        | NULL       | 2003-07-00 |
| Icoaten & Co. | WLAN        | NULL       | 2003-07-00 |
| Nittboad Inc  | WLAN        | NULL       | 2003-07-00 |
+---------------+-------------+------------+------------+
40 rows in set
```

```
+---------------+-------------+------------+------------+
| name          | name        | start      | end        |
+---------------+-------------+------------+------------+
| Lennart AG    | New CMS     | 2003-01-00 | 2003-05-00 |
| MySQL AB      | Texi2XML    | 2002-04-00 | 2003-09-00 |
| Icoaten & Co. | PDC Server  | 2003-01-00 | 2003-01-00 |
| Lennart AG    | Intranet    | 2009-02-00 | NULL       |
| Seamen's      | Intranet    | NULL       | NULL       |
| Icoaten & Co. | SMB Server  | 2003-05-00 | NULL       |
| Icoaten & Co. | WLAN        | NULL       | 2003-07-00 |
+---------------+-------------+------------+------------+
7 rows in set
```

Answer 4:

The statements will return the following result sets:

```
+----------------+--------------+--------------+--------------+
| name           | name         | start        | end          |
+----------------+--------------+--------------+--------------+
| Lennart AG     | New CMS      | 2003-01-00   | 2003-05-00   |
| MySQL AB       | Texi2XML     | 2002-04-00   | 2003-09-00   |
| Icoaten & Co.  | PDC Server  | 2003-01-00   | 2003-01-00   |
| Lennart AG     | Intranet    | 2009-02-00   | NULL         |
| Icoaten & Co.  | SMB Server  | 2003-05-00   | NULL         |
+----------------+--------------+--------------+--------------+
5 rows in set
```

```
+----------------+--------------+--------------+--------------+
| name           | name         | start        | end          |
+----------------+--------------+--------------+--------------+
| Lennart AG     | New CMS      | 2003-01-00   | 2003-05-00   |
| MySQL AB       | Texi2XML     | 2002-04-00   | 2003-09-00   |
| Icoaten & Co.  | PDC Server  | 2003-01-00   | 2003-01-00   |
+----------------+--------------+--------------+--------------+
3 rows in set
```

Answer 5:

Note: For this exercise, as for several of the following exercises, there might be more than one way to retrieve the required information. But here's one SQL statement that accomplishes the task:

```
mysql> SELECT
    -> c.name AS CLIENT, p.name AS PROJECT,
    -> p.start AS START, p.end AS END
    -> FROM client AS c
    -> LEFT JOIN project AS p
    -> USING (id)
    -> WHERE p.id IS NULL
    -> ORDER BY CLIENT
    -> ;
+--------------+---------+-------+------+
| CLIENT       | PROJECT | START | END  |
+--------------+---------+-------+------+
| Nittboad Inc | NULL    | NULL  | NULL |
+--------------+---------+-------+------+
1 row in set
```

Answer 6:

Here's one SQL statement that accomplishes the task:

```
mysql> SELECT
    -> c.name AS CLIENT, p.name AS PROJECT,
    -> p.start AS START, p.end AS END
    -> FROM client AS c
    -> LEFT JOIN project AS p
    -> USING (id)
    -> WHERE START BETWEEN '2003-01-00' AND '2003-12-31'
    -> ORDER BY START
    -> ;
+---------------+------------+------------+------------+
| CLIENT        | PROJECT    | START      | END        |
+---------------+------------+------------+------------+
| Lennart AG    | New CMS    | 2003-01-00 | 2003-05-00 |
| Icoaten & Co. | PDC Server | 2003-01-00 | 2003-01-00 |
| Icoaten & Co. | SMB Server | 2003-05-00 | NULL       |
+---------------+------------+------------+------------+
3 rows in set
```

Answer 7:

This statement accomplishes the task:

```
mysql> SELECT
    -> c.name AS CLIENT, p.name AS PROJECT,
    -> p.start AS START, p.end AS END
    -> FROM client AS c
    -> LEFT JOIN project AS p
    -> USING (id) /* or: ON c.id = p.id */
    -> WHERE p.name = 'Intranet'
    -> ;
+------------+----------+------------+------+
| CLIENT     | PROJECT  | START      | END  |
+------------+----------+------------+------+
| Seamen's   | Intranet | NULL       | NULL |
| Lennart AG | Intranet | 2009-02-00 | NULL |
+------------+----------+------------+------+
2 rows in set
```

Answer 8:

This statement accomplishes the task:

```
mysql> SELECT
    -> c.name AS CLIENT, p.name AS PROJECT,
    -> p.start AS START, p.end AS END
```

```
    -> FROM client AS c
    -> INNER JOIN project AS p
    -> USING (id) /* or: ON c.id = p.id */
    -> WHERE p.name = 'Intranet'
    -> ;
+------------+----------+------------+------+
| CLIENT     | PROJECT  | START      | END  |
+------------+----------+------------+------+
| Seamen's   | Intranet | NULL       | NULL |
| Lennart AG | Intranet | 2009-02-00 | NULL |
+------------+----------+------------+------+
2 rows in set
```

Answer 9:

This statement accomplishes the task:

```
mysql> SELECT
    -> c.name AS CLIENT, p.name AS PROJECT,
    -> p.start AS START, p.end AS END
    -> FROM client AS c, project AS p
    -> WHERE c.id = p.id
    -> AND p.name = 'Intranet'
    -> ;
+------------+----------+------------+------+
| CLIENT     | PROJECT  | START      | END  |
+------------+----------+------------+------+
| Seamen's   | Intranet | NULL       | NULL |
| Lennart AG | Intranet | 2009-02-00 | NULL |
+------------+----------+------------+------+
2 rows in set
```

Answer 10:

Here's one SQL statement that accomplishes the task:

```
mysql> SELECT
    -> c.name AS CLIENT, p.name AS PROJECT,
    -> p.start AS START, p.end AS END
    -> FROM client AS c
    -> LEFT JOIN project AS p
    -> USING (id) /* or: ON c.id = p.id */
    -> ORDER BY c.name ASC, p.start ASC
    -> ;
+---------------+------------+------------+------------+
| CLIENT        | PROJECT    | START      | END        |
+---------------+------------+------------+------------+
| Icoaten & Co. | WLAN       | NULL       | 2003-07-00 |
| Icoaten & Co. | PDC Server | 2003-01-00 | 2003-01-00 |
```

```
| Icoaten & Co. | SMB Server | 2003-05-00 | NULL       |
| Nittboad Inc  | NULL       | NULL       | NULL       |
| Lennart AG    | New CMS    | 2003-01-00 | 2003-05-00 |
| Lennart AG    | Intranet   | 2009-02-00 | NULL       |
| MySQL AB      | Texi2XML   | 2002-04-00 | 2003-09-00 |
| Seamen's      | Intranet   | NULL       | NULL       |
+---------------+------------+------------+------------+
8 rows in set
```

Answer 11:

Here's one SQL statement that accomplishes the task:

```
mysql> SELECT
    -> c.name AS CLIENT, p.name AS PROJECT,
    -> p.start AS START, p.end AS END
    -> FROM client AS c
    -> LEFT JOIN project AS p
    -> USING (id) /* or: ON c.id = p.id */
    -> WHERE p.start IS NOT NULL
    ->   AND p.end   IS NOT NULL
    -> ORDER BY c.name ASC, p.start ASC
    -> ;
+---------------+------------+------------+------------+
| CLIENT        | PROJECT    | START      | END        |
+---------------+------------+------------+------------+
| Icoaten & Co. | PDC Server | 2003-01-00 | 2003-01-00 |
| Lennart AG    | New CMS    | 2003-01-00 | 2003-05-00 |
| MySQL AB      | Texi2XML   | 2002-04-00 | 2003-09-00 |
+---------------+------------+------------+------------+
3 rows in set
```

Answer 12:

Subquery converted to a LEFT JOIN:

```
mysql> SELECT
    ->  p.pid AS `Project ID`,
    ->  p.name AS `Project Name`,
    ->  c.id AS `Client No`,
    ->  c.name AS `Client Name`
    -> FROM project AS p
    -> LEFT JOIN client AS c
    -> USING (id) /* or: ON p.id = c.id */
    -> WHERE c.name IS NOT NULL
    -> ;
+------------+--------------+-----------+---------------+
| Project ID | Project Name | Client No | Client Name   |
+------------+--------------+-----------+---------------+
```

```
|       10000 | New CMS       |       103 | Lennart AG    |
|       10010 | Texi2XML      |       110 | MySQL AB      |
|       10020 | Studyguides   |       110 | MySQL AB      |
|       10030 | PDC Server    |       115 | Icoaten & Co. |
|       10040 | Intranet      |       103 | Lennart AG    |
|       10050 | Intranet      |       101 | Seamen's      |
|       10060 | SMB Server    |       115 | Icoaten & Co. |
|       10070 | WLAN          |       115 | Icoaten & Co. |
+-------------+---------------+-----------+---------------+
8 rows in set
```

Answer 13:

Subquery converted to a RIGHT JOIN:

```
mysql> SELECT
    ->    p.pid AS `Project ID`,
    ->    p.name AS `Project Name`,
    ->    c.id AS `Client No`,
    ->    c.name AS `Client Name`
    -> FROM client AS c
    -> RIGHT JOIN project AS p
    -> USING (id) /* or: ON c.id = p.id */
    -> WHERE c.name IS NOT NULL
    -> ;
+-------------+---------------+-----------+---------------+
| Project ID  | Project Name  | Client No | Client Name   |
+-------------+---------------+-----------+---------------+
|       10000 | New CMS       |       103 | Lennart AG    |
|       10010 | Texi2XML      |       110 | MySQL AB      |
|       10020 | Studyguides   |       110 | MySQL AB      |
|       10030 | PDC Server    |       115 | Icoaten & Co. |
|       10040 | Intranet      |       103 | Lennart AG    |
|       10050 | Intranet      |       101 | Seamen's      |
|       10060 | SMB Server    |       115 | Icoaten & Co. |
|       10070 | WLAN          |       115 | Icoaten & Co. |
+-------------+---------------+-----------+---------------+
8 rows in set
```

Answer 14:

Subquery converted to an INNER JOIN:

```
mysql> SELECT
    ->    p.pid AS `Project ID`,
    ->    p.name AS `Project Name`,
    ->    c.id AS `Client No`,
    ->    c.name AS `Client Name`
    -> FROM project AS p
```

```
    -> INNER JOIN client AS c
    -> USING (id) /* or: ON p.id = c.id */
    -> ;
+------------+--------------+-----------+----------------+
| Project ID | Project Name | Client No | Client Name    |
+------------+--------------+-----------+----------------+
|      10050 | Intranet     |       101 | Seamen's       |
|      10000 | New CMS      |       103 | Lennart AG     |
|      10040 | Intranet     |       103 | Lennart AG     |
|      10010 | Texi2XML     |       110 | MySQL AB       |
|      10020 | Studyguides  |       110 | MySQL AB       |
|      10030 | PDC Server   |       115 | Icoaten & Co.  |
|      10060 | SMB Server   |       115 | Icoaten & Co.  |
|      10070 | WLAN         |       115 | Icoaten & Co.  |
+------------+--------------+-----------+----------------+
8 rows in set
```

Answer 15:

Subquery converted to a LEFT JOIN:

```
mysql> SELECT
    ->    p.pid AS `Project ID`,
    ->    p.name AS `Project Name`,
    ->    c.id AS `Client No`,
    ->    c.name AS `Client Name`
    -> FROM project AS p
    -> LEFT JOIN client AS c
    -> USING (id) /* or: ON p.id = c.id */
    -> WHERE c.name IS NULL
    -> ;
+------------+--------------+-----------+-------------+
| Project ID | Project Name | Client No | Client Name |
+------------+--------------+-----------+-------------+
|      10080 | Intranet     |      NULL | NULL        |
|      10090 | PDC Server   |      NULL | NULL        |
+------------+--------------+-----------+-------------+
2 rows in set
```

Answer 16:

Subquery converted to a RIGHT JOIN:

```
mysql> SELECT
    ->    p.pid AS `Project ID`,
    ->    p.name AS `Project Name`,
    ->    c.id AS `Client No`,
    ->    c.name AS `Client Name`
    -> FROM client AS c
```

```
    -> RIGHT JOIN project AS p
    -> USING (id) /* or: ON c.id = p.id */
    -> WHERE c.name IS NULL
    -> ;
+------------+--------------+-----------+-------------+
| Project ID | Project Name | Client No | Client Name |
+------------+--------------+-----------+-------------+
|      10080 | Intranet     |      NULL | NULL        |
|      10090 | PDC Server   |      NULL | NULL        |
+------------+--------------+-----------+-------------+
2 rows in set
```

Answer 17:

This subquery cannot be converted into an inner join because an inner join will find only matching combinations, not rows that do not match.

Answer 18:

This statement retrieves a list of the countries in South America that have a larger surface area than Paraguay:

```
mysql> SELECT
    ->    c1.Name AS 'Country',
    ->    c2.Name AS 'Other Countries',
    ->    c2.Continent AS 'Continent',
    ->    c2.SurfaceArea AS 'Surface Area'
    -> FROM Country AS c1
    -> INNER JOIN Country AS c2
    -> USING (Continent)
    -> WHERE c2.SurfaceArea > c1.SurfaceArea
    -> AND c1.Name = 'Paraguay'
    -> ;
+----------+-----------------+---------------+--------------+
| Country  | Other Countries | Continent     | Surface Area |
+----------+-----------------+---------------+--------------+
| Paraguay | Argentina       | South America |   2780400.00 |
| Paraguay | Bolivia         | South America |   1098581.00 |
| Paraguay | Brazil          | South America |   8547403.00 |
| Paraguay | Chile           | South America |    756626.00 |
| Paraguay | Colombia        | South America |   1138914.00 |
| Paraguay | Peru            | South America |   1285216.00 |
| Paraguay | Venezuela       | South America |    912050.00 |
+----------+-----------------+---------------+--------------+
```

Answer 19:

This statement retrieves a list of all countries whose population is greater than or equal to that of Germany:

```
mysql> SELECT
    ->    c1.Name AS 'Country',
    ->    c2.Name AS 'Other Countries',
    ->    c2.Population AS 'Population'
    ->  FROM Country AS c1, Country AS c2
    ->  WHERE c2.Population >= c1.Population
    ->  AND c1.Name = 'Germany'
    ->  ORDER BY c2.Population DESC
    -> ;
+---------+--------------------+------------+
| Country | Other Countries    | Population |
+---------+--------------------+------------+
| Germany | China              | 1277558000 |
| Germany | India              | 1013662000 |
| Germany | United States      |  278357000 |
| Germany | Indonesia          |  212107000 |
| Germany | Brazil             |  170115000 |
| Germany | Pakistan           |  156483000 |
| Germany | Russian Federation |  146934000 |
| Germany | Bangladesh         |  129155000 |
| Germany | Japan              |  126714000 |
| Germany | Nigeria            |  111506000 |
| Germany | Mexico             |   98881000 |
| Germany | Germany            |   82164700 |
+---------+--------------------+------------+
```

Answer 20:

This statement retrieves a list of all countries whose population and surface area are greater than or equal to that of Nepal:

```
mysql> SELECT
    ->    c1.Name AS 'Country',
    ->    c2.Name AS 'Other Countries',
    ->    LEFT(c2.Region,10) AS 'Region',
    ->    c2.Population AS 'Population',
    ->    c2.SurfaceArea AS 'Surface'
    ->  FROM Country AS c1, Country AS c2
    ->  WHERE c1.Region = c2.Region
    ->    AND c2.SurfaceArea >= c1.SurfaceArea
    ->    AND c2.Population  >= c1.Population
    ->    AND c1.Name = 'Nepal'
    ->  ORDER BY c2.Population DESC
    -> ;
+---------+-----------------+------------+------------+------------+
| Country | Other Countries | Region     | Population | Surface    |
+---------+-----------------+------------+------------+------------+
```

```
| Nepal   | India          | Southern a | 1013662000 | 3287263.00 |
| Nepal   | Pakistan       | Southern a |  156483000 |  796095.00 |
| Nepal   | Iran           | Southern a |   67702000 | 1648195.00 |
| Nepal   | Uzbekistan     | Southern a |   24318000 |  447400.00 |
| Nepal   | Nepal          | Southern a |   23930000 |  147181.00 |
+---------+----------------+------------+------------+------------+
```

9

Importing and Exporting Data

This chapter covers the following exam topics:

- The LOAD DATA INFILE statement
- Using files on the server host and the client host
- Limiting the columns and rows being imported
- The SELECT INTO OUTFILE statement
- Privileges needed for LOAD DATA INFILE and SELECT INTO OUTFILE

Questions on the material in this chapter make up approximately 5% of the exam.

MySQL includes two SQL statements that can be used to import data from files into your database or export data from your database into files:

- LOAD DATA INFILE reads data records directly from a file and inserts them into a table.
- SELECT ... INTO OUTFILE writes the result of a SELECT statement to a file.

The two statements are related in the sense that they both transfer information between MySQL and datafiles. Also, both statements use similar syntax for describing the format of datafile contents.

The mysqlimport client provides another way to load datafiles into tables. It's a command-line interface to the LOAD DATA INFILE statement. It examines its arguments to determine what you want it to do, and then constructs appropriate LOAD DATA INFILE statements and executes them on your behalf. For more information about this program, see section 3.3, "Using mysqlimport."

9.1 The LOAD DATA INFILE Statement

LOAD DATA INFILE provides an alternative to INSERT for adding new records to a table. With INSERT, you specify data values directly in the INSERT statement. LOAD DATA INFILE reads the values from a separate datafile.

The simplest form of the LOAD DATA INFILE statement specifies only the name of the datafile and the table into which to load the file:

```
LOAD DATA INFILE 'file_name' INTO TABLE table_name;
```

The filename is given as a string and must be quoted. MySQL assumes, unless told otherwise, that the file is located on the server host, that it has the default file format (tab-delimited and newline-terminated lines), and that each input line contains a value for each column in the table. However, LOAD DATA INFILE has clauses that give you control over each of those aspects of data-loading operations and more:

- Which table to load
- The name and location of the datafile
- Which columns to load
- The format of the datafile
- How to handle duplicate records
- Whether to ignore lines at the beginning of the datafile

The syntax for LOAD DATA INFILE is as follows, where optional parts of the statement are indicated by square brackets:

```
LOAD DATA [LOCAL] INFILE 'file_name'
    [IGNORE | REPLACE]
    INTO TABLE table_name
    format_specifiers
    [IGNORE n LINES]
    [(column_list)]
```

The following sections explain how the various parts of the statement work.

9.1.1 Specifying the Datafile Location

LOAD DATA INFILE can read datafiles that are located on the server host or on the client host:

- By default, MySQL assumes that the file is located on the server host. The MySQL server reads the file directly.
- If the statement begins with LOAD DATA LOCAL INFILE rather than with LOAD DATA INFILE, the file is read from the client host on which the statement is issued. In other words, LOCAL means local to the client host from which the statement is issued. In this case, the client program reads the datafile and sends its contents over the network to the server.

The rules for interpreting the filename are somewhat different for the server host and the client host.

9.1.1.1 Specifying the Location of Files on the Server Host

Without LOCAL in the LOAD DATA INFILE statement, MySQL looks for the datafile located on the server host and interprets the pathname as follows:

- If you refer to the file by its full pathname, the server looks for the file in that exact location.
- If you specify a relative name with a single component, the server looks for the file in the database directory for the default database. (This isn't necessarily the database that contains the table into which you're loading the file.)
- If you specify a relative pathname with more than one component, the server interprets the name relative to its data directory.

Suppose that the server's data directory is /var/mysql/data, the database directory for the test database is /var/mysql/data/test, and the file data.txt is located in that database directory. Using the filename interpretation rules just given, it's possible to refer to the data.txt file three different ways in a LOAD DATA INFILE statement:

- You can refer to the file by its full pathname:

```
LOAD DATA INFILE '/var/mysql/data/test/data.txt' INTO TABLE t;
```

- If test is the default database, you can refer to a file in the database directory using just the final component of its pathname:

```
LOAD DATA INFILE 'data.txt' INTO TABLE t;
```

- You can refer to any file in or under the server's data directory by its pathname relative to that directory:

```
LOAD DATA INFILE './test/data.txt' INTO TABLE t;
```

9.1.1.2 Specifying the Location of Files on the Client Host

If you use LOCAL to read a datafile located on the client host, pathname interpretation is simpler:

- If you refer to the file by its full pathname, the client program looks for the file in that exact location.
- If you specify a relative pathname, the client program looks for the file relative to its current directory. Normally, this is the directory in which you invoked the program.

Suppose that there's a datafile named data.txt located in the /var/tmp directory on the client host and you invoke the mysql program while located in that directory. You can load the file into a table t using either of these two statements:

```
LOAD DATA LOCAL INFILE '/var/tmp/data.txt' INTO TABLE t;
LOAD DATA LOCAL INFILE 'data.txt' INTO TABLE t;
```

The first statement names the file using its full pathname. The second names the file relative to the current directory. If you invoke the `mysql` program in the `/var` directory instead, you can still load the file using the same full pathname. However, the relative pathname to the file is different than when running the program in the `/var/tmp` directory:

```
LOAD DATA LOCAL INFILE 'tmp/data.txt' INTO TABLE t;
```

9.1.1.3 Specifying Filenames on Windows

On Windows, the pathname separator character is \, but MySQL treats the backslash as the escape character in strings. To deal with this issue, write separators in Windows pathnames either as / or as \\. To load a file named `C:\mydata\data.txt`, specify the filename as shown in either of the following statements:

```
LOAD DATA INFILE 'C:/mydata/data.txt' INTO TABLE t;
LOAD DATA INFILE 'C:\\mydata\\data.txt' INTO TABLE t;
```

9.1.2 Loading Specific Table Columns

By default, LOAD DATA INFILE assumes that data values in input lines are present in the same order as the columns in the table. If the datafile contains more columns than the table, MySQL ignores the excess data values. If the datafile contains too few columns, each missing column is set to its default value in the table. (This is the same way MySQL handles columns that aren't named in an INSERT statement.)

If input lines don't contain values for every table column, or the data values are not in the same order as table columns, you can add a comma-separated list of column names within parentheses at the end of the LOAD DATA INFILE statement. This tells MySQL how columns in the table correspond to successive columns in the datafile. A list of columns is useful in two ways:

- If the rows of the datafile don't contain a value for every column in the table, a column list indicates which columns are present in the file. Suppose that a table named subscriber has the following structure:

```
mysql> DESCRIBE subscriber;
+---------+------------------+------+-----+---------+----------------+
| Field   | Type             | Null | Key | Default | Extra          |
+---------+------------------+------+-----+---------+----------------+
| id      | int(10) unsigned |      | PRI | NULL    | auto_increment |
| name    | char(40)         |      |     |         |                |
| address | char(40)         |      |     |         |                |
+---------+------------------+------+-----+---------+----------------+
```

Here, id is an AUTO_INCREMENT column. If you have a file people.txt containing names and addresses and want MySQL to generate ID numbers automatically, load the file like this:

```
LOAD DATA INFILE 'people.txt' INTO TABLE subscriber (name,address);
```

For any table column that isn't assigned a value from the datafile, MySQL sets it to its default value. MySQL thus sets the `id` column to the next sequence value for each input line.

- If the order of the columns in the datafile doesn't correspond to the order of the columns in the table, a column list tells MySQL how to match up columns properly. For example, if the lines in `people.txt` contain addresses and names rather than names and addresses, the statement to load the file looks like this instead:

```
LOAD DATA INFILE 'people.txt' INTO TABLE subscriber (address,name);
```

9.1.3 Skipping Datafile Lines

To ignore the initial part of the datafile, use the `IGNORE n LINES` clause, where *n* is the number of input lines to skip. This clause is commonly used when a file begins with a row of column names rather than data values. For example, to skip the first input line, a statement might be written like this:

```
LOAD DATA INFILE 'data.txt' INTO TABLE t IGNORE 1 LINES;
```

9.1.4 LOAD DATA INFILE and Duplicate Records

When you add new records to a table with an `INSERT` or `REPLACE` statement, you can control how to handle new records containing values that duplicate unique key values already present in the table. You can allow an error to occur, ignore the new records, or replace the old records with the new ones. `LOAD DATA INFILE` affords the same types of control over duplicate records by means of two modifier keywords. However, its duplicate-handling behavior differs slightly depending on whether the datafile is on the server host or the client host, so you must take the datafile location into account.

When loading a file that's located on the server host, `LOAD DATA INFILE` handles records that contain duplicate unique keys as follows:

- By default, an input record that causes a duplicate-key violation results in an error and the rest of the datafile isn't loaded. (Records processed up to that point are loaded into the table.)
- If you specify the `IGNORE` keyword after the filename, new records that cause duplicate-key violations are ignored and no error occurs. `LOAD DATA INFILE` processes the entire file, loads all records not containing duplicate keys, and discards the rest.
- If you specify the `REPLACE` keyword after the filename, new records that cause duplicate-key violations replace any records already in the table that contain the duplicated key values. `LOAD DATA INFILE` processes the entire file and loads all its records into the table.

IGNORE and REPLACE are mutually exclusive. You can specify one or the other, but not both.

For datafiles located on the client host, duplicate unique key handling is similar, except that the default is to ignore records that contain duplicate keys rather than to terminate with an error. That is, the default is as though the IGNORE modifier were specified. The reason for this is that the client/server protocol doesn't allow transfer of the datafile from the client host to the server to be interrupted after it has started, so there's no convenient way to abort the operation in the middle.

9.1.5 Interpreting the Result of a LOAD DATA INFILE Statement

As LOAD DATA INFILE executes, it keeps track of the number of records processed and the number of data conversions that occur. Then it returns to the client an information string in the following format (the counts in each field will vary per LOAD DATA INFILE operation):

```
Records: 174  Deleted: 0  Skipped: 3  Warnings: 14
```

The fields have the following meanings:

- Records indicates the number of input records read from the file. (This is not necessarily the number of records added to the table.)
- Deleted is the number of records in the table that were replaced by input records having the same unique key value as a key already present in the table. The value may be nonzero if you use the REPLACE keyword in the statement.
- Skipped indicates the number of input records that were ignored because they contained a unique key value that duplicated a key already present in the table. The value may be nonzero if you use the IGNORE keyword in the statement.
- Warnings indicates the number of problems found in the input file. These can occur for several reasons, such as missing data values or data conversion (for example, converting an empty string to 0 for a numeric column). The warning count can be larger than the number of input records because warnings can occur for each data value in a record. LOAD DATA INFILE doesn't provide more specific information about problems with the datafile. In particular, it doesn't indicate which input records or data values resulted in warnings.

9.1.6 Privileges Needed for LOAD DATA INFILE

LOAD DATA INFILE requires that you have the INSERT privilege for the table into which you want to load data, as well as the DELETE privilege if you specify the REPLACE modifier. For a file located on the client host, you must have read access to the file, but no additional MySQL privileges are required. However, if the datafile is located on the server host, the server itself must read the file. In that case, you must also have the FILE privilege. Because

FILE is an administrative privilege, it's likely that to use LOAD DATA INFILE without LOCAL, you'll need to connect to the server as an administrative user such as root.

9.1.7 Efficiency of LOAD DATA INFILE

LOAD DATA INFILE is very efficient for a datafile that is located on the server host. The MySQL server reads the file directly, so the data values need not cross the network from the client to the server. But even for a datafile located locally on the client host, LOAD DATA INFILE is more efficient than INSERT statements because there's less overhead for parsing data values and because the rows are loaded in a single operation. (Some of the efficiency of loading multiple rows at once can be obtained with INSERT if you use its multiple-row syntax, but LOAD DATA INFILE is still more efficient.)

9.2 The SELECT … INTO OUTFILE **Statement**

A SELECT statement normally creates a result set that the server returns to the client. For example, when you issue a SELECT using the mysql client, the server returns the result and mysql writes it in tabular format when run interactively or in tab-delimited format when run in batch mode.

A variation on SELECT syntax adds an INTO OUTFILE clause. This form of SELECT writes the result set directly into a file and thus is the complement of LOAD DATA INFILE. To use SELECT in this way, place the INTO OUTFILE clause before the FROM clause. For example, to write the contents of the Country table into a file named Country.txt, issue this statement:

```
SELECT * INTO OUTFILE 'Country.txt' FROM Country;
```

The name of the file indicates the location where you want to write it. MySQL interprets the pathname using the same rules that apply to LOAD DATA INFILE for files located on the server host. For example, given the statement just shown, the server writes the file into the database directory of the default database.

Use of INTO OUTFILE in a SELECT statement results in several operational differences compared to when it isn't used:

- The output produced by a SELECT … INTO OUTFILE statement never leaves the server host. Instead of sending the result over the network to the client, the server writes it to a file on the server host. The output file must not already exist. This prevents files from being overwritten, either accidentally or maliciously.

- Because the statement causes the server to write a new file on the server host, you must have the FILE privilege.

- The file is created with permissions that make it owned by the MySQL server but world-readable.

- The output is written as a set of columns, one line per row selected by the statement. By default, data values are delimited by tab characters and lines are terminated with newlines, but you can control the output format by adding format specifiers after the filename, as described in section 9.3, "Datafile Format Specifiers."

The location and manner in which SELECT … INTO OUTFILE creates the file has several implications:

- If you want to access the file directly, you must have a login account on the server host or be otherwise able to access files on that host somehow. For some purposes, this limitation might not be a problem. For example, you don't need to access the file yourself to reload it later with LOAD DATA INFILE because the MySQL server can read it for you.

- Because the file is world-readable, anyone who has filesystem access on the server host can read it. You probably don't want to use SELECT … INTO OUTFILE to write files that contain sensitive information, unless perhaps you're the only person with access to the machine.

- Because the file is owned by the MySQL server, you might not be able to remove it after you're done with it. It might be necessary to coordinate with the server administrator to arrange for removal of the file.

9.3 Datafile Format Specifiers

LOAD DATA INFILE and SELECT … INTO OUTFILE both assume by default a datafile format in which column values are separated by tab characters and records are terminated by newlines. If a datafile to be read by LOAD DATA INFILE has different column separators or line terminators, you must indicate what the format is so that MySQL can read the file contents correctly. Similarly, if you want SELECT … INTO OUTFILE to write a file with different separators or terminators, you'll need to indicate the format to use. It's also possible to control quoting and escaping behavior.

LOAD DATA INFILE and SELECT … INTO OUTFILE don't allow you to specify anything about the characteristics of specific individual columns in the datafile, such as that column 3 is numeric or that column 17 contains dates. Instead, you define the general characteristics that apply to all column values: What characters separate column values in data rows, whether values are quoted, and whether there is an escape character that signifies special character sequences.

For LOAD DATA INFILE, any format specifiers given are listed after the table name. For SELECT … INTO OUTFILE, they follow the output filename. The syntax for format specifiers is the same for both statements and looks like this:

```
FIELDS
    TERMINATED BY 'string'
    ENCLOSED BY 'char'
```

```
    ESCAPED BY 'char'
LINES TERMINATED BY 'string'
```

The FIELDS clause defines the formatting of data values within a line and the LINES clause defines the line-ending sequence. In other words, FIELDS indicates the structure of column values within records and LINES indicates where record boundaries occur.

The TERMINATED BY, ENCLOSED BY, and ESCAPED BY parts of the FIELDS clause may be given in any order. You need not specify all three parts. Defaults are used for any that are missing (or if the FIELDS clause itself is missing):

- Data values are assumed to be terminated by (that is, separated by) tab characters. To indicate a different value, include a TERMINATED BY option.

- Data values are assumed not to be quoted. To indicate a quoting character, include an ENCLOSED BY option. For LOAD DATA INFILE, enclosing quotes are stripped from input values if they're found. For SELECT … INTO OUTFILE, output values are written enclosed within quoting characters.

  A variation on ENCLOSED BY is OPTIONALLY ENCLOSED BY. For LOAD DATA INFILE, this is the same as ENCLOSED BY. For SELECT … INTO OUTFILE, it is different: The presence of OPTION-ALLY causes output value quoting only for CHAR and VARCHAR columns, not for all values.

- The default escape character is backslash ('/'). Any occurrence of this character within a data value modifies interpretation of the character that follows it. To indicate a different escape character, include an ESCAPED BY option. MySQL understands the following special escape sequences:

Sequence	Meaning
\N	NULL value
\0	ASCII NUL byte
\b	Backspace
\n	Newline (linefeed)
\r	Carriage return
\s	Space
\t	Tab
\'	Single quote
\"	Double quote
\\	Backslash

All these sequences except \N are understood whether they appear alone or within a longer data value. \N is understood as NULL only when it appears alone.

The default line terminator is the newline (linefeed) character. To indicate a line-ending sequence explicitly, use a LINES clause. Common line-terminator specifiers are newline, carriage return, and carriage return/newline pairs. These are specified as follows:

```
LINES TERMINATED BY '\n'
LINES TERMINATED BY '\r'
LINES TERMINATED BY '\r\n'
```

Because newline is the default line terminator, it need be specified only if you want to make the line-ending sequence explicit. Newline terminators are common on Unix systems, carriage returns are common on Mac OS and Mac OS X, and carriage return/newline pairs are common on Windows.

The ESCAPED BY option controls only the handling of values in the datafile, not how you specify the statement itself. If you want to specify a datafile escape character of @, you'd write ESCAPED BY '@'. That doesn't mean you then use @ to escape special characters elsewhere in the statement. For example, you'd still specify carriage return as the line termination character using LINES TERMINATED BY '\r', not using LINES TERMINATED BY '@r'.

Suppose that a file named data.txt contains information in comma-separated values (CSV) format, with values quoted by double quote characters and lines terminated by carriage returns. To load the file into a table t, use this LOAD DATA INFILE statement:

```
LOAD DATA INFILE 'data.txt' INTO TABLE t
FIELDS TERMINATED BY ',' ENCLOSED BY '"'
LINES TERMINATED BY '\r';
```

To write information in that same format, use this SELECT … INTO OUTFILE statement:

```
SELECT * INTO OUTFILE 'data.txt'
FIELDS TERMINATED BY ',' ENCLOSED BY '"'
LINES TERMINATED BY '\r'
FROM t;
```

9.4 Importing and Exporting NULL Values

A NULL value indicates the absence of a value or an unknown value, which is difficult to represent literally in a datafile. For import and export purposes, MySQL uses the convention of representing NULL values by \N:

- For LOAD DATA INFILE, a \N appearing unquoted by itself as a column value is interpreted as NULL. MySQL users sometimes assume that an empty value in an input file will be handled as a NULL value, but that isn't true. MySQL converts an empty input value to 0, an empty string, or a "zero" temporal value, depending on the type of the corresponding table column.

- For SELECT … INTO OUTFILE, MySQL writes NULL values to the output file as \N.

9.5 Exercises

Question 1:

Assume that you have a text file containing tab-separated data that you want to load into a table named loadtest that has the following structure:

```
mysql> DESCRIBE loadtest;
+---------+---------+------+-----+---------+-------+
| Field   | Type    | Null | Key | Default | Extra |
+---------+---------+------+-----+---------+-------+
| number1 | int(11) | YES  |     | NULL    |       |
| char1   | char(1) | YES  |     | NULL    |       |
| date1   | date    | YES  |     | NULL    |       |
+---------+---------+------+-----+---------+-------+
```

One line of the file looks like this, where whitespace between values represents tab characters:

```
NULL NULL NULL
```

If you use LOAD DATA INFILE to load the file, what values will be created in the table from the values in this line? What values should the line contain if you actually want a row of NULL values to be created in the table?

Question 2:

Here's the structure of an empty table called personnel:

```
mysql> DESCRIBE personnel;
+-------+-------------------+------+-----+---------+----------------+
| Field | Type              | Null | Key | Default | Extra          |
+-------+-------------------+------+-----+---------+----------------+
| pid   | smallint(5) unsigned |   | PRI | NULL    | auto_increment |
| unit  | tinyint(3) unsigned | YES |     | NULL    |                |
| grade | tinyint(3) unsigned | YES |     | NULL    |                |
+-------+-------------------+------+-----+---------+----------------+
mysql> SELECT * FROM personnel;
Empty set
```

A file called /tmp/personnel.dat contains data that you want to load into the personnel table, using the LOAD DATA INFILE statement. The datafile contains data for the unit and grade columns and looks like this:

```
23;42
23;53
23;123
23;142
23;198
```

```
23;248
23;294
42;110
42;256
```

The lines are terminated by \r. Upon which operating system was the datafile most probably generated?

Question 3:

Here's the structure of an empty table called personnel:

```
mysql> DESCRIBE personnel;
+-------+---------------------+------+-----+---------+----------------+
| Field | Type                | Null | Key | Default | Extra          |
+-------+---------------------+------+-----+---------+----------------+
| pid   | smallint(5) unsigned |     | PRI | NULL    | auto_increment |
| unit  | tinyint(3) unsigned  | YES |     | NULL    |                |
| grade | tinyint(3) unsigned  | YES |     | NULL    |                |
+-------+---------------------+------+-----+---------+----------------+
mysql> SELECT * FROM personnel;
Empty set
```

A file called /tmp/personnel.dat contains data that you want to load into the personnel
table, using the LOAD DATA INFILE statement. The datafile contains data for the unit and
grade columns and looks like this:

```
23;42
23;53
23;123
23;142
23;198
23;248
23;294
42;110
42;256
```

The lines are terminated by \r. What statement would you issue to load the data into the
table?

Question 4:

Here's the structure of an empty table called personnel:

```
mysql> DESCRIBE personnel;
+-------+---------------------+------+-----+---------+----------------+
| Field | Type                | Null | Key | Default | Extra          |
+-------+---------------------+------+-----+---------+----------------+
| pid   | smallint(5) unsigned |     | PRI | NULL    | auto_increment |
| unit  | tinyint(3) unsigned  | YES |     | NULL    |                |
```

```
| grade | tinyint(3) unsigned | YES  |     | NULL    |               |
+-------+---------------------+------+-----+---------+---------------+
mysql> SELECT * FROM personnel;
Empty set
```

A file called /tmp/personnel.dat contains data that you want to load into the personnel table, using the LOAD DATA INFILE statement. The datafile contains data for the unit and grade columns and looks like this:

```
23;42
23;53
23;123
23;142
23;198
23;248
23;294
42;110
42;256
```

The lines are terminated by \r. What entries will be in the table if the data import succeeds?

Question 5:

Is there a MySQL client program that could be used for data import instead of the LOAD DATA INFILE statement? If so, what is it called?

Question 6:

The simplest form of the LOAD DATA INFILE statement looks like this:

```
LOAD DATA INFILE 'file_name' INTO TABLE table_name;
```

MySQL will assume a number of defaults for options that are omitted from the statement. Assuming that the filename has a single component, what will MySQL use as the default location for file_name?

Question 7:

The simplest form of the LOAD DATA INFILE statement looks like this:

```
LOAD DATA INFILE 'file_name' INTO TABLE table_name;
```

MySQL will assume a number of defaults for options that are omitted from the statement. What will MySQL use as the default separators for fields and lines?

Question 8:

The simplest form of the LOAD DATA INFILE statement looks like this:

```
LOAD DATA INFILE 'file_name' INTO TABLE table_name;
```

MySQL will assume a number of defaults for options that are omitted from the statement. What will MySQL use as the default table columns to load?

Question 9:

The simplest form of the LOAD DATA INFILE statement looks like this:

```
LOAD DATA INFILE 'file_name' INTO TABLE table_name;
```

MySQL will assume a number of defaults for options that are omitted from the statement. What will MySQL use as the default number of lines of file_name to skip?

Question 10:

The simplest form of the LOAD DATA INFILE statement looks like this:

```
LOAD DATA INFILE 'file_name' INTO TABLE table_name;
```

MySQL will assume a number of defaults for options that are omitted from the statement. What will MySQL use as the default behavior when there are lines in file_name that would duplicate unique-valued key entries? Does it make a difference if file_name is located on the client host rather than on the server host?

Question 11:

After loading data into a table, you see the following result from the LOAD DATA INFILE statement. What does it mean?

```
Query OK, 18 rows affected (0.00 sec)
Records: 9  Deleted: 9  Skipped: 0  Warnings: 2
```

Question 12:

After loading data into a table, you see the following result from the LOAD DATA INFILE statement. What does it mean?

```
Query OK, 0 rows affected (0.00 sec)
Records: 9  Deleted: 0  Skipped: 9  Warnings: 2
```

Question 13:

Consider the following table data:

```
mysql> SELECT * FROM personnel;
+-----+------+-------+
| pid | unit | grade |
+-----+------+-------+
|  46 |   23 |    42 |
|  47 |   23 |    53 |
|  48 |   23 |   123 |
|  49 |   23 |   142 |
|  50 |   23 |   198 |
```

```
|  60 |  23 |   248 |
|  70 |  23 |   255 |
|  80 |  42 |   110 |
|  90 |  42 |   255 |
+-----+------+-------+
```

Assume that you want to export the pid and unit columns for the five highest grades to a file that has Windows-like line terminators (\r\n) and that looks like this:

```
"70";"23"
"90";"42"
"60";"23"
"50";"23"
"49";"23"
```

What statement would you issue?

Answers to Exercises

Answer 1:

The actual result of the LOAD DATA statement will look like this:

```
mysql> SELECT * FROM loadtest;
+---------+-------+------------+
| number1 | char1 | date1      |
+---------+-------+------------+
|       0 | N     | 0000-00-00 |
+---------+-------+------------+
```

The import file values are interpreted as the string 'NULL', not as NULL values. For nonstring columns, these strings are converted first before they are inserted. This conversion results in values of 0 for integers and '0000-00-00' for dates. For the string column, the import string is clipped to the length of the column, resulting in a value of 'N'. If you wanted to actually insert NULL values, the import file would have to contain the \N sequence that LOAD DATA INFILE interprets as representing NULL.

Answer 2:

The datafile personnel.dat was most probably generated under Mac OS because carriage returns (\r) are a common line terminator under that operating system.

Answer 3:

This statement loads the data into the personnel table:

```
mysql> LOAD DATA
    -> INFILE '/tmp/personnel.dat'
    -> INTO TABLE personnel
    -> FIELDS TERMINATED BY ';'
    -> LINES TERMINATED BY '\r'
```

```
    -> (unit, grade)
    -> ;
Query OK, 9 rows affected (0.01 sec)
Records: 9  Deleted: 0  Skipped: 0  Warnings: 2
```

Note the two warnings.

Answer 4:

The table will contain the following data:

```
mysql> SELECT * FROM personnel;
+-----+------+-------+
| pid | unit | grade |
+-----+------+-------+
|   1 |   23 |    42 |
|   2 |   23 |    53 |
|   3 |   23 |   123 |
|   4 |   23 |   142 |
|   5 |   23 |   198 |
|   6 |   23 |   248 |
|   7 |   23 |   255 |
|   8 |   42 |   110 |
|   9 |   42 |   255 |
+-----+------+-------+
9 rows in set
```

As you would expect, the pid column values were assigned automatically due to the AUTO_INCREMENT option of the pid column. For the grade column, however, the import encountered two problem lines (7 and 9), where the provided values of 294 and 256 are out of the range of the TINYINT UNSIGNED datatype (which has a maximum value of 255). The values given were therefore truncated to the maximum value for this datatype before being inserted. MySQL gives a warning for each of the values truncated, as shown in the message displayed by the LOAD DATA INFILE statement. (See answer to previous question.)

Answer 5:

Instead of using the SQL command LOAD DATA INFILE, you could use the MySQL client program named mysqlimport. It takes arguments that correspond to the various clauses of the LOAD DATA INFILE statement.

Answer 6:

The default location of file_name is the directory of the default database.

Answer 7:

The default separator for fields is the tab character (\t). The default separator for lines is the newline character (\n).

Answer 8:

All table columns will be loaded by default. This means that `file_name` should specify a value for every table column. If lines don't contain values for all columns, each missing column is set to its default value.

Answer 9:

No lines of `file_name` will be skipped by default.

Answer 10:

If the datafile is located on the server host, the default behavior in case of duplicate unique-valued key entries is to return an error. MySQL will not insert the duplicating line, and will then skip the rest of the lines. If the datafile is located on the client host, the default behavior changes. In this case, the default is to skip lines that would duplicate records; that is, MySQL operates as if the keyword `IGNORE` had been specified.

Answer 11:

The message provides four pieces of information.

- Nine lines were read from the datafile (`Records: 9`).
- The keyword `REPLACE` was used in the `LOAD DATA INFILE` statement.
- Each one of the nine lines in the datafile has the same unique-valued key entries. The same value already exists in the table, so all nine entries were deleted and then replaced by the nine lines from the datafile (`Deleted: 9`, and `18 rows affected`).
- The warnings indicate that two problems were found in the import file (`Warnings: 2`).

Answer 12:

The message provides four pieces of information.

- Nine lines were read from the datafile (`Records: 9`).
- The keyword `IGNORE` was used in the `LOAD DATA INFILE` statement.
- Each one of the nine lines in the datafile has the same unique-valued key entries. The same value already exists in the table, so all nine entries were skipped, that is, they were not inserted (`Skipped: 9`, and `0 rows affected`).
- The warnings indicate that two problems were found in the import file (`Warnings: 2`).

Answer 13:

```
mysql> SELECT pid, unit
    ->   INTO OUTFILE 'highpers.dat'
    ->   FIELDS TERMINATED BY ';'
    ->          ENCLOSED BY '"'
    ->   LINES TERMINATED BY '\r\n'
    ->   FROM personnel
    ->   ORDER BY grade DESC
    ->   LIMIT 5
    -> ;
```

10

MySQL Architecture

A MySQL installation includes a number of programs that work together using a client/server architecture, and a data directory under which the server manages the databases in which you're storing information. This chapter describes the general characteristics of the architecture used by the server and its client programs, and the use and layout of the server's data directory. The coverage includes the following topics:

- The design architecture of MySQL; its major programs and how they work together.
- Important administrative clients and their capabilities.
- Communication protocols that clients can use to connect to the server.
- How the server uses disk and memory to do its job. Disk use includes the components of the data directory under which the server stores databases and related files such as logs. Memory use includes data structures that the server sets up to manage communication with clients and to process the contents of databases.
- The server's log files. The logs record various types of diagnostic and error messages, and information about the queries that the server processes. They can be used to assess the operational state of the server, for data recovery after a crash, and for replication purposes.
- The storage engines that the server supports. MySQL enables you to choose from any of several table types when creating a table. These table types are managed by different storage engines, each of which has specific characteristics.

Questions on the material in this chapter make up approximately 15% of the exam.

MySQL runs on many varieties of Windows, Unix, and Linux. Most of the concepts discussed here apply universally to any system on which MySQL runs. Platform-specific information is so indicated. In this guide, unless otherwise specified, *Unix* includes Linux and other Unix-like operating systems.

10.1 Client/Server Overview

MySQL operates using a client/server architecture. The server is the central program that manages database contents. The client programs connect to the server to retrieve or modify data. MySQL also includes nonclient utility programs and scripts. Thus, a complete MySQL installation consists of three general categories of programs:

- *The server.* This is the `mysqld` program that manages databases and tables. If you do not build MySQL from source, you should choose a binary (precompiled) distribution that includes a server with the capabilities you need. The types of distributions available are discussed in the "Core Study Guide."

- *Client programs.* These programs communicate with the server by sending requests to it over a network connection. The server acts on each request and returns a response to the client. For example, you can use the `mysql` client to send queries to the server, and the server returns the query results. The client programs included with MySQL distributions are character-based programs that display output to your terminal. Another client, `MySQLCC` (MySQL Control Center), provides a graphical interface for interacting with the server. `MySQLCC` is not included with MySQL distributions but can be obtained from the MySQL AB Web site. Section 10.2, "Choosing the Right Client," describes clients that are particularly important for administrative purposes.

- *Utility programs.* These programs are generally used for special purposes and do not act as clients of the server. That is, they do not connect over the network to the server. For example, `mysqld_safe` is a script for starting up and monitoring the server. It invokes the server directly. `myisamchk` is a standalone utility for table checking and repair. It accesses or modifies table files directly. Utilities such as `myisamchk` must be used with care to avoid unintended interaction with the server. If table files are used by two programs at the same time, it's possible to get incorrect results or even to cause table damage.

10.2 Choosing the Right Client

This section describes general capabilities of important administrative MySQL client programs. Each of these programs can be invoked with the `--help` option to display a help message that shows the command syntax and the other options that the program supports.

In some cases, you might be able to choose from among different clients to accomplish a given task. By understanding the purpose and capabilities of each client, you can better get your work done by selecting an appropriate client for particular tasks.

In general, you perform most administrative operations using either `mysqladmin`, `mysql`, or `MySQLCC`.

10.2.1 The mysqladmin Client

The mysqladmin client is designed specifically for administrative operations. These include (but are not limited to) the following:

- "Ping" the server to see whether it's running and accepting client connections
- Shut down the server
- Create and drop databases
- Display server configuration and version information
- Display or reset server status variables
- Set passwords
- Reload the grant tables
- Flush the log files or various server caches
- Start or stop replication slave servers
- Show information about client connections or kill connections

For a full list of mysqladmin capabilities, invoke the program with the --help option.

mysqladmin accepts multiple commands on the same command line. For example, the following command displays a brief status message, followed by the list of server system variables:

```
shell> mysqladmin status variables
```

Some mysqladmin commands are available only to MySQL accounts that have administrative privileges. For example, to shut down the server, it's necessary to connect using an administrative account such as root that has the SHUTDOWN privilege:

```
shell> mysqladmin -u root -p shutdown
```

10.2.2 The mysql Client

The mysql client sends SQL statements to the server, and thus can perform any operation that can be expressed using SQL. Some examples are

- Create and drop databases
- Create, drop, and modify tables and indexes
- Retrieve data from tables
- Modify data in tables
- Set up user accounts, grant and revoke privileges, and set passwords
- Display server configuration and version information
- Display or reset server status variables
- Reload the grant tables

- Flush the log files or various server caches
- Start or stop replication slave servers
- Show information about client connections or kill connections

You can use mysql in interactive mode, where you type in queries and see their results. mysql also can operate in batch mode, in which it reads queries stored in a text file. The mysql program is covered extensively in the "Core Study Guide."

10.2.3 The MySQLCC Client

MySQL Control Center (MySQLCC) is a graphical client with capabilities that are something like those of mysql and mysqladmin combined. MySQLCC can send SQL statements to the server, so it can do pretty much anything that mysql can do. MySQLCC also can perform administrative operations such as pinging or shutting down the server, which mysqladmin can do but mysql cannot. MySQLCC is available in precompiled form for Windows and Linux, or it can be compiled from source.

MySQLCC requires a graphical environment such as Windows or the X Window System. However, if the MySQL server is running on a host with no graphical environment, you can connect to it remotely by running MySQLCC on a client host that does have a graphical environment.

10.2.4 Other Administrative Clients

The mysqladmin, mysql, and MySQLCC programs just described are multipurpose programs. Other MySQL clients have more specialized administrative capabilities:

- mysqlcheck checks, repairs, analyzes, and optimizes tables. It can perform all these operations on MyISAM tables, and can perform some of them on InnoDB and BDB tables. It provides a command-line interface to the various SQL statements (such as CHECK TABLE and REPAIR TABLE) that instruct the server to perform these operations.
- mysqlimport provides a command-line interface to the LOAD DATA INFILE statement. It is used to load datafiles into tables without having to issue the statement yourself.
- mysqldump dumps the contents of databases and tables. It's useful for making backups or for copying databases to another machine.
- mysqlshow produces information about the structure of your databases and tables. It provides a command-line interface to various forms of the SHOW statement that list the names of your databases, tables within a database, or information about table columns or indexes.

The "Core Study Guide" provides more detail on the general use of mysqlcheck, mysqlimport, and mysqldump. The capabilities of mysqlshow are illustrated by several of the exercises at the end of this chapter.

10.2.5 Client Program Limitations

No client program does everything. It's important to understand what each client can do, but you should also know what they cannot do. For example:

- `mysqladmin` can create or drop databases, but it has no capabilities for creating or dropping individual tables or indexes. It can change passwords, but cannot create or delete user accounts. The `mysql` and `MySQLCC` programs can perform all of these operations.

- `mysqlimport` loads datafiles, but it cannot load SQL-format dump files containing `INSERT` statements produced by `mysqldump`. In this sense, `mysqlimport` is not the complement of `mysqldump`. Dump files containing SQL statements should be processed using `mysql` instead.

- None of the client programs can start the server. You invoke the server directly or by using a startup script, or you can arrange to have the operating system invoke the server as part of its system startup procedure. Server startup procedures are discussed in Chapter 11, "MySQL Installation and Configuration."

- None of the clients in the preceding discussion can shut down the server except `mysqladmin` and `MySQLCC`. For example, `mysql` cannot do so because it sends SQL statements to the server, and there is no "shut down" SQL statement. `mysqladmin` and `MySQLCC` shut down the server by using a special non-SQL capability of the client/server protocol. If you use an account that has the `SHUTDOWN` privilege, either program can shut down local or remote servers.

10.2.6 The `perror` Utility

`perror` is a handy utility that is installed with the MySQL server. The purpose of the `perror` program is to give you a textual representation of the error codes used by MySQL when operating system-level errors occur.

You can use `perror` in situations when a query results in a message such as the following being returned to you:

```
mysql> CREATE TABLE CountryCopy SELECT * FROM Country;
ERROR 1: Can't create/write to file './world/CountryCopy.frm' (Errcode: 13)
```

This error message indicates that MySQL cannot write to the file `CountryCopy.frm`, but does not report the reason. It might be due to a full disk, a permissions problem, or some other error.

Running the `perror` program results in a message indicating that the source of the problem is that someone has set the permissions incorrectly for the current database:

```
shell> perror 13
Error code  13:  Permission denied
```

10.3 Connecting the Client to the Server

A MySQL client can connect to a server running on the same machine. This is a local connection. A client can also connect to a server running on another machine, which is a remote connection.

MySQL supports connections between clients and the server using several networking protocols:

- A client can establish a local connection by using TCP/IP, by using a named pipe (on Windows NT-based systems), or by using a Unix socket file (on Unix systems).
- Remote connections are established only over TCP/IP. For remote connections, the client and the server need not be used on hosts that run the same type of operating system because TCP/IP is not operating system–dependent.

On Windows, the servers with -nt in the name (mysql-nt, mysql-max-nt) support named pipe connections. However, even for these servers, named pipes are disabled by default because on some Windows systems their use can cause server shutdown problems. To use named pipes, you must start the server with the --enable-named-pipe option. A local client can establish a named pipe connection to the server by specifying . (period) as the hostname. The client also may name no host at all; in this case, the client attempts a named pipe connection first and falls back to TCP/IP if that fails.

Client programs included with MySQL distributions (mysql, mysqladmin, and so forth) establish connections to the server using the native C client library. However, other interfaces are available. For example, ODBC-based applications can connect to a MySQL server by using MySQL Connector/ODBC. Java applications that use JDBC can connect using MySQL Connector/J. These connectors provide MySQL-specific drivers for the ODBC and JDBC protocols.

The different connection methods are not all equally efficient:

- In many Windows configurations, communication via named pipes is much slower than using TCP/IP. You should use named pipes only when you choose to disable TCP/IP (using the ---skip-networking startup parameter) or when you can confirm that named pipes are actually faster on your particular setup. A client can make sure that it connects using TCP/IP rather than a named pipe by specifying a host value of localhost, 127.0.0.1 (the address of the TCP/IP loopback interface), or the server's actual hostname or IP number.
- On Unix, a Unix socket file connection provides better performance than a TCP/IP connection. By convention, the hostname localhost is special for MySQL on Unix. It indicates that the client should connect to the server using a Unix socket file. To explicitly establish a TCP/IP connection to a local server, specify a host of 127.0.0.1 (the address of the TCP/IP loopback interface) or the server's actual hostname or IP number.

- On any platform, an ODBC connection made via Connector/ODBC is slower than a connection established directly using the native C client library. This is because ODBC adds overhead.

- On any platform, a JDBC connection made via Connector/J is likely to be roughly about the same speed as a connection established using the native C client library.

MySQL clients understand command-line options that enable you to specify the host where the server is running, your username, and password. The "Core Study Guide" discusses these options and how to use them when invoking client programs.

10.4 How MySQL Uses Disk Space

The MySQL server uses disk space in several ways, primarily for directories and files that are located in the data directory. The server uses the data directory to store all the following:

- Database directories. Each database corresponds to a single directory under the data directory, regardless of what types of tables you create in the database. For example, a given database is represented by one directory whether it contains MyISAM tables, InnoDB tables, or a mix of the two.

- Table format files (.frm files). Every table has its own .frm file, located in the appropriate database directory. This is true no matter which storage engine manages the table.

- Data and index files are created for each table by some storage engines. These files are placed in the appropriate database directory. For example, the MyISAM storage engine creates a datafile and an index file for each table. The BDB storage engine creates one file per table that includes both data and indexes.

- The InnoDB storage engine has its own tablespace and log files. The tablespace contains data and index information for all InnoDB tables, as well as the undo logs that are needed if a transaction must be rolled back. The log files record information about committed transactions and are used to ensure that no data loss occurs. By default, the tablespace and log files are located in the data directory. The default tablespace file is named ibdata1 and the default log files are named ib_logfile0 and ib_logfile1.

- General log files and status files. More information on these files is given in section 10.6, "Log and Status Files."

10.5 How MySQL Uses Memory

The MySQL server allocates memory for various kinds of information as it runs:

- Thread handlers. The server is multithreaded, and a thread is like a small process running inside the server. For each client that connects, the server allocates a thread to it to handle the connection. Thus, *thread* is roughly synonymous with *client connection*. For performance reasons, the server maintains a small cache of thread handlers. If the cache is not full when a client disconnects, the thread is placed in the cache for later reuse. If the cache is not empty when a client connects, a thread from the cache is reused to handle the connection. Thread handler reuse avoids the overhead of repeated handler setup and teardown.

- The server uses several buffers (caches) to hold information in memory for the purpose of avoiding disk access when possible. Some of these buffers are

  - Grant tables. The server loads a copy of the grant tables into memory for fast access-control checking. Client access is checked for every query, so looking up privilege information in memory rather than from the grant tables on disk results in a significant reduction of disk access overhead.

  - A key buffer is used to hold index blocks. By caching index blocks in memory, the server often can avoid reading index contents repeatedly from disk for index-based retrievals and other index-related operations such as sorts.

  - The table cache holds descriptors for open tables. For frequently used tables, keeping the descriptors in the cache avoids having to open the tables again and again.

  - The server supports a query cache that is used to speed up processing of queries that are issued repeatedly.

  - The host cache holds the results of hostname resolution lookups. These results are cached to minimize the number of calls to the hostname resolver.

  - The InnoDB storage engine logs information about current transactions in a memory buffer. When a transaction commits, the log buffer is flushed to the InnoDB log files, providing a record on disk that can be used to recommit the transaction if it's lost due to a crash. If the transaction rolls back instead, the flush to disk need not be done at all.

  There are no buffers specifically for caching table data because MySQL relies on the operating system to provide efficient caching when reading data from tables.

- The server maintains several buffers for each client connection. It uses a communications buffer for exchanging information with the client. It also maintains client-specific buffers for reading tables and for performing join and sort operations.

- The HEAP (MEMORY) storage engine creates tables that are held in memory. These tables are very fast because no transfer between disk and memory need be done to process queries on them.

- The server might create internal temporary tables in memory during the course of query processing. If the size of such a table exceeds the value of the `tmp_table_size` system variable, the server converts it to a MyISAM-format table on disk and increments its `Created_tmp_disk_tables` status variable.

Several SHOW statements enable you to check the sizes of various memory-related parameters. SHOW VARIABLES displays server system variables so that you can see how the server is set up. SHOW STATUS displays server status variables. The status indicators enable you to check the runtime state of caches, which can be useful for assessing the effectiveness with which they are being used and for determining whether you would be better off using larger (or in some cases smaller) buffers.

Server memory use can be tuned by setting buffer sizes using command-line options or in an option file that the server reads at startup time. For more information, see Chapter 16, "Advanced Server Features."

10.6 Log and Status Files

The MySQL server can write information to several types of log files. The following list briefly describes each of these logs:

- The general query log contains a record of when clients connect and disconnect, and the text of every single query received by the server (whether or not it was processed successfully). This log is useful for determining the frequency of a given type of statement or for troubleshooting queries that are not otherwise logged.

- The binary log contains a record of queries that update data. It is stored in binary format, but its contents can be viewed using the mysqlbinlog utility. The server logs only successful queries to this file, and only queries that modify data. (For example, the server logs DELETE statements to the binary log, but not SELECT statements.) The binary log is used for communication between master and slave replication servers. It can also be used for data recovery.

  The server also can write a text-format update log, but that log is deprecated in MySQL 4, and eventually will disappear entirely.

- The slow query log contains the text of queries that take a long time to execute, as well as information about their execution status. By default, *a long time* is more than 10 seconds. This can be changed by setting the long_query_time server variable. If the server is started with the --log-long-format option, it also writes to the slow query log queries for which no index was used, whether or not the queries took a long time to execute. The contents of this log are helpful for identifying queries that should be optimized.

None of the preceding logs are enabled by default. You must enable them explicitly using appropriate startup options, which are shown in the following table. Each option may be given in *--option* or *--option=file_name* form. If no filename is specified, the server uses a default name, as shown in the table:

Log Type	Option	Default Log Name
General query log	--log	*host_name*.log
Binary log	--log-bin	*host_name*-bin.*nnn*
Slow query log	--log-slow-queries	*host_name*-slow.log

By default, each log file is created under the data directory unless you specify an absolute pathname. *host_name* stands for the server hostname. *nnn* in the name means that the server writes a numbered series of logs, creating a new log each time the server starts up or the logs are flushed.

The server also produces diagnostic messages about normal startups and shutdowns, as well as about abnormal conditions. On Windows, the server logs these messages to an error log, unless you invoke it with the --console option to send the messages to the console window. On Unix, the error log is set up by the mysqld_safe startup script, which then invokes the server with its output redirected to the error log. (That is, the server itself does not directly create the error log.) The default error log name is *host_name*.err in the data directory. (Older Windows servers use the name mysql.err instead.)

Log files, particularly the general query log, can grow to be quite large. Thus, you do not necessarily want to enable them all, especially for a busy server.

All logs are written in text format except for the binary log which, as the name implies, is in binary format. Text logs can be viewed using any program capable of displaying text files. For the slow query log, another approach is to use the mysqldumpslow utility; it can summarize the log contents. To view the binary log, use the mysqlbinlog utility.

On Unix, the server records its process ID in a PID file, for use by other programs that need to send the server a signal. (Unix processes send signals to each other using process ID values.) The default PID filename is *host_name*.pid in the data directory. The name and location can be changed with the --pid-file=*file_name* option.

Unix servers create a Unix socket file so that local clients can establish socket connections. By default, this file is /tmp/mysql.sock. A different filename can be specified by starting the server with the --socket option. If you change the location, client programs also need to be started with --socket so that they know where the socket file is located.

10.7 MySQL Storage Engines

The MySQL server uses storage engines to manage data in tables. Each storage engine handles a particular table type. These storage engines have certain similarities. For example, each database is represented by a directory under the data directory, and every table in the database has a format (.frm file in the database directory). This is true no matter the table type. On the other hand, storage engines differ in such things as how they use locking to manage query contention, which has implications for query concurrency and deadlock prevention. (*Deadlock* occurs when multiple queries are blocked and cannot proceed because they're waiting for each other to finish.)

The table type characteristics and features are summarized in this section as an overview. The MyISAM and InnoDB table types are examined in more detail in later chapters. See also the *MySQL Reference Manual* for more information about table types.

The ISAM table type, which is referenced in several places in the *MySQL Reference Manual*, is not covered on the exam. It is an older table format that has been made obsolete by the newer MyISAM format that replaces it.

When you create a table, you can choose its type according to which storage engine offers features that best fit the needs of your application. Section 10.7.6, "Specifying the Storage Engine for a Table," discusses how to choose a table type when creating a table.

For any table, the DESCRIBE statement provides information about the columns in a table. However, DESCRIBE doesn't show the table type. If you want to know that, you can use either the SHOW CREATE TABLE or the SHOW TABLE STATUS statement. The latter also shows other information that might be of interest. For example, it displays when a table was created or last modified.

10.7.1 MyISAM Tables

The MyISAM storage engine manages tables that have the following characteristics:

- Each MyISAM table is represented on disk by an .frm format file, as well as an .MYD datafile and an .MYI index file. All these files are located in the database directory.
- MyISAM has the most flexible AUTO_INCREMENT column handling of all the table types.
- MyISAM tables can be used to set up MERGE tables.
- MyISAM tables can be converted into fast, compressed, read-only tables.
- MyISAM supports FULLTEXT searching.
- MySQL manages contention between queries for MyISAM table access using table-level locking. Query performance is very fast for retrievals. Multiple queries can read the same table simultaneously. For a write query, an exclusive table-level lock is used to prevent use of the table by other read or write queries, leading to reduced performance in environments with a mix of read and write queries. Deadlock cannot occur with table-level locking.

10.7.2 InnoDB Tables

The InnoDB storage engine manages tables that have the following characteristics:

- Each InnoDB table is represented on disk by an .frm format file in the database directory, as well as data and index storage in the InnoDB tablespace. This tablespace is a logical single storage area that is made up of one or more files or partitions on disk. The tablespace is shared by all InnoDB tables.

- InnoDB supports transactions (commit and rollback) with full ACID compliance.

- InnoDB provides auto-recovery after a crash of the MySQL server or the host where the server runs.

- InnoDB supports foreign keys and referential integrity, including cascaded deletes and updates.

- MySQL manages query contention for InnoDB tables using multi-versioning and row-level locking. Multi-versioning gives each transaction its own view of the database. This, combined with row-level locking, keeps contention to a minimum. The result is good concurrency even in an environment consisting of mixed reads and writes. However, it's possible for deadlock to occur.

10.7.3 MERGE Tables

The MERGE storage engine manages tables that have the following characteristics:

- A MERGE table is a collection of identically structured MyISAM tables. Each MERGE table is represented on disk by an .frm format file and an .MRG file that lists the names of the constituent MyISAM files. Both files are located in the database directory.

- Logically, a query on a MERGE table acts as a query on all the MyISAM tables of which it consists.

- A MERGE table creates a logical entity that can exceed the maximum MyISAM table size.

10.7.4 BDB (Berkeley DB) Tables

The BDB storage engine manages tables that have the following characteristics:

- Each BDB table is represented on disk by an .frm format file and a .db file that stores data and index information. Both files are located in the database directory.

- BDB supports transactions (commit and rollback) with full ACID compliance.

- BDB provides auto-recovery after a crash of the MySQL server or the host where the server runs.

- MySQL manages query contention for BDB tables using page-level locking. This locking level provides concurrency performance that's intermediate to that of row-level and table-level locking. It's possible for deadlock to occur.

10.7.5 HEAP (MEMORY) Tables

The HEAP storage engine manages tables that have the following characteristics:

- Each HEAP table is represented on disk by an .frm format file in the database directory. Table data and indexes are stored in memory.

- In-memory storage results in very good performance. A memory table is never written to disk, so reads and writes are extremely fast. (A small MyISAM table that can be cached in memory and is used primarily for reading might be as fast, but there's no guarantee that its contents will stay in the cache.)

- HEAP table contents do not survive a restart of the server. The table itself survives, but the contents are empty after a restart.

- HEAP tables use up memory, so they should not be used for large tables.

- MySQL manages query contention for HEAP tables using table-level locking. Deadlock cannot occur.

10.7.6 Specifying the Storage Engine for a Table

Every table must be created using one of the table types supported by the server. The set of table types available depends on which storage engines are present. This is determined both by how the server was compiled when it was built and by the options used at startup:

- The MyISAM, MERGE, and HEAP storage engines are always available.

- The InnoDB storage engine is included in all binary distributions. If you build MySQL from source, InnoDB is included by default unless you specify the `--without-innodb` configuration option. For a server that has the InnoDB storage engine included, support can be disabled at startup with the `--skip-innodb` option.

- The BDB storage engine is included in MySQL-Max binary distributions. If you build MySQL from source, BDB is not included unless you specify the `--with-berkeley-db` configuration option. For a server that has the BDB storage engine included, support can be disabled at startup with the `--skip-bdb` option.

To specify a table type when creating a table, include a `TYPE = type_name` option in the CREATE TABLE statement. For example:

```
CREATE TABLE t (i INT) TYPE = InnoDB;
```

To change the type of an existing table, use an ALTER TABLE statement:

```
ALTER TABLE t TYPE = MyISAM;
```

If a CREATE TABLE statement includes no TYPE option, the table is created using the default table type. The built-in default table type is MyISAM. This can be changed in several ways:

- The default table type can be specified at server startup time with the `--default-table-type` option.

- For a running server, an administrator who has the SUPER privilege can change the default table type globally for all clients by setting the `table_type` variable:

```
mysql> SET GLOBAL table_type = type_name;
```

Setting the table type this way affects any client that connects after the statement executes. Clients that are connected at the time of statement execution are unaffected.

- Any client can change its own default table type by issuing this statement:

```
mysql> SET SESSION table_type = type_name;
```

If a CREATE TABLE statement includes a *type_name* value that is one of the legal type names but the storage engine is not active, the server creates the table as a MyISAM table. This is true even if the default table type has been changed to something other than MyISAM.

10.7.7 Using TEMPORARY Tables

Each storage engine implements tables with a particular set of characteristics. One characteristic held in common by all storage engines is that by default they create tables that exist until they are removed with DROP TABLE. This behavior may be changed by using CREATE TEMPORARY TABLE rather than CREATE TABLE. A TEMPORARY table differs from a non-TEMPORARY table in the following ways:

- It's visible only to the client that created it and may be used only by that client. This means that different clients can create TEMPORARY tables that have the same name and no conflict occurs.

- The server drops a TEMPORARY table automatically when the client connection ends if the client has not already dropped it.

- A TEMPORARY table may have the same name as a non-TEMPORARY table. The non-TEMPORARY table becomes hidden to the client that created the TEMPORARY table as long as the TEMPORARY table exists.

A table created with TEMPORARY is not the same thing as a HEAP table. A HEAP table is temporary in the sense that its contents are lost if you restart the server, but the table itself continues to exist in its database. A TEMPORARY table exists only while the client that created it remains connected, and then disappears. Given that a server restart necessarily involves termination of all client connections, it also results in removal of all TEMPORARY tables.

10.8 Exercises

These exercises include several questions that ask which programs can be used to perform particular tasks. The questions require that you know only about programs developed by MySQL AB. There might be third-party programs available that have similar capabilities, but they aren't covered here.

Question 1:

Name a utility program that accesses database tables directly, without communicating with the server. Why do you have to use this type of program with extra care?

Question 2:

Name two programs that access tables by communicating with the server.

Question 3:

Does mysql allow you to create a database? Does mysqladmin?

Question 4:

Does mysql allow you to drop a table? Does mysqladmin?

Question 5:

Does mysql allow you to find out which clients are connected to the server? Does mysqladmin?

Question 6:

Does mysql allow you to restart the server? Does mysqladmin?

Question 7:

Does mysql allow you to change the contents of the my.cnf or my.ini option file? Does mysqladmin?

Question 8:

Does mysql allow you to change the password of a MySQL user? Does mysqladmin?

Question 9:

Does mysql allow you to find out whether the server is running? Does mysqladmin?

Question 10:

Using mysqlshow, what command would you issue to find out which tables in the test database have names starting with my?

Question 11:

Using mysqlshow, how can you see the indexes of the table mytable in the database test? Can you retrieve information about the indexes of multiple tables issuing a single command?

Question 12:

You can use mysqladmin to signal the local server to shut down. Does mysqladmin have any platform dependencies? Can the program also signal a remote server to shut down?

Question 13:

You can use mysql.server to signal the local server to shut down. Does mysql.server have any platform dependencies? Can the program also signal a remote server to shut down?

Question 14:

You can use MySQLCC to signal the local server to shut down. Does MySQLCC have any platform dependencies? Can the program also signal a remote server to shut down?

Question 15:

How could you find out what an error number such as 13 means?

```
Can't find file: './mysql/host.frm' (errno: 13)
```

Question 16:

Which client or utility programs can be used to create a database named `landmarks`?

Question 17:

Which client or utility programs can be used to grant all privileges to user `landm_editor` with a password of `Sakila`?

Question 18:

Which client or utility programs can be used to create the table `buildings` from a batch file `/tmp/buildings.sql` that contains a `CREATE TABLE` statement that names the table but not the database in which the table should be created?

Question 19:

Which client or utility programs can be used to display the structure of the `buildings` table, including any indexes it has?

Question 20:

Which client or utility programs can be used to populate the table `buildings` with information stored in the data file `/tmp/buildings.txt`? Assume that the contents of the file are in the default format expected by the program.

Question 21:

Consider the `FLUSH PRIVILEGES` SQL statement, which you can issue using `mysql`. What command-line program could you use to accomplish the same task? What would the command look like?

Question 22:

Consider the `SHOW PROCESSLIST` SQL statement, which you can issue using `mysql`. What command-line program could you use to accomplish the same task? What would the command look like?

Question 23:

Consider the `SHOW DATABASES` SQL statement, which you can issue using `mysql`. What command-line program could you use to accomplish the same task? What would the command look like?

Question 24:

Consider the `SHOW DATABASES LIKE 'w%'` SQL statement, which you can issue using `mysql`. What command-line program could you use to accomplish the same task? What would the command look like?

Question 25:

Consider the SHOW TABLES FROM world SQL statement, which you can issue using mysql. What command-line program could you use to accomplish the same task? What would the command look like?

Question 26:

Consider the SHOW TABLES FROM world LIKE 'C%' SQL statement, which you can issue using mysql. What command-line program could you use to accomplish the same task? What would the command look like?

Question 27:

Consider the SHOW COLUMNS FROM City FROM world SQL statement, which you can issue using mysql. What command-line program could you use to accomplish the same task? What would the command look like?

Question 28:

Consider the SHOW KEYS FROM City FROM world SQL statement, which you can issue using mysql. What command-line program could you use to accomplish the same task? What would the command look like?

Question 29:

Consider the following list of ways to connect to the MySQL server. Which are operating system–dependent? Which will work only for connections to the local server, and which will also work for remote connections to a remote server?

a. TCP/IP

b. ODBC

c. Named pipe

d. Unix socket file

Question 30:

a. Will mysql -h localhost establish a connection to a local server or a remote server?

b. What type of connection will mysql -h localhost use (Unix socket file, Windows named pipe, or TCP/IP)?

c. Will mysql -h localhost work only for a specific operating system?

Question 31:

a. Will mysql -h . establish a connection to a local server or a remote server?

b. What type of connection will mysql -h . use (Unix socket file, Windows named pipe, or TCP/IP)?

c. Will mysql -h . work only for a specific operating system?

Question 32:

a. Will mysql -h 127.0.0.1 establish a connection to a local server or a remote server?

b. What type of connection will mysql -h 127.0.0.1 use (Unix socket file, Windows named pipe, or TCP/IP)?

c. Will mysql -h 127.0.0.1 work only for a specific operating system?

Question 33:

a. Will mysql -h 192.168.10.1 establish a connection to a local server or a remote server?

b. What type of connection will mysql -h 192.168.10.1 use (Unix socket file, Windows named pipe, or TCP/IP)?

c. Will mysql -h 192.168.10.1 work only for a specific operating system?

Question 34:

a. Will mysql establish a connection to a local server or a remote server?

b. What type of connection will mysql use (Unix socket file, Windows named pipe, or TCP/IP)?

c. Will mysql work only for a specific operating system?

Question 35:

For what kinds of files and directories does MySQL use disk space?

Question 36:

For what kinds of information does the MySQL server allocate memory?

Question 37:

How would you start the server so that it logs errors? How do you access the information in the error log?

Question 38:

How would you start the server so that it logs two things: queries that take longer than 10 seconds to perform and queries that use no indexes? How can you access the information logged this way?

Question 39:

How would you start the server so that it logs all operations that change data in tables? How can you access the information logged this way?

Question 40:

You know that MyISAM is the default table type in MySQL. So, what's the explanation for the following?

```
mysql> CREATE TABLE defaulttype (id INT);
mysql> SHOW TABLE STATUS LIKE 'defaulttype';
+-------------+--------+------------+------+-
| Name        | Type   | Row_format | Rows |
+-------------+--------+------------+------+-
| defaulttype | InnoDB | Fixed      |    0 |
+-------------+--------+------------+------+-
```

Question 41:

What's the explanation for the following?

```
mysql> CREATE TABLE bdbtable (id INT) TYPE=BDB;
mysql> SHOW TABLE STATUS LIKE 'bdbtable';
+----------+--------+------------+------+-
| Name     | Type   | Row_format | Rows |
+----------+--------+------------+------+-
| bdbtable | MyISAM | Fixed      |    0 |
+----------+--------+------------+------+-
```

Question 42:

Two SQL statements tell you what table type a given table mytable has. What are they?

Question 43:

Assume that you want a table to include a column that has a FULLTEXT index. What table types could you use?

Question 44:

In an application, you expect to have a high number of reads as well as a high number of writes at the same time. Which table type is best suited to handle this?

Question 45:

How can you change the server's default table type for new tables from MyISAM to InnoDB at server startup time?

Question 46:

How can you change the server's default table type for new tables from MyISAM to InnoDB if the server is already running?

Question 47:

How can an individual client change its own default table type to InnoDB?

Answers to Exercises

Answer 1:

`myisamchk` is one example of a utility program that accesses table data directly. You have to take care when using programs that access tables directly, which usually means you have to make sure that the server won't access those tables at the same time. If two or more programs access the same tables at the same time, this could lead to incorrect results or even table damage.

Answer 2:

`mysql` and `mysqlimport` are two examples of programs that access tables by communicating with the server. There are others, such as `MySQLCC`, `mysqlcheck`, and `mysqldump`.

Answer 3:

Both programs can do this task: You can create a database with either `mysql` or `mysqladmin`. (Both programs also allow you to drop a database.)

Answer 4:

Only `mysql` can do this task. You cannot perform table operations with `mysqladmin`. To create or drop a table, use `mysql`.

Answer 5:

Both programs can do this task. To find out which clients are connected to the server using the `mysql` client program, you can issue a `SHOW PROCESSLIST` SQL statement. To perform the same task with `mysqladmin`, you can use `mysqladmin processlist`.

Answer 6:

You cannot restart the server with either program. However, `mysqladmin` will allow you to signal the server to shut down.

Answer 7:

You cannot change the contents of the `my.cnf` or `my.ini` option file with either `mysqladmin` or `mysql`. You must use a text editor or some other program that provides configuration-editing capabilities.

Answer 8:

Both programs can do this task: You can change the password of a MySQL user with either `mysql` or `mysqladmin`. Both programs allow you to change your own password, and, if you have sufficient privileges, passwords for other users as well.

Answer 9:

Only `mysqladmin` is able to explicitly do this task. Although `mysql` has no specific "is the server running?" command, you can deduce the fact by invoking `mysql`: If the server allows `mysql` to connect, the server must be running. With `mysqladmin`, you can send the server a ping request (`mysqladmin ping`). If the server is running, it will respond saying `mysqld is alive`. In both cases, only an affirmative response is definitive. Failure to get a response might indicate that the server is down, but it's possible that there are other reasons. For example, the network connection between the client and server hosts might be down.

Answer 10:

To list the tables in the `test` database starting with `my`, you would issue a `mysqlshow test my%` or `mysqlshow test my*` command. However, your command interpreter might treat the `%` or `*` character as special. It can be helpful to quote the pattern argument or to use whichever character your command interpreter does not consider special. `my*` may be used without quoting on Windows, and `my%` without quoting on Unix.

Answer 11:

The `--keys` or `-k` option instructs `mysqlshow` to display table index information in addition to column information. For the `mytable` table in the `test` database, use `mysqlshow --keys test mytable`. You can show the indexes for only one table per command.

Answer 12:

`mysqladmin` can shut down both the local server and remote servers. The program has no platform dependencies.

Answer 13:

`mysql.server` cannot be used to shut down a remote server, just the local server. The program runs under Unix-like operating systems only.

Answer 14:

MySQLCC can shut down both the local server and remote servers. The program has no platform dependencies.

Answer 15:

You could use the `perror` utility to find an error message for an error number, like this:

```
c:\mysql\bin>perror 13
Error code  13:  Permission denied
```

Answer 16:

To create the database from the command line, run `mysqladmin`:

```
shell> mysqladmin create landmarks
```

From within the `mysql` client, use the CREATE DATABASE statement:

```
mysql> CREATE DATABASE landmarks;
```

Answer 17:

There's no command-line program other than `mysql` that you could use to grant privileges to a user. However, you could use the graphical client program `MySQLCC` to accomplish that task.

Answer 18:

To create a table from a statement in a batch file, you must use `mysql`. To specify both the filename and the database name on the command line, use this command:

```
shell> mysql landmarks < /tmp/buildings.sql
```

If you're already running `mysql`, you can select the database first and then use `SOURCE` to execute the statement in the batch file:

```
mysql> USE landmarks;
mysql> SOURCE /tmp/buildings.sql;
```

Answer 19:

You can display the structure of the table and its indexes using the `mysqlshow` command:

```
shell> mysqlshow --keys landmarks buildings
```

The same can be accomplished from within the `mysql` client by using the `DESCRIBE` and `SHOW INDEX` statements:

```
mysql> DESCRIBE landmarks.buildings;
mysql> SHOW INDEX FROM landmarks.buildings;
```

Answer 20:

To populate the table from data stored in a text file, use `mysqlimport`. You must specify the database name. The table name is determined implicitly from the final component of the filename (excluding any filename extension):

```
shell> mysqlimport landmarks /tmp/buildings.txt
```

The same can be accomplished from with the `mysql` client program using the `LOAD DATA INFILE` statement. Here, you must specify the table name explicitly:

```
mysql> LOAD DATA INFILE '/tmp/buildings.txt' INTO landmarks.buildings;
```

For details about the `LOAD DATA INFILE` command, see section A.1.20, "`LOAD DATA INFILE`."

Answer 21:

You could use `mysqladmin flush-privileges` to accomplish the same task.

Answer 22:

You could use `mysqladmin processlist` to accomplish the same task.

Answer 23:

You could use `mysqlshow` to accomplish the same task.

Answer 24:

You could use `mysqlshow "w*"` to accomplish the same task.

Answer 25:

You could use `mysqlshow world` to accomplish the same task.

Answer 26:

You could use `mysqlshow world "C*"` to accomplish the same task.

Answer 27:

You could use `mysqlshow world City` to accomplish the same task.

Answer 28:

You could use `mysqlshow --keys world City` to accomplish the same task. (This command will display the table columns, too, so it's not exactly equivalent to `SHOW KEYS FROM City FROM world`. There's no way to display only the table's indexes using `mysqlshow`.)

Answer 29:

Named pipes are available only under Windows, and Unix socket files are available only under Unix-like operating systems. TCP/IP is not operating system-dependent. ODBC is not operating system–dependent in itself, but is available for MySQL only on operating systems where MySQL Connector/ODBC is supported. Any of the connection methods can be used to connect to a local server. TCP/IP and ODBC can be used to connect to a remote server.

Answer 30:

`mysql -h localhost` establishes a local connection. On Unix-like operating systems, the connection is established through a Unix socket file. Under Windows, the connection is made using TCP/IP. `mysql -h localhost` can be used on any platform.

Answer 31:

`mysql -h .` establishes a local connection using a named pipe. Named pipes are available only under Windows, so the command will work only on Windows, and only if the server was started with the `--enable-named-pipe` option.

Answer 32:

`mysql -h 127.0.0.1` establishes a local connection that uses TCP/IP on any operating system.

Answer 33:

A connection to a server running on a machine specified by an IP number will establish a connection via TCP/IP on any operating system. Whether this is a local or remote connection depends on whether 192.168.10.1 is the IP number of the local host.

Answer 34:

If no host is specified, the client will try to connect locally. Under Unix, this means it will use a Unix socket file. Under Windows, it will try to use a named pipe first, and TCP/IP if that fails.

Answer 35:

MySQL uses disk space to store the following:

- The server and client programs, and their libraries
- Log files and status files
- Databases
- Table format (.frm) files for all storage engines, and datafiles and index files for some storage engines
- InnoDB tablespace files (if the InnoDB storage engine is enabled)
- Internal temporary tables that have crossed the size threshold for being converted from in-memory tables to on-disk tables

Answer 36:

MySQL allocates memory for the following:

- Connection handlers (every connection uses memory)
- Buffers and caches
- A copy of the grant tables
- Internal temporary tables that are below the size threshold for being converted from in-memory tables to on-disk tables
- The host cache and the table cache
- The query cache
- HEAP (memory) table contents (note that each HEAP table also requires disk space to store its .frm file)

Answer 37:

On Windows, the server logs errors to a file by default. You need do nothing to enable the error log.

On Unix, the server does not create an error log. `mysqld_safe` creates the error log by starting the server with its output redirected to the log file. Therefore, to log errors, start the server using `mysqld_safe`. You can also use `mysql.server`, because that invokes `mysqld_safe`.

To see the error log, look for a file with a `.err` suffix in the data directory. The error log is written in text format and can be viewed using any program that displays text files.

Answer 38:

To log slow queries, enable the slow query log by starting the server with the `--log-slow-queries` option. This logs queries that take a long time to perform. By default, a *long time* is defined as 10 seconds. Using the `--log-long-format` option, in addition to the `--log-slow-queries` option, instructs the server to also write queries that use no indexes to the slow query log.

The slow query log is in text format and can be viewed with any program that displays text files. For convenience, you can also use `mysqldumpslow` to view the slow query log. This utility is available under Unix-like systems only.

Answer 39:

Enable the binary log by starting the server with the `--log-bin` option. The server writes to this log all queries that modify data. Its contents are in binary format, but can be viewed using the `mysqlbinlog` program.

Answer 40:

The default table type has been changed to InnoDB. For example, this could have happened at server startup (using the `--default-table-type` option).

Answer 41:

If you try to use a table type that is not compiled in or has been disabled, MySQL instead creates a MyISAM table. Because the request to create the table as a BDB table was not honored by the server, this means that the server either was not compiled with support for the BDB storage engine or that BDB was disabled at server startup time (using the `--skip-bdb` option).

Answer 42:

You can use either `SHOW CREATE TABLE mytable` or `SHOW TABLE STATUS LIKE 'mytable'`. See sections A.1.36, "SHOW CREATE TABLE," and A.1.43, "SHOW TABLE STATUS."

Answer 43:

MyISAM is the only table type that supports `FULLTEXT` indexing.

Answer 44:

InnoDB provides the best concurrency in an environment consisting of mixed reads and writes. Of the MySQL storage engines available, it provides the most fine-grained locking (row-level locking), and it also uses multi-versioning to give each transaction its own view of the database.

Answer 45:

A default table type of InnoDB can be specified at server startup time by using the --default-table-type=InnoDB option, either on the command line or in an option file. For example, you could start the server like this:

```
mysqld --default-table-type=InnoDB
```

To use an option file, put these lines in the file:

```
[mysqld]
default-table-type=InnoDB
```

Answer 46:

A MySQL user with sufficient privileges can change the server's default table type to InnoDB while the server is running by using this statement:

```
SET GLOBAL table_type=InnoDB;
```

This setting affects all clients that connect after the statement executes.

Answer 47:

Any client can change its connection-specific default table type by issuing this statement:

```
SET SESSION table_type=InnoDB;
```

This setting will not affect other client connections.

11

MySQL Installation and Configuration

This chapter discusses issues involved in setting up and configuring MySQL:

- Running MySQL on Windows
- Running MySQL on Unix and Unix-like systems such as Linux
- Selecting the proper runtime configuration options
- Reasons to compile MySQL from a source distribution rather than using a precompiled binary distribution
- Upgrading an older installation to a newer version of MySQL
- Configuring your operating system and hardware to make MySQL perform better

Questions on the material in this chapter make up approximately 20% of the exam.

This study guide covers general installation principles and procedures, not details specific to a particular variety of Windows or Unix. For those kinds of details, see the installation chapter in the *MySQL Reference Manual*.

You can get any distribution files you need from `http://www.mysql.com`, the MySQL AB Web site.

11.1 Running MySQL on Windows

This section describes MySQL installation, startup, and shutdown procedures for Windows systems.

11.1.1 Installing the MySQL Distribution

MySQL distributions for Windows come in the form of Zip files and can be installed as follows:

- Download and unpack the distribution that you want to install.

- The folder created by unpacking the distribution contains a `Setup.exe` or `.msi` installer program that runs the Setup Wizard. The program that unpacks the distribution might invoke this program automatically. If not, run it yourself to install MySQL.

- The default installation location is `C:\mysql`; this is the MySQL base directory. You can select another base directory, but if you do, you must specify this directory when you run the server. See section 11.3, "Runtime MySQL Configuration."

The Windows installer automatically sets up the data directory under the MySQL base installation directory. The default data directory is `C:\mysql\data`. Under this directory, the installer also creates a `mysql` directory for the `mysql` database that contains the initial MySQL accounts. Note that these accounts at this point have no passwords. Chapter 12, "Security Issues," discusses how to set up passwords.

11.1.2 Starting and Stopping the MySQL Server

Windows MySQL distributions include several servers. You should choose the one you want to use:

- `mysqld` is the standard server. It includes both the MyISAM and InnoDB storage engines.

- `mysqld-nt` is like `mysqld`, but includes support for Windows NT-named pipes. It is intended for NT-based systems such as Windows NT, 2000, and XP.

- `mysqld-max` and `mysql-max-nt` are like `mysqld` and `mysql-nt`, but with additional features such as support for the BDB storage engine and for symlinking database directories.

The examples in the following discussion use `mysqld` for the server name; make the appropriate substitutions to use a different server. Note that even if you use a server that supports named pipes, it will not allow named pipe connections by default. To allow that type of connection, you must start the server with the `--enable-named-pipe` option.

See section 11.3, "Runtime MySQL Configuration," for instructions on specifying any server startup options you need.

11.1.2.1 Running the Server Manually

To run a Windows MySQL server manually, invoke it from the command line of a console window:

```
shell> mysqld
```

By default, Windows servers write error messages to the file *host_name*`.err` in the data directory, where *host_name* is the MySQL server hostname. (If you have an older version of

MySQL 4, the error log might be named `mysql.err` instead.) If the server does not start properly, check the error log to see why. Alternatively, to display diagnostic output in the console window instead, invoke the server with the `--console` option:

```
shell> mysqld --console
```

Other server options may be specified on the command line or in option files. See section 11.3, "Runtime MySQL Configuration."

Note that when you invoke the server at the command prompt, the command interpreter might not display another prompt until the server exits. To invoke other MySQL programs while the server is running, open a new console window.

To stop the server, use `mysqladmin` from the command line:

```
shell> mysqladmin shutdown
```

Another way to stop the server is to use the `MySQLCC` program. It's also possible to use the Windows Task Manager, although you should avoid that if you can because the Task Manager terminates the server forcibly without giving it a chance to perform a clean shutdown. The result might be data corruption or loss.

11.1.2.2 Running the Server as a Windows Service

On Windows NT–based systems, you can run the server manually, as just described, or you can install it as a Windows service. To use the service approach, invoke the server with the `--install` option:

```
shell> mysqld --install
```

This command does not actually start the server; it tells Windows to handle the server as a service. When Windows starts up or shuts down, it starts or stops `mysqld` automatically. The service also can be started or stopped manually from the command line. To do so, use these commands:

```
shell> net start MySQL
```

```
shell> net stop MySQL
```

`MySQL` is the service name for MySQL. It can be given in any lettercase.

You can also shut down the server manually using `mysqladmin shutdown` or with `MySQLCC`.

To control the service using a graphical interface, use the Windows Services Manager. It displays a window that lists all known services and has controls for starting and stopping them.

If the server does not start properly when run as a service, check the error log or run the server manually with the `--console` option as described in section 11.1.2.1, "Running the Server Manually."

If you want to specify runtime options for a MySQL server that is to run as a service, don't give them on the `--install` command line. Instead, put the options in an option file. The server normally reads options from the [mysqld] group of the standard Windows option files when it starts up. (These files are described in section 11.3, "Runtime MySQL Configuration.") To use a specific option file, use a command like this to install the service:

```
shell> mysqld --install MySQL --defaults-file=file_name
```

In this case, when the server starts, it reads options in the [mysqld] option group of the named file, and ignores the standard option files.

To remove the MySQL service, shut down the server if it's running (using any of the means just described), and then issue the following command:

```
shell> mysqld --remove
```

11.2 Running MySQL on Unix

MySQL runs on many Unix and Unix-like systems, including those based on BSD Unix, System V Unix, and Linux. This section describes general procedures for running MySQL on them. The topics include selecting an appropriate distribution, installing it, and arranging for server startup and shutdown.

On Unix, precompiled MySQL distributions come in the form of RPM files or as compressed `tar` files. RPMs are used on Linux systems. `tar` files are available for many platforms. This section discusses installation using a precompiled binary distribution. It's also fairly common to install MySQL on Unix by building it from source, a topic discussed in section 11.4, "Compiling MySQL from a Source Distribution."

The assumption here is that you're installing MySQL on a system that doesn't already have it. This might not be true for a given machine: MySQL might already be installed because several operating system distributions now include MySQL by default or allow it to be selected during the operating system installation procedure. However, you might find on such systems that the provided version of MySQL is older than the version currently available from MySQL AB. Section 11.5, "Upgrading MySQL," describes how to upgrade an existing MySQL installation to a newer version.

11.2.1 Installing MySQL Using RPM Files

RPM installation for MySQL typically requires more than one RPM file because the distribution is split up into different RPMs. The most important RPM files are for the server and for the client programs.

To install MySQL using RPM files, follow these steps:

1. Obtain the RPM files. At a minimum, you should get the server RPM and client RPM. If you want to run a Max version of the server, you'll also need a Max server RPM, which must be installed *after* the regular server RPM.

2. Install the RPM files. You'll need to do this as `root`. The installation process sets up a login account with user and group names of `mysql` to use for administering and running the server, installs all the files, initializes the data directory and the `mysql` database that contains the initial MySQL accounts, registers a startup script, and starts the server.

A typical installation uses the server and client RPM files. If the current version of MySQL happens to be 4.0.15, the installation commands would look like this:

```
shell> rpm -i MySQL-server-4.0.15-0.i386.rpm
shell> rpm -i MySQL-client-4.0.15-0.i386.rpm
```

The MySQL accounts at this point have no passwords. Chapter 12 discusses how to set up passwords.

11.2.2 Installing MySQL Using a `tar` File

To install MySQL from a tar file distribution, use this procedure:

1. Set up a login account for administering and running the server. The commands to do this vary for different versions of Unix; assume for purposes of this guide that you create an account with user and group names set to `mysql`. You need to perform this step as `root`. Most of the following steps can be executed while logged in as the `mysql` user.

2. Obtain the tar file, place it in the location under which you want to install MySQL, and unpack it. The top-level MySQL directory created by unpacking the distribution will have a long name because the names of binary distributions include a version number and a platform name indicating the type of system for which the distribution is intended. For this reason, it's a good idea to create a symbolic link to that directory with a shorter name that is easier to refer to.

   The following example shows how to unpack a distribution and create the symbolic link, using a distribution file named `mysql-standard-4.0.17-sun-solaris2.9-sparc.tar.gz` that unpacks to create a MySQL installation directory named `mysql-standard-4.0.17-sun-solaris2.9-sparc`:

```
shell> tar zxf mysql-standard-4.0.17-sun-solaris2.9-sparc.tar.gz
shell> ln -s mysql-standard-4.0.17-sun-solaris2.9-sparc mysql
```

   Suppose that the directory in which you issue those commands is `/usr/local`. The resulting installation directory (that is, the MySQL base directory) can be referred to as `/usr/local/mysql`. One advantage of setting up a symbolic link (besides that it's shorter than the name created by the tar file) is that when you upgrade to a newer version of

MySQL, you can easily retarget the link to the new installation directory. Just delete the link and re-create it to point to the new directory.

3. `tar` file distributions do not create the data directory automatically the way Windows and RPM distributions do. To initialize the data directory, change location into the installation base directory and run the `mysql_install_db` script. For a `tar` file distribution, this script normally is located in the `scripts` directory, so you can run it like this:

```
shell> cd /usr/local/mysql
shell> scripts/mysql_install_db
```

To make sure that all directories and files that `mysql_install_db` creates have the proper ownership, run the script as just shown while logged in as the `mysql` user. Alternatively, you can run it as `root` with the `--user=mysql` option:

```
shell> cd /usr/local/mysql
shell> scripts/mysql_install_db --user=mysql
```

`mysql_install_db` creates the data directory and initializes the `mysql` and `test` databases. If you do not run this script, the server will complain when you run it later that it cannot find files in the `mysql` database. For example, the server will issue an error message such as `Can't find file: ./host.frm`.

4. Install a startup script. Choosing a script and how to install it are covered in section 11.2.3, "Starting and Stopping the MySQL Server."

The MySQL accounts at this point have no passwords. Chapter 12 discusses how to set up passwords.

The procedure for installing a `tar` file distribution involves more steps than that for RPM installation. The RPM installation handles many details for you that `tar` file installation doesn't. For example, it creates the `mysql` login account, runs the `mysql_install_db` script, and installs the startup script automatically.

11.2.3 Starting and Stopping the MySQL Server

Under Unix, it's possible to start the server using several different methods:

- You can invoke `mysqld` manually. This usually isn't done except for debugging purposes. If you invoke the server this way, error messages go to the terminal rather than to the error log.

- `mysqld_safe` is a shell script that invokes `mysqld`. The script sets up the error log and then launches `mysqld` and monitors it. If `mysqld` terminates abnormally, `mysqld_safe` restarts it.

- `mysql.server` is a shell script that invokes `mysqld_safe`. It's used as a wrapper around `mysqld_safe` for systems such as Linux and Solaris that use System V run-level directories. Typically, this script is renamed to `mysql` when it is installed in the run-level directories.

- `mysqld_multi` is a Perl script intended to make it easier to manage multiple servers on a single host. It can start or stop servers, or report on whether or not servers are running. Use of multiple servers is discussed further in Chapter 16, "Advanced Server Features."

To have the server run automatically at system startup time, install a startup script that's appropriate for your system:

- On BSD-style Unix systems, it's most common to invoke `mysqld_safe` from one of the system startup scripts, such as the `rc.local` script in the `/etc` directory.

- Linux and System V Unix variants that have run-level directories under `/etc/init.d` use the `mysql.server` script. If you install the server RPM on Linux, the installation command automatically installs `mysql.server` under the name `mysql` for the appropriate run levels. It can be invoked manually with an argument of `start` or `stop` to start or stop the server:

```
shell> /etc/init.d/mysql start
shell> /etc/init.d/mysql stop
```

The operating system startup and shutdown procedures issue those commands automatically.

If the server does not start properly, look in the error log. The default error log name on Unix is *host_name*.err in the data directory, where *host_name* is the name of your server host.

To stop the server manually, use one of the following techniques:

- The `mysqladmin` program has a `shutdown` command. It connects to the server as a client and can shut down local or remote servers.

- The `mysql.server` script can shut down the local server when invoked with an argument of `stop`.

- The `mysqld_multi` script has a `stop` command and can shut down any of the servers that it manages. It does so by invoking `mysqladmin`.

`mysqld_safe` has no server shutdown capability. You can use `mysqladmin shutdown` instead. Note that if you forcibly terminate `mysqld` by using the `kill -9` command to send it a signal, `mysqld_safe` will detect that `mysqld` terminated abnormally and will restart it. You can work around this by killing `mysqld_safe` first and then `mysqld`, but it's better to use `mysqladmin shutdown`, which initiates a normal (clean) server shutdown.

11.3 Runtime MySQL Configuration

By default, the server uses built-in values for its configuration variables when it runs. If the default values aren't suitable, you can use runtime options to tell the server to use different values:

- Several options specify the locations of important directories and files. For example, under Windows, the default value for the base installation directory is C:\mysql. If you install MySQL somewhere else, you'll need to tell the server the correct location by using the --basedir option or the server will not start. Similarly, if you use a data directory other than the directory named data under the base directory, you'll need to use a --datadir option to tell the server the correct location.

- Options also can be used to override the server's built-in values for performance-related variables, such as those that control the maximum number of simultaneous connections and the sizes of buffers and caches.

The examples in this section concentrate on options that relate to directory and file layout. Chapter 16 concentrates on performance-related options and discusses how to use them to tune the server to run more efficiently.

To change the configuration and behavior of the server, specify runtime options when you start it. Options can be given on the command line or in option files (also known as configuration files). The "Core Study Guide" provides general background on the use of option files. That discussion occurs in the context of running client programs, but the bulk of it also applies to specifying server options.

The server looks for option files in several standard locations. It uses any that exist, but it is not an error for an option file to be missing. The standard files are different for Windows and Unix.

On Windows, the search order for option files is as follows:

```
WINDIR\my.ini
C:\my.cnf
```

WINDIR represents the location of the Windows directory. Typically, this is something like C:\Windows or C:\WinNT.

On Unix, the search order includes two general option files:

```
/etc/my.cnf
DATADIR/my.cnf
```

DATADIR represents the compiled-in location of the data directory. This means that if you have two servers on the same machine, each with a different compiled-in data directory location, you can specify options specific to each server by putting them in the my.cnf file of the appropriate data directory.

The Unix option file search order also includes ~/.my.cnf; that is, the .my.cnf file located in the home directory of the person running the program. However, because ~/.my.cnf is a user-specific file, it isn't an especially suitable location for server options. Normally, you invoke the server as mysql or as root with a --user=mysql option. The user-specific file that the server would read differs in the two cases, possibly leading to inconsistent sets of options being used.

To name a specific option file, use a --defaults-file=file_name option on the command line In this case, the server reads only the named file and ignores the standard option files. When you use this option, it must be the first one named on the command line.

To find out what options the server supports, invoke it manually with the --help option:

```
shell> mysqld --help
```

Any of the server options shown in the help message may be specified on the command line. However, it's more typical to list them in an option file, for several reasons:

- By putting options in a file, you need not specify them on the command line each time you start the server. This is not only more convenient, it's less error-prone for complex options such as those used to configure the InnoDB tablespace.

- If you invoke the server using the mysql.server startup script, you cannot specify server options on the command line of the script. (It understands arguments of start or stop only.) This makes use of an option file mandatory.

- By looking at the option file, you can see immediately how you've configured the server to run.

To specify server startup options in an option file, use the [mysqld] option group. If the file does not exist, create it as a plain text file using an editor. To create or modify an option file, you must have write permission for it. The server itself needs only read access; it reads option files, but does not create or modify them.

The following examples illustrate some ways to use option files to specify server options:

- If you install MySQL on Windows, the server assumes by default that the base installation directory is C:\mysql and the data directory is named data in the base directory. If you install MySQL somewhere else, such as E:\mysql, you must tell the server the location with a --basedir option. In an option file, the following lines accomplish that:

```
[mysqld]
basedir=E:/mysql
```

If you use the data directory under E:\mysql as the data directory, that's sufficient. However, if you use a different data directory location, you must specify the --datadir option as well:

```
[mysqld]
basedir=E:/mysql
datadir=D:/mysql-data
```

Note that in this case you'll also need to copy the data directory from under the base directory to the new location of D:\mysql-data before starting the server. If the server does not find the data directory in the location you specify in the option file, it will not start.

- For any option that specifies a Windows pathname, write any backslashes in the name as slashes or as doubled backslashes. For example, to specify a basedir value of E:\mysql, you can write it using either of the following formats:

```
basedir=E:/mysql
basedir=E:\\mysql
```

- On Windows NT, the mysqld-nt and mysql-max-nt servers are capable of supporting named pipe connections but do not enable them by default, as discussed in section 10.3, "Connecting the Client to the Server." To turn on named pipe support, use this option:

```
[mysqld]
enable-named-pipe
```

- To enable logging, use the options that turn on the types of logs you want. The following options turn on the general query log, the binary log, and the slow query log:

```
[mysqld]
log
log-bin
log-slow-queries
```

Section 10.6, "Log and Status Files," discusses the logging options.

11.4 Compiling MySQL from a Source Distribution

The discussion of MySQL installation earlier in this chapter concentrates on using binary (precompiled) distributions containing ready-to-run programs. There are several advantages to using binary distributions from MySQL AB, aside from the obvious one that you need not go through a possibly somewhat lengthy build process. One significant advantage is that binaries produced by MySQL are likely to provide better performance than those you build yourself:

- MySQL AB has a great deal of experience selecting configuration options such as compiler switches that produce the most highly optimized binaries.
- In many cases, MySQL AB uses commercial compilers that produce superior quality code compared to the compilers typically available for general-purpose use.

- In some cases, MySQL AB produces binaries compiled with libraries that provide capabilities beyond those available in the standard operating system vendor libraries. For example, on Linux systems, a special C library is used that allows a higher maximum number of concurrent connections than can be achieved using the stock C library. Other times, binaries are built using special libraries that work around known bugs in vendor libraries.

Despite these advantages of precompiled distributions, there are reasons you might choose to compile MySQL yourself using a source distribution:

- There might be no binary distribution available for your platform. In this case, you have no choice but to build MySQL from source.

- You need to enable a feature that might not be available in a precompiled distribution, such as full debugging support. Or you might want to disable a feature that you don't need, to produce a server that uses less memory when it runs.

- Binary distributions are available only for released versions, not for the very latest development source code. If you want to run a server built from the current source, you must compile it yourself.

Should you decide to build MySQL from source, always remember to consult the *MySQL Reference Manual*. The manual has extensive notes and information on platform-specific issues.

11.5 Upgrading MySQL

MySQL development is ongoing, and MySQL AB releases new versions frequently. New versions add new features and correct problems found in older versions. Nevertheless, you should not upgrade to a newer version of MySQL without checking the implications and possible difficulties of doing so. Before performing any upgrade, check the *MySQL Reference Manual*:

- Always consult the section on upgrading to see whether there are any notes pertaining to the type of upgrade you're performing. If so, follow the recommended procedures described there.

- Check the change note sections for versions more recent than your current version to make sure that you're aware of what has changed since your original install. Note particularly any changes that are not backward compatible with your current version because they might require modifications to your existing applications if you upgrade.

Despite those cautionary remarks, upgrading MySQL usually is straightforward and can be done using the following procedure:

- Back up your databases.
- Stop the server.

- Install the new version of MySQL on top of the existing version.
- Start the new server.

If you install a new version on top of an existing one, you might not need to do much reconfiguring. This is common for Windows installations, RPM installations, and installations from source because those types of distributions each tend to use the same installation directory location regardless of MySQL version. (For example, the default location for Windows is always C:\mysql.) However, if you upgrade MySQL using a tar file, the new distribution likely will create a new version-specific base installation directory that differs from your existing installation directory. In this case, some reconfiguration might be necessary. If you have a symbolic link set up that points to the old base directory, you can delete the link and re-create it to point to the new base directory. Subsequent references to the new symbolic link will access the new installation.

When upgrading the server from one MySQL 4.0 version to another, you'll be able to use your old data directory without any changes for the new installation. There are no file incompatibilities when upgrading your server to a newer version.

On the other hand, the InnoDB storage engine did become enabled by default in MySQL 4.0. This does not cause any incompatibility problems, but does cause the server to use more memory by default because it allocates InnoDB-related data structures. If you upgrade from 3.23 to 4.0, but do not want to use InnoDB, you can start the server with the --skip-innodb option to save memory. Similarly, if you run a Max server that includes support for the BDB storage engine, starting the server with the --skip-bdb option saves memory if you don't need BDB tables.

11.6 Optimizing the Operating System for MySQL Use

MySQL has many configurable parameters that you can change to optimize server performance. Several of these are related to operating system resources and thus cannot be set higher than what the operating system allows. MySQL operates within the boundaries of the limits set by the OS. For example, you might request enough file descriptors to be able to open 2,000 files at once, but the effective limit is 1,000 if that's how many descriptors the operating system allows to each process. You can sometimes gain more latitude by increasing operating system limits; then the MySQL server can take advantage of the higher limits. Some of the relevant operating system limits include the following:

- The per-process limit on the number of open files. This limits the maximum size of the table cache that holds file descriptors for table files. You can tell MySQL to allocate more file descriptors with the --open-files-limit option, but that option cannot be increased beyond the per-process limit allowed by the operating system. If your operating system can be reconfigured, you might be able to increase this limit, which effectively allows a larger maximum table cache size.

- The maximum number of clients that can be connected simultaneously. This limit is controlled by the max_connections server variable. You can increase this variable, but not beyond the number of threads allowed to each process by the operating system. (Each connection is handled by a separate thread within the server.) To allow more connections than that, you must reconfigure the operating system to allow more threads.

- The number of queued network connections for clients that are waiting to connect. For a busy server with a high rate of client connections, increasing the backlog allowed by the operating system allows you to increase the value of the back_log server variable that governs the size of the server's queue.

11.7 Configuring Disks for MySQL Use

The MySQL server makes heavy use of disk resources. All storage engines except the HEAP engine store table contents on disk, and log files are recorded on disk. Consequently, the physical characteristics of your disks and disk-related subsystems strongly influence server performance:

- Physical disk characteristics are important because slow disks hinder the server. However, disk speed can be measured in various ways, and the most important parameter is seek time, not transfer rate. (It's more important for the heads to move quickly from track to track than for the platters to spin more quickly.) A RAM disk reduces seek time to near-zero because there is no physical movement at all.

- With a heavy I/O burden, a faster disk controller helps improve disk subsystem throughput. So does installing an additional controller and dividing disk assignments between controllers.

- RAID drives can improve retrieval performance, and some forms of RAID also boost write performance. Other benefits of RAID drives include data redundancy through mirroring and parity checking. Some RAID systems enable you to replace a disk without powering down the server host.

Using disks with better physical characteristics is one way to improve server performance. In addition, the way you employ your disks has a bearing on performance. The following list describes some key strategies for better using your disks:

- Distributing parts of your MySQL installation onto different disks can improve performance by splitting up database-related disk activity to distribute it more evenly. You can do this in several ways:
  - Put log files on one disk, and databases on another disk. This can be done using server options; each option that enables a log allows you to specify the log file location. To move the entire data directory, copy it to a different location and specify the new location with the --datadir option.

- Use a separate disk for temporary file storage. This can be done using the `--tmpdir` server option.

- Distribute databases among several disks. To do this for a given database, move it to a different location, and then create a symbolic link in the data directory that points to the new location of the database. Section 11.7.1, "Moving Databases Using Symbolic Links," discusses this technique.

- A strategy for distributing disk activity that's possible but not necessarily recommended is to put individual MyISAM tables on different disks. This technique is available for MyISAM tables using `CREATE TABLE` options. The technique is described in section 14.1.3, "MyISAM Table Symlinking." It has some drawbacks. Table symlinking isn't universally supported on all systems, and spreading your tables around can make it difficult to keep track of how much table storage you're using on which file systems. In addition, some filesystem commands don't understand symbolic links.

- Use a type of filesystem that is suited for the tables you have. MySQL can run on pretty much any kind of filesystem supported by your operating system, but some types of filesystems might be better for your installation than others. Two factors to consider are the maximum table size you need and the number of tables in your database.

In general, you can use larger MyISAM tables with filesystems or operating systems that allow larger files. The MyISAM storage engine has an internal file size limit of about 8TB, but MyISAM tables cannot actually use files that large unless the filesystem allows it. For example, with older Linux kernels, a common size limit is 2GB. If you use a newer Linux kernel instead, the file size limit goes up considerably and the MySQL server can create much larger MyISAM tables.

The number of tables in a database can have an effect on table-opening time and on the time to check files after a machine crash. For example, because MySQL represents a MyISAM table on disk by three files (the `.frm` format file, the `.MYD` data file, and the `.MYI` index file), that translates into many small files in the database directory if you have many small MyISAM tables in a database. For some filesystem types, this results in significantly increased directory lookup times when opening the files associated with tables. In situations like this, filesystems such as ReiserFS or ext3 can help performance. They're designed to deal well with large numbers of small files and to provide good directory lookup time. Also, the recovery time to check the filesystem after a machine crash is very good, so the MySQL server becomes available again faster.

Table use is subject to the read/write characteristics of the filesystem on which tables are located. It's most common for MySQL installations to store databases and tables on media that are readable and writable, so that both retrieval and update operations can be performed. However, it's possible to initialize a database and then modify the properties of the filesystem on which it's located to disable write access or to copy a database to read-only media such as CD-ROM. In both cases, the server must only perform retrievals from a disk-based table. Any attempt to issue a query that updates a table fails with an error. HEAP tables are an exception to this because table contents reside in memory.

Under some circumstances, MySQL can run on a completely read-only system (one that has both data and programs stored on read-only media). To do this, you must observe certain precautions:

- No logging can be enabled.
- InnoDB cannot be used because the InnoDB storage engine expects to open its log files for read/write access and writes an information stamp to the tablespace files at shutdown.
- On Unix, the server expects to create a Unix socket file and a process ID file. This does not work on read-only media. The workaround is to run the server on read-write media and keep only databases on read-only media.

11.7.1 Moving Databases Using Symbolic Links

It's possible to move individual databases under either Windows or Unix. Use the instructions in the following sections. While moving a database, be sure that the MySQL server isn't running.

11.7.1.1 Using Database Symbolic Links on Windows

To relocate a database directory under Windows, you must be using a `mysqld-max` or `mysqld-max-nt` server because only those servers are compiled with symbolic link support.

1. Move the database directory from the data directory to its new location.
2. In the data directory, create a file with the same name as the database and a `.sym` extension. The file should contain the full pathname to the new database location. The `.sym` file is the symbolic link.

11.7.1.2 Using Database Symbolic Links on Unix

To relocate a database directory under Unix, no special server support is needed.

1. Move the database directory from the data directory to its new location.
2. In the data directory, create a symbolic link with the same name as the database that points to the new database location.

11.8 Choosing Hardware for MySQL Use

MySQL can benefit from improvements to several subsystems of your hardware configuration. The following list describes the most important factors:

- Adding more memory allows larger buffers to be used. This improves caching so that disk activity can be minimized. The performance effect can be considerable because it's much faster to read information from memory than from disk. Adding memory also can reduce the amount of swapping the operating system needs to do.

- Use a 64-bit CPU rather than a 32-bit CPU. A 64-bit CPU allows certain mathematical (and other) functions to complete faster. It also allows MySQL to support larger internal cache sizes.

- Use a multiprocessor system. If MySQL uses kernel threads, it can take advantage of multiple processors.

- A faster main logic board (motherboard) improves general system throughput.

- With a faster network, the server can transfer information to clients faster. This lets the server process queries faster, reducing resource contention.

- Choose disks with better performance. Factors to consider in evaluating performance were discussed in section 11.7, "Configuring Disks for MySQL Use."

11.9 Exercises

Question 1:

Say you installed MySQL on a Linux host, using RPM files to set up the MySQL server and clients. Can you start working with MySQL right away, or are there any further steps you must perform first?

Question 2:

After installing MySQL, the server fails to start properly. How can you find out what prevented the server from starting?

Question 3:

After installing MySQL on Linux from a tar file, the server cannot be started. Looking up the error log you find that it writes `Can't find file: './mysql/host.frm' (errno: 13)` to the error log before it terminates. What's the reason for this, and how could you solve the problem?

Question 4:

Under Windows, you want to install MySQL in `D:\Programs\MySQL`. Besides installing it there using the Setup Wizard, what additional steps must you perform so that the server runs properly?

Question 5:

Name some reasons why you would compile MySQL from source, rather than using a binary distribution provided by MySQL AB.

Question 6:

Name three limits that the operating system imposes on a MySQL server, and say how these limits affect server performance.

Question 7:

What's the maximum size for a MyISAM table?

A. 2MB

B. 4GB

C. 8TB

Answers to Exercises

Answer 1:

The RPM installation gives you a MySQL system that is ready to work with, if no problems occurred during the installation procedure:

- The `mysql` login and group accounts are created
- The MySQL server and all client programs are installed
- The data directory is set up
- The grant tables are set up and initialized
- The startup script is registered
- The MySQL server is started

Note, however, that the initial MySQL accounts stored in the grant tables have no passwords and should be modified to make MySQL secure.

Answer 2:

Look in the error log, which is where the server writes error messages indicating why it couldn't start. The error log is located in the data directory and is named `host_name.err`, where `host_name` is the name of the machine on which the MySQL server is running. Another way to see error messages is to send them to the console:

- On Windows, invoke the server at the command line with the `--console` option.
- On Unix, invoke `mysqld` directly rather than by using a startup script.

Answer 3:

The error message indicates that the grant tables were not installed. The server tries to read the grant tables at startup, and if they aren't present, it reports an error for the first table file it doesn't find (`host.frm`). This can occur if the grant tables do not exist or if they exist but the server cannot read them. If the tables do not exist, run the `mysql_install_db` script to create them. If the grant tables exist, make sure that their ownership and access permissions allow the server to read them.

Answer 4:

You must set up an option file. The file can be either the `my.ini` file in the Windows directory or `C:\my.cnf`. It should contain the following lines:

```
[mysqld]
basedir=D:/Programs/MySQL
```

Answer 5:

Reasons why you might choose to compile MySQL yourself using a source distribution include the following:

- No binary distribution is available for your platform.
- You need to enable a feature that is not available in any of the precompiled distributions.
- You want to disable an unneeded feature to produce a server that uses less memory.
- You want to run a server built from the current development source.

Answer 6:

The limits to a MySQL server imposed by the operating system include the following:

- The per-process limit on number of open files. This limits the maximum size of the table cache that holds file descriptors for table files.
- The number of threads allowed to each process by the operating system. This limits the number of clients that can connect to a MySQL server at the same time.
- The backlog allowed by the operating system. This affects the maximum number of queued network connections for clients that are waiting to connect.

Answer 7:

The MyISAM storage engine has an internal file size limit of about 8TB, but MyISAM tables cannot actually use files that large unless the filesystem allows it.

12

Security Issues

Information stored in MySQL databases must be kept secure to avoid exposing data that MySQL users expect to be private. Risks to a MySQL installation come in several forms, but they can be grouped into two general categories:

- *Filesystem security risks.* Database information is stored in directories and files, and the server also maintains log files that contain information about queries that clients execute. Because these directories and files are part of the filesystem, they need to be protected so that other users who have login accounts on the server host cannot access them directly. A MySQL installation also includes the programs and scripts used to manage and access databases. Users need to be able to run some of these (such as the client programs), but should not be able to modify or replace them. This means that MySQL programs need to be protected appropriately as well.

- *Network security risks.* The MySQL server provides access to databases by allowing clients to connect and make requests. Information about client accounts is stored in the mysql database. Each account should be set up with privileges that provide access only to the data the accounts needs to see or modify. Accounts also should be assigned passwords to make it difficult for people to connect to the server using someone else's account. For example, a MySQL root account has full privileges to perform any database operation, so it's important to assign the account a password that is not easily guessed.

This chapter describes several steps that an administrator can take to maintain the integrity of a MySQL installation. It covers the following topics:

- Basic security procedures, both for the filesystem and for the initial MySQL accounts. These procedures prevent users with login accounts on the server host from attacking MySQL directories or files. They also prevent clients from connecting to the MySQL server without a password.

- How to set up MySQL accounts. This includes a discussion of the types of privileges available, and how the GRANT and REVOKE statements work.

- How the server uses the information in the grant tables to manage access control when clients connect.

Questions on the material in this chapter make up approximately 15% of the exam.

Note that usernames and passwords for MySQL accounts are unrelated to those for system login accounts. For example, on Unix, your login name need not be the same as the name that you use to identify yourself when connecting to the MySQL server.

12.1 Securing MySQL

Before you can consider a MySQL installation ready for general use, several security-related issues must be considered and addressed:

- If you're running MySQL on a multiuser system, you should protect the directories and files that are part of the installation against unauthorized access by users who are not responsible for database administration. To do this, set up a dedicated login account to use for administering MySQL and give that account ownership of the relevant files. An additional benefit of setting up this account is that you can use it to run the MySQL server, rather than running the server from the Unix root account. A server that has the privileges of the root login account has more filesystem access than necessary and constitutes a security risk.

- The initial MySQL accounts that are set up during the MySQL installation procedure have no passwords. Some of these accounts have full privileges for server access and should be assigned passwords to prevent unauthorized clients from connecting to the server and gaining complete access to it.

The directories and files of a MySQL installation can be protected by changing their ownership and access permissions before running the server, but setting passwords for the MySQL root accounts can be done only while the server is running. Consequently, before starting the server and setting passwords, you should take any actions necessary to protect MySQL-related portions of the filesystem. If you set the passwords first, before protecting the files in which the grant tables are stored, it's possible for someone with direct filesystem access on the server host to replace the grant tables. This compromises your MySQL installation and undoes the effect of setting the passwords.

12.1.1 Securing MySQL at the Filesystem Level

Under multiuser systems such as Unix, all components of a MySQL installation should be owned by a login account with proper administrative privileges. The installation should be accessible to other users only to the extent necessary.

This chapter assumes the existence of such an administrative account and that both its username and group name are mysql. However, the details of creating login accounts vary per version of Unix and are outside the scope of the exam, so they aren't discussed here. Consult the documentation for your operating system.

To have a secure MySQL installation, the following conditions should be satisfied:

- Every MySQL-related directory and file should have its user and group ownerships set to mysql. This includes the MySQL programs, the database directories and files, and the log, status, and configuration files.

  An allowable alternative to having everything owned by the mysql user is that some program and library directories and files may be owned by root. (The principle to follow is that anything the server might need to modify cannot be owned by root.)

- No files should be set to be readable by any user other than mysql except for those that client programs run by other users need to access. This includes global option files, error message files, language files, and character set files.

- In most cases, it's reasonable for client programs and other utilities to be world-executable so that other users with login accounts on the system can run them. Under certain conditions, you might want to restrict access to allow only a subset of the users on the machine to run MySQL programs.

- After you've established the proper filesystem access so that the mysql login account owns the relevant directories and files, the MySQL server should be run using this account. This is important because mysql is a regular login account that has no special filesystem privileges.

  The server should not be run as the system root user. There are many reasons for this; one is that there are operations performed by the server that involve reading or writing files in the server host filesystem. (For example, LOAD DATA INFILE and SELECT … INTO OUTFILE do so.) Running the server as root is a bad idea because that gives it root privileges and vastly increases the extent of the filesystem that the server can access or modify.

- The server program need not be executable to anyone other than mysql. Its access privileges can be set accordingly.

The following sample procedure shows how to secure the directories and files of a MySQL installation. Before using this procedure, stop the server if it's running. Also, note that some operations must be done from a privileged login account, so you'll need root login access to perform them. The chown and chgrp commands should be run as the system root user because only root can assign directory and file ownership. After directories and files have been set to be owned by mysql, you can set their access permissions by running chmod as either root or mysql.

The procedure assumes that the MySQL base installation directory is /usr/local/mysql. An installation that has the files located elsewhere can be protected by making the appropriate substitutions to the pathnames shown in the commands.

Run the following commands as root to set everything in and under the base installation directory to be owned by user mysql and group mysql:

```
shell> chown -R mysql /usr/local/mysql
shell> chgrp -R mysql /usr/local/mysql
```

Then restrict access to the base directory so that only the mysql user has permission to make changes, and so that its subdirectories are accessible only as necessary by other users. The following commands can be run either as mysql or root:

```
shell> chmod u=rwx,go=rx /usr/local/mysql
shell> chmod u=rwx,go=rx /usr/local/mysql/bin
shell> chmod u=rwx,go-rwx /usr/local/mysql/libexec
shell> chmod -R go-rwx /usr/local/mysql/data
```

These commands give complete access to the mysql user but restricted access to other users. They also make the base directory and bin directory where the client programs are installed accessible but not modifiable to other users, and make the libexec directory (where the server is installed) and the data directory inaccessible to other users.

You should also protect the global option file, /etc/my.cnf, if it exists. The mysql user should own it and have read/write access to it, but other users need only read access:

```
shell> chown mysql /etc/my.cnf
shell> chgrp mysql /etc/my.cnf
shell> chmod u=rw,go=r /etc/my.cnf
```

Before starting the server, you should arrange to have it execute with the privileges of the mysql login account. This can be done either by starting the server while logged in as mysql, or by starting it as root with a --user=mysql option to instruct it to change user from root to mysql during its startup sequence. (It's allowable to *start* the server as root, but if you do, you should use a --user option to tell the server to change user to the mysql account and give up its special root privileges. Otherwise, the server continues to execute as root, which is dangerous.)

If you have the server set to start automatically during the system boot sequence, the system invokes the server as root and does not allow you to specify any options on the command line. To reliably start the server as the mysql user, it's best to put the --user option in an option file so that the server always uses it whether you start the server manually or automatically. One way to do so is to place the following lines in /etc/my.cnf:

```
[mysqld]
user=mysql
```

12.1.2 Securing the Initial MySQL Accounts

The MySQL server controls client access using the mysql database, which contains several tables known as *grant tables*. Privileges listed in the grant tables are tied to accounts, each of which is defined by a username and a hostname. That is, a MySQL account depends not only on your username, but the client host from which you connect to the server.

The MySQL installation procedure sets up several initial accounts in the grant tables. These accounts have no passwords at first. You should assign passwords at least to those accounts that have administrative privileges. This is true no matter what platform you run MySQL on, whether Windows or Unix.

The accounts that the MySQL installation procedure creates in the `mysql` database are of two kinds:

- Accounts with a username of `root`. These are superuser accounts that have full access to the server's capabilities.

- Anonymous accounts with a blank username. An anonymous account allows a client to connect with any username if it connects from the host listed in the account record. In most cases, anonymous users have limited privileges. These accounts can access the `test` database. They also can access other databases having names that begin with `test` (on Windows) or other databases having names that begin with `test_` (on Unix). On Windows, the anonymous account for connecting from the local host actually is fully equivalent to a `root` account with respect to the privileges that it has, so it can access any database.

As already mentioned, none of the initial MySQL accounts have passwords. You should assign passwords immediately to at least the `root` accounts to prevent other people from connecting to the server as `root` and gaining complete control over it. On Windows, you should also either assign a password to the anonymous account that has superuser privileges or remove the account.

There are various ways to set up MySQL passwords:

- Use `GRANT` statements
- Use `SET PASSWORD` statements
- Use `mysqladmin password` commands
- Modify the grant tables directly with `UPDATE` statements

Generally, it's preferable to use one of the first three methods and to avoid modifying the grant tables directly. For example, after installing MySQL, a simple procedure to protect the `root` accounts by assigning them passwords is to use these two `mysqladmin password` commands, where *rootpass* represents the password and *host_name* is the hostname of your machine:

```
shell> mysqladmin -u root password 'rootpass'
shell> mysqladmin -u root -h host_name password 'rootpass'
```

However, these commands will not take care of the anonymous accounts. The following procedure secures all the initial accounts. It also serves to demonstrate how modifying the grant tables directly can be useful.

1. On the server host, connect to the server as the MySQL `root` user to access the grant tables in the `mysql` database. Initially, because the accounts have no password, you can connect as follows without specifying a password option:

   ```
   shell> mysql -u root mysql
   ```

2. Account names and passwords are stored in the `user` table of the `mysql` database. Modify the `user` table records for `root` to assign a password. The following statement represents this password as *rootpass*:

```
mysql> UPDATE user SET Password = PASSWORD('rootpass')
    -> WHERE User = 'root';
```

3. If you want to assign passwords to the anonymous accounts, do so as follows, where *anonpass* represents the anonymous-user password:

```
mysql> UPDATE user SET Password = PASSWORD('anonpass')
    -> WHERE User = '';
```

4. On Windows, one of the anonymous user accounts has `root` privileges. You should either assign it a password or remove it. To assign a password, use this statement:

```
mysql> UPDATE user SET Password = PASSWORD('rootpass')
    -> WHERE User = '' AND Host = 'localhost';
```

To delete the account instead, use this statement:

```
mysql> DELETE FROM user WHERE User = '' AND Host = 'localhost';
```

5. If you want to see what effect the preceding operations have on the `user` table, issue this statement:

```
mysql> SELECT Host, User, Password FROM user;
```

6. Finally, flush the grant tables:

```
mysql> FLUSH PRIVILEGES;
```

The reason for flushing the grant tables is that the server makes access-control decisions based on in-memory copies of the grant tables. The `FLUSH` statement tells the server to create new in-memory copies from the on-disk tables that were changed by the previous steps.

After setting the `root` account passwords, you'll need to supply the *rootpass* password whenever you connect to the server with a username of `root`. Similarly, to connect using an anonymous-user account, you'll need to specify a password of *anonpass*.

On Unix, MySQL comes with a `mysql_secure_installation` script that can perform several helpful security-related operations on your installation. This script can do any of the following:

- Set a password for the `root` account.
- Remove any remotely accessible `root` accounts. This improves security because it prevents the possibility of anyone connecting to the MySQL server as `root` from a remote host. The result is that anyone who wants to connect as `root` must first be able to log in on the server host, which provides an additional barrier against attackers.

- Remove the anonymous user accounts.
- Remove the test database. (If you remove the anonymous accounts, you might also want to remove the test database to which they have access.)

MySQL encrypts passwords in the grant tables using the PASSWORD() function. This function should be considered for use only for managing MySQL accounts, not for general user applications. One reason for this is that applications often require reversible (two-way) encryption, and PASSWORD() performs irreversible (one-way) encryption. Another reason that applications should avoid reliance on PASSWORD() is that its implementation might change. (In fact, it does change in MySQL 4.1.)

Other than the encryption of Password column values in the user table, the server performs no encryption on the contents of MySQL tables. For applications that work with data that must not be stored in unencrypted form, MySQL provides several pairs of functions to perform two-way encryption and decryption:

- ENCODE() and DECODE()
- DES_ENCRYPT() and DES_DECRYPT()
- AES_ENCRYPT() and AES_DECRYPT()

Cryptographically, AES_ENCRYPT() and AES_DECRYPT() can be considered the most secure of the pairs. DES_ENCRYPT() and DES_DECRYPT() can be used if SSL support is enabled. Other details can be found in the *MySQL Reference Manual*.

12.2 User Account Management

The MySQL access control system enables you to create MySQL accounts and define what each account can do. Several types of privileges can be assigned to an account. They should be granted according to how the account is to be used. Some examples:

- An account that needs only read access to a database can be given just the SELECT privilege.
- An account used to modify data can be given the DELETE, INSERT, and UPDATE privileges.
- Administrative accounts can be given the PROCESS or SUPER privileges for viewing client process activity or killing connections, or the SHUTDOWN privilege for stopping the server.

The MySQL server bases access control on the contents of the grant tables in the mysql database. These tables define MySQL accounts and the privileges they hold. To manage their contents, use the GRANT and REVOKE statements. These statements provide an interface to the grant tables that enables you to specify privileges without having to determine how to modify the tables directly. When you use GRANT and REVOKE to perform a privilege operation, the MySQL server determines what changes to the grant tables are needed and makes the modifications for you.

This section describes the structure and contents of the grant tables and how you set up user accounts using GRANT and REVOKE. Section 12.3, "Client Access Control," describes how the server uses the grant tables to check access privileges when clients connect.

12.2.1 Types of Privileges That MySQL Supports

You can grant several types of privileges to a MySQL account, and you can grant privileges at different levels (globally or just for particular databases, tables, or columns). For example, you can allow a user to select from any table in any database by granting the SELECT privilege at the global level. Or you might grant an account no global privileges, but give it complete control over a specific database. That allows the account to create the database and tables in it, select from the tables, and add new records, delete them, or update them.

The privileges that MySQL supports are shown in the following lists. The first names the administrative privileges and the second names the database-access privileges.

Administrative Privileges:

Privilege	Operations Allowed by Privilege
CREATE TEMPORARY TABLES	Use TEMPORARY with CREATE TABLE
FILE	Use statements that read and write files on the server host
GRANT OPTION	Grant privileges to other accounts
LOCK TABLES	Explicitly lock tables with LOCK TABLES
PROCESS	View process (thread) activity
RELOAD	Use FLUSH and RESET
REPLICATION CLIENT	Ask server for information about replication hosts
REPLICATION SLAVE	Act as a replication slave
SHOW DATABASES	See all databases with SHOW DATABASES
SHUTDOWN	Shut down the server
SUPER	Miscellaneous administrative operations

Database-Access Privileges:

Privilege	Operations Allowed by Privilege
ALTER	Modify tables with ALTER TABLE
CREATE	Create databases and tables
DELETE	Remove rows from tables
DROP	Drop databases and tables
INDEX	Create and drop indexes
INSERT	Add rows to tables
SELECT	Select records from tables
UPDATE	Modify records in tables

Some privileges not shown in these lists can be assigned to accounts but currently are unused. EXECUTE is reserved for future versions of MySQL, when stored procedures are implemented. REFERENCES may be implemented in relation to foreign key support at some point.

There are also some special privilege specifiers:

- ALL and ALL PRIVILEGES are shorthand for *all privileges except GRANT OPTION*. They're shorthand for granting all privileges except the ability to give privileges to other accounts.
- USAGE means no privileges other than being allowed to connect to the server. A record is created for the account in the user table. This causes the account to exist, and it can then be used to access the server for limited purposes such as issuing SHOW VARIABLES or SHOW STATUS statements. The account cannot be used to access databases or tables (although you could grant such privileges to the account at a later time).

Privileges can exist at different levels:

- Any privilege can be granted globally. An account that possesses a global privilege can exercise it at any time. Global privileges are therefore quite powerful and are normally granted only to administrative accounts. For example, a global DELETE privilege allows the account to remove records from any table in any database.
- Some privileges can be granted for specific databases: ALTER, CREATE, CREATE TEMPORARY TABLES, DELETE, DROP, GRANT OPTION, INDEX, INSERT, LOCK TABLES, SELECT, and UPDATE. A database-specific privilege applies to all tables in the database.
- Some privileges can be granted for specific tables: ALTER, CREATE, DELETE, DROP, GRANT OPTION, INDEX, INSERT, SELECT, and UPDATE. A table-specific privilege applies to all columns in the table.
- Some privileges can be granted for specific table columns: INSERT, SELECT, and UPDATE.

12.2.2 The Grant Tables

Four grant tables in the mysql database contain most of the access control information used by the server. They contain information to indicate what the legal accounts are and the privileges held at each access level by each account:

- The user table contains a record for each account known to the server. The user record for an account lists its global privileges. It also indicates other information about the account, such as any resource limits it's subject to, and whether client connections that use the account must be made over a secure connection using the Secure Sockets Layer (SSL). Use of SSL connections is not covered on the Professional Exam.
- The db table lists database-specific privileges for accounts.
- The tables_priv table lists table-specific privileges for accounts.
- The columns_priv table lists column-specific privileges for accounts.

Every account must have a user table record because the server uses that table's contents when determining whether to accept or reject client connection attempts. An account also will have records in the other grant tables if it has privileges at other than the global level.

Each grant table has columns that identify which accounts its records apply to:

- The server decides whether a client can connect based on the Host, User, and Password columns of the user table. An account is defined by a hostname and username, so for a client to be able to connect, some record in the user table must match the host from which the client connects and the username given by the client. In addition, the client must provide the password listed in the matching record.

- After a client connects, the server determines its access privileges based on the Host and User columns of the user, db, tables_priv, and columns_priv tables. Any privileges enabled in the matching user table record may be used globally by the client. The privileges in the matching records of the other grant tables apply in more limited contexts. For example, privileges in a db table record apply to the database named in the record, but not to other databases.

Use of the grant tables for controlling what clients can do is discussed further in section 12.3, "Client Access Control."

There is also a fifth grant table named host that exists for historical reasons. It is not affected by the GRANT and REVOKE statements, so it's discussed no further here. For more information about the host table, see the *MySQL Reference Manual*.

The grant tables are stored as MyISAM tables. The MyISAM storage engine is always guaranteed to be enabled, which is not true for storage engines such as InnoDB and BDB.

As already mentioned, the server uses the information in the grant tables to determine whether to allow clients to connect, and to determine for every statement that a connected client issues whether the client has sufficient privileges to execute it. However, the server does not actually access the on-disk grant tables each time it needs to verify client access because that would result in a great deal of overhead. Instead, the server reads the grant tables into memory during its startup sequence and uses the in-memory copies to check client access.

The server refreshes its in-memory copies of the grant tables under the following conditions:

- You modify a user account in the on-disk tables by issuing a GRANT, REVOKE, or SET PASSWORD statement.

- You tell the server to reload the tables explicitly by issuing a FLUSH PRIVILEGES statement or by executing a mysqladmin flush-privileges or mysqladmin reload command.

12.2.3 Granting and Revoking Privileges

It's possible to manage MySQL accounts by modifying the grant tables directly with SQL statements such as INSERT, DELETE, and UPDATE. The procedure described in section 12.1.2, "Securing the Initial MySQL Accounts," is an example of how UPDATE and DELETE can be used in this way. In general, however, the recommended way to set up and modify MySQL accounts is to use the GRANT and REVOKE statements because they offer these advantages:

- It's easier to use GRANT and REVOKE than to modify the grant tables directly. The syntax of GRANT and REVOKE is more natural and less cumbersome for expressing privilege operations because that's what it's designed for. When you use GRANT and REVOKE, the server determines the necessary modifications to the grant tables and makes the changes for you.

- With GRANT and REVOKE, the server automatically reloads the in-memory contents of the grant tables. If you modify the tables directly, you must explicitly tell the server to reload the tables by using a FLUSH PRIVILEGES statement or a mysqladmin flush-privileges command.

In addition to GRANT and REVOKE, the SET PASSWORD statement is useful when all you want to do is change an account's password. SET PASSWORD causes the server to automatically refresh its in-memory grant tables when you use it.

Despite the advantages of GRANT and REVOKE, it is occasionally necessary to manipulate the grant tables directly. The principal reason for this is that REVOKE does not remove records from the user table. You can use REVOKE to disable the global privileges recorded in that table, but it leaves the record in the table in case you want to assign different privileges later. If you want to eliminate all traces of an account from the grant tables, you must also use DELETE to remove its user table record.

12.2.3.1 The GRANT Statement

The syntax for the GRANT statement includes several sections. In simplest form, you specify the following:

- The privileges to be granted
- How broadly the privileges apply
- The account that should be given the privileges
- A password

As an example, the following statement grants the SELECT privilege for all tables in the world database to a user named jim, who must connect from the local host and use a password of Abc123:

```
GRANT SELECT ON world.* TO 'jim'@'localhost' IDENTIFIED BY 'Abc123';
```

The parts of the statement have the following effects:

- The statement begins with the GRANT keyword and one or more privilege names indicating which privileges are to be granted. Privilege names are not case sensitive. To list multiple privileges, separate them by commas. For example, if you want jim to be able to manipulate records in the world database, not just retrieve them, write the GRANT statement like this:

```
GRANT SELECT, INSERT, DELETE, UPDATE ON world.*
TO 'jim'@'localhost' IDENTIFIED BY 'Abc123';
```

- The ON clause specifies the level of the granted privileges (how broadly they apply). You can grant privileges globally, for a specific database, or for a specific table. The ON syntax for these levels is as follows:

```
ON *.*
ON db_name.*
ON db_name.table_name
```

For the formats that begin with db_name., it's allowable to omit the database name qualifier and specify just * or table_name. In these cases, the privileges are granted to all tables in the current database or to the named table in the current database. Be sure that you know what the current database is, to avoid granting privileges to tables in the incorrect database.

To grant privileges at a column-specific level, use an ON clause that names a particular table, and specify a comma-separated list of column names within parentheses after each privilege to be granted. The following statement indicates that the named account can retrieve three of the columns in the City table of the world database, but can update only two of them:

```
GRANT SELECT (ID, Name, CountryCode), UPDATE (Name, CountryCode)
ON world.City TO 'jim'@'localhost'
IDENTIFIED BY 'Abc123';
```

- The TO clause specifies the account to be granted the privileges. An account name consists of a username and the name of the client host from which the user must connect to the server. The account name is given in 'user_name'@'host_name' format. More detail on this format is given later, but note that the user and host parts of account names should be quoted separately. Quotes actually are necessary only for values that contain special characters such as dashes. If a value is legal as an unquoted identifier, the quotes are optional. However, quotes are always acceptable and examples shown here use them.

  Because an account name includes a hostname part, it's possible to set up separate accounts for different users who have the same username but connect from different hosts.

- The IDENTIFIED BY clause is optional. If present, it assigns a password to the account. If the account already exists and IDENTIFIED BY is given, the password replaces any old one. If the account exists but IDENTIFIED BY is omitted from the GRANT statement, the account's current password remains unchanged. If an account has no password, clients can use it to connect to the server without a password!

To specify an anonymous-user account (that is, an account that matches any username), specify an empty string for the user part of the account name:

```
GRANT SELECT ON world.* TO ''@'localhost';
```

The host part of an account name may be given in any of the following formats:

- The name localhost.
- A hostname, such as myhost.example.com.
- An IP number, such as 192.168.1.47.
- A pattern containing the % or _ wildcard characters. Patterns are useful for setting up an account that allows a client to connect from any host in an entire domain or subnet. A host value of %.example.com matches any host in the example.com domain. A host value of 192.168.% matches any host in the 192.168 subnet. A host value of % matches any host, allowing the client to connect from anywhere.
- An IP number/netmask combination. The value allows a client to connect from any host with an address that matches the IP number for all bits that are 1 in the netmask. For example, a value of 10.0.0.0/255.255.255.0 matches any host with 10.0.0 in the first 24 bits of its IP number. This format is useful for allowing an account with a given username to connect from any host in a subnet.

It's allowable to omit the host part of an account name in the GRANT statement. An account name specified as 'user_name' is equivalent to 'user_name'@'%'.

Keep the proper perspective in mind when specifying the host part of an account name in GRANT statements. When you connect to the server using a client program, you specify the host *to which* you want to connect. On the other hand, when the server checks the client against Host column values in the grant tables, it uses the host *from which* the client connects. When setting up an account with GRANT, you should specify the client host from the server's point of view. For example, if the server runs on server.example.com and you want to allow jim to connect from client.example.com, the GRANT statement should look like this:

```
GRANT ... TO 'jim'@'client.example.com' ... ;
```

Be aware that it is possible to have multiple accounts that could apply to a given client. For example, if you set up accounts for 'jim'@'localhost' and 'jim'@'%', the server could use either one when jim connects from the local host. The rules that the server employs to determine which account to use in such cases are covered in section 12.3, "Client Access Control."

If you want to give an account the capability to grant its privileges to other accounts, add a WITH GRANT OPTION clause to the statement. For example, if you want jim to have read access to the world database and to be able to create other users that have read access to that database, use this statement:

```
GRANT SELECT ON world.* TO 'jim'@'localhost'
IDENTIFIED BY 'Abc123'
WITH GRANT OPTION;
```

To find out what privileges a particular account has, use the SHOW GRANTS statement. It displays the GRANT statements that would be required to set up the account. The account name for this statement has the same 'user_name'@'host_name' format as that used with GRANT. You can always see your own privileges with SHOW GRANTS. You cannot see the privileges for other accounts unless you have the SELECT privilege for the mysql database.

Suppose that you've set up an account for a user jen who connects from the host myhost.example.com. To see this account's privileges, use the following statement:

```
mysql> SHOW GRANTS FOR 'jen'@'myhost.example.com';
+------------------------------------------------------------+
| Grants for jen@myhost.example.com                          |
+------------------------------------------------------------+
| GRANT FILE ON *.* TO 'jen'@'myhost.example.com'            |
| GRANT SELECT ON `mydb`.* TO 'jen'@'myhost.example.com'     |
| GRANT UPDATE ON `test`.`mytable` TO 'jen'@'myhost.example.com' |
+------------------------------------------------------------+
```

The output displayed here by SHOW GRANTS consists of three GRANT statements. Their ON clauses indicate that jen has privileges at the global, database, and table levels, respectively.

If the account has a password, SHOW GRANTS displays an IDENTIFIED BY PASSWORD clause at the end of the GRANT statement that lists the account's global privileges. (The word PASSWORD after IDENTIFIED BY indicates that the password value shown is the encrypted value stored in the user table, not the actual password.) If the account can grant some or all of its privileges to other accounts, SHOW GRANTS displays WITH GRANT OPTION at the end of each GRANT statement to which it applies.

SHOW GRANTS displays privileges only for the exact account specified in the statement. For example, the preceding SHOW GRANTS statement shows privileges only for 'jen'@'myhost.example.com', not for 'jen'@'%.example.com', 'jen'@'%.com', or 'jen'@'%'.

12.2.3.2 The REVOKE Statement

Use the REVOKE statement to revoke privileges from an account. Its syntax has the following sections:

- The keyword REVOKE followed by the list of privileges to be revoked
- An ON clause indicating the level at which privileges are to be revoked
- A FROM clause that specifies the account name

Suppose that jim on the local host has SELECT, DELETE, INSERT, and UPDATE privileges on the world database, but you want to change the account so that he has SELECT access only. To do this, revoke those privileges that allow him to make changes:

```
REVOKE DELETE, INSERT, UPDATE ON world.* FROM 'jim'@'localhost';
```

To revoke the GRANT OPTION privilege from an account that has it, you must revoke it in a separate statement. For example, if jill has the ability to grant her privileges for the world database to other users, you can revoke that ability as follows:

```
REVOKE GRANT OPTION ON world.* FROM 'jill'@'localhost';
```

If you use REVOKE to remove all the privileges enabled by a record in the db, tables_priv, or columns_priv tables, REVOKE removes the record entirely. However, REVOKE does not remove an account's user table record, even if you revoke all privileges for the account. It's necessary to use DELETE to remove a user record. A later example demonstrates this.

To determine what REVOKE statements are needed to revoke an account's privileges, SHOW GRANTS might be helpful. Consider again the output from SHOW GRANTS for the jen@localhost account:

```
mysql> SHOW GRANTS FOR 'jen'@'myhost.example.com';
+----------------------------------------------------------------+
| Grants for jen@myhost.example.com                              |
+----------------------------------------------------------------+
| GRANT FILE ON *.* TO 'jen'@'myhost.example.com'                |
| GRANT SELECT ON `mydb`.* TO 'jen'@'myhost.example.com'         |
| GRANT UPDATE ON `test`.`mytable` TO 'jen'@'myhost.example.com' |
+----------------------------------------------------------------+
```

This output indicates that the account has global, database-level, and table-level privileges. To remove these privileges, convert those GRANT statements to the following corresponding REVOKE statements. The privilege names, privilege levels, and account name must be the same as displayed by SHOW GRANTS:

```
mysql> REVOKE FILE ON *.* FROM 'jen'@'myhost.example.com';
mysql> REVOKE SELECT ON mydb.* FROM 'jen'@'myhost.example.com';
mysql> REVOKE UPDATE ON test.mytable FROM 'jen'@'myhost.example.com';
```

After issuing the REVOKE statements, SHOW GRANTS produces this result:

```
mysql> SHOW GRANTS FOR 'jen'@'myhost.example.com';
+-------------------------------------------------+
| Grants for jen@myhost.example.com               |
+-------------------------------------------------+
| GRANT USAGE ON *.* TO 'jen'@'myhost.example.com' |
+-------------------------------------------------+
```

This means that the account no longer has any privileges, although it does still exist and thus can be used to connect to the server. (In other words, the user table still contains a record for the account, but all the global privileges listed in the record are disabled.) To remove the last trace of the account, use a DELETE statement to remove the user table record, and then tell the server to reload the grant tables:

```
mysql> USE mysql;
mysql> DELETE FROM user WHERE User = 'jen' AND Host = 'myhost.example.com';
mysql> FLUSH PRIVILEGES;
```

After that, the account no longer exists and cannot be used to connect to the server.

12.2.3.3 When Privilege Changes Take Effect

The effects of changes to the grant tables apply to existing client connections as follows:

- Table and column privilege changes apply to all statements issued after the changes are made.
- Database privilege changes apply with the next USE statement.
- Changes to global privileges and passwords do not apply to connected clients. They apply the next time a client attempts to connect.

12.2.4 Changing Account Passwords

As discussed earlier, you can specify a password for an account by including an IDENTIFIED BY clause in a GRANT statement. If the account is new, the clause assigns its initial password. If the account already exists, the clause changes its password.

To change an existing account's password without changing any of its privileges, you have two options:

- Use the SET PASSWORD statement, specifying the account name and the new password. For example, to set the password for jim on the local host to NewPass, use this statement:

  ```
  SET PASSWORD FOR 'jim'@'localhost' = PASSWORD('NewPass');
  ```

  Any nonanonymous client can change its own password by omitting the FOR clause:

  ```
  SET PASSWORD = PASSWORD('NewPass');
  ```

- Use GRANT with the USAGE privilege specifier at the global level and an IDENTIFIED BY clause:

```
GRANT USAGE ON *.* TO 'jim'@'localhost' IDENTIFIED BY 'NewPass';
```

USAGE means *no privileges*, so the statement changes the password without granting any privileges.

Note that with SET PASSWORD, you use PASSWORD() to encrypt the password, whereas with GRANT, you do not use it.

To allow a user to connect without specifying a password, change the password to the empty string. However, you cannot revoke the password this way with REVOKE. Instead, use either of the following statements:

```
SET PASSWORD FOR 'jim'@'localhost' = '';
GRANT USAGE ON *.* TO 'jim'@'localhost' IDENTIFIED BY '';
```

Be certain that you want to do this, however. It isn't a good idea to have accounts without passwords.

12.2.5 Specifying Resource Limits

By default, there is no limit on the number of times that a client can connect to the server or the number of queries it can issue. If that is not suitable, GRANT can establish limits on an account's resource consumption for the following characteristics:

- The number of times per hour the account is allowed to connect to the server
- The number of queries per hour the account is allowed to issue
- The number of updates per hour the account is allowed to issue

Each of these resource limits is specified using an option in a WITH clause. The following example creates an account that can use the test database, but can connect to the server a maximum of only 10 times per hour. The account can issue 50 queries per hour, and at most 20 of those queries can modify data:

```
GRANT ALL ON test.* TO 'quinn'@'localhost' IDENTIFIED BY 'SomePass'
WITH MAX_CONNECTIONS_PER_HOUR 10
MAX_QUERIES_PER_HOUR 50
MAX_UPDATES_PER_HOUR 20;
```

The order in which you name the options in the WITH clause doesn't matter.

To reset an existing limit to the default of no limit, specify a value of zero. For example:

```
GRANT USAGE ON *.* TO 'quinn'@'localhost'
WITH MAX_CONNECTIONS_PER_HOUR 0;
```

12.3 Client Access Control

This section describes how the server uses account information in the grant tables to control which clients may connect and what they may do after connecting.

There are two stages of client access control:

- In the first stage, a client attempts to connect and the server either accepts or rejects the connection. For the attempt to succeed, some entry in the user table must match the host from which a client connects, the username, and the password.

- In the second stage (which occurs only if a client has already connected successfully), the server checks every query it receives from the client to see whether the client has sufficient privileges to execute it.

The server matches a client against entries in the grant tables based on the host from which the client connects and the username the client provides. However, it's possible for more than one record to match:

- Host values in grant tables may be specified as patterns containing wildcard values. If a grant table contains entries for myhost.example.com, %.example.com, %.com, and %, all of them match a client who connects from myhost.example.com.

- Patterns are not allowed for User values in grant table entries, but a username may be given as an empty string to specify an anonymous user. The empty string matches any username and thus effectively acts as a wildcard.

When the Host and User values in more than one user table record match a client, the server must decide which one to use. It does this by sorting records with the most specific Host and User column values first, and choosing the matching record that occurs first in the sorted list. Sorting takes place as follows:

- In the Host column, literal values such as localhost, 127.0.0.1, and myhost.example.com sort ahead of values such as %.example.com that have pattern characters in them. Pattern values are sorted according to how specific they are. For example, %.example.com is more specific than %.com, which is more specific than %.

- In the User column, nonblank usernames sort ahead of blank usernames. That is, nonanonymous users sort ahead of anonymous users.

The server performs this sorting at startup. It reads the grant tables into memory, sorts them, and uses the in-memory copies for access control.

Suppose that the user table contains the following values in the Host and User columns:

```
+--------------------+--------+
| Host               | User   |
+--------------------+--------+
| localhost          |        |
| %                  | james  |
| %.example.com      | jen    |
```

```
| %.com               | jobril |
| localhost           | jon    |
| myhost.example.com  | james  |
+---------------------+--------+
```

When the server reads the grant tables into memory, it sorts the user table records as follows:

- localhost and myhost.example.com are literal values, so they sort ahead of the other Host values that contain pattern characters. The Host values that contain pattern characters sort from most specific to least specific.

- The two entries that have localhost in the Host column are ordered based on the User values. The entry with the nonblank username sorts ahead of the one with the blank username.

The sorting rules result in entries that are ordered like this:

```
+---------------------+--------+
| Host                | User   |
+---------------------+--------+
| localhost           | jon    |
| localhost           |        |
| myhost.example.com  | james  |
| %.example.com       | jen    |
| %.com               | jobril |
| %                   | james  |
+---------------------+--------+
```

12.3.1 Connection Request Checking

When a client attempts to connect, the server matches the sorted records to the client using the Host values first and the User values second:

- If jon connects from the local host, the entry with localhost and jon in the Host and User columns matches first.

- If james connects from localhost, the two entries with localhost in the Host column match the host, and the entry with the blank User value matches any username. Therefore, that's the first entry that matches both the client hostname and username. (The entry with % in the Host column matches localhost as well, but the server doesn't consider it in this case because it has already found a matching record.)

- On the other hand, if james connects from pluto.example.com instead, the first entry that matches the hostname has a Host value of %.example.com. That entry's username doesn't match, so the server continues looking. The same thing happens with the entry that has a Host value of %.com: The hostname matches but the username does not. Finally, the entry with a Host value of % matches and the username matches as well.

When you attempt to determine which grant table record the server will find as the best match for a client, remember to take the sort order into account. In particular, the fact that Host matching is done before User matching leads to a property that might be surprising unless you're aware of it. Consider again the case where james connects from the local host. There are two entries with james in the User column, but neither is the first match. Host matching takes place first, so on that basis the entry that matches first is the anonymous-user entry: localhost matches the host from which james connects, and the blank User value matches any username. This means that when james connects from the local host, he will be treated as an anonymous user, not as james.

When you connect successfully to the server, the USER() function returns the username you specified and the client host from which you connected. The CURRENT_USER() function returns the username and hostname values from the User and Host columns of the user table record the server used to authenticate you. The two values may be different. If james connects from the local host, USER() and CURRENT_USER() have these values:

```
mysql> SELECT USER(), CURRENT_USER();
+----------------+----------------+
| USER()         | CURRENT_USER() |
+----------------+----------------+
| james@localhost | @localhost    |
+----------------+----------------+
```

The username part of CURRENT_USER() is empty. This occurs because the server authenticates james as an anonymous user.

If james connects from pluto.example.com instead, USER() and CURRENT_USER() have these values:

```
mysql> SELECT USER(), CURRENT_USER();
+-----------------------+----------------+
| USER()                | CURRENT_USER() |
+-----------------------+----------------+
| james@pluto.example.com | james@%      |
+-----------------------+----------------+
```

Here the host part of CURRENT_USER() is % because the server authenticates james using the user table entry that has % as the Host value.

For connection attempts that the server denies, an error message results:

- If the client attempts to connect from a host for which there is no record in the user table with a matching Host value, the error is

  ```
  Host 'host_name' is not allowed to connect to this MySQL server
  ```

- If connections from the client host are allowed by one or more user table records, but no match can be found for the User and Password values, the error is

  ```
  "Access denied for user: 'user_name'@'host_name'
  ```

12.3.2 Statement Privilege Checking

Each time the server receives a statement from a client, it checks the client's privileges to see whether it's allowed to execute the statement. For example, if you issue an UPDATE statement, you must possess the UPDATE privilege for each of the columns to be updated.

The server checks privileges in an additive fashion from the global level to the column-specific level. To check a statement, the server determines which privileges the statement requires, and then assesses whether the client possesses them by proceeding successively through the grant tables.

First, the server checks the client's global privileges in the user table. If these are sufficient, the server executes the statement. If the global privileges are not sufficient, the server adds any database-specific privileges indicated for the client in the db table and checks again. If the combined privileges are sufficient, the server executes the statement. Otherwise, it continues as necessary, checking the table-specific and column-specific privileges in the tables_priv and columns_priv tables. If, after checking all the grant tables, the client does not have sufficient privileges, the server refuses to execute the statement.

12.3.3 Resource Limit Checking

For an account that has resource limits, the server applies them to access control as follows:

- If the client has a limit on the number of times per hour it can connect to the server, that limit applies in the first stage of access control, when the server determines whether to accept the client connection.

- If the client has a limit on the number of queries or updates per hour it can issue, those limits apply in the second stage of access control. The server checks the limits for each query received before checking whether the client has the proper privileges to execute it.

12.3.4 Disabling Client Access Control

The --skip-grant-tables option tells the server not to use the grant tables to control client access. This option has the following effects:

- You can connect from anywhere with no password, and you have full privileges to do anything. That's convenient if you've forgotten the root password and need to reset it because you can connect without knowing the password. On the other hand, because anyone else can connect, running the server in this mode is dangerous. To prevent remote clients from connecting over TCP/IP, you might want to use the --skip-networking option as well. Clients then can connect only from the local host using a Windows-named pipe or a Unix socket file.

- --skip-grant-tables disables the GRANT, REVOKE, and SET PASSWORD statements. These statements require the in-memory copies of the grant tables, which aren't set up when you skip use of the tables. To make a change to the grant tables while those statements are inoperative, you must update them directly. Alternatively, when you connect to the server, you can issue a FLUSH PRIVILEGES statement to cause the server to read the tables. That will enable GRANT, REVOKE, and SET PASSWORD. (Note that if you also started the server with the --skip-networking option, you'll still need to restart it without that option to cause it to listen for TCP/IP connections again.)

12.4 Exercises

Question 1:

Which components of MySQL must you protect on the filesystem level?

Question 2:

Assume that you have three users who have login accounts on a host where a MySQL server is running. Users pablo and charlton need to communicate with the MySQL server, but user steve doesn't. How would you set the file permissions for the /usr/local/mysql/data directory so that pablo and charlton can access their databases located there but steve cannot?

Question 3:

As the root login user on a Linux host, how can you start the MySQL server so that it doesn't run as root, without having to log in as another user? How can you make sure that the server will always run as a user different from root?

Question 4:

What's the initial password of the MySQL root accounts in the grant tables that are set up during the installation procedure?

Question 5:

Having installed MySQL, you want to make sure that there's no MySQL account left that could connect to the server without specifying a password. How can you do this?

Question 6:

You want to set up a MySQL administrator account with all privileges. This administrator should be called superuser and the password should be s3creT. superuser should be able to connect only from the local host, and should be allowed to create new MySQL users. How would you create this account?

Question 7:

Which SQL functions could you use to store encrypted information? What functions could you use to retrieve the stored information unencrypted? Are there special prerequisites or requirements for using these functions?

Question 8:

What GRANT statement would you issue to set up an account for user steve, who should be able to manipulate data of tables only in the accounting database? steve should be able to connect to the server from anywhere. The account password should be some_password1.

Question 9:

What GRANT statement would you issue to set up an account for user pablo, who should be able to do all kinds of operations on the tables in the marketing database and should also be able to grant permissions to do those operations to other MySQL users? pablo should be able to connect to the server from the local network where IP numbers of all machines start with 192.168. The account password should be some_password2.

Question 10:

What GRANT statement would you issue to set up an account for user admin, who should be able to administer the database server, including performing all operations on all its databases and tables? admin should not, however, be able to grant privileges to other accounts. admin should be able to connect to the server only from the local host. The account password should be some_password3.

Question 11:

Consider the following privilege settings for the accounts associated with a given MySQL username, where the Select_priv column indicates the setting for the global SELECT privilege:

```
mysql> SELECT
    -> Host, User, Select_priv
    -> FROM mysql.user
    -> WHERE User = 'icke'
    -> ;
+-------------+------+-------------+
| Host        | User | Select_priv |
+-------------+------+-------------+
| 62.220.12.66 | icke | N           |
| 62.220.12.%  | icke | Y           |
| 62.220.%     | icke | N           |
+-------------+------+-------------+
```

The Select_priv column indicates that the SELECT privilege for the second entry has been granted on a global scope (*.*). Will user icke be able to select data from any table on the MySQL server when connecting from the following hosts:

- 62.220.12.66
- 62.220.12.43

- 62.220.42.43
- localhost

Assume that the icke accounts are not granted privileges in any of the other grant tables.

Question 12:

Assume that you set up an administrator for the MySQL server named superuser, and that this is the only account with the full set of privileges. In particular, this is the only account that can grant privileges to other accounts or shut down the server using mysqladmin shutdown. Unfortunately, you've forgotten the password for superuser. Assume that you can log on to the host where the MySQL server runs, and that you can do so as some administrative account (such as Administrator for Windows or root for Unix). What can you do to set up the MySQL superuser account with a new password, and what safety precautions would you take?

Answers to Exercises

Answer 1:

On the filesystem level, you must protect the following:

- Databases and their tables, so that unauthorized users cannot access them directly
- Log files and status files, so that unauthorized users cannot access them directly
- Configuration files, so that unauthorized users cannot replace or modify them
- Programs and scripts that manage and access databases, so that users cannot replace or modify them

Answer 2:

Neither pablo nor charlton need file system-level access to their database directories. If they want to access their databases, they should do this through the MySQL server; for example, by using the mysql client program. Therefore, the /usr/local/mysql/data directory should be accessible only to user mysql (assuming that this is the system user the server runs as).

Answer 3:

To start the server so that it runs as user mysql, you can start it with a --user option like this:

```
shell> mysqld --user=mysql
```

The mysqld_safe script also accepts a --user option. To make sure that the server will always start as that user, put the option in an option file (for example, /etc/my.cnf):

```
[mysqld]
user=mysql
```

Answer 4:

None of the MySQL accounts, not even the `root` accounts, are assigned a password by the installation procedure. You can connect to the server like this, without specifying any password option:

```
shell> mysql -u root
```

Answer 5:

To determine which accounts, if any, can be used without specifying a password, use the following statement:

```
mysql> SELECT Host, User FROM mysql.user WHERE Password = '';
```

If any such accounts exist, you can delete them as follows:

```
mysql> DELETE FROM mysql.user WHERE Password = '';
mysql> FLUSH PRIVILEGES;
```

The FLUSH PRIVILEGES statement is necessary because DELETE doesn't cause the server to reread the grant tables into memory.

Answer 6:

To create the `superuser` account, use a GRANT statement:

```
mysql> GRANT
    ->        ALL PRIVILEGES ON *.*
    ->        TO 'superuser'@'localhost'
    ->        IDENTIFIED BY 's3creT'
    ->        WITH GRANT OPTION
    -> ;
```

See section A.1.17, "GRANT."

Answer 7:

For encryption and decryption, you could use the following functions:

- ENCODE() and DECODE(); these have no special requirements.
- DES_ENCRYPT() and DES_DECRYPT(); these require SSL support to be enabled.
- AES_ENCRYPT() and AES_DECRYPT(); these have no special requirements.
- PASSWORD() can encrypt data, but has no corresponding decryption function. It should only be used for MySQL user account management.

See section A.2, "SQL Functions."

Answer 8:

This statement sets up an account for steve:

```
mysql> GRANT
    ->      SELECT, INSERT, UPDATE, DELETE
    ->      ON accounting.*
    ->      TO 'steve'@'%'
    ->      IDENTIFIED BY 'some_password1'
    -> ;
```

See section A.1.17, "GRANT."

Answer 9:

This statement sets up an account for pablo:

```
mysql> GRANT
    ->      ALL PRIVILEGES
    ->      ON marketing.*
    ->      TO 'pablo'@'192.168.%'
    ->      IDENTIFIED BY 'some_password2'
    ->      WITH GRANT OPTION
    -> ;
```

See section A.1.17, "GRANT."

Answer 10:

This statement sets up an account for admin:

```
mysql> GRANT
    ->      ALL PRIVILEGES
    ->      ON *.*
    ->      TO 'admin'@'localhost'
    ->      IDENTIFIED BY 'some_password3'
    -> ;
```

See section A.1.17, "GRANT."

Answer 11:

- 62.220.12.66 is the most specific entry that matches from which the host user icke is trying to connect. Because the SELECT privilege for that entry is N, user icke cannot select from any table on the server.

- The most specific entry that matches 62.220.12.43 is 62.220.12.%. Because the SELECT privilege for that entry is Y, user icke can select from any table on the server.

- The most specific entry that matches 62.220.42.43 is 62.220.%. Because the SELECT privilege for that entry is N, user icke cannot select from any table on the server.

- There's no entry that would match icke@localhost. Therefore, user icke cannot even connect to the server.

Answer 12:

To set up a new password for superuser, you could use the following procedure:

1. Bring down the MySQL server by means of the operating system. If you run the server as a Windows service, you can stop the service. On Unix, you might have to forcibly terminate the server by using the `kill` command.

2. Restart the server in a way that it will not read the grant tables. As a safety precaution, make sure that no clients can connect to it other than from the local host:

   ```
   shell> mysqld --skip-grant-tables --skip-networking
   ```

3. Connect to the server from the local host:

   ```
   shell> mysql
   ```

   No username is needed here because the server is not using the grant tables.

4. Update the `Password` column in the `mysql.user` table entry for the `superuser` account, and then end the `mysql` session:

   ```
   mysql> UPDATE mysql.user
       ->  SET Password = PASSWORD('NeverForget')
       ->  WHERE User = 'superuser'
       -> ;
   mysql> EXIT;
   ```

5. Shut down the server normally:

   ```
   shell> mysqladmin shutdown
   ```

   The UPDATE statement in the previous step does not cause the server to refresh the in-memory grant tables, so no password is needed here.

6. Start the server using your normal startup procedure.

7. If you had to forcibly terminate the server, it would be a good idea to check all tables:

   ```
   shell> mysqlcheck -u root -p --all-databases
   ```

Optimizing for Query Speed

This chapter discusses general principles that are useful for optimizing queries to run more efficiently. It covers the following optimization strategies:

- The primary optimization technique for reducing lookup times is to create good indexes. This is true not just for retrievals (SELECT statements); indexing reduces row lookup time for UPDATE and DELETE statements as well. You should know general principles for creating useful indexes and for avoiding unnecessary ones.

- The EXPLAIN statement provides information about how the MySQL optimizer processes queries. This is of value when you're trying to determine how to make a query run better (for example, if you suspect indexes are not being used as you think they should be).

- The way a query is written might prevent indexes from being used even if they are available. Rewriting the query often will allow the optimizer to use an index and process a query faster. Other times you can use query modifiers to give the scheduler a hint about how to execute a query.

- In some cases, query processing for a task can be improved by using a different database design. This includes techniques such as choosing a storage engine with properties that best match application requirements and using summary tables.

Questions on the material in this chapter make up approximately 15% of the exam.

Why be concerned about optimization? The most obvious reason is to make your queries run faster. Another is that optimizing your queries helps everybody who uses the server, not just you. When the server runs more smoothly and does more with less work, it performs better as a whole:

- A query that takes less time to run doesn't hold locks as long. Other clients that are waiting to update a table have to wait less time for a fast query than a slow one. This reduces the chance of a query backlog building up.

- A query might be slow because it does not use indexes and therefore MySQL must scan a table in its entirety. For a large table, that involves a lot of processing and disk activity. This extra overhead affects not only your own query, it takes machine resources that could be devoted to processing other queries. Adding effective indexes allows MySQL to read only the relevant parts of the table, which is quicker and less disk intensive.

The optimization strategies covered here are guidelines known to result in generally improved query performance. However, you must test them in specific circumstances and measure the results, particularly if you can choose from more than one technique in a given situation.

The techniques discussed in this chapter can be used by any client application to improve how the queries it issues are executed by the server. Another approach to performance improvement is to reconfigure the server itself to change its overall operation. Server tuning is addressed in Chapter 16, "Advanced Server Features."

13.1 Index Optimization and Index Usage

When you create a table, consider whether it should have indexes, because they have important benefits:

- Indexes contain sorted values. This allows MySQL to find rows containing particular values faster. The effect can be particularly dramatic for joins, which have the potential to require many combinations of rows to be examined.

- Indexes result in less disk I/O. The server can use an index to go directly to the relevant table records, which reduces the number of records it needs to read. Furthermore, if a query displays information only from indexed columns, MySQL might be able to process it by reading only the indexes and without accessing data rows at all.

13.1.1 Types of Indexes

MySQL supports four types of indexes:

- A nonunique index is one in which any key value may occur multiple times. This type of index is defined with the keyword INDEX or KEY.

- A UNIQUE index is unique-valued; that is, every key value is required to be different than all others. (The exception is that NULL values may occur multiple times.)

- A PRIMARY KEY also is a unique-valued index. It is similar to a UNIQUE index, but has additional restrictions:
  - A table may have multiple UNIQUE indexes, but at most one PRIMARY KEY.
  - A UNIQUE index can contain NULL values, whereas a PRIMARY KEY cannot.

- A FULLTEXT index is specially designed for text searching.

To define indexes when you're initially creating a table, use CREATE TABLE. To add indexes to an already existing table, use ALTER TABLE or CREATE INDEX. To drop indexes, use ALTER TABLE or DROP INDEX.

ALTER TABLE can add or drop several indexes in the same statement, which is faster than processing each one separately. CREATE INDEX and DROP INDEX allow only one index to be added or dropped at a time.

Index creation using the INDEX, UNIQUE, and PRIMARY KEY keywords is discussed in the "Core Study Guide." FULLTEXT indexes are not covered there because they are a more specialized kind of index. Instead, FULLTEXT indexing is discussed in section 13.1.4, "FULLTEXT Indexes."

13.1.2 Obtaining Table Index Information

To find out what indexes a table has, use SHOW CREATE TABLE to display the CREATE TABLE statement that corresponds to the table structure, including its indexes.

For more detailed information about the indexes, use SHOW INDEX. For example, SHOW INDEX produces the following output for the Country table of the world database:

```
mysql> SHOW INDEX FROM Country\G
*************************** 1. row ***************************
        Table: Country
   Non_unique: 0
     Key_name: PRIMARY
 Seq_in_index: 1
  Column_name: Code
    Collation: A
  Cardinality: NULL
     Sub_part: NULL
       Packed: NULL
         Null:
   Index_type: BTREE
      Comment:
```

The output indicates that the table has a single index, a primary key on the Code column. The output for the City table is similar except that it indicates the ID column is the primary key:

```
mysql> SHOW INDEX FROM City\G
*************************** 1. row ***************************
        Table: City
   Non_unique: 0
     Key_name: PRIMARY
 Seq_in_index: 1
  Column_name: ID
    Collation: A
  Cardinality: NULL
     Sub_part: NULL
       Packed: NULL
         Null:
```

```
     Index_type: BTREE
       Comment:
```

For the CountryLanguage table, the output has two rows because the primary key includes two columns, Country and Language:

```
mysql> SHOW INDEX FROM CountryLanguage\G
*************************** 1. row ***************************
        Table: CountryLanguage
   Non_unique: 0
     Key_name: PRIMARY
 Seq_in_index: 1
  Column_name: Country
    Collation: A
  Cardinality: NULL
     Sub_part: NULL
       Packed: NULL
         Null:
   Index_type: BTREE
      Comment:
*************************** 2. row ***************************
        Table: CountryLanguage
   Non_unique: 0
     Key_name: PRIMARY
 Seq_in_index: 2
  Column_name: Language
    Collation: A
  Cardinality: NULL
     Sub_part: NULL
       Packed: NULL
         Null:
   Index_type: BTREE
      Comment:
```

The Seq_in_index values show the order of the columns within the index. They indicate that the primary key columns are Country first and Language second. This information corresponds to the following PRIMARY KEY declaration:

```
PRIMARY KEY (Country, Language)
```

13.1.3 Using Indexes

An index helps MySQL perform retrievals more quickly than if no index is used. But indexes can be used with varying degrees of success, so you should keep several index-related considerations in mind when designing tables:

- Declare an indexed column NOT NULL if possible. Although NULL values can be indexed, NULL is a special value that requires additional decisions when performing comparisons on key values. An index without NULL can be processed more simply and thus faster.

- Avoid overindexing; don't index a column just because you can. If you never refer to a column in comparisons (such as in WHERE, ORDER BY, or GROUP BY clauses), there's no need to index it. Another reason to avoid unnecessary indexing is that every index you create slows down table updates. If you insert or delete a row, an entry must be added to or removed from each of the table's indexes. If you update a row, any change to indexed columns require the appropriate indexes to be updated as well.

- One strategy the MySQL optimizer uses is that if it appears an index will return a large percentage of the records in the table, it will be just as fast to scan the table as to incur the overhead required to process the index. As a consequence, an index on a column that has very few distinct values is unlikely to do much good. Suppose that a column is declared as ENUM('Y', 'N') and the values are roughly evenly distributed such that a search for either value returns about half of the records. In this case, an index on the column is unlikely to result in faster queries.

- Choose unique and nonunique indexes appropriately. The choice might be influenced by the type of a column. If the column is declared as an ENUM, there is a fixed number of distinct column values that can be stored in it. This number is equal to the number of enumeration elements, plus one for the '' (empty string) element that is used when you attempt to store an illegal value. Should you choose to index an ENUM column, you likely should create a nonunique index. A PRIMARY KEY allows only as many rows as the number of distinct enumeration values. A UNIQUE index enforces a similar restriction, except that unless the column is declared NOT NULL, the index allows NULL values.

- Index a column prefix rather than the entire column. MySQL caches index blocks in memory to avoid whenever possible reading them from disk repeatedly. Shortening the length of indexed values can improve performance by reducing the amount of disk I/O needed to read the index and by increasing the number of key values that fit into the key cache. This technique is discussed further in section 13.1.3.1, "Indexing Column Prefixes."

- Avoid creating multiple indexes that overlap (have the same initial columns). This is wasteful because MySQL can use a multiple-column index even when a query uses just the initial columns for lookups. For more information, see section 13.1.3.2, "Leftmost Index Prefixes."

13.1.3.1 Indexing Column Prefixes

Short index values can be processed more quickly than long ones. Therefore, when you index a column, it's worth asking whether it's sufficient to index partial column values rather than complete values. This technique, known as indexing a column prefix, can be applied to string column types.

Suppose that you're considering creating a table using this definition:

```
CREATE TABLE t
(
    name CHAR(255),
    INDEX (name)
);
```

If you index all 255 bytes of the values in the name column, index processing will be relatively slow:

- It's necessary to read more information from disk.
- Longer values take longer to compare.
- The index cache is not as effective because fewer index values fit into it at a time.

It's often possible to overcome these problems by indexing only a prefix of the column values. For example, if you expect column values to be distinct most of the time in the first 15 bytes, index only that many bytes of each value, not all 255 bytes.

To specify a prefix length for a column, follow the column name in the index definition by a number in parentheses. The following table definition is the same as the previous one, except that the index uses just the first 15 bytes of each column value:

```
CREATE TABLE t
(
    name CHAR(255),
    INDEX (name(15))
);
```

Indexing a column prefix can speed up query processing, but works best when the prefix values tend to have about the same amount of uniqueness as the original values. Don't use such a short prefix that you produce a very high frequency of duplicate values in the index. It might require some testing to find the optimal balance between long index values that provide good uniqueness versus shorter values that compare more quickly but have more duplicates. To determine the number of records in the table, the number of distinct values in the column, and the number of duplicates, use this query:

```
SELECT
    COUNT(*) AS 'Total Rows',
    COUNT(DISTINCT name) AS 'Distinct Values',
    COUNT(*) - COUNT(DISTINCT name) AS 'Duplicate Values'
FROM t;
```

That gives you an estimate of the amount of uniqueness in the name values. Then run a similar query on the prefix values:

```
SELECT
    COUNT(DISTINCT LEFT(name,n)) AS 'Distinct Prefix Values',
```

```
       COUNT(*) - COUNT(DISTINCT LEFT(name,n)) AS 'Duplicate Prefix Values'
FROM t;
```

That tells you how the uniqueness characteristics change when you use an *n*-byte prefix of the name values. Run the query with different values of *n* to determine an acceptable prefix length.

Note that when an index on a full column is a PRIMARY KEY or UNIQUE index, you might have to change the index to be nonunique if you decide to index prefix values instead. If you index partial column values and require the index to be unique, that means the prefix values must be unique, too.

13.1.3.2 Leftmost Index Prefixes

In a table that has a composite (multiple column) index, MySQL can use leftmost index prefixes of that index. A leftmost prefix of a composite index consists of one or more of the initial columns of the index. MySQL's capability to use leftmost index prefixes enables you to avoid creating unnecessary indexes.

The CountryLanguage table in the world database provides an example of how a leftmost prefix applies. The table has a two-part primary key:

```
mysql> SHOW INDEX FROM CountryLanguage\G
*************************** 1. row ***************************
        Table: CountryLanguage
   Non_unique: 0
     Key_name: PRIMARY
 Seq_in_index: 1
  Column_name: CountryCode
    Collation: A
  Cardinality: 246
     Sub_part: NULL
       Packed: NULL
         Null:
   Index_type: BTREE
      Comment:
*************************** 2. row ***************************
        Table: CountryLanguage
   Non_unique: 0
     Key_name: PRIMARY
 Seq_in_index: 2
  Column_name: Language
    Collation: A
  Cardinality: 984
     Sub_part: NULL
       Packed: NULL
         Null:
```

```
Index_type: BTREE
   Comment:
```

The index on the `CountryCode` and `Language` columns allows records to be looked up quickly based on a given country name and language. However, MySQL also can use the index given just a country code. Suppose that you want to determine which languages are spoken in France:

```
SELECT * FROM CountryLanguage WHERE CountryCode = 'FRA';
```

MySQL can see that `CountryCode` is a leftmost prefix of the primary key and use it as though it were a separate index. This means there's no need to define a second index on the `CountryCode` column alone.

On the other hand, if you want to perform indexed searches using just the `Language` column of the `CountryLanguage` table, you do need to create a separate index because `Language` is not a leftmost prefix of the existing index.

Note that a leftmost prefix of an index and an index on a column prefix are two different things. A leftmost prefix of an index consists of leading columns in a multiple-column index. An index on a column prefix indexes the leading bytes of values in the column.

13.1.4 FULLTEXT Indexes

`FULLTEXT` indexes are designed to make text searching fast and easy. They have the following characteristics:

- `FULLTEXT` indexes currently are supported only for MyISAM tables.

- Each column must be either `CHAR` or `VARCHAR` without the `BINARY` option, or one of the `TEXT` types. You cannot use a binary string column type such as `CHAR BINARY`, `VARCHAR BINARY`, or `BLOB`.

- `FULLTEXT` indexes are not case sensitive. This is a consequence of the fact that the index can include only nonbinary string columns.

- The syntax for defining a full-text index is much like that for other indexes: An index-type keyword (`FULLTEXT`), an optional index name, and a parenthesized list of one or more column names to be indexed. A `FULLTEXT` index may be created with `CREATE TABLE`, added to a table with `ALTER TABLE` or `CREATE INDEX`, and dropped from a table with `ALTER TABLE` or `DROP INDEX`. The following are all legal statements for `FULLTEXT` index manipulation:

```
CREATE TABLE t (name CHAR(40), FULLTEXT (name));
ALTER TABLE t ADD FULLTEXT name_idx (name);
ALTER TABLE t DROP INDEX name_idx;
CREATE FULLTEXT INDEX name_idx ON t (name);
DROP INDEX name_idx ON t;
```

- Column prefixes are not applicable for FULLTEXT indexes, which always index entire columns. If you specify a prefix length for a column in a FULLTEXT index, MySQL ignores it.

- FULLTEXT index indexes can be constructed on multiple columns, allowing searches to be conducted simultaneously on all the indexed columns. However, leftmost index prefixes are not applicable for FULLTEXT indexes. You must construct one index for every column or combination of columns you want to search. Suppose that you want to search for text sometimes only in column c1 and sometimes in both columns c1 and c2. You must construct two FULLTEXT indexes: one on column c1 and another on columns c1 and c2.

To perform a FULLTEXT search, use MATCH and AGAINST(). For example, to search the table t for records that contain 'Wendell' in the name column, use this query:

```
SELECT * FROM t WHERE MATCH(name) AGAINST('Wendell');
```

The MATCH operator names the column or columns you want to search. As mentioned earlier, there must be a FULLTEXT index on exactly those columns. If you want to search different sets of columns, you'll need one FULLTEXT index for each set. If a table people has name and address columns and you want to search them either separately or together, three FULLTEXT indexes are needed:

```
CREATE TABLE people
(
    name    CHAR(40),
    address CHAR(40),
    FULLTEXT (name),         # index for searching name only
    FULLTEXT (address),      # index for searching address only
    FULLTEXT (name,address)  # index for searching name and address
);
```

The indexes allow queries such as the following to be formulated:

```
SELECT * FROM people WHERE MATCH(name) AGAINST('string');
SELECT * FROM people WHERE MATCH(address) AGAINST('string');
SELECT * FROM people WHERE MATCH(name,address) AGAINST('string');
```

The preceding discussion summary of FULLTEXT indexing and searching is very brief. More information may be found in the *MySQL Reference Manual*.

13.2 Using EXPLAIN to Analyze Queries

When a SELECT query does not run as quickly as you think it should, use the EXPLAIN statement to ask the MySQL server for information about how the query optimizer processes the query. This information is useful in several ways:

- EXPLAIN can provide information that points out the need to add an index.
- If a table already has indexes, you can use EXPLAIN to find out whether the optimizer is using them. (To see what indexes a table has, use SHOW INDEX, as described in section 13.1.2, "Obtaining Table Index Information.")
- If indexes exist but aren't being used, you can try writing a query different ways. EXPLAIN can tell you whether the rewrites are better for helping the server use the available indexes.

When using EXPLAIN to analyze a query, it's helpful to have a good understanding of the tables involved. If you need to determine a table's structure, remember that you can use DESCRIBE to obtain information about a table's columns, and SHOW INDEX for information about its indexes.

This section describes how EXPLAIN works. Later in the chapter, section 13.3, "General Query Enhancement," discusses some general query-writing principles that help MySQL use indexes more effectively. You can apply those principles in conjunction with EXPLAIN to determine the best way of writing a query.

13.2.1 Identifying Candidates for Query Analysis

EXPLAIN can be used to analyze any SELECT query, but some query performance characteristics make it especially likely that EXPLAIN will be helpful:

- When a query that you issue (for example, using the mysql client) clearly takes a long time.
- When a query appears in the slow query log, particularly if it appears consistently each time it is issued.

Recognize that "slow" can be a relative term. You don't want to waste time trying to optimize a query that seems slow but is so only for external reasons and is not inherently slow:

- Queries in the slow log are determined to be slow using wallclock time. Queries will appear more often in the log when the server host is heavily loaded than when it is not, so you should evaluate query execution time against general system activity on that host.
- A query might appear slow if the machine is very busy, but otherwise perform acceptably. For example, if filesystem backups are taking place, they'll incur heavy disk activity that impedes the performance of other programs, including the MySQL server. The machine might be processing a heavy load for other reasons, such as if you have a very active Web server running on the same host.

Keeping in mind the preceding considerations, you have a good indicator that a query might be in need of being optimized if you find that it is consistently slow in comparison to other queries no matter when you run it, and you know the machine isn't just generally bogged down all the time.

Another factor to recognize is that the mere presence of a query in the slow query log does not necessarily mean that the query is slow. If the server is run with the `--long-log-format` option, the slow query log also will contain queries that execute without using any index. In some cases, such a query may indeed be a prime candidate for optimization (for example, by adding an index). But in other cases, MySQL might elect not to use an existing index simply because a table is so small that scanning all of its rows is just as fast as using an index.

The SHOW PROCESSLIST statement is another useful source of information about query execution. Use it periodically to get information about what queries currently are running. If you notice that a particular query often seems to be causing a backlog by making other queries block, see whether you can optimize it. If you're successful, it will alleviate the backlog. To get the most information from SHOW PROCESSLIST, you should have the PROCESS privilege. Then the statement will display queries being run by all clients, not just your own queries.

13.2.2 How EXPLAIN Works

To use EXPLAIN, write your SELECT query as you normally would, but place the keyword EXPLAIN in front of it. As a very simple example, take the following statement:

```
SELECT 1;
```

To see what EXPLAIN will do with it, issue the statement like this:

```
mysql> EXPLAIN SELECT 1;
+----------------+
| Comment        |
+----------------+
| No tables used |
+----------------+
```

In practice, it's unlikely that you'd use EXPLAIN very often for a query like that because the output doesn't tell you anything particularly interesting. However, the example does illustrate an important principle: EXPLAIN can be applied to any SELECT query. One of the implications of this principle is that you can use EXPLAIN with simple queries while you're learning how to use it and how to interpret its results. You don't have to begin with a complicated multiple-table join.

With that in mind, consider these two simple single-table queries:

```
SELECT * FROM Country WHERE Name = 'France';
SELECT * FROM Country WHERE Code = 'FRA';
```

Both queries produce the same output (information about the country of France), but they are not equally efficient. How do you know? Because EXPLAIN tells you so. When you use EXPLAIN with each of the two queries, it provides the following information about how the MySQL optimizer views them:

```
mysql> EXPLAIN SELECT * FROM Country WHERE Name = 'France'\G
*************************** 1. row ***************************
        table: Country
         type: ALL
possible_keys: NULL
          key: NULL
      key_len: NULL
          ref: NULL
         rows: 239
        Extra: Using where
mysql> EXPLAIN SELECT * FROM Country WHERE Code = 'FRA'\G
*************************** 1. row ***************************
        table: Country
         type: const
possible_keys: PRIMARY
          key: PRIMARY
      key_len: 3
          ref: const
         rows: 1
        Extra:
```

EXPLAIN produces several columns of information. In the example just shown, NULL in the possible_keys and key columns shows for the first query that no index is considered available or usable for processing the query. For the second query, the table's PRIMARY KEY column (the Code column that contains three-letter country codes) can be used, and is in fact the one that the optimizer would choose. The rows column of the EXPLAIN output shows the effect of this difference. Its value indicates the number of rows that MySQL estimates it will need to examine while processing the query:

- For the first query, the value is 239, which happens to be the number of rows in the Country table. This value indicates that MySQL would scan all rows of the table, which is inefficient.

- For the second query, only one row need be examined. This is because MySQL can use the table's primary key to go directly to the single relevant row.

This example briefly indicates the kind of useful information that EXPLAIN can provide, even for simple queries. The conclusion to draw is that, if possible, you should use the Code column rather than the Name column to look up Country table records. However, the real power of EXPLAIN lies in what it can tell you about joins—SELECT queries that use multiple tables.

EXPLAIN is especially important for join analysis because they have such enormous potential to increase the amount of processing the server must do. If you select from a table with a thousand rows, the server might need to scan all one thousand rows in the worst case. But if you perform a join between two tables with a thousand rows each, the server might need to examine every possible combination of rows, which is one million combinations. That's a much worse worst case. EXPLAIN can help you reduce the work the server must do to process such a query, so it's well worth using.

13.2.3 Analyzing a Query

The following example demonstrates how to use EXPLAIN to analyze and optimize a sample query. The purpose of the query is to answer the question, "Which cities have a population of more than eight million?" and to display for each city its name and population, along with the country name. This question could be answered using only city information, except that to get each country's name rather than its code, city information must be joined to country information.

The example uses tables created from world database information. Initially, these tables will have no indexes, so EXPLAIN will show that the query is not optimal. The example then adds indexes and uses EXPLAIN to determine the effect of indexing on query performance.

Begin by creating the initial tables, CountryList and CityList. These are derived from the Country and City tables, but need contain only the columns involved in the query:

```
mysql> CREATE TABLE CountryList
    -> SELECT Code, Name FROM Country;
Query OK, 239 rows affected (0.04 sec)
mysql> CREATE TABLE CityList
    -> SELECT CountryCode, Name, Population FROM City;
Query OK, 4079 rows affected (0.04 sec)
```

The query that retrieves the desired information in the required format looks like this:

```
mysql> SELECT CountryList.Name, CityList.Name, CityList.Population
    -> FROM CountryList, CityList
    -> WHERE CountryList.Code = CityList.CountryCode
    -> AND CityList.Population > 8000000;
```

Name	Name	Population
Brazil	São Paulo	9968485
Indonesia	Jakarta	9604900
India	Mumbai (Bombay)	10500000
China	Shanghai	9696300
South Korea	Seoul	9981619
Mexico	Ciudad de México	8591309
Pakistan	Karachi	9269265
Turkey	Istanbul	8787958
Russian Federation	Moscow	8389200
United States	New York	8008278

While the tables are in their initial unindexed state, applying EXPLAIN to the query yields the following result:

```
mysql> EXPLAIN SELECT CountryList.Name, CityList.Name, CityList.Population
    -> FROM CountryList, CityList
    -> WHERE CountryList.Code = CityList.CountryCode
    -> AND CityList.Population > 8000000\G
*************************** 1. row ***************************
        table: CountryList
         type: ALL
possible_keys: NULL
          key: NULL
      key_len: NULL
          ref: NULL
         rows: 239
        Extra:
*************************** 2. row ***************************
        table: CityList
         type: ALL
possible_keys: NULL
          key: NULL
      key_len: NULL
          ref: NULL
         rows: 4079
        Extra: Using where
```

The information displayed by EXPLAIN shows that no optimizations could be made:

- The type value in each row shows how MySQL will read the corresponding table. For CountryList, the value of ALL indicates a full scan of all rows. For CityList, the value of ALL indicates a scan of all its rows to find a match for each CountryList row. In other words, all combinations of rows will be checked to find country code matches between the two tables.

- The number of row combinations is given by the product of the rows values, where rows represents the optimizer's estimate of how many rows in a table it will need to check at each stage of the join. In this case, the product is 239 * 4,079 or 974,881.

EXPLAIN shows that MySQL would need to check nearly a million row combinations to produce a query result that contains only 10 rows. Clearly, this query would benefit from the creation of indexes that allow the server to look up information faster.

Good columns to index typically are those that you use for searching, grouping, or sorting records. The query does not have any GROUP BY or ORDER BY clauses, but it does use columns for searching. Specifically:

- The query uses `CountryList.Code` and `CityList.CountryCode` to match records between tables.
- The query uses `CityList.Population` to cull records that do not have a large enough population.

To see the effect of indexing, try creating indexes on the columns used to join the tables. In the `CountryList` table, `Code` is a primary key that uniquely identifies each row. Add the index using ALTER TABLE:

```
mysql> ALTER TABLE CountryList ADD PRIMARY KEY (Code);
```

In the `CityList` table, `CountryCode` is a nonunique index because multiple cities can share the same country code:

```
mysql> ALTER TABLE CityList ADD INDEX (CountryCode);
```

After creating the indexes, EXPLAIN reports a somewhat different result:

```
mysql> EXPLAIN SELECT CountryList.Name, CityList.Name, CityList.Population
    -> FROM CountryList, CityList
    -> WHERE CountryList.Code = CityList.CountryCode
    -> AND CityList.Population > 8000000\G
*************************** 1. row ***************************
        table: CityList
         type: ALL
possible_keys: CountryCode
          key: NULL
      key_len: NULL
          ref: NULL
         rows: 4079
        Extra: Using where
*************************** 2. row ***************************
        table: CountryList
         type: eq_ref
possible_keys: PRIMARY
          key: PRIMARY
      key_len: 3
          ref: CityList.CountryCode
         rows: 1
        Extra:
```

Observe that EXPLAIN now lists the tables in a different order. `CityList` appears first, which indicates that MySQL will read rows from that table first and use them to search for matches in the second table, `CountryList`. The change in table processing order reflects the optimizer's use of the index information that is now available for executing the query.

MySQL still will scan all rows of the CityList table (its type value is ALL), but now the server can use each of those rows to directly look up the corresponding CountryList row. This is seen by the information displayed for the CountryList table:

- The type value of eq_ref indicates that an equality test is performed by referring to the column named in the ref field, CityList.CountryCode.

- The possible_keys value of PRIMARY shows that the optimizer sees the primary key as a candidate for optimizing the query, and the key field indicates that it will actually use the primary key when executing the query.

The result from EXPLAIN shows that indexing CountryList.Code as a primary key improves query performance. However, it still indicates a full scan of the CityList table. The optimizer sees that the index on CountryCode is available, but the key value of NULL indicates that it will not be used. Does that mean the index on the CountryCode column is of no value? It depends. For this query, the index is not used. In general, however, it's good to index joined columns, so you likely would find for other queries on the CityList table that the index does help.

The product of the rows now is just 4,079. That's much better than 974,881, but perhaps further improvement is possible. The WHERE clause of the query restricts CityList rows based on their Population values, so try creating an index on that column:

```
mysql> ALTER TABLE CityList ADD INDEX (Population);
```

After creating the index, run EXPLAIN again:

```
mysql> EXPLAIN SELECT CountryList.Name, CityList.Name, CityList.Population
    -> FROM CountryList, CityList
    -> WHERE CountryList.Code = CityList.CountryCode
    -> AND CityList.Population > 8000000\G
*************************** 1. row ***************************
        table: CityList
         type: range
possible_keys: CountryCode,Population
          key: Population
      key_len: 4
          ref: NULL
         rows: 78
        Extra: Using where
*************************** 2. row ***************************
        table: CountryList
         type: eq_ref
possible_keys: PRIMARY
          key: PRIMARY
      key_len: 3
          ref: CityList.CountryCode
         rows: 1
        Extra:
```

The output for the CountryList table is unchanged compared to the previous step. That is not a surprise; MySQL already found that it could use a primary key for lookups, which is very efficient. On the other hand, the result for the CityList table is different. The optimizer now sees two indexes in the table as candidates. Furthermore, the key value shows that it will use the index on Population to look up records. This results in an improvement over a full scan, as seen in the change of the rows value from 4,079 to 78.

The query now is optimized. Note that the product of the rows values, 78, still is larger than the actual number of rows produced by the query (10 rows). This is because the rows values are only estimates. The optimizer cannot give an exact count without actually executing the query.

To summarize:

- With unindexed tables, the rows product was 974,881.
- After indexing the join columns, the rows product dropped to 4,079, a 99.6% improvement.
- After indexing the Population column, the rows product dropped to 78, a further improvement of 98.1% over the previous step.

The example shows that using indexes effectively can substantially reduce the work required by the server to execute a query, and that EXPLAIN is a useful tool for assessing the effect of indexing.

13.2.4 EXPLAIN Output Columns

To use EXPLAIN productively, it's important to know the meaning of the columns in each row of output that it produces:

- table is the name of the table to which the information in the row applies. EXPLAIN produces one row of output for each table named in the SELECT query. The order of the tables named in these rows indicates the order in which MySQL will read the tables to process the query. This is not necessarily the order in which you name them in the FROM clause, because the optimizer attempts to determine which order will result in the most efficient processing. The example in the preceding section shows this: The table order displayed by EXPLAIN changed as indexes were added.

- type indicates the join type. The value is a measure of how efficiently MySQL can scan the table. The possible type values are described later in this section.

- possible_keys indicates which of the table's indexes MySQL considers to be candidates for identifying rows that satisfy the query. This value can be a list of one or more index names, or NULL if there are no candidates. The word PRIMARY indicates that MySQL considers the table's primary key to be a candidate.

- key indicates the optimizer's decision about which of the candidate indexes listed in possible_keys will yield most efficient query execution. If the key value is NULL, it means no index was chosen. This might happen either because there were no candidates or because the optimizer believes it will be just as fast to scan the table rows as to use any of the possible indexes. A table scan might be chosen over an index scan if the table is small, or because the index would yield too high a percentage of the rows in the table to be of much use.

- key_len indicates how many bytes of index rows are used. From this value, you can derive how many columns from the index are used. For example, if you have an index consisting of three INT columns, each index row contains three 4-byte values. If key_len is 12, you know that the optimizer uses all three columns of the index when processing the query. If key_len is 4 or 8, it uses only the first one or two columns (that is, it uses a leftmost prefix of the index).

  If you've indexed partial values of string columns, take that into account when assessing the key_len value. Suppose that you have a composite index on two CHAR(8) columns that indexes only the first 4 bytes of each column. In this case, a key_len value of 8 means that both columns of the index would be used, not just the first column.

- ref indicates which indexed column or columns are used to choose rows from the table. const means key values in the index are compared to a constant expression, such as in Code='FRA'. NULL indicates that neither a constant nor another column are being used, indicating selection by an expression or range of values. It might also indicate that the column does not contain the value specified by the constant expression. If neither NULL nor const is specified, a *table_name*.*column_name* combination will be shown, indicating that the optimizer is looking at *column_name* in the rows returned from *table_name* to identify rows for the current table.

- rows is the optimizer's estimate of how many rows from the table it will need to examine. The value is an approximation because, in general, MySQL cannot know the exact number of rows without actually executing the query. For a multiple-table query, the product of the rows values is an estimate of the total number of row combinations that need to be read. This product gives you a rough measure of query performance. The smaller the value, the better.

- Extra provides other information about the join. The possible values are described later in this section.

The type value indicates the join type, but joins may be performed with varying degrees of efficiency. The type value provides a measure of this efficiency by indicating the basis on which rows are selected from each table. The following list shows the possible values, from the best type to the worst:

- system

  The table has exactly one row.

- const

  The table has exactly one matching row. This `type` value is similar to `system`, except that the table may have other, nonmatching rows. The EXPLAIN output from the query with WHERE Code='FRA' is an example of this:

  ```
  mysql> EXPLAIN SELECT * FROM Country WHERE Code = 'FRA'\G
  *************************** 1. row ***************************
          table: Country
           type: const
  possible_keys: PRIMARY
            key: PRIMARY
        key_len: 3
            ref: const
           rows: 1
          Extra:
  ```

  The query has a `type` value of `const` because only one row out of all its rows need be read. If the table contained *only* the row for France, there would be no nonmatching rows and the `type` value would be `system` rather than `const`.

  For both `system` and `const`, because only one row matches, any columns needed from it can be read once and treated as constants while processing the rest of the query.

- eq_ref

  Exactly one row is read from the table for each combination of rows from the tables listed earlier by EXPLAIN. This is common for joins where MySQL can use a primary key to identify table rows.

- ref

  Several rows may be read from the table for each combination of rows from the tables listed earlier by EXPLAIN. This is similar to `eq_ref`, but can occur when a nonunique index is used to identify table rows or when only a leftmost prefix of an index is used. For example, the CountryLanguage table has a primary key on the CountryCode and Language columns. If you search using only a CountryCode value, MySQL can use that column as a leftmost prefix, but there might be several rows for a country if multiple languages are spoken there.

- range

  The index is used to select rows that fall within a given range of index values. This is common for inequality comparisons such as id<10.

- index

  MySQL performs a full scan, but it scans the index rather than the data rows. An index scan is preferable: The index is sorted and index rows usually are shorter than data rows, so index rows can be read in order and more of them can be read at a time.

- ALL

  A full table scan of all data rows. Typically, this indicates that no optimizations are done and represents the worst case. It is particularly unfortunate when tables listed later in EXPLAIN output have a join type of ALL because that indicates a table scan for every combination of rows selected from the tables processed earlier in the join.

The Extra column provides additional information about how the table is processed. Some values indicate that the query is efficient:

- Using index

  MySQL can optimize the query by reading values from the index without having to read the corresponding data rows. This optimization is possible when the query selects only columns that are in the index.

- Where used

  MySQL uses a WHERE clause to identify rows that satisfy the query. Without a WHERE clause, you get all rows from the table.

- Distinct

  MySQL reads a single row from the table for each combination of rows from the tables listed earlier in the EXPLAIN output.

- Not exists

  MySQL can perform a LEFT JOIN "missing rows" optimization that quickly eliminates rows from consideration.

By contrast, some Extra values indicate that the query is not efficient:

- Using filesort

  Rows that satisfy the query must be sorted, which adds an extra processing step.

- Using temporary

  A temporary table must be created to process the query.

- Range checked for each record

  MySQL cannot determine in advance which index from the table to use. For each combination of rows selected from previous tables, it checks the indexes in the table to see which one will be best. This is not great, but it's better than using no index at all.

Using filesort and Using temporary generally are the two indicators of worst performance.

To use EXPLAIN for query analysis, examine its output for clues to ways the query might be improved. Make the change, and then run EXPLAIN again to see how its output changes. Changes might involve rewriting the query or changing the structure of your tables.

The following query rewriting techniques can be useful:

- If the `keys` value is `NULL` even when there are indexes available, you can try adding a `USE INDEX` option as a hint to the optimizer which index is relevant for the query. To force MySQL to use the index, use `FORCE INDEX`. To tell MySQL to ignore an index that it chose and choose a different one instead, use `IGNORE INDEX`. Each of these options is used in the `FROM` clause, following the table name containing the index you want to control. The option is followed by parentheses containing a comma-separated list of one or more index names. `PRIMARY` means the table's primary key.

```
SELECT Name FROM CountryList USE INDEX(PRIMARY) WHERE Code > 'M';


SELECT Name FROM CountryList IGNORE INDEX(Population)
WHERE Code < 'B' AND Population > 50000000;
```

  The keyword `KEY` may be used instead of `INDEX` in all three options.

- If you want to force MySQL to join tables in a particular order, begin the query with `SELECT STRAIGHT_JOIN` rather than `SELECT`, and then list the tables in the desired order in the `FROM` clause.

- Sometimes a table in a query has an index available, but the query is written in such a way that prevents the index from being used. If you can rewrite the query into an equivalent form that allows use of the index, do so. Some rewriting techniques you can use are given in section 13.3, "General Query Enhancement."

Another way to provide the optimizer with better information on which to base its decisions is to change the structure of your tables:

- If the `possible_keys` value is `NULL` in the output from `EXPLAIN`, it means MySQL finds no applicable index for processing the query. See whether an index can be added to the columns that identify which records to retrieve. For example, if you perform a join by matching a column in one table with a column in another, but neither of the columns are indexed, try indexing them.

- Keep table index statistics up-to-date to help MySQL choose optimal indexes. If the table is a MyISAM table (or an InnoDB table, as of MySQL 4.0.13), you can update its statistics with the `ANALYZE TABLE` statement. As a table's contents change, the statistics go out of date and become less useful to the optimizer in making good decisions about query execution strategies. You should run `ANALYZE TABLE` more frequently for tables that change often than for those that are updated rarely.

13.3 General Query Enhancement

The way you write a query often affects how well indexes are used. Use the following principles to make your queries more efficient:

410 CHAPTER 13   Optimizing for Query Speed

- Don't refer to an indexed column within an expression that must be evaluated for every row in the table. Doing so prevents use of the index. Instead, isolate the column onto one side of a comparison when possible. For example, one way to select rows containing date values from the year 1994 and up is as follows:

```
SELECT * FROM t WHERE YEAR(d) >= 1994;
```

In this case, the value of YEAR(d) must be evaluated for every row in the table, so the index cannot be used. Instead, write the query like this:

```
SELECT * FROM t WHERE d >= '1994-01-01';
```

In the rewritten expression, the indexed column stands by itself on one side of the comparison and MySQL can apply the index to optimize the query.

In situations like this, EXPLAIN is useful for verifying that one way of writing a query is better than another. For the two date-selection queries just shown, for example, you might find that EXPLAIN tells you something like this:

```
mysql> EXPLAIN SELECT * FROM t WHERE YEAR(d) >= 1994\G
*************************** 1. row ***************************
        table: t
         type: ALL
possible_keys: NULL
          key: NULL
      key_len: NULL
          ref: NULL
         rows: 867038
        Extra: Using where
mysql> EXPLAIN SELECT * FROM t WHERE d >= '1994-01-01'\G
*************************** 1. row ***************************
        table: t
         type: range
possible_keys: d
          key: d
      key_len: 4
          ref: NULL
         rows: 70968
        Extra: Using where
```

These results indicate that the second query is indeed better from the optimizer's point of view. MySQL can perform a range scan using the index for the column d, drastically reducing the number of rows that need to be examined. (The rows value drops from 867,038 to 70,968.)

- When comparing an indexed column to a value, use a value that has the same datatype as the column. For example, you can look for rows containing a numeric id value of 18 with either of the following WHERE clauses:

```
WHERE id = 18
WHERE id = '18'
```

MySQL will produce the same result either way, even though the value is specified as a number in one case and as a string in the other case. However, for the string value, MySQL must perform a string-to-number conversion, which might cause an index on the id column not to be used.

- In certain cases, MySQL can use an index for pattern-matching operations performed with the LIKE operator. This is true if the pattern begins with a literal prefix value rather than with a wildcard character. An index on a name column can be used for a pattern match like this:

```
WHERE name LIKE 'de%'
```

That's because the pattern match is logically equivalent to a range search:

```
WHERE name >= 'de' AND name < 'df'
```

On the other hand, the following pattern makes LIKE more difficult for the optimizer:

```
WHERE name LIKE '%de%'
```

When a pattern starts with a wildcard character as just shown, MySQL cannot make efficient use of any indexes associated with that column. (Even if an index *is* used, the entire index must be scanned.)

13.3.1 Optimizing Queries by Limiting Output

Some optimizations can be done independently of whether indexes are used. A simple but effective technique is to reduce the amount of output a query produces.

One way to eliminate unnecessary output is by using a LIMIT clause. If you don't need the entire result set, specify how many rows the server should return by including LIMIT in your query. This helps two ways:

- Less information need be returned over the network to the client.
- In many cases, LIMIT allows the server to terminate query processing earlier than it would otherwise.

Another way to limit query output is by selecting only the columns you need, rather than using SELECT * to retrieve all columns. Suppose you want information about countries having names that begin with M. The following query produces that information:

```
SELECT * FROM Country WHERE Name LIKE 'M%';
```

However, if all you really want to know is the country names, don't write the query like that. Most of the information retrieved will be irrelevant to what you want to know, resulting in unnecessary server effort and network traffic. Instead, select only the Name column:

```
SELECT Name FROM Country WHERE Name LIKE 'M%';
```

The second query is faster because MySQL has to return less information to the client when you select just one column rather than all of them.

In addition, if an index on Name exists, you get even more improvement for two reasons:

- The index can be used to determine quickly which Name values satisfy the condition in the WHERE clause. This is faster than scanning the entire table.

- Depending on the storage engine, the server might not read the table rows at all. If the values requested by the query are in the index, by reading the index, MySQL already has the information that the client wants. For example, the MyISAM handler will read the index file to determine which values satisfy the query, and then return them to the client without reading the datafile at all. Doing so is faster than reading both the index file and the datafile.

13.3.2 Optimizing Updates

The optimizations discussed so far have been shown for SELECT statements, but optimization techniques can be used for statements that update tables, too:

- For a DELETE or UPDATE statement that uses a WHERE clause, try to write it in a way that allows an index to be used for determining which rows to delete or update. Techniques for this were discussed earlier for SELECT statements; they apply to DELETE or UPDATE as well.

- EXPLAIN is used with SELECT queries, but you might also find it helpful for analyzing UPDATE and DELETE queries. Write a SELECT statement that has the same WHERE clause as the UPDATE or DELETE and analyze that.

- Use multiple-row INSERT statements instead of multiple single-row INSERT statements. For example, instead of using three single-row statements like this:

```
mysql> INSERT INTO t (id, name) VALUES(1,'Bea');
mysql> INSERT INTO t (id, name) VALUES(2,'Belle');
mysql> INSERT INTO t (id, name) VALUES(3,'Bernice');
```

You could use a single multiple-row statement that does the same thing:

```
mysql> INSERT INTO t (id, name) VALUES(1,'Bea'),(2,'Belle'),(3,'Bernice');
```

The multiple-row statement is shorter, which is less information to send to the server. More important, it allows the server to perform all the updates at once and flush the index a single time, rather than after each of the individual inserts. This optimization can be used with any storage engine.

If you're using an InnoDB table, you can get better performance even for single-row statements by grouping them within a transaction rather than by executing them with autocommit mode enabled:

```
mysql> BEGIN;
mysql> INSERT INTO t (id, name) VALUES(1,'Bea');
mysql> INSERT INTO t (id, name) VALUES(2,'Belle');
mysql> INSERT INTO t (id, name) VALUES(3,'Bernice');
mysql> COMMIT;
```

Using a transaction allows InnoDB to flush the changes at commit time. In autocommit mode, InnoDB flushes the changes after each insert.

- For any storage engine, LOAD DATA INFILE is even faster than multiple-row INSERT statements. For MyISAM in particular, if you're loading an empty table, MySQL will even automatically disable updating nonunique indexes during the load operation to speed it up more.

- To replace existing rows, use REPLACE rather than DELETE plus INSERT.

13.3.3 Using Scheduling Modifiers

For an application that uses MyISAM tables, you can change the priority of statements that retrieve or modify data. This can be useful in situations where the normal scheduling priorities do not reflect the application's requirements.

Consider an application consisting of a logging process that uses INSERT statements to record information in a log table, and a summary process that periodically issues SELECT queries to generate reports from the log table. Normally, the server will give updates to the table priority over retrievals, so at times of heavy logging activity, report generation might be delayed. If the application places high importance on having the summary process execute as quickly as possible, it can use scheduling modifiers to alter the usual query priorities. Two approaches are possible:

- To elevate the priority of the summary queries, use SELECT HIGH_PRIORITY rather than SELECT with no modifier. This will move the SELECT ahead of pending INSERT statements that have not yet begin to execute.

- To reduce the priority of record logging statements, use INSERT with either the LOW_PRIORITY or DELAYED modifier.

Scheduling modifiers are covered further in section 14.3.2, "Query Scheduling Modifiers."

13.4 Optimizing the Logical Database Structure

This section describes techniques for organizing data that can help you achieve better query performance.

13.4.1 Choosing Appropriate Table Types

When creating a table, ask yourself what types of queries you'll use it for. Then choose a table type that uses a locking level appropriate for the anticipated query mix. MyISAM table-level locking works best for a query mix that is heavily skewed toward retrievals and includes few updates. Use InnoDB if you must process a query mix containing many updates. InnoDB's use of row-level locking and multi-versioning provides good concurrency for a mix of retrievals and updates. One query can update rows while other queries read or update different rows of the table.

If you're using MyISAM tables, choose their structure to reflect whether you consider efficiency of processing speed or disk usage to be more important. Different MyISAM storage formats have different performance characteristics. This influences whether you choose fixed-length or variable-length columns to store string data:

- Use fixed-length columns (CHAR) for best speed. Fixed-length columns allow MySQL to create the table with fixed-length rows. The advantage is that fixed-length rows all are stored in the table at positions that are a multiple of the row length and can be looked up very quickly. The disadvantage is that fixed-length values are always the same length even for values that do not use the full width of the column, so the column takes more storage space.

- Use variable-length columns (VARCHAR, TEXT, BLOB) for best use of disk space. For example, values in a VARCHAR column take only as much space as necessary to store each value and on average use less storage than a CHAR column. The disadvantage is that variable-length columns result in variable-length rows. These are not stored at fixed positions within the table, so they cannot be retrieved as quickly as fixed-length rows. In addition, the contents of variable-length rows might not even be stored all in one place, another source of processing overhead.

For InnoDB tables, it is also true that CHAR columns take more space on average than VARCHAR. But there is no retrieval speed advantage for InnoDB as there is with MyISAM, because the InnoDB engine implements storage for both CHAR and VARCHAR in a similar way. In fact, retrieval of CHAR values might be slower because on average they require more information to be read from disk.

If a MyISAM table contains a mix of fixed-length and variable-length columns, the table format will be dynamic. However, if many of the queries on the table access only its fixed-length columns, it is sometimes possible to gain advantages both of static tables (faster retrieval) and of dynamic tables (lower storage requirements) by splitting the table into two tables. Use a fixed-format table to hold the fixed-length columns and a dynamic-format table to hold the variable-length columns. To split the table into two, use this procedure:

1. Make sure that the table contains a primary key that allows each record to be uniquely identified. (You might use an AUTO_INCREMENT column, for example.)

2. Create a second table that has columns for all the variable-length columns in the original table, plus a column to store values from the primary key of the original table. (This column should be a primary key as well, but should not be an AUTO_INCREMENT column.)

3. Copy the primary key column and the variable-length columns from the original table to the second table. The second table will be dynamic.

4. Use ALTER TABLE to drop the variable-length columns (but not the primary key) from the original table. MySQL will notice that the table no longer contains any variable-length columns and convert it to static format.

After modifying the table structure this way, queries that retrieve only fixed-width columns can use the static table, and will be quicker. For queries that retrieve both fixed-width and variable-width columns, join the two tables using the primary key values to match up rows.

Another option with MyISAM tables is to use compressed read-only tables.

For more information about MyISAM table structure, see section 14.2.1, "MyISAM Storage Formats."

MERGE tables can use a mix of compressed and uncompressed tables. This can be useful for time-based records. For example, if you log records each year to a different log file, you can use an uncompressed log table for the current year so that you can update it, but compress the tables for past years to save space. If you then create a MERGE table from the collection, you can easily run queries that search all tables together.

13.4.2 Using Summary Tables

Suppose that you run an analysis consisting of a set of retrievals that each perform a complex SELECT of a set of records (perhaps using an expensive join), and that differ only in the way they summarize the records. That's inefficient because it unnecessarily does the work of selecting the records repeatedly. A better technique is to select the records once, and then use them to generate the summaries. In such a situation, consider the following strategy:

1. Select the set of to-be-summarized records into a temporary table. In MySQL, you can do this easily with a CREATE TEMPORARY TABLE … SELECT statement.

2. Create any appropriate indexes on the temporary table.

3. Calculate the summaries using the temporary table.

The following example creates a summary table containing the average GNP value of countries in each continent. Then it compares the summary information to individual countries to find those countries with a GNP much less than the average and much more than the average.

First, create the summary table:

```
mysql> CREATE TABLE ContinentGNP
    -> SELECT Continent, AVG(GNP) AS AvgGNP
    -> FROM Country GROUP BY Continent;
mysql> SELECT * FROM ContinentGNP;
+---------------+---------------+
| Continent     | AvgGNP        |
+---------------+---------------+
| Asia          | 150105.725490 |
| Europe        | 206497.065217 |
| North America | 261854.789189 |
| Africa        |  10006.465517 |
| Oceania       |  14991.953571 |
| Antarctica    |      0.000000 |
| South America | 107991.000000 |
+---------------+---------------+
```

Next, compare the summary table to the original table to find countries that have a GNP less than 1% of the continental average:

```
mysql> SELECT
    ->     Country.Continent, Country.Name,
    ->     Country.GNP AS CountryGNP,
    ->     ContinentGNP.AvgGNP AS ContinentAvgGNP
    -> FROM Country, ContinentGNP
    -> WHERE
    ->     Country.Continent = ContinentGNP.Continent
    ->     AND Country.GNP < ContinentGNP.AvgGNP * .01
    -> ORDER BY Country.Continent, Country.Name;
+-----------+-----------------------------+------------+-----------------+
| Continent | Name                        | CountryGNP | ContinentAvgGNP |
+-----------+-----------------------------+------------+-----------------+
| Asia      | Bhutan                      |     372.00 |   150105.725490 |
| Asia      | East Timor                  |       0.00 |   150105.725490 |
| Asia      | Laos                        |    1292.00 |   150105.725490 |
| Asia      | Maldives                    |     199.00 |   150105.725490 |
| Asia      | Mongolia                    |    1043.00 |   150105.725490 |
| Europe    | Andorra                     |    1630.00 |   206497.065217 |
| Europe    | Faroe Islands               |       0.00 |   206497.065217 |
| Europe    | Gibraltar                   |     258.00 |   206497.065217 |
| Europe    | Holy See (Vatican City State) |     9.00 |   206497.065217 |
| Europe    | Liechtenstein               |    1119.00 |   206497.065217 |
...
```

Use the summary table again to find countries that have a GNP more than 10 times the continental average:

```
mysql> SELECT
    ->     Country.Continent, Country.Name,
    ->     Country.GNP AS CountryGNP,
    ->     ContinentGNP.AvgGNP AS ContinentAvgGNP
    -> FROM Country, ContinentGNP
    -> WHERE
    ->     Country.Continent = ContinentGNP.Continent
    ->     AND Country.GNP > ContinentGNP.AvgGNP * 10
    -> ORDER BY Country.Continent, Country.Name;
+---------------+---------------+------------+-----------------+
| Continent     | Name          | CountryGNP | ContinentAvgGNP |
+---------------+---------------+------------+-----------------+
| Asia          | Japan         | 3787042.00 |   150105.725490 |
| Europe        | Germany       | 2133367.00 |   206497.065217 |
| North America | United States | 8510700.00 |   261854.789189 |
| Africa        | South Africa  |  116729.00 |    10006.465517 |
| Oceania       | Australia     |  351182.00 |    14991.953571 |
+---------------+---------------+------------+-----------------+
```

The technique of using a summary table has several benefits:

- Calculating the summary information a single time reduces the overall computational burden by eliminating most of the repetition involved in performing the initial record selection.

- If the original table is a type that is subject to table-level locking, such as a MyISAM table, using a summary table leaves the original table available more of the time for updates by other clients by reducing the amount of time that the table remains locked.

- If the summary table is small enough that it's reasonable to hold in memory, you can increase performance even more by making it a HEAP table. Queries on the table will be especially fast because they require no disk I/O. When the HEAP table no longer is needed, drop it to free the memory allocated for it.

- Some queries are difficult or impossible to perform without using a summary table. For example, you cannot compute a summary from a set of rows and compare each row to the summarized value within a single query. However, you can use a summary table and join it to the original table to do this.

Use of summary tables has the disadvantage that the records they contain are up-to-date only as long as the original values remain unchanged, and thus so are any summaries calculated from them. If the original table rarely or never changes, this might be only a minor concern. For many applications, summaries that are close approximations are sufficiently accurate.

The summary table technique can be applied at multiple levels. Create a summary table that holds the results of an initial summary, and then summarize that table in different ways to produce secondary summaries. This avoids the computational expense of generating the initial summary repeatedly.

When a summary consists of a single value, you need not create a table at all. Use a SQL variable to hold the value. Then you can use the value for comparison purposes in subsequent queries without having to calculate it again.

13.5 Exercises

Question 1:

Consider the following table with two indexes:

```
mysql> DESCRIBE fastindex;
+-------+----------+------+-----+
| Field | Type     | Null | Key |
+-------+----------+------+-----+
| i1    | char(10) |      | MUL |
| i2    | char(10) | YES  | MUL |
+-------+----------+------+-----+
```

With no other facts given, which of the following queries would you expect to run faster?

```
SELECT i1 FROM fastindex WHERE i1 LIKE 'mid%';

SELECT i2 FROM fastindex WHERE i2 LIKE 'mid%';
```

Question 2:

Consider the following table with indexes:

```
mysql> SHOW CREATE TABLE fastindex;
+-----------+--------------------------
| Table     | Create Table
+-----------+--------------------------
| fastindex | CREATE TABLE `fastindex` (
  `i1` char(10) NOT NULL default '',
  `i2` char(10) NOT NULL default '',
  KEY `i1` (`i1`(3)),
  KEY `i2` (`i2`)
) TYPE=MyISAM |
+-----------+--------------------------
```

With no other facts given, which of the following queries would you expect to run faster?

```
SELECT i1 FROM fastindex WHERE i1 LIKE 'mid%';

SELECT i2 FROM fastindex WHERE i2 LIKE 'mid%';
```

Question 3:

For what reason can adding indexes to a table make table operations slower?

Question 4:

Consider the following table structure, which will be used for the next four questions:

```
mysql> DESCRIBE City;
+-------------+----------+------+-----+---------+----------------+
| Field       | Type     | Null | Key | Default | Extra          |
+-------------+----------+------+-----+---------+----------------+
| ID          | int(11)  |      | PRI | NULL    | auto_increment |
| Name        | char(35) | YES  |     | NULL    |                |
| CountryCode | char(3)  | YES  |     | NULL    |                |
| District    | char(20) | YES  |     | NULL    |                |
| Population  | int(11)  | YES  |     | 0       |                |
+-------------+----------+------+-----+---------+----------------+
```

You frequently retrieve data from the City table, using queries similar to those shown here:

```
mysql> SELECT * FROM City WHERE Name BETWEEN 'E' AND 'G' ORDER BY Name;
+------+-----------------+-------------+--------------+------------+
| ID   | Name            | CountryCode | District     | Population |
+------+-----------------+-------------+--------------+------------+
|  735 | East London     | ZAF         | Eastern Cape |     221047 |
| 3963 | East Los Angeles| USA         | California    |    126379 |
| 1845 | East York       | CAN         | Ontario      |     114034 |
|  533 | Eastbourne      | GBR         | England      |      90000 |
| 1720 | Ebetsu          | JPN         | Hokkaido     |     118805 |
| ...  | ...             | ...         | ...          |      ...   |
+------+-----------------+-------------+--------------+------------+
```

```
mysql> SELECT * FROM City WHERE CountryCode >= 'Y' ORDER BY name;
+------+------------+-------------+----------------+------------+
| ID   | Name       | CountryCode | District       | Population |
+------+------------+-------------+----------------+------------+
| 1781 | Aden       | YEM         | Aden           |     398300 |
| 1784 | al-Mukalla | YEM         | Hadramawt      |     122400 |
|  721 | Alberton   | ZAF         | Gauteng        |     410102 |
|  724 | Benoni     | ZAF         | Gauteng        |     365467 |
| 1792 | Beograd    | YUG         | Central Serbia |    1204000 |
| ...  | ...        | ...         | ...            |      ...   |
+------+------------+-------------+----------------+------------+
```

How would you determine the number of rows MySQL must inspect to calculate the result sets?

Question 5:

Consider, once again, the table structure and sample queries shown for the City table in the previous question. What index or indexes would you add to the table to speed up the queries?

Question 6:

Here again are the table structure and sample queries first shown for the City table two questions previously, but with the addition of the indexes on the Name and CountryCode columns from the previous question:

```
mysql> DESCRIBE City;
+-------------+----------+------+-----+---------+----------------+
| Field       | Type     | Null | Key | Default | Extra          |
+-------------+----------+------+-----+---------+----------------+
| ID          | int(11)  |      | PRI | NULL    | auto_increment |
| Name        | char(35) | YES  | MUL | NULL    |                |
| CountryCode | char(3)  | YES  | MUL | NULL    |                |
| District    | char(20) | YES  |     | NULL    |                |
| Population  | int(11)  | YES  |     | 0       |                |
+-------------+----------+------+-----+---------+----------------+
```

```
mysql> SELECT * FROM City WHERE Name BETWEEN 'E' AND 'G' ORDER BY Name;
+------+-----------------+-------------+--------------+------------+
| ID   | Name            | CountryCode | District     | Population |
+------+-----------------+-------------+--------------+------------+
|  735 | East London     | ZAF         | Eastern Cape |     221047 |
| 3963 | East Los Angeles| USA         | California    |     126379 |
| 1845 | East York       | CAN         | Ontario      |     114034 |
|  533 | Eastbourne      | GBR         | England      |      90000 |
| 1720 | Ebetsu          | JPN         | Hokkaido     |     118805 |
| ...  | ...             | ...         | ...          |      ...   |
+------+-----------------+-------------+--------------+------------+
```

```
mysql> SELECT * FROM City WHERE CountryCode >= 'Y' ORDER BY name;
+------+------------+-------------+----------------+------------+
| ID   | Name       | CountryCode | District       | Population |
+------+------------+-------------+----------------+------------+
| 1781 | Aden       | YEM         | Aden           |     398300 |
| 1784 | al-Mukalla | YEM         | Hadramawt      |     122400 |
|  721 | Alberton   | ZAF         | Gauteng        |     410102 |
|  724 | Benoni     | ZAF         | Gauteng        |     365467 |
| 1792 | Beograd    | YUG         | Central Serbia |    1204000 |
| ...  | ...        | ...         | ...            |      ...   |
+------+------------+-------------+----------------+------------+
```

In addition to adding indexes to the City table, what else can be done, with regard to the table's columns, to improve performance?

Question 7:

Consider, once again, the new table structure and the sample queries shown for the `City` table in the previous question. How would you find out whether the new indexes on the table are actually used to resolve the queries?

Question 8:

Consider the following table:

```
mysql> DESCRIBE enumtest;
+-------+------------------------------+------+-----+---------+-------+
| Field | Type                         | Null | Key | Default | Extra |
+-------+------------------------------+------+-----+---------+-------+
| col   | enum('first','second','third') |    | PRI | first   |       |
+-------+------------------------------+------+-----+---------+-------+
mysql> SELECT * FROM enumtest;
Empty set
```

Will the following statement fail or will it insert rows? What will the contents of the enumtest table be after executing the statement?

```
mysql> INSERT INTO enumtest VALUES
    -> ('first'),('second'),('third'),('false'),('fourth');
```

Question 9:

Consider the following table, which has two single-column `FULLTEXT` indexes:

```
mysql> DESCRIBE faq;
+----------+--------------+------+-----+---------+-------+
| Field    | Type         | Null | Key | Default | Extra |
+----------+--------------+------+-----+---------+-------+
| cdate    | timestamp(14)| YES  |     | NULL    |       |
| question | char(150)    |      | MUL |         |       |
| answer   | char(250)    |      | MUL |         |       |
+----------+--------------+------+-----+---------+-------+
mysql> SHOW INDEX FROM faq;
+-------+------------+----------+-  -+-------------+-  -+------------+-
| Table | Non_unique | Key_name | ... | Column_name | ... | Index_type | ...
+-------+------------+----------+-  -+-------------+-  -+------------+-
| faq   |          1 | question | ... | question    | ... | FULLTEXT   | ...
| faq   |          1 | answer   | ... | answer      | ... | FULLTEXT   | ...
+-------+------------+----------+-  -+-------------+-  -+------------+-
```

With `MATCH … AGAINST()`, you can search the answers and the questions stored in the table. How would you search for a search term `'MySQL'` in the `question` column?

Question 10:

Consider the following table, which has two single-column FULLTEXT indexes:

```
mysql> DESCRIBE faq;
+----------+--------------+------+-----+---------+-------+
| Field    | Type         | Null | Key | Default | Extra |
+----------+--------------+------+-----+---------+-------+
| cdate    | timestamp(14)| YES  |     | NULL    |       |
| question | char(150)    |      | MUL |         |       |
| answer   | char(250)    |      | MUL |         |       |
+----------+--------------+------+-----+---------+-------+
mysql> SHOW INDEX FROM faq;
+-------+------------+----------+-    -+-------------+-    -+------------+-
| Table | Non_unique | Key_name | ... | Column_name | ... | Index_type | ...
+-------+------------+----------+-    -+-------------+-    -+------------+-
| faq   |          1 | question | ... | question    | ... | FULLTEXT   | ...
| faq   |          1 | answer   | ... | answer      | ... | FULLTEXT   | ...
+-------+------------+----------+-    -+-------------+-    -+------------+-
```

With MATCH … AGAINST(), you can search the answers and the questions stored in the table. How would you search for the search term 'Access' in either the question or the answer column?

Question 11:

Consider the following tables:

```
mysql> DESCRIBE City; DESCRIBE Country;
+-------------+----------+------+-----+---------+-------+
| Field       | Type     | Null | Key | Default | Extra |
+-------------+----------+------+-----+---------+-------+
| ID          | int(11)  |      |     | 0       |       |
| Name        | char(35) |      |     |         |       |
| CountryCode | char(3)  |      |     |         |       |
| District    | char(20) |      |     |         |       |
| Population  | int(11)  |      |     | 0       |       |
+-------------+----------+------+-----+---------+-------+
+---------------+------------------------+------+-----+---------+-------+
| Field         | Type                   | Null | Key | Default | Extra |
+---------------+------------------------+------+-----+---------+-------+
| Code          | char(3)                |      | PRI |         |       |
| Name          | char(52)               |      |     |         |       |
| Continent     | enum('Asia','Europe',..)|     |     | Asia    |       |
| Region        | char(26)               |      |     |         |       |
| SurfaceArea   | float(10,2)            |      |     | 0.00    |       |
| IndepYear     | smallint(6)            | YES  |     | NULL    |       |
| Population    | int(11)                |      |     | 0       |       |
| LifeExpectancy| float(3,1)             | YES  |     | NULL    |       |
```

GNP	float(10,2)	YES		NULL		
GNPOld	float(10,2)	YES		NULL		
LocalName	char(45)					
GovernmentForm	char(45)					
HeadOfState	char(60)	YES		NULL		
Capital	int(11)	YES		NULL		
Code2	char(2)					

The tables are related: CountryCode in City references Code in Country. What information does the following EXPLAIN statement give you regarding possible optimization of the query?

```
mysql> EXPLAIN
    -> SELECT
    -> City.Name, City.Population, Country.Name
    -> FROM City INNER JOIN Country
    -> ON City.CountryCode = Country.Code
    -> WHERE City.Population > 10000000
    -> ORDER BY City.Population DESC
    -> \G
*************************** 1. row ***************************
        table: City
         type: ALL
possible_keys: NULL
          key: NULL
      key_len: NULL
          ref: NULL
         rows: 4079
        Extra: Using where; Using filesort
*************************** 2. row ***************************
        table: Country
         type: eq_ref
possible_keys: PRIMARY
          key: PRIMARY
      key_len: 3
          ref: City.CountryCode
         rows: 1
        Extra:
```

Question 12:

Based on the information provided by the EXPLAIN in the previous question, what would you do to optimize the query performance?

Question 13:

Consider, once again, the EXPLAIN output for the Country and City tables from the previous two questions. How would you roughly "measure" the performance for the unoptimized query? For the optimized query?

Question 14:

Most of the time, the MySQL optimizer makes the right choice of indexes to use for a query. However, you suspect that, for a certain query, the optimizer is not making the right choice. How can you determine whether the optimizer is choosing the index you want it to use?

Question 15:

Most of the time, the MySQL optimizer makes the right choice of indexes to use for a query. However, you suspect that, for a certain query, the optimizer is not making the right choice. How could you rewrite the query to determine whether it runs faster without using an index?

Question 16:

Most of the time, the MySQL optimizer makes the right choice of indexes to use for a query. However, you suspect that, for a certain query, the optimizer is not making the right choice. How could you force MySQL to use an index that is different from the index which the optimizer would choose?

Question 17:

Consider the following table and its indexes:

```
mysql> DESCRIBE key1;
+-------+----------+------+-----+---------+-------+
| Field | Type     | Null | Key | Default | Extra |
+-------+----------+------+-----+---------+-------+
| col   | char(10) | YES  | MUL | NULL    |       |
+-------+----------+------+-----+---------+-------+
mysql> SHOW KEYS FROM key1;
+-------+------------+----------+--------------+-------------+-
| Table | Non_unique | Key_name | Seq_in_index | Column_name | ...
+-------+------------+----------+--------------+-------------+-
| key1  |          1 | col      |            1 | col         | ...
+-------+------------+----------+--------------+-------------+-
```

Which of the following queries will most likely perform faster, and why? How could you actually find out which query runs faster?

```
SELECT * FROM key1 WHERE col LIKE '%2%'

SELECT * FROM key1 WHERE col LIKE 'hey 2%'
```

Question 18:

Assume that you have a table that is subject to many read (SELECT) requests. Compared to the number of reads, you have only a few write (INSERT) requests taking place. Furthermore, you consider the reads more important than the write requests. What could you do to give read requests priority over write requests?

Question 19:

Consider the following table and its indexes:

```
mysql> DESCRIBE mix1;
+-------+-------------+------+-----+---------+-------+
| Field | Type        | Null | Key | Default | Extra |
+-------+-------------+------+-----+---------+-------+
| id    | int(11)     |      | PRI | 0       |       |
| name  | varchar(20) | YES  |     | NULL    |       |
| story | text        | YES  |     | NULL    |       |
+-------+-------------+------+-----+---------+-------+
mysql> SHOW KEYS FROM mix1;
+-------+------------+----------+-
| Table | Non_unique | Key_name | ...
+-------+------------+----------+-
| mix1  |          0 | PRIMARY  | ...
+-------+------------+----------+-
```

Assume that you have many seeks on the mix1 table, most of which use id or name as a search term. Searches are becoming considerably slow. What can you do to improve the situation?

Question 20:

Consider the following table and its indexes:

```
mysql> DESCRIBE mix1;
+-------+-------------+------+-----+---------+-------+
| Field | Type        | Null | Key | Default | Extra |
+-------+-------------+------+-----+---------+-------+
| id    | int(11)     |      | PRI | 0       |       |
| name  | varchar(20) | YES  |     | NULL    |       |
| story | text        | YES  |     | NULL    |       |
+-------+-------------+------+-----+---------+-------+
mysql> SHOW KEYS FROM mix1;
+-------+------------+----------+-
| Table | Non_unique | Key_name | ...
+-------+------------+----------+-
| mix1  |          0 | PRIMARY  | ...
+-------+------------+----------+-
```

Assume that you have many seeks on the mix1 table, most of which look for a search term in the story column. What can you do to speed up those searches?

Question 21:

Assume that you hit a filesystem limit on file size with a MyISAM table. That table contains a FULLTEXT index, so you cannot switch to another storage engine. Also, assume that it isn't possible to change the filesystem you're using. What else could you do to overcome the filesystem size limit?

Answers to Exercises

Answer 1:

A column or index that can contain NULL values cannot be processed as fast as one that cannot contain NULL. i1 and i2 are identical except that i1 cannot contain NULL values, so i1 should be faster to process. Therefore, this query should be faster:

```
SELECT i1 FROM fastindex WHERE i1 LIKE 'mid%';
```

Answer 2:

```
SELECT i1 FROM fastindex WHERE i1 LIKE 'mid%';
```

would probably perform faster because i1 is indexed with only the first three bytes as subpart of that index. MySQL can look up that index faster because it contains only up to three-character rows, as compared to the second index that could contain up to ten-character rows.

Answer 3:

Insert, delete, and update operations will become slower when the table has indexes, because those operations require the indexes to be updated, too.

Answer 4:

You can use EXPLAIN to determine the number of rows MySQL must inspect to calculate the result sets:

```
mysql> EXPLAIN SELECT * FROM City WHERE Name BETWEEN 'E' AND 'G'
    -> ORDER BY Name\G
*************************** 1. row ***************************
        table: City
         type: ALL
possible_keys: NULL
          key: NULL
      key_len: NULL
          ref: NULL
         rows: 4079
        Extra: Using where; Using filesort
mysql> EXPLAIN SELECT * FROM City WHERE CountryCode >= 'Y'
    -> ORDER BY Name\G
*************************** 1. row ***************************
        table: City
         type: ALL
possible_keys: NULL
          key: NULL
      key_len: NULL
          ref: NULL
         rows: 4079
        Extra: Using where; Using filesort
```

The EXPLAIN output shows that MySQL would not use indexes to process the queries. All rows (4,079) must be scanned to calculate the results. This is indicated by the ALL value in the type column as well.

See section A.1.15, "EXPLAIN."

Answer 5:

To improve performance, indexes should be added to the Name and CountryCode columns because those are the columns used in the comparisons that determine which rows to return. Also, because Name is used in the ORDER BY clause, an index on Name can speed up sorting operations.

For the Name column, the results of the queries in question indicate that an index with a prefix length that is shorter than the full column length is likely to improve performance even more. However, the prefix length should be long enough to differentiate cities that begin with words like "East Lo...", so we choose a prefix length of 10:

```
mysql> ALTER TABLE City
    -> ADD INDEX (Name(10)),
    -> ADD INDEX (CountryCode)
    -> ;
```

Answer 6:

Another means of making table lookups faster is to declare the table's columns to be NOT NULL. Assume that City must contain a city name in each row, as well as a country code for each city. To disallow NULL values in the Name and CountryCode columns, you could alter the table with this SQL statement:

```
mysql> ALTER TABLE City
    -> MODIFY Name CHAR(35) NOT NULL,
    -> MODIFY CountryCode CHAR(3) NOT NULL
    -> ;
Query OK, 4079 rows affected (0.21 sec)
Records: 4079  Duplicates: 0  Warnings: 0

mysql> DESCRIBE City;
+-------------+----------+------+-----+---------+----------------+
| Field       | Type     | Null | Key | Default | Extra          |
+-------------+----------+------+-----+---------+----------------+
| ID          | int(11)  |      | PRI | NULL    | auto_increment |
| Name        | char(35) |      | MUL |         |                |
| CountryCode | char(3)  |      | MUL |         |                |
| District    | char(20) | YES  |     | NULL    |                |
| Population  | int(11)  | YES  |     | 0       |                |
+-------------+----------+------+-----+---------+----------------+
```

See section A.1.1, "ALTER TABLE."

Answer 7:

To check whether MySQL actually uses the new indexes to resolve the queries, use EXPLAIN once again:

```
mysql> EXPLAIN SELECT * FROM City WHERE Name BETWEEN 'E' AND 'G'
    -> ORDER BY Name\G
*************************** 1. row ***************************
        table: City
         type: range
possible_keys: Name
          key: Name
      key_len: 5
          ref: NULL
         rows: 146
        Extra: Using where; Using filesort
mysql> EXPLAIN SELECT * FROM City WHERE CountryCode >= 'Y' ORDER BY Name\G
*************************** 1. row ***************************
        table: City
         type: range
possible_keys: CountryCode
          key: CountryCode
      key_len: 3
          ref: NULL
         rows: 76
        Extra: Using where; Using filesort
```

The EXPLAIN output shows that the indexes you would expect to be used actually are used by MySQL to resolve the queries. Compared to the previous results from EXPLAIN (three questions previously), the number of rows inspected drops dramatically from 4,079 to 146 and 76 due to the use of indexes.

See section A.1.15, "EXPLAIN."

Answer 8:

Table enumtest has a primary key on its only column col. Therefore, there can be only unique values in that column. Because of the ENUM column type, this means that there can be only four different values in the column (the three enumeration members and the empty string that is used for invalid values). false is an invalid value, so it is converted to '' (the empty string). The last value (fourth) is not in the ENUM list, either, so it too is converted to the error value ''. The primary key, however, prevents that same value from being stored again, which leads to a duplicate key error:

```
mysql> INSERT INTO enumtest VALUES
    -> ('first'),('second'),('third'),('false'),('fourth');
ERROR 1062: Duplicate entry '' for key 1
```

For a multiple-row INSERT statement, rows are inserted as long as no error occurs. If a row fails, that row and any following rows are not inserted. As a result, the table contents are:

```
mysql> SELECT * FROM enumtest;
+--------+
| col    |
+--------+
|        |
| first  |
| second |
| third  |
+--------+
4 rows in set
```

See section A.3, "Column Types."

Answer 9:

A search for 'MySQL' in the question column only could be performed as follows:

```
mysql> SELECT
    -> LEFT(question,20), LEFT(answer,20)
    -> FROM faq
    -> WHERE MATCH(question) AGAINST('MySQL')
    -> ;
```

The result of the query could look like this:

```
+----------------------+----------------------+
| LEFT(question,20)    | LEFT(answer,20)      |
+----------------------+----------------------+
| Does MySQL support t | Yes, as of version 3 |
| When will MySQL supp | This is on the TODO  |
| Does MySQL support f | Yes, as of version 3 |
| Does MySQL support s | Not yet, but stored  |
| Is MySQL available u | Yes, you can buy a l |
| When was MySQL relea | MySQL was first rele |
+----------------------+----------------------+
```

See sections A.1.39, "SHOW INDEX" and A.1.11, "DESCRIBE."

Answer 10:

A search for 'Access' in either the question or the answer column could be performed as follows:

```
mysql> SELECT
    -> LEFT(question,20), LEFT(answer,20)
    -> FROM faq
    -> WHERE MATCH(question) AGAINST('Access')
    -> OR MATCH(answer) AGAINST('Access')
    -> ;
```

The result of the query could look like this:

```
+--------------------+----------------------+
| LEFT(question,20)  | LEFT(answer,20)      |
+--------------------+----------------------+
| Is there a database | Access will most pro |
| Is Microsoft Access | It's sold as a datab |
+--------------------+----------------------+
```

Note that OR in the preceding query means that you're looking for the word "Access" whether it appears only in the question, only in the answer, or in both the question and the answer. To find records that contain "Access" in both the question and the answer, you would use AND instead of OR in the query.

See sections A.1.39, "SHOW INDEX," and A.1.11, "DESCRIBE."

Answer 11:

EXPLAIN provides the following information:

- For table City, EXPLAIN indicates that all table rows must be scanned to find the desired information (ALL). There are no keys on the columns that should be retrieved, nor on the column mentioned in the ORDER BY clause, so no keys are used as indicated by the NULL entries for possible_keys, key, key_len, and ref. Therefore, all 4,079 table rows are scanned. Using filesort indicates that MySQL needs to do an extra pass to find out how to retrieve the rows in sorted order.

- For table Country, EXPLAIN shows a join type of eq_ref. This is the best possible join type; it means that only one row is read from this table for each row from the previous table. This join type is possible because the index used for table Country is a primary key, as indicated by the PRIMARY entries for possible_keys and key. The primary key has the same length as the column itself (3 bytes, as indicated by key_len, too). ref shows which column is used with the key to select rows from the table: the CountryCode column of the City table. The rows entry of 1 thus indicates that MySQL must examine one row of the Country table to find the match for each CountryCode value selected from the City table.

See section A.1.15, "EXPLAIN."

Answer 12:

To optimize the query shown by the EXPLAIN in the last question, you could create an index for the Population column of the City table because it is used both in the WHERE clause to determine which rows to retrieve and in the ORDER BY clause, to sort the result:

```
mysql> ALTER TABLE City
    -> ADD INDEX (Population)
    -> ;
Query OK, 4079 rows affected (0.68 sec)
Records: 4079  Duplicates: 0  Warnings: 0
```

With the new index, EXPLAIN displays the following for the same query:

```
mysql> EXPLAIN
    -> SELECT
    -> City.Name, City.Population, Country.Name
    -> FROM City INNER JOIN Country
    -> ON City.CountryCode = Country.Code
    -> WHERE City.Population > 10000000
    -> ORDER BY City.Population DESC
    -> \G
*************************** 1. row ***************************
        table: City
         type: range
possible_keys: Population
          key: Population
      key_len: 4
          ref: NULL
         rows: 9
        Extra: Using where
*************************** 2. row ***************************
        table: Country
         type: eq_ref
possible_keys: PRIMARY
          key: PRIMARY
      key_len: 3
          ref: City.CountryCode
         rows: 1
        Extra:
```

The EXPLAIN output for the Country table is unchanged, but the output for the City table indicates a much improved search. It shows that only rows within a given range of Population values will be retrieved (type: range), using an index to select the rows. The possible key Population is actually used with its full key length (4). Due to the use of the new index, MySQL now has to inspect only nine rows to resolve the WHERE clause.

See section A.1.15, "EXPLAIN."

Answer 13:

As a rough measure of performance, take the product of the rows output of the EXPLAIN statements before and after the addition of the index: In the original, unoptimized situation, the product of the rows values is 4,079 * 1 = 4,079. With the index added to optimize the query, the product is only 9 * 1 = 9. This lower value indicates that performance is better with the new index.

Answer 14:

To find out which indexes the optimizer will use, prefix your query with EXPLAIN. For example:

```
EXPLAIN SELECT Name FROM City;
```

See section A.1.15, "EXPLAIN."

Answer 15:

To rewrite a query that forces MySQL not to use a specific index that the optimizer would otherwise choose, you would use the IGNORE INDEX (or IGNORE KEY) option. For example:

```
SELECT Name FROM City IGNORE INDEX (idx_name);
```

See section A.1.29, "SELECT."

Answer 16:

To force the optimizer to use a specific index, you would use the FORCE INDEX (or FORCE KEY) option. For example:

```
SELECT Name FROM City FORCE INDEX (idx_name);
```

Another option is USE INDEX, (or USE KEY) but this provides only a hint whereas FORCE INDEX requires the index to be used.

See section A.1.29, "SELECT."

Answer 17:

To find out which query runs faster, you could look at the query execution times the server reports to the client (for example, mysql). These values could, however, be affected by other circumstances than the actual server execution time. More reliable values could be retrieved with the query analyzer (EXPLAIN). This would show that the MySQL optimizer can use indexes more efficiently for the second query:

```
mysql> EXPLAIN SELECT * FROM key1 WHERE col LIKE '%2%'\G
*************************** 1. row ***************************
        table: key1
         type: index
possible_keys: NULL
          key: col
      key_len: 11
          ref: NULL
         rows: 3599
        Extra: Using where; Using index
1 row in set (0.05 sec)
```

```
mysql> EXPLAIN SELECT * FROM key1 WHERE col LIKE 'hey2%'\G
*************************** 1. row ***************************
        table: key1
         type: range
possible_keys: col
          key: col
      key_len: 11
          ref: NULL
         rows: 1
        Extra: Using where; Using index
1 row in set (0.27 sec)
```

The listing shows—besides other things—that MySQL will have to examine 3,783 rows for the first query, but only 221 for the second one. This occurs because MySQL can use an index for a LIKE pattern match if the pattern begins with a literal value, but not if it begins with a wildcard character.

See section A.1.15, "EXPLAIN."

Answer 18:

To give read requests higher priority than write requests, you can use either of the following strategies:

- INSERT DELAYED will cause INSERT statements to wait until there are no more pending read requests on that table.
- SELECT HIGH_PRIORITY will give a SELECT statement priority over write requests.

See section A.1.18, "INSERT."

Answer 19:

To improve searches on the id and name columns, you essentially have two choices:

- You could add an index to the name column, thus improving searches for names.
- You could split the table into two separate tables, thus avoiding disk I/O caused by the TEXT column when MySQL has to scan the table. The mix1 table could be split as shown here:

```
mysql> DESCRIBE mix1; DESCRIBE mix2;
+-------+-------------+------+-----+---------+-------+
| Field | Type        | Null | Key | Default | Extra |
+-------+-------------+------+-----+---------+-------+
| id    | int(11)     |      | PRI | 0       |       |
| name  | varchar(20) | YES  |     | NULL    |       |
+-------+-------------+------+-----+---------+-------+
+---------+---------+------+-----+---------+-------+
| Field   | Type    | Null | Key | Default | Extra |
+---------+---------+------+-----+---------+-------+
```

```
| mix1_id | int(11) |      |     | 0    |       |
| story   | text    | YES  |     | NULL |       |
+---------+---------+------+-----+---------+-------+
```

You could also combine both of the strategies just described.

See sections A.1.11, "DESCRIBE," and A.1.39, "SHOW INDEX."

Answer 20:

To improve searches on the story column, you could add a FULLTEXT index to that column, like this:

```
mysql> ALTER TABLE mix1 ADD FULLTEXT (story);
mysql> SHOW KEYS FROM mix1;
+-------+------------+----------+-    -+------------+
| Table | Non_unique | Key_name |  ... | Index_type |
+-------+------------+----------+-    -+------------+
| mix1  |          0 | PRIMARY  |  ... | BTREE      |
| mix1  |          1 | story    |  ... | FULLTEXT   |
+-------+------------+----------+-    -+------------+
```

See sections A.1.11, "DESCRIBE," A.1.39, "SHOW INDEX," and A.1.1, "ALTER TABLE."

Answer 21:

In that scenario, the only solution would be to use MERGE tables, and to split up the MyISAM tables into a number of smaller MyISAM tables, each of which will not hit the filesystem size limit.

14

MyISAM Tables

This chapter describes the MyISAM table type that is supported by the MyISAM storage engine. It covers the following topics:

- Features of the MyISAM storage engine that are especially useful or that are unique to MyISAM tables
- Table processing optimizations you can use with MyISAM tables
- How MySQL handles locking for MyISAM tables
- Backup and recovery options for MyISAM tables
- How to check, repair, and maintain MyISAM tables

Questions on the material in this chapter make up approximately 10% of the exam.

MyISAM tables use the indexed sequential access method for indexing, as did the older ISAM table format. But MyISAM offers better performance and more features than ISAM (for example, you can index columns that include NULL values, and the maximum table size is larger). For these reasons, MyISAM should be preferred over ISAM. Should you want to convert an older ISAM table to MyISAM format, it's very easy; just use ALTER TABLE as follows:

```
ALTER TABLE table_name TYPE = MyISAM;
```

MyISAM was introduced in MySQL 3.23.0 and has been the default table type since. Because MyISAM is the default type, the MyISAM storage engine is always available and cannot be disabled.

On disk, MySQL represents an MyISAM table using three files: a format file that stores the definition of the table structure, a datafile that stores the contents of table rows, and an index file that stores any indexes on the table. These files are distinguished from one another by their suffixes. For example, the format, data, and index files for a table named mytable are called mytable.frm, mytable.MYD, and mytable.MYI. MySQL normally stores all three files in the database directory for the database that contains the table, although some variation is possible through the use of symlinking and RAID options.

14.1 Special MyISAM Features

MyISAM tables have certain important characteristics that are described in this section. MyISAM is the default table type, but understanding these features helps you know when to choose MyISAM deliberately rather than some other table type. MyISAM characteristics include the following:

- The table storage format is portable, allowing table files to be copied directly to another host and used by a server there.

- MyISAM tables can be converted to compressed read-only format to save space.

- You can tell MySQL the maximum number of rows that the table must be able to hold, which allows the server to adjust the table's internal row pointer size accordingly.

- On systems that support appropriate symlinking capabilities, tables can be placed in a different location than the default (which is the database directory).

- The rows of a MyISAM table normally are stored in a single datafile. MyISAM supports the option of setting up a "software RAID array" such that the datafile is implemented as a set of files. This can be advantageous when a table's datafile size is limited by the filesystem's maximum file size. Setting up a RAID array allows the file size limit to be circumvented.

- When loading data into an empty MyISAM table, you can disable updating of nonunique indexes and enable the indexes after loading. This is faster than updating the indexes for each row inserted. In fact, when LOAD DATA INFILE is used for loading an empty MyISAM table, it automatically disables and enables index updating. LOAD DATA INFILE is faster than INSERT anyway, and this optimization speeds it up even more.

- You can influence the scheduling mechanism for queries that use MyISAM tables by using a query modifier such as LOW_PRIORITY or HIGH_PRIORITY. Inserts into a table can be buffered on the server side until the table isn't busy by using INSERT DELAYED; this allows the client to proceed immediately instead of blocking until the insert operation completes.

- If you run out of disk space while adding rows to a MyISAM table, no error occurs. The server suspends the operation until space becomes available, and then completes the operation.

14.1.1 MyISAM Table Portability

MyISAM tables generally are binary portable. This means they are machine independent and that you can directly copy the files for a MyISAM table from one MySQL server to another on a different machine and the second server will be able to access the table with no problems. Were this not the case, the only option for transferring tables between servers would be to dump them into some text format (for example, with mysqldump) and reload them into the destination server.

For a MyISAM table to be binary portable from one host to another, two conditions must be met:

- Both machines must use two's-complement integer arithmetic.
- Both machines must use IEEE floating-point format, or else the table must contain no floating-point columns (FLOAT or DOUBLE).

In practice, these conditions pose little restriction. Two's-complement integer arithmetic and IEEE floating-point format are the norm on modern hardware.

When you copy a table directly to another server, the table must not be in use by other programs (including the server) while the table files are being copied. If you stop the server while copying the table, there will be no problem of server interaction. If you leave the server running, use an appropriate locking protocol to prevent server access to the table. For example, to copy the Country table in the world database, lock the table and flush any pending changes like this:

```
mysql> USE world;
mysql> LOCK TABLES Country READ;
mysql> FLUSH TABLES Country;
```

Then (with the table still locked) use your operating system's file copy command to copy the table files. After the copy operation completes, release the lock on the table:

```
mysql> UNLOCK TABLES;
```

Note that Windows file-locking behavior is such that you might not be able to copy table files for tables that are locked by the server. In that case, you'll need to stop the server before copying table files.

If the conditions for binary portability are not satisfied, you can copy a MyISAM table from one server to another by using mysqldump. This process is described in section 14.4.1, "Using mysqldump."

14.1.2 Specifying MyISAM Maximum Row Count

Internally, the MyISAM storage engine represents pointers to rows within a table using values that take from 2 to 8 bytes each. The size is determined at table-creation time based on estimates that the server makes about how big the table might become. To give the server a hint when you create the table, you can specify an option in the CREATE TABLE statement that indicates how many rows the table must be able to hold. You can change the option later with ALTER TABLE should the table need to become larger.

If a table reaches the row limit allowed by its row pointer size, a data file full error occurs and you cannot add any more rows. This error is unrelated to running of out disk space or reaching the maximum file size allowed by MyISAM or the filesystem. To "pre-size" a table when you create it, use a MAX_ROWS option to indicate how many rows the table must be able to hold. The following statement indicates to MySQL that the table must be able to contain two million rows:

```
CREATE TABLE t (i INT) MAX_ROWS = 2000000;
```

To set or change the MAX_ROWS value for an existing table, use ALTER TABLE:

```
ALTER TABLE t MAX_ROWS = 4000000;
```

When you expect a table to contain many rows, MAX_ROWS is useful for telling MySQL that it needs to use larger internal row pointers. Conversely, if you know a table will be small, specifying a small MAX_ROWS value tells MySQL to use smaller pointers. This saves space and improves table processing efficiency.

A related option, AVG_ROW_LENGTH, also gives the server information that it can use to estimate how large the table may become. This option is unnecessary for tables with fixed-length rows because the server knows how long each row is. The option might be helpful for tables with variable-length rows.

The two options may be used separately or together. For example, if a table has a BIGINT column (8 bytes each) and a VARCHAR(255) column where you expect the average string length to be 100 bytes, you can specify an AVG_ROW_LENGTH value of 108. If you also want to make sure that the table can hold four million rows, create it like this:

```
CREATE TABLE t (i BIGINT, c VARCHAR(255))
AVG_ROW_LENGTH = 108 MAX_ROWS = 4000000;
```

Note that using MAX_ROWS and AVG_ROW_LENGTH does not allow the size of MyISAM table files to be expanded beyond the limit of what the filesystem allows. For example, if you create a MyISAM table on a filesystem that only allows file sizes up to 2GB, you cannot add more rows once the datafile or index file reach 2GB, no matter what value you set MAX_ROWS to.

To find the values of MAX_ROWS and AVG_ROW_LENGTH for a table, use SHOW TABLE STATUS and check the Create_options field of the output:

```
mysql> SHOW TABLE STATUS LIKE 't'\G
*************************** 1. row ***************************
           Name: t
           Type: MyISAM
     Row_format: Dynamic
           Rows: 0
 Avg_row_length: 0
    Data_length: 0
Max_data_length: 4294967295
   Index_length: 1024
      Data_free: 0
 Auto_increment: NULL
    Create_time: 2003-10-28 11:36:04
```

```
   Update_time: 2003-10-28 11:36:04
    Check_time: NULL
Create_options: max_rows=4000000 avg_row_length=108
       Comment:
```

14.1.3 MyISAM Table Symlinking

By default, a MyISAM table for a given database is created in the database directory under the data directory. This means that the .frm, .MYD, and .MYI files are created in the database directory. It's possible to create the table such that the datafile or index file (or both) are located elsewhere. You might do this to distribute storage for the table to a filesystem with more free space, for example. If the filesystem is on a different physical disk, moving the files has the additional effect of distributing database-related disk activity, which might improve performance.

To relocate a table's datafile or index file, use the DATA DIRECTORY or INDEX DIRECTORY options in the CREATE TABLE statement. For example, to put both files for a table t in the directory /var/mysql-alt/data/test, use a statement like this:

```
CREATE TABLE t (i INT)
DATA DIRECTORY = '/var/mysql-alt/data/test'
INDEX DIRECTORY = '/var/mysql-alt/data/test';
```

This statement puts the data and index files in the same directory. To put the files in different directories, specify different pathnames for each option. You can also relocate one file only and leave the other in its default location (the database directory) by omitting either the DATA DIRECTORY or the INDEX DIRECTORY other from the CREATE TABLE statement. Directory names for DATA DIRECTORY and INDEX DIRECTORY must be specified as full (absolute) pathnames, not as relative pathnames.

The server implements datafile or index file relocation by creating the file in the directory that you specify and placing in the database directory a symbolic link to the file. You can do the same thing manually to relocate an existing MyISAM table's datafile or index file, as long as the server does not have the table open and is not using it. For each file to be relocated, use this procedure:

- Move the file to a different directory.
- Create a symlink in the database directory that points to the new location of the moved file.

Table symlinking is subject to the following restrictions:

- It does not work on Windows.
- On Unix, the operating system must have a working realpath() system call, and must have thread-safe symlinks.

Relocating MyISAM datafiles and index files as just described makes it somewhat more difficult to keep track of just where your table files are located or how table storage space is distributed among your filesystems. Thus, although it's possible to relocate MyISAM tables using symlinking, it isn't necessarily recommended as an everyday technique. If you're thinking about relocating several MyISAM tables in a database, consider the simpler alternative of relocating the entire database directory and replacing the original database directory under the data directory with a symbolic link that points to the new location. This is just as effective as moving many tables individually, but requires only a single symlink. The server should not be running while you relocate a database directory. For instructions, see section 11.7.1, "Moving Databases Using Symbolic Links."

14.1.4 Using MyISAM RAID Tables

The MyISAM storage engine supports splitting a table's datafile into a set of files. Using a set of files for table data allows the amount of table data to exceed the maximum size of a single file. This is useful on systems that have a small maximum file size.

To create a MyISAM table that has a split data file, use the following table options:

- RAID_TYPE = *type*

  This option identifies the table as a RAID table. *type* can be set to 1, STRIPED, or RAID0. All three values are synonymous.

- RAID_CHUNKS = *n*

  n indicates the number of files to use for storing table data.

- RAID_CHUNKSIZE = *n*

  n indicates the amount of space to allocate for each file, in MB.

The following statement creates a RAID table for which MySQL allocates 100 files of size 2,000MB each:

```
CREATE TABLE big_table ( ... )
RAID_TYPE = 1 RAID_CHUNKS = 100 RAID_CHUNKSIZE = 2000;
```

The RAID options apply only to the datafile, not to the index file. The indexes are still stored in a single file, so if a table's size is limited by the index file size, reconfiguring the table as a RAID table will not help.

To use MyISAM RAID tables, your server must have been configured with the --with-raid option when it was built. To find out whether a server supports RAID tables, issue the following statement:

```
mysql> SHOW VARIABLES LIKE 'have_raid';
+---------------+-------+
| Variable_name | Value |
+---------------+-------+
```

```
| have_raid     | YES   |
+---------------+-------+
```

14.2 MyISAM-Specific Optimizations

Some of the features of MyISAM tables enable you to optimize how you use them. These optimizations include the following:

- The MyISAM storage engine supports several different table storage formats that have differing characteristics. You can take advantage of these characteristics by choosing the storage format that best matches how you intend to use a table. For example, if you have a table that you'll only read and never update, you can make it a compressed table. It will take less disk space, and internal index optimizations might make retrievals faster. Section 14.2.1, "MyISAM Storage Formats," provides more details on the properties of these formats.

- You can disable index updating when loading data into an empty MyISAM table to speed up the operation. LOAD DATA INFILE does this automatically for nonunique indexes if the table is empty; it disables index updating before loading and enables it again after loading.

- Use scheduling modifiers such as LOW_PRIORITY or DELAYED to change how the server assigns query priorities.

- Use the OPTIMIZE TABLE and ANALYZE TABLE statements to update internal table index statistics and allow the query optimizer to make better decisions about how to execute queries.

- To distribute disk activity, move some of your MyISAM tables to different disks than the one where the data directory is located. Section 14.1.3, "MyISAM Table Symlinking," describes how to use table symlinking.

14.2.1 MyISAM Storage Formats

For MyISAM tables, the table storage format has an impact on query efficiency. The three allowable formats are static, dynamic, and compressed:

- Static tables have fixed-length rows, so every row in the table's datafile is stored at a position that is a multiple of the row size. This makes it easier to look up rows, with the result that MySQL typically can process static tables more quickly than dynamic tables. However, static tables on average take more space than dynamic tables. MyISAM can use static table format only if every column has a fixed width. If the table contains VARCHAR, BLOB, or TEXT columns, it cannot be static.

- Dynamic tables use a variable amount of storage for each row. Rows are not stored at fixed positions with datafiles. Each row has extra information that indicates how long the row is, and it's also possible for a row to be stored noncontiguously with different pieces in different locations. This makes retrievals more complex, and thus slower. Dynamic tables generally take less space than static tables. However, if a table is updated frequently, this storage format can result in fragmentation and wasted space. It can be useful to run OPTIMIZE TABLE from time to time to defragment the table. Dynamic format is used if the table contains VARCHAR, BLOB, or TEXT columns, or if it is declared with a ROW_FORMAT = DYNAMIC option.

- Compressed tables are packed to save space and stored in optimized form that allows quick retrievals. Compressed tables are read-only, so this table format cannot be used for tables that will be updated. To create a compressed table, use the myisampack utility. It can create compressed tables from either static or dynamic MyISAM tables, and can compress columns of any type.

To find out what storage format a table has, use the SHOW TABLE STATUS statement and examine the value of the Row_format field:

```
mysql> SHOW TABLE STATUS LIKE 'Country'\G
*************************** 1. row ***************************
           Name: Country
           Type: MyISAM
     Row_format: Fixed
           Rows: 239
 Avg_row_length: 261
    Data_length: 62379
Max_data_length: 1120986464255
   Index_length: 5120
      Data_free: 0
 Auto_increment: NULL
    Create_time: 2003-06-06 16:44:16
    Update_time: 2003-06-06 16:44:16
     Check_time: 2003-09-12 17:44:26
 Create_options:
        Comment:
```

The Row_format value will be Fixed, Dynamic, or Compressed.

14.2.2 Using Compressed MyISAM Tables

A MyISAM table may be converted to compressed form to save storage space. In many cases, compressing a table improves lookup speed as well, because the compression operation optimizes the internal structure of the table to make retrievals faster.

A compressed table is read-only, so a MyISAM table should be compressed only if its content will not change after it has been populated. If you *must* modify a compressed table, you can uncompress it, modify it, and compress it again. But if you have to do this often, the extra processing tends to negate the benefits of using a compressed table, especially because the table is unavailable for querying during the uncompression and recompression operations.

To compress a MyISAM table, use the `myisampack` utility. It's also necessary to use `myisamchk` afterward to update the indexes. The following example demonstrates how to perform this procedure, using the tables in the `world` database:

- Back up the tables, just in case:

```
shell> mysqldump --opt world > world.sql
```

- Bring down the server so that it won't use the tables while you're packing them.
- Change location into the database directory where the `world` tables are stored, and then use `myisampack` to compress them:

```
shell> myisampack Country City CountryLanguage
Compressing Country.MYD: (239 records)
- Calculating statistics
- Compressing file
73.01%
Compressing City.MYD: (4079 records)
- Calculating statistics
- Compressing file
70.94%
Compressing CountryLanguage.MYD: (984 records)
- Calculating statistics
- Compressing file
71.42%
Remember to run myisamchk -rq on compressed tables
```

`myisampack` also understands index filenames as arguments:

```
shell> myisampack *.MYI
```

This does not affect the way `myisampack` works. It simply gives you an easier way to name a group of tables, because you can use filename patterns.

- As the final line of `myisampack` output points out, you should run `myisamchk` to rebuild the indexes. Like `myisampack`, `myisamchk` understands index filename arguments for naming tables, so you can rebuild the indexes as follows:

```
shell> myisamchk -rq *.MYI
```

The equivalent long-option command is:

```
shell> myisamchk --recover --quick *.MYI
```

- Restart the server.

If you want to assess the effectiveness of the packing operation, use `SHOW TABLE STATUS` before and after packing the tables. (The server must be running when you use this statement.) The `Data_length` and `Index_length` values should be smaller afterward, and the `Row_format` value should change from `Fixed` or `Dynamic` to `Compressed`. The following examples show the results for the `City` table.

Before packing:

```
mysql> SHOW TABLE STATUS FROM world LIKE 'City'\G
*************************** 1. row ***************************
           Name: City
           Type: MyISAM
     Row_format: Fixed
           Rows: 4079
 Avg_row_length: 67
    Data_length: 273293
Max_data_length: 287762808831
   Index_length: 35840
      Data_free: 0
 Auto_increment: 4080
    Create_time: 2002-12-20 17:17:55
    Update_time: 2002-12-20 17:17:56
     Check_time: NULL
  Create_options:
        Comment:
```

After packing:

```
mysql> SHOW TABLE STATUS FROM world LIKE 'City'\G
*************************** 1. row ***************************
           Name: City
           Type: MyISAM
     Row_format: Compressed
           Rows: 4079
 Avg_row_length: 19
    Data_length: 79418
Max_data_length: 4294967295
   Index_length: 30720
      Data_free: 0
 Auto_increment: 4080
    Create_time: 2002-12-20 17:17:55
    Update_time: 2002-12-20 17:17:56
     Check_time: 2003-03-17 12:56:53
  Create_options:
        Comment:
```

To uncompress a compressed table, use myisamchk in the database directory where the table files are located:

```
shell> myisamchk --unpack table_name
```

A table must not be in use by other programs (including the server) while you compress or uncompress it. The easiest thing to do is to bring down the server while using myisampack or myisamchk.

If you do not run myisampack or myisamchk in the database directory where the table files are located, you must specify the pathname to the files, using either absolute pathnames or pathnames relative to your current directory.

Another way to uncompress a table is to dump it, drop it, and re-create it. Do this while the server is running. For example, if world.Country is compressed, you can uncompress it with the following commands:

```
shell> mysqldump --opt world Country > dump.sql
shell> mysql world < dump.sql
```

The --opt option to mysqldump causes it to include a DROP TABLE statement in the output written to the dump file. When you process the file with mysql, that statement drops the compressed table, and the rest of the dump file re-creates the table in uncompressed form.

14.3 MyISAM Locking Strategies

When multiple clients attempt to access a table at the same time, it's necessary to coordinate them. This avoids problems such as one client changing rows while another client is reading them, or two clients making changes to the same row simultaneously. MySQL solves this problem for MyISAM tables using a locking mechanism.

MyISAM locking occurs at the table level. This is not as desirable as page or row locking for concurrency in a mixed read/write environment. However, deadlock cannot occur with table locking as it can with page or row locking. For example, with row-level locking, two clients might each acquire a lock on different rows. If each then tries to modify the row that the other has locked, neither client can proceed. This is called "deadlock." With table locking, the server can determine what locks are needed before executing a statement, so deadlock never occurs.

When processing queries on MyISAM tables, the server manages contention for the tables by simultaneous clients by implicitly acquiring any locks it needs. You can also lock tables explicitly with the LOCK TABLES and UNLOCK TABLES statements. Acquiring locks yourself can be advantageous in certain situations:

- Implicit locks last for the duration of a single query only. Should you want to perform a multiple-statement update that requires no interference by other clients, you can acquire an explicit lock, which remains in effect until you release it.

- Multiple-statement locking can improve performance. For example, multiple INSERT statements executed using implicit locking result in index flushing for each statement. If you lock a table explicitly and then perform all the inserts, index flushing occurs only once when you release the lock. This results in less disk activity. It also eliminates the need to acquire the implicit lock for each statement.

14.3.1 MyISAM Locking Characteristics

Only the client that holds a lock acquired with LOCK TABLES can release the lock. Another client cannot release it. In other words, if you acquire a lock, it's yours until you give it up. Another client cannot force you to release it. Locks are released when you issue an UNLOCK TABLES or LOCK TABLES statement. Locks cannot be maintained across connections; if a client has any unreleased locks when its connection to the server terminates, the server implicitly releases its locks. An administrator with the appropriate privilege can terminate a client connection with the KILL statement, which causes release of locks held by the client.

Locks fall into two general categories: read locks and write locks. For each type of lock, there are also options to modify lock behavior somewhat.

If you need to lock several tables at the same time, you must do so with a single LOCK TABLES statement. The following statement acquires a read lock on Country and a write lock on City:

```
LOCK TABLES Country READ, City WRITE;
```

A read lock locks a table for read queries such as SELECT that retrieve data from the table. It does not allow write operations such as INSERT, DELETE, or UPDATE that modify the table. A read lock prevents a write lock from being placed on the table, but does not prevent other clients from acquiring read locks. That is, when a table is locked for reading, other clients can still read from the table at the same time, but no client can write to it. A client that wants to write to a table that is read-locked must wait until all clients currently reading from it have finished and released their locks.

A write lock is an exclusive lock. It can be acquired only when a table is not being used. Once acquired, only the client holding the write lock can read from or write to the table. Other clients can neither read from nor write to it. No other client can lock the table for either reading or writing.

A concurrent insert is a special exception to the "readers block writers" principle. If a MyISAM table has no holes in the middle resulting from deleted records, inserts always take place at the end of the table. In that case, a client that is reading from a table can lock it with a READ LOCAL lock to allow other clients to insert into the table while the client holding the read lock reads from it. If a table does have holes, concurrent inserts cannot be performed. However, you can remove the holes by using OPTIMIZE TABLE to defragment the table. (Note that a record deleted from the end of the table does not create a hole and does not prevent concurrent inserts.)

A normal write lock request is satisfied when no other clients are using the table. If other clients are using the table when the request is made, it waits until those clients have finished. However, a LOW_PRIORITY WRITE lock may be requested instead, which also waits for any new read requests that arrive while the lock request is pending.

14.3.2 Query Scheduling Modifiers

By default, the server schedules queries for execution as follows:

- Write requests (such as UPDATE and DELETE statements) take priority over read requests (such as SELECT statements).
- The server tries to perform write requests in the order that it receives them.

However, if a table is being read from when a write request arrives, the write request cannot be processed until all current readers have finished. Any read requests that arrive after the write request must wait until the write request finishes, even if they arrive before the current readers finish. That is, a new read request by default does not jump ahead of a pending write request.

When working with MyISAM tables, certain scheduling modifiers are available to change the priority of requests:

- The LOW_PRIORITY modifier may be applied to statements that update tables (INSERT, DELETE, REPLACE, or UPDATE). A low-priority write request waits not only until all current readers have finished, but for any pending read requests that arrive while the write request itself is waiting. That is, it waits until there are no pending read requests at all. It is therefore possible for a low-priority write request never to be performed, if read requests keep arriving while the write request is waiting.
- HIGH_PRIORITY may be used with a SELECT statement to move it ahead of updates and ahead of other SELECT statements that do not use the HIGH_PRIORITY modifier.
- DELAYED may be used with INSERT (and REPLACE). The server buffers the rows in memory and inserts them when the table is not being used. Delayed inserts increase efficiency because they're done in batches rather than individually. While inserting the rows, the server checks periodically to see whether other requests to use the table have arrived. If so, the server suspends insertion of delayed rows until the table becomes free again. Using DELAYED allows the client to proceed immediately after issuing the INSERT statement rather than waiting until it completes.

If you use DELAYED, keep the following points in mind:

- If a crash occurs while the server is buffering delayed rows in memory, those rows are lost.
- Delayed rows tend to be held for a longer time on a very busy server than on a lightly loaded one.

The implication is that DELAYED is more suitable for applications where loss of a few rows is not a problem, rather than applications for which each row is critical. For example, DELAYED can be appropriate for an application that logs activity for informational purposes only.

14.4 MyISAM Backup and Recovery

The following list indicates available methods for backing up MyISAM tables:

- Use the mysqldump program, which runs on any platform supported by MySQL. It can tell the server to send backups to the client in the form of SQL statements or to write data directly to files on the server host.

- Use the mysqlhotcopy script. This is a Perl script; it requires the DBI module and is available on Unix and NetWare. mysqlhotcopy is very fast, but can be used with the local server only.

- Use the BACKUP TABLE and RESTORE TABLE statements. BACKUP TABLE makes copies of the MySQL format file and datafile on the server host. RESTORE TABLE restores them and rebuilds the index file.

- Use the SELECT … INTO OUTFILE statement to save the contents of a table into a file on the server host. More information about this statement is available in the "Core Study Guide."

Except for mysqlhotcopy, any of the methods just listed can be used with either local or remote servers. mysqlhotcopy can be used only with a local server.

Some of the preceding backup methods also can be used for InnoDB tables, as discussed in section 15.5, "InnoDB Backup and Recovery."

14.4.1 Using mysqldump

The mysqldump client program dumps table contents to files. It is useful for making database backups or for transferring database contents to another server. mysqldump can produce SQL-format dump files that contain CREATE TABLE and INSERT statements for re-creating the dumped files, or it can produce tab-delimited datafiles. The "Core Study Guide" discusses general mysqldump operation for producing SQL-format dump files, and it is assumed here that you're familiar with that material. This section discusses how to produce tab-delimited datafiles.

Normally, mysqldump generates output as a set of SQL statements. These take the form of CREATE TABLE statements that create the dumped tables, and INSERT statements that load them. However, when you use the --tab=dir_name (or -T dir_name) option, mysqldump writes each dumped table as a tab-delimited text file in the dir_name directory. It also writes a file containing a CREATE TABLE statement that you can use to re-create the table.

Using --tab to produce tab-delimited dump files is much faster than creating SQL-format files, but you should keep in mind the following points:

- The CREATE TABLE statement for each table *table_name* is sent by the server to mysqldump, which writes it to a file named *table_name*.sql in the dump directory on the client host. The .sql files are owned by you.

- The table contents are written directly by the server into a file named *table_name*.txt in the dump directory on the server host. The .txt files are owned by the server.

- Using --tab can be confusing because some files are created by the client and some by the server, and because the .sql files have different ownerships than the .txt files. To minimize confusion, run mysqldump on the server host, specify the dump directory using a full pathname so that mysqldump and the server both interpret it as the same location, and specify a dump directory that is writable both to you and to the server.

- You must have the FILE privilege because the dump operation causes the server to write datafiles on the server host.

- To write only the data files and not the .sql files, use the --no-create-info option.

The default datafile format produced by the --tab option consists of tab-delimited lines with newline terminators. To control the format of the datafiles that mysqldump generates, use the following options:

- --lines-terminated-by=*string*

  string specifies the character sequence that each input line should end with. The default is \n (linefeed, also known as newline). Other common line terminators are \r (carriage return) and \r\n (carriage return/linefeed pairs).

- --fields-terminated-by=*string*

  string specifies the delimiter to write between data values within input lines. The default delimiter is \t (tab).

- --fields-enclosed-by=*char* or --fields-optionally-enclosed-by=*char*

  char indicates a quoting character that should be written surrounding data values. By default, values are not quoted. A common value for *char* is double quote. With --fields-enclosed-by, all values are quoted. With --fields-optionally-enclosed-by, only values from CHAR and VARCHAR columns are quoted.

- --fields-escaped-by=*char*

  By default, special characters in data values are written preceded by \ as an escape character, and NULL values are written as \N. Use this option to specify a different escape character. To turn escaping off (no escape character), specify an empty value for *char*.

You cannot use --tab with the --all-databases or --databases option. With --tab, mysqldump writes the files for all dumped tables to a single directory. You would have no way to tell which files correspond to tables in each database.

14.4.1.1 Reloading `mysqldump` Output

To reload a SQL-format dump file produced by `mysqldump`, read it with `mysql`. For example:

```
shell> mysqldump --opt world Country > dump.sql
shell> mysql world < dump.sql
```

`mysql` can read from a pipe, so you can combine the use of `mysqldump` and `mysql` into a single command. One use for this is for copying a database over the network to another server. If you have a MySQL account for the server on another host, you can pipe the output to that server like this:

```
shell> mysqldump world Country | mysql -h other.host.com mysql world
```

If a dump file contains very long `INSERT` statements, they might exceed the default size of the communications buffer (1MB). You can increase the buffer size for both `mysqldump` and `mysql` with the `--max-allowed-packet` option. The option value may be given in bytes or followed by `K`, `M`, or `G` to indicate a size in kilobytes, megabytes, or gigabytes. For example, `--max-allowed-packet=32M` specifies a size of 32MB. The server must also be run with a `--max-allowed-packet` value that increases its own communications buffer to be large enough.

If you use the `--tab` option to produce tab-delimited datafiles, reloading the files requires a different approach. Suppose that you dump the table `City` from the `world` database using the `/tmp` directory as the output directory:

```
shell> mysqldump --opt --tab=/tmp world City
```

The output will consist of a `City.sql` file containing the `CREATE TABLE` statement for the table, and a `City.txt` file containing the table data. To reload the table, change location into the dump directory, process the `.sql` file using `mysql`, and load the `.txt` file using `mysqlimport`:

```
shell> cd /tmp
shell> mysql world < City.sql
shell> mysqlimport world City.txt
```

If you combine the `--tab` option with format-control options such as `--fields-terminated-by` and `--fields-enclosed-by`, you should specify the same format-control options with `mysqlimport` so that it knows how to interpret the datafiles.

14.4.2 Using `mysqlhotcopy`

The `mysqlhotcopy` script copies MyISAM tables to a backup directory. It is a Perl script and requires the DBI module to be installed. It runs on Unix and NetWare.

`mysqlhotcopy` is fast because it copies table files directly rather than backing them up over the network. It's also more convenient than issuing statements to the server to lock the tables and flush any pending changes to disk, because it handles those operations for you.

mysqlhotcopy must be run on the server host so that it can copy table files while the table locks are in place. It must be run while the server is running because it must connect to the server to lock and flush the tables.

mysqlhotcopy has many options, which you can see by invoking the script with the --help option. The following examples present some simple ways to use the script:

- Back up the world database to a directory named world_copy in the server's data directory:

  ```
  shell> mysqlhotcopy world
  ```

- Back up the world database to a directory named world in the /var/archive directory:

  ```
  shell> mysqlhotcopy world /var/archive
  ```

14.4.3 Using BACKUP TABLE and RESTORE TABLE

BACKUP TABLE and RESTORE TABLE save and reload a copy of one or more MyISAM tables. (In both statements, TABLE or TABLES can be used.) These statements require that you have the FILE privilege because they create and read files on the server host.

To save a copy of a table with BACKUP TABLE, name the table and the full pathname of the directory on the server host where the copy should be written. The following statement saves the City table into the /var/archive directory:

```
BACKUP TABLE City TO '/var/archive';
```

To back up several tables, name them as a comma-separated list:

```
BACKUP TABLES City, Country, CountryLanguage TO '/var/archive';
```

For each file to be saved, BACKUP TABLE locks it to prevent changes and copies its .frm and .MYD files to the backup directory. The .MYI file is not copied because it can be rebuilt from the other two files when the table is restored.

BACKUP TABLE locks each table individually while copying it. To lock the tables as a group, lock them explicitly:

```
LOCK TABLES City READ, Country READ, CountryLanguage READ;
BACKUP TABLES City, Country, CountryLanguage TO '/var/archive';
UNLOCK TABLES;
```

To restore a saved copy of a table, use RESTORE TABLE:

```
RESTORE TABLE City FROM '/var/archive';
```

RESTORE TABLE copies the .frm and .MYD files from the named directory into the database directory, and then rebuilds the .MYI file.

BACKUP TABLE fails if a table already has been saved in the named directory. RESTORE TABLE fails if the table to be restored already exists.

14.5 Checking and Repairing MyISAM Tables

MySQL provides two programs that help you check MyISAM tables for problems and repair damage if it occurs:

- mysqlcheck is a client program that connects to the server and instructs it to perform table checking and repair operations.
- myisamchk is a standalone utility that accesses MyISAM table files directly. Because myisamchk operates independently of the server, you must ensure that while you are using it, the server does not access the table's files.

Brief instructions for using mysqlcheck and myisamchk are given in the following discussion. More detailed information may be found in the "Core Study Guide."

To check or repair a table with mysqlcheck, use these commands:

```
shell> mysqlcheck db_name table_name
shell> mysqlcheck --repair db_name table_name
```

mysqlcheck acts as a command-line interface to the CHECK TABLE and REPAIR TABLE statements. You can issue these statements directly from within the mysql client or from other applications that send statements to the server. By using these statements, you can write your own administrative applications that perform table checking and repair operations.

A recommended table-checking strategy is to run mysqlcheck with no options. If any errors occur, run it again, first with the --repair and --quick options to attempt a quick repair. If that fails, run mysqlcheck with --repair for a normal repair, and then if necessary with --repair and --force.

To check or repair a table with myisamchk, first make sure that the server will not access the table. (One way to do this is to stop the server.) Then change location into the database directory of the database that contains the table and use the following commands:

```
shell> myisamchk db_name table_name
shell> myisamchk --recover db_name table_name
```

If a repair operation performed with --recover encounters problems that it cannot fix, try using the --safe-recover option. --safe-recover can fix some problems that --recover cannot.

An administrator who is responsible for server operation can instruct the server to check and repair tables automatically. To do this, use the --myisam-recover option. The option value can consist of a comma-separated list of one or more of the following values:

- DEFAULT is the same as using no --myisam-recover option at all.
- BACKUP tells the server to make a backup of any table that it must change.
- FORCE causes table recovery to be performed even if it would cause loss of more than one row of data.
- QUICK performs quick recovery: Tables that have no holes resulting from deletes or updates are skipped.

For example, to tell the server to perform a forced recovery but make a backup of any table it changes, you can put the following lines in an option file:

```
[mysqld]
myisam-recover=FORCE,BACKUP
```

14.6 MyISAM Table Maintenance

MyISAM tables can be analyzed and optimized. These are operations that you might want to perform periodically to keep your MyISAM tables performing at their best:

- When MyISAM analyzes a table, it updates the index statistics. The MySQL optimizer uses these statistics when processing queries to make better decisions about how best to look up records in the table and the order in which to read tables in a join.
- When the MyISAM storage engine optimizes a table, it defragments the datafile to reclaim unused space, sorts the indexes, and updates the index statistics. Periodic defragmenting is useful for speeding up table access for tables that contain variable-length columns such as VARCHAR, BLOB, or TEXT. Inserts and deletes can result in many gaps in such tables, particularly those that are modified frequently. Defragmenting eliminates these gaps.

Index analysis and optimization are operations that you can perform once on a table that is fully populated and that will not change thereafter. For tables that continue to be updated, the benefits of analysis and optimization diminish the more the table's contents change, so you might want to repeat these operations periodically.

You can analyze a table several ways. The following examples show how to analyze the Country table in the world database:

- Use the ANALYZE TABLE statement:

  ```
  mysql> ANALYZE TABLE world.Country;
  ```

- Use mysqlcheck or myisamchk with the --analyze option.

Optimize a table as follows:

- Use the OPTIMIZE TABLE statement:

  ```
  mysql> OPTIMIZE TABLE world.Country;
  ```

- Use `mysqlcheck`:

  ```
  shell> mysqlcheck --optimize world Country
  ```

- `myisamchk --sort-index` sorts a table's indexes, which speeds up some read operations.

If you use `myisamchk` to analyze or optimize a MyISAM table, be sure that the server is not using the table at the same time. You can guarantee this by stopping the server first.

14.7 Exercises

Question 1:

To copy a MyISAM table to another database server on another host, you can either copy the table files directly, or you can use `mysqldump` to dump the table contents into a file and then import that file into the other server. Suppose that a table named `mytable` exists in the `test` database of server 1, but not server 2. You want to copy the table from server 1 to server 2 without stopping either server for the copy operation. How might you do that?

Question 2:

On a Windows server host, you want to compress the MyISAM table `City`, found in the `GuideProf` database. Assuming that MySQL is installed in `C:\mysql` and that MySQL's data directory is in the default location, what commands would you issue to compress the table if your current location is the `C:\mysql\bin` directory?

Question 3:

On a Windows server host, you want to compress the MyISAM table `City`, found in the `GuideProf` database. After you've done so, how would you verify that the table has actually been compressed?

Question 4:

On a Windows server host, you want to compress the MyISAM table `City`, found in the `GuideProf` database. What operations will you no longer be able to perform on `City` after the table has been compressed?

Question 5:

On a Windows server host, you want to compress the MyISAM table `City`, found in the `GuideProf` database.

a. After you've done so, how can you unpack the compressed table?

b. What alternatives to using `myisamchk --unpack` could you use to unpack the table after it has been compressed?

Question 6:

You want to compress and then unpack the MyISAM table City, found in the GuideProf database. After you've unpacked the compressed table, how would you verify that the table has actually been unpacked?

Question 7:

Why would you specify the MAX_ROWS option for a table?

Question 8:

Where does MySQL store the format, data, and index files for a MyISAM table by default? What options do you use to tell the server to place the files in locations different than the default? Are there restrictions to the use of these options?

Question 9:

Which of the following alternatives correctly describes what the server does when it finds that the disk is full during an update operation on a MyISAM table?

   a. It cancels the update operation silently.

   b. It cancels the update operation with an error message.

   c. It waits until free space becomes available.

   d. It deletes rows in the table until there's enough free space to complete the operation.

   e. It replaces existing rows with the data the update operation would insert or change.

Question 10:

Assume that you've locked the City table with a READ lock. If you now try to select data from the table, what will happen?

Question 11:

Assume that you've locked the City table with a READ lock. If another client now tries to select data from the table, what will happen?

Question 12:

Assume that you've locked the City table with a READ lock. If you now try to insert data into the table, what will happen?

Question 13:

Assume that you've locked the City table with a READ lock. If another client now tries to insert data into the table, what will happen?

Question 14:

Assume that you've locked the City table with a READ lock. Who can release the lock?

Question 15:

Assume that a client has locked the City table with a READ lock in a connection with ID 2098. Both the client with connection ID 2098 and a client with connection ID 2099 have tried to insert data into City. What will happen when the lock is released?

Question 16:

The connection with ID 2098 requests a WRITE lock on the table City. However, the connection with ID 2099 has already obtained a READ lock on the same table. Which of the following statements correctly describes how the server handles the WRITE lock request?

  a. The WRITE lock request results in an error.

  b. The server automatically releases the READ lock of connection 2099 and gives connection 2098 a WRITE lock.

  c. The server makes the WRITE lock request of connection 2098 wait until connection 2099 releases its READ lock.

  d. Connection 2098 cannot obtain the WRITE lock as long as connection 2099 has the READ lock, so the server silently converts the WRITE lock request by connection 2098 to a READ lock request.

Question 17:

Under what circumstances is a lock on a table released?

Question 18:

Are there circumstances under which an INSERT LOW_PRIORITY statement might never be performed?

Question 19:

What table or tables will the following statements lock, if any?

```
mysql> LOCK TABLES City READ; LOCK TABLES Country WRITE;
```

Question 20:

You want to use INSERT to add data into a table, but you suspect that the table is locked by a lock request of another client. You're using an interactive client (for example mysql), so you would have to wait for that lock to be released before you can continue with your work. How can you solve this problem, and still insert the data?

Question 21:

According to the following session listing, it appears that the SELECT query took longer than two minutes to execute. What is the most probable reason for that?

```
mysql> INSERT DELAYED INTO City (ID, name) VALUES (20000, 'Delayne');
Query OK, 1 row affected (0.00 sec)
mysql> SELECT ID, name FROM City WHERE ID = 20000;
+-------+---------+
| ID    | name    |
+-------+---------+
| 20000 | Delayne |
+-------+---------+
1 row in set (2 min 5.61 sec)
```

Question 22:

Assume that you have the following tables in the project database:

```
mysql> SHOW TABLES;
+------------------+
| Tables_in_project |
+------------------+
| auth             |
| lang             |
| project          |
+------------------+
3 rows in set (0.00 sec)
```

You backed up all tables in that database as follows:

```
shell> mysqldump project --tab=/tmp
```

Someone accidentally dropped that database. Using mysql (and no other program), what statements do you have to issue to restore the database and its tables?

Question 23:

Which backup programs and backup strategies require the server to be running, and which do not?

Question 24:

Which backup programs and backup strategies work when used on the local host? Which can be used from a remote host?

Question 25:

What does the SQL statement BACKUP TABLE do?

Question 26:

How can you restore tables backed up with BACKUP TABLE? What limitations must you observe when using this restore method?

Question 27:

Assume that you want to back up all tables in the project database using mysqldump on the local host. You do not want to dump the table structure, just the data. The data should be stored in text files in the /tmp directory, with columns separated by tabs and records separated by \r\n. What command would you issue?

Question 28:

Assume that you've issued the following command to back up all table data in the project database:

```
shell> mysqldump --no-create-info --tab=/tmp --lines-terminated-by="\r\n" project
```

Could you use a similar command to back up all table data for multiple databases?

Question 29:

Assume that you've issued the following command to back up all table data in the project database:

```
shell> mysqldump --no-create-info --tab=/tmp --lines-terminated-by="\r\n" project
```

How would you restore the tables?

Question 30:

The test database contains tables named tbl1 and tbl2. Assume that you want to back up the data contained in the tables. The data should be written into text files in the /backup directory. In the text files, you want columns to be separated by commas and lines to be separated by DOS line endings (\r\n). What command do you issue? What will be the names of the resulting output files?

Question 31:

Assume that you've issued the following command to back up the data contained in the test database's tbl1 and tbl2 tables:

```
shell> mysqldump --tab=/backup --fields-terminated-by=,
         --lines-terminated-by="\r\n" test tbl1 tbl2
```

Can you use a similar, single command to back up the data of all databases on the server? If so, how?

Question 32:

What SQL statement would you use to update a table's index statistics?

Question 33:

What command-line program would you use to update a table's index statistics?

Question 34:

What is the effect of a table analysis?

Question 35:

What precautions should you observe when analyzing a table?

Question 36:

What does it mean to optimize a MyISAM table, and how would you do it?

Answers to Exercises

Answer 1:

Two methods for copying the `mytable` table to another server are shown here. Other methods are possible.

- To copy `mytable` directly, you have to make sure that the server (and any other program) doesn't access the table files, and that the table is entirely flushed to disk. This would be done by issuing these statements:

```
mysql> LOCK TABLES mytable READ;
mysql> FLUSH TABLES;
```

  Now, you can copy the table files (`mytable.frm`, `mytable.MYD`, and `mytable.MYI`) to the other server host. The location to copy them to would be the `test` directory in that server's data directory. Afterward, you have to unlock the table on the first server:

```
mysql> UNLOCK TABLES;
```

- Using `mysqldump`, you would issue this command:

```
shell> mysqldump test mytable > mytabledump.sql
```

  After that, you can copy `mytabledump.sql` to the other server host, and import it by issuing this statement:

```
shell> mysql test < mytabledump.sql
```

  This assumes that `mytabledump.sql` is located in the directory from which you invoke `mysql`.

See sections A.1.21, "LOCK TABLES," and A.1.16, "FLUSH TABLES."

Answer 2:

The `City` table is located in the `GuideProf` directory under the MySQL data directory, `C:\mysql\data`. To refer to that directory from within the `C:\mysql\bin` directory, you can use either the absolute pathname `C:\mysql\data\GuideProf` or the relative pathname `..\data\GuideProf`. The commands shown here use the latter.

To compress the `City` table, bring down the server, and then issue this command:

```
shell> myisampack ..\data\GuideProf\City.MYI
Compressing ..\data\GuideProf\City.MYD: (4079 records)
- Calculating statistics
- Compressing file
70.94%
Remember to run myisamchk -rq on compressed tables
```

As indicated by the last output line, you should now run `myisamchk` with the `--recover` (or `-r`) and `--quick` (or `-q`) options:

```
shell> myisamchk --recover --quick ..\data\GuideProf\City.MYI
- check key delete-chain
- check record delete-chain
- recovering (with sort) MyISAM-table '..\data\GuideProf\City.MYI'
Data records: 4079
- Fixing index 1
```

Now you can restart the server.

Answer 3:

The `City` table is located in the `GuideProf` directory under the MySQL data directory, `C:\mysql\data`. To refer to that directory from within the `C:\mysql\bin` directory, you can use either the absolute pathname `C:\mysql\data\GuideProf` or the relative pathname `..\data\GuideProf`. The commands shown here use the latter.

To verify that the table has actually been compressed, you could issue this command:

```
shell> mysql -e "SHOW TABLE STATUS LIKE 'City'" GuideProf
+------+--------+------------+------+----------------+-------------+-
| Name | Type   | Row_format | Rows | Avg_row_length | Data_length | ...
+------+--------+------------+------+----------------+-------------+-
| City | MyISAM | Compressed | 4079 |             19 |       79419 | ...
+------+--------+------------+------+----------------+-------------+-
```

See section A.1.43, "SHOW TABLE STATUS."

Answer 4:

You can read from a compressed table, but you can no longer modify it, as these examples show:

```
mysql> USE GuideProf;
mysql> INSERT INTO City (ID, name) VALUES (10000, 'Test City');
ERROR 1036: Table 'City' is read only
mysql> ALTER TABLE City ADD testcolumn INT;
ERROR 1036: Table 'City' is read only
```

See section A.1.1, "ALTER TABLE."

Answer 5:

The `City` table is located in the `GuideProf` directory under the MySQL data directory, `C:\mysql\data`. To refer to that directory from within the `C:\mysql\bin` directory, you can use either the absolute pathname `C:\mysql\data\GuideProf` or the relative pathname `..\data\GuideProf`. The commands shown here use the latter.

- To unpack the compressed table, use this command:

```
shell> myisamchk --unpack ..\data\GuideProf\City.MYI
- recovering (with keycache) MyISAM-table '..\data\GuideProf\City.MYI'
Data records: 4079
```

- There are also other ways to unpack the table. One alternative is to use `mysqldump` to dump the table, followed by `mysql` to reimport it, as shown here:

```
shell> mysqldump --opt GuideProf City > CityDump.sql
shell> mysql GuideProf < CityDump.sql
```

Another alternative is to execute these statements with `mysql`:

```
mysql> CREATE TABLE CityCopy TYPE=MyISAM SELECT * FROM City;
Query OK, 4079 rows affected (0.03 sec)
Records: 4079  Duplicates: 0  Warnings: 0
mysql> DROP TABLE City;
Query OK, 0 rows affected (0.01 sec)
mysql> ALTER TABLE CityCopy RENAME TO City;
Query OK, 0 rows affected (0.00 sec)
```

See sections A.1.9, "CREATE TABLE," A.1.1, "ALTER TABLE," and A.1.14, "DROP TABLE."

Answer 6:

To verify that the table has actually been uncompressed, use SHOW TABLE STATUS, as shown here:

```
shell> mysql -e "SHOW TABLE STATUS LIKE 'City'" GuideProf
+------+--------+------------+------+----------------+-------------+-
| Name | Type   | Row_format | Rows | Avg_row_length | Data_length | ...
+------+--------+------------+------+----------------+-------------+-
| City | MyISAM | Fixed      | 4079 |             67 |      273293 | ...
+------+--------+------------+------+----------------+-------------+-
```

See section A.1.43, "SHOW TABLE STATUS."

Answer 7:

Reasons to specify MAX_ROWS for a table are as follows:

- For a MyISAM table, specifying MAX_ROWS allows the server to make a better estimate of how large to make the table's internal row pointers. A large MAX_ROWS value is useful when you expect a table to become very large and to contain more rows than the default pointer size will allow. For a table that you know will remain small, a small MAX_ROWS value saves space because the row pointers can be smaller than the default size.

- MAX_ROWS can be used for a HEAP table to make sure that it doesn't grow unexpectedly large and use up all available memory.

See section A.1.9, "CREATE TABLE."

Answer 8:

By default, MySQL places the format, data, and index files for a MyISAM table under the data directory, in the database directory for the database that contains the table. There is no option for creating the format file anywhere else. It is always stored in the database directory. The datafile and index file can be placed elsewhere by using the table options DATA DIRECTORY='directory' and INDEX DIRECTORY='directory'. One restriction on these options is that directory must be a full pathname to the directory, not a relative path. Another is that these options work only on operating systems that support symlinks, and only when you have not started the server with the --skip-symlink option.

See section A.1.9, "CREATE TABLE."

Answer 9:

The server waits until free space becomes available.

Answer 10:

You acquired the READ lock, so you can read data from the table:

```
mysql> LOCK TABLES City READ;
mysql> SELECT * FROM City LIMIT 1;
+----+-------+---------+----------+------------+
| ID | name  | Country | District | Population |
+----+-------+---------+----------+------------+
|  1 | Kabul | AFG     | Kabol    |    1780000 |
+----+-------+---------+----------+------------+
```

See section A.1.21, "LOCK TABLES."

Answer 11:

The READ lock that you acquired does not prevent other reads. All other clients can still read data from the table:

```
mysql> SELECT * FROM City limit 1;
+----+-------+---------+----------+------------+
| ID | name  | Country | District | Population |
+----+-------+---------+----------+------------+
|  1 | Kabul | AFG     | Kabol    |    1780000 |
+----+-------+---------+----------+------------+
```

See section A.1.21, "LOCK TABLES."

Answer 12:

Trying to insert data after acquiring a READ lock will result in an error:

```
mysql> INSERT INTO City (ID, name) VALUES (10000, 'Test City');
ERROR 1099: Table 'City' was locked with a READ lock and can't be updated
```

See section A.1.21, "LOCK TABLES."

Answer 13:

When you are holding a READ lock on a table, attempts by any other client to insert data into the table result in that client waiting for the lock to be released:

```
mysql> INSERT INTO City (ID, name) VALUES (10000, 'Test City');
(nothing happens here until you release the lock)
```

See section A.1.21, "LOCK TABLES."

Answer 14:

Only the client that acquired the lock can release it. One way to do so is with the UNLOCK TABLES statement:

```
mysql> UNLOCK TABLES;
Query OK, 0 rows affected
```

The lock also is released if the client acquires another lock with LOCK TABLES, closes the connection, or is aborted. (An administrator who has appropriate privileges can abort the connection by using a KILL statement.)

See sections A.1.21, "LOCK TABLES," and A.1.49, "UNLOCK TABLES."

Answer 15:

When the lock is released, the INSERT statement of connection 2099 will be executed.

See sections A.1.21, "LOCK TABLES," and A.1.49, "UNLOCK TABLES."

Answer 16:

The WRITE lock request of connection 2098 waits until connection 2099 releases the READ lock.

See sections A.1.21, "LOCK TABLES," and A.1.49, "UNLOCK TABLES."

Answer 17:

A lock can be released several ways:

- When the client that acquired the lock issues an UNLOCK TABLES statement.
- When the client that acquired the lock issues another LOCK TABLES statement (no matter whether for the same or different tables).

- When the client that acquired the lock is terminated (either by ending it normally, or when the client is killed by another client).
- An administrator can kill a client connection. This releases locks held by the client.

See sections A.1.21, "LOCK TABLES," and A.1.49, "UNLOCK TABLES."

Answer 18:

Yes. An INSERT LOW_PRIORITY statement waits until there are no read requests or normal-priority update requests in progress or pending on that table. This includes new requests that arrive while the INSERT LOW_PRIORITY is waiting. If a server is so busy that there is never a time when no read requests are in progress or pending, the INSERT LOW_PRIORITY might wait forever.

See sections A.1.21, "LOCK TABLES," and A.1.18, "INSERT."

Answer 19:

The first statement locks table City, but the lock is released immediately with the next lock request. As a result, table Country will be locked for read and write requests by other clients. If you want to lock both tables at the same time, you have to issue this statement:

```
mysql> LOCK TABLES City READ, Country WRITE;
```

See section A.1.21, "LOCK TABLES."

Answer 20:

You can insert the data using an INSERT DELAYED statement. This allows you to proceed immediately. The rows to be inserted will be buffered by the server and added to the table when it becomes free.

See section A.1.18, "INSERT."

Answer 21:

Most probably, there was a lock on that table obtained by another client. Only when that other client released its lock was the INSERT DELAYED statement performed. After that, the SELECT statement was performed. With no further information given, you can assume that the lock was in effect for at least two minutes and five seconds.

See sections A.1.21, "LOCK TABLES," A.1.18, "INSERT," and A.1.29, "SELECT."

Answer 22:

First, re-create the database:

```
mysql> CREATE DATABASE project;
Query OK, 1 row affected (0.00 sec)
```

Next, re-create the tables using the `.sql` files stored in /tmp:

```
mysql> SOURCE /tmp/auth.sql;
Query OK, 0 rows affected (0.00 sec)
mysql> SOURCE /tmp/lang.sql;
Query OK, 0 rows affected (0.00 sec)
mysql> SOURCE /tmp/project.sql;
Query OK, 0 rows affected (0.00 sec)
mysql> SHOW TABLES;
+-------------------+
| Tables_in_project |
+-------------------+
| auth              |
| lang              |
| project           |
+-------------------+
3 rows in set (0.00 sec)
```

Finally, load the data stored in the `.txt` files in /tmp:

```
mysql> LOAD DATA INFILE '/tmp/auth.txt' INTO TABLE auth;
Query OK, 1 row affected (0.02 sec)
Records: 1  Deleted: 0  Skipped: 0  Warnings: 0
mysql> LOAD DATA INFILE '/tmp/lang.txt' INTO TABLE lang;
Query OK, 9 rows affected (0.00 sec)
Records: 9  Deleted: 0  Skipped: 0  Warnings: 0
mysql> LOAD DATA INFILE '/tmp/project.txt' INTO TABLE project;
Query OK, 6 rows affected (0.00 sec)
Records: 6  Deleted: 0  Skipped: 0  Warnings: 0
```

By default, `mysqldump` used the same column and line formatting options as the `LOAD DATA INFILE` statement, so you don't have to specify those explicitly when reloading the tables.

See sections A.1.7, "CREATE DATABASE," A.1.44, "SHOW TABLES," and A.1.20, "LOAD DATA INFILE."

Answer 23:

- To back up data, you can use `mysql` to issue these SQL statements:
  - BACKUP TABLE
  - SELECT … INTO OUTFILE

  `mysql` requires the server to be running.
- You can also use `mysqldump` to back up data. The server must be running.
- Another way to perform data backup is to use the Perl script `mysqlhotcopy`. The server must be running for `mysqlhotcopy` to work. In addition, the script requires the Perl DBI module to be installed.

- If the server is *not* running, the only way to back up a MyISAM table is to copy its `.frm`, `.MYD`, and `.MYI` files directly.

See sections A.1.3, "BACKUP TABLE," and A.1.29, "SELECT."

Answer 24:

- `mysql`: To back up data, you can run the BACKUP TABLE or SELECT ... INTO OUTFILE statements under `mysql`. The statements can be run from any client host that can connect to the server, so you don't necessarily have to connect from the local host. The backup files, however, will always be located on the server host. This means that you must have the FILE privilege to perform backup operations using `mysql`.
- `mysqldump`: To back up data, you can also run `mysqldump`, from either a local client or from a remote client. The first of the following commands performs a dump that connects to the local server. The second command connects to a remote server.

```
shell> mysqldump test > dump_db_test.sql
shell> mysqldump test -h remote_host -u username -p > dump_db_test.sql
```

In both cases, the backup file is created on the client host where `mysqldump` is invoked.

- `mysqlhotcopy`: To back up data, you can also run the Perl script `mysqlhotcopy`. To do so, you must ensure that the script is run on the same host as the server (`mysqlhotcopy` can only run on the same host as the server itself).

Answer 25:

BACKUP TABLE performs a number of operations:

1. First, it acquires a READ lock on the table or tables to be copied.
2. It flushes any pending table changes to disk.
3. It copies the `.frm` and `.MYD` files of the specified MyISAM tables to the specified directory.
4. Finally, it releases the READ lock.

See section A.1.3, "BACKUP TABLE."

Answer 26:

To restore tables backed up with the BACKUP TABLE statement, you would use the RESTORE TABLE statement. Before doing so, you must ensure that any tables you want to restore do not already exist. Otherwise, the restore operation will fail. RESTORE TABLE uses the `.frm` and `.MYD` files to re-create the table, then rebuilds the indexes to re-create the `.MYI` index file.

See sections A.1.3, "BACKUP TABLE," and A.1.26, "RESTORE TABLE."

Answer 27:

To dump the table data to text files, you can use the `--tab` option to `mysqldump`. By default, this produces output files in which columns are separated by tabs and records are separated by \n. The tab separators match the requirements stated but the record separators do not, so a `--lines-terminated-by` option is needed. By default, `mysqldump` will also produce SQL statements that can be used to re-create table structures. With the `--tab` option, this information will be stored in `.sql` files. To prevent creation of these files, use the `--no-create-info` option. To dump only the table data in the format required, you would issue this command:

```
shell> mysqldump --no-create-info --tab=/tmp --lines-terminated-by="\r\n" project
```

Answer 28:

No, this is not possible. The `--tab` option can be used to dump only a single database. To back up multiple databases using this method, it's necessary to issue multiple `mysqldump` commands.

Answer 29:

To restore tables that have been backed up with the `--tab` option to `mysqldump`, you can use LOAD DATA INFILE. Because the records are terminated by \r\n, it will be necessary to use a LINES TERMINATED BY option. LOAD DATA INFILE must be issued for every table that was backed up. For example, to restore a table `table_1`, you would issue this statement:

```
mysql> LOAD DATA INFILE '/tmp/table_1.txt' INTO TABLE table_1 LINES TERMINATED BY
'\r\n';
```

See section A.1.20, "LOAD DATA INFILE."

Answer 30:

To back up the data as stated, you would issue this command:

```
shell> mysqldump --tab=/backup --fields-terminated-by=,
        --lines-terminated-by="\r\n" test tbl1 tbl2
```

The resulting files will be named `tbl1.sql`, `tbl1.txt`, `tbl2.sql`, and `tbl2.txt`.

Answer 31:

`mysqldump` can back up multiple databases (or even all databases), but not when invoked with the `--tab` option. This option causes the output files for all tables to be written into a single directory. That would make it impossible to tell which database each table came from.

Answer 32:

Use ANALYZE TABLE to update a table's index statistics:

```
mysql> ANALYZE TABLE City;
+----------------+---------+----------+----------+
| Table          | Op      | Msg_type | Msg_text |
+----------------+---------+----------+----------+
| GuideProf.City | analyze | status   | OK       |
+----------------+---------+----------+----------+
```

See section A.1.2, "ANALYZE TABLE."

Answer 33:

To update a table's statistics from the command line, use either mysqlcheck or myisamchk:

```
shell> mysqlcheck --analyze world City
world.City                                      OK
shell> myisamchk --analyze c:\mysql\data\GuideProf\City.MYI
Checking MyISAM file: c:\mysql\data\GuideProf\City.MYI
Data records:    4083   Deleted blocks:      0
- check file-size
- check key delete-chain
- check record delete-chain
- check index reference
```

Answer 34:

The effect of analyzing a table is twofold: A check is performed on the table and the table's index statistics are updated. Analyzing can thus help the query optimizer better process joins involving the table.

Answer 35:

- When using the ANALYZE TABLE statement or the mysqlcheck program, there are no special precautions to consider. The server automatically locks the table before performing the analysis.

- Before using myisamchk --analyze, you must ensure that no other program can access the table to be analyzed. This could be done as follows:

```
mysql> LOCK TABLES City READ;
mysql> FLUSH TABLES;
```

Alternatively, stop the server so that it isn't running when you use myisamchk.

See sections A.1.2, "ANALYZE TABLE," A.1.21, "LOCK TABLES," and A.1.16, "FLUSH TABLES."

Answer 36:

Optimizing a MyISAM table means reclaiming unused space that results when rows are deleted from the table. Deleted rows can cause wasted space within a table, thus slowing down table reads. To optimize a MyISAM table, use the OPTIMIZE TABLE statement. For example:

```
mysql> OPTIMIZE TABLE City;
+----------------+----------+----------+---------------------------+
| Table          | Op       | Msg_type | Msg_text                  |
+----------------+----------+----------+---------------------------+
| GuideProf.City | optimize | status   | Table is already up to date |
+----------------+----------+----------+---------------------------+
```

You can also use mysqlcheck --optimize.

See section A.1.22, "OPTIMIZE TABLE."

15

InnoDB Tables

This chapter describes the InnoDB table type that is supported by the InnoDB storage engine. It covers the following topics:

- The InnoDB tablespace and log files
- InnoDB support for transactions
- Optimizations that apply to working with InnoDB tables
- How the InnoDB storage engine handles locking
- Backup and recovery options for InnoDB tables
- How to check and repair InnoDB tables
- InnoDB maintenance issues, such as how to configure the tablespace

Questions on the material in this chapter make up approximately 10% of the exam.

The InnoDB storage engine is one of the table handlers that MySQL provides. InnoDB was introduced to MySQL during the 3.23 release series and is a standard feature in binary distributions as of MySQL 4. It has several notable features:

- InnoDB supports transactions, with commit and rollback. It provides full ACID (atomicity, consistency, isolation, durability) compliance. Multi-versioning is used to isolate transactions from one another. If the MySQL server or the server host crashes, InnoDB performs automatic crash recovery.
- InnoDB manages contention for tables using multi-versioning and row-level locking. This provides good query concurrency even when clients are performing a mix of reads and writes.
- InnoDB supports foreign keys and referential integrity, including cascaded deletes and updates.
- Each InnoDB table is represented on disk by an `.frm` format file in the database directory, along with data and index information stored in a tablespace that is shared among InnoDB tables. The tablespace is stored in machine-independent format. It is implemented such that table sizes can exceed the maximum file size allowed by the filesystem.

To create an InnoDB table, nothing more is necessary than to add a TYPE option to the end of the CREATE TABLE statement:

```
CREATE TABLE t (i INT) TYPE = InnoDB;
```

To convert an existing table from some other type to InnoDB, use ALTER TABLE:

```
ALTER TABLE t TYPE = InnoDB;
```

15.1 The InnoDB Tablespace and Logs

InnoDB operates using two primary disk-based resources: A tablespace for storing table contents, and a set of log files for recording transaction activity.

Each InnoDB table has a format (.frm) file in the database directory of the database to which the table belongs. This is the same as tables managed by any other MySQL storage engine, such as MyISAM. However, InnoDB manages table contents (data rows and indexes) on disk differently than does the MyISAM engine. InnoDB uses a tablespace—one or more files that form a single logical storage area. All InnoDB tables are stored together within the tablespace. There are no table-specific datafiles or index files for InnoDB the way there are for MyISAM tables. The tablespace also contains a rollback segment. As transactions modify rows, undo log information is stored in the rollback segment. This information is used to roll back failed transactions.

Although logically InnoDB treats the tablespace as a single storage area, it can consist of one file or multiple files. Each file can be a regular file or a raw partition. The final file in the tablespace can be configured to be auto-extending, in which case InnoDB expands it automatically if the tablespace fills up. Because the tablespace is shared among all databases (and thus is not database-specific), tablespace files are stored by default in the server's data directory, not within a database directory.

In MySQL 4.1, multiple tablespaces can be configured. That capability is not covered here or on the certification exams at this time. A single tablespace is assumed throughout.

In addition to the tablespace, the InnoDB storage engine manages a set of InnoDB-specific log files that contain information about ongoing transactions. As a client performs a transaction, the changes that it makes are held in the InnoDB log. The more recent log contents are cached in memory. Normally, the cached log information is written and flushed to log files on disk at transaction commit time, though that may also occur earlier.

If a crash occurs while the tables are being modified, the log files are used for auto-recovery: When the MySQL server restarts, it reapplies the changes recorded in the logs, to ensure that the tables reflect all committed transactions.

For information about configuring the tablespace and log files, see section 15.7, "InnoDB Maintenance."

15.1.1 InnoDB Tablespace Portability

Binary portability for InnoDB means that you can directly copy the tablespace files from a MySQL server on one machine to another server on a different machine and the second server will be able to access the tablespace with no problems. Because all InnoDB tables managed by a server are stored together in the tablespace, portability of the tablespace is a function of whether all individual InnoDB tables are portable. If even one table is not, neither is the tablespace.

Two conditions that determine whether the InnoDB tablespace is binary portable from one host to another are similar to the conditions for MyISAM portability:

- Both machines must use two's-complement integer arithmetic.
- Both machines must use IEEE floating-point format, or else none of the InnoDB tables in the tablespace must contain any floating-point columns (FLOAT or DOUBLE).

In practice, these conditions pose little restriction. Two's-complement integer arithmetic and IEEE floating-point format are the norm on modern hardware.

A third condition is that you should use lowercase names for databases and tables. This is because InnoDB stores these names internally in lowercase on Windows. Using lowercase names allows binary portability between Windows and Unix.

The procedure for making a binary tablespace backup can be found in section 15.5, "InnoDB Backup and Recovery."

15.2 InnoDB Transaction Support

The InnoDB storage engine provides transactional capabilities. A transaction is a logical grouping of statements that is handled by the database server as a single unit. Either all the statements execute successfully to completion or all modifications made by the statements are discarded if an error occurs. Transactional systems often are described as being ACID compliant, where "ACID" stands for the following properties:

- *Atomic*. All the statements execute successfully or are canceled as a unit.
- *Consistent*. A database that is in a consistent state when a transaction begins is left in a consistent state by the transaction.
- *Isolated*. One transaction does not affect another.
- *Durable*. All the changes made by a transaction that completes successfully are recorded properly in the database. Changes are not lost.

InnoDB satisfies the conditions for ACID compliance.

15.2.1 Performing Transactions

Multiple clients may execute transactions concurrently, but any given client performs transactions serially, one after the other. The client determines when each of its transactions begins and ends by controlling its autocommit mode. MySQL initializes each client to begin with autocommit mode enabled. This causes each statement to be committed immediately. In transactional terms, this means that each statement is a separate transaction. To group together multiple statements as a single transaction so that they succeed or fail as a unit, autocommit mode must be disabled. There are two ways to do this:

- The first method is to disable autocommit mode explicitly:

```
SET AUTOCOMMIT = 0;
```

  With autocommit disabled, any following statements become part of the current transaction until you end it by issuing a COMMIT statement to accept the transaction and commit its effects to the database, or a ROLLBACK statement to discard the transaction's effects.

  When you disable autocommit explicitly, it remains disabled until you enable it again as follows:

```
SET AUTOCOMMIT = 1;
```

- The second method is to suspend the current autocommit mode by beginning a transaction explicitly. Any of the following statements begins a transaction:

```
BEGIN;
BEGIN WORK;
START TRANSACTION;
```

  After beginning a transaction with one of those three statements, autocommit remains disabled until you end the transaction by committing it or by rolling it back. The autocommit mode then reverts to the value it had prior to the start of the transaction.

If you disable autocommit explicitly, you perform transactions like this:

```
SET AUTOCOMMIT = 0;
... statements for transaction 1 ...
COMMIT;
... statements for transaction 2 ...
COMMIT;
...
```

If you suspend autocommit by using BEGIN, you perform transactions like this:

```
BEGIN;
... statements for transaction 1 ...
COMMIT;
BEGIN;
```

```
... statements for transaction 2 ...
COMMIT;
...
```

While autocommit mode is enabled, attempts to perform multiple-statement transactions are ineffective. Each statement is committed immediately, so COMMIT is superfluous and ROLLBACK has no effect.

Under some circumstances, the current transaction may end implicitly:

- If you issue any of the following statements, InnoDB implicitly commits the preceding uncommitted statements of the current transaction and begins a new transaction:

```
ALTER TABLE
BEGIN
CREATE INDEX
DROP DATABASE
DROP INDEX
DROP TABLE
RENAME TABLE
TRUNCATE TABLE
LOCK TABLES
UNLOCK TABLES
SET AUTOCOMMIT = 1
START TRANSACTION
```

Before MySQL 4.0.13, CREATE TABLE also causes an implicit commit if the binary update log is enabled.

- If a client connection closes while the client has a transaction pending, InnoDB rolls back the transaction implicitly. This occurs regardless of whether the connection closes normally or abnormally.

Currently, the server always initializes each client connection to begin with autocommit enabled. Modifications to the autocommit mode made by a client to its connection persist only to the end of the connection. If a client disconnects and reconnects, the second connection begins with autocommit enabled, regardless of its setting at the end of the first connection.

15.2.2 Transaction Isolation Levels

As mentioned earlier, multiple transactions may be executing concurrently within the server, one transaction per client. This has the potential to cause problems: If one client's transaction changes data, should transactions for other clients see those changes or should they be isolated from them? The transaction isolation level determines level of visibility between transactions—that is, the ways in which simultaneous transactions interact when accessing the same data. This section discusses the problems that can occur and how InnoDB implements isolation levels. Note that isolation level definitions vary among database servers, so the levels as implemented by InnoDB might not correspond exactly to levels as implemented in other database systems.

When multiple clients run transactions concurrently, three problems that may result are dirty reads, nonrepeatable reads, and phantoms. These occur under the following circumstances:

- A dirty read is a read by one transaction of uncommitted changes made by another. Suppose that transaction T1 modifies a row. If transaction T2 reads the row and sees the modification even though T1 has not committed it, that is a dirty read. One reason this is a problem is that if T1 rolls back, the change is undone but T2 does not know that.

- A nonrepeatable read occurs when a transaction performs the same retrieval twice but gets a different result each time. Suppose that T1 reads some rows and that T2 then changes some of those rows and commits the changes. If T1 sees the changes when it reads the rows again, it gets a different result; the initial read is nonrepeatable. This is a problem because T1 does not get a consistent result from the same query.

- A phantom is a row that appears where it was not visible before. Suppose that T1 and T2 begin, and T1 reads some rows. If T2 inserts a new row and T1 sees that row when it reads again, the row is a phantom.

InnoDB implements four isolation levels that control the visibility of changes made by one transaction to other concurrently executing transactions:

- READ UNCOMMITTED allows a transaction to see uncommitted changes made by other transactions. This isolation level allows dirty reads, nonrepeatable reads, and phantoms to occur.

- READ COMMITTED allows a transaction to see changes made by other transactions only if they've been committed. Uncommitted changes remain invisible. This isolation level allows nonrepeatable reads and phantoms to occur.

- REPEATABLE READ ensures that if a transaction issues the same SELECT twice, it gets the same result both times, regardless of committed or uncommitted changes made by other transactions. In other words, it gets a consistent result from different executions of the same query. In some database systems, REPEATABLE READ isolation level allows phantoms, such that if another transaction inserts new rows in the interval between the SELECT statements, the second SELECT will see them. This is not true for InnoDB; phantoms do not occur for the REPEATABLE READ level.

- SERIALIZABLE completely isolates the effects of one transaction from others. It is similar to REPEATABLE READ with the additional restriction that rows selected by one transaction cannot be changed by another until the first transaction finishes.

The essential difference between REPEATABLE READ and SERIALIZABLE is that with REPEATABLE READ, one transaction cannot modify rows another has modified, whereas with SERIALIZABLE, one transaction cannot modify rows if another has merely even read them.

Isolation levels are relevant only within the context of simultaneously executing transactions. After a given transaction has committed, its changes become visible to any transaction that begins after that.

InnoDB operates by default in REPEATABLE READ mode: Each transaction sees a view of the database that consists of all changes that have been committed by the time the transaction issues its first consistent read (such as a SELECT statement), plus any changes that it makes itself. It does not see any uncommitted changes, or committed changes made by transactions that begin later than itself.

InnoDB makes transaction isolation possible by multi-versioning. As transactions modify rows, InnoDB maintains isolation between them by maintaining multiple versions of the rows, and makes available to each transaction the appropriate version of the rows that it should see. Multiple versions of a row that has been changed can be derived from the current version of the row, plus the undo logs.

With multi-versioning, each transaction sees a view of the contents of the database that is appropriate for its isolation level. For example, with a level of REPEATABLE READ, the snapshot of the database that a transaction sees is the state of the database at its first read. One property of this isolation level is that it provides consistent reads: A given SELECT yields the same results when issued at different times during a transaction. The only changes the transaction sees are those it makes itself, not those made by other transactions. For READ COMMITTED, on the other hand, the behavior is slightly different. The view of the database that the transaction sees is updated at each read to take account of commits that have been made by other transactions since the previous read.

15.2.3 Setting the Isolation Level

To set the server's default transaction isolation level at startup time, use the --transaction-isolation option. The option value should be READ-UNCOMMITTED, READ-COMMITTED, REPEATABLE-READ, or SERIALIZABLE. For example, to put the server in READ COMMITTED mode by default, put these lines in an option file:

```
[mysqld]
transaction-isolation = READ-COMMITTED
```

The isolation level may also be set dynamically for a running server with the SET TRANSACTION ISOLATION LEVEL statement. The statement has three forms:

```
SET GLOBAL TRANSACTION ISOLATION LEVEL isolation_level;
SET SESSION TRANSACTION ISOLATION LEVEL isolation_level;
SET TRANSACTION ISOLATION LEVEL isolation_level;
```

The value of *isolation_level* should be READ UNCOMMITTED, READ COMMITTED, REPEATABLE READ, or SERIALIZABLE. The first form of the statement sets the server's global isolation level. It applies to all new client connections established from that point on. Existing connections are unaffected. The second form sets the isolation level for the current client connection only and applies to transactions the client performs from that point on. The third form sets the isolation level only for the current client's next transaction.

Only clients that have the SUPER privilege may use the first form of the statement. Any client may use the second and third forms of the statement; they affect only its own transactions, so no special privilege is required.

15.3 How InnoDB Uses Locks

This section describes how InnoDB uses locks internally and some query modifiers you can use to affect locking.

InnoDB's general locking properties are as follows:

- InnoDB does not need to set locks to achieve consistent reads because multi-versioning makes them unnecessary. Transactions that modify rows see their own versions of those rows, and the undo logs allow other transactions to see the original rows. Locking reads may be performed by adding locking modifiers to SELECT statements.

- When locks are necessary, InnoDB uses row-level locking. In conjunction with multi-versioning, this results in good query concurrency because a given table can be read and modified by different clients at the same time. Row-level concurrency properties are as follows:

  - Different clients can read the same rows simultaneously.

  - Different clients can modify different rows simultaneously.

  - Different clients cannot modify the same row at the same time. If one transaction modifies a row, other transactions cannot modify the same row until the first transaction completes. Other transactions cannot read the modified row, either, unless they are using the READ UNCOMMITTED isolation level. That is, they will see the original unmodified row.

- During the course of a transaction, InnoDB may acquire row locks as it discovers them to be necessary. However, it never escalates a lock (for example, by converting it to a page lock or table lock). This keeps lock contention to a minimum and improves concurrency.

- Deadlock can occur. Deadlock is a situation in which each of two transactions is waiting for the release of a lock that the other holds. For example, if two transactions each lock a different row, and then try to modify the row locked by the other, they can deadlock. Deadlock is possible because InnoDB does not acquire locks during a transaction until they are needed. When InnoDB detects a deadlock, it terminates and rolls back one of the deadlocking transactions. It tries to pick the transaction that has modified the smallest number of rows. If InnoDB does not detect deadlock, the deadlocked transactions eventually begin to time out and InnoDB rolls them back as they do.

InnoDB supports two locking modifiers that may be added to the end of SELECT statements. They acquire shared or exclusive locks and convert nonlocking reads into locking reads:

- With LOCK IN SHARE MODE, InnoDB locks each selected row with a shared lock. Other transactions can still read the selected rows, but cannot update or delete them until the first transaction releases the locks, which happens when the transaction finishes. Also, if the SELECT will select rows that have been modified in an uncommitted transaction, IN SHARE MODE will cause the SELECT to block until that transaction commits.

- With FOR UPDATE, InnoDB locks each selected row with an exclusive lock. This is useful if you intend to select and then modify a set of rows, because it prevents other transactions from reading or writing the rows until the first transaction releases the locks, which happens when the transaction finishes.

In the REPEATABLE READ isolation level, you can add LOCK IN SHARE MODE to SELECT operations to force other transactions to wait for your transaction if they want to modify the selected rows. This is similar to operating at the SERIALIZABLE isolation level, for which InnoDB implicitly adds LOCK IN SHARE MODE to SELECT statements that have no explicit locking modifier.

15.4 InnoDB-Specific Optimizations

Several strategies may be used with InnoDB to improve performance. Some of these can be used at the application level. Others are a result of the way that the database administrator configures InnoDB itself.

Application-level optimizations may be made in terms of how you design tables or issue queries:

- Use a primary key in each table, but make the key values as short as possible. InnoDB uses the primary key to locate the table rows. Other (secondary) indexes are keyed to the primary key values, which means that there is a level of indirection to find the table rows. Thus, shorter primary key values make for quicker lookups not only for queries that use the primary key, but also for queries that use secondary indexes. Secondary indexes will also take less space because each secondary index record contains a copy of the corresponding primary key value.

- Use VARCHAR columns rather than CHAR columns in InnoDB tables. The average amount of space used will be less, resulting in less disk I/O during query processing. (This behavior differs from that of MyISAM tables, which, due to their storage format, are faster for fixed-length columns than for variable-length columns.)

- Modifications made over the course of multiple statements should be grouped into a transaction whenever it makes sense to do so. This minimizes the number of flush operations that must be performed. For example, if you need to run 100 UPDATE statements that each modify a single row based on its primary key value, it's faster to run all the statements within a single transaction than to commit each one as soon as it executes. (A corollary to this principle is that you should avoid making updates with auto-commit mode on. That causes the effects of each statement to be flushed individually.)

Administrative optimizations are possible through the way you configure InnoDB. The following list briefly mentions some of the possibilities:

- To reduce page flushing from the buffer pool, configure InnoDB to use larger log files.
- Choose a log flushing method that best matches your goals. You can opt to guarantee durability (no loss of committed changes), or to get faster performance at the possible cost of losing approximately the last second's worth of committed changes in the event of a crash.
- Use raw disk partitions in the tablespace to avoid a level of filesystem-access overhead normally incurred when using regular files.

For information on the options used to configure these aspects of InnoDB operation, see section 15.7, "InnoDB Maintenance."

15.5 InnoDB Backup and Recovery

You can back up InnoDB tables in any of the following ways:

- Use mysqldump. This method generates backups as text files and can back up individual tables. mysqldump is covered in the "Core Study Guide," with additional discussion in section 14.4.1, "Using mysqldump."
- Use the SELECT … INTO OUTFILE statement to save the contents of a table into a file on the server host. More information about this statement is available in the "Core Study Guide."
- Use InnoDB Hot Backup (ibbackup). This is a commercial product available from Innobase Oy that can back up InnoDB tables while the server is running without disturbing normal database activity.
- Perform a binary backup operation that makes a complete InnoDB backup (a backup of all InnoDB tables in the tablespace). This method is based on making exact copies of all files that InnoDB uses to manage the tablespace. For a binary backup to be successful, the conditions for binary portability that are noted in section 15.1.1, "InnoDB Tablespace Portability," must be satisfied.

To make an InnoDB binary backup, use the following procedure:

1. Shut down the server for the duration of the copy operation. The tablespace must not be in use when copying the tablespace files.
2. Make sure that the server shut down without error. Binary InnoDB backups require a clean shutdown to be certain that the server has completed any pending transactions.
3. Make a copy of each of the following components:
   - The .frm file for each InnoDB table.
   - The tablespace files.
   - The InnoDB log files.
   - Any InnoDB configuration options, such as those stored in option files. The configuration options are required in case you need to restore the backup from scratch. In that case, you'll need to know how the tablespace and log files were created originally.
4. Restart the server.

To recover an InnoDB tablespace using a binary backup, stop the server, replace all the components that you made copies of during the backup procedure, and restart the server.

If you use a binary InnoDB backup to copy the InnoDB tablespace to another server, note that the necessity of copying the tablespace as a unit means you'll need to *replace* any existing tablespace on the destination server. You cannot add one tablespace to another using a binary backup.

An alternative to making a binary backup is to use mysqldump to dump table contents in text format. This technique can be useful for copying individual InnoDB tables from one server to another or if the conditions for binary portability are not satisfied. It can also be used to add tables from one tablespace to another: Run mysqldump to dump the tables into a text file, and then load the file into the destination server using mysql.

15.6 Checking and Repairing InnoDB Tables

To check InnoDB tables for problems, use the CHECK TABLE statement:

```
mysql> CHECK TABLE table_name;
```

Another way to check InnoDB tables is to use the mysqlcheck client program, which acts as a command-line interface to the CHECK TABLE statement:

```
shell> mysqlcheck db_name table_name
```

More detailed instructions for using mysqlcheck can be found in the "Core Study Guide."

If a table check indicates that an InnoDB table has problems, you should be able to restore the table to a consistent state by dumping it with `mysqldump`, dropping it, and re-creating it from the dump file.

In the event of a crash of the MySQL server or the host on which it runs, some InnoDB tables might need repairs. Normally, it suffices simply to restart the server because the InnoDB storage engine performs auto-recovery as part of its startup sequence. In rare cases, the server might not start up due to failure of InnoDB auto-recovery. If that happens, use the following procedure:

- Restart the server with the `--innodb_force_recovery` option set to a value in the range from 1 to 6. These values indicate increasing levels of caution in avoiding a crash, and increasing levels of tolerance for possible inconsistency in the recovered tables. A good value to start with is 4.

- When you start the server with `--innodb_force_recovery` set to a nonzero value, InnoDB treats the tablespace as read-only. Consequently, you should dump the InnoDB tables and then drop them while the option is in effect. Then restart the server without the `--innodb_force_recovery` option. When the server comes up, recover the InnoDB tables from the dump files.

- If the preceding steps fail, it's necessary to restore the InnoDB tables from a previous backup.

15.7 InnoDB Maintenance

InnoDB was introduced during MySQL 3.23 development and is a standard feature in binary distributions as of MySQL 4. That is, support for InnoDB is included in MySQL 4 unless you build it from source and explicitly exclude the InnoDB storage engine using the `--without-innodb` configuration option.

If a given MySQL server has the InnoDB storage engine compiled in, but you're sure that InnoDB tables will not be needed, you can disable InnoDB support at runtime by starting the server with the `--skip-innodb` option. Disabling InnoDB reduces the server's memory requirements because it need not allocate any InnoDB-related data structures. Disabling InnoDB also reduces disk requirements because no InnoDB tablespace or log files need be allocated.

A server that has InnoDB enabled uses a default configuration for its tablespace and log files unless you provide configuration options. This section describes how to configure InnoDB explicitly, and how to obtain status information from InnoDB while the server is running.

15.7.1 Configuring the InnoDB Tablespace

The InnoDB storage engine manages the contents for all InnoDB tables in its tablespace. The tablespace stores data rows and indexes. It also contains a rollback segment consisting of undo log records for ongoing transactions, in case they need to be rolled back. The tablespace has the following general characteristics:

- It can consist of one file or multiple files.

- Each component file of the tablespace can be a regular file or a raw partition (a device file). A given tablespace can include both types of files.

- Tablespace files can be on different filesystems or physical disk drives. One reason to place the files on multiple physical drives is to distribute InnoDB-related disk activity among them.

- The tablespace size can exceed the limits that the filesystem places on maximum file size. This is true for two reasons. First, the tablespace can consist of multiple files and thus can be larger than any single file. Second, the tablespace can include raw partitions, which are not bound by filesystem limits on maximum file size. InnoDB can use the full extent of partitions, which makes it easy to configure a very large tablespace.

- The last component of the tablespace can be auto-extending, with an optional limit on how large the file can grow.

If you don't specify any tablespace configuration options at all, InnoDB creates a tablespace consisting of a single 10MB auto-extending regular file named `ibdata1` in the data directory. To control the tablespace configuration explicitly, use the `innodb_data_file_path` and `innodb_data_home_dir` options:

- `innodb_data_file_path` names each of the files in the tablespace, their sizes, and possibly other optional information. The parts of each file specification are delimited by colons. If there are multiple files, separate their specifications by semicolons. The minimum combined size of the files is 10MB.

- `innodb_data_home_dir` specifies a pathname prefix that is prepended to the pathname of each file named by `innodb_data_file_path`. By default, tablespace files are assumed to be located in the data directory. You can set the home directory to the empty value if you want filenames in `innodb_data_file_path` to be treated as absolute pathnames. This is useful when you want to place tablespace files on different filesystems or if you want to use raw partitions.

Normally, you place the settings for these options in an option file to make sure that the server uses the same tablespace configuration each time it starts. The following examples show various ways to set up an InnoDB tablespace:

- A tablespace consisting of a single 100MB file named `innodata1` located in the data directory:

```
[mysqld]
innodb_data_file_path = innodata1:100M
```

It's unnecessary to specify a value for the `innodb_data_home_dir` option in this case because the data directory is its default value.

- A tablespace like that in the previous example, except that the file is auto-extending:
  ```
  [mysqld]
  innodb_data_file_path = innodata1:100M:autoextend
  ```

- A tablespace like that in the previous example, but with a limit of 500MB on the size to which the auto-extending file may grow:
  ```
  [mysqld]
  innodb_data_file_path = innodata1:100M:autoextend:max:500M
  ```

- A tablespace consisting of two 500MB files named `innodata1` and `innodata2` located in the data directory:
  ```
  [mysqld]
  innodb_data_file_path = innodata1:500M;innodata2:500M
  ```

- A tablespace like that in the previous example, but with the files stored under the `E:\innodb` directory rather than in the data directory.
  ```
  [mysqld]
  innodb_data_home_dir = E:/innodb
  innodb_data_file_path = innodata1:500M;innodata2:500M
  ```

  Note that backslashes in Windows pathnames are written as forward slashes in option files.

- A tablespace consisting of two files stored on different filesystems. Here the home directory is set to an empty value so that the file specifications can be given as absolute pathnames on different filesystems:
  ```
  [mysqld]
  innodb_data_home_dir =
  innodb_data_file_path = E:/innodata1:500M;D:/innodata2:500M
  ```

When you first configure the tablespace, any regular files named by the configuration options must not exist. InnoDB will create and initialize them when you start the server.

Any raw partitions named in the configuration must exist but must have the modifier `newraw` listed after the size in the file specification. `newraw` tells InnoDB to initialize the partition when the server starts up. New partitions are treated as read-only after initialization. After InnoDB initializes the tablespace, stop the server, change `newraw` to `raw` in the partition specification, and restart the server. For example, to use a 10GB Unix partition named `/dev/hdc6`, begin with a configuration like this:

```
[mysqld]
innodb_data_home_dir =
innodb_data_file_path = /dev/hdc6:10Gnewraw
```

Start the server and let InnoDB initialize the tablespace. Then tell the server to shut down and change the configuration from `newraw` to `raw`:

```
[mysqld]
innodb_data_home_dir =
innodb_data_file_path = /dev/hdc6:10Graw
```

Then restart the server.

In MySQL 4.0, InnoDB does not support the use of partitions (drives) in the tablespace for Windows. That capability is added in MySQL 4.1, but it not covered here.

15.7.2 Configuring InnoDB Buffers and Logs

InnoDB uses a buffer pool to hold information read from InnoDB tables. The buffer pool serves to reduce disk I/O for information that is frequently accessed, and a larger buffer more effectively achieves this goal. To change the size of the buffer pool, set the `innodb_buffer_pool_size` option. Its default value is 8MB. If your machine has the memory available, you can set the value much higher.

The InnoDB storage engine logs information about current transactions in a memory buffer. When a transaction commits or rolls back, the log buffer is flushed to disk. If the log buffer is small, it might fill up before the end of the transaction, requiring a flush to the log file before the outcome of the transaction is known. For a committed transaction, this results in multiple disk operations rather than one. For a rolled back transaction, it results in writes that, with a larger buffer, would not need to have been made at all. To set the size of the log buffer, use the `innodb_log_buffer_size` option. The default value is 1MB. Typical values range from 1MB to 8MB. Values larger than 8MB are of no benefit.

By default, InnoDB creates two 5MB log files in the data directory named `ib_logfile0` and `ib_logfile1`. To configure the InnoDB log files explicitly, use the `innodb_log_files_in_group` and `innodb_log_file_size` options. The first controls how many log files InnoDB uses and the second how big each file is. For example, to use three log files of 50MB each, configure the log like this:

```
[mysqld]
innodb_log_files_in_group = 3
innodb_log_file_size = 50M
```

The product of the two values is the total size of the InnoDB log files. Information is logged in circular fashion, with old information at the front of the log being overwritten when the log fills up. However, the log entries cannot be overwritten if the changes they refer to have not yet been recorded in the tablespace. Consequently, a larger log allows InnoDB to run longer without having to force changes to be applied to the tablespace on disk.

The `innodb_flush_log_at_trx_commit` setting affects how InnoDB transfers log information from the log buffer in memory to the log files on disk. The buffer contains information about committed transactions, so it is important that it be written properly. However, it is one thing to perform a write operation, and another to make sure that the operating system actually has written the information to disk. Operating systems typically buffer writes in the filesystem cache briefly and do not actually perform the write to disk immediately. To ensure that buffered information has been recorded on disk, InnoDB must perform a write operation to initiate a disk transfer *and* a flush operation to force the transfer to complete.

InnoDB tries to flush the log approximately once a second in any case, but the `innodb_flush_log_at_trx_commit` option can be set to determine how log writing and flushing occurs in addition. The setting of this option is directly related to the ACID durability property and to performance as follows:

- If you set `innodb_flush_log_at_trx_commit` to 1, changes are written from the log buffer to the log file and the log file is flushed to disk for each commit. This guarantees that the changes will not be lost even in the event of a crash. This is the safest setting, and is also the required setting if you need ACID durability. However, this setting also produces slowest performance.

- A setting of 0 causes the log file to be written and flushed to disk approximately once a second, but not after each commit. On a busy system, this can reduce log-related disk activity significantly, but in the event of a crash can result in a loss of about a second's worth of committed changes.

- A setting of 2 causes the log buffer to be written to the log file after each commit, but file writes are flushed to disk approximately once a second. This is somewhat slower than a setting of 0. However, the committed changes will not be lost if it is only the MySQL server that crashes and not the operating system or server host. The reason for this is that if the machine continues to run, the changes written to the log file will be in the filesystem cache and eventually will be flushed normally.

The tradeoff controlled by the `innodb_flush_log_at_trx_commit` setting therefore is between durability and performance. If ACID durability is required, a setting of 1 is necessary. If a slight risk to durability is acceptable to achieve better performance, a value of 0 or 2 may be used.

15.7.3 Monitoring InnoDB

You can ask the InnoDB storage engine to provide information about itself by means of SHOW statements.

SHOW INNODB STATUS requires the SUPER privilege and displays extensive information about InnoDB's operation:

```
mysql> SHOW INNODB STATUS\G
*************************** 1. row ***************************
Status:
=====================================
030914 17:44:57 INNODB MONITOR OUTPUT
=====================================
Per second averages calculated from the last 35 seconds
----------
SEMAPHORES
----------
OS WAIT ARRAY INFO: reservation count 65, signal count 65
Mutex spin waits 1487, rounds 28720, OS waits 51
RW-shared spins 28, OS waits 13; RW-excl spins 1, OS waits 1
------------
TRANSACTIONS
------------
Trx id counter 0 31923
Purge done for trx's n:o < 0 21287 undo n:o < 0 0
Total number of lock structs in row lock hash table 0
LIST OF TRANSACTIONS FOR EACH SESSION:
--------
FILE I/O
--------
I/O thread 0 state: waiting for i/o request
I/O thread 1 state: waiting for i/o request
I/O thread 2 state: waiting for i/o request
I/O thread 3 state: waiting for i/o request
Pending normal aio reads: 0, aio writes: 0,
 ibuf aio reads: 0, log i/o's: 0, sync i/o's: 0
Pending flushes (fsync) log: 0; buffer pool: 0
77 OS file reads, 10959 OS file writes, 5620 OS fsyncs
0.00 reads/s, 0 avg bytes/read, 83.20 writes/s, 41.88 fsyncs/s
-------------------------------------
INSERT BUFFER AND ADAPTIVE HASH INDEX
-------------------------------------
Ibuf for space 0: size 1, free list len 0, seg size 2,
0 inserts, 0 merged recs, 0 merges
Hash table size 34679, used cells 1, node heap has 1 buffer(s)
6.06 hash searches/s, 36.68 non-hash searches/s
---
LOG
---
Log sequence number 0 1520665
Log flushed up to   0 1520665
Last checkpoint at  0 1520665
0 pending log writes, 0 pending chkp writes
```

```
10892 log i/o's done, 82.80 log i/o's/second
----------------------
BUFFER POOL AND MEMORY
----------------------
Total memory allocated 18373254; in additional pool allocated 725632
Buffer pool size    512
Free buffers        447
Database pages      64
Modified db pages   0
Pending reads 0
Pending writes: LRU 0, flush list 0, single page 0
Pages read 22, created 42, written 141
0.00 reads/s, 0.46 creates/s, 1.49 writes/s
Buffer pool hit rate 1000 / 1000
--------------
ROW OPERATIONS
--------------
0 queries inside InnoDB, 0 queries in queue
Main thread id 10836480, state: waiting for server activity
Number of rows inserted 5305, updated 3, deleted 0, read 10
41.08 inserts/s, 0.00 updates/s, 0.00 deletes/s, 0.00 reads/s
---------------------------
END OF INNODB MONITOR OUTPUT
============================
```

SHOW TABLE STATUS, when used with any InnoDB table, displays in the Comment field of the output the approximate amount of free space available in the InnoDB tablespace:

```
mysql> SHOW TABLE STATUS LIKE 'CountryList'\G
*************************** 1. row ***************************
           Name: CountryList
           Type: InnoDB
     Row_format: Fixed
           Rows: 171
 Avg_row_length: 287
    Data_length: 49152
Max_data_length: NULL
   Index_length: 0
      Data_free: 0
 Auto_increment: NULL
    Create_time: NULL
    Update_time: NULL
     Check_time: NULL
 Create_options:
        Comment: InnoDB free: 13312 kB
```

15.8 Exercises

Question 1:

Is the following statement about the InnoDB storage engine true or false?

The InnoDB storage engine keeps table data and indexes in a tablespace.

Question 2:

Is the following statement about the InnoDB storage engine true or false?

The InnoDB storage engine keeps table definitions in `.frm` files.

Question 3:

Is the following statement about the InnoDB storage engine true or false?

The InnoDB storage engine can use compressed tables.

Question 4:

Is the following statement about the InnoDB storage engine true or false?

The InnoDB storage engine has its own error log.

Question 5:

Is the following statement about the InnoDB storage engine true or false?

The InnoDB storage engine uses both its own log files and the MySQL binary log (if enabled).

Question 6:

Is the following statement about the InnoDB storage engine true or false?

The InnoDB storage engine is multi-versioned, which means that different transactions use different versions of the data.

Question 7:

Is the following statement about the InnoDB storage engine true or false?

The InnoDB storage engine is multi-versioned, which means that all versions of InnoDB can use the same datafiles.

Question 8:

InnoDB tablespace files are stored in a format that is machine independent and can be copied from one machine to another as long as certain conditions are met for both machines. Which of the following conditions must be true for the InnoDB tablespace to be machine independent?

    a. Both machines must run under the same operating system.

    b. You should create databases and tables using lowercase names.

    c. The operating systems on both machines must use the same line-ending sequence. This is why you can't copy an InnoDB tablespace from a Windows machine (where lines end with \r\n) to a Mac OS X machine (where lines end with \r).

    d. Both machines must use two's-complement integer arithmetic.

    e. Both machines must have processors from the same family, such as Intel 586.

    f. Both machines must use IEEE floating-point format, or else none of the InnoDB tables in the tablespace must contain any floating-point columns (FLOAT or DOUBLE).

Question 9:

Is the following statement about the InnoDB storage engine true or false?

Deadlock can occur with the InnoDB storage engine, unlike with the MyISAM storage engine.

Question 10:

Is the following statement about the InnoDB storage engine true or false?

The InnoDB storage engine uses row-level locking, which provides better query concurrency than page-level or table-level locking and gives better performance in environments where there are many reads and writes at the same time.

Question 11:

Is the following statement about the InnoDB storage engine true or false?

The SELECT ... FOR UPDATE SQL statement makes sense for a transactional storage engine like InnoDB, but not for a non-transactional storage engine like MyISAM.

Question 12:

Is the following statement about the InnoDB storage engine true or false?

SELECT ... LIMIT is a MySQL extension to standard SQL that cannot be used with the InnoDB storage engine.

Question 13:

What is the effect of setting the innodb_flush_log_at_trx_commit option to 1 or 0?

Question 14:

Where would you set the innodb_flush_log_at_trx_commit option? What will you have to do after setting it to cause it to take effect?

Question 15:

By default, an InnoDB tablespace is stored in a single regular file named ibdata1 in the MySQL data directory, but you can configure the tablespace to have more than one component by setting the innodb_data_file_path option in the [mysqld] section of a MySQL option file. What other kind of file can you use in a tablespace, and what would be the advantage of not using a regular file?

Question 16:

When creating an InnoDB table, how do you control which tablespace file InnoDB will use for storing that table's contents?

Question 17:

When specifying a tablespace file in a MySQL option file, you normally indicate a fixed size for it (for example, ibdata2:100M). What happens when all tablespace files are full? What could you do to make tablespace files dynamic? Give an example how you would do that.

Question 18:

For an auto-extending tablespace file, how can you prevent it from expanding to use all available space on the filesystem where it is located?

Question 19:

With InnoDB, you can create tables that exceed filesystem limits on maximum file size. Why is that so? Give an example.

Question 20:

Can an InnoDB tablespace be distributed across different filesystems?

Question 21:

Can you have a tablespace that uses regular files and raw partitions (device files) at the same time?

Question 22:

How can you view status information about InnoDB?

Question 23:

How can you check the amount of free space available in the InnoDB tablespace?

Question 24:

Is the following statement about the InnoDB rollback mechanism true or false?

InnoDB uses information in its log files to perform rollbacks.

Question 25:

Is the following comment about the InnoDB rollback mechanism true or false?

InnoDB uses a data structure called the rollback segment in the InnoDB tablespace to store transaction undo information. If your operations will require large transactions, you must ensure that the tablespace is large enough to store that information.

Question 26:

Is the following statement about the InnoDB rollback mechanism true or false?

InnoDB uses the MySQL binary log in case it has to perform a rollback.

Question 27:

Provided that the conditions for InnoDB binary portability are met, you can make a binary copy of the InnoDB tables stored on one machine and copy them to another machine. To do so, what files do you need to copy?

Question 28:

Can you make a binary copy of the InnoDB tables stored on a machine while the server is running?

Question 29:

What methods can you use to copy InnoDB tables besides making a binary copy?

Question 30:

When the MySQL server or the server host crashes, what can you do to recover your InnoDB tables, other than restoring them from backups?

Question 31:

Which programs or SQL statements can you use to check InnoDB tables?

Question 32:

Which programs or SQL statements can you use to repair InnoDB tables?

Question 33:

How would you define "multi-versioning" as used by the InnoDB storage engine?

Question 34:

After the following transaction has been ended with ROLLBACK, what will the contents of the table t be? Why?

```
mysql> CREATE TABLE t (i INT) TYPE = InnoDB;
mysql> CREATE TABLE t2 (i INT) TYPE = InnoDB;
mysql> BEGIN WORK;
mysql> INSERT INTO t SET i = 1;
mysql> DROP TABLE t2;
mysql> ROLLBACK;
```

Question 35:

Consider the following session listing for one client:

```
mysql> BEGIN WORK;
mysql> SELECT * FROM trans;
```

```
Empty set
mysql> INSERT INTO trans VALUES (1),(2),(3);
Query OK, 3 rows affected
Records: 3  Duplicates: 0  Warnings: 0
```

Now, a second client issues the following statements:

```
mysql> SELECT * FROM trans;
```

How many rows will the second client see if both clients are running with an InnoDB isolation level of REPEATABLE READ?

Question 36:

Suppose that CountryList is an InnoDB table. Consider the following session listing:

```
mysql> SELECT COUNT(*) FROM CountryList;
+----------+
| COUNT(*) |
+----------+
|      192 |
+----------+
mysql> BEGIN WORK;
mysql> DELETE FROM CountryList;
mysql> SELECT COUNT(*) FROM CountryList;
+----------+
| COUNT(*) |
+----------+
|        0 |
+----------+
mysql> ROLLBACK;
```

How many rows will the table have after the ROLLBACK statement has been issued?

Question 37:

Consider the following InnoDB table and the session listing:

```
mysql> DESCRIBE CountryList;
+-----------+-------------+------+-----+---------+-------+
| Field     | Type        | Null | Key | Default | Extra |
+-----------+-------------+------+-----+---------+-------+
| Code      | char(3)     |      |     |         |       |
| Name      | char(52)    |      |     |         |       |
| IndepYear | smallint(6) | YES  |     | NULL    |       |
+-----------+-------------+------+-----+---------+-------+
mysql> SELECT * FROM CountryList;
Empty set (0.00 sec)
mysql> SET AUTOCOMMIT=0;
mysql> INSERT INTO CountryList VALUES('XXX','XLand',2003);
```

```
Query OK, 1 row affected (0.00 sec)
mysql> ROLLBACK;
```

What are the contents of CountryList after the ROLLBACK statement has been issued?

Question 38:

Consider the following InnoDB table and the session listing:

```
mysql> DESCRIBE CountryList;
+-----------+-------------+------+-----+---------+-------+
| Field     | Type        | Null | Key | Default | Extra |
+-----------+-------------+------+-----+---------+-------+
| Code      | char(3)     |      |     |         |       |
| Name      | char(52)    |      |     |         |       |
| IndepYear | smallint(6) | YES  |     | NULL    |       |
+-----------+-------------+------+-----+---------+-------+
mysql> SELECT * FROM CountryList;
Empty set (0.01 sec)
mysql> SET AUTOCOMMIT=0;
mysql> INSERT INTO CountryList VALUES('XXX','XLand',2003);
Query OK, 1 row affected (0.00 sec)
mysql> BEGIN WORK;
mysql> INSERT INTO CountryList VALUES('YYY','YLand',2004);
Query OK, 1 row affected (0.00 sec)
mysql> ROLLBACK;
```

What are the contents of CountryList after the ROLLBACK statement has been issued?

Question 39:

Consider the following InnoDB table and the session listing:

```
mysql> DESCRIBE CountryList;
+-----------+-------------+------+-----+---------+-------+
| Field     | Type        | Null | Key | Default | Extra |
+-----------+-------------+------+-----+---------+-------+
| Code      | char(3)     |      |     |         |       |
| Name      | char(52)    |      |     |         |       |
| IndepYear | smallint(6) | YES  |     | NULL    |       |
+-----------+-------------+------+-----+---------+-------+
mysql> SELECT * FROM CountryList;
Empty set (0.01 sec)
mysql> SET AUTOCOMMIT=0;
mysql> BEGIN WORK;
mysql> BEGIN WORK;
mysql> INSERT INTO CountryList VALUES('XXX','XLand',2003);
Query OK, 1 row affected (0.00 sec)
mysql> COMMIT;
```

```
mysql> INSERT INTO CountryList VALUES('YYY','YLand',2004);
Query OK, 1 row affected (0.00 sec)
mysql> ROLLBACK;
```

What are the contents of CountryList after the ROLLBACK statement has been issued?

Question 40:

Consider the following InnoDB table and the session listing:

```
mysql> DESCRIBE CountryList;
+-----------+-------------+------+-----+---------+-------+
| Field     | Type        | Null | Key | Default | Extra |
+-----------+-------------+------+-----+---------+-------+
| Code      | char(3)     |      |     |         |       |
| Name      | char(52)    |      |     |         |       |
| IndepYear | smallint(6) | YES  |     | NULL    |       |
+-----------+-------------+------+-----+---------+-------+
mysql> SELECT * FROM CountryList;
Empty set (0.01 sec)
mysql> SET AUTOCOMMIT=0;
mysql> INSERT INTO CountryList VALUES('XXX','XLand',2003);
Query OK, 1 row affected (0.00 sec)
mysql> INSERT INTO CountryList VALUES('YYY','YLand',2004);
Query OK, 1 row affected (0.00 sec)
mysql> ROLLBACK;
```

What are the contents of CountryList after the ROLLBACK statement has been issued?

Question 41:

Can you undo a ROLLBACK or a COMMIT? If so, how would you do that?

Question 42:

Suppose that a client is in the middle of performing a transaction. How does the server handle the transaction under the following conditions:

a. The client loses the connection before ending the transaction.

b. The client itself closes the connection before ending the transaction.

Answers to Exercises

Answer 1:

The statement is true.

Answer 2:

The statement is true.

Answer 3:

False. Compressed tables are a feature of the MyISAM storage engine, not of InnoDB.

Answer 4:

False. The MySQL error log is used to store errors, but it is not InnoDB-specific.

Answer 5:

True. InnoDB records transaction activity in the InnoDB log, and MySQL records statements for all table types in the binary log if they modify data.

Answer 6:

The statement is true.

Answer 7:

False. Multi-versioning means that different transactions use different versions of the data.

Answer 8:

The conditions for a machine-independent InnoDB tablespace are similar to those the MyISAM storage engine:

- Both machines must use two's-complement integer arithmetic.
- Both machines must use IEEE floating-point format, or else none of the InnoDB tables in the tablespace must contain any floating-point columns (FLOAT or DOUBLE).

In addition, you should create databases and tables using lowercase names.

The other conditions stated are not required for machine independence of the tablespace.

Answer 9:

True. Deadlock can occur with InnoDB because it uses row-level locking and it might determine that additional locks are necessary during the course of query processing. The MyISAM storage engine uses table-level locking; this cannot lead to deadlock because the server can determine all necessary locks before executing a query.

Answer 10:

True. When there are many reads and writes at the same time, row-level locking provides superior performance over table-level locking.

Answer 11:

True. SELECT ... FOR UPDATE is used to select a set of rows that you also intend to update. It makes sense for InnoDB, which allows individual rows to be locked. It does not make sense for the MyISAM storage engine, which locks the entire table even if only some of its rows will be updated.

See section A.1.29, "SELECT."

Answer 12:

False. `SELECT ... LIMIT` is a MySQL extension to standard SQL, but it works with all MySQL storage engines.

See section A.1.29, "`SELECT`."

Answer 13:

With an `innodb_flush_log_at_trx_commit` setting of 1, InnoDB writes and flushes the log buffer to the log files after each commit, making the transaction changes permanent in the database. With a setting of 0, InnoDB writes and flushes the log buffer about once a second, but not after each commit. It is possible with a setting of 0 for about a second's worth of committed transactions to be lost if a crash occurs.

See section A.4, "Server System Variables."

Answer 14:

The `innodb_flush_log_at_trx_commit` setting should be given in the [mysqld] section of the MySQL option file, or on the command line. Putting it in the option file is advisable because you don't have to remember it each time you start the server.

To cause the change to take effect, restart the server.

See section A.4, "`Server System Variables`."

Answer 15:

You can specify a raw partition (a device file) for an InnoDB tablespace. This will avoid a level of overhead normally incurred when using regular files in a filesystem. Raw partitions also are not bound by file size limits; InnoDB can use the entire partition.

See section A.4, "Server System Variables."

Answer 16:

You cannot control that. InnoDB is free to store table contents anywhere in the tablespace that it finds available space. It will use any or all files in the tablespace, if necessary.

Answer 17:

When there is no more free space in a fixed size tablespace, InnoDB rolls back the next statement that tries to add data. (The application is expected to detect this error and perform a `ROLLBACK` operation to roll back the entire transaction.) To avoid running out of space, you can add the `autoextend` attribute to the specification of the last file in the tablespace. For example, to create a tablespace from two 100MB files in the data directory and make the second one auto-extending, you could put something like this in your `C:\my.cnf` file:

```
[mysqld]
innodb_data_file_path = ibdata1:100M;ibdata2:100M:autoextend
```

Answer 18:

To limit the size to which InnoDB allows an auto-extending file to grow, add a `max` specifier after `autoextend`. To allow `ibdata2` to grow to a maximum of 500MB, configure the tablespace like this:

```
[mysqld]
innodb_data_file_path = ibdata1:100M;ibdata2:100M:autoextend:max:500M
```

You can also limit the maximum size of a tablespace file indirectly if your operating system provides a quota system. This involves procedures that are not covered in this study guide.

Answer 19:

You can create an InnoDB tablespace from multiple files if you want. Any regular file that is part of the tablespace is subject to the size limitations of the filesystem, but InnoDB will store tables using more than one file if necessary. For example, if your filesystem imposes a limit of 2GB as the maximum size of a file, you can create the InnoDB tablespace from multiple files that are 2GB in size. To store a table that has 5GB of data, InnoDB could then use three such files, thus exceeding the filesystem's limitation. Another way to overcome file size limits is to use raw partitions that InnoDB can access directly (that is, not through the filesystem). The size of a raw partition that InnoDB can handle in a tablespace is constrained only by InnoDB's internal size limit (four billion database pages, where each page is 16KB by default).

Answer 20:

Yes. For example, you could have one tablespace file on a ReiserFS filesystem partition, and another tablespace file on an ext3 filesystem partition.

Answer 21:

Yes. You can use a mix of regular files and raw partitions in the same tablespace.

Answer 22:

The SHOW INNODB STATUS statement displays information about the status of InnoDB. For example, you can issue the statement using the `mysql` client program:

```
mysql> SHOW INNODB STATUS\G
*************************** 1. row ***************************
Status:
=====================================
030322 20:54:14 INNODB MONITOR OUTPUT
=====================================
Per second averages calculated from the last 7 seconds
----------
SEMAPHORES
----------
OS WAIT ARRAY INFO: reservation count 11, signal count 11
```

```
Mutex spin waits 9, rounds 160, OS waits 1
RW-shared spins 18, OS waits 9; RW-excl spins 1, OS waits 1
------------
TRANSACTIONS
------------
Trx id counter 0 244754
Purge done for trx's n:o < 0 244747 undo n:o < 0 0
Total number of lock structs in row lock hash table 0
LIST OF TRANSACTIONS FOR EACH SESSION:
---TRANSACTION 0 244753, not started, OS thread id 1500
MySQL thread id 2, query id 881 localhost 127.0.0.1 superuser
SHOW INNODB STATUS
--------
FILE I/O
--------
I/O thread 0 state: wait Windows aio
I/O thread 1 state: wait Windows aio
I/O thread 2 state: wait Windows aio
I/O thread 3 state: wait Windows aio
Pending normal aio reads: 0, aio writes: 0,
...
```

(The output has been shortened.)

See section A.1.40, "SHOW INNODB STATUS."

Answer 23:

Issue a SHOW TABLE STATUS statement that includes output for at least one InnoDB table. The approximate amount of available space in the tablespace is displayed in the Comment field for every InnoDB table shown in the output. For example:

```
mysql> SHOW TABLE STATUS LIKE 't%';
+----------+--------+------------+-  -+-----------------------+
| Name     | Type   | Row_format | ... | Comment               |
+----------+--------+------------+-  -+-----------------------+
| t        | InnoDB | Fixed      | ... | InnoDB free: 179200 kB |
| test     | InnoDB | Fixed      | ... | InnoDB free: 179200 kB |
+----------+--------+------------+-  -+-----------------------+
```

See section A.1.43, "SHOW TABLE STATUS."

Answer 24:

False. InnoDB uses the rollback segment of the tablespace to perform rollbacks.

Answer 25:

True. The rollback segment contains undo information that is used to roll back transactions.

Answer 26:

False. With respect to InnoDB, the binary log is used to record only committed transactions. Transactions that roll back never appear in the binary log.

Answer 27:

To make a binary copy of the InnoDB tablespace, you need to copy:

- All tablespace files
- All InnoDB log files
- The .frm file for each of your InnoDB tables
- The InnoDB tablespace and log configuration information stored in your MySQL option file (that is, the settings for innodb_data_home_dir, innodb_data_file_path, and perhaps other InnoDB options)

Answer 28:

You cannot make a binary copy of InnoDB tables while the server is running. Unlike the options available when using MyISAM tables (lock the tables, flush them to disk, and then copy them), you must tell the server to stop before making a copy of InnoDB files. This is necessary to ensure that InnoDB has completed any pending transactions before the copy is made.

Answer 29:

You can also copy InnoDB tables with the following programs and SQL statements:

- mysqldump
- InnoDB Hot Backup (ibbackup)
- SELECT … INTO OUTFILE

See section A.1.29, "SELECT."

Answer 30:

Normally, you don't have to do anything after a crash except restart the server. InnoDB will recognize that it was not shut down correctly and perform an automatic recovery.

Answer 31:

To check an InnoDB table, you can use either of the following:

- The CHECK TABLE SQL statement
- The mysqlcheck program

See section A.1.5, "CHECK TABLE."

Answer 32:

To repair an InnoDB table, you cannot use REPAIR TABLE or the myisamchk program (which, as its name indicates, is for MyISAM tables only). The method to use is to dump the InnoDB table and then reload it.

See section A.1.24, "REPAIR TABLE."

Answer 33:

In InnoDB, multi-versioning means that as transactions modify rows, InnoDB maintains isolation between them by maintaining multiple versions of the rows, and makes available to each transaction the appropriate version of the rows that it should see.

Answer 34:

The table t will contain the row added by the INSERT statement:

```
mysql> SELECT i FROM t;
+------+
| i    |
+------+
|    1 |
+------+
```

The reason for this is that DROP TABLE is one of the statements that causes an implicit commit of preceding uncommitted statements in the transaction.

See section A.1.28, "ROLLBACK."

Answer 35:

The second client will see no rows because the first client has not issued a COMMIT. If the first client does issue a COMMIT, the second client then will see the three newly inserted rows.

See sections A.1.4, "BEGIN," A.1.6, "COMMIT," and A.1.29, "SELECT."

Answer 36:

The table will have its original 192 rows. ROLLBACK rolls back the DELETE statement.

Answer 37:

CountryList will contain no rows. Setting AUTOCOMMIT to 0 causes MySQL to treat the following SQL statements as a transaction. That transaction can be (and was) rolled back. To commit it instead of rolling it back, you would either have to issue COMMIT explicitly or issue another SQL statement that would commit the transaction implicitly.

See sections A.1.4, "BEGIN," A.1.6, "COMMIT," A.1.28, "ROLLBACK," and A.1.29, "SELECT."

Answer 38:

The table CountryList will contain the following row:

```
mysql> SELECT * FROM CountryList;
+------+-------+-----------+
| Code | Name  | IndepYear |
+------+-------+-----------+
| XXX  | XLand |      2003 |
+------+-------+-----------+
```

The BEGIN WORK statement causes an implicit commit of the preceding uncommitted INSERT statement, thus the first row is inserted. The second INSERT, however, is within a transaction that is rolled back.

See sections A.1.4, "BEGIN," and A.1.29, "SELECT."

Answer 39:

The table CountryList will contain the following row:

```
mysql> SELECT * FROM CountryList;
+------+-------+-----------+
| Code | Name  | IndepYear |
+------+-------+-----------+
| XXX  | XLand |      2003 |
+------+-------+-----------+
```

The explanation is *not* that the session has "nested" transactions. The second BEGIN WORK statement actually commits the first transaction implicitly and starts another transaction. COMMIT ends that transaction. Because the session is not running in autocommit mode, however, the next statement also begins a new transaction and it is unnecessary to issue an explicit BEGIN WORK. As a result, ROLLBACK rolls back the second INSERT statement.

See sections A.1.4, "BEGIN," A.1.6, "COMMIT," A.1.28, "ROLLBACK," and A.1.29, "SELECT."

Answer 40:

The table CountryList will contain no rows. In non-autocommit mode, everything is regarded as a transaction that is committed only when a COMMIT statement is issued. Thus, all statements are rolled back with ROLLBACK.

See sections A.1.4, "BEGIN," A.1.28, "ROLLBACK," and A.1.29, "SELECT."

Answer 41:

A ROLLBACK cannot be undone. You must repeat your transaction. A COMMIT also cannot be undone.

See sections A.1.6, "COMMIT," and A.1.28, "ROLLBACK."

Answer 42:

In either case (whether the connection closes abnormally or normally), the server treats connection termination as if the client had issued a ROLLBACK statement, so the transaction is rolled back.

16

Advanced Server Features

A MySQL administrator is responsible for several aspects of a MySQL installation that have not been addressed by the previous chapters. These include optimizing the server for better performance and managing multiple servers (either on the same host or, in a replication setup, on different hosts). This chapter covers the following topics:

- How to obtain and interpret information that the mysqld server provides about its configuration and operation
- Setting server system variables to tune its performance
- Using the query cache to increase performance of queries that clients issue repeatedly
- Running multiple servers on a single host
- Replicating databases from one server to another

Questions on the material in this chapter make up approximately 15% of the exam.

16.1 Interpreting mysqld Server Information

The main purpose of the MySQL server is to perform queries on behalf of clients that need access to databases. However, the server also keeps track of information that is useful to administrators, and you can ask the server to report this information by using various forms of the SHOW statement:

- SHOW VARIABLES displays server system variables. These indicate such things as directory locations, server capabilities, and sizes of caches and buffers. You can set system variables to control how the server operates. They can be set at server startup time, and many of them can be changed while the server is running. Also, the built-in value for many system variables can be specified at compile time if you build MySQL from source.
- SHOW STATUS displays server status variables that indicate the extent and types of activities the server is performing. These variables provide information such as how long the server has been running, number of queries processed, amount of network traffic, and

statistics about the query cache. You can use status information to assess how much of a load your server is processing and how well it is handling the load. This information provides useful feedback for assessing whether system variables should be changed to improve server performance.

This chapter discusses several representative system and status variables, but many more exist. The *MySQL Reference Manual* provides a full list of variable names and meanings.

16.1.1 Accessing Server Configuration Information

Many aspects of server operation are controlled by means of a set of system variables that reflect server configuration. To display these variables, use the SHOW VARIABLES statement:

```
mysql> SHOW VARIABLES;
+------------------------+------------------+
| Variable_name          | Value            |
+------------------------+------------------+
| back_log               | 50               |
| basedir                | /usr/local/mysql/ |
| binlog_cache_size      | 32768            |
| bulk_insert_buffer_size | 8388608         |
| character_set          | latin1           |
...
```

To display only those variables with names that match a given pattern, add a LIKE pattern-matching clause. The pattern is not case sensitive and may contain the % and _ wildcard pattern metacharacters. For example, the sizes for many of the server's buffers can be displayed as follows:

```
mysql> SHOW VARIABLES LIKE '%buffer_size';
+------------------------+---------+
| Variable_name          | Value   |
+------------------------+---------+
| bulk_insert_buffer_size | 8388608 |
| innodb_log_buffer_size | 1048576 |
| join_buffer_size       | 131072  |
| key_buffer_size        | 8388600 |
| myisam_sort_buffer_size | 8388608 |
| read_buffer_size       | 131072  |
| read_rnd_buffer_size   | 262144  |
| sort_buffer_size       | 2097144 |
+------------------------+---------+
```

If the pattern contains no metacharacters, the statement displays only the named variable:

```
mysql> SHOW VARIABLES LIKE 'datadir';
+---------------+-----------------------+
| Variable_name | Value                 |
+---------------+-----------------------+
| datadir       | /usr/local/mysql/data/ |
+---------------+-----------------------+
```

System variables can be displayed in other ways as well. mysqladmin variables provides command-line access to the complete list of system variables. The MySQLCC graphical client provides access to them in its server administration window. Both clients implement this capability by sending a SHOW VARIABLES statement to the server and displaying the results.

System variables can be set at server startup time using options on the command line or in option files. For example, on a Unix machine, you can put the following lines in the /etc/my.cnf option file to specify a data directory of /var/mysql/data and a key buffer size of 16MB:

```
[mysqld]
datadir = /var/mysql/data
key_buffer_size = 16M
```

Numeric option values can have a suffix letter of K, M, or G to indicate units of kilobytes, megabytes, or gigabytes, respectively.

Some server system variables are static and can *only* be set at startup time. (You need not know which for the exam.) For example, you can specify the data directory by means of a datadir startup option, but you cannot tell a server that's running to use a different data directory. Other variables are dynamic and can be changed while the server is running. For example, either of the following statements tells the server to change the size of the key buffer to 24MB:

```
mysql> SET GLOBAL key_buffer_size = 24*1024*1024;
mysql> SET @@global.key_buffer_size = 24*1024*1024;
```

With a SET statement, you cannot use a suffix of K, M, or G to indicate units for the value, but you can use an expression.

The key_buffer_size variable is (as the preceding statements indicate) a global server variable. Some variables exist in both global and session forms:

- The global form applies server-wide and is used to initialize the corresponding session variable for new client connections. Each client may subsequently change its own session variable value.

- The session form is session-specific and applies only to a particular client connection.

To set a global variable, you must have the SUPER privilege. Any client may set its own session variables.

An example of the type of variable that has both forms is table_type, which controls the default table type used for CREATE TABLE statements that do not specify a table type explicitly. The global table_type value is used to set the session table_type variable for each client when the client connects, but the client may change its session variable value to use a different default table type.

Session variables are set using syntax similar to that for setting global variables. For example, the default table type may be set either globally or only for the current connection using the following statements:

```
mysql> SET GLOBAL table_type = MyISAM;
mysql> SET @@global.table_type = MyISAM;

mysql> SET SESSION table_type = InnoDB;
mysql> SET @@session.table_type = InnoDB;
```

LOCAL is a synonym for SESSION. Also, if you do not indicate explicitly whether to set the global or session version of a variable, MySQL sets the session variable. Each of these statements sets the session table_type variable:

```
mysql> SET LOCAL table_type = InnoDB;
mysql> SET @@local.table_type = InnoDB;
mysql> SET table_type = InnoDB;
mysql> SET @@table_type = InnoDB;
```

To explicitly display global or session variable values, use SHOW GLOBAL VARIABLES or SHOW SESSION VARIABLES. Without GLOBAL or SESSION, the SHOW VARIABLES statement displays session values.

It's also possible to use SELECT to display the values of individual global or session values:

```
mysql> SELECT @@global.table_type, @@session.table_type;
+---------------------+----------------------+
| @@global.table_type | @@session.table_type |
+---------------------+----------------------+
| MYISAM              | INNODB               |
+---------------------+----------------------+
```

If @@ is not followed by a global or session scope specifier, the server returns the session variable if it exists and the global variable otherwise:

```
mysql> SELECT @@table_type;
+--------------+
| @@table_type |
+--------------+
| INNODB       |
+--------------+
```

The *MySQL Reference Manual* indicates which variables are dynamic and whether they have global or session forms.

16.1.2 Accessing Server Status Information

The server tracks many aspects of its own operation using a set of status variables. It makes the current values of these variables available through the SHOW STATUS statement, which you use much like SHOW VARIABLES:

```
mysql> SHOW STATUS;
+-------------------------------+------------+
| Variable_name                 | Value      |
+-------------------------------+------------+
| Aborted_clients               | 160        |
| Aborted_connects              | 6          |
| Bytes_received                | 34971464   |
| Bytes_sent                    | 43375040   |
| Com_admin_commands            | 15004      |
...
```

To display only those variables with names that match a given pattern, add a LIKE pattern-matching clause. The pattern is not case sensitive and may contain the % and _ wildcard pattern metacharacters. For example, all query cache status variable names begin with Qcache and may be displayed as follows:

```
mysql> SHOW STATUS LIKE 'qcache%';
+-----------------------+--------+
| Variable_name         | Value  |
+-----------------------+--------+
| Qcache_queries_in_cache | 360  |
| Qcache_inserts        | 12823  |
| Qcache_hits           | 21145  |
| Qcache_lowmem_prunes  | 584    |
| Qcache_not_cached     | 10899  |
| Qcache_free_memory    | 231008 |
| Qcache_free_blocks    | 98     |
| Qcache_total_blocks   | 861    |
+-----------------------+--------+
```

If the pattern contains no metacharacters, the statement displays only the named variable:

```
mysql> SHOW STATUS LIKE 'Uptime';
+---------------+---------+
| Variable_name | Value   |
+---------------+---------+
| Uptime        | 5084640 |
+---------------+---------+
```

Status variables may be obtained in other ways as well. `mysqladmin extended-status` provides command-line access to the complete list of status variables, and `mysqladmin status` displays a brief summary. The `MySQLCC` graphical client provides access to status information in its server administration window.

The following list indicates some of the ways you can use status information:

- Several status variables provide information about how many connections the server is handling, including the number of successful and unsuccessful connection attempts, and also whether successful connections terminate normally or abnormally. From these variables, you can determine the following information:

  - The total number of connection attempts (both successful and unsuccessful):

    `Connections`

  - The number of unsuccessful connection attempts:

    `Aborted_connects`

  - The number of successful connection attempts:

    `Connections - Aborted_connects`

  - The number of successful connections that terminated abnormally (for example, if the client died or the network went down):

    `Aborted_clients`

  - The number of successful connections that terminated normally:

    `Connections - Aborted_connects - Aborted_clients`

  - The number of clients currently connected to the server:

  `Threads_connected`

- The `Com` variables give you a breakdown of the number of queries the server has executed by statement type. You can see all these variables with the following statement:

  ```
  mysql> SHOW STATUS LIKE 'Com%';
  +-----------------------+-------+
  | Variable_name         | Value |
  +-----------------------+-------+
  | Com_admin_commands    | 0     |
  | Com_alter_table       | 2     |
  | Com_analyze           | 0     |
  | Com_backup_table      | 0     |
  | Com_begin             | 1     |
  | Com_change_db         | 629   |
  | Com_change_master     | 0     |
  ...
  ```

Or you can name specific variables:

```
mysql> SHOW STATUS LIKE 'Com_delete';
+---------------+-------+
| Variable_name | Value |
+---------------+-------+
| Com_delete    | 315   |
+---------------+-------+
mysql> SHOW STATUS LIKE 'Com_update';
+---------------+-------+
| Variable_name | Value |
+---------------+-------+
| Com_update    | 10691 |
+---------------+-------+
mysql> SHOW STATUS LIKE 'Com_select';
+---------------+-------+
| Variable_name | Value |
+---------------+-------+
| Com_select    | 23727 |
+---------------+-------+
```

`Com_select` does not include the number of queries processed using the query cache because those queries are not executed in the usual sense. Their results are pulled directly from the query cache without consulting any tables. The number of such queries is given by the `Qcache_hits` status variable. See section 16.3, "Using the Query Cache."

- The server caches open file descriptors when possible to avoid repeated file-opening operations, but a cache that's too small will not hold all the file descriptors you need. The `Opened_tables` variable indicates the number of times the server had to open files to access tables. It provides a measure of whether your table cache is large enough. See section 16.2, "Tuning Memory Parameters."

- `Bytes_received` and `Bytes_sent` show the amount of traffic sent over the network.

Status information can help you determine how smoothly the server is running or how well it's performing. Section 16.1.3, "Measuring Server Load," discusses some ways to use status variables to assess server load.

16.1.3 Measuring Server Load

Status information that the server provides can be used to assess how hard it's working:

- Several status variables displayed by `SHOW STATUS` provide load information. For example, `Questions` indicates the number of queries the server has processed and `Uptime` indicates the number of seconds the server has been running. Combining these, the ratio `Questions/Uptime` tells you how many queries per second the server has processed.

- `Slow_queries` indicates the number of queries that take a long time to process. Ideally, its value should increase slowly or not at all. If it increases quickly, you might have a problem with certain queries. The slow query log shows the text of slow queries and provides information about how long they took. Restart the server with the slow query log enabled, let it run for a while, and then take a look at the log to see which queries turn up there. You can use this log to identify queries that might need optimizing, as discussed in section 13.2.1, "Identifying Candidates for Query Analysis."

- `SHOW PROCESSLIST` displays information about the activity of each currently connected client. For example, the presence of a large number of blocked queries might indicate that another connection is running a query that's inefficient and should be examined to see whether it can be optimized. The `SHOW PROCESSLIST` statement always shows your own queries. If you have the `PROCESS` privilege, it also shows queries being run by other accounts.

- To get a concise report of the server's load status, invoke the `mysql` client program and use its `STATUS` (or `\s`) command to display a general snapshot of the current connection state. The last part of the output provides some information about the server load:

```
mysql> STATUS;
--------------
mysql  Ver 12.22 Distrib 4.0.16, for intel-linux (i686)

Connection id:          34816
Current database:       world
Current user:           myname@localhost
SSL:                    Not in use
Current pager:          stdout
Using outfile:          ' '
Server version:         4.0.16-log
Protocol version:       10
Connection:             Localhost via UNIX socket
Client characterset:    latin1
Server characterset:    latin1
UNIX socket:            /tmp/mysql.sock
Uptime:                 51 days 3 hours 40 min 37 sec

Threads: 4  Questions: 216232  Slow queries: 5  Opens: 652
Flush tables: 6  Open tables: 64  Queries per second avg: 0.050
--------------
```

For a discussion of ways to reduce server load by helping it work more effectively, see sections 16.2, "Tuning Memory Parameters," and 16.3, "Using the Query Cache."

16.1.4 Accessing Server Error Messages

The preceding sections describe how to obtain information that the server provides during the course of its normal operation. The server also provides diagnostic information about exceptional conditions in the form of error messages:

- On Windows, the server opens an error log file, which by default is named *host_name*.err in the data directory. (Older versions use the name mysql.err.) If you start the server from the command line with the --console option, it writes error information to the console window rather than to the error log.

- On Unix, if you invoke mysqld directly, it sends diagnostics to its standard error output, which normally is your terminal. If you invoke the server using mysqld_safe (or mysql.server, which in turn invokes mysqld_safe), diagnostic output is redirected to an error log. By default, the error log name is *host_name*.err in the server's data directory.

Diagnostic output produced by the server includes information about normal startup and shutdown. It also includes messages about abnormal execution conditions, such as the following:

- Unrecognized startup options. If the server attempts to start up but quits almost immediately, you might have a bad option listed in an option file. The error log can tell you this.

- Failure of the server to open its network interfaces: the TCP/IP port, the Windows named pipe, or the Unix socket file. The server cannot use an interface that is already in use by another server.

- Storage engine initialization failure. This might occur due to incorrect configuration of the storage engine (for example, if a file specified as part of the InnoDB tablespace cannot be opened), or detection of conditions that make it impossible to continue (for example, if a storage engine detects table corruption but cannot correct it automatically).

- Failure to find SSL certificate or key files that are named by startup options.

- Inability of the server to change its user ID on Unix. This can happen if you specify a --user option but do not start the server as root so that it can relinquish root privileges and change to a different user.

- Problems related to replication.

On Unix, if the server was started by the mysqld_safe script, mysqld_safe itself may write information to the error log. For example, if mysqld_safe detects that the server has died, it automatically restarts the server after writing mysqld restarted to the log.

16.2 Tuning Memory Parameters

As the server runs, it opens files, reads information from tables to process queries, and sends the results to clients. In many cases, the server processes information that it has accessed earlier. If the server can buffer or cache this information in memory rather than reading it from disk repeatedly, it runs more efficiently and performs better. By tuning server parameters appropriately using system variables, you can control what information the server attempts to keep in memory. Some buffers are used globally and affect server performance as a whole. Others apply to individual clients, although they're still initially set to a default value controlled by the server.

Memory is a finite resource and you should allocate it in ways that make the most sense for your system. For example, if you run lots of complex queries using just a few tables, it doesn't make sense to have a large table cache. You're likely better off increasing the key buffer size. On the other hand, if you run simple queries from many different tables, a large table cache will be of much more value.

Keep in mind that increasing the value of a server parameter increases system resource consumption by the server. You cannot increase parameter values beyond what's available, and you should not allocate so much memory to MySQL that the operating system suffers in its own performance. (Remember that the operating system itself requires system resources.)

In general, the server's default parameter settings are conservative and have small values. This enables the server to run even on modest systems with little memory. If your system has ample memory, you can allocate more of it to MySQL to tune it to the available resources.

Typically, you set parameter values using options in the [mysqld] section of an option file so that the server uses them consistently each time it starts. For system variables that are dynamic, you can change them while the server runs to test how the changes affect performance. After you determine optimum values this way, record them in the option file for use in subsequent server restarts.

To get an idea of appropriate settings for systems of various sizes, look at the sample option files that MySQL distributions include. They're located in the main directory of your MySQL distribution on Windows, or in the scripts directory on Unix. The files are named my-small.cnf, my-medium.cnf, my-large.cnf, and my-huge.cnf. Each includes comments that indicate the typical kind of system to which it applies. For example, a small system may use options with small values:

```
[mysqld]
key_buffer_size = 16K
table_cache = 4
sort_buffer_size = 64K
```

For a larger system, you can increase the values and also allocate memory to the query cache:

```
[mysqld]
key_buffer_size = 256M
table_cache = 256
sort_buffer_size = 1M
query_cache_type = ON
query_cache_size = 16M
```

The material in this section is oriented toward server-side tuning. Client-side techniques can be applied to optimize the performance of individual queries, as discussed in Chapter 13, "Optimizing for Query Speed."

16.2.1 Global (Serverwide) Variables

This section discusses server parameters for resources that affect server performance as a whole or that are shared among clients. When tuning server parameters, there are three factors to consider:

- The resource that the server manages.
- The system variable that controls the size of the resource.
- Status variables that relate to the resource. These enable you to determine how well the resource is configured.

For example, the key buffer that the server uses to cache index blocks is a resource. The size of the key buffer is set using the key_buffer_size system variable, and the effectiveness of the key buffer can be measured using the Key_reads and Key_read_requests status variables.

This section covers the following memory-related resources:

- The maximum number of simultaneous client connections the server supports.
- The table cache that holds information about tables that storage engines have open.
- The key buffer that holds MyISAM index blocks.
- The InnoDB buffer pool that holds InnoDB table data and index information, and the InnoDB log buffer that holds transaction information before it's flushed to the InnoDB log file.

16.2.1.1 Maximum Connections Allowed

The MySQL server uses a multithreaded architecture that allows it to service multiple clients simultaneously. A thread is like a small process running inside the server. For each client that connects, the server allocates a thread handler to service the connection, so the term *thread* in MySQL is roughly synonymous with *connection*.

The max_connections system variable controls the maximum allowable number of simultaneous client connections. The default value is 100. If your server is very busy and needs to handle many clients at once, the default might be too small. However, each active connection handler requires some memory, so you don't necessarily want to set the number as high as the number of threads your operating system allows.

To see how many clients currently are connected, check the value of the Threads_connected status variable. If its value often is close to the value of max_connections, it might be good to increase the value of the latter to allow more connections. If clients that should be able to connect to the server frequently cannot, that's another indication that max_connections is too small.

16.2.1.2 The Table Cache

When the server opens a table, it maintains information about that table in the table cache, which is used to avoid reopening tables when possible. The next time a client tries to access the table, the server can use it immediately without opening the table again if it is found in the cache. However, if the cache is full and a client tries to access a table that isn't found there, an open table must be closed to free an entry in the cache for the new table. The table that is closed then must be reopened the next time a client accesses it.

The table_cache system variable controls the size of the table cache. Its default value is 64. The goal when configuring the table cache is to make it large enough that the server need not repeatedly open frequently accessed tables. Against this goal you must balance the fact that with a larger table cache the server requires more file descriptors. Operating systems place a limit on the number of file descriptors allowed to each process, so the table cache cannot be made arbitrarily large. However, some operating systems do allow the per-process file descriptor limit to be reconfigured.

To determine whether the cache is large enough, check the Open_tables and Opened_tables status variables. Open_tables indicates how many tables currently are open, and Opened_tables indicates how many table-opening operations the server has performed since it started. If Open_tables usually is at or near the value of table_cache and the value of Opened_tables increases steadily, it indicates that the table cache is being used to capacity and that the server often has to close tables in the cache so that it can open other tables. This is a sign that the table cache is too small and that you should increase the value of table_cache.

16.2.1.3 The Key Buffer

The key buffer (key cache) is a resource in which the server caches index blocks read from MyISAM tables. Indexes speed up retrievals, so if you can keep index values in memory and reuse them for different queries rather than rereading them from disk, performance is even better. When MySQL needs to read an index block, it checks first whether the block is in the key buffer. If so, it can satisfy the read request immediately using a block in the buffer. If not, it reads the block from disk first and puts it in the key buffer. The frequency of these two actions is reflected by the Key_read_requests and Key_reads status variables. If the key buffer is full when a block needs to be read, the server discards a block already in the buffer to make room for the new block.

The ideal situation is for MySQL to consistently find the index blocks that it needs in the buffer without having to read them from disk. In other words, Key_reads should remain as low as possible relative to Key_read_requests.

You can use the two status variables to assess the effectiveness of the key buffer in terms of keys either missing or present in the buffer. These values are the key buffer miss rate and its efficiency. The miss rate is calculated as follows:

```
Key_reads / Key_read_requests
```

The complementary value, key buffer efficiency, is calculated like this:

```
1 - (Key_reads / Key_read_requests)
```

Suppose that the status variables have the following values:

```
mysql> SHOW STATUS LIKE 'Key_read%';
+-------------------+--------+
| Variable_name     | Value  |
+-------------------+--------+
| Key_read_requests | 539614 |
| Key_reads         | 6133   |
+-------------------+--------+
```

From those values, the key buffer miss rate and efficiency can be calculated:

```
miss rate = 6133 / 539614 = .0114
efficiency = 1 - (6133 / 539614) = .9886
```

You want the miss rate to be as close as possible to 0 and the efficiency as close as possible to 1. By that measure, the values just calculated are reasonably good. If the values for your server are not so good and you have memory available, you can improve the key buffer's effectiveness by increasing the value of the key_buffer_size system variable. Its default value is 8MB.

16.2.1.4 InnoDB Buffers

Two memory-related InnoDB resources are the buffer pool and the log buffer:

- The InnoDB buffer pool caches data and index information for InnoDB tables. Making the buffer pool larger reduces disk I/O for frequently accessed InnoDB table contents. The buffer pool size is controlled by the innodb_buffer_pool_size system variable. Its default value is 8MB. On a machine dedicated to MySQL, you can set this variable anywhere from 50% to 80% of the total amount of memory. However, the setting should take into account how large you set the key_buffer_size value.

- The InnoDB log buffer holds information about modifications made during transaction processing. Ideally, you want a transaction's changes to be held in the buffer until the transaction commits, at which point they can be written to the InnoDB log file all at once. If the buffer is too small, changes might have to be written several times before commit time, resulting in additional disk activity. The log buffer size is controlled by the `innodb_log_buffer_size` system variable. Typical values range from 1MB to 8MB. The default is 1MB.

16.2.1.5 Selecting Storage Engines

If you need to save memory, one way to do so is to disable unneeded storage engines. Some of the compiled-in storage engines can be enabled or disabled at runtime. Disabling an unneeded storage engine reduces the server's memory requirements because it need not allocate buffers and other data structures associated with the engine. You can disable the InnoDB and BDB engines this way with the `--skip-innodb` and `--skip-bdb` options at server startup time.

It's also possible to disable InnoDB or BDB entirely by compiling the server without them. For example, you can disable the InnoDB storage engine using the `--without-innodb` configuration option. BDB is enabled only if you use the `--with-berkeley-db` configuration option, so to leave BDB support disabled, just omit the option. Consult the installation chapter of the *MySQL Reference Manual* for further instructions.

The MyISAM storage engine is always compiled in and cannot be disabled at runtime. This ensures that the server always has a reliably available storage engine, no matter how it might otherwise be configured.

16.2.2 Per-Client Variables

Resources such as the table cache and key buffer are shared globally among all clients, but the server also allocates a set of buffers for each client that connects. The variables that control their sizes are collectively known as *per-client variables*.

Be cautious when increasing the value of a per-client variable. For each per-client buffer, the potential amount of server memory required is the size of the buffer times the maximum allowed number of client connections. Parameters for these buffers normally are set to 1MB or 2MB, at most, to avoid causing exorbitant memory use under conditions when many clients are connected simultaneously.

Per-client buffers include the following:

- MySQL uses a record buffer to perform sequential table scans. Its size is controlled by the `read_buffer_size` system variable. Increasing the size of this buffer allows larger chunks of the table to be read at one time, which can speed up scanning by reducing the number of disk seeks required. A second record buffer also is allocated for use in reading records after an intermediate sort (such as might be required by an ORDER BY clause) or for nonsequential table reads. Its size is controlled by the `read_rnd_buffer_size` variable, which defaults to the value of `read_buffer_size` if you don't set it explicitly. This means that changing `read_buffer_size` potentially can actually result in double the effective memory increase.

- The sort buffer is used for operations such as ORDER BY and GROUP BY. Its size is controlled by the sort_buffer_size system variable. If clients execute many queries that sort large record sets, increasing the sort buffer size can speed up sorting operations.

- The join buffer is used to process joins. Its size is controlled by the join_buffer_size system variable. Increase the value if clients tend to perform complex joins.

- The server allocates a communication buffer for exchanging information with the client. If clients tend to issue very long queries, the queries will fail if the communication buffer isn't large enough to handle them. The buffer size is controlled by the max_allowed_packet parameter. For example, to allow clients to send up to 128MB of information at a time, configure the server like this:

```
[mysqld]
max_allowed_packet = 128M
```

Note that unlike a parameter such as read_buffer_size, it's generally safe to set the value of max_allowed_packet quite high. The server does not actually allocate a communication buffer that large as soon as a client connects. It begins with a buffer of size net_buffer_length bytes and increases it as necessary, up to a maximum of max_allowed_packet bytes.

Although these buffers are client-specific, it isn't necessarily the case that the server actually allocates each one for every client. No sort buffer or join buffer is allocated for a client unless it performs sorts or joins.

One scenario in which very long queries can occur is when you dump tables with mysqldump and reload them with mysql. If you run mysqldump with the --opt option to create a dump file containing long multiple-row INSERT statements, those statements might be too long for the server to handle when you use mysql later to send the contents of the file back to the server to be reloaded. Note that it might be necessary to set the client-side value of max_allowed_packet in both cases as well. mysqldump and mysql both support a --max_allowed_packet option for setting the client-side value.

16.3 Using the Query Cache

MySQL supports a query cache that greatly increases performance if the server's query mix includes SELECT statements that are processed repeatedly and return the same results each time. If you enable the query cache, the server uses it as follows:

- The server compares each SELECT query that arrives to any already in the cache. If the query is already present and none of the tables that it uses have changed since the result was cached, the server returns the result immediately without executing the query.

- If the query is not present in the cache or if any of the tables that it uses have changed (thus invalidating the saved result), the server executes the query and caches its result.

- The server determines whether a query is in the cache based on exact case-sensitive comparison of query strings. That means the following two queries are not considered the same:

```
SELECT * FROM table_name;
```

```
select * from table_name;
```

The server also takes into account any factor that distinguishes otherwise identical queries. Among these are the character set used by each client and the default database. For example, two SELECT * FROM table_name queries might be lexically identical but are semantically different if each applies to a different default database.

The query cache is global, so a query result placed in the cache can be returned to any client. Using the query cache can result in a tremendous performance boost and reduction in server load, especially for disk- or processor-intensive queries.

Three system variables control query cache operation:

```
mysql> SHOW VARIABLES LIKE 'query_cache%';
+-------------------+---------+
| Variable_name     | Value   |
+-------------------+---------+
| query_cache_limit | 1048576 |
| query_cache_size  | 0       |
| query_cache_type  | ON      |
+-------------------+---------+
```

The default value of query_cache_type is ON (caching allowed). However, the cache is not operational unless its size is set larger than the default value of zero. To enable the query cache, set the value of query_cache_size to a nonzero size in bytes to indicate how much memory to allocate to it. You may optionally set the query_cache_limit variable as well. It places an upper bound on how large an individual query result can be and still be eligible for caching. The default limit is 1MB.

Typically, you set the query cache variables in an option file where you list the server's start-up options. For example, to allocate 10MB of memory to the query cache and allow individual query results up to 2MB to be cached, put the following lines in the option file and restart the server:

```
[mysqld]
query_cache_size = 10M
query_cache_limit = 2M
```

If you have the SUPER privilege, you can change these variables for a running server without restarting it by using the following statements:

```
SET GLOBAL query_cache_size = 10485760;
SET GLOBAL query_cache_limit = 2097152;
```

If you set the variables that way, the changes will be lost at the next server restart, so SET is useful primarily for testing cache settings. When you find suitable values, record them in the option file.

The server provides information about the operation of the query cache by means of a set of status variables. To view these variables, use the following statement:

```
mysql> SHOW STATUS LIKE 'Qcache%';
+-------------------------+--------+
| Variable_name           | Value  |
+-------------------------+--------+
| Qcache_queries_in_cache | 360    |
| Qcache_inserts          | 12823  |
| Qcache_hits             | 21145  |
| Qcache_lowmem_prunes    | 584    |
| Qcache_not_cached       | 10899  |
| Qcache_free_memory      | 231008 |
| Qcache_free_blocks      | 98     |
| Qcache_total_blocks     | 861    |
+-------------------------+--------+
```

Qcache_inserts is the total number of queries that have been put in the cache. Qcache_queries_in_cache indicates the number of queries currently registered in the cache. The difference between the two values indicates how many cached queries were displaced to make room for newer queries. Qcache_hits indicates how many times a query did not have to be executed because its result could be served from the cache.

16.4 Using Multiple Servers

It's common to run a single MySQL server on a host, but it's possible to run multiple servers. Managing multiple servers is of course a more complex undertaking than running a single server because you must make sure that the servers don't interfere with each other. None of the servers can share resources that must be used exclusively by a single server. These resources include the following:

- Each server must have its own network interfaces, including the TCP/IP port, the named pipe (for Windows), and the Unix socket file (for Unix). One server cannot use network interfaces that are used by another server; it will not even start up properly if it discovers that its network interfaces are already in use. Note that it isn't necessary to set up multiple hostnames for the server host. All the MySQL servers running on a given host can share the same hostname. They can also share the same IP address as long as they listen on different TCP/IP port numbers.

- Under Windows NT, servers that are run as services must each use a unique service name.

- Each server must have its own log files. Multiple servers writing to the same log files results in unusable logs. This is also true for status files such as the PID file in which a server records its process ID.

- InnoDB tablespace files cannot be shared by multiple servers. Each server that uses InnoDB must have its own tablespace. The same is true of the InnoDB log files.

- Each server normally manages its own data directory, although it's possible for servers to share a data directory under certain circumstances:

  - If the data directory is located on read-only media, there won't be a problem of multiple servers attempting updates of the same data simultaneously. (This precludes use of InnoDB tables because InnoDB currently cannot be used on read-only media.)

  - On read-write media, external locking must be enabled so that servers can cooperate for access to database files. However, external locking does not work on all systems, is disabled by default as of MySQL 4, and does not apply to the InnoDB storage engine anyway.

You can ensure that each server uses its own network interfaces by starting each with a unique value for the --port and --socket options. Similarly, to make sure that each server manages a different data directory, start each one with a unique value for the --datadir option. Normally, having distinct data directories is sufficient to ensure distinct sets of log files as well because logs are created by default in the data directory if you specify their names using relative pathnames.

To set up Windows servers with distinct service names, follow the --install option of the service installation command with a service name. For example:

```
shell> mysqld --install mysql1
shell> mysqld --install mysql2
```

Installed that way, these servers will read options from the [mysql1] and [mysql2] groups, respectively, in the standard option files.

Another way to install MySQL as a service is to follow the service name with an option naming the file from which the server should read options when it starts:

```
shell> mysqld --install mysql1 --defaults-file=C:\mysql1.cnf
shell> mysqld --install mysql2 --defaults-file=C:\mysq2.cnf
```

In this case, each server will ignore the standard option files and will instead read options only from the [mysqld] group of the option file named by the --defaults-file option.

On Unix, some administrative assistance is available for controlling multiple servers. mysqld_multi is a Perl script intended to make it easier to manage multiple servers on a single host. It can start or stop servers, or report on whether servers are running. mysqld_multi can either start servers directly, or indirectly by invoking mysqld_safe. (An advantage of using `mysqld_safe` is that it sets up the error log and monitors the server.) `mysqld_multi` requires installation of the Perl DBI module.

16.5 Replication

MySQL supports replication capabilities that allow the contents of databases on one server to be made available on another server. MySQL replication uses a master/slave architecture:

- The server that manages the original databases is the master.
- Any server that manages a copy of the original databases is a slave.
- A given master server can have many slaves, but a slave can have only a single master.

A replication slave is set up initially by transferring an exact copy of the to-be-replicated databases from the master server to the slave server. Thereafter, each replicated database is kept synchronized to the original database. The basis for communication is the master server's binary log:

- When the master server makes modifications to its databases, it records the changes in its binary log files.
- Changes recorded in the binary log are sent to each slave server, which makes the changes to its copy of the replicated databases. Slave servers that aren't connected to the master when a statement is recorded receive the statement the next time they connect.

By default, the master server logs updates for all databases, and the slave server replicates all updates that it receives from the master. For more fine-grained control, it's possible to tell a master which databases to log updates for, and to tell a slave which of those updates that it receives from the master to apply. You can either name databases to be replicated (in which case those not named are ignored), or you can name databases to ignore (in which case those not named are replicated). The master host options are `--binlog-do-db` and `--binlog-ignore-db`. The slave host options are `--replicate-do-db` and `--replicate-ignore-db`.

The following example illustrates how this works, using the options that enable replication for specific databases. Suppose that a master server has three databases named a, b, and c. You can elect to replicate only databases a and b when you start the master server by placing these options in an option file read by that server:

```
[mysqld]
binlog-do-db = a
binlog-do-db = b
```

With those options, the master server will log updates only for the named databases to the binary log. Thus, any slave server that connects to the master will receive information only for databases a and b.

A slave that wants to filter the updates received may do so. A slave that takes no such action will replicate databases a and b. For a slave that should replicate only database a, you can start it with these lines in an option file:

```
[mysqld]
replicate-do-db = a
```

For a slave that should replicate only database b, you can start it with these lines in an option file:

```
[mysqld]
replicate-do-db = b
```

Note that these options apply only when the given database happens to be the default database. Statements that name a database explicitly are always written to the binary log.

16.6 Exercises

Question 1:

Using programs available from MySQL AB, there are three ways to access server status information. What are they?

Question 2:

Using programs available from MySQL AB, there are three ways to access server system variables. What are they?

Question 3:

What can you learn from server status information and server system variables? Give an example for each type of variable.

Question 4:

Assume that you've just installed MySQL, but you're not sure where the installation and data directories are located. However, you can connect to the server using mysql. What SQL statement or statements would you issue to find out that information?

Question 5:

In your MySQL option file, you want to have the following settings for the server:

- The installation directory should be set to D:\mysql.
- The data directory should be set to D:\mysql\data.
- The key buffer size should be 24MB.

What are the appropriate entries in your option file?

Question 6:

You can set server parameters (system variables) in a number of ways:

- With options in MySQL option files
- With options on the command line at server startup
- With a SET GLOBAL statement
- With a SET SESSION (or SET LOCAL) statement

Assume that you choose to set server parameters using options in MySQL option files. What's the lifetime of the settings? What's the scope within which each setting applies? How would you set the sort_buffer_size variable to a value of 512000?

Question 7:

Assume that you choose to set server parameters using options on the command line at server startup. What's the lifetime of the settings? What's the scope within which each setting applies? How would you set the sort_buffer_size variable to a value of 512000?

Question 8:

Assume that you choose to set server parameters using a SET GLOBAL statement. What's the lifetime of the settings? What's the scope within which each setting applies? How would you set the sort_buffer_size variable to a value of 512000?

Question 9:

Assume that you choose to set server parameters using a SET SESSION (or SET LOCAL) statement. What's the lifetime of the settings? What's the scope within which each setting applies? How would you set the sort_buffer_size variable to a value of 512000?

Question 10:

What SQL statement will display the status variables that tell you how many times the server has executed each type of SQL statement?

Question 11:

You want to see the errors reported by the server at startup. Under Windows, how would you direct that output to your terminal rather than to the error log?

Question 12:

You want to see the errors reported by the server at startup. Under Unix, how would you direct that output to your terminal rather than to the error log?

Question 13:

What kinds of errors might the server report in its diagnostic output?

Question 14:

Besides the status variables, what other sources of information are available for checking server load and performance?

Question 15:

How would you disable the InnoDB and the BDB storage engines? Why might you want to do that?

Question 16:

Name three server parameters that affect the performance of SELECT statements.

Question 17:

What might the following session listing indicate about server configuration? If further analysis would point out there is in fact a problem, how could you identify and solve it?

```
mysql> SHOW STATUS LIKE 'Opened_tables';
+---------------+-------+
| Variable_name | Value |
+---------------+-------+
| Opened_tables | 110   |
+---------------+-------+
mysql> SELECT * FROM faq LIMIT 1;
+---------------+----------------------
| cdate         | question          ...
+---------------+----------------------
| 20030318160028 | What is the name of t ...
+---------------+----------------------
mysql> SHOW STATUS LIKE 'Opened_tables';
+---------------+-------+
| Variable_name | Value |
+---------------+-------+
| Opened_tables | 111   |
+---------------+-------+
mysql> SELECT * FROM t LIMIT 1;
+------+
| i    |
+------+
|    6 |
+------+
mysql> SHOW STATUS LIKE 'Opened_tables';
+---------------+-------+
| Variable_name | Value |
+---------------+-------+
| Opened_tables | 112   |
+---------------+-------+
```

Question 18:

What does *key cache efficiency* mean?

Question 19:

What values are necessary to calculate the key cache efficiency?

Question 20:

How would you retrieve the values needed to calculate the key cache efficiency?

Question 21:

How can you improve key cache efficiency for better server performance?

Question 22:

How could you determine the number of clients that connected successfully?

Question 23:

How could you determine the number of clients that tried to connect, but failed?

Question 24:

How could you determine the number of clients that closed their connections properly?

Question 25:

How could you determine the number of clients that either aborted their connections or were killed?

Question 26:

Name MySQL's per-client buffers.

Question 27:

How would you determine the sizes of MySQL's per-client record buffers?

Question 28:

How would you determine the size of MySQL's per-client join buffer?

Question 29:

How would you determine the size of MySQL's per-client sort buffer?

Question 30:

How would you determine the size of MySQL's per-client communications buffer?

Question 31:

The server's query cache can speed up SELECT queries. How would you check the server system variables for the query cache?

Question 32:

Using the server system variables for the query cache, how could you determine whether the query cache is enabled?

Question 33:

The server's query cache can speed up SELECT queries. How would you determine the extent to which the query cache is effective?

Question 34:

When running two servers on the same host, you'll have to make sure that they don't share resources they need exclusively. What are those resources?

Question 35:

Assume that you want to run two MySQL servers on one Windows machine (NT family). You've set up two system services called MySQL_Development and MySQL_Production. What would the absolute minimum of entries in the C:\Windows\my.ini option file look like for those two servers?

Question 36:

How many masters can a replication slave have?

Question 37:

How many slaves can a replication master have?

Question 38:

How does a master replication server communicate database changes to slave servers?

Answers to Exercises

Answer 1:

You can access server status information using any of these methods:

- With the mysql client program:

  ```
  mysql> SHOW STATUS;
  ```

- With the mysqladmin program:

  ```
  shell> mysqladmin extended-status
  ```

- With the MySQLCC graphical client:

  - Open a connection to the server.
  - Double-click Server Administration in the MySQL Servers panel.
  - Choose the Status tab in the Administration Panel window that appears.

Answer 2:

You can access server system variables using any of these methods:

- With the `mysql` client program:

  ```
  mysql> SHOW VARIABLES;
  ```

- With the `mysqladmin` program:

  ```
  shell> mysqladmin variables
  ```

- With the MySQLCC graphical client:

    - Open a connection to the server.
    - Double-click Server Administration in the MySQL Servers panel.
    - Choose the Variables tab in the Administration Panel window that appears.

Answer 3:

The server system variables provide configuration details of the server. For example, you can determine the location of the data directory like this:

```
mysql> SHOW VARIABLES LIKE 'datadir';
+---------------+----------------------+
| Variable_name | Value                |
+---------------+----------------------+
| datadir       | /usr/local/mysql/data/ |
+---------------+----------------------+
```

The server status variables provide information about the activities of the server. For example, you can check how many clients are connected to the server:

```
mysql> SHOW STATUS LIKE 'Threads_connected';
+-------------------+-------+
| Variable_name     | Value |
+-------------------+-------+
| Threads_connected | 17    |
+-------------------+-------+
```

See sections A.1.45, "SHOW VARIABLES," and A.1.42, "SHOW STATUS."

Answer 4:

The server stores the base installation and data directory locations in its `basedir` and `datadir` system variables, which you can display using the SHOW VARIABLES statement:

```
mysql> SHOW VARIABLES LIKE 'basedir'; SHOW VARIABLES LIKE 'datadir';
+---------------+-----------+
| Variable_name | Value     |
+---------------+-----------+
```

```
| basedir       | c:\mysql\ |
+--------------+-----------+
+--------------+----------------+
| Variable_name | Value         |
+--------------+----------------+
| datadir       | c:\mysql\data\ |
+--------------+----------------+
```

See section A.1.45, "SHOW VARIABLES."

Answer 5:

The entries should be made in the [mysqld] option group like this:

```
[mysqld]
basedir = D:/mysql
datadir = D:/mysql/data
key_buffer_size = 24M
```

See section A.4, "Server System Variables."

Answer 6:

Each time the server is started, it reads settings in option files. Settings specified in these files therefore pertain to each invocation of the server. For any given invocation, the settings have global scope and persist until the server shuts down. Example:

```
[mysqld]
sort_buffer_size=512000
```

See section A.4, "Server System Variables."

Answer 7:

When the server is invoked with parameter settings specified on the command line, those settings pertain only to that particular invocation. The settings have global scope and persist until the server is shut down. Example:

```
shell> mysqld --sort_buffer_size=512000
```

See section A.4, "Server System Variables."

Answer 8:

Using SET GLOBAL requires the SUPER privilege. You would specify a global option like this:

```
mysql> SET GLOBAL sort_buffer_size=512000;
```

As the statement indicates, the scope is global; it applies to any clients that connect after the variable is set. An alternative syntax for setting the option value is as follows:

```
mysql> SET @@global.sort_buffer_size=512000;
```

See sections A.4, "Server System Variables," and A.1.30, "SET."

Answer 9:

Using SET SESSION (or SET LOCAL) sets the variable to a value that applies only to the current connection (and thus not to other connected users). This is called a *session scope*. Example:

```
mysql> SET SESSION sort_buffer_size=512000;
```

An alternative syntax is as follows:

```
mysql> SET @@session.sort_buffer_size=512000;
```

See sections A.4, "Server System Variables," and A.1.30, "SET."

Answer 10:

To find out how many times the server has executed each type of statement, examine the status variables that begin with Com:

```
mysql> SHOW STATUS LIKE 'Com%';
+-----------------------+-------+
| Variable_name         | Value |
+-----------------------+-------+
| Com_admin_commands    | 0     |
| Com_alter_table       | 0     |
| Com_analyze           | 0     |
| Com_backup_table      | 0     |
| Com_begin             | 0     |
| Com_change_db         | 3     |

   ...                     ...

| Com_show_status       | 26    |
| Com_show_innodb_status| 1     |
| Com_show_tables       | 3     |
| Com_show_variables    | 18    |
| Com_slave_start       | 0     |
| Com_slave_stop        | 0     |
| Com_truncate          | 0     |
| Com_unlock_tables     | 0     |
| Com_update            | 0     |
+-----------------------+-------+
```

This will not list the number of SELECT statements that were processed using the query cache. You can obtain that number from the Qcache_hits status variable:

```
mysql> SHOW STATUS LIKE 'Qcache_hits';
+---------------+-------+
| Variable_name | Value |
+---------------+-------+
| Qcache_hits   | 11019 |
+---------------+-------+
```

See section A.1.42, "SHOW STATUS."

Answer 11:

Under Windows, you would start the server with the `--console` option:

```
shell> mysqld --console
```

Answer 12:

Under Unix, you would start the server directly (that is, without using a startup script such as `mysqld_safe` or `mysql.server`):

```
shell> mysqld
```

The server will send its diagnostics to the standard error output location (normally your terminal).

Answer 13:

The errors reported by the server include the following:

- Unrecognized startup options
- Failure to open its network interfaces (TCP/IP port, Windows named pipe, Unix socket file)
- Storage engine initialization failure
- Failure to find SSL certificate or key files
- Inability of the server to change its user ID
- Problems related to replication

Answer 14:

In addition to the server's status variables, sources of server load and performance information include the following:

- The *error log* provides information also about errors that aren't fatal but might affect server performance (such as aborted connections).
- The *slow query log* provides information about queries that take a long time to perform. By default, *a long time* is defined as more than 10 seconds. If the `--log-long-format` option is specified, the slow query log also includes queries that do not use indexes.
- The STATUS command of the `mysql` client programs displays some statistical information about the server load; for example, the total number of queries (called Questions), the average number of queries per second, and the number of tables that were opened (called Opens).

Answer 15:

To disable the InnoDB and BDB storage engines, you could either put the settings in a MySQL option file or start the server with the appropriate options. In your option file, you would have these lines:

```
[mysqld]
skip-bdb
skip-innodb
```

The preceding is the preferred way to disable the storage engines. To disable them only for the next time the server starts, you would use the options on the command line rather than putting them in an option file:

```
shell> mysqld --skip-bdb --skip-innodb
```

Disabling an unneeded storage engine reduces the server's memory requirements because it need not allocate buffers and other data structures associated with the engine. Note that there is no provision for disabling the MyISAM storage engine.

It's also possible to disable the InnoDB and BDB storage engines entirely by compiling the server without them.

Answer 16:

`key_buffer_size` affects index-related operations, `sort_buffer_size` affects sorting operations (`ORDER BY`, `GROUP BY`), and `join_buffer_size` affects join performance.

See section A.4, "Server System Variables."

Answer 17:

The session listing seems to indicate that `Opened_tables` is incremented with each table that is accessed. This does not necessarily indicate there is a problem because these queries could have been the first ones that accessed those two tables since the server started. However, if you find `Opened_tables` being incremented steadily even when using tables that have been opened before, it might indicate a table cache that's too small. To see the size of the cache, check the value of the `table_cache` variable:

```
mysql> SHOW VARIABLES LIKE 'table_cache';
+---------------+-------+
| Variable_name | Value |
+---------------+-------+
| table_cache   | 1     |
+---------------+-------+
```

That output shows an extremely small value that is definitely too low. You can set it higher while the server is running by issuing a SET statement:

```
mysql> SET GLOBAL table_cache=64;
mysql> SHOW VARIABLES LIKE 'table_cache';
+---------------+-------+
| Variable_name | Value |
+---------------+-------+
| table_cache   | 64    |
+---------------+-------+
```

But more likely you would set the value in an appropriate option file. Then the setting would take effect each time you restart the server.

See section A.4, "Server System Variables."

Answer 18:

The key cache efficiency provides information about the number of index reads from the cache, relative to index reads that need to be done from disk. The value should be as close to 1 as possible, so a value of .9 is good, but a value of .99 is much better.

Answer 19:

The key cache efficiency is calculated from two status variables using this formula:

```
1 - (Key_reads / Key_read_requests)
```

See section A.4, "Server System Variables."

Answer 20:

To retrieve the values necessary for calculating key cache efficiency, you would issue this statement:

```
mysql> SHOW STATUS LIKE 'key_read%';
+-------------------+--------+
| Variable_name     | Value  |
+-------------------+--------+
| Key_read_requests | 280944 |
| Key_reads         | 5827   |
+-------------------+--------+
```

The values shown in this example give this efficiency:

```
1 - (5827 / 280944) = .98
```

That value is close to 1 and is reasonably efficient.

See sections A.4, "Server System Variables," and A.1.42, "SHOW STATUS."

Answer 21:

To improve server performance, check the value of key_buffer_size. If the value is small and memory is available, increase the key buffer size. The following example sets the size to 16MB:

```
mysql> SHOW VARIABLES LIKE 'key_buffer_size';
+-----------------+--------+
| Variable_name   | Value  |
+-----------------+--------+
| key_buffer_size | 512000 |
+-----------------+--------+
```

```
mysql> SET GLOBAL key_buffer_size=16777216;
mysql> SHOW VARIABLES LIKE 'key_buffer_size';
+-----------------+----------+
| Variable_name   | Value    |
+-----------------+----------+
| key_buffer_size | 16777216 |
+-----------------+----------+
```

See sections A.4, "Server System Variables," and A.1.45, "SHOW VARIABLES."

Answer 22:

The information can be determined using status information available from SHOW STATUS. The number of successful connections can be calculated as the number of connection attempts minus the number of unsuccessful connection attempts:

```
mysql> SHOW STATUS LIKE 'Connections';
+---------------+-------+
| Variable_name | Value |
+---------------+-------+
| Connections   | 18220 |
+---------------+-------+
mysql> SHOW STATUS LIKE 'Aborted_connects';
+------------------+-------+
| Variable_name    | Value |
+------------------+-------+
| Aborted_connects | 6     |
+------------------+-------+
```

In this case, it is 18220-6, or 18214 successful connections made.

See section A.1.42, "SHOW STATUS."

Answer 23:

The information can be determined using status information available from SHOW STATUS. To get the number of unsuccessful connection attempts, you would use this statement:

```
mysql> SHOW STATUS LIKE 'Aborted_connects';
+------------------+-------+
| Variable_name    | Value |
+------------------+-------+
| Aborted_connects | 6     |
+------------------+-------+
```

See section A.1.42, "SHOW STATUS."

Answer 24:

The information can be determined using status information available from SHOW STATUS. The number of connections that were closed properly can be calculated as the number of connection attempts, minus the number of unsuccessful attempts, minus the number of aborted clients:

```
mysql> SHOW STATUS LIKE 'Connections';
+-----------------+-------+
| Variable_name   | Value |
+-----------------+-------+
| Connections     | 18222 |
+-----------------+-------+
mysql> SHOW STATUS LIKE 'Aborted_connects';
+-----------------+-------+
| Variable_name   | Value |
+-----------------+-------+
| Aborted_connects | 99   |
+-----------------+-------+
mysql> SHOW STATUS LIKE 'Aborted_clients';
+-------------------+-------+
| Variable_name     | Value |
+-------------------+-------+
| Aborted_clients   | 4     |
+-------------------+-------+
```

In this case, it is 18222-99-4, or 18119 connections properly closed.

See section A.1.42, "SHOW STATUS."

Answer 25:

The information can be determined using status information available from SHOW STATUS. To get the number of connections that were improperly closed (aborted), you would use this statement:

```
mysql> SHOW STATUS LIKE 'Aborted_clients';
+-----------------+-------+
| Variable_name   | Value |
+-----------------+-------+
| Aborted_clients | 99    |
+-----------------+-------+
```

See section A.1.42, "SHOW STATUS."

Answer 26:

The MySQL server uses these per-client buffers:

- Record buffers are used for sequential table scans (read_buffer_size) and when reading rows in sorted order after a sort, usually with the ORDER BY clause (read_rnd_buffer_size).
- The join buffer is used to perform table joins.

- The sort buffer is used for sorting operations.
- The communications buffer is used for exchanging information with the client. It begins with a size of `net_buffer_length`, but the server expands it up to a size of `max_allowed_packet` as necessary.

See section A.4, "Server System Variables."

Answer 27:

Record buffers are used for sequential table scans (`read_buffer_size`), and when reading rows in sorted order after a sort, usually with the `ORDER BY` clause (`read_rnd_buffer_size`). To get their sizes, you would issue this statement:

```
mysql> SHOW VARIABLES LIKE 'read%buffer_size';
+---------------------+--------+
| Variable_name       | Value  |
+---------------------+--------+
| read_buffer_size    | 131072 |
| read_rnd_buffer_size | 262144 |
+---------------------+--------+
```

See sections A.4, "Server System Variables," and A.1.45, "SHOW VARIABLES."

Answer 28:

The join buffer is used to perform table joins. To get its size, you would issue this statement:

```
mysql> SHOW VARIABLES LIKE 'join_buffer_size';
+------------------+--------+
| Variable_name    | Value  |
+------------------+--------+
| join_buffer_size | 131072 |
+------------------+--------+
```

See sections A.4, "Server System Variables," and A.1.45, "SHOW VARIABLES."

Answer 29:

The sort buffer is used for sorting operations. To get its size, you would issue this statement:

```
mysql> SHOW VARIABLES LIKE 'sort_buffer_size';
+------------------+--------+
| Variable_name    | Value  |
+------------------+--------+
| sort_buffer_size | 524280 |
+------------------+--------+
```

See sections A.4, "Server System Variables," and A.1.45, "SHOW VARIABLES."

Answer 30:

The communications buffer is used for exchanging information with the client. It begins with a size of net_buffer_length, but the server expands it up to a size of max_allowed_packet as necessary. To get the sizes of these buffers, issue the following statements:

```
mysql> SHOW VARIABLES LIKE 'net_buffer_length';
+-------------------+-------+
| Variable_name     | Value |
+-------------------+-------+
| net_buffer_length | 16384 |
+-------------------+-------+
+-------------------+---------+
mysql> SHOW VARIABLES LIKE 'max_allowed_packet';
+--------------------+---------+
| Variable_name      | Value   |
+--------------------+---------+
| max_allowed_packet | 1048576 |
+--------------------+---------+
```

See sections A.4, "Server System Variables," and A.1.45, "SHOW VARIABLES."

Answer 31:

You can display the server variables that show how the query cache is configured by issuing this statement:

```
mysql> SHOW VARIABLES LIKE 'query%';
+-------------------+----------+
| Variable_name     | Value    |
+-------------------+----------+
| query_cache_limit | 1048576  |
| query_cache_size  | 67108864 |
| query_cache_type  | ON       |
+-------------------+----------+
```

See sections A.4, "Server System Variables," and A.1.45, "SHOW VARIABLES."

Answer 32:

If query_cache_type is not OFF and the value of query_cache_size is greater than zero, the query cache is enabled.

See section A.4, "Server System Variables."

Answer 33:

To check the server's usage of the query cache, examine the appropriate status variables:

```
mysql> SHOW STATUS LIKE 'Qcache%';
+-------------------------+----------+
| Variable_name           | Value    |
```

```
+------------------------+----------+
| Qcache_queries_in_cache | 179      |
| Qcache_inserts          | 7598     |
| Qcache_hits             | 11546    |
| Qcache_lowmem_prunes    | 21       |
| Qcache_not_cached       | 5511     |
| Qcache_free_memory      | 67099960 |
| Qcache_free_blocks      | 77       |
| Qcache_total_blocks     | 505      |
+------------------------+----------+
```

See sections A.4, "Server System Variables," and A.1.42, "SHOW STATUS."

Answer 34:

The following resources cannot be shared among MySQL servers:

- The network interfaces (TCP/IP port, Windows named pipe, or Unix socket file)
- The Windows service name
- The log files
- The Unix process ID file
- The InnoDB tablespace files

In addition, although it's sometimes possible for servers to share a data directory, doing so isn't recommended.

Answer 35:

Running two MySQL servers on one host under Windows requires settings for at least the TCP/IP port and the data directory. An example might look like this:

```
[MySQL_Development]
port=3306
datadir=C:/mysql_1/data

[MySQL_Production]
port=3307
datadir=C:/mysql_2/data
```

By assigning a different port for each server, you make sure that they listen on different ports (otherwise, the second server wouldn't even start). By assigning a different datadir value, you make sure that the servers use different databases. If nothing else is specified, this will also make sure that the servers use different log files and InnoDB tablespace files because those will be created in the respective data directories by default.

Answer 36:

In MySQL, a replication slave can only have one master.

Answer 37:

In MySQL, a master can have an unlimited number of replication slaves, although in practice the number is limited by the max_connections variable. If that variable's value is low compared to the number of slaves and if there are many other concurrent connections to the server, a slave might have to wait a very long time for a replication connection.

Answer 38:

The master replication server communicates changes to slaves using the binary log. The master writes statements that change data into the binary log, and sends those statements to replication slaves that connect to it.

A

Quick Reference

This Quick Reference briefly covers the syntax and use of the SQL statements, functions, column types, and server variables discussed in this study guide. It is adapted from the corresponding sections in the *MySQL Reference Manual*. For the full text, see the *MySQL Reference Manual*, which is available in book form and online in several formats at http://www.mysql.com/documentation.

A.1 SQL Statements

A.1.1 ALTER TABLE

```
ALTER [IGNORE] TABLE table_name alter_spec [, alter_spec ...]

alter_spec:
    ADD [COLUMN] create_definition [FIRST | AFTER column_name ]
  | ADD [COLUMN] (create_definition, create_definition,...)
  | ADD INDEX [index_name] (index_column_name,...)
  | ADD PRIMARY KEY (index_column_name,...)
  | ADD UNIQUE [index_name] (index_column_name,...)
  | ADD FULLTEXT [index_name] (index_column_name,...)
  | ALTER [COLUMN] column_name {SET DEFAULT literal | DROP DEFAULT}
  | CHANGE [COLUMN] old_column_name create_definition
            [FIRST | AFTER column_name]
  | MODIFY [COLUMN] create_definition
            [FIRST | AFTER column_name]
  | DROP [COLUMN] column_name
  | DROP PRIMARY KEY
  | DROP INDEX index_name
  | RENAME [TO] new_table_name
  | ORDER BY col
  | table_options
```

ALTER TABLE allows you to change the structure of an existing table. For example, you can add or delete columns, add or delete indexes, change the type of existing columns, or rename columns or the table itself. You can also change the comment for the table and the type of the table.

- To use ALTER TABLE, you need ALTER, INSERT, and CREATE privileges on the table.

- You can issue multiple ADD, ALTER, DROP, and CHANGE clauses in a single ALTER TABLE statement. This is a MySQL extension to ANSI SQL-92, which allows only one of each clause per ALTER TABLE statement.

- CHANGE column_name, DROP column_name, and DROP INDEX are MySQL extensions to ANSI SQL-92.

- MODIFY is an Oracle extension to ALTER TABLE.

- The word COLUMN is optional and can be omitted.

- create_definition clauses use the same syntax for ADD and CHANGE as for CREATE TABLE. Note that this syntax includes the column name, not just the column type.

- You can rename a column using a CHANGE old_column_name create_definition clause. To do so, specify the old and new column names and the type that the column currently has.

- If you want to change a column's type but not the name, CHANGE syntax still requires an old and new column name, even if they are the same. However, you can also use MODIFY to change a column's type without renaming it.

- When you change a column type using CHANGE or MODIFY, MySQL tries to convert data to the new type as well as possible.

- You can use FIRST or ADD … AFTER column_name to add a column at a specific position within a table row. The default is to add the column last. From MySQL Version 4.0.1, you can also use the FIRST and AFTER keywords in CHANGE or MODIFY.

- ALTER COLUMN specifies a new default value for a column or removes the old default value. If the old default is removed and the column can be NULL, the new default is NULL. If the column cannot be NULL, MySQL assigns a default value.

- DROP INDEX removes an index. This is a MySQL extension to ANSI SQL-92.

- If columns are dropped from a table, the columns are also removed from any index of which they are a part. If all columns that make up an index are dropped, the index is dropped as well.

- If a table contains only one column, the column cannot be dropped. If what you intend is to remove the table, use DROP TABLE instead.

- DROP PRIMARY KEY drops the primary index. If no such index exists, it drops the first UNIQUE index in the table. (MySQL marks the first UNIQUE key as the PRIMARY KEY if no PRIMARY KEY was specified explicitly.) If you add a UNIQUE INDEX or PRIMARY KEY to a table, this is stored before any not UNIQUE index so that MySQL can detect duplicate keys as early as possible.

- ORDER BY enables you to create the new table with the rows in a specific order. Note that the table will not remain in this order after inserts and deletes. In some cases, it might make sorting easier for MySQL if the table is in order by the column that you want to order it by later. This option is mainly useful when you know that you are mostly going to query the rows in a certain order; by using this option after big changes to the table, you might be able to get higher performance.

A.1.2 ANALYZE TABLE

ANALYZE TABLE *table_name*[,*table_name*...]

Analyzes and stores the key distribution for the table. During the analysis, the table is locked with a read lock. This works on MyISAM and BDB tables.

This is equivalent to running myisamchk -a on the table.

MySQL uses the stored key distribution to decide in which order tables should be joined when you perform a join on something other than a constant.

The command returns a table with the following columns:

- Table: Table name
- Op: Always analyze
- Msg_type: One of status, error, info, or warning
- Msg_text: The message

You can check the stored key distribution with the SHOW INDEX command.

If the table hasn't changed since the last ANALYZE TABLE command, the table will not be analyzed again.

A.1.3 BACKUP TABLE

BACKUP TABLE *table_name*[,*table_name*...] TO '*/path/to/backup/directory*'

Copies to the backup directory the minimum number of table files needed to restore the table, after flushing any buffered changes to disk. Currently works only for MyISAM tables. For MyISAM tables, copies the .frm (definition) and .MYD (data) files. The .MYI (index) file can be rebuilt from those two files.

During the backup, a read lock will be held for each table, one at time, as they are being backed up. If you want to back up several tables as a snapshot, you must first issue a LOCK TABLES statement to obtain a read lock for each table in the group.

A.1.4 BEGIN

```
BEGIN [WORK]
```

BEGIN [WORK] is a synonym for START TRANSACTION. See section A.1.46, "START TRANSACTION," in this appendix.

When you issue a BEGIN statement (or BEGIN WORK, which is a synonym), the current transaction autocommit mode is suspended, and autocommit is disabled. The following statements form a single transaction. To submit (or confirm) the transaction, issue a COMMIT statement. To cancel the transaction, use ROLLBACK instead. When the transaction ends, the autocommit mode reverts to its state prior to the BEGIN statement.

Transactions are implicitly committed if you issue certain other statements, such as CREATE TABLE. That behavior is covered in detail in Chapter 15, "InnoDB Tables."

The autocommit mode can be enabled or disabled explicitly by setting the AUTOCOMMIT server variable to 1 or 0. See section A.1.31, "SET AUTOCOMMIT," for details. When autocommit is disabled, it is unnecessary to use BEGIN to start a transaction. Just terminate each transaction with COMMIT or ROLLBACK. See sections A.1.6, "COMMIT," and A.1.28, "ROLLBACK," for details.

A.1.5 CHECK TABLE

```
CHECK TABLE table_name[, table_name...] [check_type [check_type...]]

check_type = QUICK | FAST | MEDIUM | EXTENDED | CHANGED
```

CHECK TABLE works only on MyISAM and InnoDB tables. On MyISAM tables, it's the same thing as running myisamchk --medium-check table_name on the table.

If you don't specify any check_type option, MEDIUM is used.

CHECK TABLE checks the table or tables for errors. For MyISAM tables, the key statistics are updated. The command returns a table with the following columns:

- Table: Table name
- Op: Always check
- Msg_type: One of status, error, info, or warning
- Msg_text: The message

Note that the statement might produce many rows of information for each checked table. The last row will have a Msg_type of status and should normally have a Msg_text of OK. If you don't get OK or Table is already up to date, you should normally run a repair of the table. Table is already up to date means that the storage manager for the table indicated that there was no need to check the table.

check_type indicates the type of table-checking operation to perform. The different check types are as follows:

- QUICK: Don't scan the rows to check for incorrect links.
- FAST: Only check tables that haven't been closed properly.
- CHANGED: Only check tables that have been changed since the last check or that haven't been closed properly.
- MEDIUM: Scan rows to verify that deleted links are okay. This also calculates a key checksum for the rows and verifies this with a calculated checksum for the keys.
- EXTENDED: Do a full key lookup for all keys for each row. This ensures that the table is 100% consistent, but will take a long time.

For dynamically sized MyISAM tables, a started check will always do a MEDIUM check. For statically sized rows, we skip the row scan for QUICK and FAST because the rows are very seldom corrupted.

You can combine check options, as in the following example, which does a quick check on the table to see whether it was closed properly:

```
CHECK TABLE test_table FAST QUICK;
```

Note that in some cases CHECK TABLE will change the table! This happens if the table is marked as corrupted or not closed properly but CHECK TABLE didn't find any problems in the table. In this case, CHECK TABLE will mark the table as OK.

If a table is corrupted, it's most likely that the problem is in the indexes and not in the data part. All the preceding check types check the indexes thoroughly and should thus find most errors.

If you just want to check a table that you assume is okay, you should use no check options or the QUICK option. The latter should be used when you're in a hurry and can take the very small risk that QUICK didn't find an error in the datafile. (In most cases MySQL should find, under normal usage, any error in the data file. If this happens then the table will be marked as 'corrupted,' in which case the table can't be used until it's repaired.)

FAST and CHANGED are mostly intended to be used from a script (for example, to be executed from cron) if you want to check your table from time to time. In most cases, FAST is to be preferred over CHANGED. (The only case when it isn't is when you suspect you have found a bug in the MyISAM code.)

EXTENDED is to be used only after you've run a normal check but still get strange errors from a table when MySQL tries to update a row or find a row by key. (This is very unlikely if a normal check has succeeded!)

Some things reported by CHECK TABLE can't be corrected automatically:

Found row where the auto_increment column has the value 0. This means that you have a row in the table where the AUTO_INCREMENT index column contains the value 0. (It's possible to create a row where the AUTO_INCREMENT column is 0 by explicitly setting the column to 0 with an UPDATE statement.) This isn't an error in itself, but could cause trouble if you decide to dump the table and restore it or do an ALTER TABLE on the table. In this case, the AUTO_INCREMENT column will change value according to the rules of AUTO_INCREMENT columns, which could cause problems such as a duplicate-key error. To get rid of the warning, just execute an UPDATE statement to set the column to some value other than 0.

A.1.6 COMMIT

By default, MySQL runs with autocommit mode enabled. This means that as soon as you execute an update, MySQL will store the update on disk.

If you're using transaction-safe tables (like InnoDB, BDB), you can disable autocommit mode with the following statement:

```
SET AUTOCOMMIT=0
```

After this, you must use COMMIT to store your changes to disk or ROLLBACK if you want to ignore the changes you've made since the beginning of your transaction.

If you want to enable autocommit mode for one series of statements, you can use the START TRANSACTION, BEGIN, or BEGIN WORK statement:

```
START TRANSACTION;
SELECT @A:=SUM(salary) FROM table1 WHERE type=1;
UPDATE table2 SET summary=@A WHERE type=1;
COMMIT;
```

START TRANSACTION was added to MySQL 4.0.11. This is the recommended way to start an ad-hoc transaction because this is SQL-99 syntax.

Note that if you are not using transaction-safe tables, any changes will be stored at once, regardless of the status of autocommit mode.

If you do a ROLLBACK after updating a non-transactional table, you will get an error (ER_WARNING_NOT_COMPLETE_ROLLBACK) as a warning. All transaction-safe tables will be restored, but any non-transaction-safe table will not change.

If you're using START TRANSACTION or SET AUTOCOMMIT=0, you should use the MySQL binary log for backups instead of the older update log. Transactions are stored in the binary log in one chunk, upon COMMIT, to ensure that transactions that are rolled back are not stored.

The following commands automatically end a transaction (as if you had done a COMMIT before executing the command):

- ALTER TABLE
- BEGIN

- CREATE INDEX
- DROP DATABASE
- DROP INDEX
- DROP TABLE
- LOAD MASTER DATA
- LOCK TABLES
- RENAME TABLE
- SET AUTOCOMMIT=1
- TRUNCATE

UNLOCK TABLES also ends a transaction if any tables currently are locked.

You can change the isolation level for transactions with SET TRANSACTION ISOLATION LEVEL.

A.1.7 CREATE DATABASE

CREATE DATABASE [IF NOT EXISTS] *db_name*

CREATE DATABASE creates a database with the given name. An error occurs if the database already exists and you didn't specify IF NOT EXISTS.

Databases in MySQL are implemented as directories containing files that correspond to tables in the database. Because there are no tables in a database when it is initially created, the CREATE DATABASE statement only creates a directory under the MySQL data directory.

A.1.8 CREATE INDEX

CREATE [UNIQUE|FULLTEXT] INDEX *index_name*
        ON *table_name* (*column_name*[(*length*)],…)

CREATE INDEX is mapped to an ALTER TABLE statement to create indexes. Normally, you create all indexes on a table at the time the table itself is created with CREATE TABLE. CREATE INDEX enables you to add indexes to existing tables.

A column list of the form *(col1,col2,…)* creates a multiple-column index. Index values are formed by concatenating the values of the given columns.

For CHAR and VARCHAR columns, indexes can be created that use only part of a column, using *column_name(length)* syntax to index the first *length* bytes of each column value. (For BLOB and TEXT columns, a prefix length is required; *length* may be a value up to 255.)

FULLTEXT indexes can index only CHAR, VARCHAR, and TEXT columns, and only in MyISAM tables.

A.1.9 CREATE TABLE

```
CREATE [TEMPORARY] TABLE [IF NOT EXISTS] table_name
    [(create_definition,…)]
    [table_options]
```

create_definition:
```
    column_name type
       [NOT NULL | NULL] [DEFAULT default_value]
       [AUTO_INCREMENT] [PRIMARY KEY]
 | PRIMARY KEY (index_column_name,…)
 | KEY [index_name] (index_column_name,…)
 | INDEX [index_name] (index_column_name,…)
 | UNIQUE [INDEX] [index_name] (index_column_name,…)
 | FULLTEXT [INDEX] [index_name] (index_column_name,…)
```

type:
```
    TINYINT[(length)] [UNSIGNED] [ZEROFILL]
 | SMALLINT[(length)] [UNSIGNED] [ZEROFILL]
 | MEDIUMINT[(length)] [UNSIGNED] [ZEROFILL]
 | INT[(length)] [UNSIGNED] [ZEROFILL]
 | INTEGER[(length)] [UNSIGNED] [ZEROFILL]
 | BIGINT[(length)] [UNSIGNED] [ZEROFILL]
 | REAL[(length, decimals)] [UNSIGNED] [ZEROFILL]
 | DOUBLE[(length, decimals)] [UNSIGNED] [ZEROFILL]
 | FLOAT[(length, decimals)] [UNSIGNED] [ZEROFILL]
 | DECIMAL(length, decimals) [UNSIGNED] [ZEROFILL]
 | NUMERIC(length, decimals) [UNSIGNED] [ZEROFILL]
 | CHAR(length) [BINARY]
 | VARCHAR(length) [BINARY]
 | DATE
 | TIME
 | TIMESTAMP
 | DATETIME
 | TINYBLOB
 | BLOB
 | MEDIUMBLOB
 | LONGBLOB
 | TINYTEXT
 | TEXT
 | MEDIUMTEXT
 | LONGTEXT
 | ENUM(value1, value2, value3,…)
 | SET(value1, value2, value3,…)
```

index_column_name:
```
        column_name [(length)]
```

```
table_options:
    TYPE = {BDB | HEAP | ISAM | InnoDB | MERGE | MRG_MYISAM | MYISAM }
  | AUTO_INCREMENT = #
  | AVG_ROW_LENGTH = #
  | CHECKSUM = {0 | 1}
  | COMMENT = 'string'
  | MAX_ROWS = #
  | MIN_ROWS = #
  | PACK_KEYS = {0 | 1 | DEFAULT}
  | DELAY_KEY_WRITE = {0 | 1}
  | ROW_FORMAT = { DEFAULT | DYNAMIC | FIXED | COMPRESSED }
  | RAID_TYPE = { 1 | STRIPED | RAID0 } RAID_CHUNKS=#  RAID_CHUNKSIZE=#
  | UNION = (table_name,[table_name…])
  | INSERT_METHOD = { NO | FIRST | LAST }
  | DATA DIRECTORY = 'absolute path to directory'
  | INDEX DIRECTORY = 'absolute path to directory'
```

CREATE TABLE creates a table with the given name in the current database. An error occurs if there is no current database or if the table already exists. The table name can be specified as *db_name.table_name* to create the table in a specific database. You can use the keywords IF NOT EXISTS so that an error does not occur if the table already exists. Note that there is no verification that the existing table has a structure identical to that indicated by the CREATE TABLE statement.

Keep the following considerations in mind when declaring columns and indexes:

- If neither NULL nor NOT NULL is specified, the column is treated as though NULL had been specified.

- An integer column may have the additional attribute AUTO_INCREMENT. When you insert a value of NULL (recommended) or 0 into an indexed AUTO_INCREMENT column, the column is set to the next sequence value. Typically this is *value+1*, where *value* is the largest value for the column currently in the table. AUTO_INCREMENT sequences begin with 1. If you delete all rows in the table with DELETE FROM *table_name* (without a WHERE), the sequence starts over from 1 for all table types except InnoDB. The InnoDB table handler guarantees that auto-generated values will be unique for a table, even when all rows have been deleted.

- NULL values are handled differently for TIMESTAMP columns than for other column types. You cannot store a literal NULL in a TIMESTAMP column; setting the column to NULL sets it to the current date and time. Because TIMESTAMP columns behave this way, the NULL and NOT NULL attributes do not apply in the normal way and are ignored if you specify them. On the other hand, to make it easier for MySQL clients to use TIMESTAMP columns, the server reports that such columns may be assigned NULL values (which is true), even though TIMESTAMP never actually will contain a NULL value. Note that setting a TIMESTAMP column to 0 is not the same as setting it to NULL, because 0 is a valid TIMESTAMP value.

- A DEFAULT value must be a constant; it cannot be a function or an expression. If no DEFAULT value is specified for a column, MySQL automatically assigns one, as follows. If the column may take NULL as a value, the default value is NULL. If the column is declared as NOT NULL, the default value depends on the column type:
  - For numeric types other than those declared with the AUTO_INCREMENT attribute, the default is 0. For an AUTO_INCREMENT column, the default value is the next value in the sequence.
  - For date and time types other than TIMESTAMP, the default is the appropriate zero value for the type. For the first TIMESTAMP column in a table, the default value is the current date and time.
  - For string types other than ENUM, the default value is the empty string. For ENUM, the default is the first enumeration value.

- A PRIMARY KEY is a unique key with the extra constraint that all key columns must be defined as NOT NULL. In MySQL, the key is named PRIMARY. A table can have only one PRIMARY KEY. If you don't have a PRIMARY KEY and some applications ask for the PRIMARY KEY in your tables, MySQL will return the first UNIQUE key that doesn't have any NULL columns as the PRIMARY KEY.

- A PRIMARY KEY can be a multiple-column index. However, you cannot create a multiple-column index using the PRIMARY KEY key attibute in a column specification. Doing so will mark only that single column as primary. You must use a separate PRIMARY KEY(index_column_name, …) clause.

- A UNIQUE index is one in which all values in the index must be distinct. The exception to this is that if a column in the index is allowed to contain NULL values, it may contain multiple NULL values. This exception does not apply to BDB tables, which allow only a single NULL.

- If you don't assign a name to an index that is not a PRIMARY KEY, the index will be assigned the same name as the first index_column_name, with an optional suffix (_2, _3, …) to make it unique.

- With column_name(length) syntax in an index specification, you can create an index that uses only the first length bytes of a CHAR or VARCHAR column. This can make the index file much smaller.

- Only the MyISAM table type supports indexing on BLOB and TEXT columns. When putting an index on a BLOB or TEXT column, you *must* always specify the length of the index, up to 255 bytes.

- When you use ORDER BY or GROUP BY with a TEXT or BLOB column, the server sorts values using only the initial number of bytes indicated by the max_sort_length server variable.

- You can also create special FULLTEXT indexes. They are used for full-text search. Only the MyISAM table type supports FULLTEXT indexes. They can be created only from CHAR, VARCHAR, and TEXT columns. Indexing always happens over the entire column; partial indexing is not supported.
- Each NULL column takes one bit extra, rounded up to the nearest byte.

The TYPE option for specifying the table type takes the following values:

- BDB or BerkeleyDB: Transaction-safe tables with page locking.
- HEAP: The data for this table is only stored in memory.
- ISAM: The original storage engine.
- InnoDB: Transaction-safe tables with row locking.
- MERGE: A collection of MyISAM tables used as one table.
- MRG_MyISAM: An alias for MERGE tables.
- MyISAM: The binary portable storage engine that is the replacement for ISAM.

If a storage engine is specified and that particular engine is not available, MySQL uses MyISAM instead. For example, if a table definition includes the TYPE=BDB option but the MySQL server does not support BDB tables, the table is created as a MyISAM table, and no warning is issued.

The other table options are used to optimize the behavior of the table. In most cases, you don't have to specify any of them. The options work for all table types unless otherwise indicated:

- AUTO_INCREMENT: The next AUTO_INCREMENT value you want to set for your table (MyISAM only; to set the first auto-increment value for an InnoDB table, insert a dummy row with a value one less, and delete the dummy row).
- AVG_ROW_LENGTH: An approximation of the average row length for your table. You need to set this only for large tables with variable size records.
- CHECKSUM: Set this to 1 if you want MySQL to maintain a checksum for all rows. It makes the table a little slower to update, but it also makes it easier to find corrupted tables. (MyISAM only).
- COMMENT: A comment for your table (60 characters maximum).
- MAX_ROWS: The maximum number of rows you plan to store in the table.
- MIN_ROWS: The minimum number of rows you plan to store in the table.
- PACK_KEYS: Set this to 1 if you want to have a smaller index. This usually makes updates slower and reads faster (MyISAM and ISAM only). Setting this to 0 disables all packing of keys. Setting this to DEFAULT (MySQL 4.0) tells the storage engine to pack only long CHAR/VARCHAR columns.

- DELAY_KEY_WRITE: Set this to 1 if you want to delay key table updates until the table is closed (MyISAM only).

- ROW_FORMAT: Defines how the rows should be stored. Currently, this option only works with MyISAM tables, which support the DYNAMIC and FIXED row formats.

- RAID_TYPE: Helps to exceed the 2GB or 4GB limit for the MyISAM datafile (not the index file) on operating systems that don't support big files. Note that this option is not recommended for a filesystem that supports big files. You can get more speed from the I/O bottleneck by putting RAID directories on different physical disks. RAID_TYPE will work on any operating system, as long as you have configured MySQL with --with-raid. For now, the only allowed RAID_TYPE is STRIPED (1 and RAID0 are aliases for this). If you specify RAID_TYPE=STRIPED for a MyISAM table, MyISAM creates RAID_CHUNKS sub-directories named 00, 01, 02 in the database directory. In each of these directories, MyISAM creates a table_name.MYD. When writing data to the datafile, the RAID handler maps the first RAID_CHUNKSIZE *1024 bytes to the first file, the next RAID_CHUNKSIZE *1024 bytes to the next file and so on.

- UNION: Used when you want to use a collection of identical tables as one. This works only with MERGE tables. For the moment, you need to have SELECT, UPDATE, and DELETE privileges on the tables you map to a MERGE table. All mapped tables must be in the same database as the MERGE table.

- INSERT_METHOD: If you want to insert data in a MERGE table, you have to specify with INSERT_METHOD into which table the row should be inserted. INSERT_METHOD is an option useful for MERGE tables only. In the created table, the PRIMARY key will be placed first, followed by all UNIQUE keys, and then the normal keys. This helps the MySQL optimizer to prioritize which key to use and also more quickly to detect duplicated UNIQUE keys.

- DATA DIRECTORY/INDEX DIRECTORY: By using DATA DIRECTORY='directory' or INDEX DIRECTORY='directory' you can specify where the storage engine should put its datafile and index file. Note that the directory should be a full path to the directory (not a relative path). This only works for MyISAM tables when you aren't using the --skip-symlink option.

A.1.10 DELETE

```
DELETE FROM table_name
       [WHERE where_definition]
       [ORDER BY …]
       [LIMIT rows]
or (as of MySQL 4.0.0)
DELETE table_name[.*] [, table_name[.*] …]
       FROM table-references
       [WHERE where_definition]
or (as of MySQL 4.0.2)
DELETE FROM table_name[.*] [, table_name[.*] …]
       USING table-references
       [WHERE where_definition]
```

DELETE deletes rows from *table_name* that satisfy the condition given by *where_definition*, and returns the number of records deleted.

If you issue a DELETE with no WHERE clause, all rows are deleted.

If an ORDER BY clause is used (available as of MySQL 4.0), the rows will be deleted in that order. This is really useful only in conjunction with LIMIT. The MySQL-specific LIMIT rows option to DELETE tells the server the maximum number of rows to be deleted before control is returned to the client. This can be used to ensure that a specific DELETE command doesn't take too much time. You can simply repeat the DELETE command until the number of affected rows is less than the LIMIT value.

From MySQL 4.0, you can specify multiple tables in the DELETE statement to delete rows from one or more tables depending on a particular condition in multiple tables. However, you cannot use ORDER BY or LIMIT in a multi-table DELETE.

A.1.11 DESCRIBE

{DESCRIBE | DESC} *table_name* {*column_name* | *wild*}

DESCRIBE is a shortcut for SHOW COLUMNS FROM. It provides information about a table's columns. *column_name* may be a column name or a string containing the SQL **%** and _ wildcard characters to obtain output only for the columns with names matching the string. DESCRIBE is provided for Oracle compatibility.

A.1.12 DROP DATABASE

DROP DATABASE [IF EXISTS] *db_name*

DROP DATABASE drops all tables in the database and deletes the database. If you do a DROP DATABASE on a symbolic linked database, both the link and the original database are deleted. Be *very* careful with this command!

DROP DATABASE returns the number of files that were removed from the database directory. For MyISAM tables, this is three times the number of tables because each table normally corresponds to a .MYD file, a .MYI file, and a .frm file.

You can use the keywords IF EXISTS to prevent an error from occurring if the database doesn't exist.

A.1.13 DROP INDEX

DROP INDEX *index_name* ON *table_name*

DROP INDEX drops the index named index_name from the table table_name. DROP INDEX is mapped to an ALTER TABLE statement to drop the index (see section A.1.1, "ALTER TABLE").

A.1.14 DROP TABLE

```
DROP [TEMPORARY] TABLE [IF EXISTS] table_name [, table_name,…]
```

DROP TABLE removes one or more tables. All table data and the table definition are removed, so be careful with this command!

You can use the keywords IF EXISTS to prevent an error from occurring for tables that don't exist.

A.1.15 EXPLAIN

```
    EXPLAIN table_name
or  EXPLAIN SELECT select_options
```

EXPLAIN table_name is a synonym for DESCRIBE table_name or SHOW COLUMNS FROM table_name.

When you precede a SELECT statement with the keyword EXPLAIN, MySQL explains how it would process the SELECT, providing information about how tables are joined and in which order.

With the help of EXPLAIN, you can see when you must add indexes to tables to get a faster SELECT that uses indexes to find the records.

For details regarding the output of EXPLAIN, for details about that command, and for examples of its use please refer to the *MySQL Reference Manual*.

A.1.16 FLUSH TABLES

```
FLUSH TABLES
```

This command forces all tables to be closed and reopened.

A.1.17 GRANT

```
GRANT priv_type [(column_list)] [, priv_type [(column_list)] …]
    ON {table_name | * | *.* | db_name.*}
    TO user_name [IDENTIFIED BY [PASSWORD] 'password']
        [, user_name [IDENTIFIED BY [PASSWORD] 'password'] …]
    [REQUIRE
        NONE |
        [{SSL| X509}]
        [CIPHER cipher [AND]]
        [ISSUER issuer [AND]]
        [SUBJECT subject]]
    [WITH [GRANT OPTION | MAX_QUERIES_PER_HOUR # |
                          MAX_UPDATES_PER_HOUR # |
                          MAX_CONNECTIONS_PER_HOUR #]]
```

The GRANT command enables database administrators to create users and grant rights to MySQL users at four privilege levels:

- Global level: Global privileges apply to all databases on a given server. These privileges are stored in the `mysql.user` table.

- Database level: Database privileges apply to all tables in a given database. These privileges are stored in the `mysql.db` and `mysql.host` tables.

- Table level: Table privileges apply to all columns in a given table. These privileges are stored in the `mysql.tables_priv` table.

- Column level: Column privileges apply to single columns in a given table. These privileges are stored in the `mysql.columns_priv` table.

For details, particularly on the privileges you can grant, see the *MySQL Reference Manual*.

A.1.18 INSERT

```
    INSERT [LOW_PRIORITY | DELAYED] [IGNORE]
        [INTO] table_name
        [(column_name,…)]
        VALUES ((expression | DEFAULT),…),(…),…
or  INSERT [LOW_PRIORITY | DELAYED] [IGNORE]
        [INTO] table_name
        [(column_name,…)]
        SELECT …
or  INSERT [LOW_PRIORITY | DELAYED] [IGNORE]
        [INTO] table_name
        SET column_name=(expression | DEFAULT), …
```

INSERT inserts new rows into an existing table. The INSERT … VALUES form of the statement inserts rows based on explicitly specified values.

table_name is the table into which rows should be inserted. The column name list or the SET clause indicates which columns the statement specifies values for:

- If you specify no column list for INSERT … VALUES, values for all columns in the table must be provided in the VALUES() list or by the SELECT.

- Any column not explicitly given a value is set to its default value. For example, if you specify a column list that doesn't name all the columns in the table, unnamed columns are set to their default values.

- An expression may refer to any column that was set earlier in a value list.

- If you specify the keyword DELAYED, the server puts the row or rows to be inserted into a buffer, and the client issuing the INSERT DELAYED statement then may continue on. If the table is busy, the server holds the rows. When the table becomes available for inserts, the server begins inserting rows, checking periodically to see whether there are new read requests for the table. If there are, the delayed row queue is suspended until the table becomes free again.

- If you specify the keyword LOW_PRIORITY, execution of the INSERT is delayed until no other clients are reading from the table. This includes other clients that began reading while existing clients are reading, and while the INSERT LOW_PRIORITY statement is waiting. It is possible, therefore, for a client that issues an INSERT LOW_PRIORITY statement to wait for a very long time (or even forever) in a read-heavy environment. (This is in contrast to INSERT DELAYED, which lets the client continue at once.) Note that LOW_PRIORITY should normally not be used with MyISAM tables as this disables concurrent inserts.

- If you specify the keyword IGNORE in an INSERT with many rows, any rows that duplicate an existing PRIMARY or UNIQUE key in the table are ignored (are not inserted). If you do not specify IGNORE, the insert is aborted if there is any row that duplicates an existing key value.

With INSERT … SELECT, you can quickly insert many rows into a table from one or many tables. The following conditions hold true for an INSERT … SELECT statement:

- Prior to MySQL 4.0.14, the target table of the INSERT statement cannot appear in the FROM clause of the SELECT part of the query.

- AUTO_INCREMENT columns work as usual.

- To ensure that the binary log can be used to re-create the original tables, MySQL will not allow concurrent inserts during INSERT … SELECT.

You can also use REPLACE instead of INSERT to overwrite old rows. REPLACE is the counterpart to INSERT IGNORE in the treatment of new rows that contain unique key values that duplicate old rows: The new rows are used to replace the old rows rather than being discarded.

A.1.19 JOIN

MySQL supports the following JOIN syntaxes for use in SELECT statements:

```
table_reference, table_reference
table_reference [CROSS] JOIN table_reference
table_reference INNER JOIN table_reference join_condition
table_reference STRAIGHT_JOIN table_reference
table_reference LEFT [OUTER] JOIN table_reference join_condition
table_reference LEFT [OUTER] JOIN table_reference
table_reference NATURAL [LEFT [OUTER]] JOIN table_reference
{ OJ table_reference LEFT OUTER JOIN table_reference ON conditional_expr }
table_reference RIGHT [OUTER] JOIN table_reference join_condition
table_reference RIGHT [OUTER] JOIN table_reference
table_reference NATURAL [RIGHT [OUTER]] JOIN table_reference
```

table_reference is defined as:

```
table_name [[AS] alias]
```

`join_condition` is defined as:

```
ON conditional_expr | USING (column_list)
```

You should generally not have any conditions in the ON part that are used to restrict which rows you have in the result set (there are exceptions to this rule). If you want to restrict which rows should be in the result, you have to do this in the WHERE clause.

The last LEFT OUTER JOIN syntax shown in the preceding list exists only for compatibility with ODBA.

- A table reference may be aliased using `table_name` AS `alias_name` or `table_name` `alias_name`.
- The ON conditional is any conditional of the form that may be used in a WHERE clause.
- If there is no matching record for the right table in the ON or USING part in a LEFT JOIN, a row with all columns set to NULL is used for the right table. You can use this fact to find records in a table that have no counterpart in another table.
- The USING `(column_list)` clause names a list of columns that must exist in both tables.
- The NATURAL [LEFT] JOIN of two tables is defined to be semantically equivalent to an INNER JOIN or a LEFT JOIN with a USING clause that names all columns that exist in both tables.
- INNER JOIN and , (comma) are semantically equivalent in the absence of a join condition. Both produce a Cartesian product of the tables used. Normally, you specify how the tables should be linked in the WHERE condition.
- RIGHT JOIN works analogously to LEFT JOIN. To keep code portable across databases, it's recommended to use LEFT JOIN instead of RIGHT JOIN.
- STRAIGHT_JOIN is identical to JOIN, except that the left table is always read before the right table. This can be used for those (few) cases in which the join optimizer puts the tables in the wrong order.

A.1.20 LOAD DATA INFILE

```
LOAD DATA [LOCAL] INFILE 'file_name'
    [REPLACE | IGNORE]
    INTO TABLE table_name
    [FIELDS
        [TERMINATED BY '\t']
        [[OPTIONALLY] ENCLOSED BY '']
        [ESCAPED BY '\\' ]
    ]
    [LINES TERMINATED BY '\n']
    [IGNORE number LINES]
    [(column_name,…)]
```

The LOAD DATA INFILE statement reads rows from a text file into a table at a very high speed. If the LOCAL keyword is specified, it is interpreted with respect to the client end of the connection. When LOCAL is specified, the file is read by the client program on the client host and sent to the server. If LOCAL is not specified, the file must be located on the server host and is read directly by the server.

For security reasons, when reading text files located on the server, the files must either reside in the database directory or be readable by all. Also, to use LOAD DATA INFILE on server files, you must have the FILE privilege on the server host.

Using LOCAL will be a bit slower than letting the server access the files directly because the contents of the file must be sent over the connection by the client to the server. On the other hand, you do not need the FILE privilege to load local files.

You can also load datafiles by using the mysqlimport utility; it operates by sending a LOAD DATA INFILE command to the server. The --local option causes mysqlimport to read datafiles from the client host.

When locating files on the server host, the server uses the following rules:

- If an absolute pathname is given, the server uses the pathname as is.
- If a relative pathname with one or more leading components is given, the server searches for the file relative to the server's data directory.
- If a filename with no leading components is given, the server looks for the file in the database directory of the current database.

Note that these rules mean a file named as ./myfile.txt is read from the server's data directory, whereas the same file named as myfile.txt is read from the database directory of the current database.

The REPLACE and IGNORE keywords control handling of input records that duplicate existing records on unique key values. If you specify REPLACE, input rows replace existing rows that have the same unique key value. If you specify IGNORE, input rows that duplicate an existing row on a unique key value are skipped. If you don't specify either option, the behavior depends on whether or not the LOCAL keyword is specified. Without LOCAL, an error occurs when a duplicate key value is found, and the rest of the text file is ignored. With LOCAL, the default behavior is the same as if IGNORE is specified; this is because the server has no way to stop transmission of the file in the middle of the operation.

LOAD DATA INFILE is the complement of SELECT … INTO OUTFILE. To write data from a table to a file, use SELECT … INTO OUTFILE. To read the file back into a table, use LOAD DATA INFILE. The syntax of the FIELDS and LINES clauses is the same for both commands. Both clauses are optional, but FIELDS must precede LINES if both are specified.

If you specify a FIELDS clause, each of its subclauses (TERMINATED BY, [OPTIONALLY] ENCLOSED BY, and ESCAPED BY) is also optional, except that you must specify at least one of them.

If you don't specify a FIELDS clause, the defaults are the same as if you had written this:

```
FIELDS TERMINATED BY '\t' ENCLOSED BY '' ESCAPED BY '\\'
```

If you don't specify a LINES clause, the default is the same as if you had written this:

```
LINES TERMINATED BY '\n'
```

Note that to write FIELDS ESCAPED BY '\\', you must specify two backslashes for the value to be read as a single backslash.

The IGNORE *number* LINES option can be used to ignore lines at the start of the file. For example, you can use IGNORE 1 LINES to skip over an initial header line containing column names.

Any of the field or line handling options may specify an empty string (' '). If not empty, the FIELDS [OPTIONALLY] ENCLOSED BY and FIELDS ESCAPED BY values must be a single character. The FIELDS TERMINATED BY and LINES TERMINATED BY values may be more than one character.

FIELDS [OPTIONALLY] ENCLOSED BY controls quoting of fields. For output (SELECT … INTO OUTFILE), if you omit the word OPTIONALLY, all fields are enclosed by the ENCLOSED BY character. If you specify OPTIONALLY, the ENCLOSED BY character is used only to enclose CHAR and VARCHAR fields.

FIELDS ESCAPED BY controls how to write or read special characters. If the FIELDS ESCAPED BY character is not empty, it is used to prefix the following characters on output:

- The FIELDS ESCAPED BY character
- The FIELDS [OPTIONALLY] ENCLOSED BY character
- The first character of the FIELDS TERMINATED BY and LINES TERMINATED BY values
- ASCII 0 (what is actually written following the escape character is ASCII '0', not a zero-valued byte)

If the FIELDS ESCAPED BY character is empty, no characters are escaped. It is probably not a good idea to specify an empty escape character, particularly if field values in your data contain any of the characters in the previous list (such as ASCII 0).

For input, if the FIELDS ESCAPED BY character is not empty, occurrences of that character are stripped and the following character is taken literally as part of a field value. The exceptions are an escaped 0 or N (for example, \0 or \N if the escape character is \). These sequences are interpreted as ASCII NUL (a zero-valued byte) and NULL.

If you want to load only some of a table's columns, specify a field list.

You must also specify a field list if the order of the fields in the input file differs from the order of the columns in the table. Otherwise, MySQL cannot tell how to match up input fields with table columns.

If a row has too few fields, the columns for which no input field is present are set to their default values.

TIMESTAMP columns are set to the current date and time only if there is a NULL value for the column (that is, \N), or (for the first TIMESTAMP column only) if the TIMESTAMP column is omitted from the field list when a field list is specified.

If an input row has too many fields, the extra fields are ignored and the number of warnings is incremented.

LOAD DATA INFILE regards all input as strings, so you can't use numeric values for ENUM or SET columns the way you can with INSERT statements. All ENUM and SET values must be specified as strings.

Warnings occur under the same circumstances as when values are inserted via the INSERT statement, except that LOAD DATA INFILE also generates warnings when there are too few or too many fields in the input row.

A.1.21 LOCK TABLES

```
LOCK TABLES table_name [AS alias] {READ [LOCAL] | [LOW_PRIORITY] WRITE}
            [, table_name [AS alias] {READ [LOCAL] | [LOW_PRIORITY] WRITE}] …
```

To use LOCK TABLES, you need the global LOCK TABLES privilege and a SELECT privilege on the involved tables.

The main reasons to use LOCK TABLES are for emulating transactions or getting more speed when updating tables.

If a thread obtains a READ lock on a table, that thread (and all other threads) can only read from the table. If a thread obtains a WRITE lock on a table, only the thread holding the lock can read from or write to the table. Other threads are blocked.

The difference between READ LOCAL and READ is that READ LOCAL allows nonconflicting INSERT statements to execute while the lock is held. However, this can't be used if you're going to manipulate the database files outside MySQL while you hold the lock.

When you use LOCK TABLES, you must lock all tables that you're going to use and you must use the same alias that you're going to use in your queries. If you're using a table multiple times in a query (with aliases), you must get a lock for each alias.

WRITE locks normally have higher priority than READ locks to ensure that updates are processed as soon as possible. This means that if one thread obtains a READ lock and then another thread requests a WRITE lock, subsequent READ lock requests will wait until the WRITE thread has gotten the lock and released it. You can use LOW_PRIORITY WRITE locks to allow other threads to obtain READ locks while the thread is waiting for the WRITE lock. You should use LOW_PRIORITY WRITE locks only if you are sure that there will eventually be a time when no threads will have a READ lock.

LOCK TABLES works as follows:

1. Sort all tables to be locked in an internally defined order (from the user standpoint, the order is undefined).
2. If a table is locked with a read and a write lock, put the write lock before the read lock.
3. Lock one table at a time until the thread gets all locks.

This policy ensures that table locking is deadlock free. There are, however, other things you need to be aware of with this schema:

If you're using a LOW_PRIORITY WRITE lock for a table, it means only that MySQL will wait for this particlar lock until there are no threads that want a READ lock. When the thread has gotten the WRITE lock and is waiting to get the lock for the next table in the lock table list, all other threads will wait for the WRITE lock to be released. If this becomes a serious problem with your application, you should consider converting some of your tables to transaction-safe tables.

You can safely kill a thread that is waiting for a table lock with KILL.

Note that you should *not* lock any tables that you are using with INSERT DELAYED. This is because, in this case, the INSERT is done by a separate thread.

Normally, you don't have to lock tables because all single UPDATE statements are atomic; no other thread can interfere with any other currently executing SQL statement. There are a few cases when you would like to lock tables anyway:

- If you're going to run many operations on multiple tables, it's much faster to lock the tables you are going to use. The downside is that no other thread can update a READ-locked table and no other thread can read a WRITE-locked table.

  The reason some things are faster under LOCK TABLES is that MySQL will not flush the key cache for the locked tables until UNLOCK TABLES is called (normally the key cache is flushed after each SQL statement). This speeds up inserting, updating, and deleting on MyISAM tables.

- If you're using a storage engine in MySQL that doesn't support transactions, you must use LOCK TABLES if you want to ensure that no other thread comes between a SELECT and an UPDATE. The example shown here requires LOCK TABLES to execute safely:

```
mysql> LOCK TABLES trans READ, customer WRITE;
mysql> SELECT SUM(value) FROM trans WHERE customer_id=some_id;
mysql> UPDATE customer SET total_value=sum_from_previous_statement
    ->          WHERE customer_id=some_id;
mysql> UNLOCK TABLES;
```

Without LOCK TABLES, there is a chance that another thread might insert a new row in the trans table between execution of the SELECT and UPDATE statements.

By using incremental updates (UPDATE customer SET *value=value+new_value*) or the LAST_INSERT_ID() function, you can avoid using LOCK TABLES in many cases.

You can also solve some cases by using the user-level lock functions GET_LOCK() and RELEASE_LOCK().

You can lock all tables in all databases with read locks with the FLUSH TABLES WITH READ LOCK command. This is a very convenient way to get backups if you have a filesystem, such as Veritas, that can take snapshots in time.

Note that LOCK TABLES is not transaction-safe and will automatically commit any active transactions before attempting to lock the tables.

The counterpart to the LOCK TABLES command is UNLOCK TABLES (section A.1.49, "UNLOCK TABLES").

A.1.22 OPTIMIZE TABLE

OPTIMIZE TABLE *table_name*[,*table_name*]...

At the moment, OPTIMIZE TABLE works only on MyISAM and BDB tables. For BDB tables, OPTIMIZE TABLE is currently mapped to ANALYZE TABLE (see section A.1.2, "ANALYZE TABLE"). You can get OPTIMIZE TABLE to work on other table types by starting mysqld with --skip-new or --safe-mode, but in this case OPTIMIZE TABLE is just mapped to ALTER TABLE (see section A.1.1, "ALTER TABLE").

OPTIMIZE TABLE should be used if you've deleted a large part of a table or if you've made many changes to a table with variable-length rows (tables that have VARCHAR, BLOB, or TEXT columns). Deleted records are maintained in a linked list and subsequent INSERT operations reuse old record positions. You can use OPTIMIZE TABLE to reclaim the unused space and to defragment the datafile.

OPTIMIZE TABLE works the following way:

- If the table has deleted or split rows, repair the table.
- If the index pages are not sorted, sort them.
- If the statistics are not up-to-date (and the repair couldn't be done by sorting the index), update them.

OPTIMIZE TABLE for a MyISAM table is equivalent to running myisamchk --quick --check-only-changed --sort-index --analyze on the table.

Note that the table is locked during the time OPTIMIZE TABLE is running.

A.1.23 RENAME TABLE

RENAME TABLE *table_name* TO *new_table_name*[, *table_name2* TO *new_table_name2*,...]

Assigns *new_table_name* to the table *table_name*.

A.1.24 REPAIR TABLE

```
REPAIR TABLE table_name[,table_name...] [QUICK] [EXTENDED] [USE_FRM]
```

REPAIR TABLE works only on MyISAM tables and is the same as running myisamchk -r `table_name` on the table.

Normally, you should never have to run this command, but if disaster strikes, you're very likely to get back all your data from a MyISAM table with REPAIR TABLE. If your tables get corrupted often, you should try to find the reason for it to eliminate the need to use REPAIR TABLE.

REPAIR TABLE repairs a possibly corrupted table. The command returns a table with the following columns:

- Table: Table name
- Op: Always repair
- Msg_type: One of status, error, info, or warning
- Msg_text: The message

Note that the statement might produce many rows of information for each repaired table. The last row will have a Msg_type of status and should normally have a Msg_text of OK. If you don't get OK, you should try repairing the table with myisamchk --safe-recover because REPAIR TABLE does not yet implement all the options of myisamchk. In the near future, we'll make it more flexible.

If QUICK is given, REPAIR TABLE tries to repair only the index tree.

If you use EXTENDED, MySQL creates the index row by row instead of creating one index at a time with sorting. This might be better than sorting on fixed-length keys if you have long CHAR keys that compress very well. EXTENDED repair is like that done by myisamchk --safe-recover.

Use USE_FRM mode for REPAIR if the .MYI file is missing or if its header is corrupted. In this mode, MySQL will re-create the table using information from the .frm file. This kind of repair cannot be done with myisamchk.

A.1.25 REPLACE

```
    REPLACE [LOW_PRIORITY | DELAYED]
            [INTO] table_name
            [(column_name,...)]
            VALUES (expression,...),(...),...
or  REPLACE [LOW_PRIORITY | DELAYED]
            [INTO] table_name
            SET column_name=expression, column_name=expression,...
```

REPLACE works exactly like INSERT, except that if an old record in the table has the same value as a new record on a UNIQUE index or PRIMARY KEY, the old record is deleted before the new record is inserted.

To be able to use REPLACE, you must have INSERT and DELETE privileges for the table.

When you use a REPLACE statement, the affected-rows count is 2 if the new row replaced an old row. This is because one row was inserted after the duplicate was deleted. This fact makes it easy to determine whether REPLACE added or replaced a row: check whether the affected-rows value is 1 (added) or 2 (replaced).

Note that unless the table has a UNIQUE index or PRIMARY KEY, using a REPLACE command makes no sense. It becomes equivalent to INSERT because there is no unique-valued index to be used to determine whether a new row duplicates another.

A.1.26 RESTORE TABLE

RESTORE TABLE tbl_name[,tbl_name…] FROM '/path/to/backup/directory'

Restores the table or tables from the backup that was made with BACKUP TABLE. Existing tables will not be overwritten; if you try to restore over an existing table, you'll get an error. Restoring will take longer than backing up due to the need to rebuild the index. The more keys you have, the longer it will take. Just as BACKUP TABLE, RESTORE TABLE currently works only for MyISAM tables.

A.1.27 REVOKE

REVOKE priv_type [(column_list)] [, priv_type [(column_list)] …]
    ON {table_name | * | *.* | db_name.*}
    FROM user_name [, user_name …]

Revokes privileges granted to a user by using the GRANT command. When using REVOKE to revoke privileges on the column level, you must specify the same columns that were granted.

See also section A.1.17, "GRANT."

A.1.28 ROLLBACK

ROLLBACK

After disabling autocommit mode by setting the AUTOCOMMIT variable to zero, you must use COMMIT to store your changes to disk or ROLLBACK if you want to ignore the changes you've made since the beginning of your transaction. See section A.1.6, "COMMIT," for details.

A.1.29 SELECT

```
SELECT [STRAIGHT_JOIN]
       [SQL_SMALL_RESULT] [SQL_BIG_RESULT] [SQL_BUFFER_RESULT]
       [SQL_CACHE | SQL_NO_CACHE] [SQL_CALC_FOUND_ROWS] [HIGH_PRIORITY]
       [DISTINCT | DISTINCTROW]
    select_expression,…
    [INTO OUTFILE 'file_name' export_options
    | INTO DUMPFILE 'file_name']
    [FROM table_references
      [WHERE where_definition]
      [GROUP BY {unsigned_integer | column_name | formula} [ASC | DESC], …]
      [HAVING where_definition]
      [ORDER BY {unsigned_integer | column_name | formula} [ASC | DESC] ,…]
      [LIMIT [offset,] row_count]
      [PROCEDURE procedure_name]
      [FOR UPDATE | LOCK IN SHARE MODE]]
```

SELECT is used to retrieve rows selected from one or more tables. A *select_expression* indicates a column you want to retrieve. SELECT may also be used to retrieve rows computed without reference to any table.

All clauses used must be given in exactly the order shown in the syntax description. For example, a HAVING clause must come after any GROUP BY clause and before any ORDER BY clause.

- A SELECT expression may be given an alias using AS *alias_name*. The alias is used as the expression's column name and can be used with ORDER BY or HAVING clauses. The AS keyword is optional when aliasing a SELECT expression.

- You aren't allowed to use a column alias in a WHERE clause because the column value might not yet be determined when the WHERE clause is executed.

- The FROM *table_references* clause indicates the tables from which to retrieve rows. If you name more than one table, you're performing a join. Joins are discussed further in the "Core Study Guide."

- A table reference may be aliased using *table_name* AS *alias_name*. The AS keyword is optional.

- Columns selected for output may be referred to in ORDER BY and GROUP BY clauses using column names, column aliases, or column positions. Column positions begin with 1. To sort in reverse order, add the DESC (descending) keyword to the name of the column in the ORDER BY clause that you're sorting by. The default is ascending order; this may be specified explicitly using the ASC keyword.

- In the WHERE clause, you can use any of the functions that MySQL supports, except for aggregate (summary) functions.

- The HAVING clause can refer to any column or alias named in the *select_expression*. It is applied nearly last, just before items are sent to the client, with no optimization.

(LIMIT is applied after HAVING.) Don't use HAVING for items that should be in the WHERE clause.

- The DISTINCT and DISTINCTROW options specify that duplicate rows in the result set should be removed.

- STRAIGHT_JOIN, HIGH_PRIORITY, and options beginning with SQL, are MySQL extensions to SQL-99.

  - HIGH_PRIORITY will give the SELECT higher priority than a statement that updates a table. You should use this only for queries that are very fast and must be done at once. A SELECT HIGH_PRIORITY query will run if the table is locked for reading even if there is an update statement that is waiting for the table to be free.

  - SQL_BIG_RESULT can be used with GROUP BY or DISTINCT to tell the optimizer that the result set will have many rows. In this case, MySQL will directly use disk-based temporary tables if needed. MySQL will also, in this case, prefer sorting to doing a temporary table with a key on the GROUP BY elements.

  - SQL_BUFFER_RESULT forces the result to be put into a temporary table. This helps MySQL free the table locks early and helps in cases where it takes a long time to send the result set to the client.

  - SQL_SMALL_RESULT can be used with GROUP BY or DISTINCT to tell the optimizer that the result set will be small. In this case, MySQL uses fast temporary tables to store the resulting table instead of using sorting.

  - SQL_CALC_FOUND_ROWS tells MySQL to calculate how many rows there would be in the result, disregarding any LIMIT clause. The number of rows then can be obtained with SELECT FOUND_ROWS().

  - SQL_CACHE tells MySQL to store the query result in the query cache if you're using QUERY_CACHE_TYPE=2 (DEMAND).

  - SQL_NO_CACHE tells MySQL not to store the query result in the query cache.

  - STRAIGHT_JOIN forces the optimizer to join the tables in the order in which they are listed in the FROM clause. You can use this to speed up a query if the optimizer joins the tables in non-optimal order.

- If you use GROUP BY, the output rows will be sorted according to the GROUP BY as if you had an ORDER BY over all the fields in the GROUP BY. MySQL has extended the GROUP BY clause so that you can also specify ASC and DESC after columns named in the clause.

- The LIMIT clause can be used to constrain the number of rows returned by the SELECT statement. LIMIT takes one or two numeric arguments, which must be integer constants. With one argument, the value specifies the number of rows to return from the beginning of the result set. With two arguments, the first argument specifies the offset of the first row to return, and the second specifies the maximum number of rows to return. The offset of the initial row is 0 (not 1).

- The SELECT ... INTO OUTFILE 'file_name' form of SELECT writes the selected rows to a file. The file is created on the server host and cannot already exist (among other things, this prevents database tables and files such as /etc/passwd from being destroyed). You must have the FILE privilege on the server host to use this form of SELECT. The SELECT ... INTO OUTFILE statement is intended primarily to let you very quickly dump a table on the server machine. If you want to create the resulting file on some other host than the server host, you can't use SELECT ... INTO OUTFILE. In that case, you should instead use a client program such as mysqldump to generate the file. SELECT ... INTO OUTFILE is the complement of LOAD DATA INFILE; the syntax for the export_options part of the statement consists of the same FIELDS and LINES clauses that are used with the LOAD DATA INFILE statement. Note that any file created by INTO OUTFILE will be writable by all users on the server host. The reason is that the MySQL server can't create a file that is owned by anyone else than the user it's running as (you should never run mysqld as root). The file thus must be world-writable so that you can manipulate its contents.

- If you use INTO DUMPFILE instead of INTO OUTFILE, MySQL will only write one row into the file, without any column or line terminations and without performing any escape processing. This is useful if you want to store a BLOB value in a file.

- If you use FOR UPDATE on a table handler with page or row locks, the examined rows are write-locked until the end of the current transaction.

A.1.30 SET

```
SET [GLOBAL | SESSION] sql_variable=expression
    [, [GLOBAL | SESSION] sql_variable=expression] ...
```

SET sets various options that affect the operation of the server or your client.

The following examples show the different syntaxes one can use to set variables:

LOCAL can be used as a synonym for SESSION.

If you set several variables on the same command line, the last used GLOBAL | SESSION mode is used.

The @@variable_name syntax is supported to make MySQL syntax compatible with some other databases.

Some of the system variables you can set are described in the system variable section of this appendix. See section A.4, "Server System Variables."

If you're using SESSION (the default), the option you set remains in effect until the current session ends or until you set the option to a different value. If you use GLOBAL, which requires the SUPER privilege, the option is remembered and used for new connections until the server restarts. If you want to make an option permanent, you should set it in one of the MySQL option files.

To avoid incorrect usage, MySQL will produce an error if you use SET GLOBAL with a variable that can only be used with SET SESSION, or if you attempt to set a a global variable without specifying GLOBAL.

If you want to set a SESSION variable to the GLOBAL value or a GLOBAL value to the MySQL default value, you can set it to DEFAULT.

See also the SHOW VARIABLES section in this appendix (A.1.45, "SHOW VARIABLES").

A.1.31 SET AUTOCOMMIT

SET AUTOCOMMIT = {0 | 1}

If you're using transaction-safe tables (such as InnoDB or BDB), you can disable autocommit mode with the following statement:

SET AUTOCOMMIT=0

To enable autocommit mode, use the following statement:

SET AUTOCOMMIT=1

By default, autocommit mode is enabled.

A.1.32 SET PASSWORD

SET PASSWORD FOR 'user'[@'host']=PASSWORD('new_password')

Sets the password for the specified user. Note that the password needs to be encrypted using the PASSWORD() function.

A.1.33 SET TRANSACTION ISOLATION LEVEL

SET [GLOBAL | SESSION] TRANSACTION ISOLATION LEVEL
{ READ UNCOMMITTED | READ COMMITTED | REPEATABLE READ | SERIALIZABLE }

Sets the transaction isolation level for the global, whole session, or the next transaction.

The default behavior is to set the isolation level for the next (not started) transaction. If you use the GLOBAL keyword, the statement sets the default transaction level globally for all new connections created from that point on (but not existing connections). You need the SUPER privilege to do this. Using the SESSION keyword sets the default transaction level for all future transactions performed on the current connection.

InnoDB supports each of these levels from MySQL 4.0.5 on. The default level is REPEATABLE READ.

You can set the default global isolation level for mysqld with --transaction-isolation.

A.1.34 SHOW

```
    SHOW COLUMNS FROM table_name [FROM db_name] [LIKE 'pattern']
|   SHOW CREATE TABLE table_name
|   SHOW DATABASES [LIKE 'pattern']
|   SHOW INDEX FROM table_name [FROM db_name]
|   SHOW INNODB STATUS
|   SHOW [FULL] PROCESSLIST
|   SHOW STATUS [LIKE 'pattern']
|   SHOW TABLE STATUS [FROM db_name] [LIKE 'pattern']
|   SHOW TABLES [FROM db_name] [LIKE 'pattern']
|   SHOW VARIABLES [LIKE 'pattern']
```

SHOW provides information about databases, tables, columns, or status information about the server. If the LIKE 'pattern' part is used, the 'pattern' string can contain the SQL % and _ wildcard characters.

A.1.35 SHOW COLUMNS

```
SHOW COLUMNS FROM table_name [FROM db_name] [LIKE 'pattern']
```

Lists the columns in a given table. SHOW FIELDS is a synonym for SHOW COLUMNS.

A.1.36 SHOW CREATE TABLE

```
SHOW CREATE TABLE table_name
```

Shows a CREATE TABLE statement that will create the given table.

A.1.37 SHOW DATABASES

```
SHOW DATABASES [LIKE 'pattern']
```

Lists the databases on the MySQL server host. If you don't have the global SHOW DATABASES privilege, you'll see only those databases for which you have some kind of privilege.

A.1.38 SHOW FIELDS

SHOW FIELDS is a synonym for SHOW COLUMNS. See section A.1.35, "SHOW COLUMNS."

A.1.39 SHOW INDEX

```
SHOW INDEX FROM table_name [FROM db_name]
```

Returns index information about a table. Here are some of the columns that are returned:

- Non_unique: 0 if the index can't contain duplicates, 1 if it can
- Key_name: Name of the index

- Column_name: Column name
- Sub_part: Number of indexed characters if the column is only partly indexed; NULL if the entire key is indexed
- Null: Contains YES if the column may contain NULL

A.1.40 SHOW INNODB STATUS

SHOW INNODB STATUS

The InnoDB storage engine includes InnoDB Monitors that print information about the InnoDB internal state. The SHOW INNODB STATUS statement fetches the output of the standard InnoDB Monitor to the SQL client. The information is useful in performance tuning. If you're using the mysql interactive SQL client, the output is more readable if you replace the usual semicolon statement terminator by \G:

SHOW INNODB STATUS\G

A.1.41 SHOW PROCESSLIST

SHOW [FULL] PROCESSLIST

SHOW [FULL] PROCESSLIST shows you which threads are running. You can also get this information using the mysqladmin processlist command. If you have the SUPER privilege, you can see all threads. Otherwise, you can see only your own threads. If you don't use the FULL option, only the first 100 characters of each query are shown.

Starting from 4.0.12, MySQL reports the hostname for TCP/IP connections in hostname:client_port format to make it easier to determine which client is doing what.

This command is very useful if you get a too many connections error message and want to find out what's going on. MySQL reserves one extra connection for a client with the SUPER privilege to ensure that you should always be able to log in and check the system (assuming that you aren't giving this privilege to all your users).

A.1.42 SHOW STATUS

SHOW STATUS [like 'pattern']

SHOW STATUS provides server status information (like mysqladmin extended-status). For the variables and their values that this command displays, see the *MySQL Reference Manual*.

A.1.43 SHOW TABLE STATUS

SHOW TABLE STATUS [FROM db_name] [LIKE 'pattern']

This statement has syntax similar to SHOW TABLES, but provides a lot of information about each table.

A.1.44 SHOW TABLES

```
SHOW TABLES [FROM db_name] [LIKE 'pattern']
```

Lists the tables in a given database.

A.1.45 SHOW VARIABLES

```
SHOW [GLOBAL | SESSION] VARIABLES [LIKE 'pattern']
```

SHOW VARIABLES shows the values of some MySQL system variables. With GLOBAL, you'll get the values that will be used for new connections to MySQL. With SESSION, you'll get the values that are in effect for the current connection. If you don't specify either option, SESSION is used.

You can also get this information using the mysqladmin variables command.

If the default variable values are unsuitable, you can set most of them using command-line options when mysqld starts. It's also possible to change most variables with the SET statement.

For some of the variables and their values that this statement displays, see the system variables section in this appendix (A.4, "Server System Variables"). For a full list, see the *MySQL Reference Manual*.

A.1.46 START TRANSACTION

```
START TRANSACTION
```

If you want to disable autocommit mode for a single series of statements, you can use the START TRANSACTION statement, as follows:

```
START TRANSACTION;
SELECT @A:=SUM(salary) FROM table1 WHERE type=1;
UPDATE table2 SET summary=@A WHERE type=1;
COMMIT;
```

BEGIN and BEGIN WORK can be used instead of START TRANSACTION to initiate a transaction. START TRANSACTION was added in MySQL 4.0.11; it is SQL-99 syntax and is the recommended way to start an ad-hoc transaction.

Note that if you aren't using transaction-safe tables, any changes will be stored at once, regardless of the status of autocommit mode.

A.1.47 TRUNCATE TABLE

```
TRUNCATE TABLE table_name
```

TRUNCATE TABLE deletes all rows in a table. It differs from DELETE FROM … in the following ways:

- Truncate operations drop and re-create the table, which is much faster than deleting rows one by one.
- Truncate operations are not transaction-safe; you'll get an error if you have an active transaction or an active table lock.
- The number of deleted rows is not returned.
- As long as the table format file `table_name.frm` is valid, the table can be re-created this way, even if the data or index files have become corrupted.

TRUNCATE TABLE is an Oracle SQL extension.

A.1.48 UNION

SELECT … UNION [ALL] SELECT … [UNION SELECT …]

UNION is used to combine the result from many SELECT statements into one result set.

The columns listed in the *select_expression* portion of the SELECT (see section A.1.29, "SELECT") should have the same type. The column names used in the first SELECT query will be used as the column names for the results returned.

If you don't use the keyword ALL for the UNION, all returned rows will be unique, as if you had done a DISTINCT for the total result set. If you specify ALL, you'll get all matching rows from all the used SELECT statements.

A.1.49 UNLOCK TABLES

UNLOCK TABLES

UNLOCK TABLES releases any locks held by the current thread. See also the LOCK TABLES section in this appendix (A.1.21, "LOCK TABLES").

A.1.50 UPDATE

```
    UPDATE table_name
        SET column_name1=expr1 [, column_name2=expr2 …]
        [WHERE where_definition]
        [ORDER BY …]
        [LIMIT row_count]
or  UPDATE table_name [, table_name …]
        SET column_name1=expr1 [, column_name2=expr2 …]
        [WHERE where_definition]
```

UPDATE updates columns in existing table rows with new values. The SET clause indicates which columns to modify and the values they should be given. The WHERE clause, if given, specifies which rows should be updated. Otherwise, all rows are updated. If the ORDER BY clause is specified, the rows will be updated in the order that is specified.

If you access a column from *table_name* in an expression, UPDATE uses the current value of the column (for example, for calculations with the column value).

UPDATE returns the number of rows that were actually changed. If you set a column to the value it currently has, MySQL notices this and doesn't update it.

You can use LIMIT *row_count* to ensure that only a given number of rows are changed.

Starting with MySQL Version 4.0.4, you can also perform UPDATE operations that cover multiple tables. *Note:* You cannot use ORDER BY or LIMIT with multi-table UPDATE.

A.2 SQL Functions

A.2.1 ABS()

ABS(*num*)

Returns the absolute value of *num*. This function is safe to use with BIGINT values.

A.2.2 AES_DECRYPT()

AES_DECRYPT(*string*,*key_string*)

This function allows decryption of data using the official AES (Advanced Encryption Standard) algorithm, previously known as Rijndael. Encoding with a 128-bit key length is used, but you can extend it up to 256 bits by modifying the source. We chose 128 bits because it is much faster and it is usually secure enough. The input arguments may be any length. If either argument is NULL, the result of this function is also NULL. Because AES is a block-level algorithm, padding is used to encode uneven length strings and so the result string length may be calculated as 16*(trunc(*string_length*/16)+1). If AES_DECRYPT() detects invalid data or incorrect padding, it returns NULL. However, it is possible for AES_DECRYPT() to return a non-NULL value (possibly garbage) if the input data or the key is invalid.

AES_DECRYPT() was added in version 4.0.2, and can be considered the most cryptographically secure decryption function currently available in MySQL.

A.2.3 AES_ENCRYPT()

AES_ENCRYPT(*string*,*key_string*)

This function allows encryption of data using the official AES (Advanced Encryption Standard) algorithm, previously known as Rijndael. Encoding with a 128-bit key length is used, but you can extend it up to 256 bits by modifying the source. We chose 128 bits because it is much faster and it is usually secure enough. The input arguments may be any length. If either argument is NULL, the result of this function is also NULL. Because AES is a block-level algorithm, padding is used to encode uneven length strings and so the result string length may be calculated as 16*(trunc(*string_length*/16)+1). You can use AES_ENCRYPT to store data in an encrypted form by modifying your queries, for example:

```
INSERT INTO t VALUES (1,AES_ENCRYPT('text','password'));
```

You can get even more security by not transferring the key over the connection for each query, which can be accomplished by storing it in a server-side variable at connection time. For example:

```
SELECT @password:='my password';
INSERT INTO t VALUES (1,AES_ENCRYPT('text',@password));
```

AES_ENCRYPT() was added in version 4.0.2, and can be considered the most cryptographically secure encryption function currently available in MySQL.

A.2.4 BIN()

BIN(*num*)

Returns a string representation of the binary value of *num*, where *num* is a longlong (BIGINT) number. This is equivalent to CONV(num,10,2). Returns NULL if *num* is NULL.

A.2.5 CEILING()

CEILING(*num*)

Returns the smallest integer value not less than *num*. A synonym is CEIL().

A.2.6 CHAR()

CHAR(*num*, [, *num* [, …]])

Interprets the arguments as integers and returns a string consisting of the characters given by the ASCII code values of those integers. NULL values are skipped.

A.2.7 CHAR_LENGTH()

CHAR_LENGTH(*str*)

Returns the length of the string *str*, measured in characters.

A.2.8 CHARACTER_LENGTH()

CHARACTER_LENGTH(*str*)

Returns the length of the string *str*, measured in characters.

A.2.9 CONCAT()

CONCAT(*str* [, *str* [, …]])

Returns the string that results from concatenating the arguments. Returns NULL if any argument is NULL. May have more than two arguments. A numeric argument is converted to its equivalent string form.

A.2.10 CONCAT_WS()

CONCAT_WS(*separator*, *str* [, *str* [, …]])

CONCAT_WS() stands for CONCAT With Separator and is a special form of CONCAT(). The first argument is the separator for the rest of the arguments. The separator is added between the strings to be concatenated. The separator can be a string as can the rest of the arguments. If the separator is NULL, the result is NULL. The function skips any NULL values after the separator argument.

A.2.11 CONV()

CONV(*N*, *from_base*, *to_base*)

Converts numbers between different number bases. Returns a string representation of the number N, converted from base *from_base* to base *to_base*. Returns NULL if any argument is NULL. The argument N is interpreted as an integer, but may be specified as an integer or a string. The minimum base is 2 and the maximum base is 36. If *to_base* is a negative number, N is regarded as a signed number. Otherwise, N is treated as unsigned. (CONV) works with 64-bit precision.

A.2.12 CURRENT_DATE()

CURRENT_DATE()

Returns the current date as a value in 'YYYY-MM-DD' or YYYYMMDD format, depending on whether the function is used in a string or numeric context. CURRENT_DATE and CURDATE() are synonyms.

A.2.13 CURRENT_TIME()

CURRENT_TIME()

Returns the current time as a value in 'HH:MM:SS' or HHMMSS format, depending on whether the function is used in a string or numeric context. CURRENT_TIME and CURTIME() are synonyms.

A.2.14 DATE_ADD()

DATE_ADD(*date*, INTERVAL *expr type*)

Performs date arithmetiA.

INTERVAL *expr type* also can be used in arithmetic expressions. INTERVAL *expr type* is allowed on either side of the + operator if the expression on the other side is a date or date-time value. For the - operator, INTERVAL *expr type* is allowed only on the right side because it makes no sense to subtract a date or datetime value from an interval. *date* is a DATETIME or DATE value specifying the starting date. *expr* is an expression specifying the interval value to be added or subtracted from the starting date. *expr* is a string; it may start with a - for negative intervals. *type* is a keyword indicating how the expression should be interpreted.

A.2.15 DATE_FORMAT()

DATE_FORMAT(*date*, *format*)

Formats the *date* value according to the *format* string. A large number of specifiers may be used in the *format* string. See the *MySQL Reference Manual* for details.

A.2.16 DATE_SUB()

DATE_SUB(*date*, INTERVAL *expr type*)

Performs date arithmetiA.

INTERVAL *expr type* also can be used in arithmetic expressions. INTERVAL *expr type* is allowed on either side of the + operator if the expression on the other side is a date or date-time value. For the - operator, INTERVAL *expr type* is allowed only on the right side because it makes no sense to subtract a date or datetime value from an interval. *date* is a DATETIME or DATE value specifying the starting date. *expr* is an expression specifying the interval value to be added or subtracted from the starting date. *expr* is a string; it may start with a - for negative intervals. *type* is a keyword indicating how the expression should be interpreted.

A.2.17 DAYNAME()

DAYNAME(*date*)

Returns the name of the weekday for *date*.

A.2.18 DAYOFMONTH()

DAYOFMONTH(*date*)

Returns the day of the month for *date*, in the range 1 to 31.

A.2.19 DAYOFWEEK()

DAYOFWEEK(*date*)

Returns the weekday index for *date* (1 = Sunday, 2 = Monday, ... 7 = Saturday). These index values correspond to the ODBC standard.

A.2.20 DAYOFYEAR()

DAYOFYEAR(*date*)

Returns the day of the year for *date*, in the range 1 to 366.

A.2.21 DECODE()

DECODE(*crypt_str*, *pass_str*)

Decrypts the encrypted string *crypt_str* using *pass_str* as the password. *crypt_str* should be a string returned from ENCODE() (see section A.2.25, "ENCODE()").

A.2.22 DES_DECRYPT()

DES_DECRYPT(*string_to_decrypt* [, *key_string*])

Decrypts a string encrypted with DES_ENCRYPT() (see section A.2.23, "DES_ENCRYPT()"). Note that this function works only if MySQL has been configured with SSL support.

If no *key_string* argument is given, DES_DECRYPT() examines the first byte of the encrypted string to determine the DES key number that was used to encrypt the original string, and then reads the key from the *des-key-file* to decrypt the message. For this to work, the user must have the SUPER privilege.

If you pass this function a *key_string* argument, that string is used as the key for decrypting the message.

If the *string_to_decrypt* doesn't look like an encrypted string, MySQL will return the given *string_to_decrypt*.

On error, this function returns NULL.

A.2.23 DES_ENCRYPT()

DES_ENCRYPT(*string_to_encrypt* [, (*key_number* | *key_string*)])

Encrypts the string with the given key using the Triple-DES algorithm. Note that this function works only if MySQL has been configured with SSL support. The encryption key to use is chosen the following way:

- Only one argument: The first key from *des-key-file* is used.
- Key number: The given key (0-9) from the *des-key-file* is used.
- String: The given *key_string* will be used to crypt *string_to_encrypt*.

The return string will be a binary string where the first character will be CHAR(128 | *key_number*). The 128 is added to make it easier to recognize an encrypted key. If you use a string key, *key_number* will be 127.

On error, this function returns NULL.

The string length for the result will be *new_length = orig_length + (8-(orig_length % 8))+1*.

A.2.24 ELT()

ELT(*num, str1* [, *str2* [, …]])

Returns *str1* if *num* = 1, *str2* if *num* = 2, and so on. Returns NULL if *num* is less than 1 or greater than the number of arguments. ELT() is the complement of FIELD() (see section A.2.27, "FIELD()").

A.2.25 ENCODE()

ENCODE(*str, pass_str*)

Encrypts *str* using *pass_str* as the password. To decrypt the result, use DECODE() (see section A.2.21, "DECODE()").

The result is a binary string of the same length as *str*. If you want to save it in a column, use a BLOB column type.

A.2.26 EXPORT_SET()

EXPORT_SET(*bits, on, off, [separator, [number_of_bits]]*)

Returns a string in which for every bit set in *bit*, you get an *on* string and for every reset bit, you get an *off* string. Each string is separated by *separator* (default ',') and only *number_of_bits* (default 64) of *bits* is used.

A.2.27 FIELD()

FIELD(*str, str1* [, *str2* [, …]])

Returns the index of *str* in the *str1, str2, str3, …* list. Returns 0 if *str* is not found. FIELD() is the complement of ELT() (see section A.2.24, "ELT()").

A.2.28 FIND_IN_SET()

FIND_IN_SET(*str*, *strlist*)

Returns a value 1 to *N* if the string *str* is in the list *strlist* consisting of *N* substrings. A string list is a string composed of substrings separated by ',' characters. If the first argument is a constant string and the second is a column of type SET, the FIND_IN_SET() function is optimized to use bit arithmetiA. Returns 0 if *str* is not in *strlist* or if *strlist* is the empty string. Returns NULL if either argument is NULL. This function will not work properly if the first argument contains a comma (,).

A.2.29 FLOOR()

FLOOR(*num*)

Returns the largest integer value not greater than *num*.

A.2.30 FROM_DAYS()

FROM_DAYS(*num*)

Given a day number *num*, the function returns a DATE value.

A.2.31 FROM_UNIXTIME()

FROM_UNIXTIME(*unix_timestamp* [, *format*])

Returns a representation of the *unix_timestamp* argument as a value in 'YYYY-MM-DD HH:MM:SS' or YYYYMMDDHHMMSS format, depending on whether the function is used in a string or numeric context. If *format* is given, the result is formatted according to the *format* string. *format* may contain the same specifiers as those listed in the entry for the DATE_FORMAT() function.

A.2.32 GREATEST()

GREATEST(*num1* [, *num2* [, …]])

Returns the largest (maximum-valued) argument. The arguments are compared using the same rules as for LEAST. See section A.2.38, "LEAST()."

A.2.33 HEX()

HEX(*N_or_S*)

If *N_OR_S* is a number, returns a string representation of the hexadecimal value of *N*, where *N* is a longlong (BIGINT) number. This is equivalent to CONV(*N*,10,16). See section A.2.11,

"CONV()." If *N_OR_S* is a string, returns a hexadecimal string of *N_OR_S* where each character in *N_OR_S* is converted to two hexadecimal digits.

A.2.34 HOUR()

HOUR(*time*)

Returns the hour for *time*. The range of the return value will be 0 to 23 for time-of-day values. However, the range of TIME values actually is much larger, so HOUR can return values greater than 23.

A.2.35 INSERT()

INSERT(*str*, *xpos*, *len*, *newstr*)

Returns the string *str*, with the substring beginning at position *pos* and *len* characters long replaced by the string *newstr*. This function is multi-byte safe.

A.2.36 INSTR()

INSTR(*str*, *substr*)

Returns the position of the first occurrence of substring *substr* in string *str*. This is the same as the two-argument form of LOCATE(), except that the arguments are swapped. This function is multi-byte safe. This function is case sensitive if either argument is a binary string. Otherwise, it is not case sensitive.

A.2.37 LCASE()

LCASE(*str*)

Synonym for LOWER(). See section A.2.43, "LOWER()."

A.2.38 LEAST()

LEAST(*num1* [, *num2* [, …]])

With two or more arguments, returns the smallest (minimum-valued) argument. The arguments are compared using the following rules:

- If the return value is used in an INTEGER context or all arguments are integer-valued, they are compared as integers.
- If the return value is used in a REAL context or all arguments are real-valued, they are compared as reals.

- If any argument is a case-sensitive string, the arguments are compared as case-sensitive strings.
- In other cases, the arguments are compared as case-insensitive strings.

A.2.39 LEFT()

LEFT(*str*, *len*)

Returns the leftmost *len* characters from the string *str*. This function is multi-byte safe.

A.2.40 LENGTH()

LENGTH(*str*)

Returns the length of the string *str*, measured in bytes.

A.2.41 LOAD_FILE()

LOAD_FILE(*filename*)

Reads the file and returns the file contents as a string. The file must exist on the server host, you must specify the full pathname to the file, and you must have the FILE privilege. The file must be world-readable and be smaller than max_allowed_packet bytes (see section A.4, "Server System Variables"). If any of these conditions are not satisfied, the function returns NULL.

A.2.42 LOCATE()

LOCATE(*substr*, *str*)

A synonym for POSITION(), although with a slightly different syntax. See section A.2.57, "POSITION()."

A.2.43 LOWER()

LOWER(*str*)

Returns the string *str* with all characters changed to lowercase according to the current character set mapping. A synonym is LCASE() (see section A.2.37, "LCASE()").

A.2.44 LPAD()

LPAD(*str*, *len*, *padstr*)

Returns the string *str*, left-padded with the string *padstr* to a length of *len* characters. If *str* is longer than *len*, the return value is shortened to *len* characters.

A.2.45 LTRIM()

LTRIM(*str*)

Returns the string *str* with leading space characters removed.

A.2.46 MAKE_SET()

MAKE_SET(*bits*, *str1* [, *str2* [,...]])

Returns a set (a string containing substrings separated by , characters) consisting of the strings that have the corresponding bit in *bits* set. *str1* corresponds to bit 0, *str2* to bit 1, and so on. NULL values in *str1*, *str2*, ... are not appended to the result.

A.2.47 MID()

MID(*str*, *pos*, *len*)

Returns a substring *len* characters long from string *str*, starting at position *pos*. A synonym is SUBSTRING() (see section A.2.72, "SUBSTRING()").

A.2.48 MINUTE()

MINUTE(*time*)

Returns the minute for *time*, in the range 0 to 59.

A.2.49 MOD()

MOD(*N*, *M*)

Modulo (like the % operator in C). Returns the remainder of *N* divided by *M*.

A.2.50 MONTH()

MONTH(*date*)

Returns the month for *date*, in the range 1 to 12.

A.2.51 MONTHNAME()

MONTHNAME(*date*)

Returns the name of the month for *date*.

A.2.52 NOW()

NOW()

Returns the current date and time as a value in 'YYYY-MM-DD HH:MM:SS' or YYYYMMDDHHMMSS format, depending on whether the function is used in a string or numeric context. Synonyms are SYSDATE(), CURRENT_TIMESTAMP, CURRENT_TIMESTAMP(), LOCALTIME, LOCALTIME(), LOCALTIMESTAMP, and LOCALTIMESTAMP().

A.2.53 OCT()

OCT(num)

Returns a string representation of the octal value of num, where num is a longlong number. This is equivalent to CONV(num,10,8). See section A.2.11, "CONV()." Returns NULL if num is NULL.

A.2.54 PASSWORD()

PASSWORD(str)

Calculates a password string from the plaintext password str. This function is used for encrypting MySQL passwords for storage in the Password column of the user grant table. The encryption that this function produces is irreversible. Note that it does not perform password encryption in the same way that Unix passwords are encrypted. This function is for use by the authentication system in the MySQL Server. You should *not* use it in your own applications. Use MD5() or SHA1() instead. Also see RFC-2195 for more information about handling passwords and authentication securely in your application.

A.2.55 PERIOD_ADD()

PERIOD_ADD(P, N)

Adds N months to period P (in the format YYMM or YYYYMM). Returns a value in the format YYYYMM. Note that the period argument P is *not* a date value.

A.2.56 PERIOD_DIFF()

PERIOD_DIFF(P1, P2)

Returns the number of months between periods P1 and P2. P1 and P2 should be in the format YYMM or YYYYMM. Note that the period arguments P1 and P2 are *not* date values.

A.2.57 POSITION()

POSITION(substr IN str)

Returns the position of the first occurrence of substring *substr* in string *str*. Returns 0 if *substr* is not in *str*. This function is multi-byte safe. This function is case sensitive if either argument is a binary string. Otherwise, it is not case sensitive. A synonym, although with a slightly different syntax, is LOCATE (see section A.2.42, "LOCATE()").

A.2.58 POW()

POW(*X*, *Y*)

A synonym for POWER() (see section A.2.59, "POWER()").

A.2.59 POWER()

POWER(*X*, *Y*)

Returns the value of *X* raised to the power of *Y*. A synonym is POW() (see section A.2.58, "POW()").

A.2.60 QUARTER()

QUARTER(*date*)

Returns the quarter of the year for *date*, in the range 1 to 4.

A.2.61 QUOTE()

QUOTE(*str*)

Quotes a string to produce a result that can be used as a properly escaped data value in an SQL statement. The string is returned surrounded by single quotes and with each instance of single quote ('), backslash (\), ASCII NUL, and Control-Z preceded by a backslash. If the argument is NULL, the return value is the word "NULL" without surrounding quotes.

A.2.62 RAND()

RAND() | RAND(*num*)

Returns a random floating-point value in the range 0 to 1.0. If an integer argument *num* is specified, it is used as the seed value (producing a repeatable sequence).

A.2.63 REPLACE()

REPLACE(*str*, *from_str*, *to_str*)

Returns the string *str* with all occurrences of the string *from_str* replaced by the string *to_str*. This function is multi-byte safe.

A.2.64 REVERSE()

REVERSE(*str*)

Returns the string *str* with the order of the characters reversed. This function is multi-byte safe.

A.2.65 RIGHT()

RIGHT(*str*, *len*)

Returns the rightmost *len* characters from the string *str*. This function is multi-byte safe.

A.2.66 ROUND()

ROUND(*X*) | ROUND(*X*, *D*)

Returns the argument *X*, rounded to the nearest integer. With two arguments, rounded to a number to *D* decimals. Note that the behavior of ROUND() when the argument is halfway between two integers depends on the C library implementation. Some round to the nearest even number, always up, always down, or always toward zero. If you need one kind of rounding, you should use a well-defined function such as TRUNCATE() or FLOOR() instead.

A.2.67 RPAD()

RPAD(*str*, *len*, *padstr*)

Returns the string *str*, right-padded with the string *padstr* to a length of *len* characters. If *str* is longer than *len*, the return value is shortened to *len* characters.

A.2.68 RTRIM()

RTRIM(*str*)

Returns the string *str* with trailing space characters removed. This function is multi-byte safe.

A.2.69 SEC_TO_TIME()

SEC_TO_TIME(*seconds*)

Returns the *seconds* argument, converted to hours, minutes, and seconds, as a value in 'HH:MM:SS' or HHMMSS format, depending on whether the function is used in a string or numeric context.

A.2.70 SECOND()

SECOND(*time*)

Returns the second for *time*, in the range 0 to 59.

A.2.71 SIGN()

SIGN(*num*)

Returns the sign of the argument as -1, 0, or 1, depending on whether *num* is negative, zero, or positive.

A.2.72 SUBSTRING()

SUBSTRING(*str*, *pos*, *len*) | SUBSTRING(*str* FROM *pos* FOR *len*)

Returns a substring *len* characters long from string *str*, starting at position *pos*. The variant form that uses FROM is SQL-92 syntax. A synonym is MID() (see section A.2.47, "MID()").

A.2.73 SUBSTRING_INDEX()

SUBSTRING_INDEX(*str*, *delim*, *count*)

Returns the substring from string *str* before *count* occurrences of the delimiter *delim*. If *count* is positive, everything to the left of the final delimiter (counting from the left) is returned. If *count* is negative, everything to the right of the final delimiter (counting from the right) is returned. This function is multi-byte safe.

A.2.74 TIME_FORMAT()

TIME_FORMAT(*time*, *format*)

This is used like the DATE_FORMAT() function (see section A.2.15, "DATE_FORMAT()"), but the *format* string may contain only those format specifiers that handle hours, minutes, and seconds. Other specifiers produce a NULL value or 0. If the *time* value contains an hour part that is greater than 23, the %H and %k hour format specifiers produce a value larger than the usual range of 0..23. The other hour format specifiers produce the hour value modulo 12.

A.2.75 TIME_TO_SEC()

TIME_TO_SEC(*time*)

Returns the *time* argument, converted to seconds.

A.2.76 TO_DAYS()

TO_DAYS(*date*)

Given a date *date*, returns a daynumber (the number of days since year 0). TO_DAYS() is not intended for use with values that precede the advent of the Gregorian calendar (1582) because it doesn't take into account the days that were lost when the calendar was changed.

A.2.77 TRIM()

TRIM([[BOTH | LEADING | TRAILING] [*remstr*] FROM] *str*)

Returns the string *str* with all *remstr* prefixes and/or suffixes removed. If none of the specifiers BOTH, LEADING or TRAILING is given, BOTH is assumed. If *remstr* is not specified, spaces are removed. This function is multi-byte safe.

A.2.78 TRUNCATE()

TRUNCATE(*X*, *D*)

Returns the number *X*, truncated to *D* decimals. If *D* is 0, the result will have no decimal point or fractional part. All numbers are rounded toward zero. If *D* is negative, the whole part of the number is zeroed out. Note that decimal numbers are normally not stored as exact numbers in computers, but as double-precision values.

A.2.79 UCASE()

UCASE(*str*)

Synonym for UPPER(). See section A.2.81, "UPPER()."

A.2.80 UNIX_TIMESTAMP()

UNIX_TIMESTAMP([*date*])

If called with no argument, returns a Unix timestamp (seconds since '1970-01-01 00:00:00' GMT) as an unsigned integer. If UNIX_TIMESTAMP() is called with a *date* argument, it returns the value of the argument as seconds since '1970-01-01 00:00:00' GMT. *date* may be a DATE string, a DATETIME string, a TIMESTAMP, or a number in the format YYMMDD or YYYYMMDD in local time. When UNIX_TIMESTAMP is used on a TIMESTAMP column, the function returns the internal timestamp value directly, with no implicit "string-to-Unix-timestamp" conversion. If you pass an out-of-range date to UNIX_TIMESTAMP(), it returns 0, but please note that only basic checking is performed (year 1970-2037, month 01-12, day 01-31). If you want to subtract UNIX_TIMESTAMP() columns, you might want to cast the result to a signed integer.

A.2.81 UPPER()

UPPER(*str*)

Returns the string *str* with all characters changed to uppercase according to the current character set mapping. This function is multi-byte safe. A synonym is UCASE() (see section A.2.79, "UCASE()").

A.2.82 WEEK()

WEEK(*date* [, *start*])

With a single argument, returns the week for *date*, in the range 0 to 53 (yes, there could be the beginnings of a week 53), for locations where Sunday is the first day of the week. The two-argument form of WEEK() enables you to specify whether the week starts on Sunday or Monday and whether the return value should be in the range 0-53 or 1-52.

A.2.83 WEEKDAY()

WEEKDAY(*date*)

Returns the weekday index for *date* (0 = Monday, 1 = Tuesday, … 6 = Sunday).

A.2.84 YEAR()

YEAR(*date*)

Returns the year for *date*, in the range 1000 to 9999.

A.2.85 YEARWEEK()

YEARWEEK(*date* [, *start*])

Returns the year and week for a date. The *start* argument works exactly like the *start* argument to WEEK() (see section A.2.82, "WEEK()"). Note that the year in the result may be different from the year in the date argument for the first and the last week of the year. Note that the week number is different from what the WEEK() function would return (0) for optional argument 0 or 1 because WEEK() returns the week in the context of the given year.

A.3 Column Types

MySQL supports a number of column types, which may be grouped into three categories: numeric types, date and time types, and string (character) types. This section first gives an overview of the types available and summarizes the storage requirements for each column type, and then provides a more detailed description of the properties of the types in each category. The overview is intentionally brief. More detailed descriptions should be consulted for additional information about particular column types, such as the allowable formats in which you can specify values.

The column types supported by MySQL follow. The following code letters are used in the descriptions:

- *M*: Indicates the maximum display size. The maximum legal display size is 255.
- *D*: Applies to floating-point types and indicates the number of digits following the decimal point. The maximum possible value is 30, but should be no greater than *M*-2.

Square brackets ([and]) indicate parts of type specifiers that are optional.

Note that if you specify ZEROFILL for a column, MySQL automatically adds the UNSIGNED attribute to the column.

Warning: You should be aware that when you use subtraction between integer values where one is of type UNSIGNED, the result will be unsigned.

- TINYINT[(*M*)] [UNSIGNED] [ZEROFILL]: A very small integer. The signed range is -128 to 127. The unsigned range is 0 to 255.
- BIT, BOOL: These are synonyms for TINYINT(1).
- SMALLINT[(*M*)] [UNSIGNED] [ZEROFILL]: A small integer. The signed range is -32768 to 32767. The unsigned range is 0 to 65535.
- MEDIUMINT[(*M*)] [UNSIGNED] [ZEROFILL]: A medium-size integer. The signed range is -8388608 to 8388607. The unsigned range is 0 to 16777215.
- INT[(*M*)] [UNSIGNED] [ZEROFILL]: A normal-size integer. The signed range is -2147483648 to 2147483647. The unsigned range is 0 to 4294967295.
- INTEGER[(*M*)] [UNSIGNED] [ZEROFILL]: This is a synonym for INT. BIGINT[(*M*)] [UNSIGNED] [ZEROFILL]: A large integer. The signed range is -9223372036854775808 to 9223372036854775807. The unsigned range is 0 to 18446744073709551615.
- FLOAT(precision) [UNSIGNED] [ZEROFILL]: A floating-point number. precision can be less than or equal to 24 for a single-precision floating-point number and between 25 and 53 for a double-precision floating-point number. These types are like the FLOAT and DOUBLE types described immediately following. FLOAT(X) has the same range as the corresponding FLOAT and DOUBLE types, but the display size and number of decimals are undefined. Note that using FLOAT might give you some unexpected problems because all calculations in MySQL are done with double precision.
- FLOAT[(*M,D*)] [UNSIGNED] [ZEROFILL]: A small (single-precision) floating-point number. Allowable values are -3.402823466E+38 to -1.175494351E-38, 0, and 1.175494351E-38 to 3.402823466E+38. If UNSIGNED is specified, negative values are disallowed. The *M* is the display width and *D* is the number of decimals. FLOAT without arguments or FLOAT(X) where X is less than or equal to 24 stands for a single-precision floating-point number.

- DOUBLE[(*M*,*D*)] [UNSIGNED] [ZEROFILL]: A normal-size (double-precision) floating-point number. Allowable values are -1.7976931348623157E+308 to -2.2250738585072014E-308, 0, and 2.2250738585072014E-308 to 1.7976931348623157E+308. If UNSIGNED is specified, negative values are disallowed. The *M* is the display width and *D* is the number of decimals. DOUBLE without arguments or FLOAT(X) where X is between 25 and 53 stands for a double-precision floating-point number.

- DOUBLE PRECISION[(*M*,*D*)] [UNSIGNED] [ZEROFILL], REAL[(*M*,*D*)] [UNSIGNED] [ZEROFILL]: These are synonyms for DOUBLE.

- DECIMAL[(*M*[,*D*])] [UNSIGNED] [ZEROFILL]: An unpacked floating-point number. Behaves like a CHAR column: "unpacked" means the number is stored as a string, using one character for each digit of the value. The decimal point and, for negative numbers, the - sign, are not counted in *M* (but space for these is reserved). If *D* is 0, values will have no decimal point or fractional part. The maximum range of DECIMAL values is the same as for DOUBLE, but the actual range for a given DECIMAL column may be constrained by the choice of *M* and *D*. If UNSIGNED is specified, negative values are disallowed. If *D* is omitted, the default is 0. If *M* is omitted, the default is 10.

- DEC[(*M*[,*D*])] [UNSIGNED] [ZEROFILL], NUMERIC[(*M*[,*D*])] [UNSIGNED] [ZEROFILL]: These are synonyms for DECIMAL.

- DATE: A date. The supported range is '1000-01-01' to '9999-12-31'. MySQL displays DATE values in 'YYYY-MM-DD' format, but allows you to assign values to DATE columns using either strings or numbers.

- DATETIME: A date and time combination. The supported range is '1000-01-01 00:00:00' to '9999-12-31 23:59:59'. MySQL displays DATETIME values in 'YYYY-MM-DD HH:MM:SS' format, but allows you to assign values to DATETIME columns using either strings or numbers.

- TIMESTAMP[(*M*)]: A timestamp. The range is '1970-01-01 00:00:00' to sometime in the year 2037.

  In MySQL 4.0 and earlier, TIMESTAMP values are displayed in YYYYMMDDHHMMSS, YYMMDDHH-MMSS, YYYYMMDD, or YYMMDD format, depending on whether *M* is 14 (or missing), 12, 8, or 6, but allows you to assign values to TIMESTAMP columns using either strings or numbers.

  From MySQL 4.1, TIMESTAMP is returned as a string with the format 'YYYY-MM-DD HH:MM:SS'. If you want to have this as a number, you should add +0 to the timestamp column. Different timestamp lengths are not supported. From version 4.0.12, the --new option can be used to make the server behave as in version 4.1.

  A TIMESTAMP column is useful for recording the date and time of an INSERT or UPDATE operation because it is automatically set to the date and time of the most recent operation if you don't give it a value yourself. You can also set it to the current date and time by assigning it a NULL value. The *M* argument affects only how a TIMESTAMP column is displayed; its values always are stored using 4 bytes each.

- TIME: A time. The range is '-838:59:59' to '838:59:59'. MySQL displays TIME values in 'HH:MM:SS' format, but allows you to assign values to TIME columns using either strings or numbers.

- YEAR[(2|4)]: A year in two- or four-digit format (default is four-digit). The allowable values are 1901 to 2155, 0000 in the four-digit year format, and 1970-2069 if you use the two-digit format (70-69). MySQL displays YEAR values in YYYY format, but allows you to assign values to YEAR columns using either strings or numbers.

- [NATIONAL] CHAR(M) [BINARY]: A fixed-length string that is always right-padded with spaces to the specified length when stored. The range of M is 0 to 255 characters. Trailing spaces are removed when the value is retrieved. CHAR values are sorted and compared in case-insensitive fashion according to the default character set unless the BINARY keyword is given. NATIONAL CHAR (or its equivalent short form, NCHAR) is the SQL-99 way to define that a CHAR column should use the default character set. This is the default in MySQL. CHAR is shorthand for CHARACTER. MySQL allows you to create a column of type CHAR(0). This is mainly useful when you have to be compliant with some old applications that depend on the existence of a column but that do not actually use the value. This is also quite nice when you need a column that can take only two values: A CHAR(0) that is not defined as NOT NULL will occupy only 1 bit and can take two values: NULL or '' (the empty string).

- CHAR: This is a synonym for CHAR(1).

- [NATIONAL] VARCHAR(M) [BINARY]: A variable-length string. *Note*: Trailing spaces are removed when the value is stored (this differs from the SQL-99 specification). The range of M is 0 to 255 characters (1 to 255 prior to MySQL Version 4.0.2). VARCHAR values are sorted and compared in case-insensitive fashion unless the BINARY keyword is given. VARCHAR is a shorthand for CHARACTER VARYING.

- TINYBLOB, TINYTEXT: A BLOB or TEXT column with a maximum length of 255 characters.

- BLOB, TEXT: A BLOB or TEXT column with a maximum length of 65535 characters.

- MEDIUMBLOB, MEDIUMTEXT: A BLOB or TEXT column with a maximum length of 16777215 characters.

- LONGBLOB, LONGTEXT: A BLOB or TEXT column with a maximum length of 4294967295 characters. The maximum allowed length of LONGBLOB or LONGTEXT columns depends on the configured maximum packet size in the client/server protocol and available memory.

- ENUM('value1','value2',…): An enumeration. A string object that can have only one value, chosen from the list of values 'value1', 'value2', …, NULL or the special '' error value. An ENUM column can have a maximum of 65535 distinct values.

- SET('value1','value2',…): A set. A string object that can have zero or more values, each of which must be chosen from the list of values 'value1', 'value2', … A SET column can have a maximum of 64 members.

A.4 Server System Variables

This section covers the server variables that are discussed in the study guide. There are many more system variables that are not shown here. For a full list, see the *MySQL Reference Manual*. Also note that the exam might not be limited to the variables discussed here.

- `back_log`: The number of outstanding connection requests MySQL can have. This comes into play when the main MySQL thread gets very many connection requests in a very short time. You need to increase this only if you expect a large number of connections in a short period of time.

- `datadir`: The location of the data directory.

- `innodb_buffer_pool_size`: The size of the memory buffer InnoDB uses to cache data and indexes of its tables. The larger you set this, the less disk I/O is needed to access data in tables. On a dedicated database server, you may set this parameter up to 80% of the machine physical memory size. Do not set it too large, though, because competition for physical memory might cause paging in the operating system.

- `innodb_flush_log_at_trx_commit`: Normally you set this to 1, meaning that at a transaction commit, the log is flushed to disk and the modifications made by the transaction become permanent, and survive a database crash. If you're willing to compromise this safety, and you're running small transactions, you may set this to 0 or 2 to reduce disk I/O to the logs. A value of 0 means that the log is only written to the log file and the log file flushed to disk approximately once per second. A value of 2 means the log is written to the log file at each commit, but the log file is only flushed to disk approximately once per second. The default value is 1 starting from MySQL 4.0.13; previously it was 0.

- `innodb_log_file_size`: Size of each log file in a log group in megabytes. Sensible values range from 1MB to 1/n-th of the size of the buffer pool (see earlier discussion), where n is the number of log files in the group. The larger the value, the less checkpoint flush activity is needed in the buffer pool, saving disk I/O. But larger log files also mean that recovery will be slower in case of a crash. The combined size of log files must be less than 4GB on 32-bit computers. The default value is 5MB.

- `join_buffer_size`: The size of the buffer that is used for joins that do not use indexes. The buffer is allocated one time for each such join between two tables. Increase this value to get a faster join when adding indexes is not possible. (Normally, the best way to get fast joins is to add indexes.)

- `key_buffer_size`: Index blocks are buffered and are shared by all threads. `key_buffer_size` is the size of the buffer used for index blocks.

  Increase the value of `key_buffer_size` to as much as you can afford to get better index handling. 64MB on a 256MB machine that mainly runs MySQL is quite common. However, if you make this too large (for example, more than 50% of your total memory), your system might start to page and become extremely slow. Remember that because MySQL does not cache data reads, you'll have to leave some room for the operating system filesystem cache.

You can check the performance of the key buffer by issuing a SHOW STATUS statement and examining the variables Key_read_requests, Key_reads, Key_write_requests, and Key_writes. The Key_reads/Key_read_request ratio should normally be less than 0.01. The Key_write/Key_write_requests ratio is usually near 1 if you're using mostly updates and deletes, but might be much smaller if you tend to do updates that affect many rows at the same time, or if you're using DELAY_KEY_WRITE.

- long_query_time: How long a query can take in seconds before it is considered slow. Slow queries are written to the slow query log.

- max_allowed_packet: The maximum size of one packet. The message buffer is initialized to net_buffer_length bytes, but can grow up to max_allowed_packet bytes when needed. This value is small by default to catch big (possibly wrong) packets. You must increase this value if you're using big BLOB columns. It should be as big as the biggest BLOB you want to use. The protocol limit for max_allowed_packet is 1GB.

- max_connections: The number of simultaneous clients allowed. Increasing this value increases the number of file descriptors that mysqld requires.

- max_heap_table_size: Doesn't allow the creation of HEAP tables that are bigger than the value of this variable.

- query_cache_limit: The maximum size of individual query results that can be cached.

- query_cache_size: The memory allocated to store results from previously issued queries. If this is 0 (default), the query cache is disabled.

- query_cache_type: This may be set to one of the following values:

  - 0 or OFF: Don't cache or retrieve results

  - 1 or ON: Cache all results except SELECT SQL_NO_CACHE … queries

  - 2 or DEMAND: Cache only SELECT SQL_CACHE … queries

- read_buffer_size: Each thread that does a sequential scan allocates a buffer of this size for each table it scans. If you do many sequential scans, you might want to increase this value.

- read_rnd_buffer_size: When reading rows in sorted order after a sort, the rows are read through this buffer to avoid disk seeks. It can improve ORDER BY by a lot if set to a high value. This is a thread-specific variable, so you should not set the value large globally, but just change it when running some specific large queries.

- sort_buffer_size: Each thread that needs to do a sort allocates a buffer of this size. Increase this value for faster ORDER BY or GROUP BY operations.

- table_cache: The maximum number of open tables for all threads. Increasing this value increases the number of file descriptors that mysqld requires.

You can find out whether you need to increase the table cache by checking the Opened_tables variable. See SHOW VARIABLES (section A.1.45, "SHOW VARIABLES"). If this variable is big and you don't issue FLUSH TABLES a lot (which just forces all tables to be closed and reopened), you should increase the value of this variable.

For more information about the table cache, see the *MySQL Reference Manual*.

- `table_type`: The default table type.

- `tmp_table_size`: If an in-memory temporary table exceeds the value of this variable, MySQL will automatically convert it to an on-disk MyISAM table. Increase the value of `tmp_table_size` if you do many advanced GROUP BY queries and you have lots of memory.

B

MySQL Certification Candidate Guide

Note: *The information contained in this guide is informative in nature. MySQL AB reserves the right to change the content, without notice.*

This copy of the candidate guide was accurate as of the beginning of 2004. You're strongly encouraged to check the latest version on the MySQL Web site before going to the exam.

B.1 What Is a MySQL Certification?

A MySQL™ certification is the credential that validates your knowledge, experience, and skills with the MySQL server and related products.

B.1.1 Benefits to Individuals

As a professional, holding one or more certifications shows your commitment to keeping your technical skills current and upgraded at all times. A certification is the recognized proof you need to show that you have the skills, and credibility to move upward in your organization, handling greater responsibilities, managing larger projects, and getting better pay. Several independent studies prove that certified individuals are, on average, placed higher in the organization and each month bring home a larger paycheck than their noncertified colleagues.

If you're an independent contractor, a MySQL certification title on your business card is sure to increase your value in the eyes and minds of your customers. They'll see the title as a guarantee that your skills are current and your knowledge up-to-date, before allowing you access to their data.

B.1.2 Benefits to Companies

Knowing the certification level of individual employees makes it easier for management to identify differences in experience and knowledge, when planning who will be doing what in existing and upcoming projects. The task of hiring new employees is also made easier because each individual candidate's level of certification will provide the information needed to judge how well he or she will fit into his or her new team.

Certification is also a proven method of testing the effectiveness of the training given to each candidate. Training might have been obtained on the job or through one of the many training courses provided by MySQL AB and its training partners (see `http://www.mysql.com/training`).

MySQL training partners may be found in the portals section of the MySQL AB Web site (see `http://www.mysql.com/portal`).

If the company's line of business is selling MySQL-related products, having MySQL certified employees not only inspires more customer confidence in your services and products, it's also a proof of the company's commitment to make sure that all employees are kept current with the latest breakthroughs in the technology.

B.2 Other Sources of Information

This candidate guide is the primary source of information on the MySQL Certification program. There are three more sources of which you should be aware:

- The certification area of the MySQL Web site (`http://www.mysql.com/certification`) is always the first place you should go to find the latest news on MySQL certifications. Of special interest on the Web site is the Certification FAQ, which answers most common questions not answered in this guide.

- To make sure that you're kept current on all things going on in the world of MySQL certifications, subscribe to the certification mailing list provided by MySQL AB. This is a low-volume list, on which announcements are sent out every few weeks with the latest news on the certification program. To subscribe to this mailing list, send an email to `certification-subscribe@lists.mysql.com`. You'll then need to answer a confirmation email that is sent to you.

- In 2004, MySQL AB will publish a *Study Guide* for both the Core and the Professional exams. When they are available, this will be announced on the MySQL Web site and the certification mailing list.

B.3 The MySQL Certification Program

The MySQL Certification program is about much more than passing a number of exams: To pass each exam, you've worked hard on gaining both the required knowledge and skills, as well as gaining some practical experience. When you certify, all your efforts are immediately repaid with a number of benefits.

Before taking an exam, you should check section B.5, "Preparing for the Exams," to ensure that you have all the necessary prerequisites in place. The details of the exam-taking process are described in section B.6, "How the Exams ProceeB."

When you're certified, you not only get the benefits already described earlier, you also receive a welcome package and access to even more material from MySQL. Section B.7, "After the Exam" later in this guide describes this in more detail.

B.3.1 The MySQL Certification Levels

Note: MySQL Certifications are *version specific*. All certifications published so far are specific to the MySQL v. 4.x line of products.

Currently, the MySQL Certification program consists of a main track of two certification levels, the *MySQL Core Certification* and the *MySQL Professional Certification*. MySQL AB also plans to add a *MySQL Certified PHP Developer* certification to the existing program.

The exams in the main track must be passed in order; the MySQL Core Certification is a prerequisite for the MySQL Professional Certification.

Each level is focused on specific areas of interest, expertise, and job skills. As you gain more experience with the MySQL database, make sure to certify for the expertise level relevant for you. This will help both you and your employer in proving that you have the skills sought by many companies.

If you're planning to pursue a career as MySQL developer and/or administrator, MySQL AB recommends that you attain at least the level of the MySQL Professional Certification.

In sections B.10, "MySQL 4 Core Certification" and B.11, "Certified MySQL 4 Professional," the knowledge and skills required to pass the MySQL Core Certification and MySQL Professional Certification exams are described in detail.

B.4 Registering for Exams

B.4.1 Exam Prices

The price for taking the *MySQL Core Certification* exam is the local equivalent of U.S. $200 plus any local taxes. Please check the *Pearson VUE* Web site or call your regional *Pearson VUE* test center for exact information on pricing in your area. (Addresses and telephone numbers are listed in section B.12, "*Pearson VUE* Contact Information" at the end of this guide.)

The price for taking the *MySQL Professional Certification* exam is the local equivalent of U.S. $250 plus any local taxes.

Each certification level consists of a single exam.

If your organization has many employees wanting to certify for one or more levels of MySQL certification, you might consider using vouchers to pre-pay for exams and obtain volume discounts. Contact your regional *Pearson VUE* office for further information (see the list of contact addresses and telephone numbers in section B.12, "*Pearson VUE* Contact Information," of this guide).

B.4.2 Beta Exams

At times, MySQL AB might announce the possibility of taking part in beta testing of new or updated certification exams. Beta exams will be offered at a discounted price.

Just as regular exams, beta exams count toward certification. However, instead of receiving an immediate response, results of beta tests must first be evaluateB. For that reason, you won't receive the result of a beta exam until 3-4 months after the exam has taken place.

Details of upcoming beta exams are published on the MySQL certification Web site and on the certification mailing list, as information becomes available.

B.4.3 How to Register for or Reschedule Exams

All MySQL AB certification exams are delivered through *Pearson VUE*. There are three ways to register for exams:

- On the *Pearson VUE* Web site: `http://www.vue.com/mysql`
- By registering directly at a test center
- By calling a *Pearson VUE* call center

You can find more contact information for *Pearson VUE* at the end of this guide.

Subject to test center availability, you may register for an exam as late as the day on which you want to take the exam. The *Pearson VUE* FAQ page has additional information (see `http://www.vue.com/faqs`). This is also the place to look if you need to reschedule an exam.

B.4.4 Retaking Exams

Exams may be retaken at any time. However, we strongly recommend that you spend at least two weeks doing extra studies for each of the exams before retaking. All exams are created on-the-fly from a large pool of questions. It's unlikely that you'll be presented with any of the questions you answered in the first try.

B.5 Preparing for the Exams

Make sure that you carefully read through the exam description for your exam, later in this guide.

For each subject, read and make sure that you understand the corresponding sections in the manual, as well as some of the many tutorials for the MySQL products available on the Web.

You might want to consider taking one of the many courses offered by MySQL AB and its partners. The course structure corresponds to the contents of the certification exams.

B.6 How the Exams Proceed

Note that all exams are designed to be "closed book" exams; you aren't allowed to (and will not need to) bring books or any other materials into the testing room. The test center will provide you with a pen and note paper (which you must leave behind you when you leave the testing station).

On the day of your exam, make sure that you arrive at the test center well ahead of the appointed time. When you arrive, the test center will inform you how much time you should expect to spend to complete all steps necessary for testing.

Before taking the test, you will be required to show two forms of identification. One of these must be a photo ID (driver's license, passport, company ID, and so on).

After you've registered, you'll be taken to your testing station. When the test begins, you must first read and confirm that you understand and will adhere to the *MySQL AB Certification Non-Disclosure Agreement and Logo Usage Agreement*. This document is also presented at the end of this guide; it is strongly recommended that you read it and make sure you understand it before going to the exam. That way, you don't have to spend time reading it at the exam itself.

The test session length is 90 minutes. During this time, you're presented with 70 questions. You should attempt to answer all questions because an unanswered question will count as a wrong answer. You can move back and forth between questions, so initially you can skip the ones you're unsure of, and return to them as time permits.

For multiple-choice questions, you can either use a mouse to click on the correct answer or type the corresponding key on the keyboarB. The lower-left part of the screen tells you whether only one answer is possible or if several answers may be correct. Note that you can mark a question for review—all questions marked are presented when you have completed the last question, allowing you to go back and review any questions you have markeB.

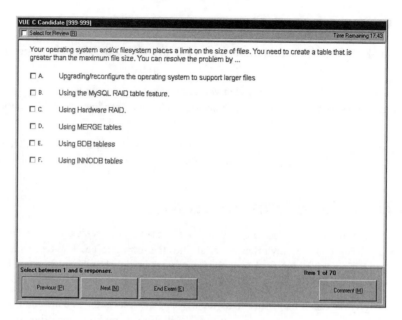

An example of the question display screen.

The question types you will be presented with during the exams are as follows:

- Multiple-choice questions with a single correct answer
- Multiple-choice questions, in which one or more answers are correct
- Text answers, in which you must provide for example a command name or an SQL statement

Currently, the language used in all MySQL certification exams is English.

Unless you are taking part in a Beta exam, after you've completed your test, you'll receive immediate notification whether you've passed or faileB.

B.7 After the Exam

When you complete a certification exam, you immediately get a printed report from the test center where you take the test. MySQL AB is notified of all results from the individual test centers within a few days.

After we've received notice of your results, we send a letter to you with details on how to access the Certification Candidate part of the MySQL Web site.

If you passed the exam, the package will also contain your certificate and instructions on how to obtain logos for use on your business cards, stationary, and so on. With these proofs of knowledge at your disposal, you're well equipped to enhance your career path.

B.8 Staying Updated

Passing exams and obtaining certification diplomas for the MySQL Core and Professional certifications are important steps in your career path toward becoming a MySQL Certified DBA, but it doesn't stop there.

First of all, the MySQL server and associated products are continually evolving, new features are being added, and so on. As these changes take place, so does the certification program change to assist you in always being able to show proof that your knowledge is up-to-date. New and specialized certifications will be added over time, so you should check back on the MySQL certification Web site at regular intervals to keep updateB. You can also keep yourself informed by subscribing to the MySQL Newsletter, which keeps you updated on MySQL-related news items.

Staying updated is not just a question of working with the MySQL server; you need to plan to work with the subjects of each exam, to get the experience required for passing. In an ideal situation, your employer will take an interest in your training needs and make sure you get to work on projects related to your next exam. However, this will not always be possible even for the best of employers. Allocate time to try things out on your own, and plan this carefully so you gain sufficient experience in time for your next exam.

B.9 How Long Are the Certifications Valid?

MySQL certifications are tied to the major version numbers of the MySQL server and related products. A change in the major version number is made by MySQL AB when significant new features are introduced in MySQL server.

As older versions become outdated, MySQL AB will retire the certifications related to these versions. Candidates will be notified well in advance when such a retirement will take place.

At MySQL AB, we believe that although certifications help you prove your knowledge, certification is no substitute for experience. Nonetheless, prospective employers are likely to look more favorably at candidates who continuously keep updated on their knowledge, and recertifying will help you with that proof.

B.10 MySQL 4 Core Certification

This certification is the first tier on your road to full MySQL certification. Whatever your future certification path, you must first pass the exam for the MySQL Core Certification before moving on.

With the Core Certification in hand, you have proof that you're capable of creating and using databases and tables, inserting, modifying, deleting, and retrieving data from a MySQL database, all based on a number of criteria like those that occur in real-world situations.

The job role of a person holding the MySQL Core Certification will typically be to maintain data in company databases, performing data analysis, importing and exporting data, and so forth.

For most candidates, the Core Certification is the first step toward obtaining the much desired title of Certified MySQL Professional. To move on to the Professional Certification, you must first pass the Core exam.

B.10.1 When Should I Certify?

The MySQL Core Certification is aimed at users:

- Who have used the MySQL server for one man-month (150 hours) or more
- Who often find themselves in situations where they need to pull data from a MySQL database, or perform operations such as importing large amounts of data into the database
- Who have done some semi-advanced reporting using features such as LIMIT, WHERE, joins, aggregate functions, and the like

B.10.2 What Knowledge Is Tested?

The MySQL Core Certification is achieved by passing a single exam. The sections covered by the test are listed below, along with the relative weight of each section in the final scoring. The weight also indicates how many questions you should expect to be asked for each section.

The test consists of approximately 70 questions, and you have 1 1/2 hours in which to answer them.

B.10.3 Exam Contents—MySQL Core Certification

- MySQL and MySQL AB (10%)
    - The difference between MySQL and MySQL AB
    - How MySQL AB operates
    - MySQL core values
    - MySQL dual licensing
    - Organization and structure of the *MySQL Reference Manual*
    - The MySQL mailing lists

- MySQL Software (10%)
    - Major program components used in MySQL
    - Major operating system families supported by MySQL

- Differences between major MySQL distributions
- Available MySQL client interfaces

- Using MySQL Client Programs (10%)
  - Invoking command-line client programs
  - Specifying command-line options
  - The `mysql` client
    - Using `mysql` interactively
    - Using script files with `mysql`
    - `mysql` client commands and SQL statements
    - Using the `--safe-updates` option
  - Using `mysqlimport`
  - Using `mysqldump` and reloading the dump
  - Checking tables with `mysqlcheck` and `myisamchk`
  - Using `MySQLCC`
  - Using MySQL Connector/ODBC and MySQL Connector/J

- Data Definition Language (20%)
  - General database and table properties
  - Storage engines and table types
  - Limits on number and size of database components
  - Identifier syntax
  - `CREATE DATABASE`, `DROP DATABASE`
  - `CREATE TABLE`, `ALTER TABLE`, `DROP TABLE`
  - `CREATE INDEX`, `DROP INDEX`; specifying indexes at table-creation time
  - Creating and using primary keys
  - Column types
  - Using `AUTO_INCREMENT`
  - String and number formats
  - Using `SHOW` and `DESCRIBE` to review table structures

- `SELECT` Statements (10%)
  - Selecting which columns to display
  - Restricting a selection using `WHERE`
  - Using `ORDER BY` to sort query results

- Limiting a selection using LIMIT
- Aggregate functions, GROUP BY, and HAVING
- Using DISTINCT to eliminate duplicates
- Concatentating SELECT results with UNION

- Basic SQL (10%)
  - Using SQL expressions and functions
  - Using LIKE for pattern matching
  - Using IN() to test membership
  - Case sensitivity in string comparisons
  - Case sensitivity in database, table, column, and function names
  - Using reserved words as identifiers
  - NULL values in SELECT statements
  - Comments in SQL statements

- Update Statements (10%)
  - INSERT and REPLACE
  - UPDATE
  - DELETE and TRUNCATE
  - Handling duplicate key values
  - Using ORDER BY and LIMIT with UPDATE and DELETE statements

- Joins (15%)
  - Writing inner joins using INNER JOIN and the comma (',') operator
  - Writing outer joins using LEFT JOIN and RIGHT JOIN
  - Converting subqueries to inner and outer joins
  - Resolving name clashes using qualifiers and aliases
  - Multiple-table UPDATE and DELETE statements

- Importing and Exporting Data (5%)
  - LOAD DATA INFILE
  - Using files on the server and the client host
  - Limiting the columns and rows being imported
  - SELECT INTO OUTFILE
  - Privileges needed for LOAD DATA INFILE and SELECT INTO OUTFILE

B.11 Certified MySQL 4 Professional

The MySQL Professional Certification is the second tier of the MySQL Certification program. When you've achieved the MySQL Core Certification and have gained enough experience, the time has come to prove your abilities in basic installation, setup, and management of a MySQL server.

With the title of Certified MySQL Professional (MySQL-Prof) on your resume, you have proof that you master more complex issues, such as installing a server from scratch, keeping the server running smoothly at all times, using the new table types, using more advanced SQL, and analyzing the trouble spots of other users' queries.

The typical job role of a MySQL-Prof is in setting up and managing one or more MySQL servers in an organization, often managing a team of one or more users and programmers of MySQL products.

B.11.1 When Should I Certify?

Professional Certification is for users who have passed the MySQL Core Certification exam and have managed to move beyond the skills required for that exam by doing the following:

- Installing a MySQL server without assistance
- Troubleshooting queries that take too long to run
- Granting other users access to some of the databases on the server in a secure manner
- Having gained knowledge of the internals of the MyISAM and InnoDB table types and advanced server features

B.11.2 What Knowledge Is Tested?

MySQL Professional Certification is achieved by passing a single exam. The sections covered by the exam are listed below, along with the relative weight of each section in the final scoring. The weight also indicates how many questions you should expect to be asked for each section.

The test consists of approximately 70 questions, and you have 1 ½ hours in which to answer them.

B.11.3 Exam Contents—Certified MySQL Professional

- MySQL Architecture (15%)
  - Client-server overview
  - Choosing the right client
  - Connecting the client to the server

- Hard disk footprint
- Memory footprint
- Log and status files
- Table types in MySQL

- MySQL Installation and Configuration (20%)
    - Installing MySQL on Windows
    - Startup and shutdown on Windows
    - Installing MySQL on Unix
    - Startup and shutdown on Unix
    - Configuring MySQL
    - Compiling MySQL
    - Upgrading MySQL
    - Optimizing the operating system for MySQL use
    - Configuring disks for MySQL use
    - Choosing hardware for MySQL use

- Security Issues (15%)
    - Securing MySQL
    - User account management
    - Client access control

- Optimizing for Query Speed (15%)
    - Index optimization and index usage
    - Using EXPLAIN to analyze queries
    - General query enhancement
    - Optimizing the logical database structure

- MyISAM Tables (10%)
    - MyISAM-specific optimizations
    - Locking strategies
    - Backup and recovery
    - Checking and repairing tables
    - Table maintenance

- InnoDB Tables (10%)
    - Special InnoDB features (ACID compliance, transaction model, versioning, con-currency, and isolation levels)
    - InnoDB-specific optimizations

- Locking strategies
- Backup and recovery
- Checking and repairing tables
- Table maintenance

- Advanced Server Features (15%)

    - Interpreting `mysqld` server information
    - Measuring server load
    - Tuning memory parameters
    - Using the query cache
    - Using multiple servers
    - Replication

B.12 Pearson VUE Contact Information

There are three ways to register for MySQL AB exams at *Pearson VUE*:

- On the *Pearson VUE* Web site: `http://www.vue.com/mysql`
- By registering directly at a test center
- By calling a *Pearson VUE* call center (see the following information)

MySQL AB strongly recommends that you register through the *Pearson VUE* Web site at `http://www.vue.com/mysql`. Note that if you aren't already registered as a MySQL candidate at *Pearson VUE*, your registration might take up to 24 hours to complete.

If you want to register directly at a test center, you can find a list of test centers at `http://www.vue.com/mysql`. Click on the Test Centers link about halfway down the page.

Lastly, you can call one of the *Pearson VUE* call centers to register for an exam. Use one of the following telephone numbers to reach the *Pearson VUE* call center in your area.

Americas

- Canada: (800) 247-8715, option 4
- United States: (800) 247-8715, option 4
- From outside Canada or USA: +1 952 681-3807, option 4

Asia-Pacific Region

- Australia: 1-800-356-022
- Hong Kong: 800-930-988
- Japan: 0120-355-173
- Korea, South: 00308-610-021

- Malaysia: 1800-808-578
- New Zealand: 0800-445-884
- Philippines: 1800-1611-0155
- Singapore: 800-6161-888
- Taiwan 0080-611-289
- From outside one of the listed countries: +612-9487-5425

Europe, Middle East, Africa

- Austria: 0800-292150
- Belgium - Dutch: 0800-74174
- Belgium - French: 0800-74175
- France: 0800-904757
- Germany: 0800-0826499
- Ireland: 1-800-552131
- Israel: 1-800-9453797
- Italy: 800-790521
- Netherlands: 0800-0235323
- Portugal: 800-831429
- South Africa: 0800-995044
- Spain: 900-993190
- Sweden: 020-798690
- Switzerland: 0800-837550
- Turkey: 0080031929149
- United Kingdom: 0800-7319905
- From outside one of the listed countries: +31-30-287-4962

B.13 MySQL AB Certification NDA and LUA

Before taking any test for the certification program, you are required to accept the combined MySQL AB Certification Non-Disclosure Agreement (NDA) and Certification Logo Usage Agreement (LUA).

Below is a copy of the text, which you'll be required to accept at the test center as the first action after the test has been starteB.

We strongly suggest that you read through and make sure that you understand the document now, so that you do not spend valuable time on this after the test has begun.

B.13.1 MySQL AB Certification Non-Disclosure and Logo Usage Agreement

B.13.1.1 Introduction

Before taking any test under the MySQL AB Certification Program (a "Certification Exam"), you will be required to accept the terms of this MySQL AB Certification Non-Disclosure and Logo Usage Agreement (this "Agreement").

In addition, before using any Certification Logo (as defined below), you will be required to pass a Certification Exam, and you must receive electronic or written notice from MySQL AB stating that you may use that particular Certification Logo.

This Agreement is created to protect your certification. By adhering to this Agreement (that is, keeping questions, answers and other information related to the Certification Exams confidential and by ensuring that the Certification Logos are used only by you), you help maintain the integrity of the MySQL AB Certification Program. This helps maintain the value of your Certification(s).

By clicking the NEXT button below, you agree that the terms and conditions of this Agreement shall be valid and binding upon you.

B.13.2 Agreement

B.13.2.1 1 Non-Disclosure Agreement

I understand that the MySQL AB Certification Program and Certification Exam(s) are proprietary to MySQL AB. Therefore, I agree to the following terms and conditions:

1. I will not copy, disclose, publish or transmit to any person or entity any details of any Certification Exam, or information pertaining to it, in any form or by any means.

2. I alone must complete in full all the requirements for MySQL AB certification and/or assessment.

3. All work submitted in connection with the MySQL AB Certification Program will be my own, and not the work of any other individual, group or entity.

4. All MySQL AB certification information, including (without limitation) exams, questions, answers and related information, is made available to me strictly for the purpose of certification. All such information is proprietary material that is wholly owned by MySQL AB and protected under copyright, trade secret and other laws.

B.13.2.2 2 Logo Usage Agreement

I understand that MySQL AB may, from time to time, develop a logo for limited use by those individuals who have passed a particular Certification Exam (a "Certification Logo"). Therefore, I agree to the following terms and conditions:

1. This Agreement permits me to use only the Certification Logos expressly identified in an electronic or written notice provided to me by MySQL AB, and only in the manner described herein.

2. I may only use a Certification Logo that pertains to a Certification level that I, as an individual, have achieved, and only on printed, personal business cards, printed, personal letterheads and printed, personal resumes. I may not use a Certification Logo, or any imitation thereof, in any other place, such as on product packaging or a Web site. My certification is personal and does not apply to or benefit any company or organization that I may own, or for whom I may work or otherwise be associateB.

3. I may not alter a Certification Logo in any way, including (without limitation) by resizing, translating, or altering the colors used in, the Certification Logo. A Certification Logo may be scaled proportionally in order to adhere to the conditions of this Agreement.

4. My certification will expire as published by MySQL AB from time to time. In the event that my certification expires or is otherwise terminated, I will immediately discontinue my usage of the applicable Certification Logo.

5. I may not display or use the Certification Logo in a manner that suggests that I am an employee or other representative of MySQL AB, or that either my company or I are affiliated with, or endorsed by, MySQL AB. Moreover, everywhere I use a Certification Logo, my name, or the name of my company, must appear more prominently than, and clearly distinguished from, the Certification Logo.

6. My use of any and all Certification Logos shall further be restricted by, and subject to, the MySQL Trademark Policy ("The Trademark Policy") posted on the MySQL AB Web site (www.mysql.com, the "Web site"). MySQL AB may from time to time change the Trademark Policy, and I agree to check the Web site for changes to the Trademark Policy on a periodic basis. I shall be deemed to have knowledge of any changes to the Trademark Policy as soon as they are posted on the Web site. MySQL AB reserves any and all rights not expressly granted herein. I agree that any and all goodwill pertaining to my use of a Certification Logo shall inure to the exclusive benefit of MySQL AB.

B.13.2.3 3 Miscellaneous

1. I hereby declare that: (a) I am the individual registered and authorized to complete the Certification Exam, identified by such unique information as my MySQL AB Certification user id and password, electronic mail address, given and family names, or such other means used by MySQL AB to uniquely identify an individual; and (b) I am at least eighteen (18) years old and competent to sign this Agreement.

2. I understand that violation of any of the terms of this Agreement will result in: (a) the immediate revocation of any existing MySQL AB certification; (b) my permanent ineligibility to obtain any MySQL certification; and/or (c) other punitive or legal action deemed appropriate by MySQL AB.

3. If the test center at which I am accepting this Agreement is located in the United States of America, then this Agreement shall be deemed to have been executed in the United States of America and shall be governed by the laws of the State of Delaware, without regard to the conflict of laws provisions thereof. If the test center at which I am signing this Agreement is located anywhere other than the United States of America, then this Agreement shall be deemed to have been executed in Sweden and shall be governed by the laws of Sweden, without regard to the conflict of laws provisions thereof. I have agreed to execute this Agreement in the English language. In the event of any dispute in connection with this Agreement, the English language version of the Agreement will control for all purposes. Any action brought under this Agreement shall be conducted in the English language.

4. By clicking the "NEXT" button displayed below, I am confirming that I understand and accept all of the terms and conditions of this Agreement. I understand that I am under no obligation to accept these terms, but that my acceptance is required to proceed with this Certification Exam.

You must accept the above terms and click "NEXT" in order to proceed with the exam.

If you do not accept the above terms, click "END EXAM". You will not be able to proceed with the exam.

Index

D

E

How can we make this index more useful? Email us at indexes@samspublishing.com

O

obtaining information about tables, 102
OCT() function, 581
ODBC driver, 26, 30, 53
online documentation, 19
OpenBSD, 25
operating system optimization, 354-355
operating systems supported, 24-25
operators
  , (comma), 258-264
  IS NOT NULL, 198
  IS NULL, 198
  LIKE, 190-193
  <= (less than or equal to), 198
  MATCH, 397
  OR, 193
OPTIMIZE TABLE statement, 453, 560
optimizing
  InnoDB, 479-480
  MyISAM tables, 441, 453-454
  operating system, 354-355
  queries
    database structure, 414-418
    EXPLAIN statements, 397-409
    general enhancements, 409-411
    indexes, 390-397
    limiting output, 411-412
    strategy overview, 389-390
  table updates, 412-413
option files (client programs), 34-36, 350-352
options (client programs), 31-32
OR operator, 193
ORDER BY clause
  DELETE statements, 242, 277
  SELECT statements, 146-149
  UPDATE statements, 240-241, 277
outer joins, 265-270
output column names, 144
output formats, 41

P

PASSWORD() function, 367, 581
passwords
  changing, 376-377
  encryption, 367
  server connections, 33-34
  setting, 365-366
pattern matching, 190-193
Pearson VUE
  call centers, 605-606
  Web site, 595, 605
per-client variables, 516-517
PERIOD_ADD() function, 581
PERIOD_DIFF() function, 581
perror utility, 321
philosophy of free software, 18
PID file, 326
POSITION() function, 581
POW() function, 582
POWER() function, 582
pre-alpha versions, 26
preparing for exams, 597
PRIMARY KEY indexes, 73, 75-77, 231, 390
privileges
  accounts, 371
  administrative, 368
  database access, 368
  grant tables, 369-370
  granting, 371-374
  levels, 369
  LOAD DATA INFILE, 304-305
  overview, 367
  revoking, 371, 374-376
  special specifiers, 369
  statement privilege checking, 381
  viewing, 374
  when they take effect, 376
process ID (PID) file, 326
production versions, 26

Professional Certification. *See* MySQL
  Professional Certification
professional services, 16
prompts (mysql client program), 39-40

Q

qualifiers for table and column names, 65
QUARTER() function, 582
queries
  concatenating SELECT results, 164-166
  converting subqueries to joins, 270-273
  identifying databases, 144-145
  identifying what values to display,
    142-144
  mysql prompts, 39-40
  optimizing
    database structure, 414-418
    EXPLAIN statements, 397-409
    general enhancements, 409-411
    indexes, 390-397
    limiting output, 411-412
    strategy overview, 389-390
  output column names, 144
  scheduling, 447-448
  script files, 40-41
  sorting results, 146-149
  statement terminators, 39
  writing, 409-411
query cache, 324, 517-519
query_cache_limit system variable, 591
query_cache_size system variable, 591
query_cache_type system variable, 591
query log, 325
QUOTE() function, 582

R

RAID drives, 355
RAID tables, 440
RAND() function, 190, 582
read-only systems, 357
read_buffer_size system variable, 591

read_rnd_buffer_size system variable, 591
records (tables)
  adding, 231-235, 299-304
  deleting, 231, 241-242
  duplicates, 303-304
  eliminating duplicates, 162-164
  grouping, 160-162
  replacing, 231, 235-237
  retrieving from multiple tables, 145
  selecting
      limiting selections, 152-153
      restricting selections, 145-146
  updating, 231, 238-241
recovering backups, 481
Red Hat Linux, 25
registering to take exams, 596, 605-606
reloading SQL-format dump file, 48-49
RENAME TABLE statement, 560
renaming tables, 72
REPAIR TABLE statement, 561
repairing
  InnoDB tables, 482
  MyISAM tables, 452-453
  tables, 49-51
REPLACE statement, 231, 235-237,
  561-562
REPLACE() function, 582
replacing records, 231, 235-237
replicating databases, 521-522
rescheduling exams, 596
reserved words, 194-196
resolving name clashes, 273-276
resource limits (accounts), 377, 381
RESTORE TABLE statement, 448, 451-
  452, 562
result sets, writing to files, 305-306
retaking exams, 596
retrieving records from multiple tables,
  145
REVERSE() function, 583
reviewing table structure, 100
REVOKE statement, 371, 374-376, 562

How can we make this index more useful? Email us at indexes@samspublishing.com

X – Y – Z

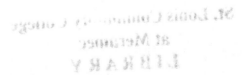

How can we make this index more useful? Email us at indexes@samspublishing.com

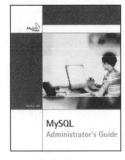